IF FOUND, please notify and arrange return to owner. The owner of this text is preparing for the Certified Management Accountant Examination and/or the Certified in Financial Management Examination.

Name of CMA/CFM Candidate ______________________________

Address ______________________________

City, State, Zip ______________________________

Telephone (   ) ______________ E-mail ______________

Additional Gleim *CMA/CFM Review* books, software, and other accounting study materials are available directly from

Gleim Publications, Inc.
P.O. Box 12848
University Station
Gainesville, Florida 32604

(800) 87-GLEIM
(352) 375-0772
FAX: (352) 375-6940

E-mail: admin@gleim.com
Internet: www.gleim.com

AF712616

This is *CMA/CFM Review: Part 1, Economics, Finance, and Management*, 8th ed., available for $22.95. Also available are

CFM Review: Part 2CFM, Corporate Financial Management, 8th ed. $22.95
CMA Review: Part 2CMA, Financial Accounting and Reporting, 8th ed. 22.95
CMA/CFM Review: Part 3, Mgmt. Reporting, Analysis, and Behavioral Issues, 8th ed. . . 22.95
CMA/CFM Review: Part 4, Decision Analysis and Information Systems, 8th ed. 22.95

CMA/CFM Test Prep software ($35 per section) is also available to complement your study.

Other review manuals available are

CPA Review: Financial $24.50
CPA Review: Auditing 24.50
CPA Review: Business Law 24.50
CPA Review: TAX-MAN-GOV 24.50

CPA Test Prep software ($35 per section) and *CPA Review* audiotapes ($75 per section) are also available to complement your study.

Order forms for these and all of our other publications are provided at the back of this book.

All orders must be prepaid. Shipping and handling charges will be added to all orders. Library and company orders may be purchased on account. Add applicable sales tax to shipments within Florida. All payments must be in U.S. funds and payable on a U.S. bank. Please write or call for prices and availability of all foreign country shipments. Orders will usually be shipped the day after your request is received. Allow 10 days for delivery in the United States. Please contact us if you do not receive your shipment within 2 weeks.

Gleim Publications, Inc. guarantees the immediate refund of all resalable texts and unopened software and audiotapes purchased directly from Gleim Publications, Inc. if they are returned within 30 days. Shipping and handling charges are nonrefundable. Returns of books purchased from bookstores and other resellers should be made to the respective bookstore or reseller.

Groundwood Paper and Highlighters -- This book is printed on high quality groundwood paper. It is lightweight and easy-to-recycle. We recommend that you purchase a highlighter specifically designed to be non-bleed-through (e.g., Avery *Glidestick*™) at your local office supply store.

REVIEWERS AND CONTRIBUTORS

Grady M. Irwin, J.D., University of Florida Holland Law Center, has taught in the University of Florida College of Business. Mr. Irwin provided many answer explanations and extensive editorial assistance throughout.

Karen Louviere, B.A., University of Florida, is our book production coordinator. Ms. Louviere coordinated the production staff and provided production assistance throughout the project.

Travis Moore, M.B.A., University of Florida, provided technical and editorial assistance, reviewed the final manuscript, and prepared the page layout.

Nancy Raughley, B.A., Tift College, is our editor. Ms. Raughley reviewed the entire manuscript and assisted in all phases of production.

Brian Soltis, M.Acc., University of Florida, provided editorial assistance throughout the project.

A PERSONAL THANKS

This manual would not have been possible without the extraordinary effort and dedication of Jim Collis, Terry Hall, and Gail Luparello, who typed the entire manuscript and all revisions as well as prepared the camera-ready pages.

The authors appreciate the proofreading and production assistance of Shannon Bunker, Lana Cox, Eric Hall, Jennifer Johnson, and Jordi Kraft.

The authors also appreciate the editorial assistance of Rusty Helton and Shana Robbins.

Finally, we appreciate the encouragement and tolerance of our families throughout the project.

EIGHTH EDITION

CMA/CFM REVIEW

for PART 1
ECONOMICS, FINANCE, AND MANAGEMENT

by Irvin N. Gleim, Ph.D., CPA, CIA, CMA, CFM

and

Dale L. Flesher, Ph.D., CPA, CIA, CMA, CFM

ABOUT THE AUTHORS

Irvin N. Gleim is Professor Emeritus in the Fisher School of Accounting at the University of Florida and is a member of the American Accounting Association, Academy of Legal Studies in Business, American Institute of Certified Public Accountants, Association of Government Accountants, Florida Institute of Certified Public Accountants, Institute of Internal Auditors, and the Institute of Management Accountants. He has had articles published in the *Journal of Accountancy, The Accounting Review,* and *The American Business Law Journal* and is author/coauthor of numerous accounting and aviation books and CPE courses.

Dale L. Flesher is the Arthur Andersen Alumni Professor in the School of Accountancy at the University of Mississippi and has written over 180 articles for business and professional journals, including *Management Accounting, Journal of Accountancy,* and *The Accounting Review,* as well as numerous books. He is a member of the Institute of Management Accountants, American Institute of Certified Public Accountants, Institute of Internal Auditors, American Accounting Association, and American Taxation Association. He is a past editor of *The Accounting Historians' Journal* and is a trustee and past president of the Academy of Accounting Historians.

Gleim Publications, Inc.
P.O. Box 12848
University Station
Gainesville, Florida 32604
(352) 375-0772
(800) 87-GLEIM
FAX: (352) 375-6940
E-mail: admin@gleim.com
Internet: www.gleim.com

ISSN: 1093-2542

ISBN 0-917539-76-1

Copyright © 1997, 1998 by Gleim Publications, Inc.

Second Printing: April 1998

This is the second printing of the eighth edition of
CMA/CFM Review: Part 1.
Please e-mail update@gleim.com with CMA/CFM Part 1 8-2 included in the subject or text. You will receive our current update as a reply.

EXAMPLE:

To: update@gleim.com
From: your e-mail address
Subject: CMA/CFM Part 1 8-2

ALL RIGHTS RESERVED. No part of this material may be reproduced in any form whatsoever without express written permission from Gleim Publications, Inc.

ACKNOWLEDGMENTS

The authors are indebted to the Institute of Certified Management Accountants for permission to use problem materials from past CMA examinations. Questions and unofficial answers from the Certified Management Accountant Examinations, copyright © 1976 through 1997 by the Institute of Certified Management Accountants, are reprinted and/or adapted with permission.

The authors are also indebted to The Institute of Internal Auditors, Inc. for permission to use Certified Internal Auditor Examination Questions and Suggested Solutions, copyright © 1980 through 1997 by The Institute of Internal Auditors, Inc.

This publication is designed to provide accurate and authoritative information with regard to the subject matter covered. It is sold with the understanding that the publisher is not engaged in rendering legal, accounting, or other professional service.

If legal advice or other expert assistance is required, the services of a competent professional person should be sought.

(From a declaration of principles jointly adopted by a Committee of the American Bar Association and a Committee of Publishers.)

PREFACE FOR CMA/CFM CANDIDATES

The purpose of this book is to help YOU prepare YOURSELF to pass Part 1 of the CMA/CFM examinations. The overriding consideration is an inexpensive, effective, and easy-to-use study program. This manual

1. Defines topics tested on Part 1 of the CMA/CFM exams.
2. Explains how to optimize your exam score by analyzing how the CMA/CFM exams are constructed, administered, and graded.
3. Outlines all of the subject matter tested on Part 1 of the CMA/CFM exams in 10 easy-to-use study units.
4. Presents multiple-choice questions to prepare you to answer questions on Part 1 of the CMA/CFM exams. The answer explanations are presented to the immediate right of the questions for your convenience. You MUST cover these answers until you commit to the correct answer. Use the bookmark provided at the back of this book.
5. Illustrates **individual question answering techniques** to minimize selecting incorrect answers and to maximize your exam score.
6. Suggests **exam-taking techniques** to help you maintain control and achieve success.

This is the Eighth Edition of *CMA/CFM Review* for Part 1, which covers only Part 1 of the CMA/CFM exams. Recall that the only difference between the CFM exam and the CMA exam is Part 2. Part 2CFM is "Corporate Financial Management." Part 2CMA is "Financial Accounting and Reporting."

Now is the time to take and pass the CMA/CFM exams. The CMA examination has been administered since 1972. The number of CMA candidates has increased from 410 in 1972 to almost 10,000 in 1996. The pass rates for each section of the CMA/CFM exams average over 40%. This higher (compared to other certifications) pass rate is consistent with the more mature CMA/CFM candidate (average age 30+) and the professional development nature of the CMA/CFM programs.

To maximize the efficiency of your review program, begin by **studying** (not reading) pages 1 through 22 in this book. "Preparing for and Taking the CMA/CFM Exams" is very short but very important. It has been carefully organized and written to provide you with important information to assist you in successfully completing Part 1 of the CMA/CFM examinations.

The outline format and spacing and the question and answer formats are designed to facilitate learning and readability. While this book constitutes a complete self-study program for Part 1 of the CMA/CFM exams, candidates should consider enrolling in a formal review program. Local colleges and universities as well as IMA chapters throughout the country have coordinated CMA review programs in the past and will continue to do so, as well as add CFM reviews.

Thank you for your interest in our review materials. We very much appreciate the thousands of letters and suggestions received from CIA, CMA/CFM, and CPA candidates since 1974. Please give us feedback concerning this book. The last page has been designed to help you note corrections and suggestions throughout your study process. Please tear it out and mail or fax it to us with your comments.

We also want you to e-mail, fax, or mail us feedback immediately after you take the exam. Do NOT disclose information about individual questions beyond subject matter not covered in our books. Tell us which part and which topics were NOT covered or inadequately covered.

Good Luck on the Exam,

Irvin N. Gleim
Dale L. Flesher

April 1998

TABLE OF CONTENTS

PUBLISHER'S NOTE:
This is the second printing of the eighth edition of ***CMA/CFM Review: Part 1***. Please help. Use the form on pages 487-488 to send us corrections and suggestions for improvement (please send after you take Part 1 of the CMA/CFM exams). FAX the emergency support form on page vii or e-mail irvin@gleim.com for inquiries about errors, omissions, etc.

For updates and information on this and other Gleim books, please see our web page (www.gleim.com/updates.html), or send e-mail to update@gleim.com with "CMA/CFM Part 1 8-2" in the subject line.

Gleim's *CMA/CFM Review* Support via Fax

If you fax us inquiries about errors, omissions, etc., before 1:00 p.m. eastern time, we will respond by fax the following business day. If we have trouble faxing our response, it will be mailed. Technical support is also available via e-mail (support@gleim.com). Please include your e-mail address on the fax form below if you wish to receive a response to your request by e-mail (required if you are outside the United States).

Please photocopy this *CMA/CFM Review* Support Request fax form. It must be completed as requested so we can address the issues and questions you have. All items should refer to a specific page number and outline letter/number or question number.

Wait until after you take the CMA/CFM exam to send us the separate evaluation form provided on pages 487 and 488. Please DO NOT duplicate items via fax that you will be sending to us on the evaluation form.

Gleim Publications, Inc. FAX (352) 375-6940

***CMA/CFM REVIEW* SUPPORT REQUEST**

Complete this form and attach additional pages as necessary.

Your name ______________________ Your Fax # ( ) _______-__________

Address: ____

____

City: ______________________ State: ______ Zip: __________

E-mail: ____

Inquiry: ____

____

____

____

____

____

____

____

____

____

After Completing Each Study Unit...

Test yourself further with hundreds of questions not in the Gleim books by using

CMA/CFM Test Prep Software --

Another powerful tool in the Gleim Knowledge Transfer System

Each of our four disks contains 1,000+ questions for one section of the exam.

Improve your study process and test yourself in an interactive environment with actual CMA/CFM questions.

ORDER TODAY!*

($35 per disk)

Ensure Your Success On The CMA/CFM Exams!

*Download a free DEMO from our home page: www.gleim.com.

PREPARING FOR AND TAKING THE CMA/CFM EXAMS

ABOUT THE CMA/CFM EXAMS

INTRODUCTION

CMA is the acronym for Certified Management Accountant. CFM is an acronym for Certified in Financial Management. The CFM exam is an offshoot of the CMA. The two exams are identical except that the Part 2CFM exam is "Corporate Financial Management," while the Part 2CMA exam is "Financial Accounting and Reporting."

The CMA examination has been, and the CMA/CFM exams will continue to be, developed and offered by the Institute of Certified Management Accountants (ICMA) in over 175 locations in the U.S. as well as in San Juan, Puerto Rico; Amman, Jordan; Amsterdam; Bahrain; Cairo; Dhahran, Saudi Arabia; Hong Kong; London; Taipei; and Zurich. International availability will begin May 1, 1998.

Both the CMA and the CFM are computer-administered, on-demand exams. Each part consists of 120 multiple-choice questions with a 3-hour time limit. The exam is administered at Sylvan testing centers.

CMA/CFM Review: Part 1 contains this 22-page introduction and 10 study units of outlines and multiple-choice questions that cover all of the material tested on Part 1 of the CMA/CFM exams. This introduction discusses exam content, pass rates, administration, organization, background information, preparing for the CMA/CFM exams, and taking the CMA/CFM exams. We urge you to read the next 20 pages carefully because they will help you dramatically improve your study and test-taking procedures.

CORPORATE MANAGEMENT ACCOUNTANTS AND FINANCIAL MANAGERS

1. Objective: Maximize the value of the firm by optimizing
    a. Long-term investment strategies
    b. The capital structure, i.e., how these long-term investments are funded
    c. Short-term cash flow management
2. Corporate financial management involves a financial manager, usually a vice-president/chief financial officer, who is assisted by the
    a. Treasurer -- cash, credit, capital outlay management
    b. Controller -- financial, cost, tax accounting
3. All accounting and finance personnel are beneficiaries of CFM and/or CMA participation.
4. The CMA/CFM tools are set forth in the ICMA's Content Specification Outlines for the CMA/CFM exams.
5. The diagram below illustrates an entity combining the factors of production into finished goods (arrows to the right) with money flowing to the left.

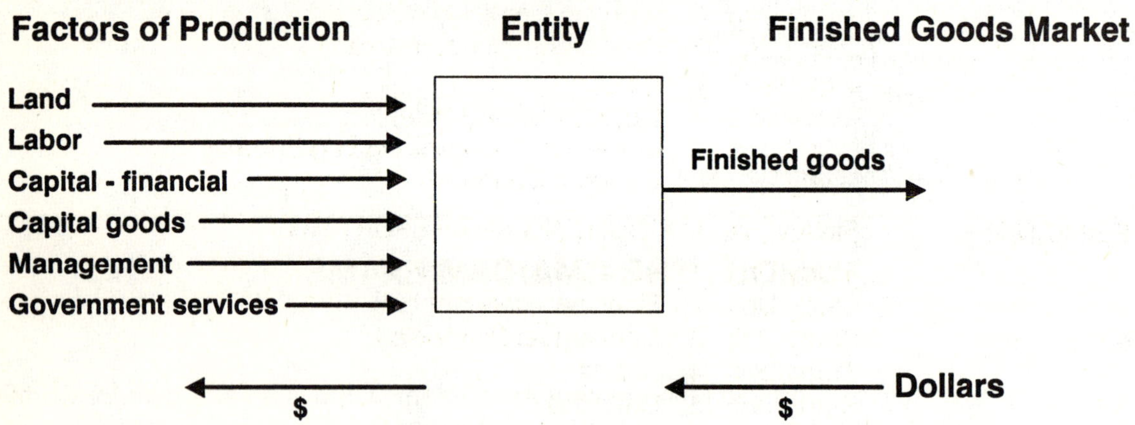

6. Put CMA and CFM in perspective of goods or services production in our capitalistic society. An entity combines the factors of production into finished goods.
    a. Note that the CMA/CFM programs focus on financial capital and the other factors of production as well as the finished goods market. The CEO (chief operations officer) has overall responsibility for the entity's operations.

OBJECTIVES AND CONTENT OF THE CMA/CFM EXAMINATIONS

The primary purpose of the CMA/CFM examination programs are "to establish an objective measure of an individual's knowledge and competence in the fields of management accounting and financial management." Three other objectives set forth by the ICMA are to

1. "Establish management accounting and financial management as recognized professions by identifying the role of the professional, the underlying body of knowledge, and a course of study by which such knowledge is acquired"
2. "Encourage higher educational standards in the management accounting and financial management fields"
3. "Encourage continued professional development"

The exams test the candidates' knowledge and ability with respect to the current state of the art in the fields of management accounting and financial management.

We have arranged the subject matter tested on the CMA/CFM examinations into 10 study units for each part. Each part is presented in a separate book. For CMA/CFM Parts 1, 3, and 4, study the corresponding *CMA/CFM Review* book. For Part 2CMA, study *CMA Review: Part 2CMA* and, for Part 2CFM, study *CFM Review: Part 2CFM*. All contain review outlines and prior CMA/CFM exam questions and answers. The 50 study units are organized as follows:

CMA/CFM Part 1: ECONOMICS, FINANCE, AND MANAGEMENT*

Study Unit 1: Microeconomics
Study Unit 2: Macroeconomics
Study Unit 3: International Business Environment
Study Unit 4: Domestic Institutional Environment of Business
Study Unit 5: Working Capital Finance
Study Unit 6: Capital Structure Finance
Study Unit 7: Risk
Study Unit 8: Organizational Theory
Study Unit 9: Motivation and the Directing Process
Study Unit 10: Communication

Part 2CMA: FINANCIAL ACCOUNTING AND REPORTING

Study Unit 1: Accounting Standards
Study Unit 2: Financial Statements
Study Unit 3: Conceptual Framework
Study Unit 4: Assets
Study Unit 5: Liabilities
Study Unit 6: Shareholders' Equity
Study Unit 7: Other Income Items
Study Unit 8: Other Reporting Issues
Study Unit 9: Financial Statement Analysis
Study Unit 10: External Auditing

***WARNING!!!**

About 25% of Part 1 test questions will require mathematical calculations. All other parts are approximately 50% computational questions. Practice computational questions to prepare for exam success!

Part 2CFM: CORPORATE FINANCIAL MANAGEMENT

Study Unit 1: Financial Statements and Annual Reports
Study Unit 2: Financial Statements: Special Topics
Study Unit 3: Long-Term Capital Financing
Study Unit 4: Financial Markets and Interest Rates
Study Unit 5: Investment Banking and Commercial Banking
Study Unit 6: Financial Statement Analysis
Study Unit 7: Business Combinations and Restructurings
Study Unit 8: Risk Management
Study Unit 9: External Financial Environment
Study Unit 10: Accounting Standard Setting

CMA/CFM Part 3: MANAGEMENT REPORTING, ANALYSIS, AND BEHAVIORAL ISSUES

Study Unit 1: Cost and Managerial Accounting Definitions
Study Unit 2: Product Costing and Related Topics
Study Unit 3: Cost Behavior
Study Unit 4: Statements on Management Accounting
Study Unit 5: Planning
Study Unit 6: Budgeting
Study Unit 7: The Controlling Process
Study Unit 8: Standard Costs and Variance Analysis
Study Unit 9: Responsibility Accounting
Study Unit 10: Behavioral Issues

CMA/CFM Part 4: DECISION ANALYSIS AND INFORMATION SYSTEMS

Study Unit 1: Decision Analysis
Study Unit 2: Cost-Volume-Profit Analysis
Study Unit 3: Capital Budgeting
Study Unit 4: Decision Making Under Uncertainty
Study Unit 5: Quantitative Methods I
Study Unit 6: Quantitative Methods II
Study Unit 7: Information Systems I
Study Unit 8: Information Systems II
Study Unit 9: Internal Control
Study Unit 10: Internal Auditing

Recap: The only difference between the CFM exam and the CMA exam is Part 2. This book covers Part 1 of the CMA/CFM exam.

The *CMA/CFM Review* study unit titles and organization differ somewhat from the subtopic titles used by the ICMA in its content specification outlines for the CMA/CFM exams. The detailed ICMA Content Specification Outline for Part 1 is presented in Appendix D beginning on page 444. The selection of study units in *CMA/CFM Review: Part 1* is based on the types and number of questions that have appeared on past CMA and CFM exams as well as the extensiveness of past and expected future exam coverage.

CONTENT SPECIFICATION OUTLINES

The ICMA has developed content specification outlines and has committed to follow them on each examination. A complete CSO is presented in Appendix D beginning on page 444. Thus, each examination will cover the major topics specified below; e.g., microeconomics will constitute 10% to 15% of Part 1 on each examination.

Candidates for the CMA/CFM designations are expected to have a minimum level of business knowledge that transcends all examination parts. This minimum level includes knowledge of basic financial statements, time value of money concepts, and elementary statistics. Specific discussion of the ICMA's Levels of Performance (A, B, and C) is provided on the next page.

CMA/CFM Part 1: Economics, Finance, and Management

- A. Microeconomics--10%-15% (Level B)
- B. Macroeconomics--10%-15% (Level A)
- C. International Business Environment--10%-15% (Level B)
- D. Domestic Institutional Environment of Business--10%-15% (Level A)
- E. Working Capital Policy and Management--10%-15% (Level C)
- F. Long-term Finance and Capital Structure--10%-15% (Level B)
- G. Organizational Structures, Management, and Communication--20%-30% (Level B)

Part 2CMA: Financial Accounting and Reporting

- A. Development of Accounting Standards--10%-15% (Level A)
- B. Advanced Topics on the Preparation of Financial Statements--50%-70% (Level C)
- C. Interpretation and Analysis of Financial Statements--10%-15% (Level C)
- D. External Auditing--10%-15% (Level A)

Part 2CFM: Corporate Financial Management

- A. Use of Financial Statements--10%-20% (Level B)
- B. Advanced Topics in Corporate Financial Management--50%-70% (Level C)
- C. Risk Management--10%-15% (Level C)
- D. External Financial Environment--10%-20% (Level A)
- E. Accounting Standard Setting Environment--5%-10% (Level A)

CMA/CFM Part 3: Management Reporting, Analysis, and Behavioral Issues

- A. Cost Measurement--20%-30% (Level C)
- B. Planning--20%-30% (Level C)
- C. Control and Performance Evaluation--20%-30% (Level C)
- D. Behavioral Issues--20%-30% (Level B)

CMA/CFM Part 4: Decision Analysis and Information Systems

- A. Decision Theory and Operational Decision Analysis--20%-30% (Level C)
- B. Investment Decision Analysis--20%-30% (Level C)
- C. Quantitative Methods for Decision Analysis--10%-15% (Level B)
- D. Information Systems--20%-30% (Level B)
- E. Management Controls--10%-15% (Level B)

LEVEL OF PERFORMANCE REQUIRED

All parts of the exams appear to be tested at the skill level of a final examination for the appropriate course at a good school of business. The ICMA has specified three levels of coverage as reproduced below and indicated in its content specification outlines. You will evaluate and compare the difficulty of each part of the CMA/CFM exams as you work the questions in this book.

Authors' Note: Rely on the questions at the back of each study unit in each *CMA/CFM Review* book and *CMA/CFM Test Prep* software.

Level A: Requiring an appreciation of the broad nature and fundamentals, the ability to recognize the existence of special features and problems in various business transactions, and the ability to apply this knowledge in new and concrete situations, i.e., requiring the skill levels of knowledge and comprehension.

Level B: Requiring a sound understanding of the broad aspects of practices and procedures and awareness of the problems relating to more detailed aspects, the ability to apply such broad knowledge in new and concrete situations, the ability to analyze the components of the material and their relationships, and the ability to reformulate the components into a new whole, i.e., requiring the skill levels of knowledge, comprehension, application and analysis.

Level C: Requiring a sound understanding of principles, practices, and procedures, the ability to analyze material so that its organizational structure can be understood, the proficiency to apply such knowledge to situations likely to be encountered, the ability to deal with all aspects of the situation without extensive recourse to technical research and assistance, and the ability to judge the value of material for a given purpose, i.e., requiring all six skill levels.

Authors' Note: The number of Level C questions will be relatively small, even as low as 5 to 10% because Level C questions are so difficult to construct. Thus, for example, the ICMA Content Specification Outlines indicate "working capital policy and management" in Part 1 at Level C with 10 to 15% coverage. Expect 12 to 18 questions on working capital policy and management, but as few as 1 or 2 might be Level C with the remainder being Levels A and B.

HOW ETHICS AND TAXES ARE TESTED

Ethics will probably be tested on every exam within the context of a specific subject area tested on that part. Appendix A beginning on page 419 covers ethics.

Federal income taxes are tested as (1) accounting for income taxes and (2) tax implications for business decisions. Accounting for income taxes including the proper treatment of deferred income taxes is tested in Part 2CMA, Financial Accounting and Reporting, and Part 2CFM, Corporate Financial Management.

The tax code provisions that impact business decisions will be contained in (1) questions that require decision analysis regarding debt versus equity issues in CMA/CFM Part 1, Economics, Finance, and Management; (2) questions in Part 2CFM, Corporate Financial Management; and (3) the decision analysis questions in CMA/CFM Part 4, Decision Analysis and Information Systems.

REQUIREMENTS TO ATTAIN THE CMA/CFM DESIGNATIONS

The CMA and/or the CFM designations are granted only by the ICMA. Candidates must complete five steps to become a CMA and/or CFM:

1. Become a member of the Institute of Management Accountants.
2. File an application for admission with the ICMA and register for the CMA/CFM examinations.
3. Pass all four parts of the CMA or CFM examination.* To attain both designations, CMAs in good standing need only pass Part 2CFM; CFMs in good standing need only pass Part 2CMA.
4. Meet the CMA/CFM experience requirement.
5. Comply with the Standards of Ethical Conduct.

*NEW EXAM CREDIT RULE: The ICMA has changed its policy on time limits for retaining credit for passed exam parts. The new policy no longer requires successful completion of all exam parts in a 3-year period. Instead, only "continuous candidacy" is required to retain credit after successful completion of one or more parts. "Continuous candidacy" includes

1. IMA membership
2. 20 hours of CPE annually
3. At least one examination part attempted every 2 years

Credit can be retained indefinitely as long as these requirements are fulfilled.

Once a designation is earned, the CMA and/or CFM is a member of the Institute of Certified Management Accountants and must comply with the program's CPE requirement and maintain IMA membership in good standing. The certificate of a CMA or CFM delinquent in these requirements will be subject to recall.

THE INSTITUTE OF MANAGEMENT ACCOUNTANTS (IMA)

Conceived as an educational organization to develop the individual management accountant professionally and to provide business management with the most advanced techniques and procedures, the IMA was founded as the National Association of Accountants in 1919 with 37 charter members. It grew rapidly, with 2,000 applications for membership in the first year, and today it is the largest management accounting association in the world, with approximately 80,000 members and more than 300 chapters in the U.S. and abroad.

The IMA has made major contributions to business management through its continuing education program, with courses and seminars conducted in numerous locations across the country; the monthly magazine *Management Accounting*; other literature, including research reports, monographs, and books; a technical inquiry service; a library; the annual international conference; and frequent meetings at chapter levels.

Membership in the IMA is open to all persons interested in advancing their knowledge of accounting or financial management. It is required for CMA/CFM candidates and CMAs/CFMs.

IMA Dues in the USA and Canada

1. **Regular**: 1 year, $135
2. **Associate**: $45.00 (2nd year, $90.00); must apply within 2 years of completing full-time studies; automatic transfer to regular dues at end of second year
3. **Academic member**: $37.50; must be a full-time faculty member
4. **Student**: $27.00; not less than 6 equivalent hours per semester

Membership application forms may be obtained by writing the Institute of Management Accountants, 10 Paragon Drive, Montvale, NJ 07645-1760, or calling (201) 573-9000 or (800) 638-4427. A sample of the two-page form appears in Appendix C on pages 439 and 440.

THE INSTITUTE OF CERTIFIED MANAGEMENT ACCOUNTANTS (ICMA)

The ICMA is located at the IMA headquarters in Montvale, New Jersey. The only function of the ICMA is to offer and administer the CFM and CMA designations. The staff consists of the senior director, the director of examinations, and three associates (all of whom are professional accountants), plus support personnel. The ICMA occupies about 4,000 square feet of office space in the IMA headquarters. This office is where the examinations are prepared and graded and where all records are kept.

ICMA BOARD OF REGENTS AND STAFF

The ICMA Board of Regents is a special committee of the IMA established to direct the CFM and CMA programs for financial managers and management accountants through the ICMA.

The Board of Regents consists of nine regents, one of whom is designated as chair by the president of the IMA. The regents are appointed by the president of the IMA to serve 3-year terms. Membership on the Board of Regents rotates, with one-third of the regents being appointed each year.

The regents usually meet four times a year for 1 or 2 days. The Board is divided into the following committees:

1. The Promotion and Publicity Committee consults with the staff on how to promote and market the CMA and CFM designations. Three regents serve on this committee.
2. The Credentials Committee reviews the admission standards for the CFM and CMA programs. Two regents serve on this committee.
3. The Continuing Education Committee sets continuing education standards for CFMs and CMAs and advises the staff on implementation of the CPE monitoring process. Two regents serve on this committee.
4. The Examination Policy Committee is concerned with the overall content, grading, and administration of the CFM and CMA exams. Three regents serve on this committee.
5. An Examination Review Committee consisting of two regents and two outside CMAs or CFMs exists for each of the four parts of the CFM and CMA exams. The committee reviews the content specification and grading basis of each specific exam.

The managing director of the ICMA (currently Ms. Priscilla Payne), the director of examinations (currently Ms. Terri Funk), and the ICMA staff are located at the ICMA office in Montvale, NJ. They undertake all of the day-to-day work with respect to the CFM and CMA programs.

ADMISSION TO THE CMA/CFM PROGRAMS

Candidates seeking admission to the CMA/CFM programs must

1. Hold a baccalaureate degree, in any area, from an accredited college or university. (Students may apply when they attain senior standing and will be permitted to take the examination pending receipt of a degree. Degrees from foreign institutions must be evaluated by an independent agency approved by the ICMA.) Alternatively, candidates may qualify for admission if they achieve a score in the 50th percentile or higher on either the Graduate Management Admissions Test (GMAT) or the Graduate Record Examination (GRE).
2. Be a member of the Institute of Management Accountants or submit an IMA application when applying to the ICMA

3. Be employed or expect to be employed in a position that meets the experience requirement
4. Submit the names of two character references. They will be confirmed on a random basis.
5. Be of good moral character
6. Abide by the Standards of Ethical Conduct

CMA/CFM WORK EXPERIENCE REQUIRED

Two continuous years of professional experience in financial management and/or management accounting are required any time prior to, or within 7 years of, passing the examination.

1. Professional experience shall be defined as full-time continuous experience at a level where judgments are regularly made that employ the principles of financial management and/or management accounting, e.g.,
   a. Financial analysis
   b. Budget preparation
   c. Management information systems analysis
   d. Management accounting in government, finance, or industry
   e. Auditing in government, finance, or industry
   f. Management consulting
   g. Audit work in public accounting (3 years required)
   h. Research, teaching, or consulting related to management accounting (for teaching, a significant portion required to be above the principles level)
2. Employment in functions that require the occasional application of financial management or management accounting principles but are not essentially management accounting oriented will not satisfy the requirement, e.g.,
   a. Computer operations
   b. Sales and marketing
   c. Manufacturing
   d. Engineering
   e. Personnel
   f. Employment in trainee, clerical, or nontechnical positions

If you have any questions about the acceptability of your work experience or baccalaureate degree, please write or call the ICMA. Include a complete description of your situation. You will receive a response from the ICMA as soon as your request is evaluated.

Institute of Certified Management Accountants
10 Paragon Drive
Montvale, NJ 07645-1759
(201) 573-9000
(800) 638-4427

HOW TO (1) APPLY AND (2) REGISTER FOR THE CMA/CFM EXAMS

First, you are required to **apply** both for membership in the IMA (see sample application form in Appendix C on pages 439 and 440) and for admission into the ICMA (see sample application form in Appendix C on pages 441 and 442). Thus, two applications are required if you are not already an IMA member. Apply to join the IMA and the ICMA **today** -- it only takes a few minutes. Application to the ICMA requires education, employment, and reference data. The educational experience requirements are discussed on page 8. You must provide two references: one from your employer and the second from someone other than a family member or fellow employee. Character reference forms are sent by the ICMA with your application forms. An official transcript providing proof of graduation is also required. There is a $50 application fee (waived for students and faculty). Once a person has become a candidate, there is no participant's fee other than IMA membership dues.

Second, it is necessary to **register** each time you wish to sit for the exams. The exam registration form (see page 443) is very simple (it takes about 2 minutes to complete). The registration fee for each part of the exam is $80. There is an additional $40 processing fee for candidates taking the examination at an international site. But graduating seniors and full-time graduate students are charged a one-time special rate of $40 per part. Full-time faculty are permitted to take the exam one time at no cost and thereafter pay $40 per part.

A sample of the first page of the ICMA registration form available to candidates from the ICMA appears on page 443. Order a registration booklet and IMA membership application form from the ICMA at (800) 638-4427, extension 303.

SPECIAL STUDENT EXAMINATION FEE

Seniors and full-time graduate students may take five examination parts at $40 per part (versus the normal $80). The procedure is to apply and register at the same time. This procedure requires completion and submittal of the following:

1. Name of someone who confirms your student status
2. The standard ICMA application form
3. A completed examination registration form
4. A check for $27 (IMA membership) plus $40 per part for the number of parts to be taken

FEES FOR FULL-TIME PROFESSORS

Full-time faculty members are permitted to take five examination parts once at no charge. The fee for any parts that must be retaken is 50% of the normal fee. The $50 application fee is also waived. To qualify, a faculty member must submit a letter on school stationery affirming his/her full-time status. Faculty should sit for the CMA/CFM examinations because a professor's status as a CMA/CFM encourages students to enter the program. Full-time doctoral students who plan to pursue a teaching career are treated as faculty members for purposes of qualifying for the free examination.

ICMA REFUND POLICY

In general, fees paid to the ICMA are nonrefundable. However, a candidate withdrawing from the examination within 30 days of registration may receive a credit for the examination fee less a $25 processing charge. Failure to take the examination within the assigned 60-day authorization period will result in the loss of examination fees; there will be no refund or credit available.

PASS/FAIL AND GRADE REPORTS

Immediately upon completion of your test, you will receive a grade report of pass or fail. In addition to pass or fail, you are given a "scaled score" between 200 and 700, with 500 being the passing mark. This provides information about how close, above or below, you were to passing. The "scaled score" is necessary to be able to quote the various versions of the test.

The IMA pass rate varies between 40 to 50% for the 5 parts of the exam. We believe the passing score is in the 60 to 70% range and varies with the specific test that you take; there are several versions, all very similar.

MAINTAINING YOUR CMA/CFM DESIGNATIONS

Membership in the IMA is required to maintain your CMA/CFM certificates. The general membership fee is $135. There is no additional participant fee.

Continuing professional education is required of CMAs/CFMs to maintain their proficiency in the fields of managerial accounting and financial management. Every 3 years, 90 hours of CPE must be completed, which is about 4 days per year. Qualifying topics include management accounting, finance, corporate taxation, mathematics and statistics, computer science, systems analysis, economics, management skills, production, marketing, business law, insurance, and behavioral science.

Credit for hours of study will be given for participation in programs sponsored by businesses, educational institutions, or professional and trade associations at either the national or local level. Programs conducted by an individual's employer must provide for an instructor or course leader. There must be formal instructional training material. On-the-job training does not qualify. An affidavit from the employer is required to attest to the hours of instruction. The programs may be seminars, workshops, technical meetings, or college courses under the direction of an instructor. The method of instruction may include lecture, discussion, case studies, and teaching aids such as training films and cassettes.

Credit for hours of study may be given for technical articles published in business, professional, or trade journals, and for major technical talks given for the first time before business, professional, or trade organizations. The specific hours of credit in each case will be determined by the Institute.

Gleim offers a multitude of self-study CPE programs that allow you to earn your credits in the comfort of your home or office. Many accounting professionals find this option more attractive than out-of-town travel. Call (800) 87-GLEIM for more information.

CMA/CFM TEST PREPARATION

The ICMA has developed thousands of multiple-choice questions from which each test of 120 questions will be selected. Each test will conform to the content specification outlines, which for CMA/CFM Part 1 are

A. Microeconomics--10%-15% (Level B)
B. Macroeconomics--10%-15% (Level A)
C. International Business Environment--10%-15% (Level B)
D. Domestic Institutional Environment of Business--10%-15% (Level A)
E. Working Capital Policy and Management--10%-15% (Level C)
F. Long-term Finance and Capital Structure--10%-15% (Level B)
G. Organizational Structures, Management, and Communication--20%-30% (Level B)

Questions will be refined, rewritten, etc., as the ICMA gains experience with the questions. The multiple-choice questions will have four answer choices.

CMA/CFM TEST ADMINISTRATION AND GRADING

The ICMA will send you authorization to take Part 1, which will have a 60-day window. A pilot period will exist for CMA/CFM Parts 1, 3, and 4 and Part 2CMA from December 1, 1997 to February 28, 1998, during which you must take your exam. The authorization will instruct you to call the National Sylvan registration office (800) 967-1100 and register for your test at a local Sylvan testing center.

After on-demand testing begins on May 1, 1998, your test will be graded by the computer as soon as you complete the test. This is **not** true for persons taking the CMA/CFM Parts 1, 3, and 4 and Part 2CMA exams between December 1, 1997 and February 28, 1998 because the ICMA wants to assess the difficulty of the test and curve the scores during this initial pilot period. We expect a high pass rate during this initial test period to encourage participation in the CMA/CFM programs and in computer-based testing.

COMPUTER TESTING PROCEDURES

When you arrive at the computer testing center, you will be required to provide positive proof of identification and your ICMA authorization to take the test. The identification presented must include your photograph, signature, and actual residential address, if different from the mailing address. This information may be presented in more than one form of identification. You then will sign in on the testing center's daily log.

Next, you will be taken into the testing room and seated at a computer terminal. A person from the testing center will assist you in logging on the system, and you will be asked to confirm your personal data (e.g., name, Social Security number, etc.). Then you will be prompted and given an online introduction to the computer testing system and you will take a sample test.

CONCEPTUAL VS. CALCULATION QUESTIONS

About 25% of Part 1 test questions will be calculations (e.g., compute to present value, etc.) in contrast to conceptual questions. When you take the test, it will appear that more than 25% of the questions are calculation-type because they take longer and are "more difficult." This book contains about 15% calculation-type questions. Thus, expect more on your exam.

If you have used our ***CMA/CFM Test Prep*** software, you will be conversant with the computer testing methodology and environment, and you will probably want to skip the sample test and begin the actual test immediately. Once you begin your test, you will be allowed 3 hrs. to complete the actual test. This is 1.5 minutes per question. After May 1, 1998, a computer test report will be printed and given to you when you have completed your exam. If you take the exam between December 1, 1997 and February 28, 1998, you will receive your grade in April 1998. Before you leave the testing center, you will be required to sign out on the testing center's daily log.

During the exam, you are permitted to step out of the testing room to stretch, get a drink of water, use the restroom, etc. You will be required to sign out and then back in each time.

PREPARING FOR THE CMA/CFM EXAMS

HOW MANY PARTS TO TAKE

We suggest that you take one part at a time. Currently, you have 3 years within which to pass all four parts of either the CMA or the CFM exam. If you pass parts after the June 1997 exam, you will be given credit until 3 years after these parts were passed.

CMA/CFM Part 1:	Economics, Finance, and Management
Part 2CMA:	Financial Accounting and Reporting
Part 2CFM:	Corporate Financial Management
CMA/CFM Part 3:	Management Reporting, Analysis, and Behavioral Issues
CMA/CFM Part 4:	Decision Analysis and Information Systems

Parts 2 and 3 cover many of the accounting and finance topics included in typical undergraduate accounting/finance programs. Part 1 covers the material found in management, microeconomics, macroeconomics, and corporate finance courses. Part 4 covers computer systems, quantitative methods, and statistics courses.

STEPS TO EXAM SUCCESS (THEY REALLY WORK!)

1. Study this "Introduction" carefully. Then study each of the 10 study units one at a time.
2. Using *CMA/CFM Test Prep* software, in test mode, create and answer a 20-question "assessment" test from each study unit before studying the study unit.
3. Study the knowledge transfer outline in this book for that study unit.
4. Take two or three more 20-question tests in test mode after studying knowledge transfer outlines.
5. After EACH of these 20-question test sessions, immediately switch to study mode and select questions "missed on last session" so you can analyze why you answered each question incorrectly.
6. Continue the process until you reach your desired proficiency on each study unit, e.g., 75%.
7. Modify the process to suit your individual learning process.
8. Attend and plan on passing your CMA/CFM exams.

STUDY PLAN, TIME BUDGET, AND CALENDAR

Complete one study unit at a time. Initially, budget 3 to 4 hours per study unit (1 to 2 hours studying the outline and 1 to 2 minutes each on all the multiple-choice questions).

This Introduction	2
10 study units at 3.5 hours each	35
General review	3
Total Hours	40

Each week you should evaluate your progress and review your preparation plans for the time remaining prior to the exam. The CMA/CFM calendar on page 15 will assist you in preparing for the pilot testing period which begins December 1, 1997 and ends February 28, 1998. Review your commitments, e.g., out-of-town assignments, personal responsibilities, etc., and note them on your calendar. This precaution will assist you in keeping to your schedule.

CONTROL

You have to be in control to be successful during exam preparation and execution. Control can also contribute greatly to your personal and other professional goals. Control is a process whereby you

1. Develop expectations, standards, budgets, and plans.
2. Undertake activity, production, study, and learning.
3. Measure the activity, production, output, and knowledge.
4. Compare actual activity with expected, or budgeted.
5. Modify the activity, behavior, or production to better achieve the desired outcome.
6. Revise expectations and standards in light of actual experience.
7. Continue the process.

The objective is to be confident that the best possible performance is being generated. Most accountants study this process in relation to standard costs, i.e., establish cost standards and compute cost variances.

Every day you rely on control systems implicitly. When you groom your hair, you have expectations about the desired appearance of your hair and the time required to style it. You monitor your progress and make adjustments as appropriate, e.g., brush it a different way or speed up.

Develop and enforce standards in all of your endeavors. Exercise control, implicitly or explicitly. Most endeavors will improve with explicit control. This is particularly true with certification examinations and other academic tests.

1. Practice your question answering techniques (and develop control) as you prepare answers/solutions to practice questions/problems during your study program.
2. Develop explicit control over your study programs based on the control process discussed previously.
3. Think about using more explicit control systems over any and all of your endeavors.
4. Seek continuous improvement to meet your needs given a particular situation or constraint. Additional practice will result in further efficiencies.

1997-1998 CMA/CFM CALENDAR

	Sun	Mon	Tues	Wed	Thurs	Fri	Sat
SEPT		1	2	3	4	5	6
	7	8	9	10	11	12	13
	14	15	16	17	18	19	20
	21	22	23	24	25	26	27
OCT	28	29	30	1	2	3	4
	5	6	7	8	9	10	11
	12	13	14	15	16	17	18
	19	20	21	22	23	24	25
NOV	26	27	28	29	30	31	1
	2	3	4	5	6	7	8
	9	10	11	12	13	14	15
	16	17	18	19	20	21	22
	23	24	25	26	27	28	29
DEC	30	1 Pilot Testing Period Begins	2	3	4	5	6
	7	8	9	10	11	12	13
	14	15	16	17	18	19	20
	21	22	23	24	25	26	27
JAN	28	29	30	31	1	2	3
	4	5	6	7	8	9	10
	11	12	13	14	15	16	17
	18	19	20	21	22	23	24
	25	26	27	28	29	30	31
FEB	1	2	3	4	5	6	7
	8	9	10	11	12	13	14
	15	16	17	18	19	20	21
	22	23	24	25	26	27	28 Pilot Testing Period Ends

SYLVAN TECHNOLOGY CENTERS: Part of the Sylvan Learning Center Network

ALABAMA
Birmingham
Decatur
Mobile
Montgomery

ALASKA
Anchorage

ARIZONA
Tucson
Phoenix
  Chandler

ARKANSAS
Ft. Smith
Little Rock

CALIFORNIA
Fresno
Los Angeles
  Diamond Bar
  Rancho Cuc.
  Redlands
  Riverside
  Santa Monica
  Torrance
  Westlake
Orange County
  Anaheim Hills
  Brea/Fullerton
  Garden Grove
  Irvine
Sacramento
  Fair Oaks
San Diego
  La Jolla
San Francisco
  Burlingame
  Oakland
  Walnut Creek
San Jose
Santa Rosa

COLORADO
Boulder
Colorado Sprgs
Denver
  Littleton
Pueblo

CONNECTICUT
Hartford
  Glastonbury
New Haven
  Hamden

DELAWARE
Dover

FLORIDA
Daytona Beach
  Ormond Bch
Gainesville
Jacksonville
Miami Metro
  Davie
  Miami Lakes

FLORIDA (cont'd)
West Palm Beach
  Wellington
Sarasota
Tallahassee
Tampa
  Temple Terr.
Orlando
  Winter Park

GEORGIA
Atlanta Metro
  Jonesboro
  Smyrna
Augusta
Macon
Savannah

HAWAII
Oahu
  Kailua
Maui
  Wailuku

IDAHO
Boise

ILLINOIS
Bloomington
Carbondale
Chicago Metro
  Carpentersville
  Chicago
  Homewood
  Northbrook
  Westchester
Peoria
Springfield

INDIANA
Evansville
Ft. Wayne
Merrillville
Indianapolis
Layfayette
South Bend
  Mishawaka

IOWA
Bettendorf
Cedar Rapids
W. Des Moines

KANSAS
Topeka
Wichita

KENTUCKY
Lexington
Louisville

LOUISIANA
Baton Rouge
Shreveport
  Bossier City
New Orleans

MAINE
South Portland

MARYLAND
Baltimore Metro
  Columbia
  Pikesville
Bethesda
Frederick

MASSACHUSETTS
Boston Metro
  Boston
  Woburn
Springfield
Worcester

MICHIGAN
Ann Arbor
Grand Rapids
Lansing
Detroit Metro
  Troy
  Utica
  Livonia

MINNESOTA
Duluth
Minn-St. Paul
  Bloomington
  Maplewood

MISSISSIPPI
Jackson

MISSOURI
Kansas City
  Gladstone
Springfield
St. Louis
  Ballwin
  Creve Coeur

MONTANA
Billings
Helena

NEBRASKA
Lincoln
Omaha

NEVADA
Las Vegas
Reno

NEW HAMPSHIRE
Concord

NEW JERSEY
East Brunswick
Newark Metro
  Verona
Toms River
Trenton
  Hamilton Town

NEW MEXICO
Albuquerque

NEW YORK
Albany
Buffalo
  Amherst
Long Island
  Garden City
New York City
  Queens
  Staten Island
Poughkeepsie
  Wappgrs Falls
Rochester
Syracuse
  Fayetteville
  Vestal

NORTH CAROLINA
Asheville
Charlotte
Greensboro
Greenville
Raleigh

NORTH DAKOTA
Bismarck

OHIO
Akron
Cincinnati-North
Cleveland Metro
  Mentor
  Solon
  Strongsville
Columbus
  Reynoldsburg
Dayton
Toledo
Youngstown
  Niles

OKLAHOMA
Oklahoma City
Tulsa

OREGON
Eugene
Portland

PENNSYLVANIA
Allentown
Erie
Harrisburg
Philadelphia
  Center City
Pittsburgh
  North Hills
Scranton
North Wales

RHODE ISLAND
Providence
  Cranston

SOUTH CAROLINA
Charleston
Irmo
Greenville

SOUTH DAKOTA
Sioux Falls

TENNESSEE
Chattanooga
Knoxville
Memphis
Nashville
  Madison

TEXAS
Amarillo
Austin
Beaumont
Corpus Christi
Dallas Metro
  Arlington
  Fort Worth
  Mesquite
El Paso
Houston
  Clearlake
  West Univ.
Longview
Lubbock
Midland
San Antonio
Waco

UTAH
Orem
Salt Lake City

VERMONT
Williston

VIRGINIA
Arlington
Richmond
Roanoke
Newport News

WASHINGTON
Seattle
  Lynnwood
Spokane
Tacoma
  Puyallup

WASHINGTON, DC

WEST VIRGINIA
Charleston
Morgantown

WISCONSIN
Madison
Milwaukee
  Brookfield

WYOMING
Casper

After you register to take each part of the CMA/CFM exams and pay $80, the ICMA will send you a letter with an authorization number and instructions on contacting Sylvan to schedule your test. Call your local Sylvan testing center a day or two before your test to confirm your time and obtain directions to the testing center. A listing of Sylvan testing centers is presented on page 16.

INSTRUCTIONS TO CANDIDATES

The letter accompanying these instructions is your authorization to schedule the taking of CMA/CFM Part 1 with Sylvan Technologies. If you registered for additional parts of the CMA/CFM Examinations, information regarding these parts will be sent to you under separate cover. Questions regarding your registration with ICMA should be directed to 800-638-4427, ext. 301.

Scheduling with Sylvan Technologies

The interval dates shown on your authorization letter represent the 60-day window during which you are authorized to take CMA/CFM Part 1. To schedule your examination, please call Sylvan Technologies at 800-479-6370 at least 48 hours before you would like to take the examination. Be sure you have your authorization number from the accompanying letter handy when you call as you will be required to provide this number. In addition, please choose a Sylvan Technology Center from the list shown on the reverse of this sheet. You must schedule your examination during this 60-day period as your authorization will lapse at the end of the period, and your fees will be forfeited.

General Instructions

- Be sure to arrive at the Sylvan Technology Center on time. If you are more than 30 minutes late, you may lose your scheduled sitting and be required to reschedule at a later date.
- You will be required to sign the Sylvan Log Book when you enter the center.
- You are required to present a photo identification with signature for examination admission. Approved IDs are a passport, driver's license, military ID, credit card with photo, or company ID. Student IDs are **not** acceptable. You will not be permitted into the examination without proper photo identification.
- Lockers are available at the test centers for personal belongings. Items such as purses, briefcases, and jackets will not be allowed in the testing room.
- Small battery or solar powered electronic calculators restricted to a maximum of six functions - addition, subtraction, multiplication, division, square root, and percent - are allowed. The calculator must be non-programmable and must not use any type of tape. Memory must erase when the calculator is turned off. Candidates **will not** be allowed to use calculators that do not comply with these restrictions.
- On request, candidates will be provided with scrap paper which will be counted by the test center personnel when given to candidates and will also be counted when collected from candidates. Candidates should bring pencils or pens to the test center for use in making calculations, etc., on scrap paper.
- The staff at the Sylvan Technology Centers are not involved in grading your examination. Please do not contact them for information about your performance. Examination results will be mailed from the ICMA in April 1998 for CFM Parts 1, 3, and 4 and CMA Parts 1 through 4 taken from December 1, 1997 through February 28, 1998. On-demand testing of all parts will begin on May 1, 1998.

PURPOSE OF ANSWERING PRACTICE QUESTIONS

You are attempting to improve your question answering skills, NOT to learn the answers to all of the Gleim/Flesher questions (which will probably NOT appear in your test). Keep track of your progress with 20-question "tests" in *CMA/CFM Test Prep* software. Immediately after each practice test, switch from "test mode" to "study mode" and create a study session to analyze why you missed each question you answered incorrectly. This is essential: Make and understand your mistakes while studying SO YOU AVOID MISTAKES WHEN YOU TAKE YOUR EXAM.

MULTIPLE-CHOICE QUESTION ANSWERING TECHNIQUE

1. **Budget your time.**
   a. We make this point with emphasis. Just as you should fill up your gas tank prior to reaching empty, you should finish your exam before time expires.
   b. You have 180 minutes to answer 120 questions, i.e., 1.5 minutes per question. We suggest you attempt to answer eight questions every 10 minutes, which is 1.25 minutes per question. This would result in completing 120 questions in 150 minutes to give you 30 minutes to review questions that you have marked. (See 3.c.2) for a brief discussion of marking questions at Sylvan.)
   c. On your Sylvan computer screen, the time remaining (starting with 150 minutes) appears at the upper right of your screen.
2. **Answer the questions in chronological order.**
   a. Do **not** agonize over any one question. Stay within your time budget.
   b. It is not necessary to "mark" unanswered questions. Sylvan provides options to review both unanswered questions and marked questions.
3. **For each question**
   a. **Read the question** stem carefully (the part of the question that precedes the answer choices) to determine the precise requirement.
      1) Focusing on what is required enables you to ignore extraneous information and to proceed directly to determining the correct answer.
         a) Be especially careful to note when the requirement is an **exception**; e.g., "When markets are perfectly competitive, all of the following are true **except**:."
   b. **Determine the correct answer** before reading the answer choices. The objective is to avoid allowing the answer choices to affect your reading of the question.
      1) When four answer choices are presented, three of them are incorrect. They are called **distractors** for a very good reason.
      2) **Read each answer choice** with close attention.
         a) Even if answer (A) appears to be the correct choice, do **not** skip the remaining answer choices. Answer (B), (C), or (D) may be better.
         b) Treat each answer choice as a true-false question.
   c. **Select the best answer**. The answer is selected by either pressing the answer letter on your keyboard or by using your mouse. Select the most likely or best answer choice. If you are uncertain, make an educated guess.
      1) The CMA/CFM does not penalize guessing because your score is determined by the number of correct responses. Thus, you should answer every question.
      2) As you answer a question, you can mark it by pressing "M" or unmark a marked question by pressing "M." After you have answered, marked, or looked at and not answered all 120 questions, you will be presented with a summary screen that shows how many questions you did not answer and how many you marked. You then have the option of revisiting all of the unanswered questions and "marked" questions.

4. **Questions answered incorrectly.** Learning from questions you answer incorrectly is very important. Each question you answer incorrectly is an opportunity to avoid missing actual test questions on your CMA/CFM exam. This study technique is clearly the difference between passing and failing for CMA/CFM candidates.

   You **must** determine why you answered questions incorrectly and learn how to avoid the same error in the future. Reasons for missing questions include

   a. Misreading the requirement (stem)
   b. Not understanding what is required
   c. Making a math error
   d. Applying the wrong rule or concept
   e. Being distracted by one or more of the answers
   f. Incorrectly eliminating answers from consideration
   g. Not having any knowledge of the topic tested
   h. Employing bad intuition (Why?) when guessing

5. Sylvan Computer Screen Layout

Question 10 of 120	YOUR NAME	Time remaining: 02:51

The sky is ______________

O A. blue

O B. brown

O C. green

O D. silver

Directions: Select the best answer

← Previous   Next →   Mark   ? Help

NOTE: A menu offering a number of options is displayed at the bottom of the question screen. The options enable you to view the previous question or the next question, mark a question to be revisited, or request help. You may select an option by pressing the appropriate symbol key or highlighted letter on your keyboard or by clicking on the symbol or letter with your mouse.

1) View the previous question by indicating the letter **P** or the left arrow key.
2) View the next question by indicating the letter **N** or the right arrow key.
3) Mark a question by indicating the letter **M**.
4) Request help by indicating the question mark.

USE GLEIM *CMA/CFM TEST PREP* SOFTWARE. It emulates the SYLVAN testing procedures and environment including computer screen layout, software operation, etc.

TAKING THE CMA/CFM EXAMS

CMA/CFM EXAMINATIONS CHECKLIST

1. Acquire your study materials. Rely on this book and *CMA/CFM Test Prep* software. It's all you need!
2. **Apply** for membership in the IMA (see pages 440 and 441) and for admission to the ICMA (pages 442 and 443).
3. **Register** to take the desired part of the exam using the examination registration form (page 444) and send it with your applications to the ICMA. Take one part at a time. When you register and pay $80 for a part, you have 60 days to take the part. Upon receipt of authorization to take the exam, call SYLVAN to schedule your test.
4. Plan your preparation process. It's easy. You have 10 study units to complete.
5. Orderly, controlled preparation builds confidence, reduces anxiety, and produces success!
6. PASS THE EXAMINATION (study this Introduction)!

LOGISTICAL AND HEALTH CONCERNS

As soon as the ICMA sends you a computer-based test authorization, call and schedule your test at a convenient time and convenient Sylvan testing center. In almost all cases, you should be able to drive to your testing site, take the test, and return home in one day. If the exam is not being given within driving distance of your home, call Sylvan Technology Centers to inquire about accommodations. Stay by yourself at a hotel to be assured of avoiding distractions. The hotel should be soundproof and have a comfortable bed and desk suitable for study. If possible, stay at a hotel with recreational facilities you normally use, e.g., a swimming pool.

Proper exercise, diet, and rest in the weeks before you take your exam are very important. High energy levels, reduced tension, and an improved attitude are among the benefits. A good aerobic fitness program, a nutritious and well-balanced diet, and a regular sleep pattern will promote your long-term emotional and physical well-being as well as contribute significantly to a favorable exam result. Of course, the use of health-undermining substances should be avoided.

EXAM PSYCHOLOGY

Plan ahead and systematically prepare. Then go to the exam and give it your best: neither you nor anyone else can expect more. Having undertaken a systematic preparation program, you will do fine.

Maintain a positive attitude and do not become depressed if you encounter difficulties either before or during the exam. An optimist will usually do better than an equally well-prepared pessimist. Remember, you have reason to be optimistic because you will be competing with many less qualified persons who have not prepared as well as you have.

CALCULATORS

Calculators **are** permitted on the CMA/CFM exams. Only simple six-function calculators are permitted (i.e., addition, subtraction, multiplication, division, square root, percent). You should be thoroughly experienced in the operations of your calculator. Make sure it has fresh batteries just prior to the examination.

1. Consider bringing a backup calculator with you.
2. The calculator must be small, quiet, and battery- or solar-powered so it will not be distracting to other candidates.
3. The calculator may have a memory. However, the memory must be temporary and erase when the memory is cleared or the calculator is turned off.
4. The calculator must not use any type of tape.
5. The calculator must be nonprogrammable.
6. Nonconforming calculators and calculator instruction books are **not** permitted.
7. The CMA/CFM examinations will continue to be designed so that a calculator is not necessary for solving the problems within the estimated time.

EXAMINATION TACTICS

1. Remember to bring your authorization and entry cards and a valid photo ID to the exam site. The photo ID requirement is **strictly** enforced.
2. Arrive at the site a few minutes early to have a margin of safety. Your appointment may be canceled if you are 30 minutes late.
3. Dressing for exam success means emphasizing comfort, not appearance. Be prepared to adjust for changes in temperature, e.g., to remove or put on a sweater.
4. Do not bring notes, this text, other books, etc., into the Sylvan testing center. You will only make yourself nervous and confused by trying to cram the last 5 minutes before the exam. Books are not allowed in the testing room, anyway. You should, however, bring an appropriate calculator.
5. Adequate scratch paper and pencils are provided. You must turn in your scratch paper as you leave the exam site. Any breath mints, gum, etc., should be in your pocket as they may distract other persons taking the test.
6. As soon as you complete the exam, we would like you to e-mail, fax, or write to us with your comments on our books and software. We are particularly interested in which topics need to be added or expanded in our books and software. We are NOT asking about specific CMA/CFM questions; rather we are asking for feedback on our books and software.

RECAP OF CMA/CFM PART 1 EXAM COVERAGE*

ICMA Major Topics and Percent Coverage	Gleim/Flesher Study Units
A. Microeconomics--10%-15% (Level B)]	1. Microeconomics
B. Macroeconomics--10%-15% (Level A)	2: Macroeconomics
C. International Business Environment--10%-15% (Level B)	3: International Business Environment
D. Domestic Institutional Environment of Business--10%-15% (Level A)	4: Domestic Institutional Environment of Business
E. Working Capital Policy and Management--10%-15% (Level C) F. Long-term Finance and Capital Structure--10%-15% (Level B)	5: Working Capital Finance 6: Capital Structure Finance 7: Risk
G. Organizational Structures, Management, and Communication--20%-30% (Level B)	8: Organizational Theory 9: Motivation and the Directing Process 10: Communication

GO FOR IT!
IT'S YOURS TO PASS!

***WARNING!!!**

About 25% of Part 1 test questions will require mathematical calculations. All other parts are approximately 50% computational questions. Practice computational questions to prepare for exam success!

Study Unit 1: MICROECONOMICS

21 pages of outline
60 multiple-choice questions

Microeconomics is the study of the individual economic units in the economy. The focus is on the consumer (as buyer of finished goods and seller of labor, entrepreneurial services, and capital) and the firm (as seller of finished goods and buyer of labor, entrepreneurial services, and capital). Microeconomics also includes the operation of markets.

The relative weight range assigned to microeconomics in Part 1 is 10% to 15%. Expect 12 to 18 questions.

A. Overview of Economics

1. **Economics** is the social science addressing the allocation of scarce resources among competing or alternative ends.
    a. Individuals face an economic problem when deciding how to spend limited income to maximize satisfaction.
    b. The economy faces an economic problem in deciding how to allocate fixed resources (land, labor, capital, and entrepreneurial ability) to achieve maximum social welfare.
2. Economics is based on
    a. The unlimited nature of human wants
    b. Scarcity of resources or means to satisfy wants, i.e., the law of scarcity
3. Every economic system (capitalistic, socialistic, etc.) must answer the following questions:
    a. What goods and services should be produced?
    b. How much of these goods and services should be produced?
    c. How should these goods and services be produced?
    d. For whom should these goods and services be produced?
4. **Macroeconomics Distinguished from Microeconomics**
    a. **Macroeconomics** -- the study of economic aggregates and an overview of the economy, including levels of national income, employment, and prices and the effects of monetary and fiscal policies. Macroeconomics is covered in the next study unit.
    b. **Microeconomics** -- the study of the individual economic units in the economy. Again, focus is on the consumer (as buyer of finished goods and seller of labor, entrepreneurial services, and capital) and the firm (as seller of finished goods and buyer of labor, entrepreneurial services, and capital).
5. Stop and review! You have completed the outline for this subunit. There are no multiple-choice questions in this subunit.

B. Demand

1. Demand -- the Buyer's Side of the Market

a. Demand is the quantity of a good or service that consumers are willing and able to purchase at various prices during a period of time. Thus, demand is a schedule of amounts that will be purchased at various prices.

b. **The law of demand**. The price of a product and the quantity demanded are inversely (negatively) related; i.e., the lower the price, the higher the quantity demanded.

   1) **Substitution effect**. With a price decrease, new buyers will enter the market. The good will be cheaper relative to other goods and is substituted for them.

   2) **Income effect**. Individuals buy more when prices are lower.

c. The determinants of demand are variables that affect the amount of a product purchased.

   1) Consumer income

      a) **Normal goods** -- commodities for which demand is positively (directly) related to income, e.g., steak, clothes, leisure time

      b) **Inferior goods** -- commodities for which demand is negatively (inversely) related to income, e.g., potatoes, bread

   2) Consumer taste and preference
   3) Prices of closely related goods (cross-elasticity of demand)

      a) **Substitutes**. If products A and B are substitutes, a price increase in A will generate an increase in the demand for B. For example, when beef prices rise, the demand for chicken increases.

      b) **Complements**. If products A and B are complements, a price increase in A will generate a decrease in the demand for B. For example, if the price of bread increases, the demand for jelly decreases.

   4) Consumer expectations. Do consumers expect incomes and prices to rise or fall?

   5) Number of consumers

d. The demand schedule is a relationship between the prices of a commodity (on the vertical axis) and the quantity demanded at the various prices (horizontal axis), holding other determinants of the quantity demanded constant.

   1) A movement along an existing demand curve occurs when the price is changed.

   2) **Demand curve shift**. A change in quantity demanded must be distinguished from a shift in the demand curve itself. The latter occurs when one of the determinants changes. The graph on the following page illustrates an increase in demand; i.e., the demand curve shifts from D to D_1.

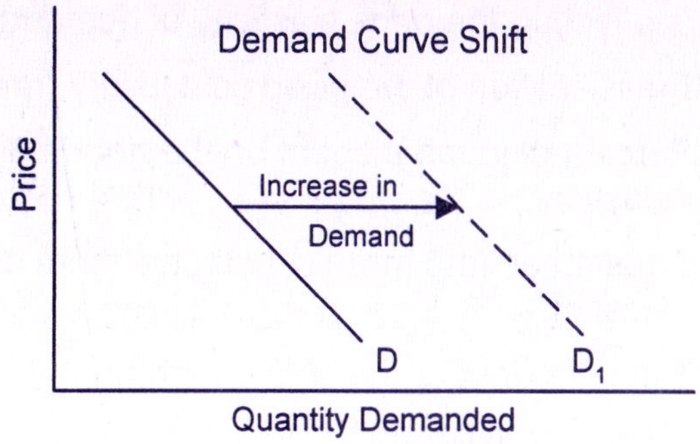

e. Such an increase in demand for commodity A (a shift in the demand schedule outward or to the right) can be caused by

1) A favorable change in the tastes and preferences of consumers toward commodity A (e.g., resulting from a successful advertising campaign)
2) An increase in consumer income, if A is a normal good
3) A decrease in consumer income, if A is an inferior good
4) An increase in the price of commodity Y, if Y is a substitute for A
5) A decrease in the price of commodity X, if X is a complement for A
6) The expectation of future price increases
7) The end of a group boycott

f. A decrease in demand for commodity A (a shift in the demand schedule inward or to the left) can be caused by the opposite of the factors listed above.

2. **Elasticity**

a. **Price elasticity of demand** (E_d) is the percentage change in quantity demanded divided by the percentage change in price.

1) $$E_d = \frac{\textit{Percentage change in quantity demanded}}{\textit{Percentage change in price}}$$

2) It measures responsiveness of a change in quantity demanded to a change in the price of a product. For a demand schedule obeying the law of demand (downward sloping), the elasticity coefficient (E) is negative, but when interpreting E_d, the absolute value is ordinarily used.

3) But the numerator and denominator are computed as the change over the average, which results in the same percentage regardless of whether there is an increase or a decrease.

$$\frac{\%\Delta Q}{\%\Delta P} = \frac{(Q_1 - Q_2) \div \dfrac{(Q_1 + Q_2)}{2}}{(P_1 - P_2) \div \dfrac{(P_1 + P_2)}{2}}$$

4) Factors affecting the price elasticity of demand are
   a) Classification of the good as a luxury (more elastic) or a necessity
   b) Percent of income spent on the goods (the larger the %, the more elastic)
   c) Substitutes (the more substitutes there are for a good, the more elastic)
   d) Time (the longer the time period analyzed, the more elastic)
5) If the elasticity coefficient is
   a) Greater than one, demand is classified as elastic.
   b) Less than one, demand is classified as inelastic.
   c) Equal to one, demand is classified as having unitary elasticity.
   d) Equal to zero, demand is classified as being perfectly inelastic.
6) In other words, if demand is elastic, it will change considerably relative to the size of a price change.
7) The relationship between price changes and total revenue (TR) changes is TR = price x quantity. It is summarized in the following table:

	E > 1	E < 1	E = 1
Price up	TR down	TR up	TR same
Price down	TR up	TR down	TR same

   a) EXAMPLE: Roxy's Bar sells 100 pitchers of beer a night at $2 each. One night Roxy decides to run a sale on beer and charges only $1 per pitcher. At that price, she sells 300 pitchers. The coefficient of elasticity, as determined by the formula, is

$$\frac{\textit{Percentage change in quantity demanded}}{\textit{Percentage change in price}} = \frac{1}{2/3} = \frac{3}{2} = 1.5$$

   because

$$\frac{300\ \textit{pitchers} - 100\ \textit{pitchers}}{200\ \textit{pitchers}} = 1 \qquad \frac{\$2 - \$1}{\$1.50} = \frac{2}{3}$$

   Since the coefficient is 1.5, demand at that point is said to be elastic. So, if the price is lowered to $1, total revenue will increase.
8) The concept of price elasticity is of considerable practical concern to the management accountant because a knowledge of the elasticity of the price of a particular product tells the accountant whether a price increase or decrease is required to increase total revenue.
9) Increases in sales and excise taxes, etc., are most easily passed on to the buyer when demand is inelastic.

b. **Cross-elasticity of demand** measures the percentage change of one commodity demanded with a given percentage change in price of another commodity.

1) The cross-elasticity coefficient (E_{xy}) is found by using the following equation:

$$E_{xy} = \frac{\%\Delta Q_x}{\%\Delta P_y} = \frac{\textit{Percentage change in Quantity demanded of good X}}{\textit{Percentage change in Price of good Y}}$$

2) If the coefficient is

   a) Positive, the two commodities are substitutes (see the example below).

   b) Negative, the two commodities are complements.

   c) Zero, they are unrelated.

3) EXAMPLE: The price of orange soda goes up 20%, and the demand for root beer increases 10%. Therefore, orange soda and root beer are substitutes.

$$E_{xy} = \frac{10\%}{20\%} > 0$$

4) Cross-elasticity of demand can be used to define a market and determine appropriate marketing strategy. In addition, the information can be used to determine what and how much to produce.

c. **Income elasticity of demand** measures percentage change in quantity demanded for a given percentage change in income. The income elasticity (E_I) is found using the following equation:

$$E_I = \frac{\%\Delta Q}{\%\Delta I} = \frac{\textit{Percentage change in Quantity demanded}}{\textit{Percentage change in Income}}$$

1) If the coefficient is

   a) Greater than zero, the good is considered a normal good. This means that if income rises, consumption of the good rises.

   b) Less than zero, the good is considered an inferior good. This means that if income rises, consumption of the good decreases.

2) EXAMPLE: Income goes up 20%, and the demand for diamonds goes up 15%. Diamonds are normal goods; i.e., as people earn more, they purchase more diamonds.

$$E_I = \frac{15\%}{20\%} > 0$$

3. **Utility Theory**

a. Utility theory helps to explain why the demand curve is downward sloping. A rational individual's objective is to maximize total utility from his/her income. This result is reached when the utility obtained from the last dollar spent on each commodity purchased is the same.

b. Utility maximization can be expressed mathematically as

$$\frac{\textit{Marginal utility of A}}{\textit{Price of A}} = \frac{\textit{Marginal utility of B}}{\textit{Price of B}}$$

c. When the utility maximization formula holds, an individual has consumed in an optimal fashion. Given a certain or fixed income, higher utility could not have been achieved.

d. There are two ways to measure utility:

1) **Cardinal** -- numerically assign values of utils received from any good. A "util" is any arbitrary unit of worth.

2) **Ordinal** -- establish a ranking among goods, without assigning specific units of worth

e. **Principle of diminishing marginal utility**. Equal increments of additional consumption of a good result in successively smaller additions of utility to the consumer. Thus, when a person is thirsty, the first glass of water tastes great, the second less so, and the third even less.

f. **Indifference curves** are all combinations of goods X and Y (e.g., wine and cheese) that give equal utility to a consumer. The farther the indifference curve is from the origin, the higher the level of utility. Hence, any point on I_3 below represents greater utility than any point on I_1 or I_2

1) Indifference curves are nonlinear because of the principle of diminishing marginal utility. If consumers obtained equal amounts of utility from equal amounts consumed, irrespective of the ratio of X to Y, the indifference curves would be straight lines.

2) Indifference curves cannot intersect, are negatively sloped, and are convex to the origin.

3) The graph below depicts indifference curves (continuums of indifference points for bundles of goods).

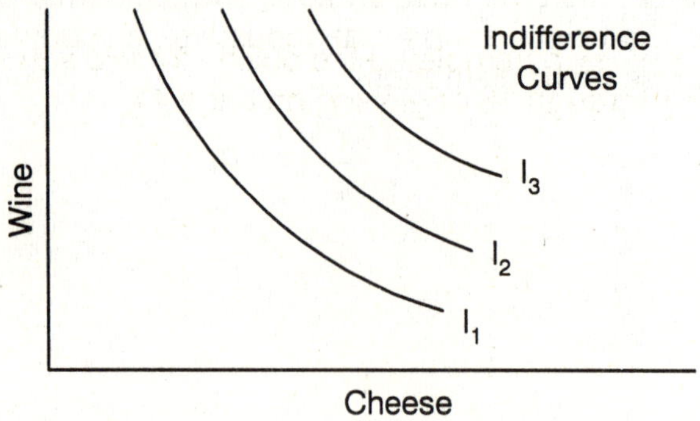

g. A **budget constraint line** depicts all combinations of two goods that can be purchased with a given income at the given prices of the two goods.

1) The budget constraint is a straight line because its slope is constant.

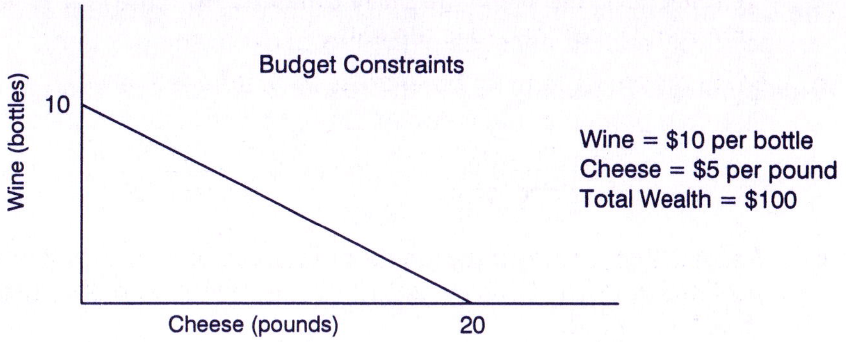

2) Properties of budget constraints include the following:

a) A change in income causes a parallel shift in the budget constraint.

b) A change in the price of one or both goods causes a change in slope of the budget constraint.

c) If the relative prices of both goods change proportionately, a parallel shift in the budget line occurs.

h. Utility is maximized when the budget line is tangent to the highest possible indifference curve. At that point, the individual receives the highest level of utility possible, given a fixed income.

1) In the following diagram, utility is maximized at point E, where the budget constraint line is tangent to the indifference curve.

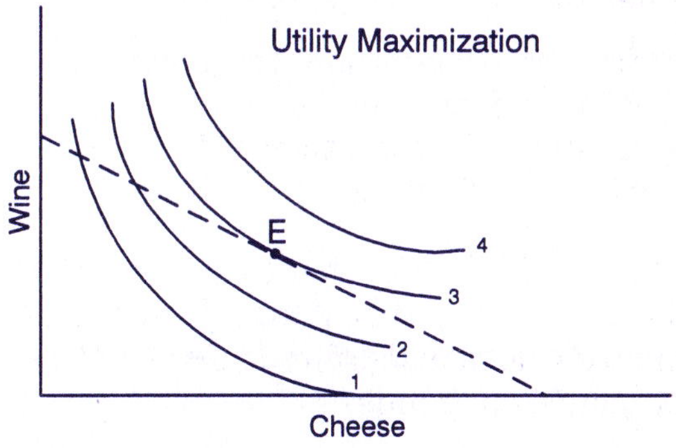

4. Stop and review! You have completed the outline for this subunit. Study multiple-choice questions 1 through 16 beginning on page 44.

C. Supply

1. **Supply** is the amounts of a good or service that producers are willing and able to offer to the market at various prices during a specified period of time.
2. **The Law of Supply**. In the short run, the price of the product and the quantity supplied are positively related because of the law of diminishing returns.
3. **Price elasticity of supply** (E_s) is the responsiveness of a change in the quantity supplied to a percentage change in the price of the commodity.
   a. $$E_s = \frac{\textit{Percentage change in quantity supplied}}{\textit{Percentage change in price}}$$
   b. Factors that affect supply elasticity include
      1) Cost and feasibility of storage
         a) EXAMPLE: A high cost of storage results in low elasticity because, as the price of carrying a good increases, the tendency to hold that good decreases.
      2) Characteristics of the production process
         a) EXAMPLE: The supply elasticity of a joint product may be affected by the demand for the other joint products.
      3) Time
         a) EXAMPLE: Production of goods, i.e., the ability to supply them, becomes more elastic with time.
   c. A perfectly inelastic supply curve has an elasticity of zero. Thus, it occurs only when a firm cannot vary the quantity it supplies. A perfectly inelastic supply curve is depicted as a vertical line.
4. The **determinants of supply** are the variables that affect the amount supplied.
   a. Production prices
   b. Technology
   c. Prices of other goods
   d. Price expectations
   e. Taxes and subsidies
5. The **supply schedule** is a relationship between the price of a good (on the vertical axis) and the quantity supplied to the market (horizontal axis) at each price, holding other determinants of the quantity supplied constant. A change in the price of a commodity is represented as a movement along the supply schedule.
   a. **Supply curve shift.** A change in the quantity supplied must be distinguished from a shift in the supply curve itself. The latter is caused by a change in one of the determinants. The graph illustrates an increase in supply, which shifts the line from S to S_1.

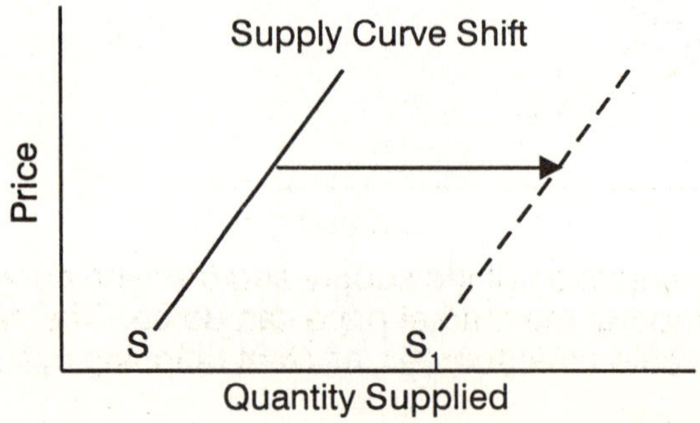

6. An increase in supply for commodity A (a shift in the supply schedule to the right) can be caused by changes in the determinants.
   a. A decrease in a factor of the production price
   b. An improvement in technology
   c. A decrease in the demand for another commodity (B), inducing firms to divert resources from the production of B to A
   d. The expectation of future price decreases
   e. A decrease in taxation of a good or an increase in subsidization
7. A decrease in supply can be caused by the opposite of the above determinants.
8. In the short run, certain costs are fixed regardless of output. Given that fixed costs are incurred even if the firm shuts down, the firm gains in the short run by continuing to operate if revenues exceed variable costs. Accordingly, the firm's short-run supply curve is derived from the marginal cost curve (the firm produces until MR = MC). It consists of the part of the marginal cost curve above the average variable cost curve.
9. **Market supply** is the sum of the individual supply curves of all sellers in the market.
10. **Economic Rent**. If any input is paid a higher amount than it would receive from the next highest bidder for that input, economic rent is said to be earned. When economic rent is earned, an input is being paid more than is necessary to keep the input employed in production. For example, a $5,000,000-a-year baseball player is earning economic rent of $4,950,000 if the player could earn only $50,000 per year in another occupation.
    a. But if the supply of a resource is fixed (e.g., land), the entire price paid is deemed to be a surplus (economic rent) because a change in price will not affect total supply (the productive potential of the economy).
11. Stop and review! You have completed the outline for this subunit. Study multiple-choice questions 17 through 23 beginning on page 49.

D. Market Equilibrium and Pricing

1. The market is the interaction of buyers and sellers brought into contact with one another to engage in purchases and sales of economic goods.
2. **Equilibrium** between price and output is the point at which the demand and supply curves intersect. The graph illustrates the concept of market equilibrium, i.e., the intersection of a supply and demand curve.

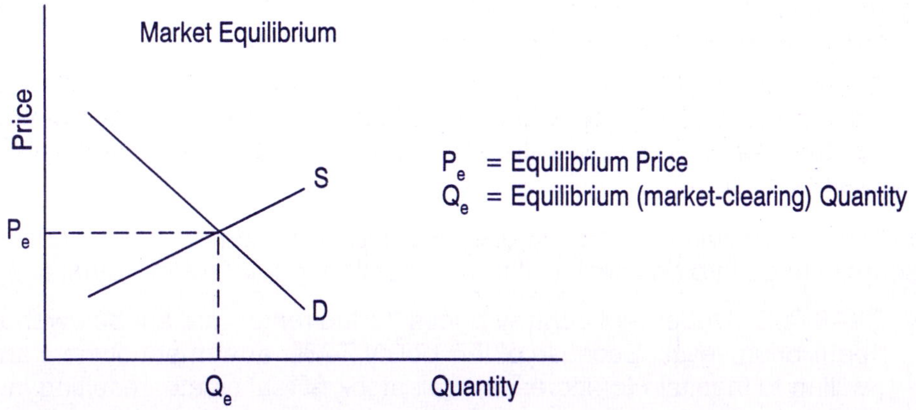

3. At the point of intersection of the supply and demand curves, anyone wishing to purchase the good at the market price can do so. The market forces of supply and demand thus create an automatic, efficient rationing system.

a. Economic goods are scarce resources because they are demanded by the consumer, but exist in insufficient supply to satisfy all demands for them.

4. **Price fixing** is the setting of mandatory or artificial prices. It often interferes with the free operation of the market. Attempts to alter the output and price can have an effect on equilibrium.

   a. **Price ceiling**. Price is established below the equilibrium price, causing shortages to develop (e.g., rent control). The usual result is nonprice competition among buyers (waiting lines are one form), which allocates the quantity that is supplied.

      1) The graph below depicts a shortage resulting from an artificially low price.

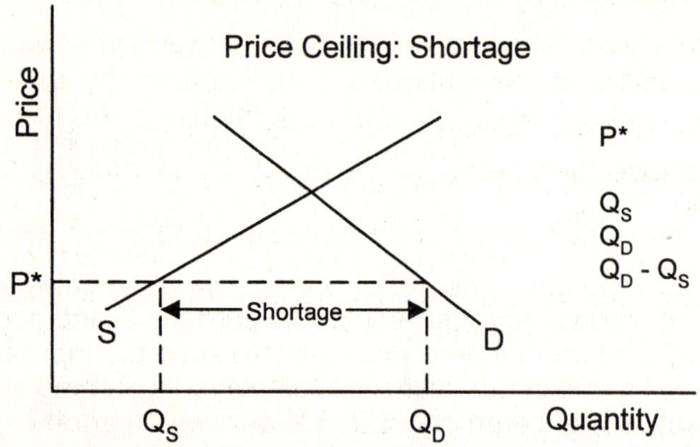

P* = Artificial ceiling set by government (price not allowed to go above this ceiling)
Q_S = Quantity supplied at P*
Q_D = Quantity demanded at P*
$Q_D - Q_S$ = Amount of shortage

   b. **Price floor**. A minimum price is set above the equilibrium price, causing surpluses to develop (e.g., many agricultural products).

      1) The graph below illustrates a surplus because of an artificially high price.

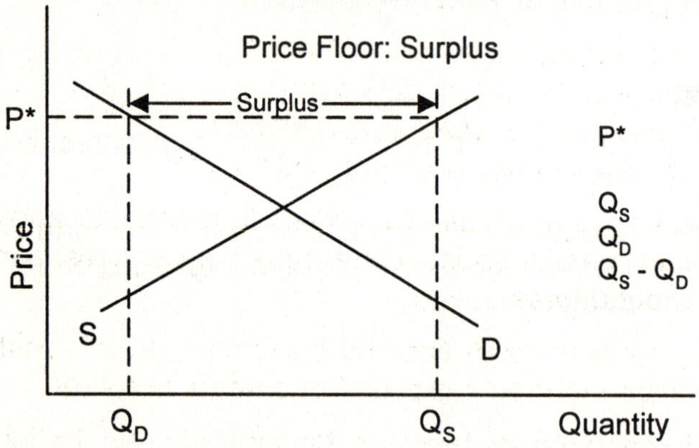

P* = Artificial price floor set by government (price not allowed to go below the floor)
Q_S = Quantity supplied at P*
Q_D = Quantity demanded at P*
$Q_S - Q_D$ = Amount of surplus

5. The pricing system acts to efficiently allocate economic goods to consumers willing to pay for them. When a shortage exists, the market price will rise and the quantity demanded will decrease, eliminating the shortage.

6. Attempts to circumvent the market often interfere with market forces, causing too many resources to go into one sector of the economy and too few into others.

   a. EXAMPLE: Under rent control, prices (to the renter) are set below their true equilibrium level. Because of this policy, fewer apartment owners are likely or willing to maintain (or increase) their stock of real estate, resulting in under-investment in the housing sector.

7. **The Impact on Equilibrium of Shifts in the Supply and Demand Schedules**
   a. An increase in supply (demand held constant) will decrease the equilibrium price and increase the equilibrium quantity.
   b. A decrease in supply (demand held constant) will increase the equilibrium price and decrease the equilibrium quantity.
   c. An increase in demand (supply held constant) will increase the equilibrium price and increase the equilibrium quantity.
   d. A decrease in demand (supply held constant) will decrease the equilibrium price and the equilibrium quantity.
   e. Simultaneous shifts in supply and demand and their resulting effects on equilibrium can be summed up as follows:
      1) An increase (decrease) in demand and supply will cause the equilibrium quantity to increase (decrease), but the effect on the equilibrium price is indeterminable.
      2) An increase (decrease) in demand and a decrease (increase) in supply will cause the equilibrium price to increase (decrease), but the effect on the equilibrium quantity is indeterminable.
8. Stop and review! You have completed the outline for this subunit. Study multiple-choice questions 24 through 29 beginning on page 51.

E. Production and Costs of Economic Resources

1. **Production and Costs in the Short Run**
   a. Factors of production (inputs) are often classified as follows:
      1) Land, which receives the return called **rent**
      2) Labor, which receives the return called **wages**
      3) Capital, which receives the return called **interest**
      4) Management, which receives the return called **profit**
   b. Other factors of production, which can be derived from the four above, include governmental services, capital goods, entrepreneurial services, and research and development expenditures.
   c. The short-run supply curve is determined by the firm's marginal cost curve because fixed costs are incurred if production is not undertaken.
   d. The distinction in microeconomics between the short run and the long run
      1) The short run is a time period so brief that a firm has insufficient time to vary the amount of all inputs. Thus, the quantity of one or more inputs is fixed.
      2) The long run is a time period long enough for all inputs, including plant capacity, to be varied.

e. Economic decisions are based on marginal analyses of output, revenue, profit, etc.

1) **Marginal revenue (MR)** is the additional revenue obtained by increasing output by one unit.

2) **Marginal cost (MC)** is the addition to total cost as a result of increasing production by one unit.

3) **Marginal profit** is marginal revenue minus marginal cost.

4) **Marginal product** (or marginal physical product) is the additional output obtained by adding one extra input (e.g., additional oranges picked by adding one more worker).

5) **Marginal resource cost (MRC)** is the change in the total cost of a resource used divided by the change in quantity.

6) **Marginal revenue product (MRP)** equals the change in total revenue from using one more unit of a resource.

f. **The law of diminishing returns.** If increasing amounts of a variable input are applied to a fixed input, beyond some point additional units of the variable input will contribute less and less to the total product (marginal product will decline).

1) The law of diminishing returns governs the optimal (profit-maximizing) use of variable inputs.

a) A firm should produce the output for which MR equals MC. Similarly, a firm should demand additional resources until MRP equals MRC. Moreover, the MRP schedule for a resource is the firm's demand curve for that resource. The curve slopes downward because of diminishing marginal productivity.

2) The following is a graph of returns to an input:

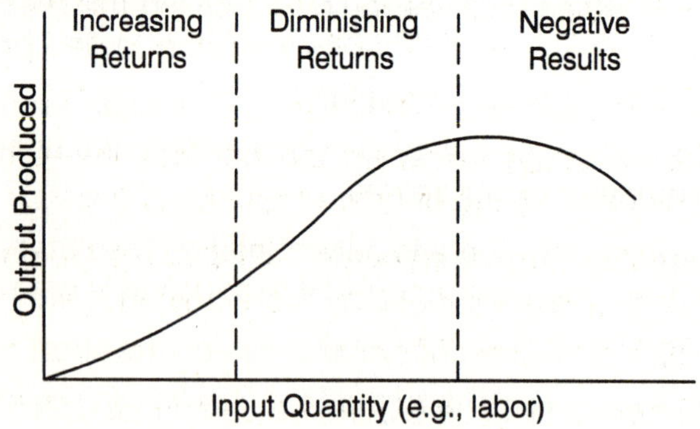

g. Classification of costs

1) **Fixed costs** -- costs that do not change with the level of output
2) **Variable costs** -- costs that vary with output
3) **Total cost** -- the sum of fixed and variable costs
4) **Average fixed costs** -- total fixed costs divided by output
5) **Average variable costs** -- total variable costs divided by output
6) **Average total costs** -- the sum of average fixed costs and average variable costs for a given output
7) **Explicit (historical) costs** -- (as determined by accountants) the actual expenditures made in producing a product
8) **Implicit costs** -- the amounts that would have been received if self-owned resources had been used outside the firm's business. Thus, the lease payments forgone by not renting the firm's building to others is an implicit cost.
9) **Opportunity costs** -- amounts of any activity or product that must be forgone to perform the chosen activity or produce the chosen product
10) **Normal profit** -- the implicit cost of keeping entrepreneurial skills in the organization
11) **Economic cost** -- the payments a firm must make or the incomes the firm must provide to a supplier to attract a resource away from an alternative use. The payments or incomes may be either explicit or implicit.
    a) Total revenue minus all economic costs equals **economic profit (pure profit)**.
12) **Sunk costs** -- previously committed costs not relevant to future costs
13) **Technological efficiency** -- the relationship between the physical output of a given technology and the maximum output that is possible

2. **Production and Costs in the Long Run**

a. Because all inputs are variable in the long run, the relationship between input and output is dictated by the degree of returns to scale.

1) **Increasing returns to scale** -- if all inputs are changed by the same factor (k), but output changes by more than (k) (e.g., if all inputs are doubled and output more than doubles)
2) **Decreasing returns to scale** -- if all inputs are changed by the same factor (k), but output changes by less than (k)
3) **Constant returns to scale** -- if all inputs are changed by the same factor (k) and output also changes by the same factor (k)

b. The long-run average-cost curve is U-shaped because of economies and diseconomies of scale.

1) **Economies of scale**. Initially, as most firms expand output, average costs of production tend to decline. Some of the reasons are
    a) Increased specialization and division of labor
    b) Better use and specialization of management
    c) Use of more efficient machinery and equipment

2) **Diseconomies of scale**. Eventually, as most firms continue to expand output, the marginal cost of production tends to increase. The most frequent reason given for diseconomies of scale is the difficulty of managing a large-scale enterprise.

3) The following graph illustrates a long-run average-cost curve:

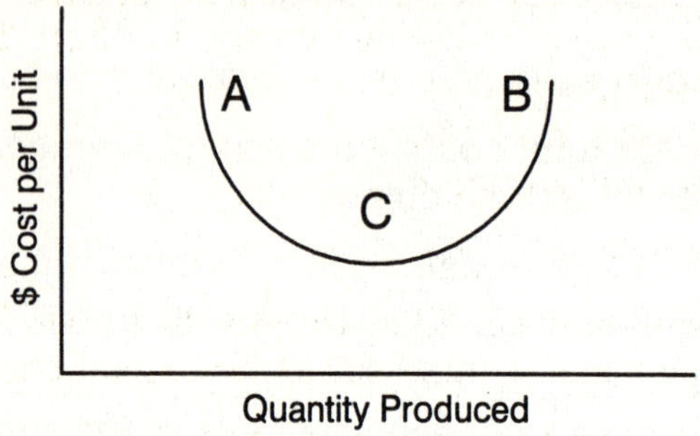

a) A represents increasing returns to scale (or decreasing marginal cost).
b) B represents decreasing returns to scale (or increasing marginal cost).
c) C represents constant returns to scale (or constant marginal cost).

c. Relationships of marginal cost and average cost

1) When average cost is rising, marginal cost is above it.

2) When average cost is falling, marginal cost is below it.

3) Average cost = marginal cost whenever average cost is at a minimum or a maximum.

4) The following graph shows these relationships:

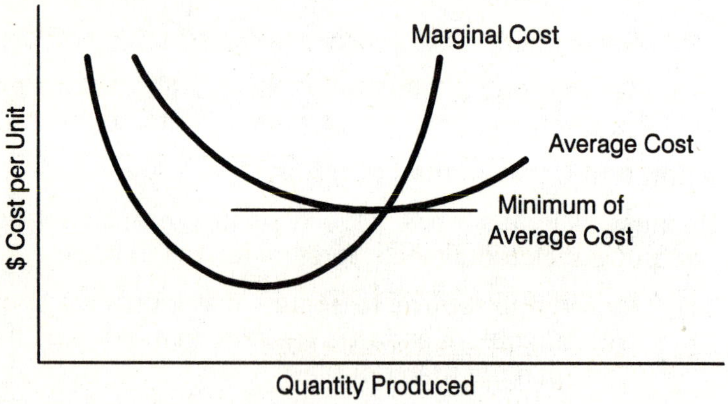

d. Technological changes result in higher costs and lower profits in older plants.

1) Technological efficiency is impaired when the ratio of the physical output of a given technology and the maximum output that is possible declines.

e. An important consideration in the **minimum efficient scale**, which is the output at which long-run average cost is minimized. When great economies of scale are possible, long-run average cost is minimized only at very high levels of output. Hence, efficiency will be achieved only by a few very large firms. In contrast, if economies of scale are easily attained, and diseconomies of scale quickly occur, the industry will usually consist of many small firms.

3. Stop and review! You have completed the outline for this subunit. Study multiple-choice questions 30 through 41 beginning on page 53.

F. Market Structure

1. Pure (Perfect) Competition

a. Assumptions

1) Large number of buyers and sellers acting independently
2) Homogeneous or standardized product
3) Firms having free entry into and exit from the market (no barriers to entry)
4) Perfect information
5) No control over prices
6) No nonprice competition

b. Short-run analysis

1) The demand schedule is perfectly elastic (horizontal) because the firm is a price taker. It must sell at the market price.

2) For profit maximization, the firm equates price and marginal cost. If price is less than average variable cost, the firm should shut down (to minimize losses).

c. The following graph shows a competitive firm in the short run:

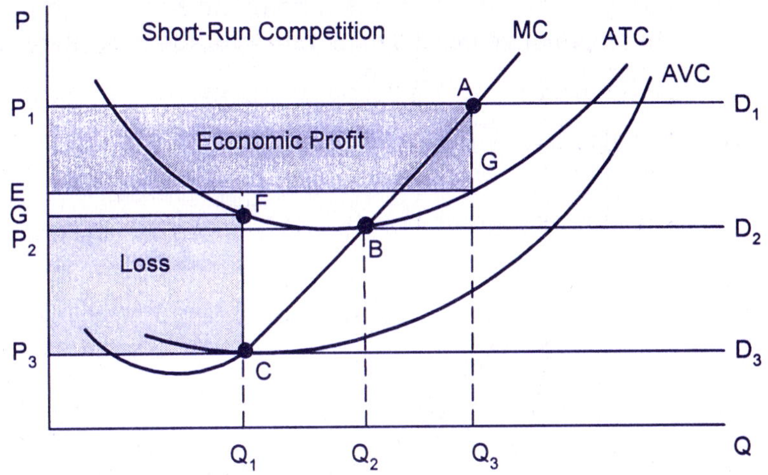

1) MC = marginal cost

2) ATC = average total cost

3) AVC = average variable cost

4) D = demand

5) P_1 P_2 P_3 represent alternative prices.
   D_1 D_2 D_3 represent resulting demand.
   Q_1 Q_2 Q_3 represent related quantities produced.

6) Point A represents maximum profit given price P_1.

7) Point B represents the breakeven point where fixed and variable costs are covered.

8) Q_2 is the long-run equilibrium quantity.

9) C is the point below which the firm must close down because it will not recover its variable costs.

d. Long-run analysis

1) On the graph on the previous page, the firm is making an economic profit [(P_1 – ATC) per unit x Q_3, that is, the area P_1AGE] given demand at D_1 and price at P_1. In the long run, because profits are available, more firms will enter, eventually driving the price down to P_2, where no economic profits occur. If the demand is at D_3, the firm is taking a loss [(ATC – P_3) per unit x Q_1, that is, the area P_3GFC], which will lead to firms dropping out of the industry, eventually causing price to rise to P_2 again.

2) The standard theory assumes that all firms are equally efficient. This means that the minimum point on the average total cost curve is the same for all firms. Consequently, when entry causes price to equal the minimum of the average total cost, no firms are earning economic profits. However, if there are more efficient producers with lower average total cost curves, these will earn economic profits in the long run.

3) Because price equals marginal cost, allocation of resources is optimal.

4) Firms produce the ideal output, the output at which average cost is lowest.

5) Price is lower and output greater than in any other market structure.

6) The following graph shows a competitive firm in long-run equilibrium. Because price equals minimum average cost at the optimal output, no economic profit is earned.

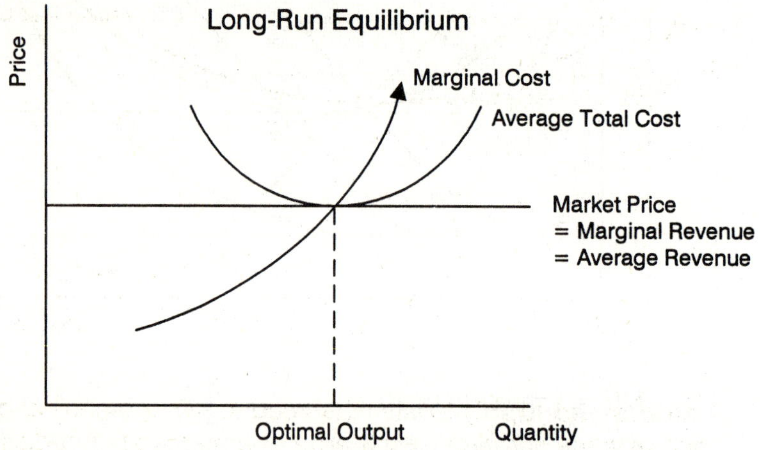

2. **Pure Monopoly**

a. Assumptions

1) Single firm
2) Unique product with no close substitutes
3) Blocked entry of other firms
4) Significant price control
5) Goodwill advertising

b. The demand curve is negatively sloped. Thus, marginal revenue lies below demand and is negatively sloped.

c. For profit maximization, the firm equates marginal revenue with marginal cost unless price is less than average variable cost (the shutdown case).

d. Blocked entry allows the monopolist to earn an economic profit in the long run, given sufficiently low costs and adequate demand.

e. Price exceeds marginal cost. Thus, resources are underallocated.

f. The firm produces less than the ideal output.

g. Price is higher and output lower than in pure competition.

h. The following compares monopoly with pure competition. The monopolist, by setting MR equal to MC (point M), earns an economic profit in the long run (area P_MAGE). The competitor sets P_C (MR in pure competition) equal to MC (point C) and earns no economic profit in the long run.

Monopoly vs. Competition

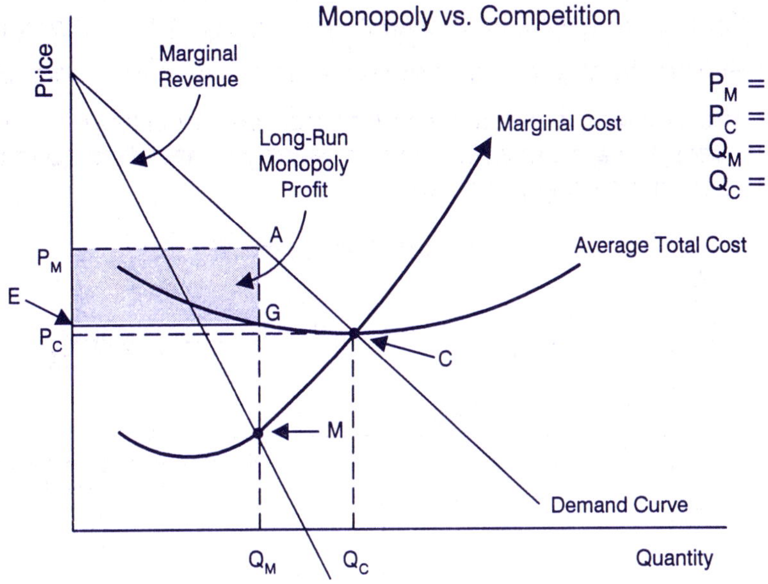

P_M = Monopoly Price
P_C = Competitive Price
Q_M = Monopoly Output
Q_C = Competitive Output

i. A **natural monopoly** exists when economic or technical conditions permit only one efficient supplier. Very large operations are needed to achieve low unit costs and prices (economies of scale are great). Thus, the long-term average cost of meeting demand is minimized when the industry has one firm.

3. **Monopolistic Competition**

   a. Assumptions

      1) Large number of firms that act noncollusively
      2) Differentiated products
      3) Relatively easy entry into market
      4) Some price control
      5) Large amounts of nonprice competition (advertising, brands, etc.)

   b. The demand curve is negatively sloped and MR lies below demand and is also negatively sloped.

   c. For profit maximization, the firm equates MR and MC, unless price is less than average variable cost (the shutdown case).

   d. Firms may incur losses or earn economic profits in the short run. In the long run, firms tend to earn a normal profit.

   e. Price exceeds marginal cost. Thus, resources are underallocated.

   f. Price exceeds average total cost, indicating productive inefficiency (output does not reach the lowest-unit-cost level).

   g. Firms produce less than the ideal output, and the industry is populated by too many firms that are too small. These conditions are often referred to as the waste of monopolistic competition.

   h. Price is higher and output less than in pure competition.

4. **Oligopoly**

   a. Assumptions. The oligopoly model is much less specific than the previous three market structures, but the following are common assumptions:

      1) Few firms. The decisions of rivals do not go unnoticed.

      2) Products can be differentiated (autos) or standardized (steel).

      3) Prices tend to be rigid (sticky) because of the interdependence among firms.

      4) Entry is difficult because of entry barriers, which can be

         a) Natural, e.g., an absolute cost advantage
         b) Created, e.g., ongoing advertising, patents

   b. The short-run and long-run analyses are indeterminate because of the effect of each company on the other companies.

   c. The price rigidity normally found in oligopolistic markets can be explained in part by the **kinked demand curve** theory. Because competitors respond to price changes by one of the firms in an oligopolistic industry, the demand curve for an oligopolist tends to be kinked.

      1) If other firms do not match a price decrease by an oligopolist, it will capture more of the market. If other firms match the price decrease, less of the market will be captured.

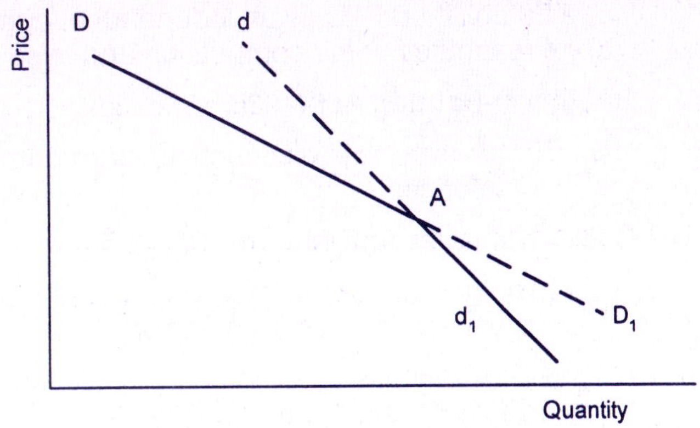

If: DD_1 is the firm's demand curve when competitors do not respond to changes in the current price (A).

dd_1 is the firm's demand curve when competitors match any price changes.

Dd_1 is the firm's demand curve when competitors do not respond to increases in the current price but do respond to price decreases.

d. **Price leadership** is typical in oligopolistic industries. Under price leadership, price changes are announced first by a major firm in the industry. Once the industry leader has spoken, everyone else in the industry matches the price charged by the leader.

e. A **cartel** arises when a group of oligopolistic firms join together for price-fixing purposes. This practice is illegal except in international markets. For example, the international diamond cartel DeBeers has successfully maintained the market price of diamonds for many years by incorporating into the cartel almost all major diamond-producing sources.

f. Oligopolistic industries include automobiles and steel.

5. **Government's Role in Maintaining Market Structure and Performance**

a. The two evils of monopoly power are

1) Higher price for the product (compared to perfect competition)
2) Lower quantity produced (compared to perfect competition)

b. Monopoly power decreases as the number of firms increases. Therefore, antitrust policy seeks to limit monopoly power and promote competition.

c. The following laws form the basis of public control in the United States:

1) **Sherman Act** (1890)

a) Prohibits restraint of trade and monopolies in interstate and foreign trade, e.g., price fixing, boycotts, dividing markets, restrictions on resale, etc.

2) **Clayton Act** (1914)

a) Prohibits the acquisition of stock of competitors (merger) if the result might be a tendency to lessen competition

b) Prohibits price discrimination

c) Keeps directors of one company from sitting on the board of a competitor

3) **Federal Trade Commission Act** (1914)

a) Established FTC as an independent agency
b) Prosecutes unfair competition and false or misleading advertising

4) **Robinson-Patman Act** (1936)

a) Prohibits special discounts to large purchasers unless based on cost differences

5) **Celler-Kefauver Anti-Merger Act** (1950)

a) Prohibits any corporation from acquiring the assets of another if the effect is to reduce competition

6) Also see the discussion of antitrust regulation in Study Unit 4, Domestic Institutional Environment of Business.

d. The effect of the size of a business on competition is a much-debated topic. Arguments for and against big business include the following:

1) For big business

a) A larger scale operation is necessary for innovation (e.g., a large company can afford more research and development).

b) Economies of scale

2) Against big business

a) Inequitable flow of wealth to firms with market power

b) Expansion of output restrictions

c) Lack of incentive for innovation by a large company that may be able to afford it

e. One major way firms become large is through mergers. The three types are

1) **Vertical mergers** -- union of two companies, one of which supplies inputs (e.g., raw materials) for the other

2) **Horizontal mergers** -- union of two companies that engage in the same or similar activities

3) **Conglomerate mergers** -- union of two unrelated companies

f. Two approaches to formulating and implementing antitrust policy are

1) Performance

a) Market performance
b) Rate of technological growth
c) Efficiency and profit

2) Industry market structure

a) Number and size of competitors
b) Distribution of buyers and sellers
c) Ease of entry
d) Product differentiation

g. **Concentration ratio** is the percentage of an industry's output produced by its four largest firms. Statistical studies often rely on the concentration ratio as a measure of monopoly market power in an industry. One disadvantage of the concentration ratio is that it does not measure the allocation of market power when an industry consists of only a few firms.

1) The **Herfindahl index** addresses this issue. It equals the sum of the squared market shares of the firms in the industry. The larger the index, the greater the market power in the industry.

h. **Taxes**

1) License fee -- a lump-sum tax that must be paid if a firm is to operate

a) **Short-run effect**. The tax raises average cost but does not change marginal cost. Thus, the firm's output decision remains unchanged.

b) **Long-run effect**. In a competitive industry, firms are not making profits after the tax. Some firms leave the industry. The industry price is higher, and total industry output is lower.

2) Profits tax. This tax does not change the firm's revenue or cost functions. This implies that the output to maximize pretax profits also maximizes after-tax profits. Hence, a firm's optimal output is unchanged.

3) Per-unit tax. This tax, e.g., sales, excise, and value-added taxes, creates a difference between demand price (what consumers are willing to pay) and the price a firm receives. The effect is to decrease marginal revenue. The firm's response is to lower the quantity produced by moving down the marginal cost curve.

i. Governmental action is sometimes anticompetitive. Examples are

1) Patent, copyright, trademark, and trade name protection

2) Price supports, such as for certain agricultural commodities, or price ceilings, e.g., on utility rates

3) Licensing of television and radio stations

4) Tariffs, import quotas, and other restrictions on foreign producers' access to domestic markets

5) Costs driven up by governmental regulation

6) Larger, more established companies benefiting by governmental spending

6. Stop and review! You have completed the outline for this subunit. Study multiple-choice questions 42 through 60 beginning on page 57.

MULTIPLE-CHOICE QUESTIONS AND ANSWER EXPLANATIONS

A. Overview of Economics -- no multiple-choice questions

B. Demand

1. The local video store's business increased by 12% after the movie theater raised its prices from $6.50 to $7.00. This is an example of

A. Substitute goods.

B. Superior goods.

C. Complementary goods.

D. Public goods.

The correct answer is (A). *(CMA, adapted)*

REQUIRED: The type of goods for which sales increase when the price of another good is raised.

DISCUSSION: The increase in prices at the movie theater caused consumers to demand fewer movies at the theater and more movies at the video store (where prices were unchanged). Thus, cross-elasticity of demand existed because the percentage change in quantity demanded of videos was correlated with the percentage change in the price of movie theater tickets. The correlation was positive, so the goods are substitutes.

Answer (B) is incorrect because superior (normal) goods are defined as those for which demand is positively correlated with income. Answer (C) is incorrect because sales of a complementary good are negatively correlated with changes in the price of its complement. For example, sales of tennis balls decrease with an increase in tennis racquet prices. Answer (D) is incorrect because public goods are characterized by the difficulty of excluding individuals from their benefits. Examples are national defense and public parks.

2. All of the following are complementary goods except

A. Margarine and butter.

B. Cameras and rolls of film.

C. VCRs and video cassettes.

D. Razors and razor blades.

The correct answer is (A). *(CMA, adapted)*

REQUIRED: The pair that does not represent complementary goods.

DISCUSSION: Goods or services are complements if the price change of one has an inverse relationship to the demand for the other. For example, when the price of one good increases, the demand for a complementary good decreases. Margarine and butter, however, are substitutes and their relationship is direct. When the price of one good increases, demand for a substitute good also increases.

Answers (B), (C), and (D) are incorrect because cameras and rolls of film, VCRs and video cassettes, and razors and razor blades are all examples of complementary products. For instance, when the price of VCRs decreases, people demand more video cassettes.

3. A decrease in the price of a complementary good will

A. Shift the demand curve of the joint commodity to the left.

B. Increase the price paid for a substitute good.

C. Shift the supply curve of the joint commodity to the left.

D. Shift the demand curve of the joint commodity to the right.

The correct answer is (D). *(CMA, adapted)*

REQUIRED: The effect of a decrease in the price of a complementary good.

DISCUSSION: A decrease in the price of a complementary good (e.g., gasoline) will cause the demand curve of the joint commodity (e.g., automobiles) to shift to the right (increase). The lower price results in greater demand by consumers at each price level. A movement along an existing demand curve occurs when the price for the product is changed but demand is constant.

Answer (A) is incorrect because a shift to the left (a decrease in demand) would occur if the price of a complementary product increased. Answer (B) is incorrect because demand for a substitute would decrease, thereby lowering its equilibrium price. Answer (C) is incorrect because the demand curve will shift to the right, but the supply curve will not change.

4. The demand curve for a normal good is

A. Upward sloping because firms produce more at higher prices.

B. Upward sloping because higher-priced goods are of higher quality.

C. Vertical.

D. Downward sloping because of the income and substitution effects of price changes.

The correct answer is (D). *(CMA, adapted)*

REQUIRED: The true statement about the demand curve for a normal good.

DISCUSSION: The demand curve for a consumer good (normal or inferior) is downward sloping to the right. At high prices, the amount demanded is relatively low. As prices decrease, the quantity demanded increases. The substitution effect is the change in the cost of a good relative to others that will cause a cheaper good to be substituted for more expensive ones. The income effect is the change in purchasing power experienced by consumers as a result of a price change (real income increases or decreases). Both of these effects cause the price of a product and the quantity demanded to be inversely related.

Answers (A) and (B) are incorrect because the demand curve is downward sloping. Answer (C) is incorrect because a vertical demand curve signifies that the quantity demanded does not change with price.

5. The Waymand family typically ate hamburger as a staple in their diet. In the last few years, the family's income has doubled, and they have now replaced hamburger with steak as a staple in their diet. This is an example in which the demand for hamburger

A. Is relatively elastic.

B. Is perfectly elastic.

C. Is relatively inelastic.

D. Responds as an inferior good.

The correct answer is (D). *(CMA, adapted)*

REQUIRED: The true statement about a change in the demand for hamburger as income rises.

DISCUSSION: Consumers purchase more (less) of a normal good (such as steak) at every price when income levels increase (decrease). The opposite is true of inferior goods (such as hamburger). These effects result because normal goods have a positive income elasticity of demand and inferior goods have a negative income elasticity. Income elasticity of demand equals the percentage change in quantity demanded divided by the percentage change in income.

Answers (A), (B), and (C) are incorrect because no information is given about the effects of changes in the price.

6. Which one of the following would cause the demand curve for a commodity to shift to the left?

A. A rise in the price of a substitute product.

B. A rise in average household income.

C. A rise in the price of a complementary commodity.

D. A change in consumers' tastes in favor of the commodity.

The correct answer is (C). *(CMA, adapted)*

REQUIRED: The event causing the demand curve to shift to the left.

DISCUSSION: The demand curve is the relationship between the prices of a commodity (vertical axis) and the quantity demanded at the various prices (horizontal axis), holding other determinants of demand constant. A movement along an existing demand curve occurs when the price is changed. A shift in a demand curve may occur when one of the determinants changes. A shift to the left represents a decline in demand. A leftward shift may be caused by an unfavorable change in the tastes and preferences of consumers, a decline in consumer income (if the commodity is a normal good), a decrease in the price of a substitute good, an increase in the price of a complementary product, or the expectation of future price decreases.

Answers (A), (B), and (D) are incorrect because a rise in the price of a substitute, a rise in income, and a favorable change in consumers' tastes cause the demand curve to shift to the right.

7. The movement along the demand curve from one price-quantity combination to another is called a(n)

A. Change in demand.

B. Shift in the demand curve.

C. Change in the quantity demanded.

D. Increase in demand.

The correct answer is (C). *(CMA, adapted)*

REQUIRED: The term for a movement along a demand curve from one price-quantity combination to another.

DISCUSSION: The demand curve represents the relationship between the prices of a commodity and the quantity demanded at those prices, holding other determinants of the quantity demanded constant. Movement along a demand curve reflects a change (increase or decrease) in the quantity demanded.

Answers (A) and (D) are incorrect because a change in demand (increase or decrease) causes the demand curve to shift. Changes in demand can occur as a result of changes in consumer income, in the price of substitute or complementary products, in the number of consumers, or in the tastes and preferences of consumers. Answer (B) is incorrect because a shift in the demand curve represents changes attributable to something other than price.

8. If a group of consumers decide to boycott a particular product, the expected result would be

A. An increase in the product price to make up lost revenue.

B. A decrease in the demand for the product.

C. An increase in product supply because of increased availability.

D. That demand for the product would become completely inelastic.

The correct answer is (B). *(CMA, adapted)*

REQUIRED: The expected result of a consumer boycott of a particular product.

DISCUSSION: A group boycott will decrease the demand for a product (shift the demand curve to the left). This decrease in demand should lead to a lower price for the product assuming that supply is constant (the supply curve does not shift).

Answer (A) is incorrect because reduced demand will drive the price downward. Answer (C) is incorrect because supply remains unchanged in the short run. Answer (D) is incorrect because, if demand is inelastic, customers will continue buying the product regardless of the price; a boycott, however, means that consumers will stop buying the product.

9. Long Lake Golf Course has raised greens fees for a nine-hole game due to an increase in demand.

	Previous Rate	New Rate	Average Games Played at Previous Rate	Average Games Played at New Rate
Regular weekday	$10	$11	80	70
Senior citizen	6	8	150	82
Weekend	15	20	221	223

Which one of the following is correct?

A. The regular weekday and weekend demand is inelastic.

B. The regular weekday and weekend demand is elastic.

C. The senior citizen demand is elastic, and weekend demand is inelastic.

D. The regular weekday demand is inelastic, and weekend demand is elastic.

The correct answer is (C). *(CMA, adapted)*

REQUIRED: The true statement about the elasticity of greens fees as indicated by changes in demand related to higher rates.

DISCUSSION: The price elasticity of demand is the percentage change in quantity demanded divided by the percentage change in price. If the elasticity coefficient is greater than one, demand is elastic. If the coefficient is less than one, demand is inelastic. If elasticity is calculated as the change over the average, the ccefficient for senior citizens indicates that demand is elastic.

$$\frac{(150 - 82) \div [(150 + 82) \div 2]}{(8 - 6) \div [(8 + 6) \div 2]} = 2.05$$

The coefficient for weekends indicates that demand is inelastic.

$$\frac{(223 - 221) \div [(223 + 221) \div 2]}{(20 - 15) \div [(20 + 15) \div 2]} = .03$$

Answer (A) is incorrect because weekday demand is elastic. Answer (B) is incorrect because weekend demand is inelastic. Answer (D) is incorrect because weekday demand is elastic, and weekend demand is inelastic.

10. In a competitive market for labor in which demand is stable, if workers try to increase their wage,

A. Employment must fall.

B. Government must set a maximum wage below the equilibrium wage.

C. Firms in the industry must become smaller.

D. Product supply must decrease.

The correct answer is (A). *(CMA, adapted)*

REQUIRED: The effect in a competitive labor market of an increase in wages.

DISCUSSION: In a competitive market for labor in which demand is stable, total wages cannot increase. If some workers do increase their wages, the increases can occur only if some workers are laid off. Given a stable demand curve for labor, a higher price for this resource will result in a decrease in the amount of labor demanded (a movement up the demand curve).

Answer (B) is incorrect because a maximum wage that is lower than the equilibrium wage will not allow workers to increase their wages. Answer (C) is incorrect because firms may choose to become more capital intensive rather than smaller. Answer (D) is incorrect because supply will not decrease if workers are more productive after gaining an increase in wages.

11. If a diabetic must have insulin no matter what the cost, the diabetic's demand is considered to be

A. Perfectly elastic.

B. Perfectly inelastic.

C. Relatively inelastic.

D. Indifferent.

The correct answer is (B). *(CMA, adapted)*

REQUIRED: The elasticity of the demand for insulin.

DISCUSSION: Price increases can most easily be passed along to consumers when demand is inelastic. If the demand coefficient is less than 1.0, the percentage change in quantity demanded is less than the percentage change in price. If demand does not change at all (i.e., an elasticity of zero), as may be true of insulin, the demand for the product is perfectly inelastic.

Answer (A) is incorrect because demand is elastic when the coefficient exceeds 1.0. Answer (C) is incorrect because demand is relatively inelastic when the coefficient is greater than 0.0 but less than 1.0. Answer (D) is incorrect because the appropriate technical term is perfectly inelastic.

12. If a product has a price elasticity of demand of 2.0, the demand is considered to be

A. Perfectly elastic.

B. Perfectly inelastic.

C. Relatively elastic.

D. Relatively inelastic.

The correct answer is (C). *(CMA, adapted)*

REQUIRED: The meaning of a price elasticity of demand of 2.0.

DISCUSSION: The price elasticity of demand measures the responsiveness of a change in quantity demanded to a change in the price of a product. It equals the percentage change in quantity demanded divided by the percentage change in price. If the demand coefficient is greater than 1.0, demand is elastic. If the coefficient is less than 1.0, demand is inelastic. If the elasticity coefficient is exactly 1.0, demand has unitary elasticity.

Answer (A) is incorrect because an elasticity of 2.0 is relatively elastic, not perfectly elastic. Answers (B) and (D) are incorrect because an elasticity coefficient greater than 1.0 is elastic.

13. As the price for a particular product changes, the quantity of the product demanded changes according to the following schedule.

Total Quantity Demanded	Price per Unit
100	$50
150	45
200	40
225	35
230	30
232	25

The price elasticity of demand for this product when the price decreases from $50 to $45 is

A. 0.20

B. 10.00

C. 0.10

D. 3.80

The correct answer is (D). *(CMA, adapted) 694 1-3)*

REQUIRED: The calculation of the price elasticity of demand.

DISCUSSION: A product's price elasticity of demand is measured as the percentage change in quantity demanded divided by the percentage change in price. If elasticity is determined by calculating percentage changes over the average, the price elasticity is

$$\frac{(150 - 100) \div [(150 + 100) \div 2]}{(\$50 - \$45) \div [(\$50 + \$45) \div 2]} = 3.8$$

Answer (A) is incorrect because 0.20 equals the 10% decline in price divided by the 50% change in quantity demanded. Answer (B) is incorrect because 10.00 assumes a 5% change in price; the correct decline in price is 10%. It also does not calculate the change over the average. Answer (C) is incorrect because 0.10 is the percentage change in price.

14. The law of diminishing marginal utility states that

A. Marginal utility will decline as a consumer acquires additional units of a specific product.

B. Total utility will decline as a consumer acquires additional units of a specific product.

C. Declining utils cause the demand curve to slope upward.

D. Consumers' wants diminish with the passage of time.

The correct answer is (A). *(CMA, adapted) 696 1-4)*

REQUIRED: The true statement about the law of diminishing marginal utility.

DISCUSSION: The principle of diminishing marginal utility states that equal increments of additional consumption of a product result in smaller additions of utility to the consumer. For example, a glass of water on a hot day tastes great, the second glass less so, and the third even less.

Answer (B) is incorrect because total utility will increase with additional units of product, but the increases are at a declining rate; the principle applies to marginal utility, not total utility. Answer (C) is incorrect because diminishing marginal utility results in a downward-sloping demand curve. Answer (D) is incorrect because the utility principle applies not to time but to additional units of product.

15. In the theory of demand, the marginal utility per dollar of a product

A. Increases when consumption expands.

B. Decreases when consumption expands.

C. Explains why short-run supply curves are upward sloping.

D. Increases as more units of a variable input are added to the production process.

The correct answer is (B). *(CMA, adapted) 1292 1-5)*

REQUIRED: The true statement about marginal utility per dollar of product.

DISCUSSION: A rational individual maximizes total utility from income. This objective can be accomplished when the utility obtained from the last dollar spent on each commodity purchased is the same. In other words, the marginal utility for each dollar spent on product A should be the same as the marginal utility for each dollar spent on product B, and so on. However, the principle of diminishing marginal utility must be considered. Under this assumption, equal increments of additional consumption of a product result in less than equal additions of utility to the consumer. For example, when a person is thirsty, the first glass of water tastes better than the second, and the third has even less utility than the second.

Answer (A) is incorrect because the principle of diminishing marginal utility states that marginal utility decreases as consumption expands. Answer (C) is incorrect because the concept of marginal utility is a measure associated with demand, not with supply. Answer (D) is incorrect because marginal utility is not associated with inputs to the production process; it is a measure associated with demand.

16. Which one of the following statements is not true of indifference curves?

A. Indifference curves slope downward to the right, indicating goods are substitutable.

B. Indifference curves indicate that more goods are preferable to fewer goods.

C. The marginal utility of a good decreases as consumption of the good increases.

D. Indifference curves cross at their equilibrium point.

The correct answer is (D). *(CMA, adapted)*

REQUIRED: The false statement regarding indifference curves.

DISCUSSION: An indifference curve represents all combinations of two commodities that give equal utility to a consumer. The farther the indifference curve is from the origin, the higher the level of utility. Indifference curves slope downward to the right and are convex to the origin because the utility of each additional unit of a good diminishes. Hence, indifference curves cannot intersect and are negatively sloped.

Answer (A) is incorrect because indifference curves have a negative slope. They reflect different combinations of goods. Answer (B) is incorrect because the farther the curve from the origin, the higher the total utility. Answer (C) is incorrect because the principle of diminishing marginal utility applies.

C. Supply

17. In the short run, the supply curve in a competitive market shows a positive relationship between price and quantity supplied because

A. Consumers will only buy more of a product at a higher price.

B. Of the law of diminishing returns.

C. As the size of a business firm increases, price must rise.

D. Increases in output imply a shift in consumer preferences, allowing a higher price.

The correct answer is (B). *(CMA, adapted)*

REQUIRED: The reason for a positive relationship between price and quantity supplied on a short-run supply curve in a competitive market.

DISCUSSION: The law of diminishing returns states that if increasing amounts of a variable input are applied to a fixed input, there is some point beyond which additional units of the variable input will contribute less and less to the total product. Thus, an input is used up to the point at which the marginal increase in revenue from that input is equal to its marginal cost. This means that adding variable inputs to a firm's fixed inputs will result in lower product costs, but only up to a point. Accordingly, a firm will increase short-run supply as long as marginal revenue (the price in a purely competitive market) exceeds marginal cost, whether because of a lower marginal cost or a higher price.

Answer (A) is incorrect because consumers will buy less of a product if prices are higher. Answer (C) is incorrect because costs decline up to a point as economies of scale are achieved. Answer (D) is incorrect because the supply curve is independent of the demand curve, which is based on consumer preferences.

18. A perfectly inelastic supply curve in a competitive market

A. Implies a vertical demand curve.

B. Exists when firms cannot vary input usage.

C. Implies a horizontal market supply curve.

D. Can exist only in the long run.

The correct answer is (B). *(CMA, adapted)*

REQUIRED: The true statement regarding a perfectly inelastic supply curve in a competitive market.

DISCUSSION: The elasticity of supply is a measure of the responsiveness of a change in the quantity supplied to a percentage change in the price of the commodity. A perfectly inelastic supply curve has an elasticity of zero. This can occur only when the numerator of the elasticity fraction, the percentage change in quantity supplied, is zero. Thus, a condition of perfect inelasticity of supply could occur only when a firm could not vary the quantity it supplies, i.e., when the firm cannot vary its input usage.

Answer (A) is incorrect because the elasticity of supply is not a measure involving the demand curve. Answer (C) is incorrect because a perfectly inelastic supply curve is vertical. The firm will supply the same quantity at all price levels. Answer (D) is incorrect because, in the long run, a firm can vary its inputs. Only in the short-run situation is input usage unchangeable. Hence, perfectly inelastic supply is a short-run condition.

19. A supply curve illustrates the relationship between

A. Price and quantity supplied.

B. Price and consumer tastes.

C. Price and quantity demanded.

D. Supply and demand.

The correct answer is (A). *(CMA, adapted)*

REQUIRED: The relationship illustrated by a supply curve.

DISCUSSION: A supply curve illustrates the relationship between price and the quantity of a good that sellers are willing to supply. As price increases, the supply will increase.

Answer (B) is incorrect because consumer tastes are reflected by the demand curve, not the supply curve. Answer (C) is incorrect because the demand curve shows the relationship between price and quantity demanded. Answer (D) is incorrect because the supply curve shows only the supply, not the demand.

20. The firm's short-run supply curve is derived from the

A. Average total cost curve.

B. Fixed cost curve.

C. Marginal cost curve.

D. Total cost curve.

The correct answer is (C). *(CMA, adapted)*

REQUIRED: The source of the firm's short-run supply curve.

DISCUSSION: In the short run, certain costs are fixed regardless of output. Given that fixed costs are incurred even if the firm shuts down, the firm gains in the short run by continuing to operate if revenues exceed variable costs. Accordingly, the firm's short-run supply curve is derived from the marginal cost curve. The firm benefits by producing until marginal cost equals marginal revenue. As long as the marginal cost is lower than the marginal revenue, the firm will recover some of its fixed costs as well as its variable costs. However, only the segment of the marginal cost curve that lies above average variable cost will constitute the short-run supply curve. At a price below the average variable cost, the firm's losses equal its fixed costs plus some of its variable costs. In this case, the firm would close down and not supply anything.

Answers (A), (B), and (D) are incorrect because the short-run supply curve is derived from the marginal cost curve, not the average total cost curve, the fixed cost curve, the total cost curve, or the difference between average total costs and fixed costs.

21. An improvement in technology that in turn leads to improved worker productivity would most likely result in

A. A shift to the right in the supply curve and a lowering of the price of the output.

B. A shift to the left in the supply curve and a lowering of the price of the output.

C. An increase in the price of the output if demand is unchanged.

D. Wage increases.

The correct answer is (A). *(CMA, adapted)*

REQUIRED: The result of improved technology and improved worker productivity.

DISCUSSION: Enhanced technology and worker productivity would cause the supply curve to shift to the right where it would intersect with the demand curve at a lower price level. The shift is caused by the producer's ability to lower costs and produce more at a given market price.

Answer (B) is incorrect because the increased productivity would cause a rightward shift in the supply curve. Answer (C) is incorrect because the rightward shift would result in an intersection with the demand curve at a lower price. Answer (D) is incorrect because the effect on wages cannot be determined from the information given.

22. When the federal government imposes health and safety regulations on certain products, one of the most likely results is

A. Greater consumption of the product.

B. Lower prices for the product.

C. Greater tax revenues for the federal government.

D. Higher prices for the product.

The correct answer is (D). *(CMA, adapted)*

REQUIRED: The effect of governmental health and safety regulations on certain products.

DISCUSSION: When government imposes health and safety regulations, production cost is likely to increase as a result of the manufacturer's efforts to comply. The increased costs are then passed on to consumers in the form of higher prices. Moreover, the amount the manufacturer is willing to supply will decrease.

Answer (A) is incorrect because consumption will either remain unchanged or decline following the increase in price. Answer (B) is incorrect because the costs of compliance will lead to higher prices. Answer (C) is incorrect because tax revenues are more likely to decline as price rises and the quantity demanded falls.

23. Economic rent is the total price paid for land and other natural resources when there is a(n)

A. Completely elastic supply function.

B. Completely fixed total supply.

C. Fixed demand schedule.

D. Artificial market price.

The correct answer is (B). *(CMA, adapted)*

REQUIRED: The condition in which economic rent is the total price paid for land and other natural resources.

DISCUSSION: Economic rent is the total price paid for land and other natural resources that have a completely fixed supply. Given this perfect inelasticity, the sole factor determining rent for land and other resources with a completely fixed total supply is demand. A higher price will not increase supply and thereby the productive potential of the economy. Thus, no part of the rent paid for such resources provides an incentive to increase supply, and the entire rent is deemed to be a surplus (economic rent) by economists.

Answer (A) is incorrect because an elastic supply function would not be fixed in total. Economic rent is paid when the supply is perfectly inelastic. Answer (C) is incorrect because a fixed supply schedule is typical of resources that receive economic rent. Answer (D) is incorrect because market price is irrelevant to the definition.

D. Market Equilibrium and Pricing

24. Price ceilings

A. Are illustrated by government price support programs in agriculture.

B. Create prices greater than equilibrium prices.

C. Create prices below equilibrium prices.

D. Result in persistent surpluses.

The correct answer is (C). *(CMA, adapted)*

REQUIRED: The true statement about price ceilings.

DISCUSSION: Government-imposed price ceilings may cause prices to be set at rates below equilibrium. Because prices are set artificially low, demand will tend to exceed the supply and shortages will occur.

Answer (A) is incorrect because price ceilings are essentially the opposite of price supports. If price is subject to a ceiling, suppliers may receive less than at the equilibrium level. But the supplier may receive more at the equilibrium rate if the price is supported. Answer (B) is incorrect because prices may be lower than at the equilibrium level. Answer (D) is incorrect because price ceilings cause shortages if consumers demand more than sellers are willing to supply.

25. The competitive model of supply and demand predicts that a surplus can arise only if there is a

A. Maximum price above the equilibrium price.

B. Minimum price below the equilibrium price.

C. Maximum price below the equilibrium price.

D. Minimum price above the equilibrium price.

The correct answer is (D). *(CMA, adapted)*

REQUIRED: The circumstance that could lead to a product surplus.

DISCUSSION: In the competitive model of supply and demand, a surplus can never occur. Pure competition leads to perfect equilibrium between supply and demand. Only when government intervenes with price controls can a surplus or shortage occur. A surplus can arise if a minimum price is set that exceeds the equilibrium price. For example, if the minimum price is $5 and the equilibrium price is $4, consumers will demand fewer goods at $5 than $4, but producers will supply more goods at $5 than $4. Thus, a surplus will occur. However, at a price of $4, supply would exactly equal demand.

Answer (A) is incorrect because a maximum price in excess of the equilibrium price creates neither a surplus nor a shortage. Answer (B) is incorrect because a minimum price below the equilibrium price creates neither a surplus nor a shortage. Answer (C) is incorrect because a maximum price (such as rent controls) set lower than the equilibrium price leads to shortages. Producers will not be willing to supply as much as consumers demand.

26. An increase in the market supply of beef would result in a(n)

A. Increase in the price of beef.

B. Decrease in the demand for beef.

C. Increase in the price of pork.

D. Increase in the quantity of beef demanded.

The correct answer is (D). *(CMA, adapted)*

REQUIRED: The effect of an increase in the market supply of beef.

DISCUSSION: If demand is constant, an increase in supply should result in a lower equilibrium price. The supply curve shifts to the right; that is, more is supplied at each price. Thus, the new intersection of the supply and demand curves is at a lower point on the demand curve. The result is an increase in the quantity demanded.

Answer (A) is incorrect because the increased supply will lead to a lower price. Answer (B) is incorrect because an increase in supply increases quantity demanded, not overall demand. Answer (C) is incorrect because pork is a substitute for beef. Hence, the lower price of beef will shift demand for pork to the left, resulting in a lower equilibrium price.

27. If the federal government regulates a product or service in a competitive market by setting a maximum price below the equilibrium price, what is the long-run effect?

A. A surplus.

B. A shortage.

C. A decrease in demand.

D. No effect on the market.

The correct answer is (B). *(CMA, adapted)*

REQUIRED: The effect of the government's setting a price below the equilibrium point in a competitive market.

DISCUSSION: Price fixing is the setting of mandatory or artificial prices. It often interferes with the free operation of the market. A price ceiling is a price below the equilibrium point. The result is a shortage because consumer demand will exceed supply.

Answer (A) is incorrect because a surplus arises when the price is set above the equilibrium point. Supply will exceed demand. Answer (C) is incorrect because a decrease in demand (a leftward shift in the demand curve) may result when future prices are expected to decline. However, given a price set below equilibrium, pressure on prices is upward. Answer (D) is incorrect because the price ceiling will cause shortages.

28. In any competitive market, an equal increase in both demand and supply can be expected to always

A. Increase both price and market-clearing quantity.

B. Decrease both price and market-clearing quantity.

C. Increase market-clearing quantity.

D. Increase price.

The correct answer is (C). *(CMA, adapted)*

REQUIRED: The result of an equal increase in both demand and supply in a competitive market.

DISCUSSION: In a competitive market, equilibrium exists when demand is exactly equal to supply. If both demand and supply increase in equal amounts, the market will still be in equilibrium, but the new price may be higher, lower, or unchanged depending upon the slopes of the demand and supply curves. Whatever the new price, the quantity of products cleared by the market should increase.

Answer (A) is incorrect because prices might decline or stay the same depending upon the slope of the demand and supply curves. For example, if the demand curve were steeper than the supply curve, prices would decline. Answer (B) is incorrect because prices might increase or stay the same depending upon the slope of the demand and supply curves. For example, if the supply curve were steeper than the demand curve, prices would increase. Answer (D) is incorrect because prices might decline or stay the same depending upon the slope of the demand and supply curves.

29. If both the supply and the demand for a good increase, the market price will

A. Rise only in the case of an inelastic supply function.

B. Fall only in the case of an inelastic supply function.

C. Not be predictable with only these facts.

D. Rise only in the case of an inelastic demand function.

The correct answer is (C). *(CMA, adapted)*

REQUIRED: The effect on market price of a simultaneous increase in both the supply and demand for a good.

DISCUSSION: If demand is constant, an increase in supply will lower the price of a good. If supply is constant, an increase in demand will raise the price. When both events occur, the effect depends on the magnitude of the changes. Thus, the market price is not predictable from the facts given.

Answers (A), (B), and (D) are incorrect because the degree of elasticity is not a sufficient predictor of the nature of the change in market price.

E. Production and Costs of Economic Resources

30. In microeconomics, the distinguishing characteristic of the long run on the supply side is that

A. Only supply factors determine price and output.

B. Only demand factors determine price and output.

C. Firms are not allowed to enter or exit the industry.

D. All inputs are variable.

The correct answer is (D). *(CMA, adapted)*

REQUIRED: The distinguishing characteristic of long-run supply.

DISCUSSION: The distinction in microeconomics between the short run and the long run is that the long run is a time period long enough that all inputs, including plant capacity, can be varied. The short run is a time period so brief that a firm has insufficient time to vary the amount of all inputs. Thus, in the short run, the quantity of one or more inputs is fixed.

Answers (A) and (B) are incorrect because both demand and supply factors determine price and output. Answer (C) is incorrect because, in the long run, firms can enter or exit an industry.

31. Marginal revenue is

A. Equal to price in monopolistic competition.

B. The change in total revenue associated with increasing prices.

C. Greater than price in pure competition.

D. The change in total revenue associated with producing and selling one more unit.

The correct answer is (D). *(CMA, adapted)*

REQUIRED: The definition of marginal revenue.

DISCUSSION: Marginal revenue is the change in total revenue resulting from producing and selling one additional unit of product. Marginal revenue is constant in pure competition but declines as output rises in other market structures. Equating marginal revenue and marginal cost is the profit-maximizing position for all firms.

Answer (A) is incorrect because marginal revenue equals price in pure competition. In monopolistic competition, no firm can affect the price. Hence, the price is the same at all levels of output. Answer (B) is incorrect because marginal revenue is the change in revenue from selling one additional unit of product, not from a change in prices. Moreover, in market structures other than pure competition, marginal revenue declines as sales increase because prices eventually must be lowered to stimulate demand. Answer (C) is incorrect because marginal revenue cannot be greater than price.

Questions 32 through 34 are based on the following information.

Number of Workers	Total Product Units	Average Selling Price
10	20	$50.00
11	25	49.00
12	28	47.50

32. The marginal physical product when one worker is added to a team of 10 workers is

A. 1 unit.

B. 8 units.

C. 5 units.

D. 25 units.

The correct answer is (C). *(CMA, adapted)*

REQUIRED: The marginal physical product.

DISCUSSION: According to the table, 11 workers can produce 25 units, which is an increase of five over the 20 units that 10 workers can produce. This additional five units is known as the marginal physical product generated by the 11th worker.

Answer (A) is incorrect because the 11th worker will cause total production to increase to 25 units, an increment of five. Answer (B) is incorrect because eight units is the marginal product of adding two workers to a team of ten workers. Answer (D) is incorrect because 25 units will be the total production by all 11 workers, not the marginal product added by the 11th.

33. The marginal revenue per unit when one worker is added to a team of 11 workers is

A. $35.00

B. $225.00

C. $105.00

D. $47.50

The correct answer is (A). *(CMA, adapted)*

REQUIRED: The marginal revenue per unit.

DISCUSSION: The total revenue produced by 11 workers would be $1,225 (25 units x $49). With 12 workers producing a total of 28 units at $47.50 each, the total revenue would be $1,330. The $1,330 of revenue represents an increment of $105 over the revenue generated by 11 workers. Dividing the $105 increment by the three incremental units (28 – 25) produces marginal revenue of $35 per unit.

Answer (B) is incorrect because $225 is the total increment when the number of workers increases from 10 to 11. Answer (C) is incorrect because $105 is the total increase in revenue for three additional units, not the marginal revenue per unit. Answer (D) is incorrect because $47.50 is the new price per unit, not the marginal revenue.

34. The marginal revenue product when one worker is added to a team of 11 workers is

A. $42.00

B. $225.00

C. $105.00

D. $47.50

The correct answer is (C). *(CMA, adapted)*

REQUIRED: The marginal revenue product.

DISCUSSION: The marginal revenue product represents the increase in total revenue resulting from the additional production of an additional worker. The total revenue produced by 11 workers would be $1,225 (25 units x $49). With 12 workers producing a total of 28 units at $47.50 each, the total revenue would be $1,330. The $1,330 of revenue represents an increment of $105 over the revenue generated by 11 workers.

Answer (A) is incorrect because $42 is the sales price variance produced by multiplying the 28 units times the $1.50 decline in price; it ignores the revenue produced by the extra units. Answer (B) is incorrect because $225 is the total increment when the number of workers increases from 10 to 11. Answer (D) is incorrect because $47.50 is the new price per unit, not the marginal revenue.

Questions 35 and 36 are based on the following information.

Total Units of Product	Average Fixed Cost	Average Variable Cost	Average Total Cost
6	$15.00	$25.00	$40.00
7	12.86	24.00	36.86
8	11.25	23.50	34.75
9	10.00	23.75	33.75

35. The total cost of producing seven units is

A. $90.02

B. $168.00

C. $258.02

D. $280.00

The correct answer is (C). *(CMA, adapted)*

REQUIRED: The total cost of producing seven units when the average cost per unit is known.

DISCUSSION: If seven units can be produced at an average cost of $36.86 each, multiplying that amount by seven produces the total cost of $258.02.

Answer (A) is incorrect because $90.02 is the total fixed cost. Answer (B) is incorrect because $168 is the total variable cost. Answer (D) is incorrect because $280 is the total cost if average total cost for seven units were $40.00.

36. The marginal cost of producing the ninth unit is

A. $23.50

B. $23.75

C. $25.75

D. $33.75

The correct answer is (C). *(CMA, adapted)*

REQUIRED: The marginal cost of producing the ninth unit.

DISCUSSION: Marginal cost is the incremental cost of producing one additional unit. Thus, the marginal cost of the ninth unit is the increment over the total cost for eight units. The total cost for eight units at $34.75 each is $278, and the total cost for nine units at $33.75 each is $303.75, so the total cost for nine units is $25.75 greater than the total for eight units. This $25.75 is the marginal cost of the ninth unit.

Answer (A) is incorrect because $23.50 is the variable cost of the eighth unit. Answer (B) is incorrect because $23.75 is the variable cost of the ninth unit. Answer (D) is incorrect because $33.75 is the average cost per unit for nine units.

37. The measurement of using resources now in lieu of alternative uses of the resources is

A. Economic efficiency.

B. Opportunity cost.

C. Comparative advantage.

D. Absolute advantage.

The correct answer is (B). *(CMA, adapted)*

REQUIRED: The measurement of using resources now in lieu of alternative uses of the resources.

DISCUSSION: Opportunity cost is the benefit forgone by using scarce resources in a given way. Thus, it is the benefit that could have been obtained from the best alternative use of the resources.

Answer (A) is incorrect because economic efficiency is a comparison measured in dollar terms. Answer (C) is incorrect because comparative advantage compares the costs of products within one country. Answer (D) is incorrect because absolute advantage compares costs among countries.

38. The definition of economic cost is

A. All the dollar costs employers pay for all inputs purchased.

B. The opportunity cost of all inputs minus the dollar cost of those inputs.

C. The difference between all implicit and explicit costs of the business firm.

D. The sum of all explicit and implicit costs of the business firm.

The correct answer is (D). *(CMA, adapted)*

REQUIRED: The definition of economic cost.

DISCUSSION: Economic cost is defined as the sum of all costs, both implicit and explicit, of a firm. Explicit costs include direct expenditures made to those outside the firm, for example, the costs of labor, materials, and equipment. Implicit costs are the payments that would have been received if self-owned resources had been used outside the firm's business. Thus, the lease payments forgone by not renting the firm's building to others is an implicit cost. The return necessary to keep resources employed in a given enterprise (normal profit) is also an implicit cost.

Answer (A) is incorrect because economic cost includes not only explicit costs (dollars paid), but implicit costs as well; implicit costs include opportunity costs. Answer (B) is incorrect because opportunity costs and dollar costs should be added, not subtracted. Answer (C) is incorrect because all explicit and implicit costs should be added, not subtracted.

39. In the long run, a firm may experience increasing returns due to

A. Law of diminishing returns.

B. Opportunity costs.

C. Comparative advantage.

D. Economies of scale.

The correct answer is (D). *(CMA, adapted)*

REQUIRED: The factor that can cause a firm to experience increasing returns in the long run.

DISCUSSION: In a competitive market, equilibrium exists when demand is exactly equal to supply. If both demand and supply increase in equal amounts, the market will still be in equilibrium, but the new price may be higher, lower, or unchanged depending upon the slopes of the demand and supply curves. Whatever the new price, the quantity of products cleared by the market should increase.

Answer (A) is incorrect because, under the law of diminishing returns, if increasing amounts of a variable input are applied to a fixed input, there is some point beyond which additional units of the variable input will contribute less and less to the total output. Answer (B) is incorrect because an opportunity cost is the benefit forgone by not choosing the next best use of a scarce resource. Answer (C) is incorrect because the principle of comparative advantage states that world output is maximized when each output is produced by the nation with the lower opportunity cost.

40. Because of the existence of economies of scale, business firms may find that

A. Each additional unit of labor is less efficient than the previous unit.

B. As more labor is added to a factory, increases in output will diminish in the short run.

C. Increasing the size of a factory will result in lower average costs.

D. Increasing the size of a factory will result in lower total costs.

The correct answer is (C). *(CMA, adapted)*

REQUIRED: The true statement about economies of scale.

DISCUSSION: As most firms expand output, average costs of production initially tend to decline. The reasons for this include increased specialization and division of labor, better use and specialization of management, and use of more efficient machinery and equipment. Consequently, increasing the size of a factory often results in lower average costs.

Answer (A) is incorrect because economies of scale refer to the savings in costs as production increases; less efficient labor would lead to higher costs. Answer (B) is incorrect because output should increase, although average productivity may or may not change. Answer (D) is incorrect because increasing factory size will normally increase total costs but result in lower average costs.

41. The long-run average total cost curve

A. Is horizontal and parallel to the demand curve.

B. Is strongly influenced by diminishing returns.

C. Is the same as the rising portion of the marginal cost curve.

D. Is ordinarily U-shaped.

The correct answer is (D). *(CMA, adapted)*

REQUIRED: The true statement about the long-run average total cost curve.

DISCUSSION: The long-run average total cost curve is normally U-shaped because the average cost per unit declines as the firm experiences economies of scale. However, beyond the point of intersection with the marginal cost curve, it will begin rising because the amount added (marginal cost) to total cost is greater than the average total cost.

Answer (A) is incorrect because the curve is not horizontal. It varies with changes in production scale. Answer (B) is incorrect because, although returns to incremental input may be diminishing and marginal cost rising, average total cost may continue to decline. Answer (C) is incorrect because the average total cost curve is a U-shaped curve that is intersected at its minimum point by the rising portion of the marginal cost curve.

F. Market Structure

42. When markets are perfectly competitive, consumers

A. Are able to avoid the problem of diminishing returns.

B. Have goods and services produced at the lowest cost in the long run.

C. Do not receive any consumer surplus unless producers choose to overproduce.

D. Must search for the lowest price for the products they buy.

The correct answer is (B). *(CMA, adapted)*

REQUIRED: The true statement about consumers in perfectly competitive markets.

DISCUSSION: Pure competition is characterized by a large number of buyers and sellers acting independently, homogeneous or standardized products, free entry into and exit of firms from the market, perfect information, no control over prices, and no nonprice competition. Because price equals marginal cost, allocation of resources is optimal. Firms produce the ideal output, the output at which average cost is lowest. Price is lower and output greater than in any other market structure.

Answer (A) is incorrect because diminishing returns can exist in any market structure. Answer (C) is incorrect because, in pure competition, the optimal output is produced. Because resource allocation is ideal, no over- or underproduction occurs, and consumer surplus (the difference between what consumers are willing to pay and what they actually pay) is nonexistent. Answer (D) is incorrect because all suppliers will charge the market price, given perfect information in the economy.

43. Which one of the following is not a key assumption of perfect competition?

A. Firms sell a homogeneous product.

B. Customers are indifferent about which firm they buy from.

C. The level of a firm's output is small relative to the industry's total output.

D. Each firm can price its product above the industry price.

The correct answer is (D). *(CMA, adapted)*

REQUIRED: The assumption not made about perfect competition.

DISCUSSION: Perfect competition is characterized by a market structure with many buyers and sellers acting independently, a homogeneous or standardized product, free entry into and exit from the market, perfect information, no control over the industry price, and the absence of nonprice competition. Moreover, customers are indifferent about which firm they buy from because price is the only difference between one seller and the next.

Answers (A), (B), and (C) are incorrect because a homogeneous product, customer indifference regarding choice of seller, and small firm output relative to the industry are key assumptions of perfect competition.

44. Which one of the following statements concerning pure monopolies is correct?

A. The demand curve of a monopolist is perfectly elastic.

B. The point of profit maximization for a monopoly is where average total revenue equals average total cost.

C. The monopolist's marginal revenue curve lies below the monopolist's demand curve.

D. The supply curve of a monopoly is perfectly inelastic.

The correct answer is (C). *(CMA, adapted)*

REQUIRED: The correct statement about pure monopolies.

DISCUSSION: A pure monopolist constitutes the industry; that is, the negatively sloped industry demand curve is the pure monopolist's demand curve. Accordingly, the pure monopolist must reduce price to increase sales, and the marginal revenue curve will also be negatively sloped. Moreover, marginal revenue will be less than price (average revenue) because the price reductions necessary to increase sales apply to all units that might otherwise have been sold at a higher price. This relationship explains why the marginal revenue curve lies below the demand curve. The latter is a function of price and quantity demanded.

Answer (A) is incorrect because the demand curve of a pure competitor is perfectly elastic. Such a firm is a price taker that can sell all of its output at the market price but none of its output at a higher price. Answer (B) is incorrect because profit is maximized when marginal revenue equals marginal cost. Answer (D) is incorrect because the supply curve is unrelated to the market structure of the producer's industry.

45. Which one of the following statements concerning pure monopolies is correct?

A. The demand curve of a monopolist is perfectly elastic.

B. The price at which a monopolist maximizes its profit is where price equals both marginal cost and marginal revenue.

C. A monopolist's marginal revenue curve lies below its demand curve.

D. For a monopolist, there is a unique relationship between the price and the quantity supplied.

The correct answer is (C). *(CMA, adapted)*

REQUIRED: The true statement concerning pure monopolies.

DISCUSSION: In a pure monopoly, the marginal revenue curve is negatively (downwardly) sloped. The reason is that the demand curve faced by the monopolist is also negatively sloped; that is, price must decrease to increase sales. However, a price cut to increase sales applies not only to the incremental units but also to all other units. Each additional unit adds its price minus the sum of the reductions on preceding units to total revenue. Thus, marginal revenue (change in total revenue) declines as output rises, and the marginal revenue curve will lie below the demand curve. If marginal revenue equaled the price change, the marginal revenue and demand curves would be the same.

Answer (A) is incorrect because the demand curve in pure competition is perfectly elastic. Answer (B) is incorrect because a monopolist's profit is maximized when price exceeds marginal revenue and marginal cost. Answer (D) is incorrect because a monopolist has no supply curve. Because a monopolist equates marginal revenue and marginal cost, but marginal revenue is not price, different demand curves may result in different prices at the same output level. Thus, price and quantity supplied do not have a unique relationship.

46. Natural monopoly conditions, which often lead to governmental regulation, exist when

A. Consumer demand for a product is perfectly elastic.

B. Marginal costs are rising.

C. Consumer demand is inversely related to the business cycle.

D. Total average costs are declining.

The correct answer is (D). *(CMA, adapted)*

REQUIRED: The time when natural monopoly conditions exist.

DISCUSSION: A natural monopoly exists because economic and technical conditions exist in the industry or economy that permit only one efficient supplier in a locale. A natural monopoly exists when economies of scale are very great, that is, when very large-scale operations are required to achieve low unit costs and prices. In a natural monopoly, the unit cost (the long-term average cost) of meeting the entire demand is minimized when the industry consists of one firm. Thus, competition would be undesirable because the presence of two or more firms would prevent the realization of the necessary economies of scale.

Answer (A) is incorrect because elasticity of demand is unrelated to market structure. Answer (B) is incorrect because, if marginal costs are rising, multiple smaller firms are preferable to a single producer. Answer (C) is incorrect because consumer demand is unrelated to the market structure of the supplier.

47. Monopolistic competition is characterized by

A. A relatively large group of sellers who produce differentiated products.

B. A relatively small group of sellers who produce differentiated products.

C. A monopolistic market where the consumer is persuaded that there is perfect competition.

D. A relatively large group of sellers who produce a homogeneous product.

The correct answer is (A). *(CMA, adapted)*

REQUIRED: The true statement about monopolistic competition.

DISCUSSION: Monopolistic competition is characterized by a large number of firms offering differentiated products. Entry into the market is relatively easy, firms have some price control, and substantial nonprice competition exists, such as advertising.

Answer (B) is incorrect because monopolistic competition is characterized by a relatively large group of sellers. Answer (C) is incorrect because the market is not monopolistic. There are many sellers. Answer (D) is incorrect because products are not homogeneous in monopolistic competition; although products may appear to be similar, they have differences in service, quality, or other attributes.

48. Economic markets that are characterized by monopolistic competition have all of the following characteristics except

A. One seller of the product.

B. Economies or diseconomies of scale.

C. Advertising.

D. Heterogeneous products.

The correct answer is (A). *(CMA, adapted)*

REQUIRED: The characteristic that does not exist in the case of monopolistic competition.

DISCUSSION: The characteristics of monopolistic competition are a large number of firms, differentiated products, relatively easy entry into the market, some price control by individual firms, and large amounts of nonprice competition. In such cases, price exceeds marginal cost and resources are underallocated. The industry is typically populated by too many firms that are too small. These conditions are often referred to as the waste of monopolistic competition. Prices are higher and output is less than with pure competition.

Answer (B) is incorrect because economies and diseconomies of scale do exist with monopolistic competition. Answer (C) is incorrect because advertising is an important element in an economy characterized by monopolistic competition. Answer (D) is incorrect because monopolistic competition is characterized by heterogeneous products.

49. Compared with firms in a perfectly competitive market, a monopolist tends to

A. Produce substantially less but charge a higher price.

B. Produce substantially more and charge a higher price.

C. Produce the same output and charge a higher price.

D. Produce substantially less and charge a lower price.

The correct answer is (A). *(CMA, adapted)*

REQUIRED: The true statement about a monopolist.

DISCUSSION: Competitive markets are preferable to other types of markets, such as monopolies, because price is lower and output greater. All firms should equate marginal revenue (MR) and marginal cost (MC). For a competitive firm, MR equals price at all output levels because the firm is a price taker. However, a monopolist must reduce price to raise sales, so its MR curve will decline with output. Assuming no difference between the MC curves of the purely competitive firm and the monopolist, the latter's downward-sloping MR curve will intersect the MC curve at a lower output level than that for a competitive firm. This lower output level corresponds to a higher point (a higher price) on the demand curve.

Answers (B), (C), and (D) are incorrect because a monopolist produces less and charges a higher price than a pure competitor.

50. The distinguishing characteristic of oligopolistic markets is

A. A single seller of a homogeneous product with no close substitute.

B. A single seller of a heterogeneous product with no close substitute.

C. Lack of entry and exit barriers in the industry.

D. Mutual interdependence of firm pricing and output decisions.

The correct answer is (D). *(CMA, adapted)*

REQUIRED: The distinguishing characteristic of oligopolistic markets.

DISCUSSION: The oligopoly model is much less specific than the other market structures, but there are typically few firms in the industry. Thus, the decisions of rival firms do not go unnoticed. Products can be either differentiated or standardized. Prices tend to be rigid because of the interdependence among firms. Entry is difficult because of either natural or created barriers. Price leadership is typical in oligopolistic industries. Under price leadership, price changes are announced first by a major firm. Once the industry leader has spoken, other firms in the industry match the price charged by the leader. The mutual interdependence of the firms influences both pricing and output decisions.

Answers (A) and (B) are incorrect because oligopolies contain several firms; a single seller is characteristic of a monopoly. Answer (C) is incorrect because oligopolies are typified by barriers to entry; that is the reason the industry has only a few firms.

51. An oligopolist faces a "kinked" demand curve. This terminology indicates that

A. When an oligopolist lowers its price, the other firms in the oligopoly will match the price reduction, but if the oligopolist raises its price, the other firms will ignore the price change.

B. An oligopolist faces a non-linear demand for its product, and price changes will have little effect on demand for that product.

C. An oligopolist can sell its product at any price, but after the "saturation point," another oligopolist will lower its price and, therefore, shift the demand curve to the left.

D. Consumers have no effect on the demand curve, and an oligopolist can shape the curve to optimize its own efficiency.

The correct answer is (A). *(CMA, adapted)*

REQUIRED: The meaning of an oligopolist's kinked demand curve.

DISCUSSION: An oligopoly consists of a few firms. Thus, the decisions of rivals do not go unnoticed. Prices tend to be rigid (sticky) because of the interdependence among firms. Because competitors respond only to certain price changes by one of the firms in an oligopolistic industry, the demand curve for an oligopolist tends to be kinked. Price decreases are usually matched by price decreases, but price increases are often not followed. If other firms do not match a lower price, a price decrease by an oligopolist would capture more of the market. If other firms match the price decrease, less of the market will be captured.

Answer (B) is incorrect because price changes will have an effect on demand for an oligopolist's product. Answer (C) is incorrect because an oligopolist must essentially match the price of other firms in the industry. Answer (D) is incorrect because an oligopolist cannot shape its demand curve.

52. Patents are granted in order to encourage firms to invest in the research and development of new products. Patents are an example of

A. Vertical integration.

B. Market concentration.

C. Entry barriers.

D. Collusion.

The correct answer is (C). *(CMA, adapted)*

REQUIRED: The true statement about patents.

DISCUSSION: Entry barriers exist in all market structures other than perfect competition. The fewer the firms in an industry, the greater the barriers tend to be. Entry barriers include the existence of substantial economies of scale (low unit costs can be achieved only by large producers). They also include barriers created by existing firms. For example, large advertising expenditures may be necessary to compete. Control of raw materials or technology is another barrier. Consequently, patents held by existing firms may serve as an entry barrier because they prevent potential competitors from using certain technology. Patents are rights granted by the federal government to inventors to allow them the exclusive use of their inventions for a specified period.

Answer (A) is incorrect because vertical integration is the combination of a company with a supplier or a customer. Answer (B) is incorrect because market concentration is the degree to which a few producers dominate an industry. Answer (D) is incorrect because a patent is a contract between the government and an inventor. There is no collusion.

53. A market with many independent firms, low barriers to entry, and product differentiation is best classified as

A. A monopoly.

B. Monopolistic competition.

C. An oligopoly.

D. Pure competition.

The correct answer is (B). *(CMA, adapted)*

REQUIRED: The market with many independent firms, low barriers to entry, and product differentiation.

DISCUSSION: Like perfect competition, monopolistic competition is characterized by a large number of firms and relative ease of market entry. However, monopolistic competition is also characterized by differentiated products, some control over price, and considerable nonprice competition, e.g., through advertising and emphasis on brand awareness.

Answer (A) is incorrect because a monopoly consists of a single seller. Answer (C) is incorrect because an oligopoly consists of a few firms. Products may be differentiated or standardized, and entry is typically difficult. Answer (D) is incorrect because products are standardized in pure competition.

54. The marginal cost curve is the supply curve for the firm in

A. Pure monopoly.

B. Monopolistic competition.

C. Pure competition.

D. Oligopoly.

The correct answer is (C). *(CMA, adapted)*

REQUIRED: The type of market structure in which the marginal cost curve is the supply curve for a firm.

DISCUSSION: Under pure competition, the portion of a firm's marginal cost (MC) curve above its average variable cost curve (the firm cannot cover its variable costs below this shutdown point) is also its supply curve. Because the firm is a price taker (the marginal revenue (MR) curve is horizontal), increases in supply can occur only at higher prices because the firm produces at the level at which MR equals MC.

Answers (A), (B), and (D) are incorrect because the marginal revenue curve is downward sloping in these cases. Thus, the point on the MC curve equal to MR indicates the profit-maximizing quantity but not the price. The price is found by extending a perpendicular line up to the demand curve from the MR = MC point. In other words, the price (vertical) coordinate of each point on the MC curve does not equal the market price at a given level of output except in pure competition. In this structure, the MR curve is the firm's demand curve.

Questions 55 and 56 are based on the following information. Karen Parker wants to establish an environmental testing company that would specialize in evaluating the quality of water found in rivers and streams. However, Parker has discovered that she needs either certification or approval from five separate local and state governmental agencies before she can commence business. Also, the necessary equipment to begin would cost several million dollars. Nevertheless, Parker believes that if she is able to obtain capital resources, she can gain market share from the two major competitors.

55. The large capital outlay necessary for the equipment is an example of a(n)

A. Entry barrier.

B. Minimum efficient scale.

C. Created barrier.

D. Production possibility boundary.

The correct answer is (A). *(CMA, adapted)*

REQUIRED: The nature of the large capital outlay necessary to enter an industry.

DISCUSSION: A large capital outlay necessary to enter an industry is an entry barrier. Entry barriers are characteristic of monopolistic competition, oligopoly, and monopoly. In these market structures, the barriers are successively more difficult to overcome, with the strongest barriers existing in a monopoly structure.

Answer (B) is incorrect because the minimum efficient scale is the lowest output at which long-term average unit cost is minimized. A natural monopoly occurs when only one firm can produce at the MES. The reason is that economies of scale can continue to be obtained at output levels in excess of the total market demand. Accordingly, the lowest unit costs are achieved when one producer exists. Answer (C) is incorrect because a barrier to entry may be created by the firms already operating in the industry. An example is an ongoing advertising campaign. Answer (D) is incorrect because the production possibility boundary is a macroeconomic concept. It depicts the short-run maximum gross domestic product obtainable given full production and full employment of existing resources (land, labor, capital, and entrepreneurial ability).

56. The market structure Karen Parker is attempting to enter is best described as

A. A natural monopoly.

B. A cartel.

C. An oligopoly.

D. Monopolistic competition.

The correct answer is (C). *(CMA, adapted)*

REQUIRED: The type of market structure that currently has two major competitors.

DISCUSSION: An oligopoly is characterized by a few firms in the industry (but more than one). Prices tend to be rigid because of the interdependence among firms. Entry is difficult because an oligopolistic industry usually has substantial economies of scale. Hence, a new entrant needs to begin as a large producer. Other barriers, such as existing firms' control of technology or raw materials, the need for substantial advertising, or costly licensing requirements, may make entry difficult.

Answer (A) is incorrect because a natural monopoly exists when economic or technical conditions permit only one efficient supplier. It arises when economies of scale are very great, that is, when very large operations are needed to achieve low unit costs and prices. Thus, the unit cost of meeting demand is minimized when the industry has one firm. Answer (B) is incorrect because a cartel is a group of oligopolistic firms that have joined together for price-fixing purposes. The practice is illegal except in international markets. Answer (D) is incorrect because monopolistic competition is characterized by a relatively large number of firms in the industry, differentiated products, relatively easy entry into the market, and large amounts of nonprice competition.

57. The manner in which cartels set and maintain price above the competitive market price is to

A. Avoid product differentiation in order to decrease demand for the product.

B. Advertise more so market demand increases.

C. Increase costs so price must rise.

D. Require cartel members to restrict output.

The correct answer is (D). *(CMA, adapted)*

REQUIRED: The means used by cartels to set and maintain prices that are above the competitive market price.

DISCUSSION: In an oligopolistic industry, a cartel can be formed to add structure to a market with a few firms. A cartel arises when a group of oligopolistic firms join together for price-fixing purposes. This practice is illegal except in international markets. Prices are fixed at an amount greater than would occur under pure competition. Members of the cartel maintain higher prices by voluntarily restricting output.

Answer (A) is incorrect because oligopolists do not attempt to decrease demand for the product. Answer (B) is incorrect because prices are maintained by restricting output. Answer (C) is incorrect because increased costs do not necessarily result in higher prices.

58. A horizontal merger is best defined as a merger of

A. Two or more firms in the same industry.

B. A manufacturing company and its supplier.

C. Two or more firms in different industries.

D. Two or more firms in different stages of the production process.

The correct answer is (A). *(CMA, adapted)*

REQUIRED: The best description of a horizontal merger.

DISCUSSION: A merger is a business combination in which an acquiring firm absorbs a second firm, and the acquiring firm remains in business as a combination of the two. A horizontal merger is the union of two or more companies that engage in the same or similar activities; in other words, two firms in the same industry.

Answer (B) is incorrect because a merger between a manufacturer and its supplier or distributor is a vertical merger. Answer (C) is incorrect because a merger between firms in different industries is a conglomerate merger. Answer (D) is incorrect because a merger between firms in different stages of the production process is vertical.

59. Which one of the following examples best describes a vertical merger?

A. A grocery store buying another grocery store in the same market.

B. A grocery store buying another grocery store in a state where the first company does not do business.

C. A hot dog producer buying a soft drink manufacturer.

D. A brewer buying a glass company.

The correct answer is (D). *(CMA, adapted)*

REQUIRED: The vertical merger.

DISCUSSION: A vertical merger is a combination of two companies, one of which supplies inputs for the other. A brewer's purchase of a glass company is an example. The glass company could supply glass for the brewer's bottles.

Answers (A) and (B) are incorrect because the purchase of a grocery store by another similar store, whether or not in the same market, is a horizontal merger, a combination of two companies that engage in the same or similar activities. Answer (C) is incorrect because a hot dog producer's purchase of a soft drink manufacturer is a conglomerate merger, a combination of companies in unrelated industries.

60. A high concentration ratio is

A. An indicator of monopolistic power.

B. An indicator of a highly competitive industry.

C. Consistent with the law of demand.

D. Consistent with monopolistic competition.

The correct answer is (A). *(CMA, adapted)*

REQUIRED: The true statement about a high concentration ratio.

DISCUSSION: The concentration ratio is the percentage of total industry sales attributable to a specified number of the largest firms. A high concentration ratio indicates that few firms are operating in an industry. Thus, a high ratio indicates monopoly power.

Answer (B) is incorrect because a highly competitive industry would have a low concentration ratio. Answer (C) is incorrect because the concentration ratio has no relationship to the law of demand. Answer (D) is incorrect because a high concentration ratio is more indicative of a monopoly than of monopolistic competition, which is characterized by the existence of many firms.

Use Gleim's ***CMA/CFM Test Prep*** for interactive testing with **over 2,000 additional multiple-choice questions!**

ADDENDUM: COMPUTATIONAL PRACTICE QUESTIONS

Questions A1 through A3 are presented below. Please see pages 172, 386, and 473 for additional questions. The study unit on which the question is based is indicated in bold after the source code for each question.

A1. The output and cost information for a firm is presented below.

Output	Total Variable Cost	Total Cost
0	$ -0-	$100
1	$150	$250
2	$260	$360
3	$350	$450

The marginal cost of the second unit of output is

A. $100

B. $110

C. $150

D. $180

The correct answer is (B). *(Publisher)* **SU 1**

REQUIRED: The marginal cost of the second unit of output.

DISCUSSION: Marginal cost is the additional cost of producing one more unit of output. Because total cost increased from $250 to $360, the marginal cost of the second unit is $110.

Answer (A) is incorrect because $100 is the fixed cost of production. Answer (C) is incorrect because $150 is the marginal cost of the first unit of production. Answer (D) is incorrect because $180 is the average cost of production for two units.

A2. A company operating in a perfectly competitive market has been paying $10 per hour for labor and $20 per hour to rent a piece of capital equipment. The firm can use labor and capital in any desired proportions to produce its product. If wages rise to $20 per hour and capital equipment rentals rise to $22 per hour, in the long run the firm will

A. Use relatively more equipment and relatively less labor in its production.

B. Use relatively more labor and relatively less equipment in its production.

C. Use less of both labor and equipment in its production, but in the same proportions as before.

D. Lower its average equipment-output ratio and raise its average labor-output ratio.

The correct answer is (A). *(Publisher)* **SU 1**

REQUIRED: The long-run effects of increases in the costs of factors of production.

DISCUSSION: A firm should employ inputs such that the marginal products per dollar of input are equal. Because the wage rate increased by more than the rental rate, the marginal product of labor was reduced with respect to the marginal product of equipment. By using more equipment and less labor, the company's marginal product for equipment will be reduced and its marginal product for labor will rise until the two are equal.

Answer (B) is incorrect because the company should use relatively less labor than before. Labor costs went up at a greater rate than equipment costs. Answer (C) is incorrect because the company should not decrease the amounts of both inputs if it wishes to maintain output and profitability. Answer (D) is incorrect because the company has an incentive to increase the equipment-output ratio.

A3. If the price elasticity of demand for a normal good is estimated to be 2.5, a 5% reduction in its price causes

A. Total revenue to fall by 5%.

B. Total revenue to fall by 12.5%.

C. Quantity demanded to rise by 12.5%.

D. Quantity demanded to decrease by 5%.

The correct answer is (C). *(Publisher)* **SU 1**

REQUIRED: The effect of a reduction in price of a normal good.

DISCUSSION: Price elasticity is the percentage change in quantity demanded divided by the percentage change in price. An elasticity of 2.5 means that the change in demand will increase by 250% of any change in price measured in absolute terms (the minus sign is ignored). Hence, a 5% price reduction increases demand by 12.5% (2.5 x 5%).

Answers (A) and (B) are incorrect because revenue should rise as the price falls when elasticity exceeds 1.0. Answer (D) is incorrect because the price decline will lead to increased demand if elasticity is greater than 1.0.

STUDY UNIT 2: MACROECONOMICS

21 pages of outline
48 multiple-choice questions

Macroeconomics is the study of economic aggregates and an overview of the economy. It includes levels of national income, employment, and prices. The relative weight range assigned to macroeconomics in Part 1 is 10% to 15%. Expect 12 to 18 questions on macroeconomics.

A. GDP and Business Cycles

1. **National income accounting** is used to measure the output and performance of a nation's economy.
   a. **Gross domestic product** (GDP) is the principal measure of national economic performance. It is the total market value of all final goods and services produced within the boundaries of the U.S., whether by domestic or foreign-owned sources, during a specified period of time (usually a year).
   b. GDP is calculated without regard to the ownership of productive resources. Thus, the value of the output of a U.S.-owned factory abroad is excluded, but the output of a foreign-owned factory in the U.S. is included.
   c. There are two equivalent approaches to the measurement of GDP.
      1) **Income approach.** GDP equals the sum of the items below, minus U.S. income earned abroad.
         a) Wages (compensation of employees)
         b) Interest
         c) Rents
         d) Proprietors' income
         e) Depreciation (consumption of fixed capital)
         f) Indirect business taxes (e.g., sales taxes)
         g) Corporate income taxes
         h) Dividends
         i) Undistributed corporate profits
      2) **Expenditure approach.** GDP is the sum of
         a) Personal consumption expenditures
         b) Gross private domestic investment
         c) Government purchases
         d) Net exports
      3) To avoid double counting in the computation of GDP, the value added to each good or service at each stage of production over the period must be summed.
         a) Alternatively, the total market value of all final goods and services may be added.

4) GDP is not an ideal measure of economic well-being.

a) GDP is a monetary measure; therefore, comparing GDP over a period of time requires adjustment for price changes, inflation, etc.

b) Increases in GDP often involve environmental damage such as noise, congestion, or pollution.

c) GDP is not adjusted for changes in the population (which changes the per capita income).

d) Changes in the value of leisure time are not considered.

e) Some nonmarket transactions are excluded, e.g., the value of homemakers' work.

f) Military expenditures are included at cost, not incremental total value.

5) Other national income concepts

a) **Net domestic product** (NDP) = GDP – depreciation

b) **National income** (NI) = NDP + U.S. net income earned abroad – indirect business taxes (e.g., sales taxes)

c) **Personal income** (PI) = NI – corporate income taxes and undistributed profits – Social Security contributions + transfer payments (public and private)

d) **Disposable income** = PI – personal income taxes

6) Disposable income is divided between

a) Consumption and interest payments
b) Savings

7) Real per capita output is GDP divided by population, adjusted for inflation. It is used as a measure of the standard of living.

2. At the macroeconomic level, prices and equilibrium quantities for specific goods and services are aggregated.

a. **Aggregate demand** reflects the real domestic output demanded at each possible price level. This is an inverse relationship, so the curve slopes downward. As the price level falls, real purchasing power increases, interest rates decline, and foreign purchases increase. The determinants of aggregate demand are changes in consumer spending, investment, government spending, and net exports.

b. **Aggregate supply** reflects the real domestic output available at each possible price level. This is a direct relationship. This curve has horizontal, upward-sloping, and vertical components. The assumption is that the price level will not rise when productive resources are substantially underused. However, at full employment, the price level will rise with no increase in real output. In the intermediate range, both the price level and real output increase. The determinants of aggregate supply are changes in input prices, productivity, and the legal and institutional environment.

3. The study of **business cycles** focuses on the periodic cycles in the economy, most of which are characterized by changes in price levels and in rates of employment.
   a. A business cycle has four stages: trough, recovery, peak, and recession.
   b. A **trough** is marked by low levels of economic activity and underuse of resources.
   c. **Recovery** is marked by increasing economic activity.
   d. The **peak** is that period when economic activity is booming.
   e. **Recession** means economic activities and employment levels contract.
      1) During the recessionary phase of a business cycle, society's resources are underused. Because of the underuse of resources, potential national income will exceed actual national income.
4. **Economic Indicators**. Economists use a variety of economic indicators to forecast turns in the business cycle. Economic indicators are variables that in the past have had a high correlation with aggregate economic activity. The best known are the composite indexes calculated by The Conference Board, a private research group with more than 2,700 corporate and other members worldwide. Indicators may lead, lag, or coincide with economic activity.
   a. The Conference Board's **leading indicators** include
      1) Average workweek for production workers
      2) Prices of 500 common stocks
      3) Average weekly initial unemployment insurance claims
      4) New orders for consumer goods and materials (1992 dollars)
      5) New orders for nondefense capital goods
      6) Building permits for homes
      7) Vendor performance (slower deliveries diffusion index)
      8) Money supply (M_2 in 1992 dollars)
      9) Index of consumer expectations (1966 base year)
      10) Interest rate spread (10-year Treasury bonds-federal funds rate)
   b. The Conference Board's **lagging indicators** include
      1) Average duration of unemployment in weeks
      2) Change in index of labor cost per unit of output
      3) Average prime rate charged by banks
      4) Ratio of manufacturing and trade inventories to sales (1992 dollars)
      5) Commercial and industrial loans outstanding (1992 dollars)
      6) Ratio of consumer installment credit outstanding to personal income
      7) Change in CPI for services
   c. The Conference Board's **coincident indicators** include
      1) Employees on nonagricultural payrolls
      2) Personal income minus transfer payments (1992 dollars)
      3) Industrial production (indexed to 1992)
      4) Manufacturing and trade sales (1992 dollars)
5. Investment expenditure is a focal point used by economists to explain business cycles.
   a. The **accelerator theory** gives a model for volatility of investment and the subsequent effects on GDP.
      1) The accelerator theory states that capital investment is related to the rate of change in GDP.
      2) It assumes a particular level of capital equipment needed to produce a given level of output.

b. Given an economy producing at capacity and a subsequent increase in product demand, an increase in capital investment is required to meet the increased demand. The demand for capital goods then creates an additional increase in demand, which in turn requires an additional investment in capital goods. In this fashion, the process of investing to meet demand continues to accelerate.

c. A positive net investment occurs when the additions to capital goods exceed the amount of depreciation on existing capital goods.

1) Negative net investment occurs when depreciation exceeds the additions to capital stock.

6. Stop and review! You have completed the outline for this subunit. Study multiple-choice questions 1 through 13 beginning on page 86.

B. Keynesian (Fiscal) Economics

In 1936, John Maynard Keynes published his theory maintaining that the economy could be in equilibrium at less than full employment. These new ideas gained acceptance because of the failure of classical economics during the Great Depression.

1. Classical Economics

a. According to classical theory, the economy is capable of generating and maintaining full employment over the long run without government intervention because of price and wage flexibility.

b. **Adjustment mechanisms**

1) **Say's Law**: Supply creates its own demand.

2) Flexible interest rates provide equality of savings and investments.

3) Flexible prices allow self-correction of surpluses or shortages in product or labor markets.

c. **Demand for money**

1) **The equation of exchange**, the fundamental, classical equation, is an identity that serves as a framework for analyzing the impact of money on the level of aggregate demand. Thus, it is also fundamental to monetarism. The equation is usually stated as

$$MV = GDP$$

or

$$MV = PQ$$

If: M = Money stock (supply)
V = Velocity (defined below)
GDP = Gross domestic product
P = Aggregate price index
Q = Aggregate output index

2) **The income velocity of money** (V) reflects the average turnover rate of the money stock in the transactions that constitute our GDP. The velocity of money can be defined as the ratio of GDP to the money supply (the number of times a dollar is spent for final goods and services).

3) A major classical proposition is that an increase in the money supply will lead to an increase in aggregate demand (as opposed to Keynes, who argued that an increase in M will be completely offset by a decrease in V, leaving PQ unchanged). A classical economist would use either of the following arguments:

a) V may be unstable, but the money supply is an important aspect of aggregate demand (thus, an increase in M is not offset by a decrease in V).

b) V is quite stable. Thus, a change in the money supply has a powerful effect on aggregate demand.

d. Unemployment does not exist in the classical model because, if people (or capital) are unemployed, downward pressure is placed on wage rates until all of the people who want to work at prevailing wage rates are working.

e. Classical economics has no well-defined position on fiscal policy and its effectiveness as a stimulant to aggregate demand. Some classical views:

1) An increase in government spending would have little effect on demand (if it were financed by debt) because it would draw from the same pool as the private (business) sector.

2) High government spending will have an effect on demand when it is financed by increasing the money supply (which in itself stimulates demand).

3) An increase in government spending will lead to an increase in velocity, resulting in an increase in aggregate demand.

2. **Three General Assumptions of Keynesian Economics**

a. The difference between savings plans and investment plans is fundamental to an understanding of changes in the level of income.

1) Keynesian analysis emphasizes that saving and investing are undertaken by different people with different motivations.

b. Price flexibility cannot be relied upon to provide full employment because prices tend to be sticky downward; i.e., they are not lowered easily.

c. Equilibrium GDP does not necessarily provide full employment.

3. **The Basic Keynesian Equation**

a. This equation reflects the aggregate expenditures approach to measurement of GDP. It equals the sum of after-tax consumption expenditures, gross investment, net exports, and government spending.

$$GDP = C + I_g + X_N + G$$

4. **Consumption and Saving**

a. The major determinant is income.

b. Propensities to consume and save (Δ means the change in.)

1) *Average propensity to consume* = *Consumption* ÷ *Income*
2) *Average propensity to save* = *Savings* ÷ *Income*
3) *Marginal propensity to consume* = Δ *Consumption* ÷ Δ *Income*
4) *Marginal propensity to save* = Δ *Savings* ÷ Δ *Income*

c. Nonincome determinants

1) Price expectations (includes expectations about availability, future prices, future incomes). Consumer expectations about price increases, or the lack of future availability, cause an increase in current purchases.

2) Interest rates. As interest rates increase, the incentive to save is increased (which leads to reduced consumption).

3) Quantity of liquid assets. If people have larger stocks of assets, they tend to spend more money at every level of disposable income.

4) Credit. If consumers are deeply in debt, they are likely to reduce their rate of growth in consumption.

5) Attitudes. If individuals believe that saving money is virtuous, aggregate consumption is lower than if the feeling is "consume for today."

6) Consumer stock of durable goods. With a high stock of durables, consumers can cease purchasing durable goods but still consume a high level (depleting the stock). No cash flow is associated with the use of durables, so spending decreases at all levels of disposable income.

5. **Investment**

a. The major determinant of investment is its profitability as expected by the business sector. Profitability is affected by the following variables:

1) Rate of growth of technology. Because new products and innovations are often profitable, firms will invest more when the technological growth rate is high.

2) Interest rates. As real interest rates increase, marginal investments are not undertaken, thus lowering total business investment.

a) The real rate is the nominal rate minus the inflation premium.

3) Stock of capital goods. The higher the stock, the lower the demand for new capital goods (until the stock is depleted).

4) Government actions. Changes in tax rates, depreciation allowances, and government spending can change the expected profitability of a given investment.

5) Acquisition and maintenance costs. The higher the purchase price and life-long operating costs of a capital good, the lower the expected profitability on the investment.

b. Components of investment

1) Plant and equipment expenditures

a) The capital consumption allowance (depreciation) is a negative component of investment.

2) Residential construction expenditures

3) Inventories

c. Autonomous investment -- investment expenditures made by businesses that are independent of the level of national income and that are undertaken for their expected profitability. The level of autonomous investment will be constant regardless of an expansion or a recession of economic activity.

d. Induced investment -- investment made as a result of increased economic activity

e. Investment tends to be the most volatile component of private spending. For that reason, it is given central importance in income determination theory. Reasons for this volatility are

1) Capital durability. Because a piece of equipment can be either repaired or scrapped, the timing option (when to purchase new capital) is usually open. Only when expectations about future business conditions are bright will new durables be purchased (only then would new debt be wise).

2) State of technology. Major breakthroughs in technology are fairly rare and irregular. However, when a breakthrough does occur, large amounts of investment are undertaken, increasing the volatility of investment expenditures.

3) Expectations. Changing expectations about future business conditions may alter business confidence. Events that may change expectations include legislation, changes in economic policy, strikes, shifts in population demographics, and important judicial decisions.

4) The variability of profits results not only in variability of incentive to invest but also in variability of the means of investment.

6. **Equilibrium GDP** is the output level at which the economy creates just enough spending to purchase the output produced. A model can be devised for determination of equilibrium GDP in a closed private economy, one without government spending and international trade.

a. In this model, equilibrium occurs when aggregate expenditures (consumption + investment) equal real aggregate domestic output.

b. The 45° line in the graph below on the right consists of a series of points representing equilibrium (C + I = GDP).

1) Equilibrium GDP also occurs at the point where aggregate savings equals aggregate investment (see graph below on the left). This alternative model has been called the leakages-injections approach to determining equilibrium GDP. Saving is a leakage of spending from aggregate expenditures, and investment is an injection of spending.

Equilibrium GDP
(Closed Economy, No Government)

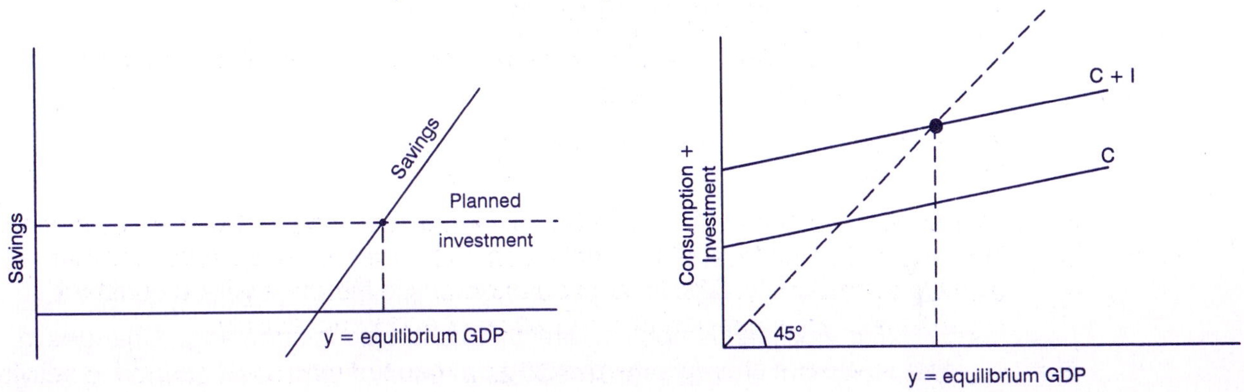

c. A model also can be devised for determination of equilibrium GDP that incorporates net exports as part of aggregate expenditures. Positive net exports increase expenditures and GDP. Negative net exports have the opposite effect. The model can be further extended to incorporate government spending. See the basic Keynesian equation on page 69.

1) In the leakages-injections equilibrium model, savings plus imports equals investment plus exports.

2) Furthermore, the leakages-injections equilibrium model can also be expanded to include government spending and taxation [(savings after taxes + imports + taxes) = (investment + exports + government spending)].

7. **The Multiplier**

a. A change (positive or negative) in investment, consumption, government spending, or net export spending will result in a multiplied change in equilibrium GDP. This multiplier phenomenon occurs because the initial change in spending has a ripple effect (the magnitude depends on the marginal propensity to consume).

b. The **marginal propensity to consume (MPC)** is the percentage of additional income that is consumed.

c. The **marginal propensity to save (MPS)** is the percentage of additional income that is saved.

1) $MPC + MPS = 1$ (Income can be either spent or saved.)
$MPS = 1 - MPC$

d. The formula for the multiplier is

$$\frac{1}{MPS} \quad \text{or} \quad \frac{1}{1 - MPC}$$

1) For example, if MPC is .8 and spending increases by \$10, the increase in equilibrium GDP is \$50 {\$10 x [1 ÷ (1 – .8)]}.

8. **Some Additional Relationships**

a. **The tax multiplier**. Changes in taxes do not affect the economy through the standard multiplier. Because changes in taxes affect the economy through changes in consumption, the tax multiplier is

$$\frac{-MPC}{1 - MPC}$$

Accordingly, the Δ GDP $= \dfrac{-MPC}{1 - MPC} \times \Delta\ taxes$

1) The reason this differs from the regular multiplier, 1÷(1–MPC), is that the regular multiplier is applied directly to changes in spending. Changes in taxes are not changes in spending but cause them.

b. **The government budget surplus (deficit)** is the excess of government tax collections over government transfers and purchases. It can either be positive (a surplus) or negative (a deficit).

c. **The full employment budget surplus** is the excess of government tax collections over government transfers and purchases that would occur if the economy were at full employment. It has the following characteristics that make it preferable to the regular budget surplus:

1) It does not change passively with output changes.

2) It is a better measure of the direction (expansionary or contractionary) of fiscal policy.

d. **The balanced budget multiplier.** The government can increase its spending and stimulate the economy without changing the budget deficit if it increases taxes and spending by the same amount. A balanced budget increase does not alter the deficit. It stimulates the economy because all of the increase in spending affects the economy, but some of the taxes are paid for out of decreased savings. The amount by which the economy is stimulated is the balanced budget multiplier. The balanced budget multiplier is 1.

9. The limit to increasing GDP in the short run is determined by the amount of resources available and can be depicted graphically. The production possibility frontier (PPF) depicts all possible combinations of output (assuming a two-good world) that a society can have, all other things held constant.

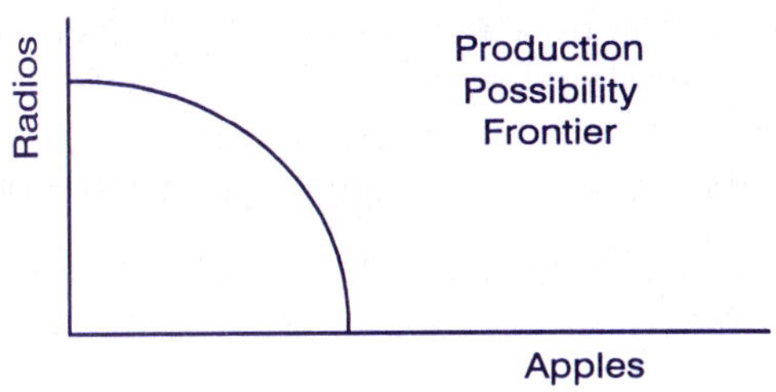

a. Assuming the society is on the outer boundary (which implies full employment and optimal use of resources for a given state of technology), the only way to have more apples is to give up some radios (or vice versa). In the long run, the frontier can be shifted (out or in). Factors causing such a shift include

1) Increases in productive resources (land, labor, and capital)
2) Technological advancements
3) International specialization and trade

b. Production at a point within the curve is attainable, but it indicates a failure to achieve full employment and full production. Production at a point outside the curve is superior to production at any point on the curve, however these points are unattainable with current resources and technologies.

c. By definition, if society is producing on the boundary of the PPF, all resources are in use and no additional output can be produced in the short run. Hence, even with an increase in aggregate demand, the production capability may not exist to supply the quantity demanded. If supply cannot be increased, consumers will bid up the prices of existing goods, creating an erosion of the price level.

d. This graph illustrates the concept of an **inflationary gap** (AB) in the closed private economy model. This gap is caused by an excess of aggregate spending (C + I) over the full employment noninflationary GDP (C'+I').

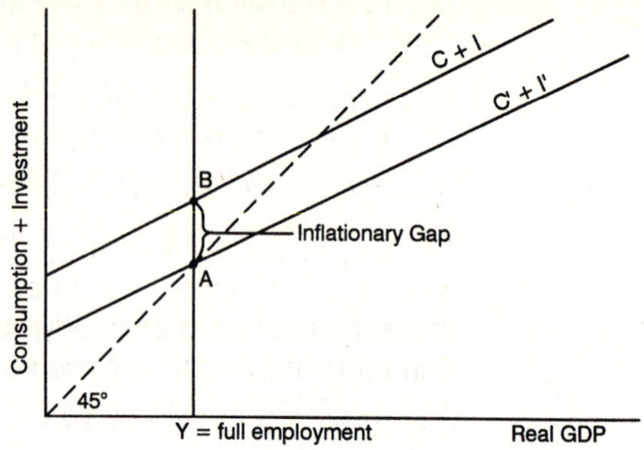

10. In Keynesian analysis, the supply and demand for money determine the interest rate.
    a. Supply of money is determined by the monetary authorities (Federal Reserve Board).
    b. Demand for money is determined by transactions demand and asset demand.
        1) Transactions demand arises from the need to use money as a medium of exchange. It varies directly with nominal GDP.
        2) Asset demand reflects money's role as a store of value. Money is the most liquid and least risky of assets. However, holding money entails an opportunity cost because it does not provide a return. Thus, asset demand is inversely related to the level of interest rates.
    c. The supply of money (fixed in the short run) and the demand for money give money market equilibrium and determine the equilibrium interest rate (price of money), I_e.
    d. The schedule below, which incorporates the above reasons for holding cash, is the demand curve for money.

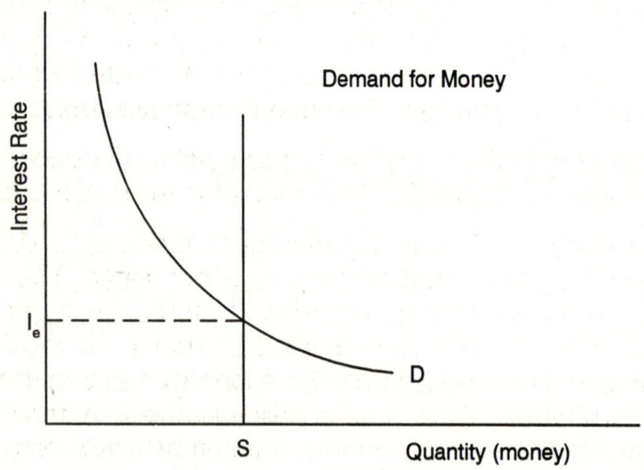

1) The function slopes downward because, at higher interest rates, people hold less cash.

2) The intersection of the money supply (fixed by the monetary authorities) and demand is the equilibrium interest rate.

3) This schedule assumes income is fixed.

e. Varying the supply of money alters the interest rate, affecting investment in society. For example, increasing the supply of money moves one down and to the right along the demand curve shown on the previous page. This decreases the interest rate and increases the amount of investment in the economy.

f. The nominal interest rate has two components.

1) Real rate (historically 2% to 4% average)
2) Inflation premium

a) The size of the premium is a function of the expected inflation rate.

b) The higher the expected inflation rate, the higher the inflation premium.

c) The higher the inflation premium, the higher the nominal interest rate.

11. **Monetarists, Supply-siders, and Others**

a. Critics believe that the Keynesian emphasis on spending and taxation (fiscal policy) overlooked the powerful effect that money supply and credit have on the economy. **Monetarists** believe that a steady, restrained growth of the money supply is more influential than budget policy on economic performance, inflation, and unemployment. The basic equation of monetarism is the equation of exchange (see page 68).

1) Monetarists believe the upward-sloping aggregate supply curve is steep, so a slight shift in aggregate demand to the right causes a large increase in the price level relative to the increase in real domestic output and employment. Thus, in the long run, inflation is caused by increases in the money supply. Excessive monetary growth will result in excessive inflation. Accordingly, inflation can be controlled only by maintaining a firm grip on the growth of the nation's money supply.

2) According to the monetarists, fiscal policy (federal taxes and spending) should not be used to counteract the turns of a business cycle.

3) Monetarists believe that government attempts to eliminate fluctuations in the economy have made them worse, not better. The monetarists' argument is that, by the time an economic disturbance is perceived and a policy is formulated and implemented to correct it, it is too late. The effects of the policy will not be felt until the economy has begun to recover from the disturbance. Thus, such a policy serves to magnify rather than to dampen fluctuations in the economy. Monetarists therefore favor letting small fluctuations work themselves out without government intervention.

b. **Supply-siders** (who hold to a philosophy popularized by the Reagan Administration) favor restoring incentives to the economy by cutting taxes to stimulate work, savings, and investment.

1) A progressive tax structure provides a strong disincentive for increasing effort and subsequent economic achievement. At higher income levels, more and more of every dollar gained is earned for government rather than for personal use. Hence, supply-siders argue that deep cuts in personal and business taxes will produce a strong recovery due not only to the increase in aggregate demand, but also to the increased motivation to achieve. It has been postulated that this recovery would offset tax losses with rising revenues, so that spending cuts might not be needed.

2) The economy will function better with new incentives to stimulate investment and production than with federal programs to redistribute wealth from rich to poor.

c. **Neo-Keynesians** represent a middle ground between Keynesians and monetarists. They continue to have confidence in the ability of aggregate demand policies (changes in government purchases, taxes, etc.) to influence economic activities. In addition, they accept that excessive monetary growth will lead inevitably to higher inflation. They believe, however, that at some levels of unemployment, money supply growth will lead primarily to increases in output and not just higher inflation. This theory is supported by an increasing number of moderate monetarists.

12. Stop and review! You have completed the outline for this subunit. Study multiple-choice questions 14 through 24 beginning on page 90.

C. Money and the Economy

1. Money functions as a medium of exchange, standard of value, and store of value.

2. **Definitions of Money**

a. **Narrow money** (M_1) **stock** includes

1) Coins and currency
2) Checking deposits (including travelers' checks)

b. The Federal Reserve's targets for monetary growth emphasize M_2, which includes

1) Coins and currency
2) Checking deposits
3) Nonchecking savings
4) Small (less than $100,000) time deposits

c. M_1 and M_2 are the most common measures of money and are reported weekly in the *Wall Street Journal*.

d. A still broader definition (M_3) includes M_2 plus large ($100,000 or more) time deposits.

e. All assets have some degree of liquidity. One group of assets is referred to as **near money**. Short-term government securities are examples of near money, as are time deposits and nonchecking savings deposits.

1) Financial assets are debt instruments, whereas real assets are productive items.

3. **Supply of Money -- Banks and Deposit Creation**

a. Commercial banks are businesses that must balance profits and liquidity.

b. A bank must have on reserve a certain percentage of its total deposits. These fractional reserve requirements are required by law in order to

1) Insure that money will be on hand to carry out transactions
2) Control the total supply of money

c. **Money multiplier**

1) If a bank's actual reserves exceed the reserves required by law, it has excess reserves with which it can (and will, if it is a profit-maximizing bank) extend loans.

2) An individual bank creates money equal to its excess reserves when it lends the excess reserves rather than investing in securities.

3) For the banking system as a whole, assuming no leakage (i.e., assuming that all the money in the economy is in the bank), money creation is measured by a multiple of excess reserves, as follows:

$D = 1 \div r$ If: D = the money multiplier
r = the legal reserve requirement

4) EXAMPLE: Assume the banking system's excess reserves increase by $100 and we want to determine how much the money supply is increased. Using the above formula (and assuming the reserve requirement is 20%), we get the following increase in the money supply:

$D = 1 \div .2 = 5$ The money supply is multiplied by 5.
$5 \times \$100 = \$500$

d. The interest rate is expressed as a percentage.

1) A basis point is one-one hundredth of 1%.

4. **Monetary Policy**

a. The **Federal Reserve Board (the Fed)** controls the money supply independently of the federal government. Any policy designed by the Fed to affect the money supply, and thus the economy, is known as monetary policy. Control of the growth of the money supply by the Fed is viewed as essential to control the availability of credit, spending, and inflation. One reason is that the money supply must grow at the same rate as the economy in order for the economy to be completely healthy.

b. Structure of the Fed

1) The Board of governors has seven members appointed by the President and confirmed by the Senate.

a) They serve fourteen-year terms, and their appointments are staggered.

b) The board of governors is responsible for administering monetary policy and running the banking system.

c) The chair and vice-chair are appointed for 4-year terms by the President and confirmed by the Senate.

2) The Federal Reserve System is divided into twelve geographical districts.

3) The federal open-market committee buys and sells bonds on the open market (changing the money supply).

c. The functions of the Federal Reserve include

1) Control of the money supply
2) Check collection
3) Serving as the fiscal agent of the U.S. government
4) Supervision of the entire banking system
5) Holding deposits (reserves) for member institutions

a) As a result, a federal funds market has developed for the lending of member banks' excess reserves to other member banks.

i) Federal funds loans are usually made for 1 day at a time.

ii) The federal funds rate is the rate paid on these overnight loans.

d. The Fed controls the money supply by using monetary policy tools.

1) Major tools

a) **Open-market operations**. Purchase and sale of government securities is the primary mechanism of monetary control.

i) Fed purchases are expansionary; they increase bank reserves and the money supply.

ii) Fed sales are contractional. Paying money into the Federal Reserve takes the money out of circulation, reduces bank reserves, and contracts the money supply.

b) **Reserves**. The legal reserve requirement is the percentage of deposits that must be kept on hand.

i) Lowering the percentage is expansionary (allowing banks to put more of their excess reserves into circulation through loans).

ii) Raising the percentage is contractional.

iii) This tool is not frequently used because it has very powerful effects on the economy.

c) **Changing the discount rate**. This rate is the interest rate at which member banks may borrow from the Fed.

i) Lowering the rate encourages borrowing and increases the money supply.

ii) Raising the rate discourages borrowing, increases saving, and decreases the money supply.

iii) Changing the federal funds rate is another way in which the Fed affects interest rates, the money supply, and economic activity.

2) Minor tools

a) Moral suasion. "Jawbone control" entails merely asking banks to hold down rates.

b) Margin requirements. The margin is the percentage of the purchase price of securities that cannot be borrowed. It determines the down payment requirements on stock purchases.

c) Selective credit controls. For example, the Fed may require a certain percentage of down payment on durable good purchases.

e. The Federal Reserve cannot stabilize interest rates and at the same time control growth in reserves and the money supply because there is an inverse relationship between (1) interest rates and bank reserves and (2) interest rates and the money supply. Thus, the Federal Reserve has adopted the pragmatic policy of sometimes targeting interest rates and sometimes targeting the money supply.

1) If the Fed wants to stabilize interest rates, more reserves must be supplied (which in turn can increase the money supply).

2) EXAMPLE: If the reserve requirement is increased (giving banks lower free reserves to lend to borrowers), banks will not be able to supply all borrowers who want loans. Interest rates will be driven up to equalize the supply and demand for loans.

5. Stop and review! You have completed the outline for this subunit. Study multiple-choice questions 25 through 35 beginning on page 93.

D. Unemployment, Inflation, and Government

1. Unemployment

a. Full employment

1) Theoretical definition: Full employment exists when all individuals willing to work at prevailing market wages are employed at tasks appropriate for their skills.

2) Policy definition: Full employment exists even though some members of the labor force are unemployed. The normal workings of the market will result in a rate of unemployment (the natural rate) of 5% to 6% when full employment is deemed to exist. The full-employment rate of unemployment equals the sum of frictional and structural unemployment.

b. Types of unemployment

1) **Frictional unemployment** is the amount of unemployment caused by the normal workings of the labor market. This definition acknowledges that some unemployment exists at any given time as workers search for jobs or wait to take jobs in the near term.

2) **Structural unemployment** exists when aggregate demand is sufficient to provide full employment, but the distribution of the demand does not correspond precisely to the composition of the labor force; e.g., some NASA engineers were unemployed at the end of the race to the moon.

3) **Cyclical unemployment** is caused by insufficient aggregate demand. During economic downturns, unemployment will occur due to lack of demand.

c. Costs of unemployment

1) Economic cost can be measured in terms of the forgone output, i.e., the gap between potential GDP under full employment and actual GDP.

2) Noneconomic costs of unemployment, such as the individual and social degradation implicit in the loss of meaningful employment and income, are equally important.

2. Inflation

a. Inflation is an increase in the general level of prices. The general price level is negatively related to the purchasing power of money. There are two basic types of inflation.

1) **Cost-push** inflation is generated by increased production costs, which are passed on to consumers in the form of higher prices. Labor unions are often considered the source of these increased costs.

a) More recently, labor unions have become relatively less powerful because of expansion of service industries relative to basic manufacturing.

2) **Demand-pull** inflation is generated by excess aggregate demand for goods and services.

a) This problem arises when the economy approaches full employment and demand continues to increase.

b) Premature inflation occurs prior to full employment. The reason is that full employment may be reached in some sectors of the economy even though most have excess capacity. Thus, bottlenecks occur and prices rise in those sectors.

b. Measuring inflation

1) **The consumer price index (CPI)** measures inflation by a monthly pricing of items on a typical household shopping list.

a) The current index uses a base year as a reference point. The price in the current year of a market basket of goods and services is determined relative to the same basket for the base year.

b) $$\frac{\textit{Price of market basket in a given year}}{\textit{Price of the same market basket in the base year}} \times 100$$

2) **The wholesale price index (WPI)** measures increases in prices at the wholesale level. It is often accepted as a proxy for future inflation.

3) **GDP deflator** includes every item produced in the economy at the price at which it entered the GDP account.

c. Costs of inflation

1) The rate is difficult to predict.
2) Usury laws may prevent borrowing if interest rates are too high.
3) Negotiating long-term contracts may be difficult.
4) The efficiency of business relationships is reduced.
5) Breach of existing contracts is encouraged.

d. Redistributive effects of inflation

1) Inflation hurts creditors, fixed-income groups, and savers.

a) But inflation benefits debtors because they pay back their debts in less valuable dollars.

2) Inflation is an arbitrary redistribution of income that does not reflect the operations of the free market or the government's attempt to alter income distribution.

3. **Inflation versus Unemployment Trade-off**

   a. Economic theory has historically treated inflation and unemployment as mutually exclusive agents.

   b. Fluctuations in aggregate demand reveal an inverse relationship between inflation and unemployment. The underlying reason for this trade-off is that the aggregate supply curve is upward sloping (i.e., more goods will be produced only at a higher price).

   c. Modern macroeconomic theory suggests there is little or no relationship between inflation and unemployment. In the long run, unemployment will be near the natural rate (5% – 6%) regardless of the inflation rate. The downward-sloping Phillips curve that postulates an inverse relationship between inflation and unemployment is true only in the short run, although this short run may last 2 or 3 years.

   d. **Phillips curve** -- an attempt to quantify the trade-off between inflation and unemployment. It is an empirical relationship showing the trade-offs between the rate of inflation and the rate of unemployment.

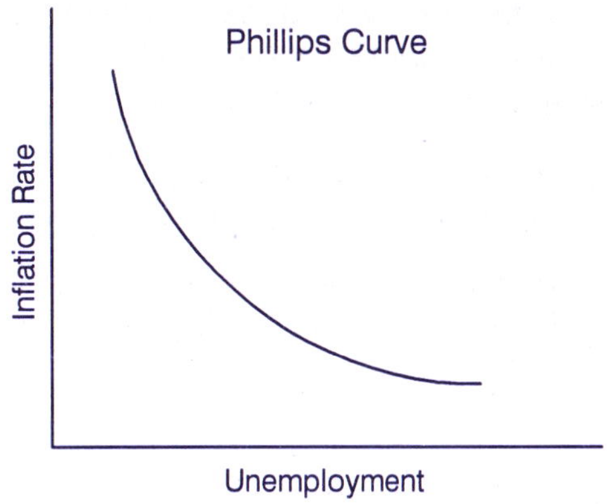

4. **The Role of Government in an Economic System**

   a. **Fiscal policy.** Government expenditures and taxation are aimed at certain socially acceptable goals (level of income, unemployment, distribution of income, etc.).

   b. With the Full Employment Act of 1946, the federal government assumed responsibility for full employment, price stability, and economic growth.

   c. Thus, government can justify entering a market in which market forces will not allocate resources efficiently.

   d. Dividing consumption goods into two categories facilitates analysis of government's role in the market place.

      1) **Public goods** are characterized by

         a) Indivisibility of services (e.g., a public park)

         b) Difficulty of excluding individuals from the benefits (e.g., national defense)

2) **Private goods**

a) One individual's consumption of a private good excludes another from consuming that particular good (e.g., only one person can consume a strawberry milkshake, but everyone benefits from national defense).

3) The relationship of government spending to private consumption and savings can be expressed graphically as shown below. The curvilinear line represents the maximum production level for the economy.

e. The market may not allocate resources efficiently with respect to public goods. Because a public good such as defense cannot be excluded from certain individuals, people often receive the benefit without paying for it. Thus, it represents a spillover benefit. See subsection h. on page 85. Also refer to the graph below.

1) At point A, total societal consumption consists of Y amount of public goods and X amount of private goods. Because point A lies on the frontier, resources are being used efficiently.

2) A society at point B has unemployment and inefficient use of its resources.

3) The combination of public and private consumption represented by point C cannot be obtained in the short run. It lies beyond the frontier, which, by definition, is set at the maximum production level in the short run.

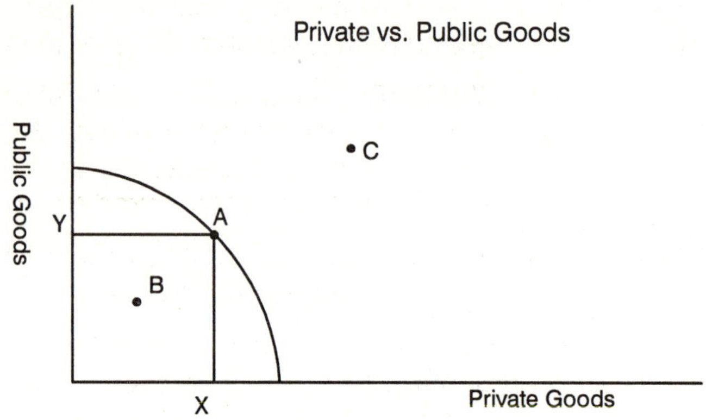

f. Government finances its expenditures by

1) **Taxation**

a) Two principles of taxation

i) Benefits received. Individuals should pay tax based on the benefits received from the services (e.g., paying for the use of a public park or swimming pool).

ii) Ability to pay. Consumers should pay taxes based on their ability to pay them (e.g., taxes on income and wealth).

b) Three classifications of taxes that may or may not reflect ability-to-pay principles

i) **Progressive**. With a higher income, individuals pay a higher percentage of their income in taxes (e.g., income tax).

ii) **Proportional**. At all levels of income, the percentage paid in taxes is constant (e.g., sales tax).

iii) **Regressive**. As income increases, the percentage paid in taxes decreases (e.g., payroll or excise taxes).

- EXAMPLE: An excise tax is regressive because its burden falls disproportionately on lower-income persons. As personal income increases, the percentage of income paid declines since an excise tax is a flat amount per quantity of the good or service purchased.

c) Taxes also may be classified as either direct or indirect.

   i) **Direct taxes** are imposed upon the taxpayer and paid directly to the government, e.g., the personal income tax.

   ii) **Indirect taxes** are levied against others and thus only indirectly on the individual taxpayer, e.g., sales and Social Security taxes paid by employers.

d) **Incidence of taxation** -- the parties who actually bear a particular tax. For example, the person who actually bears the burden of an indirect tax may not be the same one who pays the tax to the government.

   i) The incidence of taxation becomes important when a government wants to change the tax structure. Because taxation is a form of fiscal policy, the government needs to know who will actually bear the incidence of taxation, not just who will pay the tax.

   ii) EXAMPLE: Taxes such as the corporate income tax and corporate property and excise taxes are often shifted to the consumer in the form of higher prices.

   iii) EXAMPLE: Taxes such as windfall profits taxes are not shifted to the consumer via higher prices. This type of one-time-only tax levied on part of the output produced does not increase the equilibrium price of the taxed good.

e) In recent years, some authorities have supported a tax based on consumption -- a **value-added tax**.

   i) Many major industrial nations have already adopted a value-added tax.

   ii) The tax is levied on the value added to goods by each business unit in the production and distribution chain.

      - The amount of value added is measured by the difference between a firm's sales and its purchases.
      - Each firm in the chain collects the tax on its sales, takes a credit for taxes paid on purchases, and remits the difference to the government.
      - The consumer ultimately bears the incidence of the tax through higher prices.

   iii) A value-added tax encourages consumer saving because taxes are paid on consumption only, not on savings.

      - Because the value-added tax is based on consumption, people in the lower income groups would spend a greater proportion of their income on taxes.
      - The value-added tax is thus regressive.

iv) Only those businesses that make a profit have to pay income taxes. Under the value-added tax, however, all businesses have to pay taxes, regardless of income.

2) Debt -- an alternative means of financing

a) Individuals lend to the government on a voluntary basis, whereas taxation is mandatory.

b) Debt spreads the cost over time, allowing future generations to share in the payment of public goods.

i) In contrast, taxation is immediate payment for the goods.

c) **The crowding-out effect**. When the government sells bonds to finance its expenditures, it competes with corporations that are trying to sell their own shares or bonds, thereby dividing a limited market, increasing interest rates, and reducing corporate borrowing and investment.

d) **The crowding-in effect**. In times of slack economic conditions, additional government spending will increase GDP (by shifting aggregate demand), which will encourage investment.

g. Other government activities

1) The activity in which government has increased the most since 1929 is that of welfare expenditures. These **transfer payments** include Medicare, Social Security, welfare, unemployment compensation, and food stamps.

2) Through taxation, the government can alter society's distribution of income, which can be depicted by the Lorenz curve. The Lorenz curve below illustrates the inequality of income distribution. The more bowed out (convex to the X-axis) the curve, the more unequal the distribution of wealth in a country.

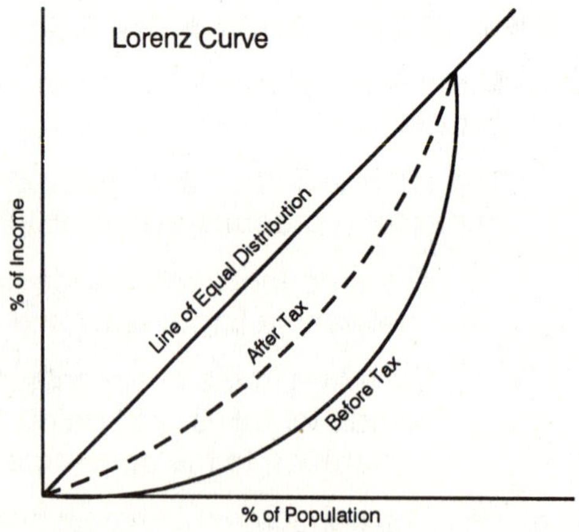

a) If all individuals had equal incomes, the Lorenz curve would lie on the 45° line. The actual income distribution may approximate the before-tax line.

b) With progressive taxation, however, the government can shift the curve closer to equal distribution of income (as shown by the broken line).

3) **Automatic stabilizers** -- elements in the economy that support aggregate demand when it would otherwise be weak (e.g., during a recession) and hold down aggregate demand when it would otherwise be increasing (e.g., during an expansionary period). They reduce the economy's sensitivity to shifts in demand.

a) Examples of automatic stabilizers

i) Income taxes
ii) Unemployment insurance
iii) Corporate profits tax
iv) Agricultural price supports

b) Income tax rates are indexed to inflation so that tax liabilities will not increase solely because of inflation. The enactment of indexation, however, has eliminated an automatic stabilizer. Thus, even though individual taxpayers have more after-tax income with indexation, inflation may get worse as a result.

h. **Externalities** (spillovers) can affect the allocation of resources. For example, pollution of Lake Michigan by an automobile manufacturer that does not clean it up results in lower costs (than if the company used pollution equipment or other purification methods) and a cheaper car to the public. Because the cars are relatively cheaper, more people buy them, encouraging still more pollution. The result is too many cars produced at too low cost with too much pollution. Government can intervene to eliminate these spillover costs by forcing the polluter to bear all of the costs of production, e.g., by enacting environmental laws or imposing specific taxes.

5. Stop and review! You have completed the outline for this subunit. Study multiple-choice questions 36 through 48 beginning on page 97.

MULTIPLE-CHOICE QUESTIONS

A. GDP and Business Cycles

1. Which one of the following would not be included in the calculation of the gross domestic product (GDP)?

A. Purchase of a new home.

B. An automotive worker's wages.

C. A doctor's fee.

D. Purchase of common stock.

The correct answer is (D). *(CMA, adapted)*

REQUIRED: The transaction not included in the gross domestic product.

DISCUSSION: GDP is the value of all final goods and services produced in the U.S., whether by domestic or foreign-owned sources, during a specified period. A common stock purchase is not a new good or service. It is instead a claim to ownership of property that already exists.

Answer (A) is incorrect because a new home is a productive good and is included in GDP. Answer (B) is incorrect because the services of an autoworker are productive and are part of GDP. Answer (C) is incorrect because the doctor's services were produced during the year and thus his/her fee is part of GDP.

2. Under the income approach, gross domestic product (GDP) is measured as

A. *Depreciation charges and indirect business taxes + Wages + Rents + Interest + Profits – Net American income earned abroad.*

B. *Wages + Rents + Interest + Profits.*

C. *Depreciation charges and indirect business taxes + Wages + Rents – Interest + Profits.*

D. *Wages + Rents + Interest – Profits + Net American income earned abroad.*

The correct answer is (A). *(CIA, adapted)*

REQUIRED: The income approach to measurement of GDP.

DISCUSSION: GDP is the total value of goods and services produced within the boundaries of the United States. It may be measured using an expenditures approach or an income approach. Under the income approach, GDP equals all income derived from the production of the year's output, with an adjustment for net U.S. income earned abroad. Two types of nonincome charges or allocations must be added to incomes (wages, rents, interest, and profits). Depreciation reflects the consumption of fixed capital during the period. It is the part of the year's receipts that must be allocated to replace the machinery, plant, etc., used up in the production of GDP. Indirect business taxes, such as sales, excise, and property taxes, are treated by businesses as a cost of production and form part of the total price of goods and services. Thus, they are not paid as wages, rents, interest, and profits. Accordingly, GDP may be measured as the sum of consumption of fixed capital, indirect business taxes, wages, rents, interest, and profits (proprietors' income, corporate taxes, dividends, and undistributed corporate profits), with an adjustment for net U.S. income earned abroad.

Answer (B) is incorrect because nonincome charges and net U.S. income earned abroad must also be included in the calculation. Answer (C) is incorrect because interest income is added, not subtracted. Also, net U.S. income earned abroad must be considered. Answer (D) is incorrect because profits are added, not subtracted. Also, nonincome charges must be included in the calculation.

3. When the addition to capital goods in an economy exceeds the capital consumption allowance, the economy has experienced

A. Negative net investment.

B. Equilibrium investment.

C. Positive gross investment.

D. Positive net investment.

The correct answer is (D). *(CMA, adapted)*

REQUIRED: The condition in which the addition to capital goods exceeds the capital consumption allowance.

DISCUSSION: When the addition to capital goods exceeds the amount of depreciation on existing capital goods, a positive net investment has occurred. In national income accounting, depreciation is referred to as the capital consumption allowance. This allowance is deducted from GDP to arrive at national income.

Answer (A) is incorrect because a negative net investment would occur when depreciation exceeded the additions to the capital stock. Answer (B) is incorrect because it presumably refers to the investment when national income is at the equilibrium point. Answer (C) is incorrect because gross investment is the total addition to capital stock without regard to depreciation.

4. When gross investment <List A> depreciation, the capital stock of the economy is <List B>.

	List A	List B
A.	Exceeds	Shrinking
B.	Equals	Shrinking
C.	Equals	Growing
D.	Is less than	Shrinking

The correct answer is (D). *(CIA, adapted)*

REQUIRED: The relationship of gross investment, depreciation, and the capital stock of the economy.

DISCUSSION: If gross investment is less than depreciation, new investment is insufficient to replace the usage of existing capital. The result is negative net investment (disinvestment). Thus, the capital stock of the economy shrinks.

Answer (A) is incorrect because, when gross investment exceeds depreciation, new investment is greater than the usage of existing capital, and the capital stock of the economy grows. Answers (B) and (C) are incorrect because, when gross investment equals depreciation, new investment is just sufficient to replace the usage of existing capital, and the capital stock of the economy is constant.

5. In national income terms, aggregate demand is the

A. Demand for money by the community in a period of full employment.

B. Total expenditure on capital goods by entrepreneurs during a period of full employment.

C. Demand that is needed if a country's economy is to operate at optimum level and the level of investment is to be raised.

D. Total expenditure on consumer goods and investment, including government and foreign expenditure, during a given period.

The correct answer is (D). *(CMA, adapted)*

REQUIRED: The definition of aggregate demand.

DISCUSSION: Aggregate demand reflects the real domestic output demanded at each possible price level. This is an inverse relationship, so the curve slopes downward. As the price level falls, real purchasing power increases, interest rates decline, and foreign purchases increase. The determinants of aggregate demand are changes in consumer spending, investment, government spending, and net exports.

Answer (A) is incorrect because the demand for money is excluded. Answer (B) is incorrect because aggregate demand includes all expenditures. Answer (C) is incorrect because the definition does not depend upon an optimum level.

Questions 6 through 9 are based on the following information. The financial transactions for a country with values stated in billions of dollars appear in the next column.

Gross domestic product (GDP)	$4,000
Transfer payments	500
Corporate income taxes	50
Social Security contributions	200
Indirect business taxes	210
Personal taxes	250
Undistributed corporate profits	25
Depreciation	500
Net income earned abroad for the country	0

6. Net domestic product is

A. $3,500

B. $3,450

C. $3,290

D. $3,475

The correct answer is (A). *(CMA, adapted)*

REQUIRED: The amount of net domestic product.

DISCUSSION: Net domestic product (NDP) is defined as gross domestic product (GDP) minus consumption of fixed capital (depreciation). GDP is the total market value of all final goods and services produced in an economy during a specified period of time. It excludes the market value of goods and services produced outside the U.S. but includes domestic production by foreign-owned resources. NDP equals $3,500 ($4,000 GDP – $500 depreciation).

Answer (B) is incorrect because corporate income taxes are not included in the NDP calculation. Answer (C) is incorrect because $3,290 equals national income. NDP equals GDP minus depreciation. Answer (D) is incorrect because undistributed corporate profits are not included in the NDP calculation.

7. National income is

A. $3,500

B. $3,290

C. $3,515

D. $3,265

The correct answer is (B). *(CMA, adapted)*

REQUIRED: The amount of national income.

DISCUSSION: National income is defined as net domestic product (NDP), plus net U.S. income earned abroad, minus indirect business taxes. NDP is GDP ($4,000) minus depreciation ($500), or $3,500. Thus, national income is $3,290 ($3,500 GDP + $0 net U.S. income earned abroad – $210 indirect business taxes).

Answer (A) is incorrect because $3,500 is the NDP. Answer (C) is incorrect because $3,515 equals personal income. Answer (D) is incorrect because $3,265 equals disposable income.

8. Personal income is

A. $3,500

B. $3,290

C. $3,265

D. $3,515

The correct answer is (D). *(CMA, adapted)*

REQUIRED: The amount of personal income.

DISCUSSION: Personal income is defined as national income, minus corporate income taxes, minus undistributed corporate profits, minus Social Security contributions, plus transfer payments. National income is $3,290 ($4,000 GDP – $500 depreciation – $210 indirect business taxes). Personal income is $3,515 ($3,290 – $50 – $25 – $200 + $500).

Answer (A) is incorrect because $3,500 equals NDP. Answer (B) is incorrect because $3,290 equals national income. Answer (C) is incorrect because $3,265 equals disposable income.

9. Disposable income is

A. $3,500

B. $3,290

C. $4,500

D. $3,265

The correct answer is (D). *(CMA, adapted)*

REQUIRED: The amount of disposable income.

DISCUSSION: Disposable income is defined as personal income minus personal income taxes. Personal income is $3,515 (see previous Discussion), and disposable income is $3,265 ($3,515 – $250).

Answer (A) is incorrect because $3,500 equals NDP. Answer (B) is incorrect because $3,290 equals national income. Answer (C) is incorrect because $4,500 equals GDP plus transfer payments.

10. For a given level of tax collections, prices, and interest rates, a decrease in governmental purchases will result in a(n)

A. Increase in aggregate demand.

B. Increase in aggregate supply.

C. Decrease in aggregate demand.

D. Decrease in aggregate supply.

The correct answer is (C). *(CIA, adapted)*

REQUIRED: The effect of a decrease in governmental purchases.

DISCUSSION: Aggregate demand includes governmental spending, consumption, investment, and net exports. A decrease in government purchases will decrease aggregate demand.

Answer (A) is incorrect because government purchases are a component of aggregate demand. If government purchases decrease, aggregate demand also decreases. Answers (B) and (D) are incorrect because government purchases do not have an effect on aggregate supply. The determinants of aggregate supply (factors that shift the aggregate supply curve) are changes in input prices, in productivity, in business taxes and subsidies, and in governmental regulation.

11. The trough of a business cycle is generally characterized by

A. Shortages of essential raw materials and rising costs.

B. Increasing purchasing power and increasing capital investments.

C. Rising costs and an unwillingness to risk new investments.

D. Unused productive capacity and an unwillingness to risk new investments.

The correct answer is (D). *(CMA, adapted)*

REQUIRED: The characteristic of the trough.

DISCUSSION: There are four phases of a business cycle: trough, recovery, peak, and recession. The trough is marked by low levels of economic activity and underuse of resources. Investors are unwilling to risk new investments in productive capacity.

Answer (A) is incorrect because the trough of a business cycle is characterized by excess resources and a lack of demand-pull inflation; thus, prices are more apt to be stable or decline during the trough. Answer (B) is incorrect because investors are unwilling to risk new investments during the trough. Answer (C) is incorrect because costs ordinarily do not rise during the trough given excess capacity.

12. During the recessionary phase of a business cycle,

A. The purchasing power of money is likely to decline rapidly.

B. The natural rate of unemployment will increase dramatically.

C. Potential national income will exceed actual national income.

D. Actual national income will exceed potential national income.

The correct answer is (C). *(CMA, adapted)*

REQUIRED: The effect of the recessionary phase.

DISCUSSION: There are four phases of a business cycle: trough, recovery, peak, and recession. During the recessionary phase of a business cycle, economic activities and employment levels contract and society's resources are underused. Because of the underuse of resources, potential national income will exceed actual national income.

Answer (A) is incorrect because, technically, the purchasing power of money is unrelated to the concept of recession; purchasing power relates to inflation. However, demand-pull inflation is unlikely during a recession. Answer (B) is incorrect because the natural rate of unemployment remains unchanged. Any increase in unemployment will be cyclical, i.e., the amount caused by inadequate aggregate demand. Answer (D) is incorrect because potential income will be greater than actual national income given the existence of idle capacity.

13. Which of the following may provide a leading indicator of a future increase in gross domestic product?

A. A reduction in the money supply.

B. A decrease in the issuance of building permits.

C. An increase in the timeliness of delivery by vendors.

D. An increase in the average hours worked per week of production workers.

The correct answer is (D). *(CIA, adapted)*

REQUIRED: The leading indicator.

DISCUSSION: An economic indicator is highly correlated with changes in aggregate economic activity. A leading indicator changes prior to a change in the direction of the business cycle. The leading indicators included in the Conference Board's index are average weekly hours worked by manufacturing workers, unemployment claims, consumer goods orders, stock prices, orders for fixed assets, building permits, timeliness of deliveries, money supply, consumer confidence, and the spread between the yield on 10-year Treasury bonds and the federal funds rate. An increase in weekly hours worked by production workers is favorable for economic growth.

Answer (A) is incorrect because a falling money supply is associated with falling GDP. Answer (B) is incorrect because a decline in the issuance of building permits signals lower expected building activity and a falling GDP. Answer (C) is incorrect because an increase in the timeliness of delivery by vendors indicates slacking business demand and potentially falling GDP.

B. Keynesian (Fiscal) Economics

14. The Keynesian analysis of monetary and fiscal policy

A. Assumes the economy is stable and self-regulating.

B. Places primary emphasis on monetary policy.

C. Assumes that velocity is stable.

D. Focuses on aggregate expenditures.

The correct answer is (D). *(CMA, adapted)*

REQUIRED: The true statement about the Keynesian analysis of monetary and fiscal policy.

DISCUSSION: Keynesians believe that equilibrium occurs when aggregate expenditures (consumption + investment + government expenditures + net exports) equals real GDP.

Answer (A) is incorrect because Keynesians believe that the lack of perfect competition weakens the market mechanism and creates a need for government intervention. Answer (B) is incorrect because emphasis is on fiscal policy, not monetary policy. Answer (C) is incorrect because Keynesian analysis assumes that the velocity of money can change.

15. Given the following data, what is the marginal propensity to consume?

Level of	
Disposable Income	Consumption
$40,000	$38,000
48,000	44,000

A. 1.33

B. 1.26

C. 0.95

D. 0.75

The correct answer is (D). *(CMA, adapted)*

REQUIRED: The marginal propensity to consume.

DISCUSSION: The marginal propensity to consume is the percentage of additional income that is consumed, not saved. Thus, if disposable income increases by $8,000 ($48,000 – $40,000), and consumption increases by $6,000 ($44,000 – $38,000), the marginal propensity to consume is 75% ($6,000 ÷ $8,000).

Answer (A) is incorrect because 1.33 equals marginal income divided by marginal consumption. Answer (B) is incorrect because 1.26 equals $48,000 divided by $38,000. Answer (C) is incorrect because 0.95 equals $38,000 divided by $40,000.

16. A consumer has the following consumption patterns at different income levels:

Level of Income	Consumption
$250	$130
$300	$160
$350	$190

At an income level of $300, this consumer has a marginal propensity to consume of <List A> and an average propensity to save of <List B>.

	List A	List B
A.	0.40	0.47
B.	0.40	0.53
C.	0.60	0.47
D.	0.60	0.53

The correct answer is (C). *(CIA, adapted)*

REQUIRED: The marginal propensity to consume and average propensity to save at a given income level.

DISCUSSION: The marginal propensity to consume is the increase in consumption divided by the increase in income. Thus, it equals [($160 – $130) ÷ ($300 – $250)], or .60. The average propensity to save equals the difference between income and consumption, divided by level of income. Thus, it equals [($300 – $160) ÷ $300], or .47.

Answer (A) is incorrect because the marginal propensity to save is .4. Answer (B) is incorrect because the marginal propensity to save is .4, and the average propensity to consume is .53. Answer (D) is incorrect because the average propensity to consume is .53.

17. If an increase in government purchases of goods and services of $20 billion causes equilibrium GDP to rise by $80 billion, and if total taxes and investment are constant, the marginal propensity to consume out of disposable income is

A. 0.75

B. 0.25

C. 1.25

D. 4.00

The correct answer is (A). *(CMA, adapted)*

REQUIRED: The marginal propensity to consume given the multiplier.

DISCUSSION: The multiplier is defined as the change in income with respect to a change in demand. With taxes and investment held constant, the multiplier is equal to one divided by an expression equal to one minus the marginal propensity to consume. The multiplier here is 4 ($80 billion ÷ $20 billion). Substituting 4 into the formula for the multiplier, a marginal propensity to consume of .75 results.

Answer (B) is incorrect because .25 is the marginal propensity to save. Answers (C) and (D) are incorrect because the marginal propensity to consume is between 0 and 1.

18. Economists and economic policy makers are interested in the multiplier effect because the multiplier explains why

A. A small change in investment can have a much larger impact on gross domestic product.

B. Consumption is always a multiple of savings.

C. The money supply increases when deposits in the banking system increase.

D. The velocity of money is less than one.

The correct answer is (A). *(CMA, adapted)*

REQUIRED: The reason economists are interested in the multiplier effect.

DISCUSSION: The multiplier effect is the increase in GDP that occurs as a result of a change in investment. A given investment can result in a much larger increase in GDP because the investment is spent several times. The multiplier is the reciprocal of the marginal propensity to save.

Answer (B) is incorrect because the consumption function relates disposable income, the marginal propensity to consume, and the amount of consumption at zero income. Answer (C) is incorrect because the multiplier is not concerned with monetary policy. Answer (D) is incorrect because the velocity of money is the ratio of GDP to the money supply. Keynes argued that changes in the money supply would be offset by a decrease in velocity.

19. The federal budget deficit is the

A. Total accumulation of the federal government's surpluses and deficits.

B. Excess of state, local, and federal spending over their revenues.

C. Amount by which the federal government's expenditures exceed its revenues in a given year.

D. Amount by which liabilities exceed assets on the federal government's balance sheet.

The correct answer is (C). *(CMA, adapted)*

REQUIRED: The definition of the federal budget deficit.

DISCUSSION: The federal budget deficit is the amount by which the federal government's expenditures (transfers and purchases) exceed its revenues (tax collections) in a given year.

Answer (A) is incorrect because the concept of a budget deficit refers to a single period of time; it is not an accumulation. Answer (B) is incorrect because state and local deficits are not included in the federal budget deficit. Answer (D) is incorrect because the federal budget deficit is a flow concept relating to a single period of time; it is not a balance sheet concept.

20.

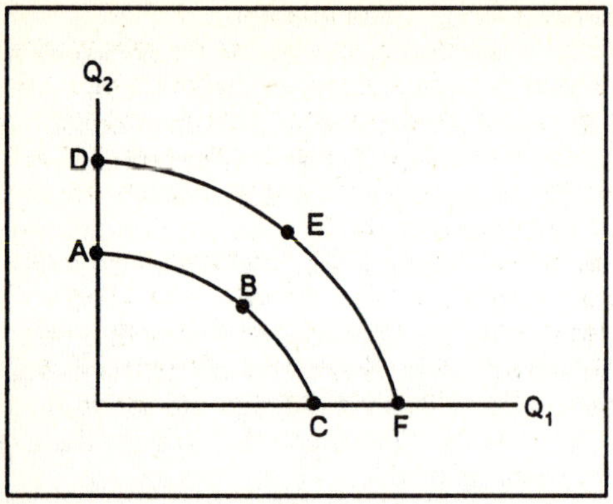

Curves ABC and DEF on the above graph represent production possibility curves for a nation. If point E on curve DEF represents the current combination of goods #1 and #2 consumed by that nation, the nation can reach point B on curve ABC by

A. Discovering more or better resources.

B. Discovering improved production techniques.

C. Incurring a trade deficit.

D. Incurring a trade surplus.

The correct answer is (D). *(CIA, adapted)*

REQUIRED: The method by which a nation can change its production possibilities curve.

DISCUSSION: If a nation's exports are greater than its imports, the combination of goods consumed will be less than the combination produced. Hence, the production possibilities curve will shift inward, for example, to point B on curve ABC.

Answer (A) is incorrect because the discovery of more or better resources causes an outward shift of the production possibilities curve. Answer (B) is incorrect because the discovery of improved production techniques causes an outward shift of the production possibilities curve. Answer (C) is incorrect because incurring a trade deficit results in consumption of a combination of goods outside the current production possibilities curve.

21. When economists are concerned about the liquidity preference function, they are interested in

A. The relationship of the demand for money and the rate of interest.

B. The proportion of liquid (cash) reserves maintained by commercial banks.

C. The preference for a currency backed by gold.

D. A bank's desire for accounts receivable as collateral.

The correct answer is (A). *(CMA, adapted)*

REQUIRED: The definition of the liquidity preference function.

DISCUSSION: The liquidity preference function is the demand curve for money. It explains the relationship between interest rates and the demand for money. If interest rates are high, individuals and businesses will be less likely to hold large amounts of cash because the earnings from investment would represent a high opportunity cost for a given level of liquidity. However, if interest rates are low, less income will be lost if consumers hold their money (remain liquid).

Answer (B) is incorrect because the reserve ratio affects money supply, not demand. Answer (C) is incorrect because the liquidity preference relates interest rates to demand for money, not the desire for a currency redeemable in a precious metal. Answer (D) is incorrect because the liquidity preference applies not only to banks but to all businesses and individuals in the economy.

22. If a government were to use only fiscal policy to stimulate the economy from a recession, it would

A. Raise consumer taxes and increase government spending.

B. Lower business taxes and government spending.

C. Increase the money supply and increase government spending.

D. Lower consumer taxes and increase government spending.

The correct answer is (D). *(CIA, adapted)*

REQUIRED: The actions taken if a government were to use only fiscal policy to stimulate the economy.

DISCUSSION: According to Keynesian economics, fiscal policy should be expansionary when the economy is in recession. Increases in government spending, decreases in taxation, or both will have a stimulative effect. To achieve this effect, the increase in spending should not be matched by a tax increase, the effect of which is contractionary. Thus, deficit spending is the result of pursuing an expansionary fiscal policy.

Answer (A) is incorrect because raising consumer taxes is contractionary. Answer (B) is incorrect because lower government spending is contractionary. Answer (C) is incorrect because increasing the supply of money involves monetary, not fiscal, policy.

23. The movement of migrant workers from a poor country to a rich country with a low unemployment rate will have which of the following effects on the receiving country?

A. GDP will increase.

B. Average wage levels will increase.

C. Business incomes will decrease.

D. The labor force will decrease.

The correct answer is (A). *(CIA, adapted)*

REQUIRED: The effect of an influx of migrant workers.

DISCUSSION: An influx of migrant workers into a rich country with low unemployment will result in increased GDP. This change occurs because of improvements in productivity arising from lower labor costs, increases in business incomes, and a larger real output.

Answer (B) is incorrect because average wage levels will decrease as the quantity of labor available increases. Answer (C) is incorrect because business incomes will increase as the cost of labor decreases. Answer (D) is incorrect because the total labor force will increase.

24. A prevailing view among many monetarists is that monetary policy should be conducted

A. Through the adoption of a monetary rule that would increase the money supply at a constant annual rate.

B. By Congress alone because its members are elected while the Board of Governors of the Federal Reserve System is appointed.

C. At the discretion of the Board of Governors of the Federal Reserve System because it has sufficient knowledge to help stabilize the economy.

D. In a way that keeps the money supply and the velocity of circulation approximately equal.

The correct answer is (A). *(CMA, adapted)*

REQUIRED: The prevailing view about monetary policy.

DISCUSSION: Monetarists favor a steady, restrained growth of the money supply, so they would be likely to favor a rule that would increase the money supply at a constant annual rate.

Answers (B) and (C) are incorrect because monetarists feel that fiscal policy should not be used to influence the economy and that government attempts at stability only make problems worse. They would therefore probably not like policy set by Congress or the Fed. Answer (D) is incorrect because money supply and velocity of circulation are totally different variables. Making them equal would be nonsensical.

C. Money and the Economy

25. The narrow definition of money supply, M_1, consists only of

A. Current and demand deposits.

B. Currency, demand deposits, other checkable deposits, and travelers' checks.

C. Currency, demand deposits, and small time deposits.

D. Currency, demand deposits, small time deposits, and Money Market Mutual Fund balances.

The correct answer is (B). *(CMA, adapted)*

REQUIRED: The narrow definition of money supply.

DISCUSSION: The narrow definition of money supply includes coins, currency, and checking account deposits (including travelers' checks).

Answer (A) is incorrect because it omits travelers' checks. Answer (C) is incorrect because it includes small time deposits. Answer (D) is incorrect because the broader definition adds small time deposits (e.g., little CDs owned by individuals) and money market funds.

26. All of the following are functions of the Federal Reserve System except

A. Acting as a lender of last resort to the business community.

B. Accepting deposits of, and making loans to, commercial banks.

C. Supplying the economy with paper money in the form of Federal Reserve notes.

D. Providing for the collection of checks.

The correct answer is (A). *(CMA, adapted)*

REQUIRED: The item not a function of the Federal Reserve System.

DISCUSSION: The Fed lends only to its member banks, not to the business community.

Answers (B), (C), and (D) are incorrect because they are legitimate functions of the Federal Reserve System.

27. Which of the following instruments of monetary policy is the most important means by which the money supply is controlled?

A. Changing the reserve ratio.

B. Open-market operations.

C. Manipulation of government spending.

D. Changing the discount rate.

The correct answer is (B). *(CIA, adapted)*

REQUIRED: The most important means of controlling the money supply.

DISCUSSION: Open-market operations permit the Federal Reserve to control the money supply. This result is obtained through the buying and selling of government securities to increase or decrease, respectively, the excess reserves of commercial banks. For example, buying securities increases lendable reserves, thereby indirectly increasing the money supply. Moreover, purchases from individuals lead to an increase in demand deposits, which directly increases the money supply.

Answer (A) is incorrect because reserve ratio changes are infrequent, offer less flexibility, and have less prompt effects than open-market operations. Answer (C) is incorrect because manipulation of government spending is an instrument of fiscal policy, not monetary policy. Answer (D) is incorrect because the amount of commercial bank reserves obtained by borrowing from the central bank is small. Furthermore, whether a change in the discount rate has much impact depends on whether the change occurs at a time when the commercial banks are inclined to alter their central bank borrowings.

28. In order for the Federal Reserve System to increase the money supply, the appropriate policy would be to

A. Encourage banks to increase their holdings of excess reserves.

B. Increase the discount rate.

C. Engage in open-market purchases of government securities.

D. Raise margin requirements on stock market purchases.

The correct answer is (C). *(CMA, adapted)*

REQUIRED: The Fed's policy to increase the money supply.

DISCUSSION: Open-market purchases of government securities would put more money into circulation. Vault cash that was previously unavailable to the public for circulation is placed into the hands of the public by the open-market purchase of government securities.

Answer (A) is incorrect because an increase in excess reserves or reserve requirements would mean that member banks could make fewer loans. Thus, less money would be introduced into the economy. Answer (B) is incorrect because, if the discount rate were raised, member banks would borrow less from the Fed to lend to their customers. Answer (D) is incorrect because an increase in margin requirements would mean that investors would borrow less.

29. The Federal Reserve System's reserve ratio is

A. The specified percentage of a commercial bank's deposit liabilities that must be deposited in the central bank.

B. The rate that the central bank charges for loans granted to commercial banks.

C. The ratio of excess reserves to legal reserves that are deposited in the central bank.

D. The specified percentage of a commercial bank's demand deposits to total liabilities.

The correct answer is (A). *(CMA, adapted)*

REQUIRED: The definition of the Federal Reserve System's reserve ratio.

DISCUSSION: The reserve ratio is the percentage of the customer deposits that banks must deposit with the Fed. These deposits are required by law to ensure the soundness of the bank and also serve as a tool for monetary policy, i.e., changes in the reserve ratio affect the money supply.

Answer (B) is incorrect because it refers to the discount rate: the amount that the Fed charges for loans granted to commercial banks. Answers (C) and (D) are incorrect because excess reserves and specified percentage are nonsense terms.

30. If the Federal Reserve Board wanted to implement an expansionary monetary policy, which one of the following actions would the Federal Reserve Board take?

A. Raise the reserve requirement and the discount rate.

B. Purchase additional U.S. government securities and lower the discount rate.

C. Reduce the reserve requirement and raise the discount rate.

D. Raise the discount rate and sell U.S. government securities.

The correct answer is (B). *(CMA, adapted)*

REQUIRED: The action by the Federal Reserve to implement an expansionary monetary policy.

DISCUSSION: The Federal Reserve affects monetary policy primarily through the purchase and sale of government securities in open-market operations. A purchase of securities is expansionary because it increases bank reserves and the money supply. However, the sale of government securities by the Federal Reserve contracts the money supply by removing resources from the economy. Lowering the legal reserve requirement (the percentage of deposits that a bank must keep on hand) also expands the money supply by increasing the lendable funds held by banks. Similarly, lowering the discount rate (the rate at which member banks may borrow from the Federal Reserve) encourages borrowing and increases the money supply.

Answers (A), (C) and (D) are incorrect because raising the reserve requirement and the discount rate and selling U.S. government securities reduce the money supply.

31. A banking system with a reserve ratio of 20% and a change in reserves of $1,000,000 can increase its total demand deposits by

A. $200,000

B. $5,000,000

C. $1,000,000

D. $800,000

The correct answer is (B). *(CMA, adapted)*

REQUIRED: The amount by which a banking system can increase its total demand deposits given the reserve ratio and the change in reserves.

DISCUSSION: Reserves represent the proportion of demand deposits that cannot be lent. Given a 20% reserve requirement and an increase of $1,000,000 in reserves, the system can increase total demand deposits by $5,000,000 ($1,000,000 ÷ .2).

Answer (A) is incorrect because the reserve is 20% of deposits, not the reverse. Answer (C) is incorrect because reserves need to be only 20% of deposits; thus, an increase in reserves will support a five-fold increase in deposits. Answer (D) is incorrect because $800,000 equals the increase in net lendable funds assuming a $1,000,000 increase in deposits.

32. The money supply in a nation's economy will decrease following

A. Open-market purchases by the nation's central bank.

B. A decrease in the discount rate.

C. An increase in the reserve ratio.

D. A decrease in the margin requirement.

The correct answer is (C). *(CIA, adapted)*

REQUIRED: The item that causes a decrease in the money supply.

DISCUSSION: The reserve ratio is the minimum percentage of its deposits that a bank must keep on deposit with the Federal Reserve or in its vault. When the reserve ratio increases, banks must maintain larger reserves, and less money is available for lending and investment. Consequently, the money supply decreases.

Answer (A) is incorrect because open-market purchases by the central bank increase the money supply by increasing commercial banks' reserves. Answer (B) is incorrect because a decrease in the rate charged to member banks for loans by the Federal Reserve (the discount rate) increases the money supply by increasing bank reserves. Answer (D) is incorrect because a decrease in the margin requirement decreases the minimum down payment that purchasers of stock must make. This credit control affects the stock market and has no direct impact on the money supply.

33. The discount rate of the Federal Reserve System is

A. The specified percentage of a commercial bank's deposit liabilities that must be deposited in the central bank.

B. The rate that the central bank charges for loans granted to commercial banks.

C. The rate that commercial banks charge for loans granted to the public.

D. The ratio of excess reserves to legal reserves that are deposited in the central bank.

The correct answer is (B). *(CMA, adapted)*

REQUIRED: The definition of the Fed's discount rate.

DISCUSSION: The discount rate is the amount the central bank charges when making loans to member banks.

Answer (A) is incorrect because it refers to the reserve ratio. Answer (C) is incorrect because it defines the prime rate. Answer (D) is incorrect because the rate described is nonsensical.

34. The creation of deposit money by U.S. commercial banks increases the

A. Real wealth of the United States.

B. Real U.S. national income.

C. U.S. money supply.

D. Purchasing power of the U.S. dollar.

The correct answer is (C). *(CMA, adapted)*

REQUIRED: The effect of the creation of deposit money by U.S. commercial banks.

DISCUSSION: As money is deposited with banks, the banks lend the money to qualified customers. Banks may only lend a certain percentage of their funds because of the reserve requirement, but the more funds they have, the more they can lend. Therefore, as the amount of money deposited increases, the amount and number of loans increase, thus increasing the money supply.

Answers (A) and (B) are incorrect because real wealth and national income are not directly affected by the creation of deposit money. Answer (D) is incorrect because the purchasing power of the dollar (amount of goods that can be bought with a dollar) may well be decreased by the expansion of the money supply.

35. The discount rate set by the Federal Reserve System is the

A. Required percentage of reserves deposited at the central bank.

B. Rate that commercial banks charge for loans to each other.

C. Rate that commercial banks charge for loans to the general public.

D. Rate that the central bank charges for loans to commercial banks.

The correct answer is (D). *(CMA, adapted)*

REQUIRED: The true statement about the Federal Reserve discount rate.

DISCUSSION: The discount rate is the interest rate at which member banks may borrow money from the Fed. A lowering of the discount rate encourages borrowing, which increases the money supply. An increase in the discount rate discourages borrowing and correspondingly increases saving, which decreases the money supply.

Answer (A) is incorrect because the required percentage of reserves deposited at the central bank is the legal reserve requirement. Answer (B) is incorrect because the discount rate is the amount the Fed charges to member banks, not what banks charge each other. Answer (C) is incorrect because the rate that commercial banks charge for loans to the general public is usually scaled upward from the prime rate, which is the rate charged to the most creditworthy customers.

D. Unemployment, Inflation, and Government

36. Unemployment that is caused by a mismatch between the composition of the labor force (in terms of skills, occupation, industries, or geographic location) and the makeup of the demand for labor is called

A. Real wage unemployment.

B. Deficient-demand unemployment.

C. Frictional unemployment.

D. Structural unemployment.

The correct answer is (D). *(CMA, adapted)*

REQUIRED: The term for unemployment caused by a mismatch between the composition of the labor force and the makeup of the demand for labor.

DISCUSSION: Structural unemployment exists when aggregate demand is sufficient to provide full employment, but the distribution of the demand does not correspond precisely to the composition of the labor force in terms of skills, industries, etc.

Answers (A) and (B) are incorrect because neither is a meaningful term in this context. Answer (C) is incorrect because frictional unemployment is defined as the amount of unemployment caused by the normal workings of the labor market. It includes, for example, unemployment resulting from time lost in changing jobs.

37. The rate of unemployment caused by changes in the composition of employment opportunities over time is referred to as the

A. Frictional unemployment rate.

B. Cyclical unemployment rate.

C. Structural unemployment rate.

D. Full employment unemployment rate.

The correct answer is (C). *(CIA, adapted)*

REQUIRED: The rate of unemployment caused by changes in the composition of employment opportunities over time.

DISCUSSION: Economists define full employment as occurring when cyclical unemployment is zero. Hence, the natural rate of unemployment (the full employment unemployment rate) equals the sum of structural and frictional unemployment. Cyclical unemployment is caused by insufficient aggregate demand. Frictional unemployment occurs when both jobs and the workers qualified to fill them are available. This definition acknowledges that there will be changing of jobs, temporary layoffs, etc. Structural unemployment exists when aggregate demand is sufficient to provide full employment, but the distribution of the demand does not correspond precisely to the composition of the labor force. This form of unemployment arises when the required job skills or the geographic distribution of jobs changes.

Answer (A) is incorrect because frictional unemployment results from imperfections in the labor market. Answer (B) is incorrect because cyclical unemployment is caused by a deficiency of aggregate spending. Answer (D) is incorrect because the full employment unemployment rate is the sum of frictional and structural unemployment.

38. A nation's unemployment rate increased from 4% to 6%. The economic cost of this increase in unemployment can be described as the amount by which

A. Actual gross domestic product falls short of potential gross domestic product.

B. Aggregate expenditures fall short of the full-employment level of net domestic product.

C. Aggregate spending exceeds the full-employment level of net domestic product.

D. Merchandise imports exceed exports.

The correct answer is (A). *(CIA, adapted)*

REQUIRED: The economic cost of an increase in unemployment.

DISCUSSION: In macroeconomic terms, the cost of unemployment is lost production. This lost output is measured in terms of the GDP gap, that is, the difference between actual and potential GDP. According to Okun's Law, a 2.5% GDP gap results from every 1% excess of the actual unemployment rate over the natural rate.

Answers (B), (C), and (D) are incorrect because the cost of unemployment is estimated in terms of the GDP gap.

39. The most effective fiscal policy program to help reduce demand-pull inflation would be to

A. Decrease the rate of growth of the money supply.

B. Increase both taxes and government spending.

C. Decrease taxes and increase government spending.

D. Increase taxes and decrease government spending.

The correct answer is (D). *(CMA, adapted)*

REQUIRED: The most effective fiscal policy for reducing demand-pull inflation.

DISCUSSION: Demand-pull inflation results when demand for goods and services exceeds supply, thereby pulling prices upward. Increasing taxes and reducing government spending will reduce the amount of money available for consumer demand. When demand is reduced, prices and inflation will decline.

Answer (A) is incorrect because monetary policy concerns changes in the supply of money. Answer (B) is incorrect because the results of such a policy would be indeterminate. Answer (C) is incorrect because it would exacerbate inflation.

40. The formula for calculating a price index for the year 1997, using the year 1980 as a reference period, is

A. $\frac{\textit{Price of 1997 market basket in 1997}}{\textit{Price of 1997 market basket in 1980}} \times 100$

B. $\frac{\textit{Price of 1980 market basket in 1997}}{\textit{Price of 1980 market basket in 1980}} \times 100$

C. $\frac{\textit{Price of 1997 market basket in 1997}}{\textit{Price of 1980 market basket in 1980}} \times 100$

D. $\frac{\textit{Price of 1980 market basket in 1980}}{\textit{Price of 1980 market basket in 1997}} \times 100$

The correct answer is (A). *(CIA, adapted)*

REQUIRED: The formula for calculating a price index.

DISCUSSION: The 1997 price index using 1980 as a reference period is the price of the 1997 market basket in 1997 relative to the price of the same basket of goods and services in 1980. In general, the price index in a given year is calculated as

$$\frac{\textit{Price of market basket in a given year}}{\textit{Price of the same market basket in the base year}} \times 100$$

Answer (B) is incorrect because the 1997 market basket is used to calculate the 1997 price index. Answer (C) is incorrect because the 1997 market basket is used in both the numerator and the denominator. The price index compares the 1997 and 1980 prices of the same market basket. Answer (D) is incorrect because the 1997 market basket is used to calculate the 1997 price index, and the convention is to calculate the 1997 price relative to the 1980 price.

41. If nominal income increases <List A> the price level, real income will <List B>.

	List A	List B
A.	Faster than	Rise
B.	Slower than	Rise
C.	At the same rate as	Fall
D.	At the same rate as	Rise

The correct answer is (A). *(CIA, adapted)*

REQUIRED: The relationship of changes in nominal and real income.

DISCUSSION: The percentage change in real income is the difference between the percentage change in nominal income and the percentage change in the price level. If nominal income increases more than the price level, real income also increases.

Answer (B) is incorrect because, if nominal income increases less than the price level, real income decreases as nominal income loses purchasing power. Answers (C) and (D) are incorrect because, if nominal income increases by the same amount as the price level, real income is constant.

42. A period of rising inflation

A. Increases the price level, which benefits those who are entitled to receive specific amounts of money.

B. Enhances the positive relationship between the price level and the purchasing power of money.

C. Will not be affected by contracts that include the indexing of payments.

D. Increases the price level, which is negatively related to the purchasing power of money.

The correct answer is (D). *(CMA, adapted)*

REQUIRED: The true statement about rising inflation.

DISCUSSION: Inflation increases the price level, which means that a static supply of dollars will purchase fewer goods. In other words, the purchasing power of money declines as the price level increases.

Answer (A) is incorrect because an increased price level hurts those who are entitled to receive specific amounts of money. Fixed amounts will purchase less than before. Answer (B) is incorrect because there is an inverse relationship between the price level and the purchasing power of money. Answer (C) is incorrect because rising inflation activates provisions in contracts for the indexing of payments.

43. Two examples of indirect taxes are

A. Taxes on business and rental property and personal income taxes.

B. Sales taxes and Social Security taxes paid by employees.

C. Sales taxes and excise taxes.

D. Social Security taxes paid by employees and personal income taxes.

The correct answer is (C). *(CMA, adapted)*

REQUIRED: The two forms of indirect taxes.

DISCUSSION: Indirect taxes are those levied against someone other than individual taxpayers, and thus only indirectly affect the individual. General sales taxes, excise taxes, customs, duties, licensing fees, and business property taxes are examples. They are levied against businesses and are then passed along to the individual purchaser.

Answers (A), (B) and (D) are incorrect because personal income taxes and Social Security taxes levied against the employee are direct taxes.

44. Which of the following is not an advantage of the value-added tax?

A. It provides an incentive for cost control.

B. It provides an incentive for saving.

C. It is beneficial to new businesses.

D. It is simple to calculate and enforce.

The correct answer is (C). *(Publisher)*

REQUIRED: The item not an advantage of a value-added tax.

DISCUSSION: A value-added tax is a tax levied on the difference between a firm's sales and its purchases. A value-added tax provides no benefits to, and imposes no costs on, a new business that are not provided to, or imposed on, already existing businesses.

Answer (A) is incorrect because lower costs mean lower taxes with a value-added tax. Answer (B) is incorrect because the tax is on consumption, not savings, so there is an incentive to save. Answer (D) is incorrect because the simplicity of the value-added tax and the ease with which it can be enforced make the tax an attractive alternative to the corporate income tax.

45. Government spending is known to affect the economy. The crowding-out effect refers to the <List A> impact of an expansionary fiscal policy on <List B>.

	List A	List B
A.	Positive	The money multiplier
B.	Positive	Investment
C.	Negative	The money multiplier
D.	Negative	Investment

The correct answer is (D). *(CIA, adapted)*

REQUIRED: The definition of the crowding-out effect.

DISCUSSION: As the government borrows to finance greater spending under an expansionary fiscal policy, interest rates rise. Higher interest rates crowd out private investment, which cancels or weakens the stimulus of the fiscal policy.

Answer (A) is incorrect because fiscal policy has no direct effect on the money multiplier, which is a relationship between the money supply and legal reserve requirements. Answer (B) is incorrect because expansionary fiscal policy results in higher interest rates and a negative effect on investment levels. Answer (C) is incorrect because fiscal policy has no direct effect on the money multiplier.

46. Government borrowing to finance large deficits increases the demand for lendable funds and

A. Increases the supply of lendable funds.

B. Exerts downward pressure on interest rates.

C. Has no impact on interest rates.

D. Puts upward pressure on interest rates.

The correct answer is (D). *(CMA, adapted)*

REQUIRED: The true statement about government borrowing to finance large deficits.

DISCUSSION: When the government borrows money, it enters into the same market as private business and competes for funds. The added demand will drive the interest rate higher. This activity produces the crowding-out effect. The result is reduced corporate borrowing and investment.

Answer (A) is incorrect because the supply of lendable funds is unaffected by government borrowing. Only the demand is affected. Answers (B) and (C) are incorrect because the increased demand for funds increases interest rates.

47. Government transfer payments

A. Reallocate the consumption of goods and services to the public sector.

B. Increase aggregate demand for private sector goods and services.

C. Reallocate the consumption of goods and services in the private sector.

D. Decrease aggregate demand for private sector goods and services.

The correct answer is (C). *(CMA, adapted)*

REQUIRED: The true statement about government transfer payments.

DISCUSSION: Government expenditures, such as those for welfare and Social Security, are not actual expenditures on goods or services. Instead, they are transfers of money from the government to households in the form of a negative tax designed to redistribute income. Through taxation and transfer payments, income redistribution is effected, and consumption in the private sector will be reallocated.

Answer (A) is incorrect because the reallocation is not to the public sector. Individuals in the private sector will decide how the money will be spent. Answers (B) and (D) are incorrect because transfer payments reallocate income; they do not increase or decrease demand, per se.

48. A societal advantage of the federal government's levying emission charges on manufacturers in order to control pollution is that such charges would

A. Become a cost of production and cause a firm to consider the cost of pollution.

B. Help equalize and even out the use of the environment, while encouraging industrial dispersion.

C. Set national standards that all firms would have to follow.

D. Discourage firms from moving to areas where local emission standards are lower.

The correct answer is (A). *(CMA, adapted)*

REQUIRED: The societal advantage of levying emission charges to control pollution.

DISCUSSION: Pollution is an externality (spillover). It is a negative externality because it imposes costs rather than benefits that are external to the market transaction. Such costs result in overallocation of resources to production of particular goods because the producer does not bear all the associated costs. One solution is to levy charges on pollution emissions so that they become costs of production. Firms then must consider the costs of pollution when making routine operating decisions.

Answer (B) is incorrect because emission charges would not necessarily even out usage. Companies with the most profitable products could afford the most emissions. Answer (C) is incorrect because standards place a limit on the amount of emissions, whereas the levying of charges allows any amount of emissions providing a payment is made. Answer (D) is incorrect because compliance with low standards may be cheaper than paying emissions charges.

Use Gleim's ***CMA/CFM Test Prep*** for interactive testing with **over 2,000 additional multiple-choice questions!**

STUDY UNIT 3: INTERNATIONAL BUSINESS ENVIRONMENT

13 pages of outline
50 multiple-choice questions

A. Advantages of Trade
B. Trade Barriers
C. Foreign Currency Rates and Markets
D. Balance of Payments
E. International Institutions and Agreements

International business environment as covered on Part 1 of the exam is both macro (e.g., principles of international supply and demand, foreign currency, etc.) and, to a lesser extent, micro (e.g., the effects of trade restrictions on individual companies). In the ICMA's content specification outlines, international economics is a subject area under the major topic of macroeconomics and international economics. The relative weight range assigned to this major topic in Part 1 is 10% to 15%. Expect 12-18 questions.

A. Advantages of Trade

1. Countries vary greatly in their efficiency in producing certain goods because of the immobility of resources. This variation can be largely attributed to differences from country to country in the following five factors:
   a. Climatic and geographical conditions
   b. Human capacities
   c. Supply and type of capital accumulation
   d. Proportions of resources
   e. Political and social climates
2. Given the above differences, it is clear that countries can mutually benefit from trade. The greatest advantage from trade is obtained when each nation specializes in producing what it can produce most efficiently. If nations specialize and then exchange with others, more is produced and consumed than if each nation tries to be self-sufficient. We know that specialization of labor is beneficial for individuals; the same principle applies to nations.
3. This principle of **comparative advantage** can be explained with the help of the following chart:

Comparative Costs of Production

	U.S.	Japan
Food (1 bushel)	1	2
Cars	1.5	1

   If the countries consume only the above two goods, is there an advantage to specializing? Yes, there will be an increase in total output if the U.S. uses its resources to grow food and Japan uses its resources to produce cars (given a fixed amount of inputs).

   a. Total output will be maximized when each nation specializes in the products in which it has the lower opportunity cost, that is, a comparative advantage.

b. EXAMPLE: Assume that the costs in the chart on the previous page are solely for labor and that labor is the only input required for the production of food and cars. Thus, for 100,000 units of labor input, the U.S. economy can produce either 100,000 bushels of food or 66,667 cars. If the labor input is divided equally, however, the U.S. economy can produce 50,000 bushels of food and 33,333 cars. At the same time, if the Japanese economy divides its efforts equally, input of 100,000 units of labor can produce 25,000 bushels of food and 50,000 cars. In the absence of world trade, the two economies together can produce 75,000 bushels of food (50,000 + 25,000) and 83,333 cars (33,333 + 50,000). But if each country concentrates on the product in which it has a comparative advantage, the total production will be 100,000 bushels of food (all produced in the U.S.) and 100,000 cars (all produced in Japan).

c. Comparative advantage is different from absolute advantage. In the above example, the U.S. has an **absolute** advantage with respect to food production because the price of food is lower in the U.S. than in Japan. Japan has an absolute advantage in car production. Along with its absolute advantage, the U.S. has a **comparative** advantage in food production because its opportunity cost for food production (cars forgone) is lower than Japan's. Similarly, Japan's opportunity cost for car production (food forgone) is lower. Hence, Japan has a comparative advantage in car production.

1) **Comparative advantage** compares costs within a single country. No matter what the costs may be elsewhere, the U.S. will always have a comparative advantage in the production of food rather than cars. Similarly, Japan has a comparative advantage in the production of cars as opposed to food.

2) **Absolute advantage** compares the costs of inputs between countries. Thus, a given country might have an absolute advantage with respect to every product compared with a specific other country.

3) In the above example, Japan would continue to have a comparative advantage with respect to cars even if its costs were 1.6. In that case, the U.S. would have an absolute advantage (1.5 is less than 1.6). Nevertheless, trade is still beneficial.

d. A nation will export goods in which it has a comparative advantage and import goods in which it has a comparative disadvantage.

1) Developing countries exporting primarily raw materials are dependent on vibrant economies in developed (importing) countries.

e. If a country has only two factors of production (labor and capital) and a relative abundance of capital, it will tend to export capital-intensive goods and import labor-intensive goods. Thus, factors of production and the varying efficiency in producing goods determine which products a country will export and import.

1) Capital-intensive goods are those requiring a high level of investment, e.g., oil refining.

2) Labor-intensive goods are those requiring a high level of labor, e.g., manufacture of fashion clothes.

f. For nations to receive the full advantages of international specialization and exchange, free trade must be allowed among all countries.

4. Stop and review! You have completed the outline for this subunit. Study multiple-choice questions 1 through 6 beginning on page 114.

B. Trade Barriers

1. Even though individuals (as a whole) are best off under free trade, governments often establish policies designed to block or restrict the importation of certain products, to encourage exports, or even to restrict exports.
   a. **Tariffs** are consumption taxes designed to restrict imports, e.g., a tax on German beer. Governments raise taxes to lower consumption.
      1) Antidumping rules prevent foreign producers from "dumping" excess goods on the U.S. market at less than cost to squeeze out competitors and gain control of the market.
      2) The agreements reached during the Uruguay Round specified the rules for levying antidumping tariffs. Most cases hinge on the definition of "cost."
      3) The Secretary of the Treasury must first determine that a class of foreign merchandise is being sold in the U.S. at less than its fair value.
   b. **Import quotas** set fixed limits on different products, e.g., French wine.
      1) In the short run, import quotas will help a country's balance of payments position by increasing domestic employment, but the prices of the products produced will also increase.
      2) An **embargo** is a total ban on some kinds of imports. It is an extreme form of the import quota.
   c. **Domestic content rules** require that at least a portion of any imported product be constructed from parts manufactured in the importing nation.
      1) This rule is sometimes used by capital-intensive nations. Parts can be produced using idle capacity and then sent to a labor-intensive country for final assembly.
   d. **Exchange controls** limit foreign currency transactions and set exchange rates. The purpose is to limit the ability of a firm selling in a country to repatriate its earnings.
   e. **Export subsidies** are payments by the government to producers in certain industries in an attempt to increase exports.
      1) A government may impose "countervailing duties" on imported goods if those goods were produced in a foreign country with the aid of a governmental subsidy.
   f. **Special tax benefits to exporters** are an indirect form of export subsidy. The best U.S. examples are Foreign Sales Corporations (FSCs). They are entities located in U.S. possessions or in countries with tax information exchange agreements with the U.S. FSCs receive an exemption of about 15% of qualified export income.
   g. The Export Trading Company Act of 1982 permits competitors to form export trading companies without regard to U.S. antitrust legislation.
   h. Certain exports may require **licenses**. For example, sales of technology with military applications are limited by western nations that are members of the Coordinating Committee for Multilateral Export Controls. The related U.S. legislation is the Export Administration Act of 1979.
   i. See discussion of the World Trade Organization and NAFTA on page 112.
2. The economic effect of tariffs and quotas on free trade is to shift workers from relatively efficient export industries into less efficient protected industries. Real wage rates will decline as a result, as will total world output.

3. A major reason for trade restrictions is that the costs of competition are direct and concentrated (people lose jobs and firms go out of business), but benefits of unrestricted trade are less noticeable and occur in the future (lower prices, higher wages, more jobs in export industries).
    a. Special-interest groups are strong and well organized, and they lobby effectively, getting legislation passed that is harmful to free trade.
    b. **Economic integration** is the joining of the markets from two or more nations into a free-trade zone. Examples of economic blocs of trading nations are the European Union and the North American Free Trade Agreement (NAFTA). Generally, the trading bloc provides trading incentives to member nations and discriminates against nonmember nations.
4. Stop and review! You have completed the outline for this subunit. Study multiple-choice questions 7 through 16 beginning on page 116.

C. Foreign Currency Rates and Markets

1. For international trade to occur, the two currencies involved must be easily converted at some prevailing exchange rate. The **exchange rate** is the price of one country's currency in terms of another country's currency.
    a. Currency appreciates when it can buy more units of another currency.
    b. Currency depreciates when it can purchase fewer units of another currency.
    c. In other words, depreciation in country A's currency is an appreciation of the currency of country B.
2. **Exchange Rate Determination**
    a. Equilibrium exchange rates in floating markets are determined by the supply of and demand for the currencies.

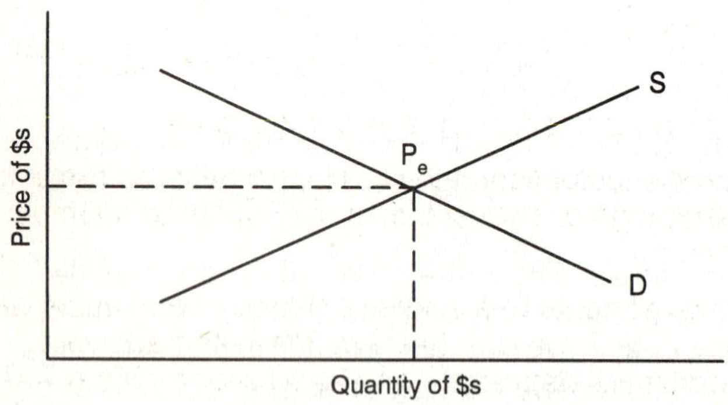

The equilibrium rate of P_e will prevail in the market. No surplus (or deficit) occurs at P_e.

1) Demand for currencies comes from international trade in goods and services, investor global trading (e.g., an American buys a French stock or bond), and international corporate activity.
2) Supply of currencies comes from reversing these transactions.

b. Fixed exchange rates are set by some outside force (e.g., the government). One traditional method of establishing rates is to require that currencies be convertible to specified amounts of gold.

1) An exchange rate set too high (in foreign currency units per dollar) tends to create a deficit U.S. balance of payments. This deficit must be financed by drawing down foreign reserves or by borrowing from the central banks of the foreign countries. This effect is short-term because at some time the country will deplete its foreign reserves.

a) A major reason for a country's devaluation is to improve its balance of payments.

2) An exchange rate set too low (in foreign currency units per dollar) tends to create a surplus U.S. balance of payments. In this case, surplus reserves build up. At some time, the country will not want any greater reserve balances and will have to raise the value of its currency.

Balance of Payments Deficit and Surplus

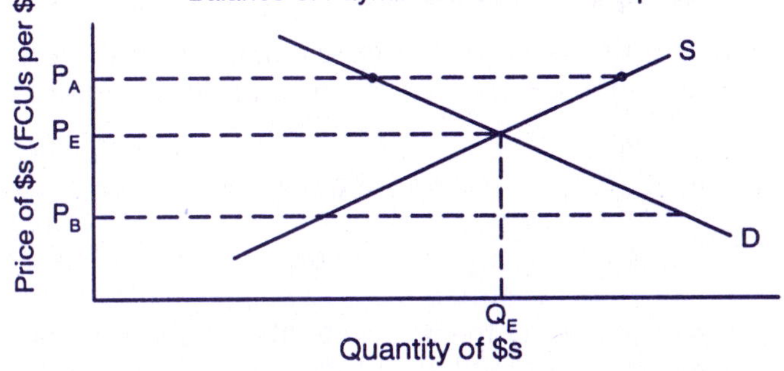

3) At exchange rate A (P_A foreign currency units per dollar), a greater quantity of dollars is supplied by U.S. interests than demanded by foreign interests (i.e., U.S. imports exceed exports). The result is a trade deficit. At exchange rate B, a smaller quantity of dollars is supplied by U.S. interests than demanded by foreign interests (i.e., U.S. exports exceed imports). The result is a trade surplus.

c. A **managed float** is the current method of exchange rate determination.

1) Supply and demand forces primarily guide exchange rates.

2) During periods of extreme fluctuation in the value of a nation's currency, intervention by governments or central banks may occur to maintain fairly stable exchange rates.

3) Floating rates permit adjustments to eliminate balance of payments deficits or surpluses. For example, if the U.S. has a deficit in its trade with country X, the U.S. dollar will depreciate relative to country X's currency. This adjustment should decrease imports from, and increase exports to, country X.

3. Floating exchange rates may fluctuate differently in the long, medium, and short term.

a. Long-term exchange rates are dictated by **the purchasing-power parity theorem.**

1) In the long run, real prices should be the same worldwide (net of government taxes or trade barriers and transportation costs) for a given good. Exchange rates will adjust until purchasing-power parity is achieved. In other words, relative price levels determine exchange rates. In the real world, exchange rates do not perfectly reflect purchasing-power parity, but relative price levels are clearly important determinants of those rates.

b. Medium-term exchange rates are dictated by the economic activity in a country.

1) When the U.S. is in a recession, spending on imports (as well as domestic goods) will decrease. This reduced spending on imports shifts the supply curve for dollars to the left, causing the equilibrium value of the dollar to increase (assuming the demand for dollars is constant); that is, at any given exchange rate, the supply to foreigners is less.

2) If more goods are exported because of an increased preference for U.S. goods, the demand curve for dollars shifts to the right, causing upward pressure on the value of the dollar.

3) An increase in imports or a decrease in exports will have effects opposite to those described above.

c. Short-term exchange rates are dictated by interest rates. Big corporations and banks invest their large reserves of cash where the real interest rate is highest. A rise in the real interest rate in a country will lead to an appreciation of the currency because it will be demanded for investment at the higher real interest rate, thereby shifting the demand curve to the right (outward).

1) The reverse holds true for a decline in real interest rates because that currency will be sold as investors move their money out of the country.

2) However, the interplay of interest rates and inflation must also be considered. Inflation of a currency relative to a second currency causes the first currency to depreciate relative to the second. Moreover, nominal interest rates increase when inflation rates are expected to increase. The effect on exchange rates of inflation reflected in nominal interest rates is expressed by the **interest-rate parity theorem.** The ratio of the current forward and spot exchange rates (expressed in units of foreign currency per dollar) equals the ratio of one plus the current nominal foreign rate to one plus the current nominal domestic rate.

$$\frac{\textit{Forward exchange rate}}{\textit{Spot exchange rate}} = \frac{1 + \textit{Foreign interest rate}}{1 + \textit{Domestic interest rate}}$$

For example, if the current nominal foreign interest rate increases, the forward rate in terms of units of the foreign currency per dollar will increase. Hence, that currency will trade at a discount in the forward market.

4. **Interaction in Foreign Currency Markets**

a. The **spot rate** is the exchange rate paid for immediate delivery of a currency.

b. The **forward exchange rate** is the future price of the currency.

1) If the forward rate in foreign currency units per dollar is greater than the spot rate, the dollar is selling at a premium; speculators expect the dollar to appreciate.

2) If the spot rate in foreign currency units per dollar is greater than the forward rate, the dollar is selling at a discount; speculators expect the dollar to depreciate.

3) The annual effect in the forward market equals

$$\frac{\textit{Forward market rate (FC)} - \textit{Spot rate (FC)}}{\textit{Spot rate (FC)}} \times \textit{Number of forward periods in a year}$$

a) FC means that the amount is denominated in foreign currency.

b) For example, if there is a 1% premium in a 30-day forward market, the annual premium is 12%.

c. The discount or premium is related to the difference between the nominal interest rates paid by foreign and domestic banks (differences in interest rates are largely related to differences in expected inflation).

1) When the foreign nominal interest rate is lower than the domestic nominal rate, the forward foreign currency sells at a premium. If this were not true, investors would borrow at the lower interest rate, invest at the higher rate, and buy a forward contract for the principal and interest.

2) If the foreign nominal rate exceeds the domestic nominal rate, the forward foreign currency sells at a discount.

d. A foreign currency will depreciate or appreciate relative to the dollar at a rate equivalent to the amount by which its inflation rate exceeds or is less than the dollar's inflation rate (everything else constant).

1) EXAMPLE: If the inflation rate in UK is 12% and the inflation rate in the U.S. is 10%, the dollar should appreciate by 2%.

e. Borrowing in a country with the lowest nominal rate is not always best because of the potential for an exchange rate loss if the borrower's currency depreciates relative to the lender's.

1) The foreign currency exchange rates equalize inflation rates.

5. **Avoidance of Exchange Rate Risk in Foreign Currency Markets**

a. The firm may **hedge** its risk by purchasing or selling forward exchange contracts.

1) A firm may buy or sell forward contracts to cover liabilities or receivables, respectively, denominated in a foreign currency.

2) Any gain or loss on the foreign payables or receivables because of changes in exchange rates is offset by the loss or gain on the forward contract.

b. The firm may choose to minimize receivables and liabilities denominated in foreign currencies.

c. Maintaining a monetary balance between receivables and payables denominated in a particular foreign currency avoids a net receivable or net liability position in that currency. Monetary items are those with fixed cash flows.

1) A firm may attempt to achieve a net monetary debtor (creditor) position in countries with currencies expected to depreciate (appreciate).

2) Large multinational corporations have established multinational netting centers as special departments to attempt to achieve balance between foreign receivables and payables.

a) They also enter into foreign currency futures contracts when necessary to achieve balance.

d. Another means of managing exchange rate risk is by the use of **trigger pricing**. Under trigger pricing, foreign funds are supplied at an indexed price but with an option to convert to a futures-based fixed price when a specified basis differential exists between the two prices.

e. A firm may seek to minimize its exchange-rate risk by diversification. If it has transactions in both strong and weak currencies, the effects of changes in rates may be offsetting.

f. A **speculative forward contract** does not hedge any exposure to foreign currency fluctuations; it creates the exposure.

6. **Analysis of Foreign Investments**
   a. Relevant cash flows are the dividends and possible future sales price of the investment paid to the investor.
   b. Cost of capital for foreign projects is higher because of the increased
      1) Exchange-rate risk
      2) Sovereignty risk arising from possible expropriation (or other restrictions), with net losses to the parent company
   c. Foreign operations are more difficult to manage than domestic operations.
7. Foreign investments are funded by
   a. Parent company resources
   b. Common stock sales in the foreign country
   c. Bond sales in the foreign country
   d. Borrowing in world financial markets
8. Stop and review! You have completed the outline for this subunit. Study multiple-choice questions 17 through 39 beginning on page 119.

D. Balance of Payments

1. The balance of payments includes all international payments made by one nation to another, including those for imports, exports, investments, unilateral transfers, and capital movements. The principal accounts are the **current account** and the **capital account**.
   a. The current account records
      1) Exports (credits) and imports (debits) of goods
         a) The **balance of trade** is the difference between total exports and total imports of goods.
      2) Exports (credits) and imports (debits) of services
         a) The **balance on goods and services** is the difference between total exports and total imports of goods and services.
      3) Interest and dividends received on investments abroad (credits) and interest and dividends paid on foreign investments in the U.S. (debits)
      4) Net unilateral transfers, e.g., foreign aid, pension payments, and remittance to relatives (credits or debits depending on whether the flow is into or out of the U.S., respectively)
      5) The balance on the current account
   b. The capital account records capital flows resulting from the purchase and sale of fixed or financial assets.
      1) Inflows of foreign capital (credits) are effectively exports of stocks and bonds and therefore result in inflows of foreign exchange.
      2) Outflows of capital (debits) use up supplies of foreign exchange.
      3) A capital account surplus therefore indicates that inflows exceeded outflows.
   c. The balance of payments deficit or surplus is the net of the current and capital account balances.

d. The references to debits and credits treat the balance of payments account as if it were a revenue or expense account. In other words, a debit is similar to an expense in that it is unfavorable for the country's balance of payments position.

   1) EXAMPLE: A debit (such as an import) is undesirable because it contributes to an unfavorable balance of payments. The U.S. has an unfavorable balance of payments when payments by the U.S. to foreign countries exceed the payments made from foreign countries to the U.S. It is also unfavorable because foreign currency reserves held by the U.S. must be given up to correct the imbalance.

   2) A credit in the balance of payments account is desirable (exports, for instance) because foreigners will be paying more to the U.S. than the U.S. is paying out. Thus, the foreign currency reserves available to the U.S. increase.

e. In addition to decreasing the reserves of foreign currencies held by the U.S., an unfavorable balance of payments can also affect the domestic economy.

   1) EXAMPLE: An excess of imports can cause an unfavorable balance of payments. At the same time, consumers may not be buying domestic products, which may result in domestic layoffs and production cutbacks. These in turn will mean less investment opportunity domestically, and investors will begin sending their investment dollars overseas. The flow of capital overseas compounds the balance of payments problem because investing in a foreign country is essentially the same as importing a product (i.e., the investor is importing foreign stocks and bonds).

   2) Steps to correct an unfavorable balance of payments

      a) Establish import quotas.

         i) One country's unfavorable balance of payments may be caused by another nation's import quotas. For example, if the U.S. has a continuing unfavorable balance of payments with Japan, it might be possible to encourage Japan to remove the trade barriers set up to keep U.S. electronics products out. The removal of Japan's trade restrictions would help the U.S. balance of payments (but might result in an unfavorable balance of payments for Japan).

      b) Provide export incentives.

         i) EXAMPLE: The tax law provisions for Domestic International Sales Corporations (DISCs) and Foreign Sales Corporations (FSCs) permit exporters to postpone or avoid income taxes on export-related income as long as that income is reinvested in export-related assets.

      c) Develop substitutes for products currently being imported.

         i) EXAMPLE: The U.S. has tried to develop substitutes or local sources for imported oil. Products such as gasohol and solar energy have grown in popularity as the government has emphasized the patriotic aspects of these new products; i.e., they contribute to a favorable balance of payments.

f. A balance of payments deficit (imbalance) must be equalized by shipments of goods or reductions in reserves.

   1) Gifts and grants are also used.

g. In the 1980s, the U.S. became the nation with the largest foreign debt. The reasons include the following:

   1) Federal budget deficits financed by foreigners
   2) Growth in the economy that attracted foreign investors
   3) High real interest rates
   4) A strengthened dollar in the early 1980s that encouraged imports
   5) The shift from a manufacturing to a service economy
   6) A decrease in exports of agricultural goods

h. The following are the actual or potential effects of the U.S.'s debt:

   1) An increase in the percentage of the GDP used for debt service
   2) Reduced reserves leading to a devalued dollar, inflation, and increased exports
   3) A decline in net imports and improvement in the trade balance
   4) Increased savings as a result of economic uncertainty
   5) Increased pressure for trade protectionism
   6) Potentially high interest rates to curtail inflation and tighten the money supply, with the consequent incentive for foreign investment

2. Stop and review! You have completed the outline for this subunit. Study multiple-choice questions 40 through 45 beginning on page 126.

E. International Institutions and Agreements

1. International Monetary System

a. In the last 50 years, international monetary crises have periodically been in the news. Economic conditions have changed rapidly. Following is a brief description of events that have helped shape today's monetary situation.

   1) The monetary system that prevailed in the post-World War II period was devised in 1944. It was a system of fixed exchange rates based on a modified gold standard. International reserves in this system included foreign currencies and the right to borrow in specified situations. The **International Monetary Fund (IMF)** was created and is still active today.

      a) Resources of the IMF consist of a pool of currency from which participating countries can draw during short-term balance of payments difficulties.

      b) The **World Bank** was created at the same time as the IMF.

         i) Its purpose is to provide credit for development purposes to underdeveloped countries.

   2) In the post-war years, the U.S. dollar became the world's key currency used for transactions and reserves.

   3) By the mid-1950s, fixed exchange rates and changing economic conditions turned the dollar shortage into a dollar glut. Holders tried to convert dollars to other currencies, causing the dollar to decline in value.

4) In the early 1970s, convertibility of gold into dollars was abolished by the U.S., breaking down the entire fixed-rate international system. Most countries agreed to allow the currencies to float to determine the new rates, but these countries would frequently intervene in support of their currencies.

5) In 1976 the leading noncommunist nations developed a system called the Jamaica Agreement. This agreement moved the world to a system of managed floating exchanges. Each country had greater autonomy in managing its exchange rate.

b. **Eurodollars** are U.S. dollars held at banks outside of the U.S., either foreign banks or branches of U.S. banks. The growth in the use of Eurodollars has been spectacular because they facilitate the exchange of goods between other nations (often the exchanges use dollars even if the U.S. is not involved in the transaction).

1) Because it is outside the direct control of the U.S. monetary authorities, the Eurodollar market has lower costs. For example, U.S. reserve requirements and FDIC premium payments do not apply in this market. A lower cost market can offer depositors higher interest rates.

2) Eurobonds are sold in one country but denominated in the currency of another country. Their advantage is that they are usually less stringently regulated than most other bonds. Thus, transaction costs are lower. They are not always denominated in Eurodollars.

2. **Multinational Corporations**

a. The home country benefits from multinational operations because of improved earnings and exports of products to foreign subsidiaries. A multinational company may also be better able to obtain scarce resources than a domestic corporation. The existence of multinationals tends to benefit everyone to the extent they foster more international trade, freer trading policies, a better international monetary system, and improved international understanding.

1) The home country, however, may suffer adverse balance of payments effects as a result of investment in foreign nations. Jobs may be lost to foreign subsidiaries, unions weakened, and tax revenues diminished. The multinational may also have a competitive advantage over domestic rivals. Furthermore, multinationals incur greater risk of expropriation and reduced flexibility of operation in a foreign political system.

b. The host country for a multinational operation reaps the advantages of the investment of capital, technology, and management abilities. Output and efficiency often improve along with exports and the balance of payments. The presence of a multinational may stimulate competition, increase tax revenues, and produce a higher standard of living.

1) But payment of royalties, dividends, and profits can result in a net capital outflow. Multinationals sometimes establish economically unreasonable transfer prices among subsidiaries so that profits will be earned where taxes are lowest or restrictions on the export of profits are least stringent. Moreover, multinationals may engage in anticompetitive activities, such as formation of cartels.

3. International trade agreements provide regulatory authority for businesses in international trade. Until recently, the broadest and most important of these agreements was the General Agreement on Tariffs and Trade (GATT). Under GATT, the signatory countries agreed to equal treatment of all member nations, multilateral negotiations to reduce tariffs, and the abolition of import quotas.

   a. However, GATT has now been replaced by the **World Trade Organization (WTO)**. The WTO, which was established on January 1, 1995, is the product of the Uruguay Round of international trade negotiations. It is a permanent body with a secretariat based in Geneva, Switzerland.

      1) The WTO Agreement is a permanent set of commitments by more than 120 nations designed to prohibit trade discrimination among member nations and between imported and domestic products. Most of the rules of GATT are still applicable with respect to trade in goods.

      2) The WTO Agreement applies to trade in services and intellectual property as well as goods. In addition to market access, the WTO's mandate also extends to antidumping rules, subsidies and countervailing measures, import licensing, rules of origin, technical barriers to trade, sanitary measures, emergency protection from imports ("safeguards"), and preshipment inspection.

      3) The WTO provides for a multilateral dispute settlement apparatus. If bilateral consultations and mediation efforts fail, a panel is established to examine the case and make recommendations. If a violation is found, trade retaliation by the complainant against an offending country may be approved if that country does not comply with the recommendations.

4. **North American Free Trade Agreement (NAFTA)**

   a. NAFTA was passed by the U.S. Congress in late 1993. The agreement basically provides for free trade among the U.S., Canada, and Mexico. The pact creates the world's largest free trade zone, stretching from the Yukon to the Yucatan. Three nations and 360 million people are linked into one economic unit.

   b. The consensus is that Mexico will benefit the most by the agreement because many U.S. firms are likely to transfer assembly operations to Mexican subsidiaries with lower labor costs.

      1) NAFTA will help correct the disparities between the open markets of the U.S. and the relatively closed markets of Mexico. U.S. companies should be able to sell more goods to Mexico because Mexicans will have greater disposable income due to new industries transferring there.

      2) The biggest fear in the U.S. is that NAFTA will cause the loss of jobs to Mexico due to the lower labor costs and the more lax environmental standards. Supporters of NAFTA claim that the pact will create 200,000 more jobs in the U.S. than it eliminates over the next two years, because of the increase in exports.

      3) The financial services industry, such as mutual funds, banks, and brokers, should benefit by NAFTA because the agreement allows U.S. financial firms, for the first time, to have easy access to Mexican investors. Also, with the opening of Mexico's financial markets, more opportunities for U.S. investors will emerge.

      4) American industries, such as shoe makers, apparel manufacturers, and farmers may be hurt by increased competition from cheaper Mexican products.

      5) High-tech firms in the U.S. may benefit because there will be few Mexican products to compete against and exports will expand.

c. With respect to transition rules, tariffs ended on about half of the more than 9,000 products covered by the agreement. Tariffs on another 15% of the goods will end in 5 years, and the rest of the products will be duty-free at the end of 15 years.

1) One of the biggest controversies during negotiations was determining the products to be protected with the longest tariff phaseouts. The U.S. won long phaseouts for such items as sneakers, household glassware, asparagus, broccoli, peanuts, and orange juice concentrate.

2) Negotiation of import and export restrictions was an important aspect of setting the transition rules for NAFTA. For example, the "infant-industry argument" contends that protective tariffs are needed to allow new domestic industries to become established.

3) An extension of the infant-industry argument is the "strategic trade policy argument," which contends that a government should use trade barriers strategically to reduce the risk of product development borne by domestic firms, particularly for products involving advanced technology.

d. The theory behind free trade zones is that they benefit consumers by lowering prices and that manufacturers and workers gain from expanded markets for the items each country produces most efficiently.

5. **International Tax Considerations**

a. Multinational corporations frequently derive income from several countries. The government of each country in which a corporation does business may enact statutes imposing one or more types of tax on the corporation.

b. **Treaties**. To avoid double taxation, two or more countries may adopt treaties to coordinate or synchronize the effects of their taxing statutes.

1) Treaties are also used to integrate other governmental goals, e.g., providing incentive for desired investment.

2) If a U.S. statute and a treaty to which the U.S. is a party conflict, the one enacted or adopted last controls.

3) A treaty might modify the rules in a country's statutes that designate to which country income is sourced or of which country a firm is a resident.

c. **Multinational corporations**

1) Most countries tax only the income sourced to that country.

2) The U.S. taxes worldwide income (from whatever source derived) of a domestic corporation. Double taxation is avoided by allowing a credit for income tax paid to foreign countries or by treaty provisions.

3) In the case of foreign corporations, the U.S. taxes only income sourced to the U.S. Ordinarily, such income is effectively connected with engaging in a trade or business of the U.S. Certain U.S. source income, e.g., gain on the sale of most stock, is not taxed by the U.S.

6. Stop and review! You have completed the outline for this subunit. Study multiple-choice questions 46 through 50 beginning on page 129.

MULTIPLE-CHOICE QUESTIONS

A. Advantages of Trade

1. One of the major consequences of international trade between nations is

A. Higher prices for consumers.

B. A decreased variety of consumer products.

C. The possibility for total world output to increase.

D. Reduced competition for businesses.

The correct answer is (C). *(CMA, adapted)*

REQUIRED: The major consequence of international trade.

DISCUSSION: Under the concept of comparative advantage, total world output will be maximized when each nation specializes in the products in which it has the lowest opportunity cost, that is, a comparative advantage. When nations specialize in what they produce most efficiently and then exchange with others, more is produced and consumed than if each nation tries to be self-sufficient. Specialization of labor is beneficial for individuals; the same principle applies to nations.

Answer (A) is incorrect because prices will be lower and greater quantities will be available with international trade. Answer (B) is incorrect because variety will be increased by international trade. Answer (D) is incorrect because competition will be increased when more producers are in the market.

2. Which one of the following statements concerning international trade and protection is true?

A. Protection is necessary in order to keep U.S. money in the United States.

B. When two nations trade, one must gain while the other must lose.

C. The United States cannot compete with nations whose labor costs are lower.

D. U.S. imports raise living standards in the United States.

The correct answer is (D). *(CMA, adapted)*

REQUIRED: The true statement about international trade and protection.

DISCUSSION: Imports can raise the standard of living because more goods are available to consumers. Tariffs, quotas, and other trade restraints are undesirable because free trade will maximize the total benefit to consumers worldwide (under the concept of comparative advantage).

Answer (A) is incorrect because U.S. investment abroad has proven to be beneficial. Answer (B) is incorrect because both nations should benefit from international trade. Under the concept of comparative advantage, no country will be worse off through international trade. Answer (C) is incorrect because the U.S. has other advantages not possessed by countries with low labor costs.

Questions 3 through 5 are based on the following information.

One Unit of Resources Can Produce

	Soybeans (tons)	Chips (units)
Taiwan	6	1,500
United States	12	1,800

3. In trade between Taiwan and the United States,

A. Taiwan has an absolute advantage in producing soybeans.

B. The United States has a comparative advantage in producing soybeans.

C. Taiwan has a comparative advantage in producing soybeans.

D. The United States has a comparative advantage in producing chips.

The correct answer is (B). *(CMA, adapted)*

REQUIRED: The true statement about comparative and absolute advantage in a two-country, two-product model.

DISCUSSION: Given two countries and two products, each country will always have a comparative advantage with respect to one of the products. Each country may or may not have an absolute advantage. In this case, the U.S. has an absolute advantage with respect to both products because with one unit of resources it can produce more soybeans (12 to 6) and more chips (1,800 to 1,500) than Taiwan. Comparatively, the U.S. has an advantage with respect to soybeans. Comparative advantage is measured by determining which product can be manufactured more cheaply (for the lower opportunity cost) in comparison to the other country. For 1 ton of soybeans, the U.S. opportunity cost is 150 units (1,800/12) of chips. The opportunity cost for Taiwan is 250 units (1,500/6) of chips.

Answer (A) is incorrect because Taiwan does not have an absolute advantage with respect to either product. Answers (C) and (D) are incorrect because the U.S. has the comparative advantage in the production of soybeans, and Taiwan has the comparative advantage in the production of chips. Taiwan's opportunity cost for the production of one unit of chips is .004 ton (6/1,500) of soybeans. U.S. chip production has an opportunity cost of .0067 ton (12/1,800) of soybeans.

4. If there were free trade between the two countries, which one of the following statements would be true?

A. Only the United States will gain from free trade.

B. The United States would specialize in the production of both chips and soybeans.

C. The United States will export chips to Taiwan.

D. Taiwan will specialize in the production of chips.

The correct answer is (D). *(CMA, adapted)*

REQUIRED: The true statement about free trade between the two countries.

DISCUSSION: Countries should specialize in the production and export of products for which they have a comparative advantage. They should import those products for which they do not have a comparative advantage. Thus, Taiwan will specialize in the production of chips, and the U.S. will specialize in the production of soybeans.

Answer (A) is incorrect because both countries will benefit from free trade. Specialization results in the optimal total output. Answer (B) is incorrect because the U.S. will specialize in the production of soybeans. Answer (C) is incorrect because Taiwan will produce chips and export them to the U.S.

5. Assuming free trade between the United States and Taiwan, the relative prices of soybeans and chips will be

A. Exactly 1 ton of soybeans for 250 chips.

B. Between 150 to 250 chips for 1 ton of soybeans.

C. Between 1.2 to 2.0 tons of soybeans for 100 chips.

D. Exactly 1 ton of soybeans for 120 chips.

The correct answer is (B). *(CMA, adapted)*

REQUIRED: The relative prices of two products assuming free trade.

DISCUSSION: Taiwan's opportunity cost for 1 ton of soybeans is 250 units of chips. The U.S.'s opportunity cost for 1 ton of soybeans is 150 units of chips (see question 3). Thus, the lowest price that the U.S. should charge is 150 units of chips per ton of soybeans. Moreover, Taiwan should not pay more than 250 units of chips for imported soybeans because they could be made domestically for that price. Therefore, the trading price must be between 150 and 250 units of chips per ton of soybeans if trade is to be advantageous.

Answer (A) is incorrect because 1 ton of soybeans for 250 chips is the opportunity cost for Taiwan. Answer (C) is incorrect because the lowest price the U.S. should charge is 150 units of chips per ton of soybeans and the maximum price that Taiwan would be willing to pay is 250 units of chips per ton of soybeans. Answer (D) is incorrect because the lowest price that the U.S. should charge is 150 units of chips per ton of soybeans. Additionally, Taiwan would not be willing to pay more than 250 units of chips per ton of soybeans.

6. All of the following are true about international trade except that

A. The gains from international trade depend on specialization with comparative advantage.

B. Absolute advantage without comparative advantage does not result in gains from international trade.

C. Absolute advantage is defined as the ability of one nation to produce a product at a relatively lower opportunity cost than another nation.

D. If there is reciprocal absolute advantage between two countries, specialization will make it possible to produce more of each product.

The correct answer is (C). *(CMA, adapted)*

REQUIRED: The false statement about international trade.

DISCUSSION: The concept of comparative advantage compares costs within a single country. It is the ability of one nation to produce a product at a relatively lower opportunity cost (benefits forgone) than another nation. Absolute advantage compares the costs of inputs between countries. One country might have an absolute advantage with respect to every product. However, total output will be maximized when each nation specializes in the products in which it has the lowest opportunity costs, that is, a comparative advantage.

Answer (A) is incorrect because world output will be maximized if each country specializes in those products in which they have a comparative advantage. Answer (B) is incorrect because comparative advantage, not absolute advantage, determines the products in which a country should specialize. Answer (D) is incorrect because, given a reciprocal absolute advantage, a corresponding comparative advantage will exist.

B. Trade Barriers

7. Which of the following is a tariff?

A. Licensing requirements.

B. Consumption taxes on imported goods.

C. Unreasonable standards pertaining to product quality and safety.

D. Domestic content rules.

The correct answer is (B). *(CIA, adapted)*

REQUIRED: The example of a tariff.

DISCUSSION: Tariffs are excise taxes on imported goods imposed either to generate revenue or protect domestic producers. Thus, consumption taxes on imported goods are tariffs.

Answer (A) is incorrect because licensing requirements limit exports, e.g., of militarily sensitive technology. Answer (C) is incorrect because unreasonable standards pertaining to product quality and safety are nontariff trade barriers. Answer (D) is incorrect because domestic content rules require that a portion of an imported good be made in the importing country.

8. Which of the following is a direct effect of imposing a protective tariff on an imported product?

A. Lower domestic prices on the imported item.

B. Lower domestic consumption of the item.

C. Reduced domestic production of the item.

D. Higher sales revenues for foreign producers of the item.

The correct answer is (B). *(CIA, adapted)*

REQUIRED: The direct effect of imposing a protective tariff on an imported product.

DISCUSSION: A protective tariff adds to the purchase price of imported goods. If an imported good's sales price is higher than a comparable, less expensive domestic good, consumers will purchase the domestic good. Thus, the direct effect of imposing a protective tariff on an imported good is lower domestic consumption.

Answer (A) is incorrect because a protective tariff can only increase the domestic price of the imported item. Answer (C) is incorrect because, as the imported item's domestic price increases, demand for domestic goods will increase. Thus, domestic production will increase, not decrease. Answer (D) is incorrect because, as the imported item's domestic price increases, demand for the item decreases. Lower sales revenues will result.

9. A direct effect of imposing a protective tariff on an item for which there are both foreign and domestic producers is that domestic producers will sell <List A> of the item while domestic consumers consume <List B> of the item.

	List A	List B
A.	More	More
B.	More	Less
C.	Less	More
D.	Less	Less

The correct answer is (B). *(CIA, adapted)*

REQUIRED: The effects of a tariff.

DISCUSSION: Domestic producers are not subject to the tariff and will therefore have a price advantage over their foreign competitors. However, absent such competition, the domestic price of the item will be higher. Domestic producers will sell more at a higher price, and domestic consumers will consume less following the price increase.

Answers (A), (C), and (D) are incorrect because domestic producers will sell more, and domestic consumers will consume less, as a result of the imposition of a protective tariff.

10. Many domestic industries, such as cars and textiles, are partially protected from foreign competition by a system of import tariffs and import quotas. A major effect of such tariffs and quotas is to

A. Raise the domestic price of cars and textiles.

B. Lower the domestic price of cars and textiles.

C. Increase the volume of international trade in cars and textiles.

D. Reduce employment in the car and textile industries in the short run.

The correct answer is (A). *(CMA, adapted)*

REQUIRED: The major effect of import tariffs and import quotas on cars and textiles.

DISCUSSION: Import tariffs and quotas cause the prices of goods to increase. Tariffs directly increase the prices paid by consumers. Quotas decrease supply and therefore indirectly raise the price. At the same time, resources will shift from relatively efficient export industries to less efficient protected industries. Price will rise as resources are misallocated to high-cost producers.

Answer (B) is incorrect because prices will increase. Answer (C) is incorrect because the volume of trade will decline as less efficient domestic producers remain in or enter the market. Total worldwide real output will also decline. Answer (D) is incorrect because employment in the protected industries will increase in the short run, but total employment may not be affected.

11. One consequence of the imposition of tariffs or quotas on imported products is

A. Lower prices for domestic products that compete with affected imports.

B. Domestic industry opposition to protection from imports.

C. Additional consumption of the affected imported products.

D. Higher prices for the affected imported products.

The correct answer is (D). *(CMA, adapted)*

REQUIRED: The consequence of the imposition of tariffs or quotas.

DISCUSSION: Tariffs lead to higher prices on imported products. Similarly, the imposition of quotas leads to higher prices through an artificial limitation on supply.

Answer (A) is incorrect because trade restricts full inflation since incentives to charge lower prices for domestic products are removed. Answer (B) is incorrect because domestic industries support protection from imports to reduce competition. Answer (C) is incorrect because consumption is reduced owing to higher prices and reduced supply.

12. Which one of the following groups would be the primary beneficiary of a tariff?

A. Domestic producers of export goods.

B. Domestic producers of goods protected by the tariff.

C. Domestic consumers of goods protected by the tariff.

D. Foreign producers of goods protected by the tariff.

The correct answer is (B). (CMA, adapted)

REQUIRED: The primary beneficiaries of a tariff.

DISCUSSION: Despite the advantages of free trade, nations often levy tariffs to discourage the importation of certain products. A tariff is a tax on imports intended to protect a domestic producer from foreign competition. For instance, a tariff on imported autos benefits U. S. auto manufacturers because it is an additional cost imposed on U.S. consumers of such products. The disadvantages of the tariff are that it may protect an inefficient domestic producer and increase prices paid by domestic consumers.

Answer (A) is incorrect because domestic producers of export goods are not benefitted. Indeed, they may be harmed by retaliatory tariffs. Answer (C) is incorrect because domestic consumers must pay higher prices for imported goods. Answer (D) is incorrect because the foreign producers will be forced to bear an additional cost.

13. In trade discussions between the United States and Japanese governments, if Japan voluntarily agrees to restrict automobile exports, which one of the following is true?

A. This restriction has no effect on the price paid by the consumer.

B. The United States government gains from these restrictions.

C. Profit margins for Japanese auto manufacturers have increased.

D. Under this agreement, the Japanese have an incentive to export less expensive cars to the United States.

The correct answer is (C). *(CMA, adapted)*

REQUIRED: The true statement about Japan's voluntary agreement to restrict automobile exports to the United States.

DISCUSSION: A voluntary agreement to restrict exports to the United States forestalls possible trade restrictions. Such an agreement is more likely if Japan's domestic profit margins are sufficiently high that its dependence on exports to the U.S. has been reduced.

Answer (A) is incorrect because this restriction increases the price to U.S. consumers. The reduced supply may not be matched by reduced demand. Answer (B) is incorrect because the government will not directly benefit from the restriction on auto imports from Japan. The restriction benefits U.S. manufacturers and helps equalize the balance of payments. Answer (D) is incorrect because Japan will want to export more expensive cars to the U.S. The higher-priced cars will have higher margins of profit.

14. The graph below depicts the domestic supply of and demand for a product that is also sold in the domestic market by foreign producers. The domestic producers are protected by a tariff of the amount P_t minus P_w. P_t is the domestic price including the tariff, and P_w is the world price for the product. The effect of the tariff is to

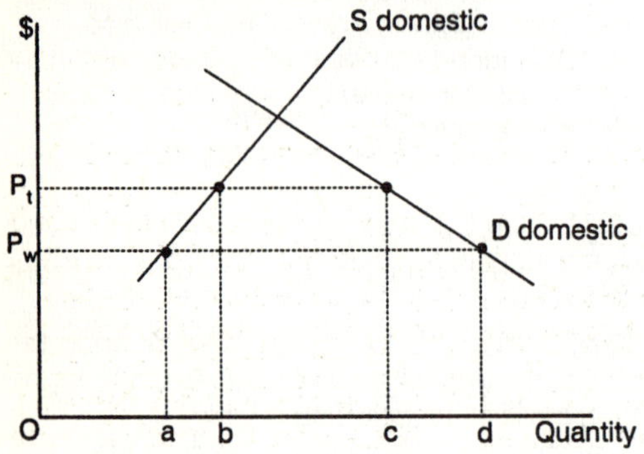

A. Reduce the domestic price from OP_w to OP_t.

B. Reduce foreign sales in the domestic market from ac to bc.

C. Increase domestic production from Ob to Oc.

D. Increase domestic production from Oa to Ob.

The correct answer is (D). *(CIA, adapted)*

REQUIRED: The effect of a tariff.

DISCUSSION: Without the tariff, domestic production is determined by the intersection of the P_w line with the domestic supply curve at the quantity Oa. Domestic production increases from Oa to Ob as a result of the introduction of the tariff. Supply intersects the P_t line at a higher price and at a greater domestic quantity, Ob.

Answer (A) is incorrect because the inclusion of the tariff increases the domestic price. Answer (B) is incorrect because foreign sales in the domestic market decline from ad to bc. Answer (C) is incorrect because domestic production increases from Oa to Ob.

15. Which of the following measures create the most restrictive barrier to exporting to a country?

A. Tariffs.

B. Quotas.

C. Embargoes.

D. Exchange controls.

The correct answer is (C). *(CIA, adapted)*

REQUIRED: The most restrictive barriers to exports to a country.

DISCUSSION: An embargo is a total ban on some kinds of imports. It is an extreme form of the import quota. Embargoes have the effect of totally excluding the exporting firm from selling in that country and are the most restrictive type of import/export law.

Answer (A) is incorrect because a tariff is a tax levied by a foreign government against certain imported products. A firm exporting to that country must accept lower profits, absorbing the tariff, or increase selling prices in the foreign country to compensate. The tariff reduces profitability or competitiveness in the foreign market but does not exclude the firm from exporting to that country. Answer (B) is incorrect because a quota is a limit on the amount of goods that an importing country will accept in certain product categories. The effect of a quota is to restrict the quantity the firm can export to that country but not to exclude the firm from selling in that market. The effect on revenues and profitability depends on market conditions in that country. Answer (D) is incorrect because exchange controls limit the amount of foreign exchange that can be transacted or the exchange rate against other currencies. These controls limit the ability of a firm selling in the country to repatriate its export earnings but do not exclude the firm from selling in that market.

16. The creation of a regional economic bloc of trading nations, such as the European Union (EU),

A. Discourages foreign investment by nonmember multinational companies.

B. Encourages trade between the member nations and nonmember nations.

C. Requires the adoption of a common monetary unit.

D. Discriminates economically against nonmember nations.

The correct answer is (D). *(CMA, adapted)*

REQUIRED: The effect of the creation of a regional economic bloc of trading nations.

DISCUSSION: A trading bloc provides trading incentives to member nations and discriminates against nonmember nations. For example, the European Union calls for abolition of internal tariffs and import quotas, free movement of capital and labor within the market, and implementation of common policies for the member nations. However, the EU also imposed a common system of tariffs on goods of nonmember nations.

Answer (A) is incorrect because foreign investment may be welcomed under the appropriate conditions. Answer (B) is incorrect because the EU provides incentives to trade with other members, not nonmembers. Answer (C) is incorrect because currencies are not affected by bloc membership.

C. Foreign Currency Rates and Markets

17. The most widely used currency in international business today is the

A. United States dollar.

B. Euro.

C. Japanese yen.

D. Swiss franc.

The correct answer is (A). *(CMA, adapted)*

REQUIRED: The most widely used currency in international business.

DISCUSSION: The U.S. dollar is the most widely used currency in international markets today. It is considered much more stable than any of the third-world currencies. Thus, many third-world countries rely on the U.S. dollar for foreign trade.

Answer (B) is incorrect because the Euro has not yet been adopted. Answers (C) and (D) are incorrect because they are not as heavily used as the U.S. dollar.

18. If the value of the U.S. dollar in foreign currency markets changes from $1 = 6 marks to $1 = 4 marks,

A. The German mark has depreciated against the dollar.

B. German imported products in the U.S. will become more expensive.

C. U.S. tourists in Germany will find their dollars will buy more German products.

D. U.S. exports to Germany should decrease.

The correct answer is (B). *(CMA, adapted)*

REQUIRED: The effect of a depreciation in the value of the dollar.

DISCUSSION: The dollar has declined in value relative to the mark. If an American had previously wished to purchase a German product that was priced at 12 marks, the dollar price would have been $2. After the decline in value, the dollar cost of the item has increased to $3. Therefore, imports from West Germany should decrease and exports increase.

Answer (A) is incorrect because the mark has appreciated (increased in value) relative to the dollar. Answer (C) is incorrect because dollars will buy fewer West German products. Answer (D) is incorrect because U.S. exports should increase. For example, if a U.S. product previously cost $3, the price to Germans would have been 18 marks. With the decline of the dollar, the Germans can now buy the $3 item for 12 marks.

19. An overvalued foreign currency exchange rate

A. Represents a tax on exports and a subsidy to imports.

B. Represents a subsidy to exports and a tax on imports.

C. Has an effect on capital flows but no effect on trade flows.

D. Has no effect on capital flows but does affect trade flows.

The correct answer is (A). *(CMA, adapted)*

REQUIRED: The effect of an overvalued exchange rate.

DISCUSSION: An overvalued exchange rate is a tax on exports because they will be overvalued in terms of the foreign currency. For example, if the true value of $1 is 5 marks but the exchange rate is $1 to 6 marks, the cost of goods priced in dollars will include a 20% tax for holders of marks. It is also a subsidy to imports because the overly high exchange rate causes the price of foreign goods and services to be undervalued. In the same example, $1 will buy 6 marks' worth of imports instead of 5, a 20% subsidy.

Answer (B) is incorrect because devaluation taxes imports and subsidizes exports. Answers (C) and (D) are incorrect because both will be affected.

20. Exchange rates are determined by

A. Each industrial country's government.

B. The International Monetary Fund.

C. Supply and demand in the foreign currency market.

D. Exporters and importers of manufactured goods.

The correct answer is (C). *(CMA, adapted)*

REQUIRED: The factor that determines foreign exchange rates.

DISCUSSION: Although currencies can be supported by various means for short periods, the primary determinant of exchange rates is the supply of and demand for the various currencies. Under current international agreements, exchange rates are allowed to "float." During periods of extreme fluctuations, however, governments and control banks may intervene to maintain stability in the market.

Answers (A), (B), and (D) are incorrect because they have only temporary influence, if any, on the setting of exchange rates.

21. Two countries have flexible exchange rate systems and an active trading relationship. If incomes <List A> in country 1, everything else equal, then the currency of country 1 will tend to <List B> relative to the currency of country 2.

	List A	List B
A.	Rise	Remain constant
B.	Fall	Depreciate
C.	Rise	Depreciate
D.	Remain constant	Appreciate

The correct answer is (C). *(CIA, adapted)*

REQUIRED: The effect of a change in incomes in one nation on its currency.

DISCUSSION: If incomes in country 1 rise, consumers in country 1 will increase their imports from country 2. The resulting increase in the supply of currency 1 will result in a tendency for it to depreciate relative to the currency of country 2.

Answer (A) is incorrect because, if incomes in country 1 rise, the result will be a tendency for it to devalue relative to the currency of country 2. Answer (B) is incorrect because, if incomes in country 1 fall, consumers in country 1 will reduce their imports. The resulting decrease in the supply of currency 1 will result in a tendency for it to appreciate relative to the currency of country 2. Answer (D) is incorrect because, if incomes in country 1 remain constant, the currency of country 1 will not tend to appreciate or depreciate relative to the currency of country 2.

22. In foreign currency markets, the phrase "managed float" refers to the

A. Tendency for most currencies to depreciate in value.

B. Discretionary buying and selling of currencies by central banks.

C. Necessity of maintaining a highly liquid asset, such as gold, to conduct international trade.

D. Fact that actual exchange rates are set by private business people in trading nations.

The correct answer is (B). *(CMA, adapted)*

REQUIRED: The meaning of the phrase "managed float."

DISCUSSION: Exchange rates "float" when they are set by supply and demand, not by agreement among countries. In a managed float, central banks buy and sell currencies at their discretion to avoid erratic fluctuations in the foreign currency market. The objective of such transactions is to "manage" the level at which a particular currency sells in the open market. For instance, if there is an oversupply of a country's currency on the foreign currency market, the central bank will purchase that currency to support the market.

Answer (A) is incorrect because currencies do not have an inherent tendency to depreciate or appreciate. Answer (C) is incorrect because currencies no longer have to be supported by gold. Answer (D) is incorrect because central banks, not private business people, manage the quantity of currency on the market.

23. The U.S. dollar has a free-floating exchange rate. When the dollar has fallen considerably in relation to other currencies, the

A. Trade account in the U.S. balance of payments is neither in a deficit nor in a surplus because of the floating exchange rates.

B. Capital account in the U.S. balance of payments is neither in a deficit nor in a surplus because of the floating exchange rates.

C. Fall in the dollar's value cannot be expected to have any effect on the U.S. trade balance.

D. Cheaper dollar helps U.S. exporters of domestically produced goods.

The correct answer is (D). *(CMA, adapted)*

REQUIRED: The true statement about the fall in the price of the dollar relative to other currencies.

DISCUSSION: A decline in the value of the dollar relative to other currencies lowers the price of U.S. goods to foreign consumers. Thus, exporters of domestically produced goods benefit. A low value of the dollar also decreases imports by making foreign goods more expensive.

Answer (A) is incorrect because the trade account still has a deficit despite the cheaper dollar. Imports continue to exceed exports because patterns of consumption are slow to change. Answer (B) is incorrect because the capital account benefits from the cheaper dollar. Foreigners can buy more dollars with fewer yen, marks, etc. Moreover, foreign capital inflow increases because of the federal government's budget deficits. Hence, the U.S. experiences a net capital inflow. Answer (C) is incorrect because the fall in the dollar has a positive effect on the nation's trade deficit. Exports increase and imports decrease.

24. The purchasing-power parity exchange rate

A. Is a fixed (pegged) exchange rate.

B. Is always equal to the market exchange rate.

C. Results in an undervalued currency of countries that are net importers.

D. Holds constant the relative price levels in two countries when measured in a common currency.

The correct answer is (D). *(CMA, adapted)*

REQUIRED: The definition of purchasing-power parity exchange rate.

DISCUSSION: The purchasing-power parity theorem states that, in the long run, the real price of a good in country A will equal the price of the same good in country B when the prices are expressed in a common currency and converted at the current exchange rate (adjustments for tariffs, taxes, or transportation costs may need to be made).

Answer (A) is incorrect because purchasing-power parity is achieved through floating exchange rates. Answer (B) is incorrect because the purchasing-power parity exchange rate is a long-run measure, but the market rate may reflect short-term or medium-term conditions. Answer (C) is incorrect because purchasing-power parity does not affect the valuation of currency.

25. If the U.S. dollar declines in value relative to the currencies of many of its trading partners, the likely result is that

A. Foreign currencies will depreciate against the dollar.

B. The U.S. balance of payments deficit will become worse.

C. U.S. exports will tend to increase.

D. U.S. imports will tend to increase.

The correct answer is (C). *(CMA, adapted)*

REQUIRED: The true statement if the U.S. dollar declines in value.

DISCUSSION: The decline in the value of the dollar reduces the prices of U.S. goods to foreigners and should increase exports. Also, foreign goods will be higher priced (in dollars) and imports from foreign countries should decrease, thus helping the U.S. balance of payments.

Answer (A) is incorrect because the dollar has depreciated against foreign currencies. Answer (B) is incorrect because the U.S. trade balance of payments should improve. Answer (D) is incorrect because U.S. imports will decline. Foreign goods will be higher priced than before.

26. If consumers in Japan decide they would like to increase their purchases of consumer products made in the United States, in foreign currency markets there will be a tendency for

A. The supply of dollars to increase.

B. The supply of dollars to decrease.

C. The Japanese yen to appreciate relative to the U.S. dollar.

D. The demand for dollars to increase.

The correct answer is (D). *(CMA, adapted)*

REQUIRED: The effect of decisions by Japanese consumers to increase their purchases of U.S. products.

DISCUSSION: The increase in demand for U.S. products will increase the demand for the dollars necessary to pay for those products.

Answers (A) and (B) are incorrect because the demand for dollars, not the supply, will be affected by the decision to purchase additional U.S. products. Answer (C) is incorrect because the dollar should appreciate relative to the yen owing to the increased demand for dollars.

27. Debt-servicing problems of less developed countries that primarily sell raw materials to the United States would be eased by

A. A recession in the United States with declines in interest rates.

B. An expanding U.S. economy with stable money supply growth.

C. An expansion of the lending authority of the World Bank.

D. A significant increase in the level of U.S. tariffs.

The correct answer is (B). *(CMA, adapted)*

REQUIRED: The means of easing debt-servicing problems of less developed countries.

DISCUSSION: An expanding U.S. economy would result in greater demand for raw materials from these countries. Also, because the money supply and interest rates are inversely proportional (when the money supply is rising, interest rates are falling), less developed nations could borrow again at lower rates. Moreover, if the money supply is rising, inflation might increase and U.S. dollars would become cheaper, thereby easing the burden of foreign debtors with obligations payable in dollars.

Answer (A) is incorrect because a recession would result in less U.S. demand for raw materials from abroad and a reduction in funds available to the underdeveloped nations to pay debts. Answer (C) is incorrect because an expansion of lending authority could only increase the debt outstanding and make it less possible for less developed countries to service their debts. Answer (D) is incorrect because tariffs would reduce exports to the U.S. and thus the funds available for debt service.

28. If the central bank of a country raises interest rates sharply, the country's currency will likely

A. Increase in relative value.

B. Remain unchanged in value.

C. Decrease in relative value.

D. Decrease sharply in value at first and then return to its initial value.

The correct answer is (A). *(CMA, adapted)*

REQUIRED: The effect on a country's currency if its central bank raises interest rates sharply.

DISCUSSION: Exchange rates fluctuate depending upon the demand for each country's currency. If a country raises its interest rates, its currency will appreciate. The demand for investment at the higher interest rates will shift the demand curve for the currency to the right. The reverse holds true for a decrease in interest rates.

Answers (B), (C), and (D) are incorrect because the currency should increase in relative value when interest rates in the country rise sharply. More investors will want to earn the higher rates of interest.

29. One U.S. dollar is being quoted at 120 Japanese yen on the spot market and at 123 Japanese yen on the 90-day forward market; hence, the annual effect in the forward market is that the

A. U.S. dollar is at a premium of 10%.

B. U.S. dollar is at a premium of 2.5%.

C. U.S. dollar is at a discount of 10%.

D. U.S. dollar is at a premium of 0.025%.

The correct answer is (A). *(CMA, adapted)*

REQUIRED: The annual effect in the forward market of the difference between the current (spot) rate and the 90-day rate.

DISCUSSION: The price difference of three yen is a difference of 2½% (3 ÷ 120) for 90 days. Annualizing this difference (multiplying by 4) produces an annual premium of 10%. Because the 90-day price of the dollar is higher than the current price, it is said that the dollar is at a premium on the 90-day forward market.

Answer (B) is incorrect because 2.5% is the premium for 90 days. Answer (C) is incorrect because the effect is a 10% premium, not discount. Answer (D) is incorrect because the 90-day effect is a 2.5% or 0.025 premium.

30. Assuming exchange rates are allowed to fluctuate freely, which one of the following factors would likely cause a nation's currency to appreciate on the foreign exchange market?

A. A relatively rapid rate of growth in income that stimulates imports.

B. A high rate of inflation relative to other countries.

C. A slower rate of growth in income than in other countries, which causes imports to lag behind exports.

D. Domestic real interest rates that are lower than real interest rates abroad.

The correct answer is (C). (CMA, adapted)

REQUIRED: The factor causing a currency to appreciate given freely fluctuating exchange rates.

DISCUSSION: Assuming that exchange rates are allowed to fluctuate freely, a nation's currency will appreciate if the demand for it is constant or increasing while supply is decreasing. For example, if the nation decreases its imports relative to exports, less of its currency will be used to buy foreign currencies for import transactions and more of its currency will be demanded for export transactions. Thus, the supply of the nation's currency available in foreign currency markets decreases. If the demand for the currency increases or does not change, the result is an increase in (appreciation of) the value of the currency.

Answer (A) is incorrect because an increase in imports drives down the value of the nation's currency. Answer (B) is incorrect because a high rate of inflation devalues a nation's currency. Answer (D) is incorrect because lower interest rates relative to those in other countries discourage foreign investment, decreases demand for the nation's currency, and reduces its value.

31. Assuming that the real rate of interest is the same in both countries, if country A has a higher nominal interest rate than country B, the currency of country A will likely be selling at a

A. Forward discount relative to the currency of country B.

B. Forward premium relative to the currency of country B.

C. Spot discount relative to the currency of country B.

D. Spot premium relative to the currency of country B.

The correct answer is (A). *(CIA, adapted)*

REQUIRED: The effect of a higher nominal interest rate.

DISCUSSION: If the real rates of interest are equal, the country with the higher nominal interest rate is expected to experience a higher rate of inflation. A higher rate of inflation is associated with a devaluing currency, so the currency of the country with the higher nominal interest rate will likely be selling at a forward discount.

Answer (B) is incorrect because the currency of country A will be selling at a forward discount. Answers (C) and (D) are incorrect because the spot relationship between the two currencies cannot be determined from the information given.

32. If the annual U.S. inflation rate is expected to be 5% while the Italian lira is expected to depreciate against the U.S. dollar by 10%, an Italian firm importing from its U.S. parent can expect its lira costs for these imports to

A. Decrease by about 10%.

B. Decrease by about 5%.

C. Increase by about 5%.

D. Increase by about 15%.

The correct answer is (D). *(CMA, adapted)*

REQUIRED: The combined effect of inflation and currency depreciation.

DISCUSSION: Assuming the original exchange rate is \$1 to 2,000 lira and that U.S. inflation is 5%, the cost in lira to purchase what once cost \$1 will now be 2,100 lira (2,000 x 1.05). However, if the lira also depreciates by 10%, the exchange rate will be \$1 to 2,200 lira. At this rate, 2,310 lira (2,200 x 1.05) will be required to purchase \$1.05. Lira costs will thus increase by just over 15% (310 ÷ 2,000).

Answers (A) and (B) are incorrect because the combined effect of U.S. inflation and the decline in value of the lira would cause the lira costs for U.S. imports to increase. Answer (C) is incorrect because 5% is the difference between the currency depreciation and the inflation rate.

33. If the exchange rate has changed from 1 U.S. dollar being worth 5 French francs to a rate of 1 U.S. dollar being worth 5.5 French francs,

A. The U.S. dollar has appreciated by 10%.

B. The U.S. dollar has depreciated by 10%.

C. The French franc has appreciated by 20%.

D. The French franc has depreciated by 20%.

The correct answer is (A). *(CIA, adapted)*

REQUIRED: The effect of a change in the exchange rate.

DISCUSSION: If the exchange rate changes from \$1 being worth 5 francs to \$1 being worth 5.5 francs, the U.S. dollar has appreciated by 10% [(5.5 – 5) ÷ 5].

Answer (B) is incorrect because the U.S. dollar has appreciated in value. It will now purchase more francs. Answer (C) is incorrect because the franc is depreciating, not appreciating. Answer (D) is incorrect because the franc has depreciated by 9.09%.

34. An American importer of English clothing has contracted to pay an amount fixed in British pounds three months from now. If the importer worries that the U.S. dollar may depreciate sharply against the British pound in the interim, it would be well advised to

A. Buy pounds in the forward exchange market.

B. Sell pounds in the forward exchange market.

C. Buy dollars in the futures market.

D. Sell dollars in the futures market.

The correct answer is (A). *(CMA, adapted)*

REQUIRED: The action to hedge a liability denominated in a foreign currency.

DISCUSSION: The American importer should buy pounds now. If the dollar depreciates against the pound in the next 90 days, the gain on the forward exchange contract would offset the loss from having to pay more dollars to satisfy the liability.

Answer (B) is incorrect because selling pounds would compound the risk of loss for someone who has incurred a liability. However, it would be an appropriate hedge of a receivable denominated in pounds. Answer (C) is incorrect because the importer needs pounds, not dollars. Answer (D) is incorrect because, although buying pounds might be equivalent to selling dollars for pounds, this is not the best answer. This choice does not state what is received for the dollars.

35. Consider a world consisting of only two countries, Canada and Italy. Inflation in Canada in 1 year was 5%, and in Italy 10%. Which one of the following statements about the Canadian exchange rate (rounded) during that year will be true?

A. Inflation has no effect on the exchange rates.

B. The Canadian dollar will appreciate by 5%.

C. The Canadian dollar will depreciate by 5%.

D. The Canadian dollar will depreciate by 15%.

The correct answer is (B). *(CMA, adapted)*

REQUIRED: The true statement about the exchange rate of a currency given domestic and foreign inflation.

DISCUSSION: Because Italy has experienced the greater inflation, its currency should depreciate in relation to Canada's. For example, if Canada trades 100 units of a product to Italy for a preinflation price of $100 (the domestic price in Canada), and Italy pays with 10,000 units of an Italian product that sells domestically for 10,000 preinflation lira, the exchange rate without regard to inflation is 100 lira per $1 (10,000 lira/$100). Allowing for the inflation, the 100 units of the Canadian product would sell for $105. The 10,000 units of the Italian product would sell for 11,000 lira. Thus, the new exchange rate will be 104.76 lira per $1 (11,000 lira/$105), and the price of the Canadian dollar will increase by 4.76% (rounded to 5%).

Answer (A) is incorrect because inflation affects exchange rates by diminishing a currency's purchasing power. Answers (C) and (D) are incorrect because the Canadian currency will appreciate relative to Italy's since Canadian inflation was lower.

36. Caroline Brown, the product manager for a U.S. computer manufacturer, is being asked to quote prices of desktop computers to be used in Kuwait. The Kuwaiti government wants the price in British pounds, for delivery next year. Brown knows that the general price level in the United States will increase by 3%. Her banker forecasts that the British pound will depreciate about 5% this year with respect to the U.S. dollar. If Brown is able to quote £700 for immediate delivery, the price that should be quoted for delivery to Kuwait next year is about

A. £735

B. £721

C. £757

D. £745

The correct answer is (C). *(CMA, adapted)*

REQUIRED: The foreign currency price to quote for a future delivery of goods.

DISCUSSION: Two factors are to be considered: (1) the 3% inflation rate and (2) the 5% decline in the pound. Considering the inflation rate first, 3% should be added to the immediate delivery price to arrive at a future price of £721. However, to allow for the foreign currency exchange-rate risk, an additional 5% should be added to the inflation-adjusted price. The bid price should be £757 [£721 + (5% x £721)].

Answer (A) is incorrect because £735 results from considering only the effect of the 5% decline in the pound. Answer (B) is incorrect because £721 results from considering only the effect of the 3% U.S. inflation rate. Answer (D) is incorrect because the effects of both the 3% U.S. inflation rate and the 5% decline in the pound need to be added to the initial £700.

37. If risk is purposely undertaken in the foreign currency market, the investor in foreign currency then becomes

A. A speculator.

B. An arbitrageur.

C. Involved in hedging.

D. An exporter.

The correct answer is (A). *(CMA, adapted)*

REQUIRED: The term for an investor who purposely undertakes risk in the foreign currency market.

DISCUSSION: An individual who purposely accepts exchange rate risk is a speculator. Speculators buy and sell foreign currencies in anticipation of favorable changes in rates.

Answer (B) is incorrect because an arbitrageur is someone who simultaneously buys foreign currency in one market and sells in another market at a slightly higher price. Thus, the arbitrageur's risk is slight. Answer (C) is incorrect because hedging avoids the risk of foreign currency transactions for those who do not seek to gain from fluctuations in exchange rates. Hedging is the sale or purchase of a forward exchange contract to offset a possible exchange rate loss. When a forward exchange contract is intended and is effective as an economic hedge against an exposed net asset or net liability position (e.g., an outstanding receivable or liability denominated in a foreign currency), any exchange gain or loss on the forward contract will offset any exchange gain or loss on the exposed net asset or net liability position. Thus, no exchange gain or loss will result. Answer (D) is incorrect because exporters and importers are likely to engage in hedging to avoid exchange-rate risk.

38. A company has a foreign-currency-denominated trade payable, due in 60 days. In order to eliminate the foreign currency exchange-rate risk associated with the payable, the company could

A. Sell foreign currency forward today.

B. Wait 60 days and pay the invoice by purchasing foreign currency in the spot market at that time.

C. Buy foreign currency forward today.

D. Borrow foreign currency today, convert it to domestic currency on the spot market, and invest the funds in a domestic bank deposit until the invoice payment date.

The correct answer is (C). *(CIA, adapted)*

REQUIRED: The means of eliminating exchange-rate risk.

DISCUSSION: The company can arrange to purchase the foreign currency today rather than in 60 days by buying the currency in the forward market. This hedging transaction will eliminate the exchange-rate risk associated with the trade payable.

Answer (A) is incorrect because a forward market sale of foreign currency is appropriate to hedge a receivable denominated in a foreign currency. Answer (B) is incorrect because waiting to buy the currency in 60 days does not eliminate the risk of an adverse exchange-rate movement. Answer (D) is incorrect because this strategy would be comparable to a future sale of the foreign currency at a rate known today, which would not provide the currency needed to pay the invoice. However, the opposite strategy would be an effective money market hedge. If the company converted domestic currency to foreign currency in the spot market today and invested in a foreign bank deposit or treasury bill, it could then use the proceeds from the foreign investment to pay the invoice in 60 days.

39. Which one of the following did not contribute to the high value of the U.S. dollar during the 1980s?

A. Relatively high, real interest rates.

B. A large demand for U.S. dollars.

C. U.S. demand for foreign goods.

D. A stable U.S. government and currency.

The correct answer is (C). *(CMA, adapted)*

REQUIRED: The event that did not contribute to the high value of the U.S. dollar during the 1980s.

DISCUSSION: Many factors influence the value of a country's currency on the international market. These factors include interest rate differentials, inflation differentials, balance of trade, balance of payments, and stability of governments. However, a demand by Americans for more foreign goods would drive down the price of the dollar because of the resulting increased demand for foreign currencies.

Answer (A) is incorrect because, in the 1980s, high real interest rates made investments in the U.S. more attractive. Thus, demand for U.S. dollars increased. Answer (B) is incorrect because a large demand for dollars drives up the price of dollars relative to other currencies. Answer (D) is incorrect because the stability of the U.S. government and its currency made the dollar a secure store of value in the eyes of many foreigners; these foreigners therefore acquired dollars to hold as a safeguard against inflation in their own countries.

D. Balance of Payments

40. In relation to the balance of trade, all international transactions involving the purchase or sale of physical products between domestic and foreign countries are reflected in

A. The balance of the capital account.

B. Official reserves held by the central banks.

C. The official financing account.

D. The trade balance in the current account.

The correct answer is (D). *(CMA, adapted)*

REQUIRED: The correct account.

DISCUSSION: The balance of payments represents all international payments made by one nation to another, including those for imports, exports, investments, unilateral transfers such as pensions and gifts, and capital movements. The principal accounts are the current account and the capital account. The current account includes a net trade balance in goods, net investment receipts or payments, net receipts or payments for services, and the balance of unilateral transfers.

Answer (A) is incorrect because the capital account includes capital movements only; the direction of capital movements is influenced by the prevailing interest rates in each nation. Answer (B) is incorrect because official reserves are assets held by central banks and are not necessarily related to current transactions. Answer (C) is incorrect because this is a nonsense answer.

41. When analyzing a country's balance of payments accounts, the

A. "Current account" refers only to merchandise exports and imports.

B. "Current account" and "trade balance" are the same.

C. "Capital account" refers to the transactions related to the international movement of financial capital.

D. Country will be in financial jeopardy unless each component in the balance of payments accounts balances at the end of the year.

The correct answer is (C). *(CMA, adapted)*

REQUIRED: The true statement about a country's balance of payments accounts.

DISCUSSION: The balance of payments accounts include all international payments made by one nation to another, including capital movements, imports, exports, and unilateral transfers. The net of exports and imports is the current account balance. The current account balance does not include capital transactions. The capital account reflects movements of financial capital (investments).

Answer (A) is incorrect because the current account includes exports and imports of services as well as goods. Answer (B) is incorrect because the trade balance concerns goods only. Answer (D) is incorrect because the various components are never in balance. In reality, the important consideration is the total, and that is more of a long-run than an annual problem.

42. The following transactions were noted for an economy whose currency is denominated in pesetas (Pta).

	Amount in Pesetas
Imports of goods	20,300
Exports of goods	15,760
Domestic long-term investment in foreign countries	6,300
Investment by foreigners in the country	1,400
Interest payments on foreign loans	3,700
Gifts received from abroad	1,240

When calculating the balance of trade for this economy, the

A. Current account has a surplus of Pta 7,000.

B. Capital account has a surplus of Pta 4,000.

C. Capital account has a deficit of Pta 7,700.

D. Current account has a deficit of Pta 7,000.

The correct answer is (D). *(CMA, adapted)*

REQUIRED: The balance of trade for the economy.

DISCUSSION: The balance of trade is the balance of imports and exports of goods. The current account also considers trade in services (none for this economy), unilateral transfers (e.g., gifts), and investment receipts and payments. It does not include capital transactions. Thus, investments by foreigners in the domestic economy and investments made in foreign countries will not be included in the current account. These transactions will be reflected in the capital account. The capital account will therefore have a deficit of 4,900 (6,300 – 1,400) pesetas, since investment in foreign countries is greater than investment by foreigners. The current account will have a deficit of 7,000 pesetas (15,760 – 20,300 + 1,240 – 3,700). This question assumes that the balance of trade is synonymous with the current account balance. But these terms are often differentiated.

Answer (A) is incorrect because the current account has a deficit, not a surplus, of Pta 7,000. Answer (B) is incorrect because investment by foreigners should be deducted from, not added to, domestic investment in foreign countries. Furthermore, interest payments on foreign loans affect the current, not the capital account, and the capital account has a trade deficit, not a surplus. Answer (C) is incorrect because investment by foreigners should be deducted from, not added to, domestic investment in foreign countries.

43. Which one of the following items represents a credit in the U.S. balance of payment accounts?

A. U.S. imports of crude oil.

B. Expenditures of American tourists abroad.

C. Earnings belonging to foreign businesses that have U.S. plants.

D. Loans to Americans by foreigners.

The correct answer is (D). *(CMA, adapted)*

REQUIRED: The item that represents a credit in the U.S. balance of payments accounts.

DISCUSSION: Basically, exports of goods and services are credited to the U.S. balance of payments accounts and imports are debited. Similarly, capital movements may be debited or credited. For example, transfers of capital from foreigners to Americans, such as loans, are credits in the accounts. In effect, these loans constitute exports of debt instruments and increase the supply of foreign exchange available for the U.S.

Answer (A) is incorrect because imports are debited. Answer (B) is incorrect because expenditures of American tourists abroad are treated as imports and are therefore debited. Answer (C) is incorrect because earnings of foreigners represent outflows of foreign exchange and are debited.

44. If a country has a freely floating exchange rate system and is experiencing an appreciation in the external value of its currency, it has

A. A current account deficit and a capital account surplus.

B. A current account surplus and a capital account deficit.

C. Shrinking official reserves.

D. No balance of payments surplus or deficit after short-run exchange-rate adjustments are complete.

The correct answer is (D). *(CIA, adapted)*

REQUIRED: The effect of an appreciation in the external value of a country's currency given floating exchange rates.

DISCUSSION: In a freely floating exchange-rate system, exchange rates automatically adjust so as to eliminate balance of payments surpluses or deficits. For example, if U.S. demand for country X's currency increases, the result is a U.S. deficit at the existing exchange rate because demand now exceeds the supply of X's currency at that rate. However, the system of floating exchange rates allows the change in the relative strength of the currencies to be reflected in their exchange rate. The appreciation of X's currency against the U.S. dollar, that is, the increase in the amount of U.S. dollars exchangeable for a unit of X's currency, makes U.S. products cheaper to buyers in country X. Furthermore, X's products are more expensive to U.S. buyers. Consequently, U.S. imports will fall, U.S. exports will rise, and the balance of payments deficit will decrease.

Answers (A) and (B) are incorrect because the total balance of payments surplus or deficit, which is the sum of the current and capital account balances, is what determines changes in official reserves and pressures for exchange rates to change. Answer (C) is incorrect because, given an appreciation of the currency, the short-run effects are likely to be a balance of payments surplus and growing official reserves.

45. The dominant reason countries devalue their currencies is to

A. Improve the balance of payments.

B. Discourage exports without having to impose controls.

C. Curb inflation by increasing imports.

D. Slow what is regarded as too rapid an accumulation of international reserves.

The correct answer is (A). *(CMA, adapted)*

REQUIRED: The dominant reason countries devalue their currencies.

DISCUSSION: Currency devaluations result in a change in the balance of payments. A devaluation means that other currencies will buy more of the devaluing nation's currency, and the prices of goods denominated in the devalued currency are therefore cheaper. A devaluation usually results in an increase in exports, a decrease in imports (caused by higher relative input prices), and an improved balance of payments.

Answer (B) is incorrect because a devaluation will encourage exports. Answer (C) is incorrect because a devaluation will discourage imports and may encourage domestic inflation. Foreign goods will be more expensive. Answer (D) is incorrect because devaluation most likely occurs when a country is losing its reserves.

E. International Institutions and Agreements

46. In the modern world economy, balance-of-payments deficits and surpluses can be eliminated

A. Through the market mechanism of flexible exchange rates.

B. If all nations adopt tight monetary policies.

C. Only if trade between nations is curtailed.

D. When the opportunity costs of production are made the same in all countries.

The correct answer is (A). *(CMA, adapted)*

REQUIRED: The means by which balance-of-payments deficits and surpluses can be eliminated.

DISCUSSION: If exchange rates are allowed to fluctuate, the value of a particular currency will be determined in accordance with the supply of and demand for that currency. For example, if U.S. exports to Japan are greater than imports, the dollar will be in great demand; thus, the dollar will be driven up in price relative to the Japanese yen. This increase in price will discourage the Japanese from buying U.S. goods. The decrease in Japanese purchases will then result, in principle, in less demand for the dollar and a movement back toward equilibrium in the export/import ratio.

Answer (B) is incorrect because tight money policies would not affect the balance of payments but would reduce economic activity generally. Answer (C) is incorrect because deficits can be overcome by less drastic and counterproductive methods than eliminating trade. Answer (D) is incorrect because demand for particular products is as important as relative costs in creating trade deficits.

47. What is the role of gold in the present international monetary system?

A. Gold is quoted in United States dollars only.

B. All of the major currencies of the world, except the United States dollar, have a fixed value in terms of gold.

C. Gold is like any other asset whose value depends upon supply and demand.

D. Gold is the reserve asset of the International Monetary Fund.

The correct answer is (C). *(CMA, adapted)*

REQUIRED: The role of gold in the present international monetary system.

DISCUSSION: Gold has no special role in the modern international monetary system. The present system is based upon managed floating currency exchange rates. Consequently, gold is treated as a commodity, the price of which depends upon supply and demand.

Answer (A) is incorrect because, although most exchanges quote the price of gold in U.S. dollars, the dollar's value is not linked to that of gold. Answer (B) is incorrect because floating exchange rates have existed since about 1973. Tying currency values to a gold standard, in effect, fixes exchange rates. Answer (D) is incorrect because the only reserves of the IMF are international currencies.

48. Interest rates received by depositors on Eurodollar deposits tend to be higher than domestic U.S. rates on equivalent instruments because

A. Borrowers pay higher rates than domestic U.S. rates on equivalent instruments.

B. The deposits involve different currencies.

C. Eurodollar deposits are for smaller amounts.

D. The Eurodollar market is outside the direct control of the U.S. monetary authorities and has lower costs.

The correct answer is (D). *(CIA, adapted)*

REQUIRED: The reason that interest rates on Eurodollar deposits exceed U.S. rates.

DISCUSSION: Eurodollars are U.S. dollars deposited in banks outside the U.S. Because it is outside the direct control of the U.S. monetary authorities, the Eurodollar market has lower costs. For example, U.S. reserve requirements and FDIC premium payments do not apply in this market. A lower cost market can offer depositors higher interest rates.

Answer (A) is incorrect because Eurodollar borrowers tend to pay lower, not higher, rates. Borrowers and depositors can both receive more favorable rates because, with its lower costs, the Eurodollar market can offer smaller spreads between borrowing and lending rates. Answer (B) is incorrect because U.S. dollars are on deposit in both cases. Answer (C) is incorrect because Eurodollar deposits tend to be for larger, not smaller, amounts. Furthermore, smaller deposits tend to earn lower, not higher, rates than larger deposits.

49. Of the following, a characteristic of Eurobonds is that they are

A. Always denominated in Eurodollars.

B. Always sold in some country other than the one in whose currency the bond is denominated.

C. Sold outside the country of the borrower but denominated in the currency of the country in which the issue is sold.

D. Generally issued as registered bonds.

The correct answer is (B). *(CIA, adapted)*

REQUIRED: The characteristic of Eurobonds.

DISCUSSION: Eurobonds are, by definition, always sold in some country other than the one in whose currency the bond issue is denominated. Their advantage is that they are customarily less stringently regulated than most other bonds. Hence, transaction costs are lower.

Answer (A) is incorrect because Eurobonds are not always denominated in Eurodollars, which are U.S. dollars deposited outside the U.S. Answer (C) is incorrect because foreign bonds are denominated in the currency of the country in which they are sold. Answer (D) is incorrect because Eurobonds are usually issued not as registered bonds but as bearer bonds, so names and nationalities of the investors are not recorded.

50. The World Trade Organization

A. Introduced fixed exchange rates among the United States, Canada, and members of the European Union.

B. Created the International Monetary Fund.

C. Encourages reductions in trade barriers between countries.

D. Introduced exchange rates that adjust in response to changes in trade deficits and surpluses.

The correct answer is (C). *(CMA, adapted)*

REQUIRED: The true statement about the World Trade Organization.

DISCUSSION: International trade agreements provide regulatory authority for businesses in international trade. The WTO, which was established on January 1, 1995, is the product of the Uruguay Round of international trade negotiations. It is a permanent body with a secretariat based in Geneva, Switzerland. The WTO Agreement is a permanent set of commitments by more than 120 nations designed to prohibit trade discrimination among member nations and between imported and domestic products.

Answers (A) and (D) are incorrect because WTO is a worldwide agreement concerning trade barriers, not exchange rates. Today, moreover, exchange rates are not pegged (fixed) but are allowed to float. Answer (B) is incorrect because the IMF was founded in 1944 to stabilize exchange rates.

Use Gleim's ***CMA/CFM Test Prep*** for interactive testing with **over 2,000 additional multiple-choice questions!**

STUDY UNIT 4: DOMESTIC INSTITUTIONAL ENVIRONMENT OF BUSINESS

19 pages of outline
63 multiple-choice questions

Part 1 of the examination tests the candidates' knowledge of major federal legislation that regulates businesses, major federal agencies, rules and regulations promulgated thereunder, reasons for the enactment of the legislation or creation of an agency, and the effects of that legislation or agency on business. The effect of regulation on firms, e.g., on costs and prices, and the rationale for regulation are embodied in microeconomic theory. Turn back to the Microeconomics outline in Study Unit 1 for review of applicable concepts, e.g., market structures. The relative weight range assigned to domestic institutional environment of business subjects in Part 1 is 10% to 15%. Expect 12 to 18 questions.

All businesses in the United States are subject to governmental regulation. Such regulation exists at federal, state, and local levels. However, only the federal level is tested on the exam (except for the structure and operation of corporations under state law). Regulation may take the form of statutes, rules, and regulations, and their ongoing enforcement by courts, agencies, and commissions.

A notable phenomenon is the explosion of social regulation. The primary reason for social regulation is that the free market provides minimal protection in areas such as workplace and product safety, environmental degradation, and fair employment practices. Social regulation is intended to benefit society as a whole. Its purpose is to reach behavior that is thought to be not purely financial or economic. The activities of such agencies as the Equal Employment Opportunity Commission, the Consumer Product Safety Commission, the Occupational Safety and Health Administration, and the Environmental Protection Agency are examples. Social regulation has increased because of heightened consumer and environmental activism, the rise of the civil rights and women's movements, and improved communications capacities. However, social regulation, like other forms of governmental intervention, has costs. The results are increased prices and inflation, reduced innovation and consumer choice, and decreased productivity. One often-expressed concern is that the marginal benefit of social regulation may not equal the marginal cost.

A. Business Regulation

1. General

a. Statutes (legislation)

1) A statute must be passed by a majority vote of both the House of Representatives and the Senate, and then be signed by the President.
   a) If the President does not sign, a statute can still be passed by a two-thirds vote of the House and Senate.
2) A statute is required for an agency or a commission to be created.

b. Agencies and commissions

1) An agency or commission may regulate some area of all industries or may regulate a specific industry.
   a) EXAMPLES:
      i) The Occupational Safety and Health Administration (OSHA) regulates labor safety in all businesses, and the Federal Trade Commission (FTC) regulates unfair business practices and competition among almost all industries.
      ii) The Federal Communications Commission (FCC) regulates use of the airwaves by broadcasters. The Federal Aviation Administration (FAA) regulates the field of aviation, and the Interstate Commerce Commission (ICC) regulates other interstate carriers.
2) Agencies and commissions may be given functions of investigation, enforcement, rule making, and adjudication.
   a) They do not have the power to impose criminal sanctions.
   b) Exam emphasis is on the promulgated rules.
3) They must act within the authority granted by the statutes authorizing their formation and function.

c. Rules and regulations

1) Administrative law is created when regulatory agencies transform statutes into regulations and enforcement procedures; however, they may not go beyond the scope of the statutes under which they are promulgated.
2) Administrative law is promulgated under general grant of authority to an agency to regulate an industry.
   a) EXAMPLE: The Federal Energy Regulatory Commission (FERC) makes rules for rate setting under its authority to regulate public utilities.
3) Administrative law may also be promulgated under specific grant of authority to an agency to make detailed rules carrying out objectives of a statute.
   a) EXAMPLE: The Internal Revenue Service (IRS) makes rules to carry out specific statutes, but it is not given the general authority to make rules for the collection of revenue.

d. **Courts** interpret statutes, regulations, and the actions of agencies when a dispute develops and one or both parties wish a judicial determination.

e. All of these programs are designed to implement social change.

f. Some rules, agencies, and legislation have **sunset provisions** that require periodic review and reenactment or they terminate.

g. Small businesses have sometimes been exempted from social regulation because Congress felt that compliance costs would be an excessive burden for small firms.

2. **Legal Forms of Business**

a. **Corporations**. A corporation is a legal entity with a legal existence separate from its owners (shareholders). The formation and existence of corporations are entirely regulated by state statute.

1) Each state has a statute governing corporations that must be complied with for a corporation to exist.

2) Once a corporation exists in one state, the other states must recognize the corporation as a legal entity, but it will usually have to register to do business in other states.

3) A corporation is owned by shareholders who elect a board of directors to manage the corporation.

a) Shares of stock are used to represent the ownership of the corporation.

i) Common stock usually entitles the owner to vote and participate in the financial success or failure of the corporation.

ii) Preferred stock may or may not entitle the owner to vote and usually provides for fixed dividends.

b) The board of directors elects officers to whom they delegate the daily management of the corporation.

c) Bondholders and other creditors normally have no management rights. Their only rights are to receive payment.

b. A **limited liability partnership (LLP)** is a favorable form of organization for professionals who have not incorporated. It is like a general partnership except that a partner's liability for professional malpractice is limited to the LLP's assets. An LLP must file a form with the secretary of state and maintain professional liability insurance.

c. **General partnerships**. A general partnership comes into being whenever a business entity meets the criteria of a functioning partnership.

1) This occurs when two or more persons associate and carry on a business as co-owners, for profit. No formalities need to be observed, and the partnership may even exist though the persons involved have not so intended.

2) Under common law, a partnership (in contrast to the corporation) is not recognized as a separate legal entity. In other words, a partnership is not regarded as being separate from its owners.

3) However, a partnership is regarded as an entity for some purposes, for example, continuation of the partnership business after dissolution, each general partner's status as an agent of the partnership, bankruptcy, filing of tax returns, and qualification as an employer under workers' compensation statutes.

d. **Limited partnerships**. A limited partnership can be created only pursuant to a statute because it is a form of business organization unknown at common law. It is useful because it permits investors to avoid personal liability and the duties of day-to-day management without submitting to the complexities of corporate formation and operation.

   1) There is no maximum limit as to the number of partners (limited or general). The only requirement is that there be at least one limited and one general partner. This differs from an S corporation, which currently has a limit of 75 shareholders.

   2) One of the principal advantages of the limited partnership is that persons who invest in the enterprise but do not take part in management have limited personal liability. A limited partner is liable only to the extent of his/her agreed-upon contribution of cash or other property.

   3) Limited and general partnerships are tax-reporting but not tax-paying entities.

   4) Limited partnership interests are considered securities, and their issuance is subject to regulation by the SEC.

e. **Limited Liability Company**. Many states statutorily provide for LLCs. The LLC combines aspects of corporations, partnerships, and limited partnerships. Investors are allowed limited liability and special tax treatment; e.g., losses pass through to investors who may be able to use them to offset other taxable income.

f. **Proprietorships**. A proprietorship is the easiest type of business to form. Only one owner is required. The disadvantages of the proprietorship form include the limited amount of capital available to a single owner and the unlimited liability to which the owner is exposed. The proprietorship is the most common form of business organization.

3. **Financial**

   a. **Securities Act of 1933**

      1) The purpose of this act is to provide complete and fair **disclosure** to potential investors. The emphasis is on disclosure.

         a) The act applies only to initial issuance of securities.

         b) Once a potential investor has complete disclosure, (s)he should be able to make a reasonable decision.

         c) Disclosure is accomplished through the requirement that a registration statement be filed with the Securities and Exchange Commission (SEC).

            i) The potential investors must receive a prospectus, the contents of which are highly regulated. It is first filed with the SEC as part of the registration.

      2) Certain securities and transactions are exempt. The major exemptions are private placement and intrastate issues.

         a) **Private placement** may be offered only to knowledgeable and sophisticated investors and to no more than 35 purchasers, and it may not be offered to the public.

         b) **Intrastate issues** may be offered and sold only to persons within one state.

b. **Securities Exchange Act of 1934**

1) Purposes of the act

a) To regulate trading of securities after initial issuance

b) To provide adequate information to investors

c) To prevent insiders from unfairly using nonpublic information

2) Securities exchanges, brokers and dealers, securities that are traded on exchanges, and high-volume securities traded over the counter must be registered.

3) Issuers must file frequent reports.

4) Insiders (officers, directors, and 10%-or-more shareholders) must turn over to the corporation any profits earned on purchases and sales that fall within 6 months of each other. They are also prohibited from buying or selling stock based on inside information not available to the public.

a) The Insider Trading and Securities Fraud Enforcement Act of 1988 increased the monetary penalties for insider trading that were established in the Insider Trading Sanctions Act of 1984. The objective was to deter multi-million-dollar cases of insider trading of the type that had occurred in the early to mid 1980s.

5) Antifraud provisions make it unlawful to use any manipulative or deceptive practices in the purchase or sale of securities.

a) It is unlawful to make a false statement of a material fact or to omit a material fact that is necessary for a statement not to be misleading.

6) The SEC was created to enforce securities laws and regulate the issuance and trading of securities.

c. The **Private Securities Litigation Reform Act of 1995** amends the 1933 and 1934 acts. Among its provisions are a prohibition on solicitation or acceptance of referral fees from an attorney by brokers, dealers, and associated persons for obtaining the representation of a customer in any implied private action; a prohibition on the payment of legal fees to private parties seeking funds disgorged solely as the result of an action brought by the SEC; modification of class action guidelines; a statute of limitations for private rights of action; and safe harbor rules for forward-looking statements. Of special interest to accountants are the act's provisions concerning audit requirements for fraud detection and disclosure and proportionate liability.

1) Audits should provide reasonable assurance of detecting illegal acts having a direct and material effect on financial statement amounts, be designed to identify material related party transactions, and include an evaluation as to whether there is a substantial doubt about the issuer's ability to continue as a going concern.

a) Accountants must report illegal acts to the appropriate level of management and the audit committee unless they are clearly inconsequential.

b) If senior management and the board fail to take action on reported material illegal acts, and this failure will result in a departure from a standard report or resignation from the audit, the accountants should report their conclusions to the board immediately. The board must then, within 1 business day, notify the SEC.

c) If the accountants do not receive a copy of the notice within the 1-day period, they must furnish the SEC with a copy of their report within 1 business day.

2) Joint and several liability is imposed only for a knowing violation of the securities laws. Otherwise, liability is proportionate to the defendant's percentage of responsibility for the total damages.

a) However, if a share of the judgment is uncollectible, each defendant is jointly and severally liable to an individual plaintiff who suffered damages exceeding 10% of his/her net worth if such plaintiff has a net worth less than $200,000.

b) With respect to other plaintiffs, the defendant is liable for the uncollectible share in proportion to its percentage of responsibility, but the defendant's liability in this regard is limited to 50% of its proportionate share of the total damages.

d. **Blue-sky laws**

1) Blue-sky laws are state laws designed to prevent fraudulent or misleading security issues.

2) The name comes from the fact that some of the earliest laws prohibited "everything under the blue skies which is fraudulent."

4. **Wages and Prices**

a. In the unregulated marketplace, price is determined by a combination of supply and demand.

1) The greater the supply, the lower the price. It is a scarcity of products that creates price; if a product were unlimited, it would be free.

a) Conversely, the higher the price, the greater the supply that will be offered.

2) The greater the demand, the higher the price. Without demand for a product, no price could be charged.

a) Conversely, the higher the price, the lower the demand. This assumes the product is not necessary or that there are substitutes.

b. Our government has undertaken to regulate the free market in certain instances when an overriding public concern exists.

1) EXAMPLES:

a) Wages have been regulated in terms of minimum wages and required overtime pay.

i) The purpose is to prevent undue exploitation of segments of society and to help reduce the welfare burden of government for those at the bottom of the pay scale.

ii) In recent years, there have been proposals that employers of teenaged workers be exempt from minimum wage laws in order to encourage firms to hire these less-qualified workers.

b) Oil and gas have been regulated presumably because they are scarce and everyone needs to use energy for heat, transportation, etc.

i) The need for conservation has overridden other concerns, and price deregulation began in the late 1970s.

c) Airlines previously were regulated with regard to prices, routes, and mergers.

i) An argument used for years was that prices had to be maintained so that airlines could afford to operate safely. Supposedly, genuine competition would threaten safety. Much of the airline industry has now been deregulated.

ii) The initial effects of deregulation have included the entry of new low-cost competitors with low operating costs that provide strong competition to established high-cost companies, and the merger or downsizing of some airlines. Under regulation, high costs (partially caused by regulatory agencies) were passed on to the public.

d) The ICC has regulated prices and routes of railroads and motor carriers throughout this century.

i) Paradoxically, it was thought regulation helped to maintain competition by saving businesses as costs changed from time to time and as one method of transportation became cheaper than the other. Here, too, deregulation is in process.

e) A phenomenon in regard to price regulation is rent control. When rents skyrocketed during inflationary periods, rent controls were instituted in some parts of the country.

i) The reasoning behind rent control is that people need to have an affordable place to live.

ii) The result has been a shortage of housing (fewer housing starts) and a greater neglect of the condition of existing housing.

c. Other industries have had price controls because they are regulated monopolies. Such industries usually have inelastic demand curves, which means regulation can help control prices.

1) EXAMPLES:

a) Public utilities are regulated monopolies under the theory that it would be inefficient and unworkable to have more than one of each type of utility in a locality. These are sometimes called natural monopolies.

i) As a result, the FERC regulates the wholesale rate of public utilities, and local commissions regulate consumers' rates.

ii) The **rate base** is the amount of assets (reduced by accumulated depreciation) used in the company's operations.

iii) Normally, rates are set so that the capital providers earn a reasonable return on their investment.

iv) Public utilities can exercise the power of eminent domain and, with advance approval, may also introduce new services or alter existing ones.

b) The regulation of the telephone system is based on the same type of reasoning as that of public utilities. However, substantial deregulation has also occurred in this industry.

5. **Political Contributions**

a. Corporations and labor unions may not contribute any money directly to a federal political campaign, candidate, or party.

b. Corporations and labor unions may make independent expenditures expressing their viewpoint or even endorsing candidates.

c. Corporations, trade associations, and unions may form political action committees (PACs) and encourage employees to participate, and company funds may be used to organize and administer the PAC.

d. The Federal Elections Commission was created to oversee federal elections and to enforce and investigate political contributions and expenditure limitations.

6. **Banks and Other Financial Institutions**

a. The banking industry is one of the most heavily regulated.

b. Most regulation aimed at banks and other financial institutions has been concerned both with the financial health of the institution and with the safety of depositors' funds.

c. Regulation Q

1) This regulation established interest rate ceilings for banks and thrifts.

2) It was one of the most important regulations affecting banks and thrift institutions established by the Federal Reserve.

3) It was a cause of credit crunches. In periods of high interest rates, deposits would be lost to instruments whose rate was not regulated.

4) Recently, these rate ceilings have been removed by deregulation to increase competition among banking institutions.

d. Government regulation of federally chartered savings and loan associations (S&Ls) saw significant changes in 1989 because of the need to bail out the capsizing savings and loan industry.

1) Congress committed $166 billion to rescue bankrupt S&Ls.

2) More than 500 insolvent S&Ls were closed or merged.

3) The previous thrift industry regulatory agency, the Federal Home Loan Bank Board, has been eliminated. Its replacement was a branch of the U.S. Treasury Department known as the Office of Thrift Supervision (OTS). The OTS was recently disbanded following completion of its oversight of the savings and loan bailout.

4) The Federal Savings and Loan Insurance Corporation (FSLIC), a bankrupt agency that formerly supplied insurance to depositors, has been replaced by the Savings Association Insurance Fund (SAIF). Both SAIF and BIF (Bank Insurance Fund) are now under the FDIC (Federal Deposit Insurance Corporation), which insures commercial bank deposits for up to $100,000 per account. Member banks provide funding through payment of deposit insurance premiums.

7. **Federal Communications Commission (FCC)**
   a. The FCC is an independent agency formed in 1934 to regulate all methods of communications over the public airwaves. FCC functions include
      1) Allocating transmission frequencies
      2) Issuing transmission licenses
      3) Fostering effective and efficient use of communication resources
      4) Regulating common communications carriers engaged in interstate and foreign operations
   b. Among the rules is a limitation on the number of television stations that can be owned by a television network.
8. **Nongovernmental Regulation**
   a. Consumer groups can boycott and otherwise pressure businesses to conform to expected social behavior.
      1) Such groups can take advantage of the corporate desire to maintain a good image to help promote sales.
   b. Environmental groups also can exert formidable pressure on individual companies and even industries through consumer actions, political pressure, and lawsuits.
   c. Financial institutions regulate businesses through lending procedures. Lenders are in the position to require borrowers to conform to specified policies.
   d. Media regulation is demonstrated by the enormous power of the news media to direct consumer and political pressure.
9. **Social Responsibility**
   a. Business accountability
      1) Corporations are legal persons and should be expected to behave as responsibly as any good citizen.
      2) If corporations expect to maintain their corporate power, they must exercise the responsibility of any powerful institution or lose their power.
      3) Because business has been responsible for creating many social problems (e.g., pollution), business should underwrite the social costs of remedying those problems.
   b. Long-run advantages to business
      1) Socially responsible behavior may lead to long-run profit maximization for a business that treats customers, owners, employees, etc., fairly and thus creates goodwill.
         a) Large corporations especially can afford to defer short-run profits in the interests of long-run profit and survival.
         b) Potential competition can be avoided if a business establishes a strong public image and customer satisfaction.
         c) EXAMPLE: A petroleum company emphasizes its socially redeeming qualities in gasoline advertisements to induce consumers to buy its gas -- a product that is often undifferentiated among consumers.

2) Governmental intrusion in decision making can be avoided by socially responsible behavior.

3) Community involvement enables a business to avoid adverse local political decisions and to build employee relations (e.g., giving funds or lending executives to local school systems can help in recruiting new outside employees and in building the educational competence of existing staff).

c. Some socially responsible activities are profitable in themselves.

1) EXAMPLE: Installing a pollution control smokestack may recapture an otherwise lost precipitated material that can be sold for profit.

2) EXAMPLE: Some investors (e.g., many pension funds and university endowment funds) will invest only in the securities of socially responsible companies. Also, in recent years mutual funds have been started that invest only in socially responsible companies. Thus, being socially responsible results in an indirect support of the market price of a corporation's securities.

d. Arguments against corporate involvement

1) The only responsibility of a business is "to use its resources and engage in activities designed to increase its profits so long as it stays within the rules of the game, which is to say, engages in open and free competition, without deception or fraud." (Milton Friedman)

2) Managers are responsible to shareholders, not to a vague public image.

3) Corporate managers are trained to make business decisions, not social welfare decisions.

4) Diverting executive energies from business concerns to social concerns is a poor use of executive time, talent, and training.

5) Business persons are rewarded for making good business decisions but are seldom held accountable for the quality of their social decisions in the way that a specifically created social institution would be.

6) Business may frequently have a potential conflict of interest with socially responsible behavior (e.g., an accounting firm may have a conflict if it donates funds to a college that buys accounting services).

7) Evidence shows that the level of socially responsible activities moves with the economic cycle. These activities tend to increase in good times and decrease in bad times when they are most needed.

8) Incurring the costs of socially responsible activities may put a firm at a competitive disadvantage.

10. The **Racketeer Influenced and Corrupt Organizations (RICO) Act** was passed in 1970 as an attempt to combat organized crime and its infiltration of legitimate enterprises.

a. Criminal penalties can be levied up to $25,000 and 20 years in jail. Moreover, the gains from the illegal activities, including legitimate business interests, can be seized. Civil penalties include the awarding of treble damages, court costs, and attorney's fees to the successful plaintiff.

b. RICO specifically makes the following unlawful:

   1) Using income derived from a pattern of racketeering activity to acquire an interest in an enterprise.

   2) Acquiring or maintaining an interest in an enterprise through a pattern of racketeering activity.

   3) Conducting or participating in, directly or indirectly, the conduct of the affairs of an enterprise through a pattern of racketeering activity.

   4) Conspiring to commit any of these acts.

c. Under RICO, the defendant must have engaged in a pattern of racketeering activity. This pattern must include at least two predicate offenses within a 10-year period that are not isolated acts. Thus, they must have some relationship and continuity. These offenses are listed in the statute. Those most pertinent to normal business transactions are wire fraud, mail fraud, securities fraud, and bribery. In a civil case, the plaintiff may prevail even though the defendant has not been criminally convicted of the predicate offenses.

d. RICO has been broadly applied not only to organized crime but to white-collar crime, improprieties by accounting firms, insider trading, and many other activities.

11. Stop and review! You have completed the outline for this subunit. Study multiple-choice questions 1 through 21 beginning on page 150.

B. Labor and Safety

1. **Norris-LaGuardia Act of 1932**

   a. Prior to the enactment of this act, courts would issue injunctions against strikes even without hearing the union's argument.

   b. The act removed the power of federal courts to issue injunctions against unions without a showing of fraud or violence.

   c. Generally, labor unions have worked for higher wages and better working conditions for their members.

2. **National Labor Relations Act (NLRA) of 1935** (also known as the Wagner Act)

   a. Prior to the enactment of this act, employees could be discharged or not hired if associated with a union, and employers could refuse to recognize or bargain with unions.

   b. Employees were given the right to

      1) Associate with, join, or form labor unions

      2) Bargain collectively with employers

      3) Engage in concerted activities for collective bargaining (in effect, exempting unions from antitrust laws)

   c. Employers were required to bargain in good faith with unions.

   d. The **National Labor Relations Board (NLRB)** was formed to administer the act.

      1) It hears grievances.

      2) After employees elect a union, the board declares the winning union to be the sole bargaining agent of the employees.

3. **Labor-Management Relations Act (Taft-Hartley Act) of 1947**
   a. After the NLRA, unions became very powerful, strikes were crippling, and employees were coerced by labor bosses.
   b. This act placed restraints on unions that resulted in a more even balance of power between labor and management.
      1) Unions could be guilty of not bargaining in good faith.
      2) The Federal Mediation and Conciliation Service was created to mediate disputes.
      3) The President was given authority to obtain an injunction against strikes for 80 days (**cooling-off period**) if national health, welfare, or security was threatened.
      4) The **closed shop** was outlawed.
         a) A closed shop required union membership as a condition of obtaining employment.
         b) However, the **union shop** is still allowed in many states. In a union shop, an employee is required to join the union after employment.
         c) Some states have right-to-work laws that allow employees to work at any job without union membership.
      5) Secondary strikes and featherbedding were prohibited.

4. **Labor Management Reporting and Disclosure Act (Landrum-Griffin Act) of 1959**
   a. Corruption was found in unions, and individuals' interests were not protected.
   b. The act extended the NLRA to the internal affairs of unions to make them more democratic and to give members more rights.
      1) Financial records were required to be retained and reports to be made to the government.

5. **Fair Labor Standards Act (Wage and Hour Law) of 1938**
   a. Low wages, long hours, and child labor were common after the Depression.
   b. The act provided for minimum wages and overtime, and prohibited child labor, except as regulated.

6. **Civil Rights Act of 1964**
   a. The act prohibits discrimination in employment on the basis of race, color, religion, sex, or national origin.
   b. The **Equal Employment Opportunity Commission (EEOC)** was created to investigate discrimination in employment.
      1) One of the primary goals is to help companies create plans providing affirmative action protection for current and future employees.
      2) The EEOC may initiate its own investigation of company practices thought to violate the Civil Rights Act. Companies found not to be in compliance face the possible loss of government contracts.
      3) Individuals who believe they have been discriminated against in hiring may request the EEOC to initiate court action.

4) Under the act, a pervasive pattern or practice of discrimination, the employer's adoption of a neutral rule having an adverse impact on a protected class, and the adoption of a neutral rule that perpetuates past discrimination are violations that often must be proved, at least in part, by statistical evidence.

a) A controversial remedy sometimes adopted in such cases is an affirmative action order, which provides preferences to members of the class that previously suffered from discrimination. Affirmative action preferences apply even though the specific persons benefited are not necessarily those who were victimized by illegal discrimination.

b) Affirmative action programs are sometimes criticized because employment preferences are often viewed as reverse discrimination. Moreover, they may not result in the hiring, retention, and promotion of the most productive workers.

c. The issue of **comparable worth** has arisen because many believe that a wage disparity between individuals in completely different occupations (different jobs needing different skills) may also be a result of sex discrimination rather than a difference in the relative worth of the activities.

7. **Occupational Safety and Health Act of 1970**

a. The act created the **Occupational Safety and Health Administration (OSHA)** to protect the health and safety of all workers.

1) OSHA has created many regulations to promote safety. All businesses that affect interstate commerce must adhere to these regulations unless specifically exempted (governmental entities and businesses regulated under other statutes are exempt).

2) Entities subject to the act must also adhere to a general standard, that is, to provide a workplace free of known hazards. OSHA encourages labor-management committees to formulate safety and health programs.

3) Various reporting, record keeping, and notice requirements are established, e.g., notice to workers of hazardous conditions.

4) OSHA may impose civil penalties and seek injunctions, and intentional violations may result in criminal sanctions. Inspections typically focus on long-term health issues.

5) OSHA provides training programs conducted by nonenforcement personnel.

8. **Employee Retirement Income Security Act (ERISA) of 1974**

a. Pension abuses were growing and employees were not adequately protected.

b. ERISA prohibits discrimination in favor of highly paid and key employees, provides uniform rules for eligibility and vesting, and requires extensive reporting to and approval by the IRS.

c. Under provisions of ERISA, an employer must fully fund the annual cost of any retirement program.

d. Employers are not required to offer pension programs, but if such a program is offered, it is fully regulated by ERISA.

9. **Americans with Disabilities Act (ADA) of 1990**

   a. The ADA bans employment discrimination against people with disabilities, provides tax incentives for compliance costs, bans discrimination against people with disabilities in transportation, and requires remodeling of facilities to provide access by individuals with disabilities.

      1) Compliance includes acquiring or modifying work equipment, providing qualified readers or interpreters, adjusting working schedules, and making existing facilities such as restrooms, telephones, and drinking fountains accessible. Automatic doors and wheelchair ramps have been the most common changes observed.

      2) Organizations with 25 or more employees are required to provide reasonable accommodations for qualified workers and job applicants with disabilities.

   b. Employers are prohibited from inquiring into a job applicant's disability with questions concerning medical history, prior workers' compensation or health insurance claims, work absenteeism due to illness, past treatment for alcoholism, or mental illness.

   c. The ADA defines a person with disabilities as an individual who

      1) Has a physical or mental impairment that limits one or more life activities
      2) Has a record of such an impairment
      3) Is regarded as having such an impairment

   d. A qualified "worker with a disability" is defined as one who can perform the essential functions of a job, with or without reasonable accommodation.

   e. No federal funds are provided for implementation of ADA by employers.

   f. Penalties for violation of the ADA can reach $500,000, and thousands of charges have already been filed.

10. **The Family and Medical Leave Act (FMLA)**

   a. The FMLA, which took effect in August 1993, mandates the availability of unpaid leave for child care and other family and personal needs.

      1) The law applies to companies with 50 or more employees. Eligible employees must have worked for the employer for an average of 25 hours a week for one year.

      2) The law provides up to 12 weeks of unpaid leave after the birth or adoption of a child. Both parents are eligible.

      3) Leave may also be taken to care for a sick spouse, child, or parent, or when an employee is too sick to work.

   b. Employers must provide health benefits during the leave period and give returning workers the same or an equivalent job in terms of pay, responsibilities, and other working conditions.

   c. In many companies, employees may substitute paid "sick leave" for unpaid leave, but this is not a requirement of the law.

11. Stop and review! You have completed the outline for this subunit. Study multiple-choice questions 22 through 31 beginning on page 157.

C. Antitrust

1. Competition is used to control private economic power. Its purpose is to promote
    a. Efficient allocation of resources (resulting in lower prices)
    b. Greater choice by consumers
    c. Greater business opportunities
    d. Fairness in economic behavior
    e. Avoidance of concentrated political power resulting from economic power
2. **Sherman Act of 1890**
    a. Section 1 makes illegal every contract, combination, or conspiracy in restraint of trade in interstate or foreign commerce.
        1) The commerce clause of the Constitution has been the basis for a considerable extension of federal power in the regulatory sphere because most businesses affect interstate commerce.
        2) The **rule of reason** is applied so usually only unreasonable restraints are illegal.
            a) EXAMPLE: A covenant not to compete is enforceable so long as it is for a reasonable time and a reasonable area.
        3) Some types of arrangements between competitors are found unreasonable without inquiry. They are called **per se violations**. These include
            a) **Price fixing** (agreeing to any price)
            b) **Division of markets** (agreeing where to sell)
            c) **Group boycotts** (agreeing not to deal with another)
            d) **Resale price maintenance** (limiting a buyer's resale price)
                i) The arrangements limit competition at the expense of the consumer.
        4) Price fixing is the most prosecuted violation under the Sherman Act.
    b. Section 2 prohibits the acts of monopolizing or attempting to monopolize.
        1) **Monopoly** -- the power to control prices or exclude competition
        2) The government must prove overwhelming market power and that the act of monopolizing, attempting to monopolize, or conspiring or combining to monopolize is a deliberate or purposeful act.
            a) Acquisition of power through superior skill, or having it thrust upon one, is not a violation.
3. **Clayton Act of 1914** prohibits
    a. Mergers or the acquisition of stock if the effect may be to lessen competition or tend to create a monopoly. The act allows the Justice Department to prevent mergers before they occur.
        1) A horizontal merger (between competitors) is most closely scrutinized by the Justice Department because it usually has the greatest tendency to lessen competition.
        2) A vertical merger (between supplier and purchaser) may also lessen competition if each controls a substantial part of the relevant market.
        3) A conglomerate merger involves different industries or different areas of business. It is the least likely to lessen competition unless the resulting company is so large that its size alone affects competition.

b. Sales that prevent the buyer from dealing with the seller's competitors

c. Tying or tie-in sales; that is, sales in which a buyer must take other products in order to buy the first product

d. Exclusive dealing, which occurs when a seller requires a buyer to purchase only the seller's products and not buy any products from the seller's competitors

e. Price discrimination between different buyers

f. A person from sitting as a director of competing corporations if one company has capital of greater than $1,000,000 and if antitrust law would be violated if the companies ceased to be competitors

4. **Federal Trade Commission Act of 1914**

   a. The act prohibits unfair methods of competition, and unfair or deceptive acts in commerce.

   b. It created the Federal Trade Commission (FTC) to enforce this act and determine what is unfair competition or deceptive acts.

      1) The basic objectives of the FTC are to initiate antitrust actions and to protect the consumer public.

      2) The FTC also has broad authority to enforce the other antitrust laws in conjunction with the antitrust division of the U.S. Justice Department.

      3) The Wheeler-Lea Amendment of 1938 prohibits deceptive practices in commerce.

5. The **Robinson-Patman Act of 1936** amended the Clayton Act with respect to price discrimination.

   a. Price discrimination is prohibited with respect to both buyers and sellers.

      1) Both buyer and seller can be found guilty if there is discrimination.

   b. Price differentiation is allowed if it is to meet a competitor's price quote or if it is based on quantity purchased and a cost savings can be shown.

   c. Rebates, commissions, discounts, etc., to special customers are prohibited.

   d. The act does not apply to export sales.

6. The **Celler-Kefauver Act of 1950** amended the Clayton Act to prohibit the acquisition of assets of another corporation if the effect could lessen competition or tend to create a monopoly.

   a. The Clayton Act originally applied only to stock acquisitions.

7. The **Antitrust Improvements Act of 1976** requires that notification be made to the Justice Department prior to a merger.

8. **Remedies for Violations of These Acts**

   a. Injunctions, forced divisions, and forced divestitures may be obtained by either the public or the government.

   b. Cease and desist orders may be issued by the FTC.

   c. Treble (triple) damages may be recovered by the public.

   d. Criminal penalties may be assessed by the government.

9. **Exemptions from Antitrust Regulation**
   a. Intrastate commerce
   b. Labor unions (not exempt if the union primarily intends to restrain trade or conspires with nonlabor groups to monopolize)
   c. Regulated utilities
   d. Reasonable noncompetition clauses between
      1) Buyers and sellers of businesses
      2) Partners in a partnership
      3) Purchasers of technology or equipment
   e. Patents and copyrights
   f. Agricultural and fishing organizations
   g. Financial institutions
   h. Transport industries
   i. Major league baseball
   j. Companies qualifying for certificates of antitrust immunity issued by the Commerce Department (after concurrence by the Justice Department) under the Export Trading Company Act
10. Stop and review! You have completed the outline for this subunit. Study multiple-choice questions 32 through 53 beginning on page 160.

D. **Consumer and Environmental Protection**

1. Several statutes and commissions already discussed are oriented toward consumer protection, e.g., the SEC and the FTC.
   a. The consumer movement developed as a result of consumer dissatisfaction with goods and services. The free market provides minimal incentive for firms to provide safety and environmental protection.
2. The **Fair Packaging and Labeling Act of 1967** prohibits deceptive packaging and labeling.
3. The **Consumer Credit Protection Act (Truth-in-Lending Act) of 1968** (as amended in 1982), in simple terms, requires the interest rate and the cost of credit to be disclosed.
   a. It resulted in greater record-keeping requirements for lenders.
   b. Also, costs of making loans increased because of the additional compliance forms required.
4. The **Consumer Product Safety Act of 1972** emphasizes safety standards for new products.
   a. Information about defects is often received from consumers.
   b. Section 15 of the act requires manufacturers to publicize defects to consumers or refund the purchase price paid for defective products.
   c. The Consumer Product Safety Commission may seek a court order to have a product banned or seized.

5. The **Fair Credit Reporting Act of 1970** gives consumers the right to obtain the information reported by credit bureaus.
6. The **Equal Credit Opportunity Act of 1974** prohibits discrimination in providing credit.
7. The **Fair Credit Billing Act of 1975** provides consumers with rights in contesting billing errors and settling disputes.
8. The **Fair Debt Collection Practices Act of 1977** prohibits certain abuses of consumers' rights by collection agencies.
9. **Equal Employment Opportunity Laws**
    a. There are several laws, but it is the Civil Rights Act that did the most to prohibit discrimination on the basis of race, color, national origin, religion, or sex.
    b. Employers may use selection procedures in hiring as long as the procedures are not discriminatory.
    c. Violation of the laws can result in loss of government contracts, court orders to correct the situation, and damage awards to aggrieved individuals.
    d. The government has set goals and timetables for large employers to bring female and minority workforces up to the appropriate percentages as they relate to the available labor pool. Companies are required to create and implement a plan of affirmative action for this. However, recent Supreme Court decisions have called into question the validity of affirmative action plans.
10. The **Magnuson-Moss Warranty Act of 1975** prohibits disclaimers of implied warranties of goods unless they are written.
11. The **Food and Drug Act of 1906** as amended by the **Food, Drug, and Cosmetic Act of 1938** and much other legislation is administered by the Food and Drug Administration (FDA).
    a. The FDA was created to help maintain the safety of drugs, food, cosmetics, etc.
    b. The FDA oversees the requirements of the Federal Hazardous Substances Labeling Act of 1960.
    c. New drugs and food additives must be thoroughly tested before they are marketed. The premarket review is based upon research supplied by the drug companies.
        1) Results in higher prices to offset increased costs
        2) The FDA can extend patent lives of pharmaceutical products to allow for time lost during the premarket FDA review.

12. **Environmental Protection Agency (EPA)**
    a. The EPA prohibits manufacturers from polluting water, land, and air.
    b. Environmental regulations apply to firms in all industries.
    c. Effluent (smoke, liquid industrial refuse, sewage, etc.) standards set the volume or quality of waste products that can be discharged into the air, water, etc. Either the EPA or individual citizens can bring suit to enforce standards.
    d. The EPA is often criticized by business as having standards that are established without considering the compliance costs.
        1) A cost-benefit analysis for environmental improvements will result in the existence of pollution because the costs of eliminating all pollution will likely outweigh the benefits. However, the cost-benefit analysis could be arranged so that only an acceptable amount of pollution remains.
    e. The setting of effluent standards has often been criticized by economists as an inefficient method of pollution control. Economists prefer a sliding tax charge based on the amount of effluent emitted. This method is preferred because
        1) As effluent discharge increases, a company's tax increases, providing a strong incentive for firms to discover new methods of controlling pollution.
        2) The tax is a less direct method of economic intervention. Rather than dictating technology, the tax allows firms to seek out the technology that is most cost-effective.
        3) The Clean Air Act of 1990 allows marketable permits for pollution that firms can buy or sell like any other commodity.
        4) Beginning in November 1994, employers in large cities with air pollution were required to begin reducing the number of people who drive to work or face fines and/or criminal penalties. The law, which affects companies employing more than 100 workers, puts the onus on companies to encourage car-pooling and mass transit.
13. The **Nuclear Regulatory Commission (NRC)** licenses nuclear facilities (such as power plants) and approves the procedures for safeguarding nuclear materials, including waste products.
14. **Consumer Tactics**. Boycotts of a manufacturer's products are the most common tactic used by consumer groups to induce a company to change its behavior or the nature of its advertising. Boycotts have sometimes been quite successful.
    a. Shareholder resolutions have also been made at shareholder meetings, but such resolutions have rarely been successful.
    b. Lobbying for new laws is also an often successful tactic.
    c. Occasionally, cooperating with the manufacturer to find common ground has been used.
15. Stop and review! You have completed the outline for this subunit. Study multiple-choice questions 54 through 63 beginning on page 168.

MULTIPLE-CHOICE QUESTIONS

A. Business Regulation

1. All of the following are criticisms generally made of federal regulatory agencies and policies except

A. Taxes imposed by agencies being too high.

B. Political considerations influencing policies and rules.

C. Regulatory rules being rigid and hard to change.

D. Regulations increasing the cost of products and services.

The correct answer is (A). *(CMA, adapted)*

REQUIRED: The item not a criticism of federal regulatory agencies and policies.

DISCUSSION: Federal administrative agencies belong to the executive branch of government. They have quasi-legislative powers (rulemaking authority pursuant to enabling statutes enacted by Congress), quasi-judicial powers (the ability to adjudicate certain disputes within their jurisdiction), and quasi-executive powers (for example, to investigate and prosecute violations). However, no federal agency has taxing authority, a power reserved to Congress. Moreover, all bills for raising revenue must originate in the House of Representatives.

Answers (B), (C), and (D) are incorrect because they are frequently heard criticisms of federal regulatory agencies and policies.

2. Social legislation, as exemplified by the Occupational Safety and Health Act and Environmental Protection Act, is frequently criticized for being inefficient because the agencies

A. Use flexible rather than rigid standards.

B. Impose compliance costs that are low compared to the benefits received by society.

C. Rely heavily on the free market to allocate resources.

D. Rarely consider the marginal benefits relative to the marginal costs.

The correct answer is (D). *(CMA, adapted)*

REQUIRED: The reason social legislation such as OSHA and EPA are often criticized as inefficient.

DISCUSSION: Economic regulation usually concerns price and service to the public and is ordinarily industry specific. Social regulation has broader objectives and more pervasive effects. It addresses quality of life issues, such as workplace and product safety, pollution, and fair employment practices, and it applies to most industries. Social regulation has been criticized on the grounds that it is costly, contributes to overregulation, may inhibit innovation, increases inflation, and may place a disproportionate burden on small companies, thereby having an anticompetitive effect. Another criticism is that regulators are perceived to have little concern for the relation of marginal benefits and costs. For example, achieving total compliance with the standards for treated wastewater may be twice as costly as attaining 95% of those standards. In other words, the relatively small improvements sometimes sought by regulators may be viewed as excessively costly by those who are regulated.

Answer (A) is incorrect because social legislation is criticized when standards are rigid. Answer (B) is incorrect because compliance costs are typically high. Answer (C) is incorrect because the free market is normally not relied upon; with certain exceptions, compliance is mandatory.

3. The primary reason for social regulation (Clean Air Act, Water Pollution Control Act, Food and Drug Act, etc.) is that

A. The free market provides minimal safety and environmental protection.

B. Consumer and environmental groups are politically powerful.

C. Social benefits from such regulations always exceed the costs.

D. Social regulation is more desirable.

The correct answer is (A). *(CMA, adapted)*

REQUIRED: The primary reason for social regulation.

DISCUSSION: Social regulation concerns quality of life issues, e.g., workplace and product safety, environmental degradation, and fair employment practices. The abuses addressed are those that are difficult for market forces to remedy. For example, consumers may purchase products on the basis of price and quality, but without regard to the environmental impact of their production, and unsafe working conditions may be tolerated by individuals who have few opportunities for other employment.

Answer (B) is incorrect because, although consumer and environmental groups may occasionally exercise some lobbying power, they are typically underfunded and would have little impact on legislatures in the absence of an obvious need for social regulation. Answer (C) is incorrect because there is great difficulty in measuring both the benefits and costs of most social regulation. Answer (D) is incorrect because no regulation is desirable, but some regulation is necessary when market forces are ineffective.

4. Social regulation is often criticized by industry as inefficient. Firms perceive this inefficiency to be a result of

A. The failure to consider the marginal benefits relative to the marginal costs.

B. Lenient enforcement policies.

C. Concern for the quality of life but not the quality of products.

D. The use of the internal revenue tax code instead of strict compliance penalties.

The correct answer is (A). *(CMA, adapted)*

REQUIRED: The perceived cause of inefficiency caused by social regulation.

DISCUSSION: The purpose of social regulation is to require behavior that is thought to be beneficial for other than purely economic considerations. However, social regulation has costs, which lead to increased prices and inflation, reduced innovation and consumer choice, and decreased productivity. Social regulation is criticized because the marginal benefits may not equal the marginal costs.

Answer (B) is incorrect because enforcement policies are rarely viewed as lenient by those to whom social legislation is directed. Answer (C) is incorrect because social legislation may show a concern for the quality of life by regulating the quality of products. Answer (D) is incorrect because social regulation often involves noncompliance penalties.

5. Which one of the following forms of law is created when regulatory agencies transform statutes into regulations and enforcement procedures?

A. Constitutional law.

B. Statutory law.

C. Administrative law.

D. Judicial law.

The correct answer is (C). *(CMA, adapted)*

REQUIRED: The law created when regulatory agencies transform statutes into regulations and enforcement procedures.

DISCUSSION: Administrative law is promulgated by the executive branch under a general grant of authority to an agency to regulate an industry. Administrative law may also be promulgated under a specific grant of authority to an agency to make detailed rules to achieve the objectives of a statute. For example, the IRS makes rules to carry out specific statutes but is not given the general authority to make rules for the collection of revenue. Administrative law may not go beyond the scope of the statutes under which it is promulgated.

Answer (A) is incorrect because constitutional law is the fundamental law of a jurisdiction. Answer (B) is incorrect because statutory law is a body of detailed enactments by the legislative branch. Answer (D) is incorrect because judicial (common) law is created by the courts through the adjudication of cases and the publication of the resulting opinions.

6. Many social regulations exempt small business from their application. This exemption has been enacted because

A. Small businesses have no significant impact on jobs and the environment.

B. There are too many small businesses, and funds provided are inadequate to regulate them effectively.

C. Compliance costs are a burden for small firms, and Congress has chosen to exempt such firms.

D. The lobby for small businesses has been so active that Congress has chosen to exempt such firms.

The correct answer is (C). *(CMA, adapted)*

REQUIRED: The reason small businesses are often exempted from the requirements of many social regulations.

DISCUSSION: Social regulation embraces a variety of government requirements related to matters such as consumer protection, environmental quality, employment discrimination, and workplace safety. Small businesses have sometimes been exempted from social regulations, because Congress has felt that compliance costs would be an excessive burden for small firms. These costs are relatively fixed and are therefore higher per unit of output for smaller firms than for larger firms. Compliance costs therefore create a competitive disadvantage for small firms relative to large firms.

Answer (A) is incorrect because small businesses do have a significant impact on jobs and the environment; however, they often cannot absorb the additional costs brought on by regulation. Answer (B) is incorrect because Congress has elected to exempt small businesses from some social regulation because of the cost burden on such firms. Answer (D) is incorrect because the cost burden is a more critical factor than small business lobbyists.

7. Sunset laws refer to

A. Protection of employees nearing retirement.

B. Federal laws that prohibit the sale of securities for companies that have not been in business for at least 3 months.

C. State laws that prohibit the sale of alcohol on Sunday.

D. A periodic review of, and a fixed termination date for, government programs.

The correct answer is (D). *(CMA, adapted)*

REQUIRED: The true statement about sunset laws.

DISCUSSION: Sunset laws are provisions that require periodic review and reenactment of specific laws. Otherwise, the legislation or agency terminates at the end of a specified period of time. For example, the first federal Cost Accounting Standards Board was established with a 10-year life. At the end of that period, the agency was terminated because Congress felt that its purpose had been accomplished.

Answer (A) is incorrect because the Age Discrimination in Employment Act provides protection for older workers. Answer (B) is incorrect because sunset laws are not concerned with securities regulation. Answer (C) is incorrect because laws that prohibit the sale of alcohol on Sundays are blue laws.

8. All of the following are legal rights of shareholders in U.S. publicly traded companies except the right to

A. Vote on major mergers and acquisitions.

B. Receive dividends if declared.

C. Vote on charter and bylaw changes.

D. Vote on major management changes.

The correct answer is (D). *(CMA, adapted)*

REQUIRED: The item not a basic legal right of shareholders in publicly traded corporations.

DISCUSSION: A corporation is owned by shareholders who elect a board of directors to manage the company. The board of directors then hires managers to supervise operations. Shareholders do not vote on major management changes because the powers of the board include selection and removal of officers and the setting of management compensation. Shareholders do have the right to vote on fundamental corporate changes, e.g., mergers and acquisitions, any changes in the corporate charter and bylaws, and dissolution.

Answers (A), (B), and (C) are incorrect because shareholders in publicly traded U. S. corporations have the right to vote on fundamental corporate changes, to receive declared dividends and annual reports, to vote, to exercise any preemptive right that may have been granted, to attend meetings, to inspect corporate records, and to bring shareholder suits.

9. A basic purpose of the securities laws in the United States is to regulate the issuance of investment securities by

A. Requiring disclosure of all relevant information so that investors can make informed decisions.

B. Prohibiting the issuance of non-investment grade securities.

C. Ensuring that all shareholders have an equal vote in the election of a board of directors.

D. Providing a regulatory framework for those states that do not have their own securities laws.

The correct answer is (A). *(CMA, adapted)*

REQUIRED: The means by which the issuance of investment securities are regulated in the United States.

DISCUSSION: The basic purpose of the federal securities laws in the United States, primarily the Securities Act of 1933 and the Securities Exchange Act of 1934, is to provide complete and fair disclosure to potential investors. The emphasis is on disclosure that allows informed investors to make intelligent decisions.

Answer (B) is incorrect because the SEC does not evaluate the merits of investments or define an investment-grade security. Answer (C) is incorrect because a corporation's by-laws provide for voting rights. For example, preferred stock rarely has a vote. Answer (D) is incorrect because the federal laws apply in all states regardless of the existence of applicable state laws.

10. A main provision of the Securities Act of 1933, as amended in 1934, is the requirement that

A. Bonds be issued only under a trust indenture approved by the Securities and Exchange Commission (SEC).

B. Public utility holding companies register with the SEC.

C. New securities offered for sale in interstate commerce be registered with the SEC.

D. All security brokers be licensed by the SEC.

The correct answer is (C). *(CMA, adapted)*

REQUIRED: The true statement about the provisions of the Securities Act of 1933, as amended in 1934.

DISCUSSION: The Securities Act of 1933 was designed to provide complete and fair disclosure to potential investors. The 1933 act applies only to the initial issuance of securities. Disclosure is accomplished through the requirement that a registration statement be filed with the SEC. Once potential investors have complete disclosure, the assumption is that they can make a reasonable decision.

Answer (A) is incorrect because the SEC does not have to approve a trust indenture. Answer (B) is incorrect because the 1933 act requires disclosure of nonexempted new issuances of securities, including those of public utility holding companies, not registration of particular entities. Answer (D) is incorrect because the Securities Exchange Act of 1934 requires registration of brokers.

11. The private placement of debt securities has all of the following advantages over offerings to the general public except that a private placement

A. Does not require Securities and Exchange Commission regulation.

B. Can be completed in less time than public offerings.

C. Has no flotation expenses.

D. Can include indentures that are "tailor-made" to the borrower's needs.

The correct answer is (C). *(CMA, adapted)*

REQUIRED: The item that is not an advantage of the private placement of securities.

DISCUSSION: Private placements in unlimited amounts are exempted from the Securities Act of 1933. A private placement may be offered only to knowledgeable and sophisticated investors, may be offered to no more than 35 nonaccredited purchasers, and may not be offered to the general public. However, the securities are restricted, and the issuer must exercise reasonable care in determining that purchasers are not underwriters and are purchasing solely for their own investment purposes. Private placement flotation expenses may be lower than with a public offering, but some flotation costs will still be incurred.

Answer (A) is incorrect because the purpose of a private placement is to avoid SEC regulation. Answer (B) is incorrect because, in the absence of federal regulation, private placements typically take less time than public offerings. Answer (D) is incorrect because a private placement of securities can be tailor-made to the borrower's needs.

12. The basic purpose of the Securities Exchange Act of 1934 was to

A. Regulate outstanding securities.

B. Regulate new issues of securities.

C. Protect investors from investment losses.

D. Ensure the public that stock market crashes like that of 1929 would not occur again.

The correct answer is (A). *(CMA, adapted)*

REQUIRED: The basic purpose of the Securities Exchange Act of 1934.

DISCUSSION: The 1934 act was designed to regulate securities after initial issuances. Other purposes of the 1934 act were to provide adequate information to investors and to prevent insiders from unfairly using their information.

Answer (B) is incorrect because the Securities Act of 1933 was designed to regulate new issues of securities. Answer (C) is incorrect because the objective is not to protect investors from losses, but to provide investors with adequate information upon which to base investment decisions. Answer (D) is incorrect because the objective was to regulate securities and provide investors with adequate information. The securities acts of 1933 and 1934 were not a direct result of the stock market crash; instead, it was the bankruptcy of Ivar Kreuger, the greatest swindler the world has ever known, that led to the passage of the securities acts.

13. A large public company that is well-known can reduce the time required to register and issue securities by using a(n)

A. Shelf registration.

B. Indenture agreement.

C. Secondary market registration.

D. Red herring registration.

The correct answer is (A). *(CMA, adapted)*

REQUIRED: The means a large company may use to reduce the time required to register and issue securities.

DISCUSSION: SEC Rule 415 allows corporations to file registration statements covering a stipulated amount of securities that may be issued over the 2-year effective period of the statement. The securities are placed on the shelf and issued at an opportune moment without the necessity of filing a new registration statement, observing a 20-day waiting period, or preparing a new prospectus. The issuer is only required to provide updating amendments or to refer investors to quarterly and annual statements filed with the SEC. Shelf registration is most advantageous to large corporations that frequently offer securities to the public.

Answer (B) is incorrect because an indenture is a contract associated with the issuance of a debt instrument. Answer (C) is incorrect because a secondary market registration does not expedite the issuance of securities. Answer (D) is incorrect because a red-herring is a preliminary prospectus issued during the 20-day waiting period before the related registration statement becomes effective.

14. All the following are functions of the Securities and Exchange Commission except the

A. Review of stock trades by corporate insiders.

B. Regulation of interstate offerings of new securities to the public.

C. Setting of rules concerning the proxy process of large public companies.

D. Determination of fair trading prices for the common stock of large public companies.

The correct answer is (D). *(CMA, adapted)*

REQUIRED: The item not a function of the SEC.

DISCUSSION: The SEC is charged with enforcement of federal securities laws. Under the Securities Act of 1933, the offer or sale of a security to the public requires registration with the SEC absent a specific exemption. However, the 1933 act is essentially a disclosure statute. The SEC does not evaluate the merits of securities. Its role is to enforce the laws ensuring the public availability of information to potential investors.

Answer (A) is incorrect because insider trading is prohibited by Section 10(b) of the Securities Exchange Act of 1934 and by the SEC's Rule 10b-5. Answer (B) is incorrect because an issuer that wishes to make an interstate offering of new securities to the public must file a registration statement with the SEC. Answer (C) is incorrect because the Securities Exchange Act of 1934 provides rules with regard to proxy solicitations and tender offers.

15. Airlines headquartered in the United States have experienced deregulation in many aspects of their business. Which one of the following aspects of the business is still subject to regulation by the federal government?

A. On-time departure standards.

B. Domestic fare schedules.

C. Collective bargaining.

D. International fare schedules.

The correct answer is (C). *(CMA, adapted)*

REQUIRED: The aspect of the U. S. airline business that is still subject to regulation by the federal government.

DISCUSSION: Airline operations have been almost fully deregulated by the U. S. government, for example, with regard to departure standards, fare schedules, and the opportunity to eliminate unprofitable routes. Despite deregulation, however, airlines are still subject to federal and state labor laws, including those governing collective bargaining. The National Labor Relations Board exercises its jurisdiction over all transportation enterprises that furnish interstate services.

Answers (A), (B), and (D) are incorrect because on-time departure standards, domestic fare schedules, and international fare schedules are aspects of the airline industry that have been deregulated.

16. The Insider Trading and Securities Fraud Enforcement Act of 1988 in conjunction with the Insider Trading Sanctions Act of 1984

A. Enacted monetary penalties for insider trading for the first time.

B. Increased monetary penalties for insider trading.

C. Enacted criminal penalties for market manipulation and securities fraud.

D. Empowered the Securities and Exchange Commission with the authority to recover gains resulting from the illegal use of insider information.

The correct answer is (B). *(CMA, adapted)*

REQUIRED: The true statement about insider trading legislation.

DISCUSSION: The Insider Trading Sanctions Act of 1984 extended the law to include those who aid and abet insider trading. It also imposed a treble-damages penalty. The 1988 act increased prison terms from 5 to 10 years, the maximum fine for individuals to $1,000,000, and the maximum fine for corporations to $2,500,000. In addition, the SEC now has authority to reward an informant with up to 10% of the fine levied against the perpetrator.

Answer (A) is incorrect because monetary penalties were imposed for insider trading before 1988. For example, the Securities Exchange Act of 1934 requires insiders to turn over to the corporation any short-swing profits on purchases and sales of corporate stock. Answer (C) is incorrect because, under section 10(b) of the 1934 act and Rule 10b-5, insider trading is a fraudulent act subject to criminal penalties. Answer (D) is incorrect because the SEC already held the right to recover gains resulting from the illegal use of insider information.

17. Blue-sky laws are

A. The detailed regulations of the Securities and Exchange Commission designed to prevent fraudulent or misleading security issues.

B. Regulations of the Securities and Exchange Commission governing the treatment of goodwill in the sale of securities.

C. State laws designed to prevent fraudulent or misleading security issues.

D. Local laws regulating the issuance of securities for companies whose operations affect the environment.

The correct answer is (C). *(CMA, adapted)*

REQUIRED: The true statement about blue-sky laws.

DISCUSSION: Blue-sky laws are state laws designed to prevent fraudulent or misleading security issues. The name comes from some of the earliest laws that prohibited "everything under the blue skies that is fraudulent."

Answer (A) is incorrect because blue-sky laws are state, not federal, financial regulatory laws. Answer (B) is incorrect because blue-sky laws are state laws and have nothing to do with goodwill. Answer (D) is incorrect because blue-sky laws apply to all companies in a given state.

18. In regulating intrastate local utilities, state public utility commissions

A. Usually approve rate schedules that set the same rates for residential, commercial, and industrial customers.

B. Use only original cost methods of rate base valuation.

C. Permit utilities to refuse service to some customers within their jurisdiction.

D. Usually set rates of return for utilities based on the cost of capital as reflected in the capital markets.

The correct answer is (D). *(CMA, adapted)*

REQUIRED: The true statement about the activities of state public utility commissions.

DISCUSSION: Public utilities are natural monopolies subject to governmental price controls. State utility commissions establish utility rates by setting rates so that capital providers earn a reasonable return on their investment (the rate base). The rate base is the amount of assets minus depreciation used in the company's operations.

Answer (A) is incorrect because users who receive different volumes of service usually pay different rates. Answer (B) is incorrect because rates are also based on other than original cost when facilities are acquired by one utility from another utility. Answer (C) is incorrect because utilities are monopolies and are not permitted to refuse to deal with paying customers.

19. Which one of the following statements is a correct characterization of current federal policy toward political action committees (PACs)?

A. Corporations may use company funds to organize and administer a PAC.

B. Corporations may make corporate contributions to PACs.

C. Unions may help organize PACs, but corporations may not.

D. Individuals may only make political contributions through PACs.

The correct answer is (A). *(CMA, adapted)*

REQUIRED: The true statement about political action committees (PACs).

DISCUSSION: Federal law prohibits business corporations from donating to political election campaigns at the federal level. Note that this does not prohibit donations to state election campaigns, although some states have such laws. Political action committees (PACs) have therefore grown in importance over the past decade as a means of circumventing this prohibition.

Answers (B) and (C) are incorrect because direct corporate contributions are not allowed. However, corporations, trade associations, and unions may form PACs and encourage employees to participate, and company funds may be used to organize and administer the PAC. Answer (D) is incorrect because individuals may give funds either directly to candidates or to PACs.

20. Corporate social responsibility is

A. Effectively enforced through the controls envisioned by classical economics.

B. Defined as the obligation to shareholders to earn a profit.

C. More than the obligation to shareholders to earn a profit.

D. Defined as the obligation to serve long-term, organizational interests.

The correct answer is (C). *(Publisher)*

REQUIRED: The true statement about corporate social responsibility.

DISCUSSION: The concept of corporate social responsibility involves more than serving the interests of the organization and its shareholders. Rather, it is an extension of responsibility to embrace service to the public interest in such matters as environmental protection, employee safety, civil rights, and community involvement.

Answer (A) is incorrect because a perfectly competitive market was envisioned by classical economics. Modern monopolies and oligopolies often must be subject to regulation to enforce their social responsibilities since the limits imposed by the market are ineffective. Answers (B) and (D) are incorrect because the concept embraces the public or societal interest.

21. A common argument against corporate involvement in socially responsible behavior is that

A. It encourages government intrusion in decision making.

B. As a legal person, a corporation is accountable for its conduct.

C. It creates goodwill.

D. In a competitive market, such behavior incurs costs that place the company at a disadvantage.

The correct answer is (D). *(Publisher)*

REQUIRED: The common argument against corporate involvement in socially responsible behavior.

DISCUSSION: Socially responsible behavior clearly has immediate costs to the entity, for example, the expenses incurred in affirmative action programs, pollution control, and improvements in worker safety. When one firm incurs such costs and its competitor does not, the other may be able to sell its products or services more cheaply and increase its market share at the expense of the socially responsible firm. The rebuttal argument is that in the long run the socially responsible company may maximize profits by creating goodwill and avoiding or anticipating governmental regulation.

Answer (A) is incorrect because such behavior may prevent governmental action. Answers (B) and (C) are incorrect because each is an argument for such behavior.

B. Labor and Safety

22. In unionized and nonunionized sectors of the economy, labor unions generally

A. Result in wage equality in both sectors.

B. Raise wages in the unionized sector.

C. Raise wages at the same rate in both sectors.

D. Lower wages in both sectors.

The correct answer is (B). *(CMA, adapted)*

REQUIRED: The true statement about labor unions.

DISCUSSION: Labor unions have typically worked for higher wages and better working conditions for their members. Through collective bargaining and restrictions on membership, unions increase the wage rates of members in comparison with those earned by nonunionized workers. Because of the greater cost of hiring unionized workers, the amount of labor demanded by employers is reduced. The workers that are unemployed as a result may then seek employment in the nonunion labor market, thereby increasing the supply and decreasing the wages in that market.

Answers (A), (C), and (D) are incorrect because unions raise wages for their members and indirectly reduce wages in the nonunionized labor market.

23. The National Labor Relations Act of 1935, also known as the Wagner Act,

A. Provides for compulsory binding arbitration in the case of national emergency.

B. Guarantees the right of self-organization and the right to collective bargaining with management.

C. Designates a list of unfair labor practices on the part of unions.

D. Requires that union officials be elected on a regular basis and that secret ballots be used.

The correct answer is (B). *(CMA, adapted)*

REQUIRED: The true statement about the National Labor Relations Act (Wagner Act) of 1935.

DISCUSSION: The Wagner Act gave employees the right to join unions, bargain collectively with employers, and engage in concerted activities for collective bargaining. In effect, labor unions were exempted from antitrust laws. The National Labor Relations Board (NLRB) was formed to administer the act.

Answer (A) is incorrect because the Taft-Hartley Act provides for an 80-day injunction against a work stoppage that might imperil national security. Answer (C) is incorrect because the Taft-Hartley Act of 1947 provides for restraints on unions to permit a more even balance of power between labor and management. Answer (D) is incorrect because the Landrum-Griffin Act of 1959 requires that union officials be elected on a regular basis and that secret ballots be used. It also requires that unions submit financial reports to the government.

24. The Labor-Management Relations Act, also known as the Taft-Hartley Act of 1947,

A. Prohibits employers from interfering with the right of employees to form unions.

B. Obligates employers to bargain in good faith with unions.

C. Outlaws yellow-dog contracts, which require employees to remain as nonunion members.

D. Prohibits unions from coercing employees to become union members.

The correct answer is (D). *(CMA, adapted)*

REQUIRED: The true statement about the Labor-Management Relations Act (Taft-Hartley Act) of 1947.

DISCUSSION: The Taft-Hartley Act places restraints on unions, resulting in a more even balance of power between labor and management. One provision prohibits unions from coercing employees to become union members. Thus, the closed shop is outlawed. The act also requires unions to bargain in good faith and provides for mediation of disputes. The President of the United States has authority to obtain an injunction against strikes or lockouts for an 80-day cooling-off period if the national health, welfare, or security is threatened. Also, secondary strikes and featherbedding are prohibited.

Answer (A) is incorrect because the Wagner Act of 1935 prohibits employers from interfering with the right of employees to form unions. Answer (B) is incorrect because the Taft-Hartley Act requires unions to bargain in good faith. Answer (C) is incorrect because the Norris-LaGuardia Act of 1932 outlaws yellow-dog contracts.

25. In relation to labor unions, a closed-shop exists when

A. Only those belonging to the union can work.

B. Belonging to the union is not necessary.

C. Collective bargaining is not permitted.

D. Workers have the right to work.

The correct answer is (A). *(CMA, adapted)*

REQUIRED: The true statement about a closed shop.

DISCUSSION: A closed shop is a workplace in which union membership is required as a condition of obtaining employment. The closed shop was outlawed by the Labor-Management Relations Act of 1947. In contrast with a closed shop, a union shop is still allowed in some states. In a union shop, an employee is required to join the union after employment. Still other states have right-to-work laws that allow employees to work at any job without union membership.

Answer (B) is incorrect because, in a closed shop, all employees must be a member of the union. Answer (C) is incorrect because collective bargaining is necessary in a closed shop. All workers are members of the union. Answer (D) is incorrect because only workers who are union members have the right to work in a closed shop.

26. A factory moves from a non-right-to-work state to a right-to-work state, and the union continues to represent the employees. In the right-to-work state,

A. The employees can be forced to join the union before they start to work.

B. The employees can be forced to join the union after thirty days on the job.

C. The employees can decide not to be involved with the union.

D. The employees can be forced to make payments to the union.

The correct answer is (C). *(CMA, adapted)*

REQUIRED: The true statement about union representation in a right-to-work state.

DISCUSSION: Some states have right-to-work laws that allow employees to work at any job without union membership. Thus, employees can decide not to be involved with a union even though the union represents the workers in the shop.

Answer (A) is incorrect because a closed shop requires an employee to be a member of the union in order to get a job. Answer (B) is incorrect because a union shop requires an employee to join the union after employment. Answer (D) is incorrect because paying dues is equivalent to the requirements of a union shop.

27. Which one of the following federal acts requires unions to retain financial records and submit financial reports to federal authorities?

A. Taft-Hartley Act of 1947.

B. Wagner Act of 1935.

C. Securities Exchange Act of 1934.

D. Landrum-Griffin Act of 1959.

The correct answer is (D). *(CMA, adapted)*

REQUIRED: The act requiring unions to retain financial records and submit financial reports to federal authorities.

DISCUSSION: The Landrum-Griffin Act of 1959 (the Labor Management Reporting and Disclosure Act) requires unions to maintain financial records and submit reports to the federal government. The intent of the act was to extend the provisions of the National Labor Relations Act to the internal affairs of unions to make the organizations more democratic and give members more rights.

Answer (A) is incorrect because the Taft-Hartley Act did not address internal affairs such as financial records and reports. Answer (B) is incorrect because the Wagner Act of 1935 gave more power to unions. Answer (C) is incorrect because the Securities Exchange Act of 1934 did not address reports by labor unions.

28. Which one of the following questions can be asked by an employer during an employment interview ensuring compliance with anti-discrimination rules?

A. "How old are you?"

B. "Do you have a disability?"

C. "Are you married?"

D. "Do you have references?"

The correct answer is (D). *(CMA, adapted)*

REQUIRED: The appropriate question during an employment interview.

DISCUSSION: The Equal Employment Opportunity Commission (EEOC) specifies several questions that cannot be asked of applicants during an employment interview. These include questions regarding age, disability, arrest record, and marital status. It is permissible to ask an applicant for references.

Answer (A) is incorrect because age may not be asked under the provisions of the Age Discrimination in Employment Act. Answer (B) is incorrect because questions about a disability may not be asked under the provisions of the Americans with Disabilities Act of 1990. Answer (C) is incorrect because marital status is not a suitable subject for questioning under the civil rights laws.

29. Violations of federal regulations on equal employment opportunity are sometimes inferred from the fact that a firm has a very small percentage of protected groups among its employees. These regulations are sometimes attacked on the grounds that they may be in conflict with the economic concept that

A. The applicant who would be most productive for the job should be hired.

B. The work force employed should be in the same proportion as the demographics of the total population.

C. Equal opportunity strengthens the seniority system.

D. Wages are inversely related to marginal productivity.

The correct answer is (A). *(CMA, adapted)*

REQUIRED: The grounds upon which equal employment opportunity laws are sometimes criticized.

DISCUSSION: Title VII of the Civil Rights Act of 1964 prohibits employment discrimination on the basis of race, color, national origin, religion, or sex. Under the act, a pervasive pattern or practice of discrimination, the employer's adoption of a neutral rule having an adverse impact on a protected class, and the adoption of a neutral rule that perpetuates past discrimination are violations that often must be proved, at least in part, by statistical evidence. A controversial remedy sometimes adopted in such cases is an affirmative action order, which provides preferences to members of the class that previously suffered from discrimination. Affirmative action preferences apply even though the specific persons benefited are not necessarily those who were victimized by illegal discrimination. Affirmative action programs are sometimes criticized because employment preferences are often viewed as reverse discrimination. Moreover, they may not result in the hiring, retention, and promotion of the most productive workers.

Answer (B) is incorrect because a work force in the same proportion as the demographics of the total population is not in conflict with the equal employment opportunity laws. Answer (C) is incorrect because even a bona fide seniority system may violate Title VII if it is found to perpetuate past discrimination. An affirmative action remedy would necessarily have the effect of weakening such a system. Answer (D) is incorrect because wages should be directly related to marginal productivity.

30. Which one of the following is not a characteristic of the Occupational Safety and Health Administration (OSHA)? OSHA

A. Encourages labor-management committees to formulate safety and health programs.

B. Inspections are primarily focused on health issues, including long-term exposure to such substances as asbestos and cotton dust.

C. Has the authority to levy monetary penalties on non-compliant employers.

D. Inspections are primarily reactionary; that is, take place after major injuries have occurred.

The correct answer is (D). *(CMA, adapted)*

REQUIRED: The item that is not a characteristic of OSHA.

DISCUSSION: OSHA is empowered to conduct surprise inspections to determine whether standards are being met. However, an employer may demand that the inspector obtain a search warrant. Thus, no precipitating event must occur prior to an inspection.

Answer (A) is incorrect because OSHA encourages labor-management committees to formulate safety and health programs. Answer (B) is incorrect because inspections are intended to determine whether OSHA standards are being followed. These standards relate to workplace safety and health. Answer (C) is incorrect because OSHA has the authority to levy civil monetary penalties of up to $1,000 per violation and up to $10,000 for a repeat offense.

31. The Americans with Disabilities Act (ADA) of 1990

A. Permits employers to inquire about a job applicant's prior health insurance claims.

B. Bans discrimination against employees with physical disabilities, but not those with mental disabilities.

C. Requires organizations with 25 or more employees to provide reasonable accommodation for employees with disabilities.

D. Provides federal funds to employers who implement its provisions.

The correct answer is (C). *(CMA, adapted)*

REQUIRED: The true statement about the Americans With Disabilities Act (ADA) of 1990.

DISCUSSION: The ADA requires organizations with 25 or more employees to provide reasonable accommodation for employees and job applicants with disabilities. The ADA bans employment discrimination against people with mental or physical disabilities, provides tax incentives for compliance costs, and requires remodeling of facilities to provide access by individuals with disabilities. Another provision of the ADA is that employers are prohibited from inquiring into a job applicant's disability with questions concerning medical history, prior workers' compensation or health insurance claims, work absenteeism due to illness, past treatment for alcoholism, or mental illness.

Answer (A) is incorrect because the ADA prohibits employers from inquiring about a job applicant's prior health insurance claims. Answer (B) is incorrect because the ADA applies to both physical and mental impairments. Answer (D) is incorrect because the ADA provides no federal funds for implementation of its provisions.

C. Antitrust

32. The Sherman Antitrust Act of 1890 prohibits

A. Price discrimination, tying contracts, anti-competitive mergers, and interlocking directorates.

B. Unfair competition and deceptive business practices.

C. Mergers without prior notification to the Justice Department.

D. Restraint of trade and monopoly.

The correct answer is (D). *(CMA, adapted)*

REQUIRED: The activity prohibited by the Sherman Antitrust Act.

DISCUSSION: The Sherman Act makes illegal every contract, combination, or conspiracy in restraint of trade in interstate or foreign commerce. Section 2 of the act prohibits monopolization or the attempt to monopolize.

Answer (A) is incorrect because the Clayton Act of 1914 makes price discrimination, tying contracts, anti-competitive mergers, and interlocking directorates illegal. Answer (B) is incorrect because unfair competition and deceptive business practices are prohibited by the Federal Trade Commission Act of 1914. Answer (C) is incorrect because the Clayton Act of 1914 allows the Justice Department to prevent mergers before they occur.

33. The impact of successful prosecution for restraint of trade violations of the Sherman Antitrust Act has been less than many proponents hoped for because

A. Only a limited number of criminal prosecutions have ever been filed under Section 1 of the Act.

B. Most companies avoid behaviors that might be construed as antitrust violations because of the likelihood of fines and even jail sentences.

C. The predominant criterion for criminal prosecution is market share; a company's intent is inconsequential.

D. The courts created in the beginning a "rule of reason" that required determining whether competition was lessened by the company's behavior.

The correct answer is (D). *(CMA, adapted)*

REQUIRED: The reason for the disappointing impact of prosecutions under the Sherman Act.

DISCUSSION: The Sherman Antitrust Act of 1890 makes illegal every contract, combination, or conspiracy in restraint of trade in interstate or foreign commerce. Successful prosecutions have been few because the courts developed a rule of reason stipulating that only unreasonable restraints of trade are illegal. Thus, courts balance the anti-competitive effects against the pro-competitive effects of a restraint of trade. Unless a restraint is unreasonable by its very nature (a per se violation), the rule of reason applies.

Answer (A) is incorrect because many cases have been filed under the Sherman Act; however, the rule of reason has limited the number of successful prosecutions. Answer (B) is incorrect because numerous companies still engage in anti-competitive conduct. Answer (C) is incorrect because intent is significant; for example, a company that has a monopoly thrust upon it is not in violation.

34. The Sherman Antitrust Act

A. Established the Federal Trade Commission.

B. Prohibits collective boycotts.

C. Prohibits price discrimination.

D. Established the concept of a patent.

The correct answer is (B). *(CMA, adapted)*

REQUIRED: The true statement about the Sherman Antitrust Act.

DISCUSSION: The Sherman Act of 1890 makes illegal every contract, combination, or conspiracy in restraint of trade in interstate or foreign commerce. Some types of arrangements between competitors are to be considered unreasonable without inquiry. These are known as per se violations. Price fixing, division of markets, group boycotts, and resale price maintenance are per se violations.

Answer (A) is incorrect because the FTC was established by the Federal Trade Commission Act of 1914. Answer (C) is incorrect because price discrimination is prohibited by the Robinson-Patman Act of 1936, which was an amendment to the Clayton Act of 1914. Answer (D) is incorrect because patent laws were in effect long before the Sherman Act of 1890. Thus, the U.S. Constitution (Article I, Section 8) grants to Congress the power "To promote the progress of science and useful arts, by securing for limited times to authors and inventors the exclusive right to their respective writings and discoveries."

35. Resale price maintenance is an example of

A. Horizontal price fixing.

B. Vertical price fixing.

C. Preemptive buying.

D. Tying arrangements.

The correct answer is (B). *(CMA, adapted)*

REQUIRED: The true statement about resale price maintenance.

DISCUSSION: Resale price maintenance agreements are a form of vertical price fixing because a manufacturer or wholesaler restricts the price that may be charged by a retailer. Such agreements are *per se* violations of the Sherman Act of 1890.

Answer (A) is incorrect because horizontal price fixing occurs between two competitors at the same level in the distribution process (e.g., between two retailers in the same industry). Answer (C) is incorrect because preemptive buying is not associated with resale price maintenance. Answer (D) is incorrect because tying arrangements require a buyer to purchase other products in addition to the one that is desired.

36. Which one of the following examples of corporate behavior would most clearly represent a violation of the Sherman Act?

A. A retailer offers quantity discounts to large institutional buyers.

B. The members of a labor union meet and agree not to work for a specific firm unless the starting wage is at least $10 per hour.

C. Two firms that are in different, unrelated industries merge.

D. Two firms in the same industry agree in a telephone conversation to submit identical bids on a government contract.

The correct answer is (D). *(CMA, adapted)*

REQUIRED: The item that would most clearly represent a violation of the Sherman Act.

DISCUSSION: The Sherman Act of 1890 makes illegal every contract, combination, or conspiracy in restraint of trade in interstate or foreign commerce. Some types of arrangements, called per se violations, are considered unreasonable without inquiry. These violations include price fixing, division of markets, group boycotts, and resale price maintenance. Agreeing to submit identical bids on a government contract would be a form of price fixing, and thus a per se violation.

Answer (A) is incorrect because quantity discounts are not prohibited by the Sherman Act. Answer (B) is incorrect because the Sherman Act does not apply to labor unions. Answer (C) is incorrect because the Sherman Act does not prohibit mergers; only those that could lead to restraint of trade are outlawed.

37. Antitrust laws

A. Set maximum allowable prices for firms in oligopolistic industries.

B. Prohibit firms from collecting price information.

C. Require firms with high earnings to provide price and quantity data to the Federal Trade Commission.

D. Prohibit firms from allocating customers.

The correct answer is (D). *(CMA, adapted)*

REQUIRED: The true statement about antitrust laws.

DISCUSSION: The Sherman Antitrust Act of 1890 was the first U.S. antitrust law. It prohibited contracts, combinations, and conspiracies in restraint of trade and made monopolizing or attempting to monopolize any part of interstate commerce a criminal offense. Allocating customers among firms within an industry, for example, by division of markets, is a per se violation of the Act.

Answer (A) is incorrect because antitrust laws do not regulate prices. However, prices may not be discriminatory or collusive. Answer (B) is incorrect because collecting price information is lawful. Answer (C) is incorrect because antitrust laws apply to all firms engaged in interstate commerce, regardless of size.

38. Which one of the following antitrust laws prohibits price discrimination, tying contracts, anticompetitive mergers, and interlocking directorates?

A. Sherman Antitrust Act.

B. Clayton Antitrust Act.

C. Antitrust Improvements Act.

D. Federal Trade Commission Act.

The correct answer is (B). *(CMA, adapted)*

REQUIRED: The antitrust law prohibiting price discrimination, tying contracts, anticompetitive mergers, and interlocking directorates.

DISCUSSION: The Clayton Act of 1914 prohibits mergers or acquisitions of stock that may lessen competition or tend to create a monopoly. Mergers can be prevented by the Justice Department before they occur. Also prohibited by the Clayton Act are sales that prevent the buyer from dealing with the seller's competitors, tying (or tie-in) sales, exclusive dealing, price discrimination among different buyers, and interlocking directorates.

Answer (A) is incorrect because the Sherman Act of 1890 did not mention tying sales or interlocking directorates. Answer (C) is incorrect because the Antitrust Improvements Act of 1976 amended the antitrust laws in various ways. Answer (D) is incorrect because the Federal Trade Commission Act of 1914 created the Federal Trade Commission to enforce the Sherman and Clayton acts.

39. Which one of the following antitrust laws prohibits price discrimination and other exclusionary practices that may give certain firms a competitive advantage over other firms in the same market?

A. Celler-Kefauver Act.

B. Federal Trade Commission Act.

C. Sherman Act.

D. Robinson-Patman Act.

The correct answer is (D). *(CMA, adapted)*

REQUIRED: The antitrust law that prohibits price discrimination.

DISCUSSION: The Robinson-Patman Act of 1936 amended the Clayton Act with respect to price discrimination. Price discrimination by both buyers and sellers is prohibited in interstate commerce of goods of like grade and quality. The purpose of the act is to protect competition. However, price differentials are allowed if justified by a cost savings to the seller or a good-faith effort to meet a competitor's lawful price.

Answer (A) is incorrect because the Celler-Kefauver Act of 1950 prohibits the acquisition of the stock or assets of another business if the effect may be to lessen competition substantially or to create a monopoly. Answer (B) is incorrect because the Federal Trade Commission Act of 1914 prohibits unfair methods of competition in or affecting interstate commerce. It also created the Federal Trade Commission, which has authority to enforce the Clayton and Robinson-Patman Acts. The FTC also is authorized to proceed against unfair or deceptive acts or practices. Answer (C) is incorrect because the Sherman Act of 1890 makes illegal every contract, combination, or conspiracy that unreasonably restrains trade in interstate or foreign commerce. It also prohibits monopolization and attempts and conspiracies to monopolize.

40. Which one of the following laws addresses the issue of insider trading?

A. Federal Trade Commission Act.

B. Securities Exchange Act.

C. Clayton Act.

D. North American Free Trade Agreement.

The correct answer is (B). *(CMA, adapted)*

REQUIRED: The law that addresses insider trading.

DISCUSSION: The Securities Exchange Act of 1934 addresses the issue of insider trading. Specifically, insiders must turn over to the corporation any profits earned on purchases and sales of their company's stock that fall within six months of each other. They are also prohibited from buying or selling stock based on inside information not available to the public.

Answer (A) is incorrect because the Federal Trade Commission Act of 1914 prohibits unfair methods of competition in or affecting interstate commerce. It also created the Federal Trade Commission, which has authority to enforce the Clayton and Robinson-Patman Acts. The FTC also is authorized to proceed against unfair or deceptive acts or practices. Answer (C) is incorrect because the Clayton Act of 1914 was intended to prevent monopolies. A probability of a significant anticompetitive effect is a basis for most violations of the act. It specifically addresses price discrimination, tying contracts, exclusive dealing arrangements, mergers, and interlocking directorates. Answer (D) is incorrect because the North American Free Trade Agreement is an agreement providing for free trade among the USA, Canada, and Mexico.

41. The Clayton Act, as amended, prohibits all of the following except

A. Tying contracts that require a customer who is buying one product to buy a related but perhaps unwanted product.

B. Price discrimination by sellers.

C. Interlocking directorates in large competing organizations.

D. Unfair and deceptive business practices, such as misleading advertising.

The correct answer is (D). *(CMA, adapted)*

REQUIRED: The item not prohibited by the Clayton Act.

DISCUSSION: The Clayton Act of 1914 prohibits (1) mergers that may lessen competition or tend to create a monopoly, (2) sales that prevent the buyer from dealing with the seller's competitors, (3) tie-in sales (requiring a buyer to take other products in order to buy the first product), (4) price discrimination, and (5) interlocking directorates (directors serve on the boards of competing firms). The Clayton Act does not address unfair and deceptive business practices such as false advertising.

Answers (A), (B), and (C) are incorrect because these are prohibited by the Clayton Act.

42. Which one of the following statements regarding the application of antitrust rules to professional fees is true?

A. Most professionals, including physicians, lawyers, engineers, and accountants, are exempt from the antitrust laws.

B. Agreements to increase fees are legal if the quality of services provided improves.

C. Fee discrimination in any form is illegal.

D. Agreements to set either minimum or maximum fees are illegal.

The correct answer is (D). *(CMA, adapted)*

REQUIRED: The true statement about the application of antitrust laws to professional fees.

DISCUSSION: Lawyers, public accountants, and other professionals have received scrutiny from the FTC in recent years concerning pricing policies. In general, professionals cannot make agreements that provide for either minimum or maximum fees since price fixing by collusion among competitors is a per se violation of the Sherman Act.

Answer (A) is incorrect because professionals and their organizations are not exempt from the antitrust laws. Answer (B) is incorrect because agreements among competitors to increase fees are illegal per se. Answer (C) is incorrect because fee discrimination is not illegal per se since many factors influence the fees that a particular professional might charge. For example, a professional might charge a lower price if a service is to be performed during a normally slow period.

43. Tie-in sales (e.g., the sale of camera and film together) are legal

A. If the tie-in is necessary to assure product quality.

B. If the tying product is patented.

C. If used to facilitate price discrimination.

D. Under all circumstances.

The correct answer is (A). *(CMA, adapted)*

REQUIRED: The situation in which tie-in sales are legal.

DISCUSSION: Tie-in sales involve a seller/lessor's requirement that the buyer/lessee purchase/lease another distinct product in order to obtain the first. They are generally prohibited under the Clayton Act of 1914 unless a small company is attempting to enter a market or the tie-in is needed to protect the firm's goodwill (e.g., by maintaining a certain quality standard).

Answers (B), (C), and (D) are incorrect because tie-in sales requirements are generally illegal if the seller has enough market power to restrict competition.

44. A franchisor's requirement that its franchisees buy inputs from a particular supplier is

A. Illegal according to the provisions of the Robinson-Patman Act.

B. Illegal according to the principles of common law.

C. Legal, but the franchisor must receive approval from the Federal Trade Commission.

D. Legal as long as such a requirement is necessary to assure product quality.

The correct answer is (D). *(CMA, adapted)*

REQUIRED: The true statement about a franchisor's requirement that franchisees buy inputs from a particular supplier.

DISCUSSION: The Clayton Act of 1914 prohibits exclusive-dealing requirements. However, a franchise relationship is contractual, and the agreement is in force for a specified period. Because the franchisee and the franchisor have a common public identity, an exclusive-dealing contract is allowable if it is necessary to assure product quality. Without the exclusive-dealing requirement, a low-quality product sold by the franchisee could reflect badly on the reputation of the franchisor.

Answer (A) is incorrect because the Robinson-Patman Act concerns price discrimination, not exclusive-dealing contracts. Answer (B) is incorrect because exclusive-dealing contracts are the subject of federal antitrust law. They are not illegal under common law. Answer (C) is incorrect because there is no requirement to seek approval from the FTC.

45. The Clayton Act of 1914 prohibits

A. Closed-shop labor unions.

B. Sellers' price discrimination.

C. Group boycotts.

D. Oligopolies.

The correct answer is (B). *(CMA, adapted)*

REQUIRED: The prohibition by the Clayton Act.

DISCUSSION: The Clayton Act of 1914 prohibits price discrimination if it directly or indirectly lessens competition such that it tends to create a monopoly. The Robinson-Patman Act amended the Clayton Act to prohibit sellers of goods from granting, and buyers from inducing, unfair discounts and other preferences. However, price differentials are justified by a cost savings to the seller or a good faith effort to meet, but not undercut, the lawful price of a competitor.

Answer (A) is incorrect because the closed shop was prohibited by the Taft-Hartley Act of 1947. Answer (C) is incorrect because group boycotts were prohibited by the Sherman Act of 1890. Answer (D) is incorrect because oligopolies are not prohibited by the Clayton Act.

46. The Federal Trade Commission Act, as amended,

A. Outlaws interlocking directorates in large competing corporations.

B. Prohibits price discrimination by sellers.

C. Forbids tying contracts that require a purchaser to buy an unwanted product to get another.

D. Forbids unfair and deceptive business practices, such as misleading advertising.

The correct answer is (D). *(CMA, adapted)*

REQUIRED: The true statement about the Federal Trade Commission Act, as amended.

DISCUSSION: The Federal Trade Commission Act of 1914, as amended by the Wheeler-Lea Amendment of 1938, prohibits unfair methods of competition and unfair or deceptive acts in commerce, including false advertising. The act also created the Federal Trade Commission (FTC) to enforce the requirements of the act. The basic objectives of the FTC are to initiate antitrust actions and to protect the consumer public.

Answer (A) is incorrect because interlocking directorates are prohibited by the Clayton Act. Answer (B) is incorrect because price discrimination is prohibited by the Clayton Act as amended by the Robinson-Patman Act. Answer (C) is incorrect because tying contracts are prohibited by the Clayton Act.

47. The two major functions of the Federal Trade Commission are

A. Antitrust actions and the regulation of foreign trade.

B. Import quality inspections and anti-dumping measures.

C. Antitrust actions and consumer protection.

D. Price discrimination and unfair trade practices.

The correct answer is (C). *(CMA, adapted)*

REQUIRED: The two major functions of the Federal Trade Commission (FTC).

DISCUSSION: The FTC Act of 1914 prohibits unfair methods of competition and unfair or deceptive acts in commerce. The basic objectives are to initiate antitrust actions and protect the consumer public.

Answers (A) and (B) are incorrect because the FTC is not concerned with the regulation of foreign trade. Answer (D) is incorrect because price discrimination and unfair trade practices are merely elements of the overall mission of the FTC.

48. The Robinson-Patman Act of 1936 prohibits price discrimination unless

A. The price is set to meet a competitor's price quote.

B. The price reflects cost increases caused by government specification.

C. The price is set in a market characterized by monopolistic competition.

D. Specific prior approval is obtained from the Justice Department.

The correct answer is (A). *(CMA, adapted)*

REQUIRED: The exception to the price discrimination prohibition under the Robinson-Patman Act.

DISCUSSION: The Robinson-Patman Act prohibits price discrimination with respect to both buyers and sellers. Price discrimination is allowed if it is to meet a competitor's price quote or if justified by the quantity purchased.

Answer (B) is incorrect because cost increases caused by government specification is not an allowable exception to the Robinson-Patman Act. Answer (C) is incorrect because the nature of a market is not a factor in price discrimination under the Robinson-Patman Act. Answer (D) is incorrect because the Justice Department does not give approval for price discrimination.

49. Which one of the following transactions would be considered a violation of the Robinson-Patman Act?

A. The sale of goods of like quality at different prices to two different wholesalers, both of whom are located outside the United States.

B. The sale of goods of like quality within the United States at different prices based on cost differences related to the method of delivery.

C. The sale of goods of like quality within the United States at different prices to two different wholesalers; all parties are located within the same state.

D. The sale of goods of like quality within the United States but across state lines at different prices to two different wholesalers in the same geographic area.

The correct answer is (D). *(CMA, adapted)*

REQUIRED: The transaction that would be in violation of the Robinson-Patman Act of 1936.

DISCUSSION: The Robinson-Patman Act of 1936, an amendment to the Clayton Act, outlaws price discrimination that would lead to restraint of trade. Both buyer and seller can be found guilty of price discrimination under the provisions of the Robinson-Patman Act. Price differentiation between customers is allowed if there is a difference in costs. For instance, quantity discounts are permitted if it can be shown that larger quantities can be shipped with a cost savings. Charging competing wholesalers different prices for similar goods would be a violation of the act.

Answer (A) is incorrect because the act does not apply to export sales. Answer (B) is incorrect because cost differences related to delivery are a justification for charging different prices. Answer (C) is incorrect because the act applies only to sales in interstate commerce.

50. The Antitrust Improvements Act of 1976

A. Requires pre-approval from the Federal Trade Commission for interlocking directorates.

B. Prohibits price discrimination.

C. Requires notification prior to a merger.

D. Prohibits restraints of trade and monopoly.

The correct answer is (C). *(CMA, adapted)*

REQUIRED: The provisions of the Antitrust Improvements Act of 1976.

DISCUSSION: The Antitrust Improvements Act of 1976 requires corporations with annual sales or assets exceeding $100,000,000 to give advance notice to the Justice Department and the FTC of any acquisition of a corporation with annual sales or assets of $10,000,000 or more.

Answer (A) is incorrect because the Clayton Act of 1914 prohibits interlocking directorates in competing companies. Answer (B) is incorrect because the Robinson-Patman Act of 1936 prohibits price discrimination. Answer (D) is incorrect because the Sherman Act of 1890 prohibits restraint of trade and monopoly.

51. One way of measuring government performance with respect to antitrust regulation is cost-benefit analysis. In the graph below, P_1 and Q_1 represent the price and quantity under a monopoly. Effective government regulation could lower the price to P_2 which could increase the quantity to Q_2.

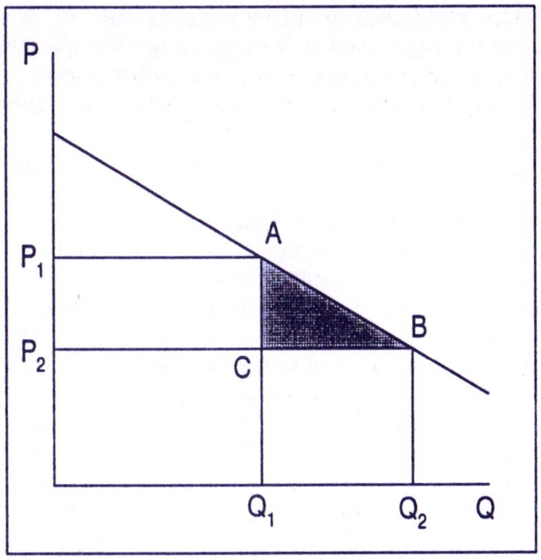

On the graph, the area ABC represents the

A. Total cost of producing the additional output.

B. Excess unsatisfied demand caused by the regulation.

C. Efficiency gain from antitrust action.

D. Total benefit generated by the change.

The correct answer is (C). *(CMA, adapted)*

REQUIRED: The meaning of the area ABC.

DISCUSSION: The area ABC represents the efficiency gain from antitrust action. It is the increase in productivity (benefits to society) from the increased quantity and lower prices resulting from the antitrust action.

Answer (A) is incorrect because no information is given regarding costs. Only selling prices and quantities are given. Answer (B) is incorrect because AC represents greater satisfied demand. Answer (D) is incorrect because total benefit is represented by the greater quantity produced (area CBQ_2Q_1).

52. Antitrust suits, particularly civil rather than criminal suits, may be brought by many different individuals or agencies. Which one of the following does not have power to bring such suits?

A. U.S. Department of Justice.

B. A state attorney general, when authorized by a state antitrust law.

C. A private party, such as a competitor.

D. U.S. Department of Commerce.

The correct answer is (D). *(CMA, adapted)*

REQUIRED: The entity that does not have power to initiate antitrust suits.

DISCUSSION: Under the Sherman Act, violations may be civil or criminal. Criminal penalties include fines and imprisonment and enforcement is by the Justice Department. Civil suits may also be brought by private parties, who may recover treble damages. The FTC also has specific authority to enforce the Clayton and Robinson-Patman Acts and implied authority to enforce the Sherman Act. State law may also provide remedies for antitrust violations. The U.S. Department of Commerce is not entitled to bring suit for violation of antitrust laws.

Answers (A), (B), and (C) are incorrect because the Justice Department, a state attorney general, and individual citizens enforce antitrust laws.

53. Over the years, various groups and activities have been exempted from coverage by the U.S. antitrust laws. Which one of the following statements regarding such exemptions is correct?

A. All sales and purchases of products by American firms outside of the U.S. are automatically exempt from coverage by the antitrust laws.

B. All resale price maintenance agreements between manufacturers and retailers selling the manufacturers' product brands are exempt from the federal antitrust laws.

C. Under certain conditions, a person who wishes to form an export trading company may obtain a certificate of antitrust immunity from the Commerce Department after concurrence by the Justice Department.

D. Water common carriers in foreign trade may enter into price fixing and market sharing treaties or agreements provided the agreements are ratified by the U.S. Senate before being put into effect.

The correct answer is (C). *(CMA, adapted)*

REQUIRED: The true statement regarding exemption from U.S. antitrust laws.

DISCUSSION: The various exemptions from antitrust laws include intrastate commerce, labor unions, regulated utilities, patents, copyrights, and reasonable noncompetition clauses between buyers and sellers of businesses, partners in a partnership, and purchasers of technology or equipment. Agricultural and fishing organizations, financial institutions, broadcasting, transportation industries, and professional baseball also have varying levels of exemption. Moreover, in 1982, Congress enacted the Export Trading Company Act. The purpose of the ETCA is to encourage export of U.S. produced goods and services. Persons who wish to form an export trading company may obtain from the Commerce Department a certificate of antitrust immunity (called a certificate of review) after concurrence by the Justice Department. This certificate is issued if certain conditions are met. These prohibit unfair export competition, substantial lessening of competition or restraint of trade in the U.S., unreasonable effects on U.S. prices, and sale or resale of the goods or services in the U.S.

Answer (A) is incorrect because the Sherman Act makes illegal every restraint of trade in interstate or foreign commerce. Answer (B) is incorrect because the Sherman Act prohibits resale price maintenance. Answer (D) is incorrect because the Sherman Act makes illegal every restraint of trade in interstate or foreign commerce.

D. Consumer and Environmental Protection

54. Which one of the following approaches to regulation best describes mandatory labeling information concerning food content and nutritional values?

A. Unregulated markets subject to antitrust enforcement.

B. Disclosure of all relevant information.

C. Changes in liability rules toward a stricter liability.

D. Creation of marketable property rights.

The correct answer is (B). *(CMA, adapted)*

REQUIRED: The approach to regulation that best describes mandatory labeling information.

DISCUSSION: Mandatory labeling follows the disclosure approach. The basis of this approach is the belief that regulation is sufficient if consumers have the information needed to make rational decisions. The assumptions are that consumers are sophisticated enough to use the information provided and that sellers will have an incentive to improve their products.

Answer (A) is incorrect because no labeling requirements exist in an unregulated market. Answer (C) is incorrect because stricter liability rules promote product quality and safety, whereas labeling requirements are primarily informational. Answer (D) is incorrect because labeling requirements do not create marketable property rights. An example of such a regulatory practice is the external trading of pollution rights.

55. Truth-in-lending is one form of price standardization that, since the adoption of the Consumer Credit Protection Act on July 1, 1969, has been provided by U.S. government regulations. The purpose of this legislation is to

A. Regulate the amount of interest that may be charged.

B. Prohibit the use of appraisal fees.

C. Allow immediate wage garnishment by creditors.

D. Disclose the finance charge and the annual percentage rate.

The correct answer is (D). *(CMA, adapted)*

REQUIRED: The purpose of truth-in-lending legislation.

DISCUSSION: The Truth-in-Lending Act applies to creditors that extend consumer credit to individual debtors (not organizations) in amounts of $25,000 or less. For a closed-end credit transaction, e.g., the typical car loan, the total finance charge, annual percentage interest rate, amount financed, late charges, security interest held by the creditor, the number and amounts of payments, due dates, and the total amount of payments must be disclosed. Open-end credit transactions, such as those involving credit cards, also have specific, detailed disclosure requirements.

Answer (A) is incorrect because the Consumer Credit Protection Act merely requires disclosure. It does not regulate interest rates. Answer (B) is incorrect because the act did not prohibit the use of appraisal fees. Answer (C) is incorrect because the act had nothing to do with wage garnishment.

56. The federal Consumer Product Safety Commission (CPSC) was created in 1972 and administers an act covering those consumer products not already regulated by the federal government. Specifically, Section 15 of the act (CPSA) requires manufacturers to take corrective steps for a product that fails to comply with a product safety rule or contains a defect that could create a substantial product hazard. This provision is included because

A. The CPSC is dependent on the manufacturers to provide information on product safety.

B. Voluntary standards are preferred to compulsory ones, and this pushes regulation back into the hands of manufacturers.

C. It encourages the CPSC to apply cost-benefit analysis in formulating and implementing consumer product safety standards.

D. The manufacturer may be compelled to publicize this defect to consumers and/or refund the purchase price.

The correct answer is (D). *(CMA, adapted)*

REQUIRED: The reason the CPSA requires manufacturers to take corrective steps for a product that fails to comply with a safety rule or contains a defect that could create a substantial hazard.

DISCUSSION: A manufacturer, retailer, or distributor must notify the CPSC if it has reason to know that a product poses a "substantial product hazard" because it violates a CPSC safety rule or for other reasons. In these circumstances, the CPSC may order the party to notify those affected, repair or replace the product, or submit its own corrective action plan.

Answer (A) is incorrect because the CPSC is not dependent upon manufacturers to provide information on product safety. Much information is obtained from consumers. Answer (B) is incorrect because standards are compulsory. Answer (C) is incorrect because cost-benefit analysis is not a consideration when products are dangerous.

57. If a product is believed to pose an imminent hazard to consumers, the Consumer Product Safety Commission (CPSC)

A. May seek a court order to have the product banned or seized.

B. May ban or seize the product upon a majority vote by the commissioners of the CPSC.

C. May ban or seize the product, but only after a notice has been published in the Federal Register for 30 days.

D. Can only ask the manufacturer voluntarily to withdraw or recall the product.

The correct answer is (A). *(CMA, adapted)*

REQUIRED: The true statement about the activities of the Consumer Product Safety Commission (CPSC).

DISCUSSION: The CPSC publishes product safety standards, issues rules banning certain hazardous products, brings federal suits to eliminate dangers presented by imminently hazardous consumer products, and requires manufacturers, distributors, and retailers to give notice if they have reason to know that their products present a substantial hazard. Remedies include injunctive relief, seizure of products, and civil and criminal penalties.

Answers (B) and (C) are incorrect because the CPSC must file suit in federal court to have a product banned or seized; it cannot ban or seize a product without a court order. Answer (D) is incorrect because the CPSC may go beyond asking for voluntary action.

58. Pharmaceutical companies must be in compliance with regulations set forth by the Food and Drug Administration (FDA). The FDA is responsible for all of the following except

A. Allowing extensions to patent lives of pharmaceutical companies in order to recover time lost during the premarket FDA regulatory review.

B. Considering benefit-risk trade-offs when evaluating the safety of drugs prior to approval.

C. Maintaining purity standards and regulations concerning drug composition and potency.

D. Approving drugs that lack substantial evidence that they will have the effects that are represented in advertisements.

The correct answer is (D). *(CMA, adapted)*

REQUIRED: The item not the responsibility of the Food and Drug Administration (FDA).

DISCUSSION: The FDA was created by the Federal Food, Drug, and Cosmetics Act of 1938 to help maintain the safety of drugs, food, cosmetics, and medicinal products and devices. It regulates the testing, distribution, and sale of drugs. Upon receiving a new drug application, the FDA conducts hearings and investigates the merits of the drug in a process that may require years. Thus, an application must be supported by substantial evidence that the drug will have the asserted effects.

Answers (A), (B), and (C) are incorrect because the FDA can extend patent lives to allow for time lost during the regulatory review; considers benefit-risk tradeoffs, and maintains purity standards.

59. Environmental policies undertaken in the United States that attempt to weigh the costs and benefits of environmental improvement

A. Will result in the elimination of all pollution.

B. Cannot work because business firms are not willing to cooperate.

C. Grant tax relief to the firms who pollute the least.

D. Would leave an acceptable amount of pollution.

The correct answer is (D). *(CMA, adapted)*

REQUIRED: The true statement about environmental policies.

DISCUSSION: If environmental policies weigh the costs and benefits of regulation, some pollution will exist because the costs of eliminating all pollution will likely outweigh the benefits. Cost-benefit considerations are reflected in, for example, the establishment of air quality standards that do not attempt to eliminate the incidence of specified pollutants and requirements for control technology that, for the most part, do not mandate use of devices that achieve the maximum pollution reduction. The drawback of a cost-benefit approach is the difficulty of quantifying benefits.

Answer (A) is incorrect because elimination of all pollution would probably be too costly for the resulting benefits. Answer (B) is incorrect because firms are more supportive of cost-benefit regulatory policies. Answer (C) is incorrect because granting tax relief to firms which pollute the least is not a cost-benefit policy.

60. The Environmental Protection Agency (EPA) might control pollution by setting effluent standards for maximum discharge or by constructing a sliding-tax charge based on the amount of effluent emitted. One advantage of the sliding-tax charge is that

A. It will totally eliminate pollution.

B. There is greater business incentive to discover new methods of controlling pollution.

C. It increases the necessity for the EPA to fully understand pollution control technology.

D. It increases the degree of direct government intervention in the economy.

The correct answer is (B). *(CMA, adapted)*

REQUIRED: The advantage of the sliding tax charge method of controlling the discharge of effluents.

DISCUSSION: The setting of effluent standards has often been criticized as an inefficient method of pollution control. Economists prefer a sliding tax charge based on the amount of effluent emitted. This method is preferred because, as effluent discharge increases, a company's tax increases, providing a strong incentive for firms to discover new methods of controlling pollution. Rather than dictating technology, the tax allows firms to seek out the technology that is the most cost effective.

Answer (A) is incorrect because pollution would not be totally eliminated. Some firms might find that a low level of pollution is more cost beneficial than total elimination. Answer (C) is incorrect because the EPA would not be directly involved in technology. Answer (D) is incorrect because the tax would be an indirect method of economic intervention.

61. An efficient way to control pollution in line with the expectations of the Clean Air Act Amendments of 1990 is to

A. Make pollution illegal.

B. Regulate the amount of pollution a firm can create.

C. Promote social awareness about the harm due to pollution.

D. Allow marketable permits for pollution that firms can buy or sell like any other commodity.

The correct answer is (D). *(CMA, adapted)*

REQUIRED: The efficient way to control pollution in line with the expectations of the Clean Air Act Amendments of 1990.

DISCUSSION: The Clean Air Act allows companies to pollute legally if they have a permit to do so. Firms can buy or sell these permits, and the result is essentially a free market that enables a firm to seek out a technology that is most cost effective. If the price of permits is too high, a firm will buy new equipment that will not pollute. If permits can be acquired at a low cost, a company may decide to continue producing with its old, high-pollution equipment.

Answer (A) is incorrect because the Clean Air Act does not make pollution illegal; it provides comprehensive regulation of air quality. Answer (B) is incorrect because regulating the amount of pollution a specific company can emit is not efficient. That is why the emphasis is on the application of air quality standards in the air quality control regions in the states. Moreover, the states are required to identify the major, not all, sources of pollution. Answer (C) is incorrect because the act does not promote social awareness about the harm due to pollution; in fact, it allows some pollution if a company is willing to pay to pollute.

62. The Clean Air Act of 1970 charged the Environmental Protection Agency (EPA) with all of the following responsibilities except

A. Setting standards without consideration for the cost of compliance to manufacturers.

B. Nullifying the right of an individual citizen to bring suit to enforce standards as such suits will now be initiated by the EPA.

C. Setting standards to prevent damage to items such as visibility, crops, and buildings.

D. Establishing minimum ambient air standards for the entire country.

The correct answer is (B). *(CMA, adapted)*

REQUIRED: The false statement about the responsibilities of the EPA.

DISCUSSION: Either the EPA or individuals can initiate or participate in civil enforcement actions. Individuals may also seek damages for personal injuries suffered as a result of violations.

Answer (A) is incorrect because the standards were established without consideration for costs of compliance. Answer (C) is incorrect because national ambient air quality standards (NAAQS) have been established to prevent damage to items such as visibility, crops, waterways, and buildings. Answer (D) is incorrect because NAAQS have been established with respect to specified pollutants to protect human health and the public welfare.

63. In recent years, governmental bodies have tried a number of devices to encourage environmental stewardship. At least fourteen major federal acts or amendments to acts were passed between 1969 and 1990. Which one of the following is not a governmental device used in recent years?

A. Direct regulation or legally enforceable environmental quality standards.

B. Pollution charges or fees for undesirable waste released by the firm.

C. Relocation of facilities to offshore sites where governmental standards are less stringent.

D. Buying and selling of pollution rights involving companies whose emissions are below the standard.

The correct answer is (C). *(CMA, adapted)*

REQUIRED: The item not a governmental device used to encourage environmental stewardship.

DISCUSSION: Environmental laws have established quality standards with respect to water, land, and air. One approach has permitted violations, but subjects violators to sliding charges depending upon the quantity of pollutants released. Companies that are below the standard for a particular pollutant can sell their rights to other firms in the industry. In addition, tax laws have provided incentives for environmental improvements, for example a tax credit for individuals who installed insulation. Similarly, windmills are encouraged by the tax laws. Moving facilities to offshore sites where governmental standards are less stringent might be undertaken by individual companies, but such action is not a governmental device.

Answer (A) is incorrect because quality standards were established by the Environmental Protection Agency. Answer (B) is incorrect because fees have been established for firms that emit pollutants. Answer (D) is incorrect because companies may buy and sell their rights to emit pollutants.

Use Gleim's ***CMA/CFM Test Prep*** for interactive testing with **over 2,000 additional multiple-choice questions!**

Addendum: Computational Practice Questions

Questions A4 through A6 are presented below. Please see pages 64, 386, and 473 for additional questions. The study unit on which the question is based is indicated in bold after the source code for each question.

A4. The high cost of short-term financing has recently caused a company to reevaluate the terms of credit it extends to its customers. The current policy is 1/10, net 60. If customers can borrow at the prime rate, at what prime rate must the company change its terms of credit in order to avoid an undesirable extension in its collection of receivables?

A. 2%

B. 5%

C. 7%

D. 8%

The correct answer is (D). *(Publisher)* **SU 5**

REQUIRED: The prime rate at which a vendor must change its terms to avoid an undesirable extension in the collection of its receivables.

DISCUSSION: Terms of 1/10, net 60 mean that a buyer can save 1% of the purchase price by paying 50 days early. In essence, not taking the discount results in the buyer's borrowing 99% of the invoice price for 50 days at a total interest charge of 1%. Because a year has 7.3 50-day periods (365 ÷ 50), the credit terms 1/10, net 60 yield an effective annualized interest charge of approximately 7.3% (7.3 × 1%). The effective interest rate is therefore 7.37% (7.3% ÷ 99% of the purchase price). If the prime rate were higher than 7.37%, the buyer would prefer to borrow from the vendor (i.e., not pay within the discount period) rather than from a bank. Consequently, an 8% prime rate could cause the vendor's receivables to increase.

Answers (A), (B), and (C) are incorrect because the prime rate must be greater than 7.37% to make the company's terms preferable to those of a bank.

A5. A company has just borrowed $2 million from a bank. The stated rate of interest is 10%. If the loan is discounted and is repayable in one year, the effective rate on the loan is approximately

A. 8.89%

B. 9.09%

C. 10.00%

D. 11.11%

The correct answer is (D). *(Publisher)* **SU 5**

REQUIRED: The effective rate of interest on a discounted loan.

DISCUSSION: If the loan is discounted, the borrower receives the face amount minus the prepaid interest. Thus, the borrower will receive proceeds of $1,800,000 [$2,000,000 – (10% × $2,000,000)]. The effective interest rate is 11.11% ($200,000 ÷ $1,800,000).

Answers (A) and (B) are incorrect because the prepayment of interest reduces the funds available, resulting in an effective interest rate greater than the contract rate. Answer (C) is incorrect because 10% is the contract rate. The effective rate is higher because the full $2 million face amount of the note will not be available to the borrower.

A6. If a firm purchases raw materials from its supplier on a 2/10, net 40, cash discount basis, the equivalent annual interest rate (using a 360-day year) of forgoing the cash discount and making payment on the 40th day is

A. 2%

B. 18.36%

C. 24.49%

D. 36.72%

The correct answer is (C). *(Publisher)* **SU 5**

REQUIRED: The equivalent annual interest charge for not taking the discount when credit terms are 2/10, net 40.

DISCUSSION: The buyer could satisfy the $100 obligation by paying $98 on the 10th day. By choosing to wait until the 40th day, the buyer is effectively paying a $2 interest charge for the use of $98 for 30 days (40-day credit period – 10-day discount period). The interest rate on what is essentially a 30-day loan is 2.04081% ($2 ÷ $98). Extrapolating this 30-day rate to a yearly rate involves multiplying by the number of periods in a year. Thus, the effective annual rate is about 24.49% [2.04081% × (360 ÷ 30 days)].

Answer (A) is incorrect because 2% is the discount rate. Answer (B) is incorrect because 18.36% is based on the 40-day credit period. Answer (D) is incorrect because 36.72% is based on a 20-day credit period.

STUDY UNIT 5: WORKING CAPITAL FINANCE

19 pages of outline
64 multiple-choice questions

This study unit and Study Unit 6, Capital Structure Finance, outline the field of managerial finance, which embraces financial analysis, planning, implementation of financial plans, and control of a firm. We have added as Study Unit 7, Risk, which covers investment risk, financing risk, and corporate insurance. The relative weight range assigned to working capital subjects in Part 1 is 10% to 15%. Expect 12 to 18 questions.

The approach is microanalysis. Managerial finance requires an applied, not a conceptual, approach and thus provides usable, everyday tools for managers of businesses and other entities. From a macro point of view, the efficient operation of individual firms promotes efficiency in our market system.

Working capital finance applies to short-term decisions, and capital structure finance to longer-term decisions. Working capital is defined as the excess of current assets over current liabilities.

The field of finance has evolved from a discipline with a descriptive approach to the analysis of the formation of firms (mergers, consolidations, etc.) and the contraction of firms (e.g., liquidations, reorganizations, etc.) to the current quantitative orientation. Managerial finance applies to both investing (left side of the balance sheet) and financing (right side of the balance sheet) decisions made by corporate managers. In addition to the investing and financing decisions that determine profitability, managers must resolve solvency issues through working capital management and prudent long-term financing.

This study unit begins with a discussion of the objectives of the firm that is also pertinent to capital structure finance.

A. Financial Management

1. The objective of the firm is to maximize the shareholders' wealth in the long term, i.e., to maximize the price per share of common stock. The market price of the stock is the result of the firm's investment and financing decisions within the context of legal and ethical bounds, including those relating to
   a. Product safety
   b. Minority hiring
   c. Pollution control
   d. Fair competition
   e. Fair advertising
2. Other objectives of the firm are less beneficial to shareholders than maximization of the per-share price of stock.
   a. Profit maximization is not the optimal objective when it is not consistent with the maximization of stock price. For example,
      1) Investing in high-risk projects may increase profits but not be commensurate with the additional risk borne by the firm.
      2) Increasing equity investment (resulting in a lower return on equity) will lower EPS and the stock price.
      3) Delaying needed maintenance may increase accounting profits, but damage to capital may more than offset this increase in short-term profit.
   b. Sales maximization is a nonoptimal objective because it does not maximize shareholders' wealth.
      1) A firm wants to increase sales only when the marginal revenue from the sale is greater than (or equal to) the marginal cost of the sale. Only at this output (sales) level is shareholders' wealth maximized.
   c. Social responsibility is an important issue, but if it were the only objective of the firm, the firm's existence would be short.
      1) However, some mutual funds invest only in socially responsible firms. Consequently, social responsibility can increase the demand for a corporation's stocks and bonds and thus increase shareholder wealth.
3. Management must make investment decisions, i.e., obtain a proper mix of productive assets, and obtain financing of these assets with the objective of maximizing shareholders' wealth.
   a. This is a dynamic process over time and requires adjusting to changes in the factors of production and finished-goods markets.
   b. It is a multifaceted process because of the large number of markets in which most businesses deal.
      1) The interrelationships among these many markets are complex.

4. The investing and financing decisions are not independent.
   a. The amount and composition of assets are directly related to the amount and composition of financing.
      1) Investing decisions are not independent of financing decisions.
   b. Given current and expected industry and overall economic conditions, the resulting mix of assets, liabilities, and capital determines the business risk.
      1) Managerial decisions and their outcomes are related to and dependent on many "outside" (**exogenous**) variables:
         a) Technological developments
         b) Weather
         c) National fiscal policies
         d) National monetary policies
         e) International relations and their effect on particular industries
         f) Competitors' actions (may not be exogenous if they are affected by the company's decisions)
5. **Taxes** (federal, state, local, and foreign) are an important consideration because they are frequently 25% to 50% of all costs.
   a. They include income, use, excise, property, legal document, payroll, and others.
   b. Thus, governmental services (national defense, fire, police, etc.) are an important and costly factor of production.
   c. Tax planning is very important in investment and financing decisions.
      1) Investment tax credits have at times provided direct reduction of taxes when assets were purchased for use in the business.
         a) The net effect is to decrease the cost of the asset.
         b) The amount of the credit and limitations on the tax credit on used equipment affect investment decisions.
         c) Investment tax credit is currently available for solar and geothermal property (business energy credit), for rehabilitation of historic structures, and for certain reforestation property.
      2) Accelerated depreciation is permitted on many types of business assets.
         a) Accordingly, in the early periods of an asset's life, depreciation is higher, taxable income is lower, and the rate of return on investment is higher.
      3) Corporate capital gains are taxed at regular rates, and the capital gains of individuals are taxed at a maximum rate of 28%.
      4) Special loss carryforward and carryback rules permit businesses to deduct net operating losses incurred in one period against income earned in other periods.

5) A dividends-received deduction makes tax free 70% to 100% of dividends received by one company from investments in the stock of another company.

   a) This prevents or reduces double taxation.

   b) It also encourages (does not discourage) one company to invest in the stock of another company.

6) Interest is a tax-deductible expense of the debtor company.

   a) But dividends on common or preferred stock are not deductible by the issuer.

d. Federal tax policy is fiscal policy that affects the overall economy, which in turn affects production and the finished-goods markets in which the company deals.

e. Government monetary policy determines the availability and cost of capital, which affect financing (and in turn, investing) decisions.

   1) Monetary policy also affects overall economic activity.

6. **Growth and expansion** are important to attract both personnel and capital. Creative people want an opportunity for advancement and challenge, and investors place a premium on growth companies.

   a. Growth can be either internal or external.

      1) Internal growth arises from earnings retained in the business.
      2) External growth occurs through issuance of equity or debt securities.

   b. Expansion occurs through

      1) New product lines

      2) Purchase of other companies

      3) Investments in other companies

      4) **Franchising**. According to the FASB in SFAS 45, *Accounting for Franchise Fee Revenue*, a franchise is a written business agreement that meets the following criteria:

         a) *The relation between the franchisor and franchisee is contractual, and an agreement, confirming the rights and responsibilities of each party, is in force for a specified period.*

         b) *The purpose is the distribution of a product or service, or an entire business concept, within a particular market area.*

         c) *Both the franchisor and the franchisee contribute resources for establishing and maintaining the franchise. The franchisor's contribution may be a trademark, a company reputation, products, procedures, manpower, equipment, or a process. The franchisee usually contributes operating capital as well as the managerial and operational resources required for opening and continuing the franchised outlet.*

         d) *The franchise agreement outlines and describes the specific marketing practices to be followed, specifies the contribution of each party to the operation of the business, and sets forth certain operating procedures that both parties agree to comply with.*

e) *The establishment of the franchised outlet creates a business entity that will, in most cases, require and support the full-time business activity of the franchisee. (There are numerous other contractual distribution arrangements in which a local businessperson becomes the "authorized distributor" or "representative" for the sale of a particular good or service, along with the many others, but such a sale usually represents only a portion of the person's total business.)*

f) *Both the franchisee and the franchisor have a common public identity. This identity is achieved most often through the use of common trade names or trademarks and is frequently reinforced through advertising programs designed to promote the recognition and acceptance of the common identity within the franchisee's market area.*

g) *The payment of an initial franchise fee or a continuing royalty fee is not a necessary criterion for an agreement to be considered a franchise agreement.*

c. Legal perspective on business combinations

1) **Merger**. Only one of the combining companies survives. The assets and liabilities of the other combining companies are merged into the surviving company.

2) **Consolidation**. A new company is organized to take over the combining companies.

3) **Acquisition**. One company exchanges its stock for the majority of the outstanding stock of another company, and both companies continue to operate separately.

d. The tax perspective on growth is to consider whether a business combination is a tax-free or a taxable event.

1) Certain exchanges of stock are tax-free exchanges, which permit the owners of one company to exchange their stock for the stock of the purchaser without paying taxes.

2) Inheritance-tax problems of owners force the sale of many closely held businesses.

e. The accounting perspective on growth must consider the type of accounting to be used for acquisition-type combinations -- either purchase or pooling accounting.

1) **Purchase accounting**. The acquisition is considered to be a purchase of net assets, and the assets and liabilities of the purchased company are recorded at their fair value on the consolidated books, usually resulting in increased depreciation charges.

a) The book value of most assets is usually less than fair value because of inflation and accounting depreciation policies.

b) The tax issues that arise when a combination is accounted for as a purchase, e.g., whether to file a consolidated return, the determination of tax bases and book values, and whether the event is taxable, are beyond the scope of this book.

2) **Pooling accounting**. The acquisition is considered to be a combining of ownership interests, and the assets of the combining companies retain their old book values.
   a) The result is usually a higher accounting income under the pooling method.
   b) Depreciation remains the same for tax purposes.

f. The financial perspective on growth is the most important, encompassing all the previously listed perspectives; the legal, tax, and accounting perspectives all have economic impact.
   1) Additional factors determining the terms of business combinations
      a) Earnings levels and growth rates
      b) Sales levels and growth rates
      c) Dividends
      d) Market values
      e) Book values
      f) Net current assets
   2) The exchanges of stock in business combinations involving public companies often result in a greater market value than the sum of the market values of the individual companies.
      a) Qualitative considerations not reflected in the historical financial data may operate to create a synergistic effect.
         i) For example, a firm needing stronger management expertise, a better distribution network, or a research and development capacity may seek a complementary merger partner.

g. **Holding companies** invest in the stock of other operating companies.
   1) The acquisition method of business combination is pertinent.
   2) Holding-company pyramiding results in control of assets with a very small percentage of ownership.
      a) The potential profits (and losses) are high.
   3) Advantages
      a) Control can often be obtained with small percentages of total stock ownership if there are no other large shareholders.
      b) Risk is isolated. If one investee has problems, it can be sold.
      c) Approval of the investment does not require the approval of shareholders or the investee's board of directors.
         i) The stock may be purchased in public markets or directly from current shareholders.
      d) Alternatively, a **tender offer** may be made to the shareholders of the potential investee with or without the approval of the potential investee's management.
         i) If the potential investee's management does not cooperate, the potential investor can advertise the offer, e.g., in the *Wall Street Journal*.

ii) A tender offer asks shareholders to tender their shares for a specified price, subject to a certain number of shares being tendered.

e) If a question of antitrust arises, liquidating a stock investment is easier than liquidating an internal operating division.

4) Disadvantage

a) If the entity meets the criteria of a personal holding company (PHC), undistributed PHC income is subject to a 39.6% tax rate. A company is a PHC if five or fewer shareholders own 50% or more of the shares and 60% or more of the adjusted ordinary gross income is PHC income (essentially, passive income). However, certain organizations are exempt from treatment as PHCs, e.g., S corporations, banks, and insurance companies.

h. There are two methods of accounting for stock investments.

1) **Equity method**. The investor must recognize the investor's share of investee income as the investee reports the income, that is, on the accrual basis.

a) Stock investments that constitute between 20% and 50% of the investee's outstanding stock are accounted for by the equity method.

b) A 20%-to-50% interest is presumed to permit substantial influence over the investee by the investor.

c) Excess of investee cost over investee book value must be amortized as an expense by the investor.

i) EXAMPLE: If 25% of a company with $7,000,000 in assets and $3,000,000 in liabilities is purchased for $1,500,000, the excess of cost over book value is $500,000. The book value of the entire company is $4,000,000 ($7,000,000 of assets – $3,000,000 of liabilities). Because 25% of $4,000,000 was purchased for $1,500,000, the excess is $500,000.

- The $500,000 must be attributed to specific assets and amortized over the estimated lives of those assets or on a straight-line basis as goodwill over a period not to exceed 40 years.
- In either case, the journal entry to record the amortization is

Investment income	XXX	
Investment in investee		XXX

2) **Cost method**. The investor reports income only when cash dividends are received from the investee.

a) The cost method accounts for investee earnings on the cash basis, that is, when received.

7. Business **contraction and liquidation** are the final stages of a corporation's life.
   a. Corporations can be perpetual, in contrast to partnerships (which terminate with the death, bankruptcy, etc., of a partner).
   b. As product demand, available supplies, etc., decline or the rate of growth in business activity declines, the business may
      1) Retrench and decline in size, although employee and capital retention may be difficult
         a) One form of contraction is **divestiture**. The types of divestiture are sale of a subunit to another company, sale of a subunit to the subunit's management, piecemeal liquidation of the subunit's assets, and a **spin-off**. This last form of divestiture is characterized by establishing a new and separate entity and transferring its newly issued stock to the shareholders of the original company.
      2) Be sold
      3) File for bankruptcy, for example, because it is unable to meet current obligations
         a) A creditor can file a petition forcing the insolvent corporation into **bankruptcy**, or the insolvent corporation can file a voluntary petition admitting itself into Chapter 7 bankruptcy.
         b) Assets are marshaled and sold by a **trustee in bankruptcy**, who is appointed by the court. Creditors are paid in statutory order of priority.
      4) Choose an alternative to bankruptcy liquidation, such as
         a) **Chapter 11 reorganization**, under which finances are restructured so the debtor may continue to operate and provide jobs, pay creditors, etc.
         b) **Compositions** with creditors, under which creditors get together voluntarily with the debtor and adjust the amount and timing of receivables
8. Working capital finance concerns the optimal level, mix, and use of current assets and current liabilities. The objective is to minimize the cost of maintaining liquidity while guarding against the possibility of technical insolvency. **Working capital** equals current assets minus current liabilities.
   a. A company that adopts a conservative working capital policy seeks to minimize liquidity risk by increasing working capital. The result is that the company forgoes the potentially higher returns available from using the additional working capital to acquire long-term assets.
   b. An aggressive policy reduces the current ratio and accepts a higher risk of short-term cash flow problems.

9. Financial Ratios to Evaluate Working Capital Management

a. **Ratio analysis** is a means of evaluating the financing and investing decisions of a business. Common ratios may be categorized as follows:

1) Solvency ratios measure the firm's ability to meet short-term obligations.
2) Activity ratios measure how effectively the firm is using its resources.
3) Leverage ratios measure the extent of debt financing.
4) Profitability ratios measure the firm's earning power.
5) Per-share ratios include EPS, yield, and book value ratios.

NOTE: Solvency and activity ratios are relevant to working capital finance. Leverage, profitability, and per-share data are relevant to capital structure finance.

b. Ratio analysis is based on norms and trends.

1) Normal or average ratios are computable for broad industrial categories.
2) Ratios for individual firms can be compared with those of competitors.
3) Changes in ratios through time provide insight about the future.
   a) Comparisons of trends in ratios of competitors are also useful.
4) Benchmarks have evolved concerning ratios.

c. **Solvency ratios** measure the short-term viability of the business, i.e., the firm's ability to continue in the short term by paying its obligations.

1) The **current ratio** equals current assets divided by current liabilities.
   a) $$\frac{\textit{Current assets}}{\textit{Current liabilities}}$$
   b) The most commonly used measure of near-term solvency, it relates current assets to the claims of short-term creditors.
   c) Benchmark: Current ratio should not be less than 2.0.
      i) Companies with an aggressive financing policy will have a low current ratio.
      ii) Conservative financing policies result in a higher current ratio.
2) The **acid test or quick ratio** equals cash, net receivables, and marketable securities divided by current liabilities.
   a) $$\frac{\textit{Cash} + \textit{Net receivables} + \textit{Marketable securities}}{\textit{Current liabilities}}$$
   b) It measures the firm's ability to pay its short-term debts from its most liquid assets.
   c) Benchmark: Quick ratio should be greater than 1.0.
      i) Liquidity is a trade-off for profitability. Liquid investments usually do not provide as high a return as productive assets.
3) **Working capital** equals current assets minus current liabilities.
   a) *Current assets – Current liabilities*
   b) It does not facilitate comparisons because it measures an absolute difference.

d. **Activity ratios** measure the firm's use of assets to generate revenue and income.

1) The **inventory turnover ratio** equals cost of sales divided by average inventories.

a) $\frac{\textit{Cost of sales}}{\textit{Average inventory}}$

b) A high turnover implies that the firm does not hold excessive stocks of inventories that are unproductive and lessen the firm's profitability.

c) A high turnover also implies that the inventory is truly marketable and does not contain obsolete goods.

d) An average inventory figure should be used.

i) If average annual inventory is cyclical, a monthly average should be used.

2) The **number of days of inventory** equals the number of days in the year divided by the inventory turnover ratio

a) $\frac{\text{365, 360, } \textit{or} \text{ 300}}{\textit{Inventory turnover}}$

b) It measures the average number of days inventory is held before sale.

i) It reflects the efficiency of inventory management.

c) The number of days in a year may be 365, 360 (a banker's year), or 300 (number of business days).

d) The lower the number of days, the better

3) The **receivables turnover ratio** equals net credit sales divided by average accounts receivable (but with net sales often used because of unavailability of credit sales data).

a) $\frac{\textit{Net credit sales}}{\textit{Average accounts receivable}}$

b) It indicates the efficiency of accounts receivable collection.

4) The **number of days of receivables** equals the number of days in the year divided by the receivables turnover ratio.

a) $\frac{\text{365, 360, } \textit{or} \text{ 300}}{\textit{Receivables turnover}}$

b) It is the average number of days to collect a receivable (collection period).

c) It may also be computed as average accounts receivable divided by average daily sales.

i) Average daily sales are net credit sales divided by the number of days in a year.

d) This ratio can be compared with the seller's credit terms to determine whether most customers are paying on time.

5) The **operating cycle** equals number of days of inventory plus number of days of receivables.

a) *Number of days of inventory + Number of days of receivables*

b) The operating cycle represents the time between the acquisition of inventory and the receipt of cash from sales of inventory.

10. Stop and review! You have completed the outline for this subunit. Study multiple-choice questions 1 through 12 beginning on page 192.

B. Cash Management

1. The **cash budget** details projected receipts and disbursements (inflows and outflows).

a. It is based on the projected sales and credit terms, collection percentages, and estimated purchases and payment terms.

b. Cash outflows are budgeted based on the level of sales.

c. Cash budgeting is an ongoing, cumulative activity.

1) One always begins with a beginning balance.
2) Budgets must be for a specified period of time.

a) The units of time must be short enough to assure that all cash payments can be met.

2. Cash is held for three reasons:

a. As a **medium of exchange**. Cash is still needed for some business transactions.

b. As a **precautionary measure**. Cash or a money-market fund can be held for emergencies. Normally, investment in high-grade, short-term securities is a better alternative to holding cash.

1) Years ago, in face of cash shortages, money was literally held, as a precaution against bank closings.

2) Today, if the banks fail, paper money will be worthless; thus, there is no precautionary reason to hoard U.S. paper dollars.

c. For **speculation**. Cash should be held only during deflationary periods when it becomes worth more. In periods of inflation, near-cash items should be held rather than cash itself.

1) If there are foreseeable future cash needs (e.g., new product lines, purchase of assets up for quick sale at low prices, etc.), money should be held as near money.

3. Cash inflows should be expedited.

a. Invoices should be mailed promptly.

b. Credit terms must be competitive but geared to encourage prompt payment.

1) See also Receivables Management on page 186.

c. A **lockbox system** may be used to expedite the receipt of funds. A company maintains mailboxes, often in numerous locations around the country, to which customers send payments. A bank checks these mailboxes several times a day, and funds received are immediately deposited to the company's account without first being processed by the company's accounting system, thereby hastening availability of the funds. In addition, having several lockboxes throughout the country reduces the time a payment is in the postal system.

1) **Concentration banking** may be useful in this context. Regional concentration banks may serve as centers for the transfer of lockbox receipts. A disbursement account at the regional center will then expedite the use of the receipts for payments in that region. Such use might be delayed if all receipts were transmitted to a national central bank.

d. Transfer of monies by wire expedites cash management.

e. **Electronic Data Interchange (EDI)** is the communication of electronic documents directly from one computer to another. **Electronic funds transfer (EFT)** and customer debit cards are applications of EDI that expedite cash inflows.

f. **Automated clearing houses (ACHs)** are electronic networks that facilitate the reading of data among banks. The 32 regional ACH associations guarantee 1-day clearing of checks. Except for the New York ACH, they are operated by the Federal Reserve.

4. Slowing cash disbursements increases available cash.

a. Payment beyond normal credit terms, however, creates vendor ill will and may incur interest charges.

b. Payments should be made within discount periods if the cost of not taking a discount exceeds the firm's cost of capital. The cost of not taking a discount (not considering compounding effects) is approximately

1) $$\frac{360}{(\textit{Total pay period} - \textit{Discount period})} \times \frac{\textit{Discount \%}}{(100\% - \textit{Discount \%})}$$

2) 2/10, net 30 means the total payment period is 30 days and the discount period is 10 days. The discount is 2%.

3) For example, 2/10, net 30 results in the following calculation:

$$(360 \div 20) \times (2 \div 98) = 36.7\% \textit{ annualized interest}$$

4) A more accurate calculation of the cost of not taking discounts considers the effects of compounding. In the example above, annualizing this cost means that 18 payments are deemed to occur during the year. The annual effective rate is

$$\textit{Rate} = [1.0 + (2 \div 98)]^{18} - 1.0 = 43.8\%$$

c. Payment by **draft** (a three-party instrument in which the drawer orders the drawee to pay money to the payee) is a means of slowing cash outflows. A check is the most common draft. **Check float** arises from the delay between an expenditure or receipt by check and the clearing of the check.

1) The effect is an interest-free loan to the payor.

2) Accordingly, companies attempt to maximize **disbursements float** (checks written but not yet deducted from the bank balance) and minimize **collections float** (checks received but not yet credited).

d. When **compensating balances** are negotiated with banks, use of average rather than absolute compensating balances frees most of the compensating balance as a contingency fund.

1) The flexible compensating balance can be used as a cushion for the days when cash demands are greatest and deposits fail to materialize.

2) The effective interest rate on loans requiring compensating balances equals total interest cost divided by total principal.

a) $\dfrac{\textit{Total interest cost}}{\textit{Total principal}}$

b) Total principal is reduced by the account's ordinary balance, and total interest cost is reduced by the amount of interest that the company would earn on its ordinary balance.

e. **Zero-balancing checking accounts** are offered by some banks. The account balance is maintained at zero until a check comes in. The resulting overdraft is covered by a transfer from an account earning a high rate of interest.

1) The disadvantage is that the bank may charge a fee for this service.

5. The amount of cash to keep on hand should be determined by cost-benefit analysis.

a. The reduction in average cash times the interest rate (cost of capital or investment yield rate) is the benefit.

b. Costs of having insufficient cash include incremental personnel cost, lost discounts, and lost vendor goodwill.

c. The **economic order quantity (EOQ)** model is applicable to cash management.

1) It can be stated in terms of the following assumptions:

a) A known demand for cash

b) A given carrying (interest) cost

c) The flat amount (cost) of converting other assets to cash, such as the broker's fee for sale of marketable securities (assumed to be constant regardless of the transaction size)

6. A firm's excess cash should be placed in an investment with a high return and little risk, such as those listed below.

a. **Treasury bills** are short-term government debt securities guaranteed explicitly by the U.S. government and exempt from state and local taxation. They are sold on a discount basis.

1) Obligations of federal agencies are not guaranteed by the U.S. government but only by the agency itself.

b. **Certificates of deposit** are a form of savings deposit that cannot be withdrawn before maturity without a high penalty. However, negotiable CDs are traded under the regulation of the Federal Reserve System.

c. **Money-market accounts** are similar to checking accounts but pay higher interest.

d. **High-grade commercial paper** consists of unsecured, short-term notes issued by large companies that are very good credit risks. However, commercial paper may yield a higher return than CDs because it is riskier.

7. Interest rate expectation theory states that long-term interest rates are usually a geometric average of expected future short-term interest rates.

8. Stop and review! You have completed the outline for this subunit. Study multiple-choice questions 13 through 31 beginning on page 196.

C. Marketable Securities Management

1. Short-term marketable securities (e.g., T-bills and CDs) are sometimes held as substitutes for cash but are more likely to be acquired as temporary investments.
   a. Most companies avoid large cash balances and prefer borrowing to meet short-term needs.
   b. As temporary investments, marketable securities may be purchased with maturities timed to meet seasonal fluctuations, to pay off a bond issue, to make tax payments, or otherwise to satisfy anticipated needs.
2. Marketable securities should be chosen with a view to the risk of default (**financial risk**).
   a. U.S. government securities are the least risky.
3. **Interest-rate risk** should be minimized given the reasons for holding marketable securities.
   a. Short-term securities are less likely to fluctuate in value because of changes in the general level of interest rates.
4. Changes in the general price level (inflation) determine the purchasing power of payments on investments (principal and interest) and thus the types of securities chosen and the rates charged.
5. The degree of marketability of a security determines its **liquidity**, that is, the ability to resell at the quoted market price.
6. The firm's tax position will influence its choice of securities; for example, a firm with net loss carryforwards may prefer a higher-yielding taxable security to a tax-exempt municipal bond.
7. Short-term marketable securities are usually chosen for reasons that make high-yield, high-risk investments unattractive. Hence, a higher return may be forgone in exchange for greater safety.
   a. Thus, speculative tactics, such as selling short (borrowing and selling securities in the expectation that their price will decline by the time they must be replaced) and margin trading (borrowing from a broker to buy securities) are avoided.
8. For typical short-term marketable securities, see Short-Term Credit on page 189.
9. Stop and review! You have completed the outline for this subunit. Study multiple-choice questions 32 through 34 beginning on page 202.

D. Receivables Management

1. The objective of managing accounts receivable is to have both the optimal amount of receivables outstanding and the optimal amount of bad debts.
   a. This balance requires a trade-off between the benefits of credit sales, such as more sales, and the costs of accounts receivable, e.g., collection, interest, and bad debt costs.
   b. Thus, a company should extend credit until the marginal benefit (profit) is zero (considering opportunity costs of alternative investments).

2. Credit terms, collection policies, etc., are frequently determined by competitors. A company must match such inducements to make sales.
3. The objective of receivables management is to maximize the accounts receivable turnover ratio, that is, to shorten the average time receivables are held.
   a. The **accounts receivable turnover ratio** equals net credit sales divided by average accounts receivable
   b. A common analytical tool is an **aging schedule** developed from a company's accounts receivable ledger. It stratifies the accounts depending on how long they have been outstanding.
   c. The **number of days of receivables** equals the number of days in the year (365, 360, or 300) divided by the receivables turnover ratio.
      1) It is the average number of days to collect a receivable (collection period).
      2) It may also be computed as average accounts receivable divided by average daily sales.
         a) Average daily sales are net credit sales divided by the number of days in a year.
      3) This ratio can be compared with the seller's credit terms to determine whether most customers are paying on time.
   d. **Average gross receivables** is calculated by multiplying average daily sales by the average collection period.
4. Other tools of credit such as bank charge cards should be evaluated as an alternative to charge accounts.
   a. Banks charge a fee equal to 3% to 5% of charge sales.
   b. Charge tickets can be deposited at the bank just like a customer check.
   c. Money is instantly available to the seller.
5. Stop and review! You have completed the outline for this subunit. Study multiple-choice questions 35 through 44 beginning on page 203.

E. Inventory Management

1. The firm should minimize total inventory costs, which include
   a. **Ordering costs** (costs of placing and receiving orders)
   b. **Carrying costs** (costs of storage, insurance, security, inventory taxes, depreciation or rent of facilities, interest, obsolescence and spoilage, and the opportunity cost of inventory investment)
   c. **Stockout costs**
2. Although the traditional approach to inventory management has been to minimize inventory and the related carrying costs, many companies find inventory a good hedge against inflation.
   a. Stockpiles of inventory also guarantee future availability of inventory.

b. The basic EOQ model minimizes the sum of ordering and carrying costs. Demand is assumed to be known and constant throughout the period. Order cost is assumed to be constant per order, and unit carrying costs are also assumed to be constant. Because demand is assumed to be deterministic, there are no stockout costs.

1) The EOQ is the square root of the quotient of twice the periodic demand multiplied by the order cost, divided by the periodic unit carrying cost.

$$X = \sqrt{\frac{2aD}{k}}$$

If: X = EOQ
a = Variable cost per purchase order
D = Periodic demand in units
k = Unit periodic carrying cost

2) EXAMPLE: Assume the periodic demand is uniform at 1,000 units. If the cost to place an order is \$4 and the cost to carry one unit in inventory for the period is \$2, then:

$$EOQ = \sqrt{\frac{2(\$4)(1{,}000)}{\$2}}$$

$$= \sqrt{4{,}000}$$

$$= 63.25 \textit{ units}$$

3. Inventory carrying costs can sometimes be transferred to either suppliers or customers.

a. If a manufacturer has good enough control of production schedules to know exactly when materials are needed, orders can be placed so that materials arrive no earlier than when actually needed.

1) This practice relies on a supplier who is willing to take the responsibility for storing the needed inventory and shipping it to arrive on time.

2) Suppliers are more willing to supply this type of service when they have many competitors who can also supply the materials.

3) **Just-in-time (JIT)** and **materials requirements planning (MRP)** are examples of systems that rely on suppliers to make deliveries just in time for the materials to enter production. The manufacturer has little or no investment in raw material inventories and minimizes inventory storage space.

b. Customers can sometimes be persuaded to carry large quantities of inventory by allowing them special quantity discounts or extended credit terms.

c. If customers are willing to accept long lead times, inventory can be manufactured to order to avoid storing large quantities.

d. Although these measures can reduce inventory carrying costs, additional costs might be incurred by adopting them.

1) Stockout costs may increase because customers are not always willing to wait for goods to be produced.

2) Production shutdowns and additional shipping costs may also keep minimization of carrying costs from being cost effective.

4. Stop and review! You have completed the outline for this subunit. Study multiple-choice questions 45 through 53 beginning on page 206.

F. **Short-Term Credit**. Short-term credit is debt scheduled to be repaid within 1 year. A discussion of the main sources of this credit follows:

1. **Trade credit** is a spontaneous source of financing because it arises automatically as part of the purchase transaction. The terms of payment are set by suppliers.
2. **Commercial banks** lend money that appears on the balance sheet of the borrower as a note payable.
   a. **Maturity** is usually in less than a year, which requires the company to roll over the debt frequently if needed.
   b. The **promissory note** states the terms of the loan and repayment policy.
   c. **Compensating balances**. Banks may require a borrower to keep a certain percentage of the face value of the loan in his/her account, which raises the real rate of interest to the borrower.
   d. A **line of credit** is the maximum loan that a bank will lend the borrower in a certain period.
      1) EXAMPLE: On January 1, a bank official may tell Company X that it may borrow up to $100,000 in the coming year.
      2) This is the most practical form of financing for most small retail businesses.
   e. Cost of bank loans
      1) **Regular interest** formula $\frac{Interest}{Borrowed\ amount}$
      2) **Discounted interest** $\frac{Interest}{Borrowed\ amount\ -\ Interest}$
      3) **Installment loan** $\frac{Interest}{Average\ borrowed\ amount}$
   f. The **prime interest rate** is the rate charged by commercial banks to their best (the largest and financially strongest) business customers. It is traditionally the lowest rate charged by banks. However, in recent years, banks have been making loans at still lower rates in response to competition from the commercial paper market.
3. **Commercial paper** consists of short-term, unsecured, notes payable issued in large denominations ($100,000 or more) by large companies with high credit ratings to other companies and institutional investors, such as pension funds, banks, and insurance companies. Maturities of commercial paper are at most 270 days. No general secondary market exists for commercial paper. Commercial paper is a lower cost source of funds than bank loans. It is usually issued at below the prime rate.
   a. Advantages
      1) Provides broad and efficient distribution
      2) Provides a great amount of funds (at a given cost)
      3) Avoids costly financing arrangements
   b. Disadvantages
      1) Impersonal market
      2) Total amount of funds available limited to the excess liquidity of big corporations

4. **Factoring.** A factor purchases a company's accounts receivable and assumes the risk of collection. The company involved receives money immediately to reinvest in new inventories. The financing cost is usually high -- about two points or more above prime, plus a fee for collection.
   a. A company that uses a factor can eliminate its credit department and accounts receivable staff.
   b. Bad debts are eliminated.
   c. These reductions in costs can more than offset the fee charged by the factor.
   d. The factor can often operate more efficiently than its clients because of the specialized nature of its service.
   e. Before the advent of computers, factoring was often considered a last-resort source of financing used only when bankruptcy was close at hand. However, the factor's computerization of receivables means it can operate a receivables department more economically than most small manufacturers. Factoring is no longer viewed as an undesirable source of financing.
   f. EXAMPLE: A typical CMA question concerns the cost to the company of a proposed factoring agreement. Assume a factor charges a 2% fee plus an interest rate of 18% on all monies advanced to the company. Monthly sales are $100,000, and the factor advances 90% of the receivables submitted after deducting the 2% fee and the interest. Credit terms are net 60 days. What is the cost to the company of this arrangement?

Amount of receivables submitted	$100,000
Minus: 10% reserve	(10,000)
Minus: 2% factor's fee	(2,000)
Amount accruing to the company	$ 88,000
Minus: 18% interest for 60 days (on $88,000)	(2,640)
Amount to be received immediately	$ 85,360

      1) The company will also receive the $10,000 reserve at the end of the 60-day period if it has not been absorbed by sales returns and allowances. Thus, the total cost to the company to factor the sales for the month is $4,640 ($2,000 factor fee + interest of $2,640). Assuming that the factor has approved the customers' credit in advance, the seller will not absorb any bad debts.
      2) The above costs should be compared with the cost of operating a credit and collection department and also the cost of borrowing monies otherwise advanced by the factor.

5. Other types of short-term funds
   a. **Bankers' acceptances** are drafts drawn on deposits at a bank. The acceptance by the bank is a guarantee of payment at maturity.
   b. **Repurchase agreements** involve sales by a dealer in government securities who agrees to repurchase at a given time for a specific price. Maturities may be very short-term. This arrangement is in essence a secured loan.
   c. Loans secured by receivables (**pledging** receivables). A bank will often lend up to 80% of outstanding receivables.

d. **Money-market mutual funds** invest in portfolios of short-term securities.

e. **Warehouse financing** uses inventory as security for the loan. A third party, a public warehouse for example, holds the collateral and serves as the creditor's agent, and the creditor receives the warehouse receipts evidencing its rights in the collateral.

f. **Agency securities** are issued by government agencies (not the Treasury), such as the Federal Home Loan Banks and other agencies that provide credit to farmers, home buyers, etc. An example is the Federal National Mortgage Association (Fannie Mae), which issues mortgage-backed securities. Agency securities may be long or short term.

g. **Treasury bills** are short-term U.S. government obligations issued by the Treasury at a discount from their face value. A T-bill is highly liquid and nearly free of risk, and it is often held as a cash substitute.

h. **Treasury notes and bonds** are long-term investments, but issues near maturity are effectively short-term securities with high liquidity.

i. State and local governmental entities issue short-term securities exempt from taxation.

j. **Eurodollars** are time deposits in banks located abroad.

k. **Chattel mortgages** are loans secured by movable personal property (e.g., equipment or livestock).

l. **Floating liens** attach to property, such as inventory, the composition of which is constantly changing.

6. Stop and review! You have completed the outline for this subunit. Study multiple-choice questions 54 through 64 beginning on page 209.

MULTIPLE-CHOICE QUESTIONS

A. Financial Management

1. Net working capital is the difference between

A. Current assets and current liabilities.

B. Fixed assets and fixed liabilities.

C. Total assets and total liabilities.

D. Shareholders' investment and cash.

The correct answer is (A). *(CMA, adapted)*

REQUIRED: The definition of net working capital.

DISCUSSION: Net working capital is defined as the difference between current assets and current liabilities. Working capital is a measure of short-term solvency.

Answer (B) is incorrect because working capital refers to the difference between current assets and current liabilities; fixed assets are not a component. Answer (C) is incorrect because total assets and total liabilities are not components of working capital; only current items are included. Answer (D) is incorrect because shareholders' equity is not a component of working capital; only current items are included in the concept of working capital.

2. Determining the appropriate level of working capital for a firm requires

A. Changing the capital structure and dividend policy of the firm.

B. Maintaining short-term debt at the lowest possible level because it is generally more expensive than long-term debt.

C. Offsetting the benefit of current assets and current liabilities against the probability of technical insolvency.

D. Maintaining a high proportion of liquid assets to total assets in order to maximize the return on total investments.

The correct answer is (C). *(CMA, adapted)*

REQUIRED: The requirement for determining the appropriate level of working capital.

DISCUSSION: Working capital finance concerns the determination of the optimal level, mix, and use of current assets and current liabilities. The objective is to minimize the cost of maintaining liquidity, while guarding against the possibility of technical insolvency. Technical insolvency is defined as the inability to pay debts as they come due.

Answer (A) is incorrect because capital structure and dividends relate to capital structure finance, not working capital finance. Answer (B) is incorrect because short-term debt is usually less expensive than long-term debt. Answer (D) is incorrect because liquid assets do not ordinarily earn high returns relative to long-term assets, so holding the former will not maximize the return on total assets.

3. As a company becomes more conservative in its working capital policy, it would tend to have a(n)

A. Decrease in its acid-test ratio.

B. Increase in the ratio of current liabilities to noncurrent liabilities.

C. Increase in the ratio of current assets to units of output.

D. Increase in funds invested in common stock and a decrease in funds invested in marketable securities.

The correct answer is (C). *(CMA, adapted)*

REQUIRED: The effect of a more conservative working capital policy.

DISCUSSION: A conservative working capital policy minimizes liquidity risk by increasing working capital (current assets – current liabilities). The result is that the company forgoes the potentially higher returns available from using the additional working capital to acquire long-term assets. A conservative working capital policy is characterized by a higher current ratio (current assets ÷ current liabilities) and acid-test ratio (quick assets ÷ current liabilities). Thus, the company will increase current assets or decrease current liabilities. A conservative policy finances assets using long-term or permanent funds rather than short-term sources.

Answer (A) is incorrect because a decrease in the acid-test ratio suggests an aggressive policy. A conservative company wants a higher acid-test ratio, that is, more liquid assets relative to liabilities. Answer (B) is incorrect because a conservative company wants working capital to be financed from long-term sources. Answer (D) is incorrect because a conservative company seeks more liquid (marketable) investments.

4. All of the following statements in regard to working capital are correct except

A. Current liabilities are an important source of financing for many small firms.

B. Profitability varies inversely with liquidity.

C. The hedging approach to financing involves matching maturities of debt with specific financing needs.

D. Financing permanent inventory buildup with long-term debt is an example of an aggressive working capital policy.

The correct answer is (D). *(CMA, adapted)*

REQUIRED: The false statement about working capital.

DISCUSSION: Financing permanent inventory buildup, which is essentially a long-term investment, with long-term debt is a moderate or conservative working capital policy. An aggressive policy uses short-term, relatively low-cost debt to finance the inventory buildup. It focuses on high profitability potential, despite high risk and low liquidity. An aggressive policy reduces the current ratio and accepts a higher risk of short-term lack of liquidity. Financing inventory with long-term debt increases the current ratio and accepts higher borrowing costs in exchange for greater liquidity and lower risk.

Answer (A) is incorrect because current liabilities, e.g., trade credit, is a major source of funds for small firms. Answer (B) is incorrect because liquid investments tend to have low returns. Answer (C) is incorrect because matching of asset and liability maturities is a moderate policy that minimizes risk. The expectation is that cash flows from the assets will be available to meet obligations for the liabilities.

5. Which one of the following transactions would increase the current ratio and decrease net profit?

A. A federal income tax payment due from the previous year is paid.

B. A stock dividend is declared.

C. Uncollectible accounts receivable are written off against the allowance account.

D. Vacant land is sold for less than the net book value.

The correct answer is (D). *(CMA, adapted)*

REQUIRED: The transaction that would increase the current ratio and decrease net profit.

DISCUSSION: The current ratio is calculated by dividing current assets by current liabilities. Thus, any transaction that will either increase current assets or decrease current liabilities will increase the current ratio. Selling vacant land for less than its book value (at a loss) would increase current assets (cash) and decrease net profit.

Answer (A) is incorrect because paying the federal tax liability from the previous year has no effect on the current year's net profit. Answer (B) is incorrect because a stock dividend (debit retained earnings, credit common stock) has no impact on either the current ratio or net profit. Answer (C) is incorrect because writing off receivables against an allowance account does not change total current assets. The allowance account is a contra account in the current asset section of the balance sheet.

6. Which one of the following transactions does not change the current ratio and does not change the total current assets?

A. A cash advance is made to a divisional office.

B. A cash dividend is declared.

C. Short-term notes payable are retired with cash.

D. A fully depreciated asset is sold for cash.

The correct answer is (A). *(CMA, adapted)*

REQUIRED: The transaction not affecting the current ratio or total current assets.

DISCUSSION: The current ratio is calculated by dividing current assets by current liabilities. Thus, any transaction that changes current assets or current liabilities changes the current ratio. A cash advance to a divisional office does not change current assets because the cash (a current asset) will be replaced by a receivable (a current asset). Current liabilities are also unaffected, so the cash advance affects neither the current ratio nor total current assets.

Answer (B) is incorrect because the declaration of a cash dividend creates a current liability, which reduces the current ratio. Answer (C) is incorrect because retiring short-term notes with cash reduces current assets and current liabilities. Answer (D) is incorrect because selling a fully depreciated asset increases cash, a current asset.

7. During 1990, Mason Company's current assets increased by $120, current liabilities decreased by $50, and net working capital

A. Increased by $70.

B. Did not change.

C. Decreased by $170.

D. Increased by $170.

The correct answer is (D). *(CMA, adapted)*

REQUIRED: The effect on net working capital of an increase in current assets and a decrease in current liabilities.

DISCUSSION: Working capital is the excess of current assets over current liabilities. An increase in current assets or a decrease in current liabilities will increase working capital. Thus, net working capital increased by $170 ($120 + $50).

Answers (A), (B), and (C) are incorrect because net working capital increased by $170.

8. MFC Corporation has 100,000 shares of stock outstanding. Below is part of MFC's Statement of Financial Position for the last fiscal year.

MFC Corporation
Statement of Financial Position - Selected Items
December 31, 1996

Cash	$455,000
Accounts receivable	900,000
Inventory	650,000
Prepaid assets	45,000
Accrued liabilities	285,000
Accounts payable	550,000
Current portion, long-term notes payable	65,000

What is the maximum amount MFC can pay in cash dividends per share and maintain a minimum current ratio of 2 to 1? Assume that all accounts other than cash remain unchanged.

A. $2.05

B. $2.50

C. $3.35

D. $3.80

The correct answer is (B). *(CMA, adapted)*

REQUIRED: The maximum dividends consistent with a specified minimum current ratio.

DISCUSSION: Before the dividend, total current assets equal $2,050,000 ($455,000 cash + $900,000 receivables + $650,000 inventory + $45,000 prepaid assets). Current liabilities total $900,000 ($285,000 accrued liabilities + $550,000 accounts payable + $65,000 current portion of long-term debt). The payment of the cash dividend will not change current liabilities, so a current ratio of 2 to 1 requires that current assets be maintained at a minimum of $1,800,000 (2 x $900,000). Thus, cash can decrease by $250,000 ($2,050,000 – $1,800,000). The maximum per-share rate is $2.50 ($250,000 ÷ 100,000 shares).

Answer (A) is incorrect because $2.05 fails to include prepaid assets (prepaid expenses) as current assets. Answer (C) is incorrect because $3.35 fails to include the current portion of long-term debt as a current liability. Answer (D) is incorrect because $3.80 fails to consider prepaid assets as a current asset and the current portion of long-term debt as a current liability.

9. Spotech Co.'s budgeted sales and budgeted cost of sales for the coming year are $212,000,000 and $132,500,000, respectively. Short-term interest rates are expected to average 5%. If Spotech could increase inventory turnover from its current 8.0 times per year to 10.0 times per year, its expected cost savings in the current year would be

A. $165,625

B. $0

C. $3,312,500

D. $828,125

The correct answer is (A). *(CMA, adapted)*

REQUIRED: The expected cost savings from increasing the inventory turnover rate from eight to ten times per year.

DISCUSSION: If cost of sales is $132,500,000, and the inventory turnover rate is 8.0 times per year, the average inventory is $16,562,500 ($132,500,000 ÷ 8). If the turnover increases to 10.0 times annually, the average inventory will decline to $13,250,000 ($132,500,000 ÷ 10), a decrease of $3,312,500. At a 5% rate, reducing working capital by $3,312,500 will save the company $165,625 (.05 x $3,312,500).

Answer (B) is incorrect because the faster turnover reduces working capital and releases funds for other uses. Answer (C) is incorrect because $3,312,500 is the decrease in average inventory. Answer (D) is incorrect because $828,125 is 5% of $16,562,500.

10. A change in credit policy has caused an increase in sales, an increase in discounts taken, a reduction in the investment in accounts receivable, and a reduction in the number of doubtful accounts. Based upon this information, we know that

A. Net profit has increased.

B. The average collection period has decreased.

C. Gross profit has declined.

D. The size of the discount offered has decreased.

The correct answer is (B). *(CMA, adapted)*

REQUIRED: The true statement about a change in credit policy that has resulted in greater sales and a reduction in accounts receivable.

DISCUSSION: An increase in discounts taken accompanied by declines in receivables balances and doubtful accounts all indicate that collections on the increased sales have been accelerated. Accordingly, the average collection period must have declined. The average collection period is a ratio calculated by dividing the number of days in a year (365) by the receivable turnover. Thus, the higher the turnover, the shorter the average collection period. The turnover increases when either sales (the numerator) increase, or receivables (the denominator) decrease. Accomplishing both higher sales and a lower receivables increases the turnover and results in a shorter collection period.

Answers (A) and (C) are incorrect because no statement can be made with respect to profits without knowing costs. Answer (D) is incorrect because the discount may have been increased, which has led to quicker payments.

11. Which one of the following statements is most correct if a seller extends credit to a purchaser for a period of time longer than the purchaser's operating cycle? The seller

A. Will have a lower level of accounts receivable than those companies whose credit period is shorter than the purchaser's operating cycle.

B. Is, in effect, financing more than just the purchaser's inventory needs.

C. Can be certain that the purchaser will be able to convert the inventory into cash before payment is due.

D. Has no need for a stated discount rate or credit period.

The correct answer is (B). *(CMA, adapted)*

REQUIRED: The true statement about extending credit for a period longer than the purchaser's operating cycle.

DISCUSSION: The normal operating cycle is defined as the period from the acquisition of inventory to the collection of the account receivable. If trade credit is for a period longer than the normal operating cycle, the seller must therefore be financing more than just the purchase of inventory.

Answer (A) is incorrect because a seller that extends long-term credit will have a higher level of receivables than a firm with a shorter credit period. Answer (C) is incorrect because the seller is not guaranteed that a purchaser will resell the merchandise. Answer (D) is incorrect because offering a discount may accelerate payment.

12. Clauson Inc. grants credit terms of 1/15, net 30 and projects gross sales for next year of $2,000,000. The credit manager estimates that 40% of their customers pay on the discount date, 40% on the net due date, and 20% pay 15 days after the net due date. Assuming uniform sales and a 360-day year, what is the projected days' sales outstanding (rounded to the nearest whole day)?

A. 20 days.

B. 24 days.

C. 27 days.

D. 30 days.

The correct answer is (C). *(CMA, adapted)*

REQUIRED: The projected days' sales outstanding.

DISCUSSION: Given that 40% of sales will be collected on the 15th day, 40% on the 30th day, and 20% on the 45th day, the days' sales outstanding can be determined by weighting the collection period for each group of receivables by its collection percentage. Hence, the projected days' sales outstanding equal 27 days [(40% x 15) + (40% x 30) + (20% x 45)].

Answer (A) is incorrect because average receivables are outstanding for much more than 20 days. Answer (B) is incorrect because 24 days assumes 40% of receivables are collected after 15 days and 60% after 30 days. Answer (D) is incorrect because more receivables are collected on the 15th day than on the 45th day; thus, the average must be less than 30 days.

B. Cash Management

13. The most direct way to prepare a cash budget for a manufacturing firm is to include

A. Projected sales, credit terms, and net income.

B. Projected net income, depreciation, and goodwill amortization.

C. Projected purchases, percentages of purchases paid, and net income.

D. Projected sales and purchases, percentages of collections, and terms of payments.

The correct answer is (D). *(CMA, adapted)*

REQUIRED: The most direct way of preparing a cash budget for a manufacturing firm.

DISCUSSION: The most direct way of preparing a cash budget requires incorporation of sales projections and credit terms, collection percentages, estimated purchases and payment terms, and other cash receipts and disbursements. In other words, preparation of the cash budget requires consideration of both inflows and outflows.

Answers (A) and (B) are incorrect because net income includes noncash elements, e.g., goodwill amortization and depreciation. Answer (C) is incorrect because collection percentages must be considered, and net income includes noncash elements.

14. RLF Corporation had income before taxes of $60,000 for the year 1997. Included in this amount was depreciation of $5,000, a charge of $6,000 for the amortization of bond discounts, and $4,000 for interest expense. The estimated cash flow for the period is

A. $60,000

B. $66,000

C. $49,000

D. $71,000

The correct answer is (D). *(CMA, adapted)*

REQUIRED: The estimated cash flow for the period.

DISCUSSION: To determine cash flow for the period, all noncash expenses should be added back to net income. Adding the $5,000 of depreciation and the $6,000 of discount amortization to the $60,000 of net income produces a cash flow of $71,000.

Answer (A) is incorrect because the cash flow for the period is greater than net income given noncash expenses in the form of depreciation and bond discount amortization. Answer (B) is incorrect because $66,000 does not reflect the noncash expense for depreciation. Answer (C) is incorrect because the $5,000 of depreciation and the $6,000 for amortization should be added back to, not subtracted from, income.

15. Shown below is a forecast of sales for Cooper Inc. for the first 4 months of 1998 (all amounts are in thousands of dollars).

	1998			
	January	February	March	April
Cash sales	$ 15	$ 24	$18	$14
Sales on credit	100	120	90	70

On average, 50% of credit sales are paid for in the month of sale, 30% in the month following the sale, and the remainder is paid 2 months after the month of sale. Assuming there are no bad debts, the expected cash inflow for Cooper in March is

A. $138,000

B. $122,000

C. $119,000

D. $108,000

The correct answer is (C). *(CMA, adapted)*

REQUIRED: The expected cash inflows for March.

DISCUSSION: Cash inflows for March would consist of 50% of March credit sales (50% x $90 = $45), plus 30% of February credit sales (30% x $120 = $36), plus 20% of January credit sales (20% x $100 = $20), plus cash sales for March of $18. Consequently, total collections equal $119,000.

Answer (A) is incorrect because $138,000 equals the sum of February credit sales and March cash sales. Answer (B) is incorrect because $122,000 equals 50% of January credit sales, 30% of February credit sales, 20% of March credit sales, and 100% of March cash sales. Answer (D) is incorrect because $108,000 is the total sales for March, not the total cash collections for March.

16. A firm has daily cash receipts of $100,000 and collection time of 2 days. A bank has offered to reduce the collection time on the firm's deposits by 2 days for a monthly fee of $500. If money market rates are expected to average 6% during the year, the net annual benefit (loss) from having this service is

A. $3,000

B. $12,000

C. $0

D. $6,000

The correct answer is (D). *(CMA, adapted)*

REQUIRED: The net annual benefit or loss.

DISCUSSION: If collection time is 2 days, and average daily receipts are $100,000, the average cash balance will increase by $200,000 if the bank's system is adopted. At a 6% interest rate, $200,000 will generate $12,000 of interest revenue annually. The $500 monthly charge by the bank will result in an annual expense of $6,000. Thus, the net annual benefit is $6,000 ($12,000 – $6,000).

Answer (A) is incorrect because $3,000 miscalculates the annual service charge. Answer (B) is incorrect because $12,000 fails to deduct the annual service charge from the interest earned. Answer (C) is incorrect because $0 results from figuring the interest earned for only one day, not two.

17. The treasury analyst for Garth Manufacturing has estimated the cash flows for the first half of next year (ignoring any short-term borrowings) as follows.

	Cash (millions)	
	Inflows	Outflows
January	$2	$1
February	2	4
March	2	5
April	2	3
May	4	2
June	5	3

Garth has a line of credit of up to $4 million on which it pays interest monthly at a rate of 1% of the amount utilized. Garth is expected to have a cash balance of $2 million on January 1 and no amount utilized on its line of credit. Assuming all cash flows occur at the end of the month, approximately how much will Garth pay in interest during the first half of the year?

A. Zero.

B. $61,000

C. $80,000

D. $132,000

The correct answer is (B). *(CMA, adapted)*

REQUIRED: The interest expense for six months.

DISCUSSION: The sum of the beginning balance and inflows exceeds the outflows for the first 2 months. At the end of March, however, Garth must use $2,000,000 of its line of credit ($2,000,000 beginning balance + $6,000,000 inflows – $10,000,000 outflows). Thus, interest for April is $20,000 (1% x $2,000,000). The net cash outflow for April (ignoring short-term borrowings) is $1,000,000 of an additional $1,000,000 of the line of credit. However, the $20,000 of interest for April must also be paid, so the amount of the line of credit used in May is $3,020,000 ($2,000,000 + $1,000,000 + $20,000). Interest for May is therefore $30,200 (1% x $3,020,000). Given the net cash inflow for May of $2,000,000 (again ignoring short-term borrowings) and the borrowing of $30,200 to pay the interest for May, the amount of the line of credit used in June is $1,050,200. Interest in June is $10,502 (1% x $1,050,200), and total interest is $60,702 ($20,000 + $30,200 + $10,502). Consequently, the closest answer is $61,000.

Answer (A) is incorrect because interest must be paid monthly when the credit line is used in April, May, and June. Answers (C) and (D) are incorrect because the company would repay the credit line at the end of months with a positive cash flow.

18. Kemple is a newly established janitorial firm, and the owner is deciding what type of checking account to open. Kemple is planning to keep a $500 minimum balance in the account for emergencies and plans to write roughly 80 checks per month. The bank charges $10 per month plus a $0.10 per check charge for a standard business checking account with no minimum balance. Kemple also has the option of a premium business checking account that requires a $2,500 minimum balance but has no monthly fees or per check charges. If Kemple's cost of funds is 10%, which account should Kemple choose?

A. Standard account, because the savings is $34 per year.

B. Premium account, because the savings is $34 per year.

C. Standard account, because the savings is $16 per year.

D. Premium account, because the savings is $16 per year.

The correct answer is (D). *(CMA, adapted)*

REQUIRED: The checking account that should be chosen.

DISCUSSION: The standard account will cost $10 per month plus $8 in check charges ($.10 x 80 checks), for a total of $18 per month or $216 per year. The premium account has no check charges, but it will require the depositor to maintain a balance of $2,000 more than desired. At a 10% cost of capital, the incremental $2,000 minimum deposit will cost $200 per year. Thus, the premium account should be selected because it is cheaper by $16 per year.

Answer (A) is incorrect because the relevant cost of the minimum premium account deposit is based on the $2,000 incremental deposit, not the full $2,500. Answers (B) and (C) are incorrect because the savings on the premium account is $16.

19. Newman Products has received proposals from several banks to establish a lockbox system to speed up receipts. Newman receives an average of 700 checks per day averaging $1,800 each, and its cost of short-term funds is 7% per year. Assuming that all proposals will produce equivalent processing results and using a 360-day year, which one of the following proposals is optimal for Newman?

A. A $0.50 fee per check.

B. A flat fee of $125,000 per year.

C. A fee of 0.03% of the amount collected.

D. A compensating balance of $1,750,000.

The correct answer is (D). *(CMA, adapted)*

REQUIRED: The optimal fee structure for a lockbox system.

DISCUSSION: Multiplying 700 checks times 360 days results in a total of 252,000 checks per year. Accordingly, under (A), total annual cost is $126,000 ($.50 x 252,000), which is less desirable than the $125,000 flat fee in (B). Given that the annual collections equal $453,600,000 ($1,800 x 700 x 360), (C) is also less desirable because the annual fee would be $136,080 (.03% x $453,600,000). The best option is therefore to maintain a compensating balance of $1,750,000 when the cost of funds is 7%, resulting in a total cost of $122,500 (.07 x $1,750,000).

Answer (A) is incorrect because the annual cost is $126,000. Answer (B) is incorrect because the annual cost is $125,000. Answer (C) is incorrect because the annual cost is $136,080.

20. Franklin Inc. is a medium-size manufacturer of toys that makes 25% of its sales to Mega Company, a major national discount retailing firm. Mega will be requiring Franklin and other suppliers to use Electronic Data Interchange (EDI) for inventory replenishment and trade payment transactions as opposed to the paper-based systems previously used. Franklin would consider all of the following to be advantages of using EDI in its dealings with Mega except

A. Access to Mega's inventory balances of Franklin's products.

B. Better status tracking of deliveries and payments.

C. Compatibility with Franklin's other procedures and systems.

D. Reduction in the payment float.

The correct answer is (C). *(CMA, adapted)*

REQUIRED: The item not an advantage of using EDI.

DISCUSSION: Electronic data interchange is the electronic transfer of documents between businesses. EDI was developed to enhance just-in-time (JIT) inventory management. Advantages include speed, reduction of clerical errors, and elimination of repetitive clerical tasks and their costs. Improved business relationships result because of the mutual benefits conferred by EDI. Accordingly, some organizations require EDI. However, EDI entails the exchange of common business data converted into standard message formats. Thus, two crucial requirements are that the participants agree on transaction formats and that translation software be developed to convert messages into a form understandable by other companies. Accordingly, establishing compatibility with Mega's procedures and systems will require Franklin to resolve issues regarding compatibility with its other procedures and systems.

Answer (A) is incorrect because access to Mega's inventory information permits better coordination of production and deliveries. Answer (B) is incorrect because EDI allows for instantaneous payment and notification of deliveries. Answer (D) is incorrect because EDI eliminates the float period when payment is by electronic funds transfer (EFT).

21. An automated clearinghouse (ACH) electronic transfer is a(n)

A. Electronic payment to a company's account at a concentration bank.

B. Check that must be immediately cleared by the Federal Reserve Bank.

C. Computer-generated deposit ticket verifying deposit of funds.

D. Check-like instrument drawn against the payor and not against the bank.

The correct answer is (A). *(CMA, adapted)*

REQUIRED: The definition of an automated clearinghouse (ACH) electronic transfer.

DISCUSSION: An ACH electronic funds transfer (EFT) is an electronic payment to a company's account at a concentration bank. A concentration bank is a large bank to which a company transfers funds from local depository banks. These local banks operate the company's lockboxes and thus serve as collection points. The transfer of funds to the concentration bank allows the company to take advantage of economies of scale in cash management. The use of an ACH facilitates concentration banking. ACHs are electronic networks operated by the Federal Reserve (except for the New York regional ACH association) that guarantee 1-day clearing.

Answer (B) is incorrect because a check is not involved in an EFT. Answer (C) is incorrect because an ACH transfer involves the actual transfer of funds electronically; it is not just a computer-generated document. Answer (D) is incorrect because an EFT is not a check-like instrument.

Questions 22 and 23 are based on the following information. CyberAge Outlet, a relatively new store, is a cafe that offers customers the opportunity to browse the Internet or play computer games at their tables while they drink coffee. The customer pays a fee based on the amount of time spent signed on to the computer. The store also sells books, tee-shirts, and computer accessories. CyberAge has been paying all of its bills on the last day of the payment period, thus forfeiting all supplier discounts. Shown below are data on CyberAge's two major vendors, including average monthly purchases and credit terms.

Vendor	Average Monthly Purchases	Credit Terms
Web Master	$25,000	2/10, net 30
Softidee	50,000	5/10, net 90

22. Assuming a 360-day year and that CyberAge continues paying on the last day of the credit period, the company's weighted-average annual interest rate for trade credit (ignoring the effects of compounding) for these two vendors is

A. 27.0%

B. 28.0%

C. 29.3%

D. 30.2%

The correct answer is (B). *(CMA, adapted)*

REQUIRED: The weighted-average annual interest rate.

DISCUSSION: If the company pays Web Master within 10 days, it will save $500 (2% x $25,000). Thus, the company is effectively paying $500 to retain $24,500 ($25,000 – $500) for 20 days (30 – 10). The annualized interest rate on this borrowing is 36.7346% [($500 ÷ $24,500) x (360 days ÷ 20 days)]. Similarly, the company is, in effect, paying Softidee $2,500 (5% x $50,000) to hold $47,500 ($50,000 – $2,500) for 80 days (90 – 10). The annualized rate on this borrowing is 23.6842% [($2,500 ÷ $47,500) x (360 days ÷ 80 days)]. The weighted average of these two rates based on average monthly purchases is 28.0% {[36.7346% x ($25,000 ÷ $75,000)] + [23.6842% x ($50,000 ÷ $75,000)]}. This calculation, however, understates the true cost of not taking the discount because it does not consider the effects of compounding.

Answer (A) is incorrect because 27.0% is based on gross purchases. Answer (C) is incorrect because 29.3% is an unweighted (simple) average based on gross purchases. Answer (D) is incorrect because 30.2% is an unweighted average of the two interest rates.

23. Should CyberAge use trade credit and continue paying at the end of the credit period?

A. Yes, if the cost of alternative short-term financing is less.

B. Yes, if the firm's weighted-average cost of capital is equal to its weighted-average cost of trade credit.

C. No, if the cost of alternative long-term financing is greater.

D. Yes, if the cost of alternative short-term financing is greater.

The correct answer is (D). *(CMA, adapted)*

REQUIRED: The true statement about the decision to use trade credit and pay at the end of the credit period.

DISCUSSION: The company is currently paying an annual rate of 28% (see previous question) to obtain trade credit and pay at the end of the credit period. This policy should be continued if trade credit is the only source of financing, or if other sources are available only at a higher rate.

Answer (A) is incorrect because the company should continue the current practice unless alternative short-term financing is available at a lower rate. Answer (B) is incorrect because the weighted-average cost of capital is usually a concern in capital budgeting and is not as important in the decision process as the marginal cost of capital. Furthermore, trade credit is just one element in the firm's financing structure. An optimal mix of financing sources may require that trade credit be obtained at less than the weighted-average cost of capital. Answer (C) is incorrect because the company should maintain its current practice if the cost of alternative long-term financing is higher.

24. Troy Toys is a retailer operating in several cities. The individual store managers deposit daily collections at a local bank in a noninterest-bearing checking account. Twice per week, the local bank issues a depository transfer check (DTC) to the central bank at headquarters. The controller of the company is considering using a wire transfer instead. The additional cost of each transfer would be $25; collections would be accelerated by 2 days; and the annual interest rate paid by the central bank is 7.2% (0.02% per day). At what amount of dollars transferred would it be economically feasible to use a wire transfer instead of the DTC? Assume a 350-day year.

A. It would never be economically feasible.

B. $125,000 or above.

C. Any amount greater than $173.

D. Any amount greater than $62,500.

The correct answer is (D). *(CMA, adapted)*

REQUIRED: The amount at which wire transfers are preferable.

DISCUSSION: Given a $25 fee and an interest rate of 0.02% per day for 2 days, the breakeven amount is $62,500 [$25 transfer fee ÷ (2 x .02% interest rate)]. Thus, the interest earned on a transfer of any amount greater than $62,500 would exceed the $25 fee.

Answer (A) is incorrect because the $25 transfer fee is covered by the interest on $62,500 for 2 days. Answer (B) is incorrect because $125,000 is required if collections are accelerated by only one day. Answer (C) is incorrect because the interest on $173 for 2 days is less than $.07.

25. A working capital technique that increases the payable float and therefore delays the outflow of cash is

A. Concentration banking.

B. A draft.

C. Electronic Data Interchange (EDI).

D. A lockbox system.

The correct answer is (B). *(CMA, adapted)*

REQUIRED: The working capital technique to increase the payable float and delay the outflow of cash.

DISCUSSION: Payment by draft, a three-party instrument in which the drawer orders the drawee to pay money to the payee, is a means of slowing cash outflows. A check is the most common type of draft. Check float arises from the delay between an expenditure and the clearing of the check through the banking system.

Answers (A) and (D) are incorrect because concentration banking, a lockbox system, and the use of a local post office box are techniques used to accelerate cash receipts. Answer (C) is incorrect because EDI is the communication of electronic documents directly from a computer in one entity to a computer in another entity. Thus, EDI expedites cash payments. The payee receives the money almost instantaneously.

26. Assume that each day a company writes and receives checks totaling $10,000. If it takes 5 days for the checks to clear and be deducted from the company's account, and only 4 days for the deposits to clear, what is the float?

A. $10,000

B. $0

C. $(10,000)

D. $50,000

The correct answer is (A). *(CMA, adapted)*

REQUIRED: The net float when checks clear more slowly than deposits.

DISCUSSION: The float period is the time between when a check is written and when it clears the payor's checking account. Check float results in an interest-free loan to the payor because of the delay between payment by check and its deduction from the bank account. If checks written require one more day to clear than checks received, the net float equals one day's receipts. The company will have free use of the money for one day. In this case, the amount is $10,000.

Answer (B) is incorrect because the company enjoys one day's net float because its checks clear more slowly than its deposits. Answer (C) is incorrect because the net float is positive. The company can write checks (up to $10,000) even when it has no money because the checks do not clear until a day after deposits clear. Answer (D) is incorrect because the net float represents the difference between when collections clear and when disbursements clear.

27. A compensating balance

A. Compensates a financial institution for services rendered by providing it with deposits of funds.

B. Is used to compensate for possible losses on a marketable securities portfolio.

C. Is a level of inventory held to compensate for variations in usage rate and lead time.

D. Is the amount of prepaid interest on a loan.

The correct answer is (A). *(CMA, adapted)*

REQUIRED: The true statement about compensating balances.

DISCUSSION: Banks sometimes require a borrower to keep a certain percentage of the face amount of a loan in a noninterest-bearing checking account. This requirement raises the effective rate of interest paid by the borrower. This greater rate compensates a bank for services provided and results in greater profitability for the financial institution. Funds kept as a compensating balance can often be withdrawn if a certain average balance is maintained.

Answer (B) is incorrect because, in financial accounting, a valuation allowance is used to reflect losses on marketable securities. Answer (C) is incorrect because safety stock is held for such purposes. Answer (D) is incorrect because interest deducted in advance is discount interest.

28. Hagar Company's bank requires a compensating balance of 20% on a $100,000 loan. If the stated interest on the loan is 7%, what is the effective cost of the loan?

A. 5.83%

B. 7.00%

C. 8.40%

D. 8.75%

The correct answer is (D). *(CMA, adapted)*

REQUIRED: The effective cost of a loan when a compensating balance is required.

DISCUSSION: Interest on the loan is $7,000 (7% x $100,000). Given that the borrower has to maintain a 20% compensating balance, only $80,000 [$100,000 – (20% x $100,000)] is available for use. Thus, the company is paying $7,000 for the use of $80,000 in funds at an effective cost of 8.75% ($7,000 ÷ $80,000).

Answer (A) is incorrect because the borrower has access to less, not more, than the face amount of the loan. Answer (B) is incorrect because the effective rate is higher than the contract rate as a result of the compensating balance requirement. Answer (C) is incorrect because 8.40% is 120% of the contract rate.

29. A company obtained a short-term bank loan of $250,000 at an annual interest rate of 6%. As a condition of the loan, the company is required to maintain a compensating balance of $50,000 in its checking account. The company's checking account earns interest at an annual rate of 2%. Ordinarily, the company maintains a balance of $25,000 in its checking account for transaction purposes. What is the effective interest rate of the loan?

A. 6.44%

B. 7.00%

C. 5.80%

D. 6.66%

The correct answer is (A). *(CMA, adapted)*

REQUIRED: The effective interest rate on a loan that requires a compensating balance of $25,000 above the company's normal working balance.

DISCUSSION: The $50,000 compensating balance requirement is partially satisfied by the company's practice of maintaining a $25,000 balance for transaction purposes. Thus, only $25,000 of the loan will not be available for current use, leaving $225,000 of the loan usable. At 6% interest, the $250,000 loan would require an interest payment of $15,000 per year. This is partially offset by the 2% interest earned on the $25,000 incremental balance, or $500. Subtracting the $500 interest earned from the $15,000 of expense results in net interest expense of $14,500 for the use of $225,000 in funds. Dividing $14,500 by $225,000 produces an effective interest rate of 6.44%.

Answer (B) is incorrect because 7.00% fails to consider that the $25,000 currently being maintained counts toward the compensating balance requirement. Answer (C) is incorrect because 5.8% fails to consider the compensating balance requirement. Answer (D) is incorrect because 6.66% fails to consider the interest earned on the incremental balance being carried.

30. A company uses the following formula in determining its optimal level of cash.

$$C^* = \sqrt{\frac{2bT}{i}}$$

If: b = fixed cost per transaction
i = interest rate on marketable securities
T = total demand for cash over a period of time

This formula is a modification of the economic order quantity (EOQ) formula used for inventory management. Assume that the fixed cost of selling marketable securities is $10 per transaction and the interest rate on marketable securities is 6% per year. The company estimates that it will make cash payments of $12,000 over a one-month period. What is the average cash balance (rounded to the nearest dollar)?

A. $1,000

B. $2,000

C. $3,464

D. $6,928

The correct answer is (D). *(CMA, adapted)*

REQUIRED: The average cash balance.

DISCUSSION: The EOQ for inventory is a function of ordering cost per order, inventory demand, and carrying cost. In the cash model, the fixed cost per sale of securities is equivalent to the ordering cost, the demand for cash is similar to the demand for inventory, and the interest rate is effectively the cost of carrying a dollar of cash for the period. Substituting in the formula yields an optimal cash balance of about $6,928.

$$\sqrt{\frac{2bT}{i}} = \sqrt{\frac{2 \times \$10 \times \$12{,}000}{6\% \div 12\ months}} = \sqrt{\frac{\$240{,}000}{.005}} = \$6{,}928$$

Answer (A) is incorrect because $1,000 results from using 24% in the denominator. Answer (B) is incorrect because $2,000 results from using 6% in the denominator. Answer (C) is incorrect because $3,464 results from using 2% in the denominator.

31. Which one of the following is not a characteristic of a negotiable certificate of deposit? Negotiable certificates of deposit

A. Have a secondary market for investors.

B. Are regulated by the Federal Reserve System.

C. Are usually sold in denominations of a minimum of $100,000.

D. Have yields considerably greater than bankers' acceptances and commercial paper.

The correct answer is (D). *(CMA, adapted)*

REQUIRED: The item not a characteristic of a negotiable certificate of deposit.

DISCUSSION: A certificate of deposit (CD) is a form of savings deposit that cannot be withdrawn before maturity without incurring a high penalty. A negotiable CD can be traded. CDs usually have a fairly high rate of return compared with other savings instruments because they are for fixed, usually long-term periods. However, their yield is less than that of commercial paper and bankers' acceptances because they are less risky.

Answer (A) is incorrect because negotiable CDs do have a secondary market (i.e., they are negotiable). Answer (B) is incorrect because negotiable CDs are regulated. Answer (C) is incorrect because negotiable CDs are typically issued in a denomination of $100,000.

C. Marketable Securities Management

32. When managing cash and short-term investments, a corporate treasurer is primarily concerned with

A. Maximizing rate of return.

B. Minimizing taxes.

C. Investing in Treasury bonds since they have no default risk.

D. Liquidity and safety.

The correct answer is (D). *(CMA, adapted)*

REQUIRED: The primary concern when managing cash and short-term investments.

DISCUSSION: Cash and short-term investments are crucial to a firm's continuing success. Sufficient liquidity must be available to meet payments as they come due. At the same time, liquid assets are subject to significant control risk. Therefore, liquidity and safety are the primary concerns of the treasurer when dealing with highly liquid assets. Cash and short-term investments are held because of their ability to facilitate routine operations of the company. These assets are not held for purposes of achieving investment returns.

Answer (A) is incorrect because most companies are not in business to earn high returns on liquid assets (i.e., they are held to facilitate operations). Answer (B) is incorrect because the holding of cash and cash-like assets is not a major factor in controlling taxes. Answer (C) is incorrect because investments in Treasury bonds do not have sufficient liquidity to serve as short-term assets.

33. All of the following are alternative marketable securities suitable for investment except

A. U.S. Treasury bills.

B. Eurodollars.

C. Commercial paper.

D. Convertible bonds.

The correct answer is (D). *(CMA, adapted)*

REQUIRED: The item that is not a marketable security.

DISCUSSION: Marketable securities are near-cash items used primarily for short-term investment. Examples include U. S. Treasury bills, Eurodollars, commercial paper, money-market mutual funds with portfolios of short-term securities, bankers' acceptances, floating-rate preferred stock, and negotiable CDs of U.S. banks. A convertible bond is not a short-term investment because its maturity date is usually more than one year in the future and its price can be influenced substantially by changes in interest rates or by changes in the investee's stock price.

Answers (A), (B), and (C) are incorrect because U.S. Treasury bills, Eurodollars, and commercial paper are short-term marketable securities.

34. The term "short selling" is the

A. Selling of a security that was purchased by borrowing money from a broker.

B. Selling of a security that is not owned by the seller.

C. Selling of all the shares you own in a company in anticipation that the price will decline dramatically.

D. Betting that a stock will increase by a certain amount within a given period of time.

The correct answer is (B). *(CMA, adapted)*

REQUIRED: The definition of "short selling."

DISCUSSION: Short selling is accomplished by borrowing securities from a broker and selling those securities. At a later time, the loan is repaid by buying securities on the open market and returning them to the broker. The seller speculates that the stock's market price will decline.

Answer (A) is incorrect because margin trading involves buying securities by borrowing money from a broker. Answer (C) is incorrect because the investor does not own the shares sold in a short sale. Answer (D) is incorrect because the short seller is betting that the stock will decrease in price.

D. Receivables Management

35. Garo Company, a retail store, is considering foregoing sales discounts in order to delay using its cash. Supplier credit terms are 2/10, net 30. Assuming a 360-day year, what is the annual cost of credit if the cash discount is not taken and Garo pays net 30?

A. 24.0%

B. 24.5%

C. 36.0%

D. 36.7%

The correct answer is (D). *(CMA, adapted)*

REQUIRED: The annual cost of credit if cash discounts are not taken when terms are 2/10, net 30.

DISCUSSION: On a $1,000 invoice, the company could save $20 by paying within the discount period. Thus, an immediate payment of $980 would save the company $20, and the interest rate charged for holding $980 an additional 20 days (30 – 10) is 2.04% ($20 ÷ $980). Because the number of 20-day periods in a year is 18 (360 ÷ 20), the annual rate is 36.7% (18 x 2.04%).

Answers (A) and (B) are incorrect because the length of the extra credit period is 20 days, not 30 days. Answer (C) is incorrect because 36.0% calculates the interest rate based on the full invoice price.

36. The sales manager at Ryan Company feels confident that, if the credit policy at Ryan's were changed, sales would increase and, consequently, the company would utilize excess capacity. The two credit proposals being considered are as follows:

	Proposal A	Proposal B
Increase in sales	$500,000	$600,000
Contribution margin	20%	20%
Bad debt percentage	5%	5%
Increase in operating profits	$75,000	$90,000
Desired return on sales	15%	15%

Currently, payment terms are net 30. The proposed payment terms for Proposal A and Proposal B are net 45 and net 90, respectively. An analysis to compare these two proposals for the change in credit policy would include all of the following factors except the

A. Cost of funds for Ryan.

B. Current bad debt experience.

C. Impact on the current customer base of extending terms to only certain customers.

D. Bank loan covenants on days' sales outstanding.

The correct answer is (B). *(CMA, adapted)*

REQUIRED: The factor not considered in an analysis of proposed credit policies.

DISCUSSION: All factors should be considered that differ between the two policies. Factors that do not differ, such as the current bad debt experience, are not relevant. Ryan must estimate the expected bad debt losses under each new policy.

Answer (A) is incorrect because the cost of funds is an obvious element in the analysis of any investment. Answer (C) is incorrect because the impact on the current customer base of extending terms to only certain customers is relevant. The current customers may demand the same terms. Answer (D) is incorrect because existing loan agreements may require Ryan to maintain certain ratios at stated levels. Thus, Ryan's ability to increase receivables and possible bad debt losses may be limited.

37. Jackson Distributors sells to retail stores on credit terms of 2/10, net 30. Daily sales average 150 units at a price of $300 each. Assuming that all sales are on credit and 60% of customers take the discount and pay on day 10 while the rest of the customers pay on day 30, the amount of Jackson's accounts receivable is

A. $1,350,000

B. $990,000

C. $900,000

D. $810,000

The correct answer is (D). *(CMA, adapted)*

REQUIRED: The amount of accounts receivable for a firm with credit terms of 2/10, net 30.

DISCUSSION: The firm has daily sales of $45,000 consisting of 150 units at $300 each. For 30 days, sales total $1,350,000. Forty percent of these sales, or $540,000, will be uncollected because customers do not take their discounts. The remaining 60%, or $810,000, will be paid within the discount period. However, by the end of 30 days, only 2/3 of the $810,000 will be collected because the sales from days 21 through 30 are still within the discount period. Therefore, an additional $270,000 ($810,000 – $540,000) will still be uncollected after the 30th day, but will be subject to a discount. In total, the average receivable balance is $810,000, consisting of $540,000 on which no discount will be taken and $270,000 that will be paid within the discount period.

Answer (A) is incorrect because 60% of the sales will be paid for within the 10-day discount period. Answers (B) and (C) are incorrect because these are based on a sales total of $1,500,000 for 30 days rather than $1,350,000.

38. The average collection period for a firm measures the number of days

A. After a typical credit sale is made until the firm receives the payment.

B. For a typical check to "clear" through the banking system.

C. Beyond the end of the credit period before a typical customer payment is received.

D. Before a typical account becomes delinquent.

The correct answer is (A). *(CMA, adapted)*

REQUIRED: The meaning of a firm's average collection period.

DISCUSSION: The average collection period measures the number of days between the date of sale and the date of collection. It should be related to a firm's credit terms. For example, a firm that allows terms of 2/15, net 30, should have an average collection period of somewhere between 15 and 30 days.

Answer (B) is incorrect because it describes the concept of float. Answer (C) is incorrect because the average collection period includes the total time before a payment is received, including the periods both before and after the end of the normal credit period. Answer (D) is incorrect because it describes the normal credit period.

39. A change in credit policy has caused an increase in sales, an increase in discounts taken, a decrease in the amount of bad debts, and a decrease in the investment in accounts receivable. Based upon this information, the company's

A. Average collection period has decreased.

B. Percentage discount offered has decreased.

C. Accounts receivable turnover has decreased.

D. Working capital has increased.

The correct answer is (A). *(CMA, adapted)*

REQUIRED: The true statement about a change in credit policy that has resulted in greater sales and a reduction in accounts receivable.

DISCUSSION: An increase in discounts taken accompanied by declines in receivables balances and doubtful accounts all indicate that collections on the increased sales have been accelerated. Accordingly, the average collection period must have declined. The average collection period is a ratio calculated by dividing the number of days in a year (365) by the receivable turnover. Thus, the higher the turnover, the shorter the average collection period. The turnover increases when either sales (the numerator) increase, or receivables (the denominator) decrease. Accomplishing both higher sales and a lower receivables increases the turnover and results in a shorter collection period.

Answer (B) is incorrect because a decrease in the percentage discount offered provides no incentive for early payment. Answer (C) is incorrect because accounts receivable turnover (sales ÷ average receivables) has increased. Answer (D) is incorrect because no information is given relative to working capital elements other than receivables. Both receivables and cash are elements of working capital, so an acceleration of customer payments will have no effect on working capital.

40. Best Computers believes that its collection costs could be reduced through modification of collection procedures. This action is expected to result in a lengthening of the average collection period from 28 days to 34 days; however, there will be no change in uncollectible accounts. The company's budgeted credit sales for the coming year are $27,000,000, and short-term interest rates are expected to average 8%. To make the changes in collection procedures cost beneficial, the minimum savings in collection costs (using a 360-day year) for the coming year would have to be

A. $30,000

B. $360,000

C. $180,000

D. $36,000

The correct answer is (D). *(CMA, adapted)*

REQUIRED: The minimum savings in collection costs that would be necessary to make the lengthened credit period beneficial.

DISCUSSION: Given sales of $27,000,000, the average amount of daily sales must be $75,000 ($27,000,000 ÷ 360 days). The increased accounts receivable balance is therefore $450,000 (6 days x $75,000). With an additional $450,000 of capital invested in receivables, the company's interest cost will increase by $36,000 per year (8% x $450,000). Thus, the company must save at least $36,000 per year to justify the change in procedures.

Answers (A), (B), and (C) are incorrect because $36,000 is the minimum savings required.

41. A company plans to tighten its credit policy. The new policy will decrease the average number of days in collection from 75 to 50 days and will reduce the ratio of credit sales to total revenue from 70% to 60%. The company estimates that projected sales will be 5% less if the proposed new credit policy is implemented. If projected sales for the coming year are $50 million, calculate the dollar impact on accounts receivable of this proposed change in credit policy. Assume a 360-day year.

A. $3,817,445 decrease.

B. $6,500,000 decrease.

C. $3,333,334 decrease.

D. $18,749,778 increase.

The correct answer is (C). *(CMA, adapted)*

REQUIRED: The dollar impact on accounts receivable of a change in credit policy.

DISCUSSION: If sales are $50 million, 70% of which are on credit, total credit sales will be $35 million. The receivables turnover equals 4.8 times per year (360 days ÷ 75-day collection period). Receivables turnover equals net credit sales divided by average receivables. Accordingly, average receivables equal $7,291,667 ($35,000,000 ÷ 4.8). Under the new policy, sales will be $47.5 million (95% x $50,000,000), and credit sales will be $28.5 million (60% x $47,500,000). The collection period will be reduced to 50 days, resulting in a turnover of 7.2 times per year (360 ÷ 50). The average receivables balance will therefore be $3,958,333 ($28,500,000 ÷ 7.2), a reduction of $3,333,334 ($7,291,667 – $3,958,333).

Answers (A) and (B) are incorrect because the decrease will be $3,333,334. Answer (D) is incorrect because receivables will decrease.

42. A company with $4.8 million in credit sales per year plans to relax its credit standards, projecting that this will increase credit sales by $720,000. The company's average collection period for new customers is expected to be 75 days, and the payment behavior of the existing customers is not expected to change. Variable costs are 80% of sales. The firm's opportunity cost is 20% before taxes. Assuming a 360-day year, what is the company's benefit (loss) on the planned change in credit terms?

A. $0

B. $28,800

C. $144,000

D. $120,000

The correct answer is (D). *(CMA, adapted)*

REQUIRED: The annual benefit or loss resulting from a change in credit terms.

DISCUSSION: The incremental sales will produce an increased contribution margin of $144,000 (20% x $720,000). However, that amount must be offset by the cost of funds invested in receivables. The variable costs associated with the incremental sales are $576,000 (80% x $720,000). Given a 75-day credit period, the average investment in receivables equals $120,000 [$576,000 x (75 ÷ 360)]. Accordingly, the cost of the investment in additional receivables is $24,000 (20% opportunity cost x $120,000), and the net benefit of the planned change in credit terms is $120,000 ($144,000 – $24,000).

Answer (A) is incorrect because the company benefits from the change in credit terms. Answer (B) is incorrect because $28,800 results from multiplying the contribution margin by the 20% interest rate. Answer (C) is incorrect because $144,000 overlooks the costs created by having funds invested in receivables for 75 days.

43. Which of the following represents a firm's average gross receivables balance?

I. Days' sales in receivables × accounts receivable turnover.

II. Average daily sales × average collection period.

III. Net sales ÷ average gross receivables.

A. I only.

B. I and II only.

C. II only.

D. II and III only.

The correct answer is (C). *(CMA, adapted)*

REQUIRED: The calculation of the average gross receivables balance.

DISCUSSION: A firm's average gross receivables balance can be calculated by multiplying average daily sales by the average collection period (days' sales outstanding). Alternatively, annual credit sales can be divided by the accounts-receivable turnover (net credit sales ÷ average accounts receivable) to obtain the average balance in receivables.

Answers (A) and (B) are incorrect because Alternative I cannot be correct. Neither of the multiplicands is a dollar figure, so the product could not be the dollar balance of receivables. Answer (D) is incorrect because Alternative III cannot be correct. It contains average gross receivables, the amount being calculated.

44. A firm averages $4,000 in sales per day and is paid, on an average, within 30 days of the sale. After they receive their invoice, 55% of the customers pay by check, while the remaining 45% pay by credit card. Approximately how much would the company show in accounts receivable on its balance sheet on any given date?

A. $4,000

B. $120,000

C. $48,000

D. $54,000

The correct answer is (B). *(CMA, adapted)*

REQUIRED: The average balance in accounts receivable given the average payment period and sales per day.

DISCUSSION: If sales are $4,000 per day and customers pay in 30 days, 30 days of sales are outstanding, or $120,000. Whether customers pay by credit card or cash, collection requires 30 days.

Answer (A) is incorrect because $4,000 is only one day's sales. Answer (C) is incorrect because invoices are outstanding for 30 days, not 12 days. Answer (D) is incorrect because $54,000 is based on the 45% of collections via credit card.

E. Inventory Management

45. Which one of the following would not be considered a carrying cost associated with inventory?

A. Insurance costs.

B. Cost of capital invested in the inventory.

C. Cost of obsolescence.

D. Shipping costs.

The correct answer is (D). *(CMA, adapted)*

REQUIRED: The item that is not a carrying cost of inventory.

DISCUSSION: Carrying costs are incurred to hold inventory. Examples include such costs as warehousing, insurance, the cost of capital invested in inventories, inventory taxes, and the cost of obsolescence and spoilage. Neither shipping costs nor the initial cost of the inventory are carrying costs.

Answers (A), (B), and (C) are incorrect because they are all examples of carrying costs.

46. An example of a carrying cost is

A. Disruption of production schedules.

B. Quantity discounts lost.

C. Handling costs.

D. Spoilage.

The correct answer is (D). *(CMA, adapted)*

REQUIRED: The inventory carrying cost.

DISCUSSION: Inventory costs fall into three categories: order or setup costs, carrying (holding) costs, and stockout costs. Carrying costs include storage costs for inventory items plus opportunity cost (i.e., the cost incurred by investing in inventory rather than making an income-earning investment). Examples are insurance, spoilage, interest on invested capital, obsolescence, and warehousing costs.

Answer (A) is incorrect because disruption of production schedules may result from a stockout. Answer (B) is incorrect because quantity discounts lost are related to ordering costs or inventory acquisition costs. Answer (C) is incorrect because shipping and handling costs are included in acquisition costs.

47. The ordering costs associated with inventory management include

A. Insurance costs, purchasing costs, shipping costs, and spoilage.

B. Obsolescence, setup costs, quantity discounts lost, and storage costs.

C. Purchasing costs, shipping costs, setup costs, and quantity discounts lost.

D. Shipping costs, obsolescence, setup costs, and capital invested.

The correct answer is (C). *(CMA, adapted)*

REQUIRED: The items included in ordering costs.

DISCUSSION: Ordering costs are costs incurred when placing and receiving orders. Ordering costs include purchasing costs, shipping costs, setup costs for a production run, and quantity discounts lost.

Answer (A) is incorrect because insurance costs are a carrying cost. Answers (B) and (D) are incorrect because obsolescence and spoilage, interest on invested capital, and storage costs are carrying costs.

48. The amount of inventory that a company would tend to hold in stock would increase as the

A. Sales level falls to a permanently lower level.

B. Cost of carrying inventory decreases.

C. Variability of sales decreases.

D. Cost of running out of stock decreases.

The correct answer is (B). *(CMA, adapted)*

REQUIRED: The reason for an increase in inventory.

DISCUSSION: Inventory management attempts to minimize the total costs of ordering, carrying inventory, and stockouts. Thus, a firm incurs carrying costs to reduce ordering and stockout costs. If the cost of carrying inventory declines, the inventory level must increase to minimize total inventory costs.

Answers (A), (C), and (D) are incorrect because permanently lower sales, more predictable sales, decreased stockout costs, and decreased inventory transit time are reasons for decreasing inventory.

49. In inventory management, the safety stock will tend to increase if the

A. Carrying cost increases.

B. Cost of running out of stock decreases.

C. Variability of the lead time increases.

D. Variability of the usage rate decreases.

The correct answer is (C). *(CMA, adapted)*

REQUIRED: The factor that will cause safety stocks to increase.

DISCUSSION: A company maintains safety stocks to protect itself against the losses caused by inventory stock-outs. These can take the form of lost sales or lost production time. Safety stock is necessary because of the variability in lead time and usage rates. As the variability in lead time increases, a company will tend to carry larger safety stocks.

Answer (A) is incorrect because an increase in inventory carrying costs makes it less economical to carry safety stocks. Thus, safety stocks will be reduced. Answer (B) is incorrect because, if the cost of stockouts declines, the incentive to carry large safety stocks is reduced. Answer (D) is incorrect because a decline in the variability of usage makes it easier to plan orders, and safety stocks will be less necessary.

50. The result of the economic order quantity formula indicates the

A. Annual quantity of inventory to be carried.

B. Annual usage of materials during the year.

C. Safety stock plus estimated inventory for the year.

D. Quantity of each individual order during the year.

The correct answer is (D). *(CMA, adapted)*

REQUIRED: The indication given by the EOQ formula.

DISCUSSION: The EOQ model is a deterministic model that calculates the ideal order (or production lot) quantity given specified demand, ordering or setup costs, and carrying costs. The model minimizes the sum of inventory carrying costs and either ordering or production setup costs.

Answer (A) is incorrect because the annual quantity of inventory demanded is an input into the formula, not the result. Answer (B) is incorrect because annual usage is a determinant of annual demand, which is an input into the formula. Answer (C) is incorrect because safety stock is not reflected in the basic EOQ formula.

51. The Stewart Co. uses the economic order quantity (EOQ) model for inventory management. A decrease in which one of the following variables would increase the EOQ?

A. Annual sales.

B. Cost per order.

C. Safety stock level.

D. Carrying costs.

The correct answer is (D). *(CMA, adapted)*

REQUIRED: The variable for which a decrease will lead to an increase in the economic order quantity (EOQ).

DISCUSSION: The EOQ model minimizes the total of ordering and carrying costs. The EOQ is calculated as follows:

$$\sqrt{\frac{2(\textit{Demand})(\textit{Order costs})}{\textit{Carrying costs per unit}}}$$

Increases in the numerator (demand or ordering costs) will increase the EOQ, whereas decreases in demand or ordering costs will decrease the EOQ. Similarly, a decrease in the denominator (carrying costs) will increase the EOQ.

Answer (A) is incorrect because a decrease in demand (annual sales), which is in the numerator, will decrease the EOQ. Answer (B) is incorrect because a decrease in ordering costs will encourage more orders, or a decrease in the EOQ. Answer (C) is incorrect because a decrease in safety stock levels will not affect the EOQ, although it might lead to a different ordering point.

52. Handy operates a chain of hardware stores across Ohio. The controller wants to determine the optimum safety stock levels for an air purifier unit. The inventory manager compiled the following data:

- The annual carrying cost of inventory approximates 20% of the investment in inventory.
- The inventory investment per unit averages $50.
- The stockout cost is estimated to be $5 per unit.
- The company orders inventory on the average of 10 times per year.
- Total cost = carrying cost + expected stockout cost.
- The probabilities of a stockout per order cycle with varying levels of safety stock are as follows:

Units		
Safety Stock	Stockout	Probability
200	0	0%
100	100	15%
0	100	15%
0	200	12%

The total cost of safety stock on an annual basis with a safety stock level of 100 units is

A. $1,750

B. $1,950

C. $550

D. $2,000

The correct answer is (A). *(CMA, adapted)*

REQUIRED: The total cost of safety stock on an annual basis for a given safety stock level.

DISCUSSION: Total cost is defined as carrying cost plus expected stockout cost. At 20% of the $50 unit inventory cost, carrying cost is $10 per unit per year. Thus, carrying cost for 100 units of safety stock is $1,000. A stockout has a 15% probability at this level of safety stock, and stockout costs are $500 (100 x $5) for each occurrence. If the firm orders 10 times per year, the expected number of stockouts is 1.5 (15% x 10). Hence, total expected stockout cost for the year is $750 ($500 x 1.5). Total cost is $1,750 per year ($1,000 + $750).

Answer (B) is incorrect because $1,950 is the sum of the expected stockout costs for stockouts of 100 units and 200 units. Answer (C) is incorrect because the carrying cost alone is $10 per unit, or $1,000 per year. Answer (D) is incorrect because $2,000 is the carrying cost of 200 units of safety stock.

53. Edwards Manufacturing Corporation uses the standard economic order quantity (EOQ) model. If the EOQ for Product A is 200 units and Edwards maintains a 50-unit safety stock for the item, what is the average inventory of Product A?

A. 250 units.

B. 150 units.

C. 125 units.

D. 100 units.

The correct answer is (B). *(CMA, adapted)*

REQUIRED: The average inventory of a product.

DISCUSSION: If safety stock is 50 units, the receipt of an order should increase the inventory to 250. That amount will decline to 50 just prior to the receipt of the next order. Thus, the average inventory would be the average of 250 and 50 [(250 + 50) ÷ 2], or 150 units.

Answer (A) is incorrect because 250 is the maximum inventory level. Answer (C) is incorrect because 125 units assumes an EOQ of 250 units and no safety stock. Answer (D) is incorrect because 100 units assumes no safety stock.

F. Short-Term Credit

54. Which one of the following provides a spontaneous source of financing for a firm?

A. Accounts payable.

B. Mortgage bonds.

C. Accounts receivable.

D. Debentures.

The correct answer is (A). *(CMA, adapted)*

REQUIRED: The item that provides a spontaneous source of financing.

DISCUSSION: Trade credit is a spontaneous source of financing because it arises automatically as part of a purchase transaction. Because of its ease in use, trade credit is the largest source of short-term financing for many firms both large and small.

Answers (B) and (D) are incorrect because mortgage bonds and debentures do not arise automatically as a result of a purchase transaction. Answer (C) is incorrect because the use of receivables as a financing source requires an extensive factoring arrangement and often involves the creditor's evaluation of the credit ratings of the borrower's customers.

55. Which one of the following statements about trade credit is correct? Trade credit is

A. Not an important source of financing for small firms.

B. A source of long-term financing to the seller.

C. Subject to risk of buyer default.

D. Usually an inexpensive source of external financing.

The correct answer is (C). *(CMA, adapted)*

REQUIRED: The true statement about trade credit.

DISCUSSION: Trade credit is a spontaneous source of financing because it arises automatically as part of a purchase transaction. The terms of payment are set by the supplier, but trade credit usually requires payment within a short period of time. Trade credit is an important source of credit for all businesses but especially for buyers, such as small businesses, that might not have access to other credit markets. Like all forms of financing, trade credit is subject to the risk of buyer default.

Answer (A) is incorrect because trade credit is an important source of financing for small firms. Answer (B) is incorrect because trade credit is ordinarily a short-term source of financing. Answer (D) is incorrect because the cost of trade credit depends on the credit terms and the price paid. A seller with generous payment terms may charge a higher price for its merchandise.

56. Assuming a 360-day year, the current price of a $100 U.S. Treasury bill due in 180 days on a 6% discount basis is

A. $97.00

B. $94.00

C. $100.00

D. $93.00

The correct answer is (A). *(CMA, adapted)*

REQUIRED: The current price of a Treasury bill issued at a discount.

DISCUSSION: The 6% discount rate is multiplied times the face amount of the Treasury bill to determine the amount of interest the lender will earn. The interest on this Treasury bill is $3 (6% x .5 year x $100); thus, the purchase price is $97 ($100 – $3).

Answer (B) is incorrect because the interest is for 180 days, not a full year. Answer (C) is incorrect because the purchase price will always be less than the face value when a Treasury bill is sold at a discount. Answer (D) is incorrect because the interest rate is 6% per year.

57. Commercial paper

A. Has a maturity date greater than 1 year.

B. Is usually sold only through investment banking dealers.

C. Ordinarily does not have an active secondary market.

D. Has an interest rate lower than Treasury bills.

The correct answer is (C). *(CMA, adapted)*

REQUIRED: The true statement about commercial paper.

DISCUSSION: Commercial paper is a form of unsecured note that is sold by only the most creditworthy companies. It is issued at a discount from its face value and has a maturity period of 270 days or less. Commercial paper usually carries a low interest rate in comparison to other means of financing. SMA 4M, *Understanding Financial Instruments*, observes that no general (active) secondary market exists for commercial paper, but that "most dealers or organizations will repurchase an issue that they have sold."

Answer (A) is incorrect because commercial paper usually has a maturity date of 270 days or less to avoid securities registration requirements. Answer (B) is incorrect because commercial paper is often issued directly by the borrowing firm. Answer (D) is incorrect because interest rates must be higher than those of Treasury bills to entice investors. Commercial paper is more risky than Treasury bills.

58. Which one of the following responses is not an advantage to a corporation that uses the commercial paper market for short-term financing?

A. This market provides more funds at lower rates than other methods provide.

B. The borrower avoids the expense of maintaining a compensating balance with a commercial bank.

C. There are no restrictions as to the type of corporation that can enter into this market.

D. This market provides a broad distribution for borrowing.

The correct answer is (C). *(CMA, adapted)*

REQUIRED: The item not an advantage of using commercial paper for short-term financing.

DISCUSSION: Commercial paper is a short-term, unsecured note payable issued in large denominations by major companies with excellent credit ratings. Maturities usually do not exceed 270 days. Commercial paper is a lower cost source of funds than bank loans, and no compensating balances are required. Commercial paper provides a broad and efficient distribution of debt, and costly financing arrangements are avoided. The market is not open to all companies because only major corporations with high credit ratings can participate.

Answers (A) (B), and (D) are incorrect because lower rates, avoidance of compensating balance requirements, and broad debt distribution are advantages of commercial paper.

59. A company enters into an agreement with a firm that will factor the company's accounts receivable. The factor agrees to buy the company's receivables, which average $100,000 per month and have an average collection period of 30 days. The factor will advance up to 80% of the face value of receivables at an annual rate of 10% and charge a fee of 2% on all receivables purchased. The controller of the company estimates that the company would save $18,000 in collection expenses over the year. Fees and interest are not deducted in advance. Assuming a 360-day year, what is the annual cost of financing?

A. 10.0%

B. 12.0%

C. 14.0%

D. 17.5%

The correct answer is (D). *(CMA, adapted)*

REQUIRED: The annual percentage cost of financing under a factoring agreement.

DISCUSSION: In an average month, the company will receive $80,000 at the time the receivables are sent to the factor. Over a year's time, the interest on this average advance of $80,000 would be $8,000 at 10% interest. In addition, the factor will charge a 2% factor fee, or $24,000 ($100,000 x 12 x .02) over the course of a year. However, this $24,000 fee is offset by the $18,000 savings in collection expenses, producing a net outlay of only $6,000. Adding the $6,000 to the $8,000 of interest produces an annual net cost of $14,000. Dividing the $14,000 cost by the $80,000 of advanced funds results in a cost of 17.5%.

Answer (A) is incorrect because 10% overlooks the factor fee. Answer (B) is incorrect because 12% overlooks the fact that the 2% fee recurs every month. Answer (C) is incorrect because 14% miscalculates the factor fee and the savings from reduced collection costs.

Questions 60 through 63 are based on the following information. The Frame Supply Company has just acquired a large account and needs to increase its working capital by $100,000. The controller of the company has identified the four sources of funds given below.

A. Pay a factor to buy the company's receivables, which average $125,000 per month and have an average collection period of 30 days. The factor will advance up to 80% of the face value of receivables at 10% and charge a fee of 2% on all receivables purchased. The controller estimates that the firm would save $24,000 in collection expenses over the year. Assume the fee and interest are not deductible in advance.

B. Borrow $110,000 from a bank at 12% interest. A 9% compensating balance would be required.

C. Issue $110,000 of 6-month commercial paper to net $100,000. (New paper would be issued every 6 months.)

D. Borrow $125,000 from a bank on a discount basis at 20%. No compensating balance would be required.

Assume a 360-day year in all of your calculations.

60. The cost of Alternative A. is

A. 10.0%

B. 12.0%

C. 13.2%

D. 16.0%

The correct answer is (D). *(CMA, adapted)*

REQUIRED: The annual percentage cost of factoring receivables.

DISCUSSION: The factor will advance $100,000 (80% x $125,000). This amount is the average balance outstanding throughout the year. Thus, annual interest will be $10,000 (10% x $100,000). In addition, the company will pay an annual fee of $30,000 (2% x $125,000 per month x 12 months), so the total annual net cost is $16,000 ($10,000 + $30,000 – $24,000 savings). Hence, the annual cost is 16% ($16,000 ÷ $100,000 loan).

Answer (A) is incorrect because 10% is the interest rate on the amount advanced. Answer (B) is incorrect because 12% is the sum of the interest rate and the fee percentage. Answer (C) is incorrect because 13.2% is the cost of option B.

61. The cost of Alternative B. is

A. 9.0%

B. 12.0%

C. 13.2%

D. 21.0%

The correct answer is (C). *(CMA, adapted)*

REQUIRED: The annual percentage cost of borrowing with a compensating balance requirement.

DISCUSSION: Even though the company will borrow $110,000, it will have use of only $100,100 because a 9% compensating balance, or $9,900, must be maintained at all times. Consequently, the effective annual interest rate is 13.2% [(12% x $110,000) ÷ $100,100].

Answer (A) is incorrect because 9% is the compensating balance requirement. Answer (B) is incorrect because 12% is the contract rate. Answer (D) is incorrect because 21% is the sum of the contract rate and the compensating balance requirement.

62. The cost of Alternative C. is

A. 9.1%

B. 10.0%

C. 18.2%

D. 20.0%

The correct answer is (D). *(CMA, adapted)*

REQUIRED: The annual percentage cost of issuing commercial paper.

DISCUSSION: By issuing commercial paper, the company will receive $100,000 and repay $110,000 every six months. Thus, for the use of $100,000 in funds, the company pays $10,000 in interest each six-month period, or a total of $20,000 per year. The annual percentage rate is therefore 20% ($20,000 ÷ $100,000).

Answer (A) is incorrect because 9.1% is the 6-month rate based on the face amount of the paper. Answer (B) is incorrect because 10% is the rate for six months. Answer (C) is incorrect because 18.2% is based on the face amount of the commercial paper.

63. The cost of Alternative D. is

A. 20.0%

B. 25.0%

C. 40.0%

D. 50.0%

The correct answer is (B). *(CMA, adapted)*

REQUIRED: The annual percentage cost of a discounted note.

DISCUSSION: The company will receive $100,000 (80% x $125,000) at an annual cost of $25,000, so the annual interest rate is 25% ($25,000 ÷ $100,000).

Answer (A) is incorrect because the effective rate must exceed the contract rate of 20%. Answer (C) is incorrect because 40% assumes no discount and a 6-month loan term. Answer (D) is incorrect because 50% assumes a 6-month loan term.

64. The following forms of short-term borrowing are available to a firm:

- Floating lien
- Factoring
- Revolving credit
- Chattel mortgages
- Bankers' acceptances
- Lines of credit
- Commercial paper

The forms of short-term borrowing that are unsecured credit are

A. Floating lien, revolving credit, chattel mortgage, and commercial paper.

B. Factoring, chattel mortgage, bankers' acceptances, and line of credit.

C. Floating lien, chattel mortgage, bankers' acceptances, and line of credit.

D. Revolving credit, bankers' acceptances, line of credit, and commercial paper.

The correct answer is (D). *(CMA, adapted)*

REQUIRED: The forms of short-term borrowing that are unsecured credit.

DISCUSSION: An unsecured loan is a loan made by a bank based on credit information about the borrower and the ability of the borrower to repay the obligation. The loan is not secured by collateral, but is made on the signature of the borrower. Unsecured credit is not backed by collateral. Revolving credit, bankers' acceptances, lines of credit, and commercial paper are all unsecured means of borrowing.

Answers (A), (B), and (C) are incorrect because a chattel mortgage is a loan secured by personal property (movable property such as equipment or livestock). Also, a floating lien is secured by property, such as inventory, the composition of which may be constantly changing. Factoring is a form of financing in which receivables serve as security.

Use Gleim's ***CMA/CFM Test Prep*** for interactive testing with **over 2,000 additional multiple-choice questions!**

STUDY UNIT 6: CAPITAL STRUCTURE FINANCE

24 pages of outline
62 multiple-choice questions

Capital structure finance concerns the amount and mixture of permanent assets used and the methods by which they are financed. In contrast, the preceding study unit, Working Capital Finance, emphasized management of current assets and short-term financing. The relative weight range assigned to capital structure finance subjects is 10% to 15% of Part 1.

Study Unit 7, Risk, includes concepts applicable to both working capital finance and capital structure finance. In addition, candidates should also keep abreast of current events in the field of capital structure finance by reading the *Wall Street Journal, Business Week,* or *Barron's*. Past exams have often tested material so recent that it does not appear in any textbook.

A. Financial Ratios to Evaluate Capital Structure Finance

1. The preceding study unit outlined the ratios relevant to working capital finance. The following types of ratios are used to evaluate capital structure, that is, investment in fixed assets and long-term financing decisions:
   a. Activity
   b. Leverage
   c. Profitability
   d. Per share
2. **Activity ratios** measure the firm's use of assets to generate revenue and income.
   a. **Fixed asset turnover** equals net sales divided by net fixed assets.
      1) $\dfrac{\textit{Net sales}}{\textit{Net fixed assets}}$
      2) It measures the level of use of productive assets.
      3) Asset turnover is largely affected by capital intensiveness.
   b. **Total asset turnover** equals net sales divided by average total assets.
      1) $\dfrac{\textit{Net sales}}{\textit{Average total assets}}$
      2) It measures the level of capital investment relative to sales volume.
3. **Leverage ratios** measure the firm's use of debt to finance assets and operations.
   a. The **debt to equity ratio** equals total debt divided by total shareholders' equity.
      1) $\dfrac{\textit{Total liabilities}}{\textit{Shareholders' equity}}$
      2) It compares the resources provided by creditors with resources provided by shareholders. A high ratio means high risk.

b. The **equity ratio** equals common shareholders' equity divided by total assets.

1) $\dfrac{\textit{Common shareholders' equity}}{\textit{Total assets}}$

2) It indicates the percentage of total assets financed by common shareholders.

c. The **debt ratio** equals total liabilities divided by total assets.

1) $\dfrac{\textit{Total liabilities}}{\textit{Total assets}}$

2) It measures the percentage of funds provided by creditors.

3) Creditors prefer this ratio to be low as a cushion against losses.

d. **Times-interest-earned** (interest coverage ratio) equals income before interest and taxes, divided by interest.

1) $\dfrac{\textit{Net income + Interest expense + Income tax expense}}{\textit{Interest expense}}$

2) It indicates the margin of safety over fixed interest charges.

3) If earnings decline sufficiently, there will be no income tax expense.

4. **Profitability ratios** measure income on a relative basis.

a. The **profit margin on sales** equals net income after taxes divided by sales.

1) $\dfrac{\textit{Net income after taxes}}{\textit{Sales}}$

2) It measures the rate of profitability on sales.

b. The **return on assets** equals net income after taxes divided by average total assets.

1) $\dfrac{\textit{Net income after taxes}}{\textit{Average total assets}}$

2) It measures the productivity of assets.

3) The book value of assets may not equal their market value.

c. The **return on shareholders' equity** equals net income after taxes divided by average common shareholders' equity

1) $\dfrac{\textit{Net income after taxes}}{\textit{Average common shareholders' equity}}$

2) It measures the rate of return on equity investment.

3) The book value of common shareholders' equity may be below or above market values.

d. The **Du Pont equation** relates the return on total assets, the total asset turnover, and the profit margin on sales.

1) $$\frac{\textit{Net income after interest and taxes}}{\textit{Average total assets}} = \frac{\textit{Net sales}}{\textit{Average total assets}} \times \frac{\textit{Net income after interest and taxes}}{\textit{Net sales}}$$

2) This formula emphasizes that ROI may be explained in terms of the efficiency of asset management and the profit margin.

3) The effects of modifying the Du Pont equation to reflect net operating income (earnings before interest and taxes) and operating assets should be understood.

5. **Per-share ratios** relate company financial information to each share.

a. **Earnings per share (EPS)** equals net income available to common shareholders divided by the average number of shares outstanding for the period.

1) $$\frac{\textit{Net income available to common shareholders}}{\textit{Average shares outstanding}}$$

2) Net income available to common shareholders is usually net income minus preferred dividends.

3) Under APB 15, primary and fully diluted EPS must be presented. Under SFAS 128 (effective for periods ending after December 15, 1997), basic and diluted EPS must be presented.

b. **Book value per share** equals the amount of net assets available to the shareholders of a given type of stock divided by the number of those shares outstanding.

1) $$\frac{\textit{Shareholders' equity}}{\textit{Shares outstanding}}$$

2) When a company has preferred as well as common stock outstanding, the computation of book value per common share must consider potential claims by preferred shareholders, such as whether the preferred stock is cumulative and in arrears, or participating. It must also take into account whether the call price (or possibly the liquidation value) exceeds the carrying amount of the preferred stock.

c. **Dividend yield** equals the annual dividend payment divided by the market value per share.

1) $$\frac{\textit{Dividends per share}}{\textit{Market value per share}}$$

2) A related ratio is the **dividend payout**, which equals dividends per common share divided by EPS.

d. **Price-earnings ratio** equals the market price per share of common stock divided by EPS.

1) $$\frac{\textit{Market Price}}{\textit{EPS}}$$

2) Most analysts prefer to use diluted EPS.

6. Other ratios are identifiable by their titles, e.g., fixed assets to long-term debt.
   a. Ratios can be identified and classified as to whether they measure solvency, activity, leverage, profitability, or per-share amounts.
   b. Ratios may be determined for a period of time or as of a moment in time.
   c. The variables may be
      1) Before or after adjustments
      2) Gross or net
      3) Average or year-end
   d. Ratios are most useful when put in context
      1) Through trend analysis of a single company
      2) By comparison with other companies or industry averages after any adjustments are made to assure that the accounting data are comparable
   e. Ratios are based on accounting data and often do not reflect current values.
7. Stop and review! You have completed the outline for this subunit. Study multiple-choice questions 1 through 16 beginning on page 237.

B. Financial Forecasting

1. Financial forecasting, an essential element of planning, is the basis for budgeting activities.
   a. The central and most important forecast is the level of activity, i.e., sales.
      1) Most other forecasts (budgets) follow from the sales forecast.
      2) Additional budgetary variables that must be forecast are
         a) The availability of the factors of production
         b) Prices of the factors of production
2. **Percent-of-sales** is the most widely used method for forecasting sales. The present level of sales is adjusted by a specified percent increase or decrease. The percent-of-sales method is
   a. A form of trend analysis
   b. Convenient and easy to apply
   c. Preferred by managers
3. Other methods of forecasting sales are described in Part 4. They include
   a. Time-series analysis
   b. Exponential smoothing
   c. Regression analysis
   d. Expected value estimation
4. **Inflation Forecasting**
   a. **Neutral inflation** is a rise in all prices by the same amount (percentage).
   b. **A nominal price change** occurs when the price of good A changes in the same direction and the same magnitude as the prices of all other commodities. For example, the price of good A may increase 20% when the price of all goods increases by 20%.

c. **A real price change** occurs when the price of commodity A changes, with the prices of all other commodities remaining constant. For example, if the price of good A declines 10% and all other prices stay the same, a real change (decrease) in the price of good A has occurred.

d. **The real risk-free rate of interest** is the return from forgoing current consumption. It assumes no fluctuations in the price level and no default risk.

e. **The nominal risk-free rate of interest** is the real risk-free rate plus an inflation premium (expected inflation for the next period)

f. The **inflation premium** is an average expected rate over the life of the security. It tends to be correlated, although not perfectly, with recent actual inflation rates.

5. The **term structure of interest rates** is the relationship between yield to maturity and time to maturity. It is graphically depicted by a yield curve.

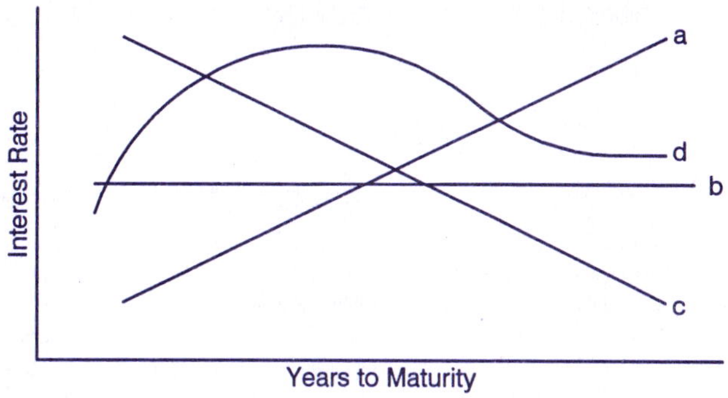

a. The graph above illustrates four common yield curves.

b. When plotting a yield curve, several factors are held constant:

   1) Default risk of instruments
   2) Taxability of the instruments
   3) Callability of the instruments
   4) Sinking fund provisions

c. The slopes of the foregoing yield curves depend on

   1) **Risk preference**

      a) **Interest rate risk** is the risk of loss associated with a change in bond prices caused by a change in interest rates. For a given change in rates, the price change will be greater the longer the term of the security. Thus, all other things being equal, short-term securities (and a lower interest rate) may be preferred by investors to long-term securities because their greater liquidity protects against a loss resulting from a rise in interest rates.

      b) Borrowers of funds prefer to borrow long-term (and pay a higher interest rate) to match the maturities of investments with the maturities of assets. Also, long-term borrowing avoids the expense of turning the debt over frequently.

2) **Future expectations concerning interest rates**

a) Most economists believe that a long-term interest rate is an average of future expected short-term interest rates. For this reason, the yield curve will slope upward if future rates are expected to rise, slope downward if interest rates are anticipated to fall, and remain flat if investors think the rate is stable. Future inflation is also incorporated into this relationship.

b) Future interest rates are determined by the same factors that determine current rates.

c) If the long-term rate is an average of future short-term rates, the manager can use the yield curve to derive the financial market's expectations of future interest rates.

d) EXAMPLE:

Years to Maturity	Rate
1	5%
2	8%
3	10%

Given this yield curve structure, the market's expectations for future interest rates can be estimated.

During year 1, the market is paying 5%.

For year 2, the market expects $\frac{(1.08)^2}{(1.05\ )} - 1 = 0.1109 = 11\%$

For year 3, the market expects $\frac{(1.10)^3}{(1.08)^2} - 1 = 0.1411 = 14\%$

6. Stop and review! You have completed the outline for this subunit. Study multiple-choice questions 17 through 22 beginning on page 243.

C. Sources of Long-Term Financing

1. A firm may have long-term financing requirements that it cannot, or does not want to, meet using retained earnings. It must therefore issue equity or debt securities.

   a. Certain hybrid forms of available financing include convertible issues and warrants. These are also used to attract long-term financing.

   b. The **primary market** is the market for new stocks and bonds; investment money flows directly to the company that will use the funds to increase productive capacity.

      1) Existing securities are traded in secondary markets such as stock exchanges.

   c. The **underwriting spread** is the difference between the price that an investment banker pays the issuer for a new security issue and the price at which that security is resold.

2. The principal issues regarding financing are the cost of each type of financing (including the question of risk) and the lender's (the investor's) view of the financing device. This discussion highlights principal components of the decision:

   a. **Common stock**. The common shareholders are the owners of the corporation, and their rights as owners, although reasonably uniform, depend on the laws of the state in which the firm is incorporated. Equity ownership involves risk because holders of common stock are not guaranteed a return and are last in priority in a liquidation. Shareholders' capital provides the cushion for creditors if any losses occur on liquidation.

      1) Advantages

         a) Common stock does not require a fixed dividend; dividends are paid from profits when available.

         b) There is no fixed maturity date for repayment of the capital.

         c) The sale of common stock increases the creditworthiness of the firm by providing more equity.

         d) Common stock is frequently more attractive to investors than debt because it grows in value with the success of the firm.

            i) The higher the common stock value, the more advantageous equity financing is compared with debt financing.

      2) Disadvantages

         a) Control (voting rights) is usually diluted as more common stock is sold.

         b) New common stock sales dilute earnings available to existing shareholders because of the greater number of shares outstanding.

         c) Underwriting costs are typically higher for common stock issues.

         d) Too much equity may raise the average cost of capital of the firm above its optimal level.

         e) Common stock cash dividends are not deductible as an expense and are after-tax cash deductions to the firm.

      3) Common shareholders ordinarily have **preemptive rights**.

         a) Preemptive rights give common shareholders the right to purchase any additional stock issuances in proportion to their current ownership percentages.

         b) If applicable state law or the corporate charter does not provide preemptive rights, the firm may nevertheless sell to the existing common shareholders in a **rights** offering. Each shareholder is issued a certificate or warrant that is an option to buy a certain number of shares at a fixed price.

i) Until the rights are actually issued, the stock trades **rights-on**; that is, the stock and the rights are not separable. After the rights are received, the stock trades **ex-rights** because the rights can be sold separately. The formula for the value of a stock right when the stock price is rights-on is

$$\frac{P - S}{N + 1}$$

If: P = value of a share rights-on
S = subscription price of a share
N = number of rights needed to buy a share

ii) The amount recorded for stock rights is based on an allocation of the cost of the shares owned based on the relative market values of the shares and the rights.

4) **Stock warrants** (certificates evidencing options to buy stock at a given price within a certain period) may be given to employees as compensation, or they may be issued with bonds or preferred stock.

a) The proceeds of securities issued with **detachable warrants** are allocated between the warrants and the securities based on their relative market values. If the fair value of one but not the other is known, the proceeds are allocated incrementally. If warrants are not detachable, they are not accounted for separately.

5) A stock's **par value** represents legal capital. It is an arbitrary value assigned to stock before the stock is issued. It also represents the maximum liability of a shareholder.

b. **Preferred stock**

1) Advantages from the issuer's (firm's) view

a) It is a form of equity and therefore builds the creditworthiness of the firm.

b) Control is still held by common shareholders.

c) Superior earnings of the firm are usually still reserved for the common shareholders.

2) Disadvantages of issuing preferred stock

a) Preferred stock cash dividends are not deductible as a tax expense and are paid with taxable income. The result is a substantially greater cost relative to bonds.

b) In periods of economic difficulty, accumulated dividends (dividends in arrears) may create major managerial and financial problems for the firm.

3) Typical provisions of preferred stock issues

a) **Priority in assets and earnings.** If the firm goes bankrupt, the preferred shareholders have priority over common shareholders.

b) **Accumulation of dividends**. All past preferred dividends must be paid before any common dividends can be paid.

c) **Convertibility**. Preferred stock issues may be convertible into common stock at the option of the shareholder.

d) **Participation.** Preferred stock participates with common in excess earnings of the company. For example, 8% participating preferred stock might pay a dividend each year greater than 8% when the corporation is extremely profitable. But nonparticipating preferred stock will receive no more than is stated on the face of the stock.

e) **Par value**. Par value is the liquidation value, and a percentage of par equals the preferred dividend.

f) **Redeemability**. Some preferred stock may be redeemed at a given time or at the option of the holder or otherwise at a time not controlled by the issuer. This feature makes preferred stock more nearly akin to debt, particularly in the case of **transient preferred stock**, which must be redeemed within a short time (e.g., 5 to 10 years). The SEC requires a separate presentation of redeemable preferred, nonredeemable preferred, and common stock.

g) **Voting rights**. These may be conferred if preferred dividends are in arrears for a stated period.

h) **Callability**. The issuer may have the right to repurchase the stock. For example, the stock may be noncallable for a stated period after which it may be called if the issuer pays a call premium (an amount exceeding par value).

i) **Maturity**. Preferred stock may have a sinking fund that allows for the purchase of a given annual percentage of the outstanding shares.

4) Holding preferred stock rather than bonds provides corporations a major tax advantage: at least 70% of the dividends received from preferred stock is tax deductible, whereas all bond interest received is taxable.

a) The **dividends-received deduction** also applies to common stock.

c. **Bonds**

1) Bonds are sold at the sum of the present values of the maturity value and the interest payments (if interest-bearing). The difference between the face value and the selling price of bonds is either a discount or a premium.

a) Bonds are sold at a discount when they sell for less than face value, that is, when the contract (stated) interest rate is less than the market (effective) interest rate.

b) Bonds are sold at a premium (in excess of face value) when the stated rate exceeds the effective rate.

c) A bond discount or premium appears as a direct deduction from or addition to the face amount of the bond payable.

2) Advantages of bonds to the issuer

   a) Basic control of the firm is not shared with the debtholder.

   b) Cost of debt is limited. Bondholders usually do not participate in the superior earnings of the firm.

   c) Ordinarily, the expected yield of bonds is lower than the cost of common stock.

   d) Interest paid on debt is tax deductible as an expense.

   e) Debt may add substantial flexibility in the financial structure of the corporation through the insertion of call provisions in the bond indenture.

3) Disadvantages of bonds to the issuing firm

   a) Debt has a fixed charge. Thus, if earnings fluctuate, the firm risks not meeting its fixed interest obligations, which could lead to its demise.

   b) Debt adds risk to a firm. Shareholders will consequently demand higher capitalization rates on equity earnings, which may result in a decline in the market price of stock.

   c) Debt usually has a maturity date.

   d) Debt is a long-term commitment, a factor that can affect risk profiles. Debt originally appearing to be profitable may become a burden and drive the firm into bankruptcy.

   e) Certain managerial prerogatives are usually given up in the contractual relationship outlined in the bond's indenture contract.

      i) For example, specific ratios must be kept above a certain level during the term of the loan.

   f) There are clear-cut limits to the amounts of debt available to the individual firm. Generally accepted standards of the investment community will usually dictate a certain debt-equity ratio for an individual firm. Beyond this limit, the cost of debt may rise rapidly, or debt may not be available.

4) Types of bonds

   a) A **mortgage bond** is a pledge of certain assets for a loan. It is usually secured by real property as a condition of the loan.

   b) A **debenture bond** is a long-term bond not secured by specific property. It is a general obligation of the borrower. Only companies with the best credit ratings can issue debentures because holders will be general creditors. They will have a status inferior to that of secured parties and creditors with priorities in bankruptcy.

   c) An **income bond** pays interest only if the issuing company has earnings. Such bonds are riskier than other bonds.

   d) **Serial bonds** have staggered maturities. These bonds permit investors to choose the maturity dates that meet their needs.

e) **Zero-coupon bonds** pay no interest but sell at a deep discount from face value. A relatively new type of bond, these instruments are very useful to investors and investees.

   i) The need to reinvest the periodic payments renders the final return available from normal coupon bonds uncertain because future reinvestment rates are uncertain. But the investor knows the exact return on a zero-coupon bond. Investors might therefore be willing to pay a premium for them, which in turn might lead firms to issue them.

   ii) The lack of interest payments means the firm faces no additional insolvency risk from the issue until it matures.

f) **Junk bonds** are very high-risk, high-yield securities issued to finance leveraged buyouts and mergers. They are also issued by troubled companies. They exploit the large tax deductions for interest payments made by entities with high debt ratios.

g) International bonds are of two types: **foreign bonds** and **Eurobonds**. Foreign bonds are denominated in the currency of the nation in which they are sold. Eurobonds are denominated in a currency other than that of the nation where they are sold.

   i) Foreign bonds issued in the United States and denominated in dollars must be registered with the SEC, but such extensive disclosure is not required in most European nations. Thus, an American company may elect to issue Eurobonds denominated in dollars in a foreign nation because of the convenience of not having to comply with governmental registration requirements.

h) **Registered bonds** are issued in the name of the owner. Interest payments are sent directly to the owner. When the owner sells registered bonds, the bond certificates must be surrendered and new certificates issued.

   i) They differ from **coupon (bearer) bonds**, which can be freely transferred and have a detachable coupon for each interest payment.

i) **Participating bonds** participate in excess earnings of the debtor as defined in the indenture.

j) **Indexed bonds** (purchasing power bonds) pay interest that is indexed to a measure of general purchasing power, such as the Consumer Price Index.

k) **Subordinated debentures** possess a feature undesirable to investors. They are subordinated to (inferior to) the claims of other general creditors as well as secured parties and persons with priorities in bankruptcy. The indenture specifies the claims (senior debt) to which these bonds are subordinate. They are usually issued only when the company has some debt instrument outstanding that prohibits the issuance of additional regular bonds. Subordinated debentures will normally pay a higher rate of interest than secured bonds.

5) Restrictive covenants in bond indentures (bond contracts) are intended to prevent the issuer from taking actions not in the bondholders' best interests. A trustee may be appointed to monitor compliance.

a) **Call provisions** give the corporation the right to call in the bond for redemption. This is an advantage to the firm but not for the investor. If interest rates decline, the company can call in the high-interest bonds and replace them with low-interest bonds. However, bonds may be **putable**, or redeemable, at the holder's option.

i) Bonds are putable if the holder has the right to exchange them for cash. This option is usually activated only if the issuer takes a stated action, for example, greatly increasing its debt or being acquired by another entity.

b) **Sinking fund** requirements provide that the firm retire a certain portion of its bonds each year or that money be set aside for repayment in the future. It increases the probability of repayment for bondholders but requires the use of capital by the firm.

c) The issuer may be required to maintain certain financial ratios, limit dividends, or restrict new bonds to a percentage of fixed assets.

d. Numerous financing arrangements are used by corporate management to increase investor interest in corporate securities. The objective is to have a lower interest rate on bonds or a higher selling price for stocks.

1) **Stock rights** evidenced by **warrants** are options that are distributed with debt or preferred stock. They permit a holder to share in a company's prosperity through a future purchase of stock at a special low price. They should be distinguished from put and call options.

a) A **put option** is a right traded in the stock market to sell stock at a given price within a specified period.

b) A **call option** is a right to purchase stock at a given price within a specified period.

c) Neither a put nor a call is issued by the company whose stock is the subject of the option.

2) **Convertibility**. Bonds or preferred stock may be exchangeable (by the investor) into common stock under certain conditions.

3) Both the issuance of rights and a conversion feature offer a corporation a means of delayed equity financing when market prices are unfavorable. When the market price rises above the conversion price, holders will presumably exercise the warrants or convert the securities.

e. **Employee stock ownership plans (ESOPs)** are established by a corporation under federal income tax laws. Under such a plan, an employee stock ownership trust (ESOT) acquires qualifying employer securities, which may be outstanding shares, treasury shares, or newly issued shares. It holds the stock in the name of the company's employees. In a typical arrangement, the trust obtains the cash to buy the stock by borrowing from a bank, and the corporation cosigns the note to the bank. Each year, the corporation makes contributions to the ESOT as deductible contributions to a qualified retirement plan. The employees may also make deposits to the ESOT.

1) The corporation receives the benefit of the bank loan by selling stock to the ESOT. Moreover, the corporation in effect repays the bank loan through deductible contributions (with pretax dollars) to the ESOT. Thus, use of a leveraged ESOP allows the corporation to obtain a deduction for the principal as well as the interest on the loan.

2) Another advantage of an ESOP is that employees should be motivated to perform better because they have a financial interest in the success of the company (although, if the market price of the stock declines, morale may be harmed).

3) Some small business owners have found that an ESOP is an effective way to transfer ownership (to employees) when no other buyer can be found.

f. **American depository receipts (ADRs)** are ownership rights in foreign corporations.

1) Foreign stocks are deposited with a large U.S. bank, which in turn issues ADRs representing ownership in the foreign shares. The ADR shares then trade on a U.S. stock exchange, whereas the company's original shares trade on a foreign stock market.

2) ADRs permit foreign companies to increase their development of a U.S. shareholder base.

3) Foreign companies want to participate in the U.S. equity market for a number of reasons, including a desire to increase liquidity of stocks, to raise equity capital without putting pressure on the stock price in the home market, and to develop a U.S. shareholder base.

g. **Dividend reinvestment plans (DRPs)**. Any dividends due to shareholders are automatically reinvested in shares of the same corporation's common stock. In recent years, many corporations have adopted such plans. Broker's fees on such purchases of stock are either zero (the costs absorbed by the corporation) or only a few cents per shareholder because only one purchase is made and the total fee is divided among all shareholders participating.

1) Initially, dividends were reinvested in stock bought by a trustee (typically a large bank) on the open market. Many plans are still of this type.

2) More recently, corporations have seen the opportunity to use DRPs as a source of financing. Thus, many plans now involve a sale of newly issued stock to the trustee to fulfill the requirements of the plan. The corporation benefits because it can issue stock at the current market value without incurring underwriting and issue costs.

h. **Intermediate-term financing** refers to debt issues having approximate maturities of greater than 1 but less than 10 years. The principal types of intermediate-term financing are term loans and lease financing. Major lenders under term agreements are commercial banks, life insurance companies, and, to some extent, pension funds.

1) **Term loans**. One possible feature of term loans is tying the interest payable on the loan to a variable rate of interest. This **floating rate**, usually stated as some percentage over the prime, creates the potential for extremely high borrowing costs.

a) This risk must be traded off against
   i) The need of the firm to obtain the loan
   ii) The flexibility inherent in term borrowing
   iii) The ability of the firm to borrow in the capital market
   iv) Other available types of debt financing
   v) The amount of privacy desired

b) Term loans are private contracts between private firms, whereas long-term debt securities quickly involve the SEC and massive disclosure.

c) Variable or floating rate loans are advantageous to lenders because they permit better matching of interest costs and revenues. Their market values tend to be more stable than those for fixed rate loans.

   i) The disadvantages include a heightened risk of default, losses of expected revenues if interest rates decline or if market rates rise above the ceiling specified in the agreement, and the difficulty of working with a more complex product.

d) Borrowers may benefit from lower initial costs of these loans but must accept increased interest rate risk, difficulty in forecasting cash flow, a possible loss of creditworthiness if interest rates are expected to rise, and the burden of more complex financing arrangements.

e) If the interest rate is variable but the monthly loan payment is fixed, an increase in the rate means that the interest component of the payment and the total interest for the loan term will be greater.

   i) The term of the loan will also be extended, and the principal balance will increase because amortization is diminished. Indeed, negative amortization may occur if the interest rate increase is great enough.

   ii) Floating or variable rate loans have an impact on monetary policy because they render analyses more complex. These loans give the Federal Reserve less control over the money supply and credit. The economy is now more sensitive to interest rate fluctuations, and political pressure to avoid rate increases will become greater.

2) **Lease financing** must be analyzed by comparing the cost of owning to the cost of leasing. Whereas the principal advantage of leasing used to be the tax advantages allowed, leasing has become a major means of financing because it offers a variety of other benefits. If leases are not accounted for as installment purchases, they provide off-balance-sheet financing. The three principal forms of leases are discussed below:

   a) A **sale-leaseback** is a financing method. A firm seeking financing sells an asset to an investor (creditor) and leases the asset back, usually on a noncancelable lease. The lease payments consist of principal and interest paid by the lessee to the lessor.

   b) **Service or operating leases** usually include both financing and maintenance services.

   c) **Financial leases**, which do not provide for maintenance services, are noncancelable and fully amortize the cost of the leased asset over the term of the basic lease contract. They are installment purchases.

i. **Maturity matching**. The desirability of maturity matching (equalizing the life of an asset acquired with the debt instrument used to finance it) is an important factor in choosing the source of funds. Financing long-term assets with long-term debt allows the company to generate sufficient cash flows from the assets to satisfy obligations as they mature.

j. **Venture capital**. Venture capital firms invest in new enterprises that might not be able to obtain funds in the usual capital markets due to the riskiness of new products. Placements of securities with venture capital firms are usually "private placements" and not subject to SEC regulation.

1) Venture capitalists risk low liquidity for their investments and high risk.
2) The payoff may be substantial if the company does succeed.

3. **Initial Public Offerings (IPOs)**. A firm's first issuance of securities to the public is an initial public offering. The process by which a closely held corporation issues new securities to the public is called **going public**. When a firm goes public, it issues its securities on a **new issue** or **initial public offering market** (a primary market).

a. Advantages of going public include

1) The ability to raise additional funds
2) The establishment of the firm's value in the market
3) An increase in the liquidity of the firm's stock

b. Disadvantages of going public include

1) Costs of the reporting requirements of the SEC and other agencies
2) Access to the company's operating data by competing firms
3) Access to net worth information of major shareholders
4) Limitations on self-dealing by corporate insiders
5) Pressure from outside shareholders for earnings growth
6) Stock prices that do not accurately reflect the true net worth of the company
7) Loss of control by management as ownership is diversified
8) Need for improved management control as operations expand
9) Increased shareholder servicing costs

c. To have its stock listed (have it traded on a stock exchange), the firm must apply to a stock exchange, pay a fee, and fulfill the exchange's requirements for membership.

1) Included in the requirements for membership is disclosure of the firm's financial data.

d. Once the decision to make an initial public offering has been made, the questions are similar to those for seasoned issues: the amount to be raised, the type of securities to sell, and the method of sale. For example, the following matters should be considered in selecting the type of securities to issue:

1) Should fixed charges be avoided? Debt creates fixed charges.
2) Is a maturity date on the security preferable?
3) Does the firm want a cushion to protect itself from losses to creditors?
4) How quickly and easily does the firm want to raise the capital?
5) Is the firm concerned about losing control of the company?
6) How does the cost of underwriting differ among the types of securities?

e. The company's next step is to prepare and file an SEC registration statement and prospectus, unless an exemption is available.

1) A **registration statement** is a complete disclosure to the SEC of all material information with respect to the issuance of the specific securities.

a) The SEC does not make any judgment on the financial health of an investment or guarantee the accuracy of the information contained in the registration statement.

2) A **prospectus** must be furnished to any interested investor. Its purpose is to supply sufficient facts to make an informed investment decision. The prospectus contains material information (financial and otherwise) with respect to the offering and the issuer.

3) The entire allotment of securities ordinarily is made available for purchase on the effective date of the registration statement. An exception is a **shelf registration**. Under the SEC's Rule 415, a master registration statement is filed for securities that the company reasonably expects to sell within 2 years. However, they are put "on the shelf" until the most opportune time for offering is determined.

a) Shelf registrations allow large, well-established issuers to respond rapidly in volatile markets and to reduce flotation costs.

4. Stop and review! You have completed the outline for this subunit. Study multiple-choice questions 23 through 50 beginning on page 246.

D. Dividend Policy

1. **Dividend policy** is the determination of what portion of a corporation's net income should be distributed to shareholders and what should be kept in the business to finance expansion.

a. A high dividend rate means a slower rate of growth.

b. A high growth rate usually means a low dividend rate.

c. Because both a high growth rate and a high dividend rate are desirable, the financial manager is in a quandary.

d. Normally, corporations try to maintain a stable level of dividends, even though profits may fluctuate considerably, because many shareholders buy stock with the expectation of receiving a certain dividend every year. Hence, management tends not to raise dividends if the payout cannot be sustained.

1) The desire for stability has led theorists to propound the **information content or signaling hypothesis**: a change in dividend policy is a signal to the market regarding management's forecast of future earnings. Thus, companies generally have an active policy strategy with respect to dividends.

e. This stability often results in a stock that sells at a higher market price because shareholders perceive less risk in receiving their dividends.

2. Various factors influence a company's dividend policy.

   a. **Legal restrictions.** Dividends ordinarily cannot be paid out of paid-in capital. A corporation must have a balance in its retained earnings account before dividends can be paid.

   b. **Stability of earnings.** A company whose earnings fluctuate greatly from year to year will tend to pay out a smaller dividend during good years so that the same dividend can be paid even if profits are much lower. For example, a company with fluctuating earnings might pay out $1 every year whether earnings per share are $10 (10% payout rate) or $1 (100% payout rate).

   c. **Rate of growth.** A company with a faster growth rate will have a greater need to finance that growth with retained earnings. Thus, growth companies usually have lower dividend payout ratios.

      1) Shareholders hope to be able to obtain larger capital gains in the future.

   d. **Cash position.** Regardless of a firm's earnings record, cash must be available before a dividend can be paid. No dividend can be declared if all of a firm's earnings are tied up in receivables and inventories.

   e. **Restrictions in debt agreements.** Restrictive covenants in bond indentures and other debt agreements often limit the dividends that a company can declare.

   f. **Tax position of shareholders.** In corporations, the shareholders may not want regular dividends because the individual owners are in such high tax brackets. They may want to forgo dividends in exchange for future capital gains or wait to receive dividends in future years when they are in lower tax brackets.

   g. Possibility of being assessed an **accumulated earnings tax**. The IRS does not like shareholders to postpone paying taxes on their dividends. It can assess an accumulated earnings tax if a corporation has accumulated retained earnings beyond its reasonably expected needs.

   h. **Residual theory of dividends.** The amount (residual) of earnings paid as dividends depends on the available investment opportunities and the debt-equity ratio at which cost of capital is minimized. The rational investor should prefer reinvestment of retained earnings when the return exceeds what the investor could earn on investments of equal risk. However, the firm may prefer to pay dividends when investment opportunities are poor and the use of internal equity financing would move the firm away from its ideal capital structure.

3. **Important Dates Concerning the Declaration of Dividends**

   a. The **date of declaration** is the date the directors meet and formally vote to declare a dividend. On this date, the dividend becomes a liability of the corporation.

   b. The **date of record** is the date as of which the corporation determines the shareholders who will receive the declared dividend. Essentially, the corporation closes its shareholder records on this date. Only those shareholders who own the stock on the date of record will receive the dividend. It typically falls anywhere from 2 to 6 weeks after the declaration date.

   c. The **date of payment** is the date on which the dividend is actually paid (when the checks are put into the mail to the investors). The payment date is usually from 2 to 4 weeks after the date of record.

d. The **ex-dividend date** is a date established by the stock exchanges, such as 4 business days before the date of record. Unlike the other dates previously mentioned, it is not established by the corporate board of directors. The period between the ex-dividend date and the date of record gives the stock exchange members time to process any transactions so that new shareholders will receive the dividends to which they are entitled. An investor who buys a share of stock before the ex-dividend date will receive the dividend that has been previously declared. An investor who buys the stock after the ex-dividend date (but before the date of record or payment date) will not receive the declared dividend. Instead, the individual who sold the stock will receive the dividend because (s)he owned it on the ex-dividend date.

1) Usually, a stock price will drop on the ex-dividend date by the amount of the dividend because the new investor will not receive it.

4. Stock dividends and splits involve issuance of additional shares to existing shareholders.

a. Shareholders do not really receive any increase in the value of their holdings. The previous holdings are simply divided into more pieces (additional shares).

b. A **stock dividend** is an issuance of stock and entails the transfer of a sum from the retained earnings account to a paid-in capital account.

1) Usually, the corporation wants to give something to the shareholders but without paying out a cash dividend because the funds are needed in the business.

2) Casual investors may believe they are receiving something of value when in essence their previous holdings are merely being divided into more pieces.

3) Stock dividends are often used by growing companies that wish to retain earnings in the business while placating shareholders.

c. A **stock split** does not involve any accounting entries. Instead, the existing shares are divided into more pieces so that the market price per share will be reduced.

1) EXAMPLE: If a corporation has 1 million shares outstanding, each of which sells for $90, a 2-for-1 stock split will result in 2 million shares outstanding, each of which sells for about $45.

2) **Reverse stock splits** reduce the shares outstanding.

d. Advantages of issuing stock splits and dividends

1) Because more shares will be outstanding, the price per share will be lower. The lower price per share will induce more small investors to purchase the company's stock. Thus, because demand for the stock is greater, the price may increase.

a) EXAMPLE: In the example above, the additional investors interested in the company at the lower price may drive the price up to $46 or $47, or slightly higher than the theoretically correct price of $45. Consequently, current shareholders will benefit from the split (or dividend) after all.

2) A dividend or split can be a publicity gesture. Because shareholders may believe they are receiving something of value (and may be indirectly), they will have a better opinion of their company.

3) Moreover, the more shares a corporation has outstanding, the larger the number of shareholders, who are usually good customers for their own company's products.

e. On rare occasions, a company will have a reverse stock split in an attempt to raise the market price per share. For example, a 1-for-10 stock split would require shareholders to turn in ten old shares in order to receive one new share.

5. Stop and review! You have completed the outline for this subunit. Study multiple-choice questions 51 through 59 beginning on page 256.

E. Business Contraction/Expansion

1. Financing after a Business Failure

a. A financially troubled business can restructure its debts under **Chapter 11 of the Federal Bankruptcy Act.**

1) This is a voluntary alternative to liquidation proceedings in bankruptcy (Chapter 7 of the Federal Bankruptcy Act).

2) The corporation submits a plan of reorganization to restructure its debts and take any other appropriate action, including a change in management.

3) The corporation remains in business and does not lose all its assets.

4) The plan of reorganization must be approved by the court. First, a majority of creditors of each class of debt must approve the plan, or only one class of creditors need approve the plan if it is fair and equitable.

b. An alternative to the bankruptcy proceedings is a **composition among creditors.**

1) It is simply an agreement between the debtor and the creditors.

2) The creditors agree to extend time for payment, take lesser sums in satisfaction of the debts owed, or accept some other plan of financial adjustment.

3) The debtor continues in business under this method also unless the parties agree to a liquidation.

2. Treasury Stock

a. **Treasury stock** is a corporation's own stock that it has reacquired. It is usually purchased on the open market at the current market price.

1) Treasury stock is not an asset of a corporation.

a) A corporation cannot own itself.

2) Treasury stock is shown as a reduction of shareholders' equity (a contra-equity account). Such stock is considered issued, but not outstanding.

b. A corporation might buy back its own stock for a number of reasons:

1) To have sufficient stock on hand to meet employee stock option and bonus plan requirements

2) To buy out a particular shareholder when the stock cannot be sold on the open market (or when such a sale would be so large that the market price would be adversely affected)

3) To attempt to support the market for the company's stock

4) To reduce the size of the business

5) To acquire stock needed to undertake a merger

6) To decrease the number of shares outstanding in hopes of increasing the earnings per share on the remaining shares

   a) Thus, the purchase of treasury stock may be the best investment opportunity available to the company, especially when management believes that the company's stock is undervalued.

7) To increase the book value per share of the remaining shares outstanding

   a) The market value must be less than the book value.

8) To hold the shares until the market rises, at which time the stock will be resold

   a) Management thereby treats the treasury stock as a stock market investment.

   b) Again, management must believe that the stock is undervalued.

9) To provide a quick and simple means of adjusting a firm's capital structure

   a) A repurchase of shares using debt financing is an even more dramatic way of quickly changing the relationship between debt and equity in the capital structure.

c. Dividends are not paid on treasury stock.

d. Treasury stock does not have any voting rights.

e. The purchase of treasury stock is sometimes criticized as being a selective dividend to shareholders who sell their stock.

   1) Like a dividend, purchase of treasury stock decreases shareholders' equity.

   2) Such dividends are usually not taxed as dividends but rather as capital gains. This is an advantage if the capital gains rate is less than the marginal tax rate of the shareholder.

f. Disadvantages of buying treasury stock include

   1) A higher debt-equity ratio, which may increase the difficulty of obtaining loans

   2) An increase in the company's susceptibility to acquisition by another corporation because fewer shares are outstanding. But a treasury stock purchase can thwart a hostile takeover. If the price is above market, this practice is known as **greenmail**.

   3) Liquidity problems because cash is being paid out to shareholders

g. To prohibit a corporation from using all of its capital (including borrowed capital) to buy treasury stock and then liquidating once all stock has been acquired, most states stipulate that legal capital (paid-in capital) cannot be reduced by treasury stock purchases.

   1) A company can buy treasury stock only to the extent it has retained earnings.

h. In addition to buying treasury stock on the open market, a corporation planning a large purchase may make a tender offer for a certain number of shares. The tender offer may specify a specific price, or it may be effected by a Dutch auction.

1) A tender offer asks shareholders to offer their shares for sale.

2) Some shareholders may prefer regular tender offers over regular dividends in that those owners in need of money can tender some of their shares and receive cash at favorable tax rates. Those shareholders who do not need cash can ignore the tender offer.

3) In a Dutch auction involving a solicitation to buy stock, each seller specifies the number of shares (s)he wishes to sell and a minimum price. Given the number of shares tendered and the prices offered by the selling shareholders, the lowest price that enables the buyer to acquire the requisite total of shares is set as the purchase price.

a) One variation is for the tender offer to specify a range of acceptable prices.

3. **Combinations of Firms**

a. A **merger** is a business transaction in which an acquiring firm absorbs a second firm, and the acquiring firm remains in business as a combination of the two merged firms. A merger is legally straightforward; however, approval of the shareholders of each firm is required. A **consolidation** is similar to a merger, but a new company is formed and neither of the merging companies survives.

b. An **acquisition** is the purchase of all of another firm's assets or a controlling interest in its stock. An acquisition of all of a firm's assets requires a vote of that firm's shareholders. It also entails the costly transfer of legal title, but it avoids the minority interest that may arise if the acquisition is by purchase of stock.

c. An **acquisition by stock purchase** is advantageous because it can be effected when management and the board of directors are hostile to the combination, and it does not require a formal vote of the firm's shareholders. If the acquiring firm's offer is rejected by the acquiree's management, a tender offer may be made directly to the acquiree's shareholders to obtain a controlling interest.

1) A **tender offer** is a general invitation by an individual or a corporation to all shareholders of another corporation to tender their shares for a specified price. In 1968, Congress enacted the Williams Act to extend reporting and disclosure requirements under the Securities and Exchange Act of 1934 to tender offers.

a) Any person or group that acquires more than 5% of a class of registered securities is required, within 10 days of the tender, to file a statement with the SEC and the issuing company.

b) The tender offer may be friendly (acceptable to the target corporation's management) or hostile. If it is the latter, the target must also file a statement with the SEC. The target has 10 days in which to respond to the bidder's tender offer. Moreover, a tender offer must be kept open for at least 20 business days.

2) Direct solicitation of shareholders when management and the board resist the combination has been called a **Saturday night special** or a **hostile takeover**. This solicitation may be by advertisement in the media or, when a shareholder list can be obtained, by a general mailing.

3) An acquisition of stock may eventually result in a merger or consolidation.

d. **Takeover** is a broad term often used in the description of business combinations. It signifies a shift of control from one set of shareholders to another and may be **friendly** or **hostile**. A takeover includes not only mergers and acquisitions but also proxy contests and going private.

   1) A **proxy contest** is an attempt by dissident shareholders to gain control of the corporation, or at least to gain influence, by electing directors. A proxy is a power of attorney given by a shareholder that authorizes the holder to exercise the voting rights of the shareholder.

      a) Ten days prior to mailing a proxy statement to shareholders, the issuer must file a copy with the SEC.

      b) SEC rules require the solicitor of proxies to furnish shareholders with all material information concerning the matter subject to vote.

      c) A form by which shareholders may indicate their agreement or disagreement must be provided.

      d) Proxies solicited for the purpose of voting for directors must be accompanied by an annual report.

   2) **Going private** entails the purchase of the publicly owned stock of a corporation by a small group of private investors, usually including senior managers. Accordingly, the stock is delisted (if it is traded on an exchange) because it will no longer be traded. Such a transaction is usually structured as a leveraged buyout.

e. A **leveraged buyout (LBO)** is a financing technique by which a company is purchased using very little equity. The cash-offer price is financed with large amounts of debt, and the target company's assets serve as collateral for a loan to finance the purchase. An LBO is often used when a company is sold to management or some other group of employees, but it is also used in hostile takeovers.

   1) Junk bonds are often issued in an LBO. They are high-risk and therefore high-yield securities that are normally issued when the debt ratio is very high. Thus, the bondholders will have as much risk as the holders of equity securities.

   2) The tax deductibility of interest paid by the restructured company is an advantage of an LBO. Given a high debt ratio (greater financial leverage), after-tax cash flows increase.

   3) In addition to greater financial leverage, the firm may benefit from an LBO because of savings in administrative costs from no longer being publicly traded. Furthermore, if the managers become owners, they have greater incentives and greater operational flexibility.

   4) Characteristics of firms that are candidates for an LBO include

      a) An established business with proven operating performance
      b) Stable earnings and cash flows
      c) Very little outstanding debt
      d) A quality asset base useful as collateral for a new loan
      e) Stable technology that will not require large R&D costs

   5) The high degree of risk in LBOs results from the fixed charges for interest on the loan and the lack of cash for expansion.

f. A merger is usually a negotiated arrangement between a single bidder and the acquired firm. Payment is most frequently in stock. Moreover, the bidder is often a cash-rich firm in a mature industry and is seeking growth possibilities. The acquired firm is usually growing and in need of cash.

g. Takeovers effected through tender offers may be friendly or hostile.

   1) When the takeover is friendly, the target is usually a successful firm in a growth industry, payment may be in cash or stock, and management of the target often has a high percentage of ownership.

   2) When the takeover is hostile, the target is usually in a mature industry and is underperforming, more than one bidder may emerge, management ownership is likely to be low, payment is more likely to be in cash, and the initial bidder is probably a corporate raider.

4. **Defenses against Takeovers**

   a. **Greenmail** or a targeted repurchase is a defensive tactic used to protect against takeover after a bidder buys a large number of shares on the open market and then makes (or threatens to make) a tender offer. If management and the board are opposed to the takeover (a hostile tender offer), the potential acquirer is offered the opportunity to sell his/her already acquired shares back to the corporation at an amount substantially above market value (i.e., paying greenmail).

      1) In conjunction with greenmail, management may reach a **standstill agreement** in which the bidder agrees not to acquire additional shares.

   b. **Staggered election of directors** requires new shareholders to wait several years before being able to place their own people on the board.

      1) Another **antitakeover amendment** to the corporate charter may require a **supermajority** (e.g., 80%) for approval of a combination.

   c. **Golden parachutes** are provisions passed by a board of directors requiring large payments to specified executives if their employment is terminated by the acquiring firm following a takeover. A 1984 change in the tax law created a 20% excise tax on such payments and nondeductibility by the corporation. It was specifically designed to reduce the use of golden parachutes.

   d. **Fair price provisions** (shareholder rights plans) have become popular. Warrants are issued to shareholders that permit purchase of stock at a small percentage (often half) of market price in the event of a takeover attempt.

      1) The plan is intended to protect shareholder interests if the corporation is confronted by a coercive or unfair takeover attempt. The objective is not to deter takeovers but to ensure that all shareholders are treated equally.

      2) In the event of a friendly tender offer, the outstanding stock rights (warrants) may be repurchased by the corporation for a few cents per share, thus paving the way for the takeover. In many cases, these rights are not even issued in certificate form to shareholders because they are not immediately exercisable and are not traded separately from the common stock.

   e. **Going private** and **LBOs** are defensive tactics that have been previously discussed.

f. **Poison pill**. A target corporation's charter, bylaws, or contracts may include a wide variety of provisions that reduce the value of the target to potential tender offerors. For example, a valuable contract may terminate by its terms upon a specified form of change of ownership of the target. A poison pill is typically a right to purchase shares, at a reduced price, in the merged firm resulting from a takeover.

g. **Flip-over rights**. The charter of a target corporation may provide for its shareholders to acquire in exchange for their stock (in the target) a relatively greater interest (e.g., twice the shares of stock of equivalent value) in an acquiring entity.

h. **Flip-in rights**. Acquisition of more than a specified ownership interest (e.g., 25%) in the target corporation by a raider is a contingency, the occurrence of which triggers additional rights in the stock other than the stock acquired by the raider; e.g., each share becomes entitled to two votes.

i. **Issuing stock**. The target corporation significantly increases the amount of outstanding stock.

j. **Reverse tender**. The target corporation may respond with a tender offer to acquire control of the tender offeror.

k. **ESOP**. The trustees of an ESOP are usually favorable to current management. Thus, they are likely to vote the shares allocated to the ESOP against a raider, who will probably destabilize the target corporation's current structure.

l. **White knight merger**. Target management arranges an alternative tender offer with a different acquirer more favorable to incumbent management and shareholders.

m. **Crown jewel transfer**. The target corporation sells or otherwise disposes of one or more assets that made it a desirable target.

n. **Legal action**. A target corporation may challenge one or more aspects of a tender offer. Delays increase costs to the raider and enable defensive action.

5. **Other Restructurings**

a. A **spin-off** is the creation of a new separate entity from another entity, with the new entity's shares being distributed on a pro rata basis to existing shareholders of the parent entity. Existing shareholders will have the same proportion of ownership in the new entity as in the parent. A spin-off is a type of dividend to existing shareholders.

b. A **divestiture** involves the sale of an operating unit of a firm to a third party.

1) Some writers define the term divestiture to include spin-offs and liquidations.

c. A **liquidation** of assets of an operating unit occurs when they are sold piecemeal.

d. A **leveraged cash-out** entails borrowing heavily to issue a very large dividend that serves as a poison pill.

e. An **equity carve-out** involves the sale of a portion of the firm through an equity offering of shares in the new entity to outsiders.

f. Reasons for spin-offs and divestitures include governmental antitrust litigation, refocusing of a firm's operations, and raising capital for the core business operation.

6. Stop and review! You have completed the outline for this subunit. Study multiple-choice questions 60 through 62 beginning on page 260.

MULTIPLE-CHOICE QUESTIONS

A. Financial Ratios to Evaluate Capital Structure Finance

1. A company has the following income statements:

	1997	1996
Sales	$1,500,000	$1,400,000
Cost of goods sold	800,000	750,000
Gross profit	$ 700,000	$ 650,000
Selling and admin expense	62,000	60,000
Depreciation expense	50,000	50,000
Earnings before interest and taxes	$ 688,000	$ 540,000
Interest expense	100,000	100,000
Earnings before taxes	$ 588,000	$ 440,000
Income tax (50%)	294,000	220,000
Net income	$ 294,000	$ 220,000

Selected balance sheet items are as follows:

	1997 Year-end	1996 Year-end
Accounts receivable	$300,000	$200,000
Accounts payable	250,000	275,000

Assume a 365-day year in any calculations. The company had an interest-coverage ratio in 1996 of

A. 2.20 times.

B. 2.94 times.

C. 5.40 times.

D. 6.88 times.

The correct answer is (C). *(CIA, adapted)*

REQUIRED: The interest-coverage ratio in 1996.

DISCUSSION: The interest-coverage (times-interest-earned) ratio equals earnings before interest and taxes divided by interest charges. For 1996, the ratio is 5.40 times ($540,000 ÷ $100,000).

Answer (A) is incorrect because 2.20 times uses net income instead of earnings before interest and taxes. Answer (B) is incorrect because 2.94 times uses 1997 information and also uses net income instead of earnings before interest and taxes. Answer (D) is incorrect because 6.88 times is the interest-coverage ratio for 1997.

2. If Company A has a higher rate of return on assets than Company B, this could be because Company A has a <List A> profit margin on sales, or a <List B> asset-turnover ratio, or both.

	List A	List B
A.	Higher	Higher
B.	Higher	Lower
C.	Lower	Higher
D.	Lower	Lower

The correct answer is (A). *(CIA, adapted)*

REQUIRED: The reason for a higher rate of return on assets.

DISCUSSION: The return on assets equals the product of the profit margin and the asset turnover.

Return on assets = Profit margin × Asset turnover

$$\frac{\text{Net income}}{\text{Assets}} = \frac{\text{Net income}}{\text{Sales}} \times \frac{\text{Sales}}{\text{Assets}}$$

If one company has a higher return on assets than another, it may have a higher profit margin, a higher asset turnover, or both.

Answers (B), (C), and (D) are incorrect because a higher profit margin on sales or a higher asset-turnover ratio may explain a higher return on assets.

Questions 3 and 4 are based on the following information. A company has common and preferred shares outstanding with the following characteristics:

	Common Shares	Preferred Shares
Number of shares outstanding	50,000	25,000
Dividends paid during the year	$100,000	$50,000
Year-end market price per share	$10	$5
Book value of equity	$500,000	$250,000

For the year just ended, the company had the following statement of income:

Sales revenue	$1,000,000
Cost of goods sold	300,000
Depreciation expense	100,000
Earnings before interest and tax	$ 600,000
Interest expense	100,000
Earnings before tax	$ 500,000
Tax expense	250,000
Net income	$ 250,000

3. The company has earnings per share of

A. $2.67

B. $3.33

C. $4.00

D. $5.00

The correct answer is (C). *(CIA, adapted)*

REQUIRED: The company's EPS.

DISCUSSION: EPS equals the income available for distribution to common shareholders divided by the number of common shares outstanding, or $4.00 [($250,000 NI – $50,000 preferred dividends) ÷ 50,000 common shares].

Answer (A) is incorrect because $2.67 includes all outstanding shares, common and preferred, in the denominator. Answer (B) is incorrect because $3.33 fails to deduct the preferred dividends from the numerator and includes all outstanding shares in the denominator. Answer (D) is incorrect because $5.00 fails to deduct the preferred dividends from the numerator.

4. The company has a rate of return on common equity of

A. 26.67%

B. 33.33%

C. 40.00%

D. 50.00%

The correct answer is (C). *(CIA, adapted)*

REQUIRED: The rate of return on common equity.

DISCUSSION: The return on common equity equals the net income available to the common shareholders divided by the book value of the common shares, or 40% [($250,000 NI – $50,000 preferred dividends) ÷ $500,000].

Answer (A) is incorrect because 26.67% includes the book value of preferred shares in the denominator. Answer (B) is incorrect because 33.33% includes the book value of preferred shares in the denominator and fails to subtract the preferred dividends from the numerator. Answer (D) is incorrect because 50.00% fails to subtract the preferred dividends from the numerator.

5. Everything else being equal, a <List A> highly leveraged firm will have <List B> earnings per share.

	List A	List B
A.	More	Lower
B.	More	Less volatile
C.	Less	Less volatile
D.	Less	Higher

The correct answer is (C). *(CIA, adapted)*

REQUIRED: The effect of leverage on EPS.

DISCUSSION: Earnings per share is less volatile in less highly leveraged firms. Lower fixed costs result in less variable earnings when sales fluctuate.

Answer (A) is incorrect because higher leverage is associated with higher, not lower, EPS when sales exceed the breakeven point. Answer (B) is incorrect because earnings per share is more volatile in more highly leveraged firms. Answer (D) is incorrect because less leverage is associated with lower, not higher, EPS when sales exceed the breakeven point.

6. A company had 150,000 shares outstanding on January 1, 1995. On March 1, 1995, 75,000 additional shares were issued through a stock dividend. Then on November 1, 1995, the company issued 60,000 shares for cash. The number of shares to be used in the denominator of the EPS calculation for 1995 is

A. 222,500 shares.

B. 225,000 shares.

C. 235,000 shares.

D. 285,000 shares.

The correct answer is (C). *(CIA, adapted)*

REQUIRED: The number of shares to be used in the denominator of the EPS calculation.

DISCUSSION: The weighted average of shares outstanding during the year is used in the EPS denominator. Shares issued in a stock dividend are assumed to have been outstanding as of the beginning of the earliest accounting period presented. Thus, the 75,000 shares issued on March 1 are deemed to have been outstanding on January 1. The EPS denominator equals 235,000 shares {[150,000 x (12 months ÷ 12 months)] + [75,000 x (12 months ÷ 12 months)] + [60,000 x (2 months ÷ 12 months)]}.

Answer (A) is incorrect because 222,500 is the weighted-average number of shares if the stock dividend is not treated as retroactive. Answer (B) is incorrect because 225,000 ignores the November 1 issuance. Answer (D) is incorrect because 285,000 is the year-end number of outstanding shares.

7. In calculating fully diluted earnings per share when a company has convertible bonds outstanding, the number of common shares outstanding must be <List A> to adjust for the conversion feature of the bonds, and the net income must be <List B> by the amount of interest expense on the bonds, net of tax.

	List A	List B
A.	Increased	Increased
B.	Increased	Decreased
C.	Decreased	Increased
D.	Decreased	Decreased

The correct answer is (A). *(CIA, adapted)*

REQUIRED: The appropriate calculation of FDEPS.

DISCUSSION: The weighted-average number of shares outstanding must be increased to reflect the shares into which the bonds could be converted. Also, the effect of the bond interest on net income must be eliminated. In this way, earnings per share is calculated as if the bonds had been converted into common shares as of the start of the year.

Answer (B) is incorrect because the net income must be increased. Answers (C) and (D) are incorrect because the weighted-average number of shares outstanding must be increased, and the net income must be increased.

Questions 8 and 9 are based on the following information. Presented below are partial year-end financial statement data for companies A and B.

	Company A	Company B
Cash	$100	$200
Accounts receivable	unknown	100
Inventories	unknown	100
Net fixed assets	200	100
Accounts payable	100	50
Long-term debt	200	50
Common stock	100	200
Retained earnings	150	100

	Company A	Company B
Sales	$600	$5,800
Cost of goods sold	300	5,000
Administrative expenses	100	500
Depreciation expense	100	100
Interest expense	20	10
Income tax expense	40	95
Net income	40	95

8. The degree of financial leverage of Company B, to two decimal places, is

A. 1.03

B. 1.05

C. 1.12

D. 1.25

The correct answer is (B). *(CIA, adapted)*

REQUIRED: The degree of financial leverage for Company B.

DISCUSSION: The degree of financial leverage for Company B may be calculated as earnings before interest and taxes, divided by EBIT minus interest. EBIT is $200 ($95 NI + $10 interest + $95 tax expense). Thus, the DFL is 1.05 [$200 ÷ ($200 – $10)].

Answer (A) is incorrect because 1.03 results if depreciation expense is omitted from the calculation of EBIT. Answer (C) is incorrect because 1.12 results if net income is used instead of EBIT. Answer (D) is incorrect because 1.25 is the degree of financial leverage for Company A.

9. If Company A has 60 common shares outstanding, it has a book value per share, to the nearest cent, of

A. $1.67

B. $2.50

C. $4.17

D. $5.00

The correct answer is (C). *(CIA, adapted)*

REQUIRED: The book value per share of Company A.

DISCUSSION: The book value per share for Company A equals the sum of common stock and retained earnings, divided by the number of shares, or $4.17 [($100 + $150) ÷ 60].

Answer (A) is incorrect because $1.67 results if retained earnings is omitted from the numerator. Answer (B) is incorrect because $2.50 results if common stock is omitted from the numerator. Answer (D) is incorrect because $5.00 is the book value per share for Company B.

10. All else being equal, a company with a higher dividend-payout ratio will have a <List A> debt-to-assets ratio and a <List B> current ratio.

	List A	List B
A.	Higher	Higher
B.	Higher	Lower
C.	Lower	Higher
D.	Lower	Lower

The correct answer is (B). *(CIA, adapted)*

REQUIRED: The implications of a higher dividend payout ratio.

DISCUSSION: A company with a higher dividend-payout ratio is distributing more of its earnings as dividends to common shareholders. It will have less cash and less total assets than a comparable firm with a lower payout ratio. The debt-to-assets ratio will be higher because total assets are lower, and the current ratio will be lower because cash is lower.

Answer (A) is incorrect because the current ratio will be lower. Answer (C) is incorrect because the debt-to-assets ratio will be higher, and the current ratio will be lower. Answer (D) is incorrect because the debt-to-assets ratio will be higher.

Questions 11 through 13 are based on the following information. A company's financial statements for the current year are as follows.

Balance Sheet

Cash	$100
Accounts receivable	200
Inventory	50
Net fixed assets	600
Total	$950
Accounts payable	$140
Long-term debt	300
Capital stock	260
Retained earnings	250
Total	$950

Statement of Income and Retained Earnings

Sales	$3,000
Cost of goods sold	1,600
Gross profit	$1,400
Operations expenses	970
Operating income	$ 430
Interest expense	30
Income before tax	$ 400
Income tax	200
Net income	$ 200
Plus Jan. 1 retained earnings	150
Minus dividends	100
Dec. 31 retained earnings	$ 250

11. The company has a dividend-payout ratio of

A. 19.6%

B. 28.6%

C. 40.0%

D. 50.0%

The correct answer is (D). *(CIA, adapted)*

REQUIRED: The dividend-payout ratio.

DISCUSSION: The dividend-payout ratio is the ratio of dividends paid to net income for the period. Hence, it equals 50.0% ($100 dividends ÷ $200 NI).

Answer (A) is incorrect because 19.6% is the ratio of dividends paid to the December 31 book value of common equity. Answer (B) is incorrect because 28.6% is the ratio of dividends paid to the sum of beginning retained earnings and net income. Answer (C) is incorrect because 40.0% is the ratio of dividends paid to the December 31 retained earnings.

12. The company has return on assets of

A. 21.1%

B. 39.2%

C. 42.1%

D. 45.3%

The correct answer is (A). *(CIA, adapted)*

REQUIRED: The return on assets.

DISCUSSION: The return on assets is the ratio of net income to total assets. It equals 21.1% ($200 NI ÷ $950 total assets).

Answer (B) is incorrect because 39.2% is the ratio of net income to common equity. Answer (C) is incorrect because 42.1% is the ratio of income before tax to total assets. Answer (D) is incorrect because 45.3% is the ratio of income before interest and tax to total assets.

13. The company has a profit margin of

A. 6.67%

B. 13.33%

C. 14.33%

D. 46.67%

The correct answer is (A). *(CIA, adapted)*

REQUIRED: The profit margin.

DISCUSSION: The profit margin is the ratio of net income to sales. It equals 6.67% ($200 NI ÷ $3,000 sales).

Answer (B) is incorrect because 13.33% is the ratio of income before tax to sales. Answer (C) is incorrect because 14.33% is the ratio of income before interest and taxes to sales. Answer (D) is incorrect because 46.67% is the ratio of gross profit to sales.

14. A firm's financial risk is a function of how it manages and maintains its debt. Which one of the following sets of ratios characterizes the firm with the greatest amount of financial risk?

A. High debt-to-equity ratio, high interest-coverage ratio, volatile return on equity.

B. High debt-to-equity ratio, high interest-coverage ratio, stable return on equity.

C. Low debt-to-equity ratio, low interest-coverage ratio, volatile return on equity.

D. High debt-to-equity ratio, low interest-coverage ratio, volatile return on equity.

The correct answer is (D). *(CMA, adapted)*

REQUIRED: The set of ratios that characterizes the firm with the greatest financial risk.

DISCUSSION: A firm with high risk will have a higher debt-to-equity ratio than a low-risk firm, a lower interest coverage, and a volatile return on equity. A higher debt-to-equity ratio poses a greater risk of insolvency. Debtholders must be paid regardless of whether the firm is profitable. Low interest coverage means that the margin of safety of earnings before interest and taxes is small. A volatile return on equity signifies that earnings are unpredictable. Lack of predictability increases risk.

Answers (A) and (B) are incorrect because high interest coverage suggests lower risk. Also, stable returns on equity indicate a low level of risk. Answer (C) is incorrect because a low debt-to-equity ratio indicates a low level of risk.

15. A company has 100,000 outstanding common shares with a market value of $20 per share. Dividends of $2 per share were paid in the current year, and the company has a dividend-payout ratio of 40%. The price-to-earnings ratio of the company is

A. 2.5

B. 4

C. 10

D. 50

The correct answer is (B). *(CIA, adapted)*

REQUIRED: The P-E ratio.

DISCUSSION: The P-E ratio equals the share price divided by EPS. If the dividends per share equaled $2 and the dividend-payout ratio was 40%, EPS must have been $5 ($2 ÷ .4). Accordingly, the P-E ratio is 4 ($20 share price ÷ $5 EPS).

Answer (A) is incorrect because 2.5 equals EPS divided by dividends per share. Answer (C) is incorrect because 10 equals share price divided by dividends per share. Answer (D) is incorrect because 50 equals price per share divided by the dividend-payout percentage.

16. Which of the following financial statement analyses is most useful in determining whether the various expenses of a given company are higher or lower than industry averages?

A. Horizontal.

B. Vertical.

C. Activity ratio.

D. Defensive-interval ratio.

The correct answer is (B). *(CIA, adapted)*

REQUIRED: The analysis most useful in determining whether various expenses of a company are higher or lower than industry averages.

DISCUSSION: Vertical analysis is the expression of each item on a financial statement in a given period in relation to a base figure. On the income statement, each item is stated as a percentage of sales. Thus, the percentages for the company in question can be compared with industry norms.

Answer (A) is incorrect because a horizontal analysis indicates the proportionate change over a period of time and is useful in trend analysis of an individual entity. Answer (C) is incorrect because activity ratio analysis includes the preparation of turnover ratios such as those for receivables, inventory, and total assets. Answer (D) is incorrect because the defensive-interval ratio is part of a liquidity analysis.

B. Financial Forecasting

17. Identify the statement below that represents a required underlying assumption for using the percentage-of-sales technique to develop pro forma financial statements.

A. Economies of scale exist in the use of assets.

B. Current levels of all assets are optimal for the current sales level.

C. Technological considerations dictate that fixed assets be added in large, discrete amounts.

D. Actual sales-to-asset ratios for the firm in any given period vary with different stages of the economic cycle.

The correct answer is (B). *(CIA, adapted)*

REQUIRED: The assumption underlying the use of the percentage of sales technique.

DISCUSSION: This method states balance sheet amounts as percentages of sales and then multiplies future sales by these percentages to develop pro forma financial statements. Thus, a greater amount of assets will be required for a greater amount of sales (e.g., receivables and cash requirements will increase). The asset-to-sales ratios must be constant when applying the percentage-of-sales forecasting method. If the current levels of assets are considered to be optimal for the current sales level, that is, if assets are efficiently used, the asset-to-sales ratios are constant.

Answer (A) is incorrect because, if economies of scale exist in the use of assets, the ratios of assets to sales are not constant. Answer (C) is incorrect because, if fixed assets must be added in large, discrete amounts, the ratios are not constant. Answer (D) is incorrect because, if ratios vary with economic cycles, the percentage-of-sales method is inappropriate.

18. A company had sales last year of $10 million, with net income equal to 6% of sales. This year the sales are expected to be $11.2 million. The accounts receivable balance was $1.5 million at the end of last year. Using the percentage-of-sales method, the accounts receivable balance at the end of this year is forecasted to be

A. $1.572 million.

B. $1.68 million.

C. $2.172 million.

D. $2.7 million.

The correct answer is (B). *(CIA, adapted)*

REQUIRED: The accounts receivable balance at the end of this year.

DISCUSSION: In financial analysis, pro forma financial statements reflect a forecast of actual events if certain assumptions are realized. One method of preparing pro forma statements is to state certain balance sheet amounts as percentages of expected sales. Items that vary directly with sales (inventory, receivables, accounts payable, plant assets, etc.) are estimated in this way. Other balance sheet amounts that do not necessarily vary directly with sales (notes payable, marketable equity securities, common stock, etc.) are taken from the most recent financial statements. This method is based on the assumptions that most balance sheet amounts directly correlate with sales and that the current levels of all assets are optimal for the current sales level. Thus, given that last year's receivables equaled 15% of sales ($1,500,000 ÷ $10,000,000), this year's ending receivables balance is expected to be $1,680,000 (15% x $11,200,000).

Answer (A) is incorrect because $1,572,000 is based on adding the percentage increase in net income to the previous amount of receivables {[6% x ($11,200,000 – $10,000,000)] + $1,500,000}. Answer (C) is incorrect because $2,172,000 is based on adding profit as a percentage of sales to last year's receivables [$1,500,000 + (6% x $11,200,000)]. Answer (D) is incorrect because $2,700,000 equals past receivables plus the additional sales.

19. A company had $500,000 of sales for the year just ended and is projecting sales of $600,000 for the coming year. For every $1 increase in sales, 38 cents of additional financing is required for the purchase of additional assets. The projected profit margin is 20%, and 60% of profits will be retained for reinvestment in the company. The amount of additional external financing needed by the company in the coming year is

A. $0

B. $38,000

C. $86,000

D. $110,000

The correct answer is (A). *(CIA, adapted)*

REQUIRED: The amount of additional external financing needed.

DISCUSSION: The projected sales increase of $100,000 requires $38,000 of additional asset financing. Profits for the year are projected to be 20% of sales, or $120,000 (20% x $600,000), of which 60%, or $72,000 (60% x $120,000), is available for reinvestment. No new external financing will be required.

Answer (B) is incorrect because $38,000 results if internally generated funds are not considered as a source of financing. Answer (C) is incorrect because $86,000 results if the dividend payment is considered to be a use of cash and internally generated funds are not considered. Answer (D) is incorrect because $110,000 results if internally generated funds available for reinvestment are treated as a use, rather than a source, of financing.

20. Short-term interest rates are

A. Usually lower than long-term rates.

B. Usually higher than long-term rates.

C. Lower than long-term rates during periods of high inflation only.

D. Not significantly related to long-term rates.

The correct answer is (A). *(CMA, adapted)*

REQUIRED: The true statement about short-term interest rates.

DISCUSSION: Historically, one facet of the term structure of interest rates (the relationship of yield and time to maturity) is that short-term interest rates have ordinarily been lower than long-term rates. One reason is that less risk is involved in the short run. Moreover, future expectations concerning interest rates affect the term structure. Most economists believe that a long-term interest rate is an average of future expected short-term interest rates. For this reason, the yield curve will slope upward if future rates are expected to rise, slope downward if interest rates are anticipated to fall, and remain flat if investors think the rate is stable. Future inflation is incorporated into this relationship. Another consideration is liquidity preference: investors in an uncertain world will accept lower rates on short-term investments because of their greater liquidity, whereas business debtors often prefer to pay higher rates on long-term debt to avoid the hazards of short-term maturities.

Answer (B) is incorrect because short-term rates are usually lower than long-term rates. Answer (C) is incorrect because short-term rates are more likely to be greater than long-term rates if current levels of inflation are high. Answer (D) is incorrect because long-term rates may be viewed as short-term rates adjusted by a risk factor.

21.

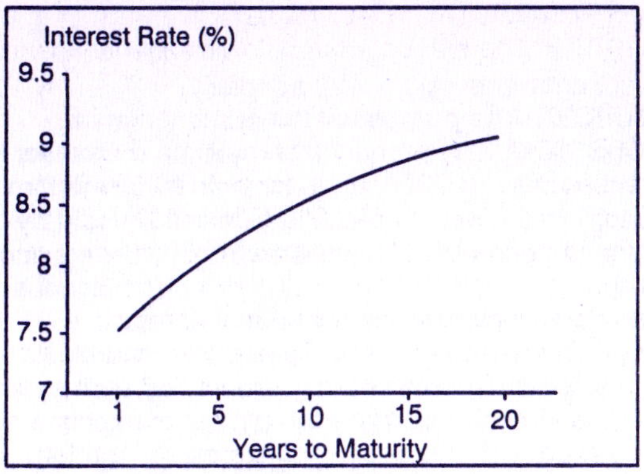

The yield curve shown above implies that the

A. Credit risk premium of corporate bonds has increased.

B. Credit risk premium of municipal bonds has increased.

C. Long-term interest rates have a higher annualized yield than short-term rates.

D. Short-term interest rates have a higher annualized yield than long-term rates.

The correct answer is (C). *(CIA, adapted)*

REQUIRED: The implication of the yield curve.

DISCUSSION: The term structure of interest rates is the relationship between yield to maturity and time to maturity. This relationship is depicted by a yield curve. Assuming the long-term interest rate is an average of expected future short-term rates, the curve will be upward sloping when future short-term interest rates are expected to rise. Furthermore, the normal expectation is for long-term investments to pay higher rates because of their higher risk. Thus, long-term interest rates have a higher annualized yield than short-term rates.

Answers (A) and (B) are incorrect because the yield curve does not reflect the credit risk premium of bonds.
Answer (D) is incorrect because long-term interest rates should be higher than short-term rates.

22. A downward-sloping yield curve depicting the term structure of interest rates implies that

A. Interest rates have declined over recent years.

B. Interest rates have increased over recent years.

C. Prevailing short-term interest rates are lower than prevailing long-term interest rates.

D. Prevailing short-term interest rates are higher than prevailing long-term interest rates.

The correct answer is (D). *(CIA, adapted)*

REQUIRED: The implication of a downward-sloping yield curve.

DISCUSSION: The term structure of interest rates is the relationship between long- and short-term interest rates, that is, between yield to maturity and time to maturity. It is graphically depicted by a yield curve with a rate of return on the vertical axis and time to maturity on the horizontal axis. If short-term rates are higher than long-term rates, the curve will be downward sloping. If the reverse is true, the curve will be upward sloping.

Answer (A) is incorrect because the yield curve does not reflect past interest rate trends. Answer (B) is incorrect because the yield curve does not reflect past interest rate trends. Answer (C) is incorrect because the downward-sloping yield curve implies that prevailing short-term interest rates are higher than prevailing long-term interest rates.

C. Sources of Long-Term Financing

23. In capital markets, the primary market is concerned with the provision of new funds for capital investments through

A. New issues of bond and stock securities.

B. Exchanges of existing bond and stock securities.

C. The sale of forward or future commodities contracts.

D. New issues of bond and stock securities and exchanges of existing bond and stock securities.

The correct answer is (A). *(CMA, adapted)*

REQUIRED: The purpose of the primary market.

DISCUSSION: The primary market is the market for new stocks and bonds. In this market, wherein investment money flows directly to the issuer, securities are initially sold by investment bankers who purchase them from issuers and sell them through an underwriting group. Later transactions occur on securities exchanges or other markets.

Answer (B) is incorrect because existing securities are traded on a secondary market (e.g., securities exchanges). Answer (C) is incorrect because the futures market is where commodities contracts are sold, not the capital market. Answer (D) is incorrect because exchanges of existing securities do not occur in the primary market.

24. The term "underwriting spread" refers to the

A. Commission percentage an investment banker receives for underwriting a security issue.

B. Discount investment bankers receive on securities they purchase from the issuing company.

C. Difference between the price the investment banker pays for a new security issue and the price at which the securities are resold.

D. Commission a broker receives for either buying or selling a security on behalf of an investor.

The correct answer is (C). *(CMA, adapted)*

REQUIRED: The definition of underwriting spread.

DISCUSSION: An investment banker performs an underwriting or insurance function when it purchases an issue of securities and then resells them. The risk of price fluctuations during the distribution period is borne entirely by the investment banker. Investment banking is also an efficient vehicle for marketing the securities because investment bankers are specialists in such activities. The profit earned is the underwriting spread, or the difference between the purchase and resale prices of the securities (effectively, the wholesale and retail prices).

Answers (A) and (D) are incorrect because the underwriting spread is not based on a commission. The underwriter actually buys the new securities and resells them at a price that is expected to result in a profit. Answer (B) is incorrect because the underwriting spread is not a genuine discount; it is simply the difference between the price paid and the price received for a new security.

25. In general, it is more expensive for a company to finance with equity capital than with debt capital because

A. Long-term bonds have a maturity date and must therefore be repaid in the future.

B. Investors are exposed to greater risk with equity capital.

C. The interest on debt is a legal obligation.

D. Equity capital is in greater demand than debt capital.

The correct answer is (B). *(CMA, adapted)*

REQUIRED: The reason equity financing is more expensive than debt financing.

DISCUSSION: Providers of equity capital are exposed to more risk than are lenders because the firm is not obligated to pay them a return. Also, in case of liquidation, creditors are paid before equity investors. Thus, equity financing is more expensive than debt because equity investors require a higher return to compensate for the greater risk assumed.

Answer (A) is incorrect because the obligation to repay at a specific maturity date reduces the risk to investors and thus the required return. Answer (C) is incorrect because the existence of a legal obligation is but one reason that debt poses less risk to investors. Thus, (C) is a more limited answer than (B). Answer (D) is incorrect because the demand for equity capital is directly related to its greater cost to the issuer.

Questions 26 and 27 are based on the following information. The equity section of Smith Corporation's Statement of Financial Position is presented below.

Preferred stock, $100 par	$12,000,000
Common stock, $5 par	10,000,000
Paid-in capital in excess of par	18,000,000
Retained earnings	9,000,000
Net worth	$49,000,000

26. The book value of Smith Corporation's common stock is

A. $18.50

B. $5.00

C. $14.00

D. $100

The correct answer is (A). *(CMA, adapted)*

REQUIRED: The book value per share of common stock.

DISCUSSION: The book value per common share equals the net assets (equity) attributable to common shareholders divided by the common shares outstanding, or $18.50 [($10,000,000 common stock + $18,000,000 additional paid-in capital + $9,000,000 RE) ÷ ($10,000,000 ÷ $5 par)].

Answer (B) is incorrect because $5 is the par value per share. Answer (C) is incorrect because $14.00 fails to include retained earnings in the portion of equity attributable to common shareholders. Answer (D) is incorrect because $100 is the par value of a preferred share.

27. The common shareholders of Smith Corporation have preemptive rights. If Smith Corporation issues 400,000 additional shares of common stock at $6 per share, a current holder of 20,000 shares of Smith Corporation's common stock must be given the option to buy

A. 1,000 additional shares.

B. 3,774 additional shares.

C. 4,000 additional shares.

D. 3,333 additional shares.

The correct answer is (C). *(CMA, adapted)*

REQUIRED: The new shares that a shareholder may buy given preemptive rights.

DISCUSSION: Common shareholders usually have preemptive rights, which means they have first right to purchase any new issues of stock in proportion to their current ownership percentages. The purpose of a preemptive right is to allow shareholders to maintain their current percentages of ownership. Given that Smith had 2,000,000 shares outstanding ($10,000,000 ÷ $5 par), an investor with 20,000 shares has a 1% ownership. Hence, this investor must be allowed to purchase 4,000 (1% x 400,000 shares) of the additional shares.

Answer (A) is incorrect because the investor would be allowed to purchase 1% of any new issues. Answers (B) and (D) are incorrect because preferred shareholders do not share in preemptive rights.

28. The formula for determining the value of one stock right when the price of the stock is rights-on is

$$R_{on} = \frac{P_{on} - S}{N + 1}$$

If: R_{on} = market value of one right when the stock is selling rights-on.

P_{on} = market value of one share of stock with rights-on.

N = number of rights necessary to purchase one share of stock.

S = subscription price per share.

If the market price of a stock is $50 per share, the subscription price is $40 per share, and three rights are necessary to buy an additional share of stock, the theoretical market value of one right used to buy the stock prior to the ex-rights date is

A. $2.00

B. $2.50

C. $10.00

D. $40.00

The correct answer is (B). *(CMA, adapted)*

REQUIRED: The theoretical value of one right prior to the ex-rights date.

DISCUSSION: Plugging the amounts into the formula produces a theoretical value of $2.50 per right:

($50 – $40) ÷ (3 + 1) = $2.50

To check the answer, assume that an investor purchases three rights at $2.50 each (a total of $7.50) and uses them to buy a share of stock for $40. The total investment is $47.50. Similarly, a person holding a $50 share of stock before the rights are issued will have a basis of $47.50 after selling the right for $2.50. Thus, the value of the stock ex-rights is $47.50, and the value of the right is $2.50.

Answer (A) is incorrect because the right is worth $2.50. Answer (C) is incorrect because $10 is the difference between the price of the stock with rights ($50) and the exercise price ($40). Answer (D) is incorrect because $40 is the exercise price of the new issue.

29. The market value of a share of stock is $50, and the market value of one right prior to the ex-rights date is $2.00 after the offering is announced but while the stock is still selling rights-on. The offer to the shareholder is that it will take three rights to buy an additional share of stock at a subscription price of $40 per share. If the theoretical value of the stock when it goes ex-rights is $47.50, the shareholder

A. Does not receive any additional benefit from a rights offering.

B. Receives an additional benefit from a rights offering.

C. Merely receives a return of capital.

D. Should redeem the right and purchase the stock before the ex-rights date.

The correct answer is (A). *(CMA, adapted)*

REQUIRED: The true statement about the effect on the value of stock when it goes ex-rights.

DISCUSSION: Plugging the amounts into the formula given in the preceding question produces a theoretical value of $2.50 per right, which leaves a theoretical value of $47.50 for the stock:

($50 – $40) ÷ (3 + 1) = $2.50

However, if the stock declines to $47.50 when the right is worth only $2, the original investor is worse off then before the rights issuance; i.e., the investor would have only $49.50 worth of investments. Hence, the original shareholder receives no benefit from the issuance of the rights.

Answer (B) is incorrect because the shareholder would be worse off after the rights offering ($49.50) than before the rights offering ($50). Answer (C) is incorrect because the shareholder receives only a certificate granting the right to make an additional investment. Answer (D) is incorrect because an investor cannot redeem a right before the ex-rights date, i.e., while the stock is still rights-on.

Questions 30 and 31 are based on the following information. A company's stock trades rights-on for $50.00 and ex-rights for $48.00. The subscription price for rights holders is $40.00, and four rights are required to purchased one share of stock.

30. The value of a right while the stock is still trading rights-on is

A. $0.40

B. $0.50

C. $1.60

D. $2.00

The correct answer is (D). *(CMA, adapted)*

REQUIRED: The value of a right when the stock is still trading rights-on.

DISCUSSION: Until rights are actually issued, the stock trades rights-on, meaning that the stock and rights are inseparable. If P is the value of a share rights-on, S is the subscription price of a new share, and N is the number of rights needed to buy a new share, the value of a right when the stock is selling rights-on is (P – S) ÷ (N + 1). Thus, the value of a right when the stock is selling rights-on is $2.00 [($50 – $40) ÷ (4 + 1)].

Answer (A) is incorrect because $0.40 is the rights-on value if P is $50 and S is $48. Answer (B) is incorrect because $0.50 is the ex-rights value if P is $50 and S is $48. Answer (C) is incorrect because $1.60 is the rights-on value if P is $48 and S is $40.

31. The value of a right when the stock is trading ex-rights is

A. $0.40

B. $0.50

C. $2.00

D. $2.50

The correct answer is (C). *(CMA, adapted)*

REQUIRED: The value of a right when the stock is trading ex-rights.

DISCUSSION: If a stock can be purchased for $48 on the open market, or for $40 with four rights, each right must be worth $2.00 ($8 savings ÷ 4 rights).

Answer (A) is incorrect because $0.40 is the rights-on value if P is $50 and S is $48. Answer (B) is incorrect because $0.50 is the ex-rights value if P is $50 and S is $48. Answer (D) is incorrect because $2.50 is the ex-rights value if P is $50 and S is $40.

Questions 32 and 33 are based on the following information. The Dawson Corporation projects the following for the year 1998.

Earnings before interest and taxes	$35 million
Interest expense	$ 5 million
Preferred stock dividends	$ 4 million
Common stock dividend-payout ratio	30%
Common shares outstanding	2 million
Effective corporate income tax rate	40%

32. The expected common stock dividend per share for Dawson Corporation for 1998 is

A. $2.34

B. $2.70

C. $1.80

D. $2.10

The correct answer is (D). *(CMA, adapted)*

REQUIRED: The expected common stock dividend per share.

DISCUSSION: The company's net income is $18,000,000 [($35,000,000 EBIT – $5,000,000 interest) x (1.0 – .4 tax rate)]. Thus, the earnings available to common shareholders equal $14,000,000 ($18,000,000 – $4,000,000 preferred dividends), and EPS is $7 ($14,000,000 ÷ 2,000,000 common shares). Given a dividend-payout ratio of 30%, the dividend to common shareholders is expected to be $2.10 per share (30% x $7).

Answer (A) is incorrect because $2.34 results from treating preferred dividends as tax deductible. Answer (B) is incorrect because $2.70 ignores the effect of preferred dividends. Answer (C) is incorrect because $1.80 is based on a 60% effective tax rate and ignores the effect of preferred dividends.

33. If Dawson Corporation's common stock is expected to trade at a price-earnings ratio of eight, the market price per share (to the nearest dollar) would be

A. $104

B. $56

C. $72

D. $68

The correct answer is (B). *(CMA, adapted)*

REQUIRED: The market price per share given the P-E ratio.

DISCUSSION: Net income is $18,000,000 [($35,000,000 EBIT – $5,000,000 interest) x (1.0 – .4 tax rate)], and EPS is $7 [($18,000,000 NI –$4,000,000 preferred dividends) ÷ 2,000,000 common shares]. Consequently, the market price is $56 ($7 EPS x $8 P-E ratio).

Answer (A) is incorrect because $104 ignores income taxes. Answer (C) is incorrect because $72 ignores the effect of preferred dividends. Answer (D) is incorrect because $68 ignores the deductibility of interest.

34. The par value of a common stock represents

A. The estimated market value of the stock when it was issued.

B. The liability ceiling of a shareholder when a company undergoes bankruptcy proceedings.

C. The total value of the stock that must be entered in the issuing corporation's records.

D. A theoretical value of $100 per share of stock with any differences entered in the issuing corporation's records as discount or premium on common stock.

The correct answer is (B). *(CMA, adapted)*

REQUIRED: The amount represented by the par value of common stock.

DISCUSSION: Par value represents a stock's legal capital. It is an arbitrary value assigned to stock before it is issued. Par value represents a shareholder's liability ceiling because, as long as the par value has been paid in to the corporation, the shareholders obtain the benefits of limited liability.

Answer (A) is incorrect because par value is rarely the same as market value. Normally, market value will be equal to or greater than par value, but there is no relationship between the two. Answer (C) is incorrect because all assets received for stock must be entered into a corporation's records. The amount received is very rarely the par value. Answer (D) is incorrect because par value can be any amount more or less than $100.

35. Each share of nonparticipating, 8%, cumulative preferred stock in a company that meets its dividend obligations has all of the following characteristics except

A. Voting rights in corporate elections.

B. Dividend payments that are not tax deductible by the company.

C. No principal repayments.

D. A superior claim to common stock equity in the case of liquidation.

The correct answer is (A). *(CMA, adapted)*

REQUIRED: The item that is not characteristic of nonparticipating, cumulative preferred stock.

DISCUSSION: Dividends on cumulative preferred stock accrue until declared; that is, the book value of the preferred stock increases by the amount of any undeclared dividends. Participating preferred stock participates with common shareholders in excess earnings of the company. In other words, 8% participating preferred stock might pay a dividend each year greater than 8% when the corporation is extremely profitable. Hence, nonparticipating preferred stock will receive no more than is stated on the face of the stock. Preferred shareholders rarely have voting rights. Voting rights are exchanged for preferences regarding dividends and liquidation of assets.

Answer (B) is incorrect because a corporation does not receive a tax deduction for making dividend payments on any type of stock. Answer (C) is incorrect because preferred stock normally need not be redeemed as long as the corporation remains in business. Answer (D) is incorrect because preferred shareholders do have priority over common shareholders in a liquidation.

36. If a $1,000 bond sells for $1,125, which of the following statements are correct?

I. The market rate of interest is greater than the coupon rate on the bond.

II. The coupon rate on the bond is greater than the market rate of interest.

III. The coupon rate and the market rate are equal.

IV. The bond sells at a premium.

V. The bond sells at a discount.

A. I and IV.

B. I and V.

C. II and IV.

D. II and V.

The correct answer is (C). *(CMA, adapted)*

REQUIRED: The true statements about a bond that sells at more than its face value.

DISCUSSION: The excess of the price over the face value is a premium. A premium is paid because the coupon rate on the bond is greater than the market rate of interest. In other words, because the bond is paying a higher rate than other similar bonds, its price is bid up by investors.

Answer (A) is incorrect because, if a bond sells at a premium, the market rate of interest is less than the coupon rate. Answers (B) and (D) are incorrect because a bond sells at a discount when the price is less than the face amount.

37. Debentures are

A. Income bonds that require interest payments only when earnings permit.

B. Subordinated debt and rank behind convertible bonds.

C. Bonds secured by the full faith and credit of the issuing firm.

D. A form of lease financing similar to equipment trust certificates.

The correct answer is (C). *(CMA, adapted)*

REQUIRED: The true statement about debentures.

DISCUSSION: Debentures are unsecured bonds. Although no assets are mortgaged as security for the bonds, debentures are secured by the full faith and credit of the issuing firm. Debentures are a general obligation of the borrower. Only companies with the best credit ratings can issue debentures because only the company's credit rating and reputation secure the bonds.

Answer (A) is incorrect because debentures must pay interest regardless of earnings levels. Answer (B) is incorrect because debentures are not subordinated except to the extent of assets mortgaged against other bond issues. Debentures are a general obligation of the borrower and rank equally with convertible bonds. Answer (D) is incorrect because debentures have nothing to do with lease financing. Debentures are not secured by assets.

38. Which one of the following characteristics distinguishes income bonds from other bonds?

A. The bondholder is guaranteed an income over the life of the security.

B. By promising a return to the bondholder, an income bond is junior to preferred and common stock.

C. Income bonds are junior to subordinated debt but senior to preferred and common stock.

D. Income bonds pay interest only if the issuing company has earned the interest.

The correct answer is (D). *(CMA, adapted)*

REQUIRED: The characteristic of income bonds.

DISCUSSION: An income bond is one that pays interest only if the issuing company has earned the interest, although the principal must still be paid on the due date. Such bonds are riskier than normal bonds.

Answer (A) is incorrect because bondholders will receive an income only if the issuing company earns sufficient income to pay the interest. Answer (B) is incorrect because all bonds have priority over preferred and common stock. Answer (C) is incorrect because subordinated debt is junior to nonsubordinated debt.

39. Serial bonds are attractive to investors because

A. All bonds in the issue mature on the same date.

B. The yield to maturity is the same for all bonds in the issue.

C. Investors can choose the maturity that suits their financial needs.

D. The coupon rate on these bonds is adjusted to the maturity date.

The correct answer is (C). *(CMA, adapted)*

REQUIRED: The reason serial bonds are attractive to investors.

DISCUSSION: Serial bonds have staggered maturities; that is, they mature over a period (series) of years. Thus, investors can choose the maturity date that meets their investment needs. For example, an investor who will have a child starting college in 16 years can choose bonds that mature in 16 years.

Answer (A) is incorrect because serial bonds mature on different dates. Answer (B) is incorrect because bonds maturing on different dates may have different yields, or they may be the same. Usually, the earlier date maturities carry slightly lower yields than the later maturities. Answer (D) is incorrect because the coupon rate is the same for all bonds; only the selling price and yield differ.

40 The best advantage of a zero-coupon bond to the issuer is that the

A. Bond requires a low issuance cost.

B. Bond requires no interest income calculation to the holder or issuer until maturity.

C. Interest can be amortized annually by the APR method and need not be shown as an interest expense to the issuer.

D. Interest can be amortized annually on a straight-line basis but is a noncash outlay.

The correct answer is (D). *(CMA, adapted)*

REQUIRED: The best advantage of a zero-coupon bond to the issuer.

DISCUSSION: Zero-coupon bonds do not pay periodic interest. The bonds are sold at a discount from their face value, and the investors do not receive interest until the bonds mature. The issuer does not have to make annual cash outlays for interest. However, the discount must be amortized annually and reported as interest expense.

Answer (A) is incorrect because the issuance costs are no lower than for any other bond issue. Answer (B) is incorrect because interest income and expense must be calculated annually based on the amount of the initial discount that is amortized. Answer (C) is incorrect because the annual amortization must be shown as interest expense. APR means "annual percentage rate."

41. Junk bonds are

A. Securities rated at less than investment grade.

B. Worthless securities.

C. Securities that are highly risky but offer only low yields.

D. Considered illegal since the collapse of the Drexel Burnham Lambert firm.

The correct answer is (A). *(CMA, adapted)*

REQUIRED: The definition of junk bonds.

DISCUSSION: Junk bonds are high-risk and therefore high-yield securities that are normally issued when the debt ratio is very high. Thus, the bondholders have as much risk as the holders of equity securities. Such bonds are not highly rated by credit evaluation companies. Junk bonds have become accepted because of the tax deductibility of the interest paid.

Answer (B) is incorrect because junk bonds are not yet worthless; they simply bear high interest rates and high risk. Answer (C) is incorrect because junk bonds typically offer high yields. Answer (D) is incorrect because Drexel Burnham was not the only underwriter to package junk bonds, and they were never illegal.

42. The best reason corporations issue Eurobonds rather than domestic bonds is that

A. These bonds are denominated in the currency of the country in which they are issued.

B. These bonds are normally a less expensive form of financing because of the absence of government regulation.

C. Foreign buyers more readily accept the issues of both large and small U.S. corporations than do domestic investors.

D. Eurobonds carry no foreign exchange risk.

The correct answer is (B). *(CMA, adapted)*

REQUIRED: The best reason for issuing Eurobonds instead of domestic bonds.

DISCUSSION: International bonds are of two types: foreign bonds and Eurobonds. Foreign bonds are denominated in the currency of the nation in which they are sold. Eurobonds are denominated in a currency other than that of the nation where they are sold.

Foreign bonds issued in the United States and denominated in dollars must be registered with the SEC, but such extensive disclosure is not required in most European nations. Thus, an American company may elect to issue Eurobonds denominated in dollars in a foreign nation because of the convenience of not having to comply with governmental registration requirements.

Answer (A) is incorrect because Eurobonds are not denominated in the currency of the nation in which they are sold. The difference is a possible disadvantage because of exchange rate risk. Nevertheless, many foreign bonds are denominated in U.S. dollars. Answer (C) is incorrect because foreign nationals are often hesitant about buying bonds issued by small companies with which they are not familiar. Answer (D) is incorrect because Eurobonds carry foreign exchange risk. The foreign lender may suffer a loss if the dollar declines relative to its domestic currency.

43. Which one of the following statements is correct when comparing bond financing alternatives?

A. A bond with a call provision typically has a lower yield to maturity than a similar bond without a call provision.

B. A convertible bond must be converted to common stock prior to its maturity.

C. A call provision is generally considered detrimental to the investor.

D. A call premium requires the investor to pay an amount greater than par at the time of purchase.

The correct answer is (C). *(CMA, adapted)*

REQUIRED: The true statement comparing bond financing alternatives.

DISCUSSION: A callable bond can be recalled by the issuer prior to maturity. A call provision is detrimental to the investor because the issuer can recall the bond when market interest rates decline. It is usually exercised only when a company wishes to refinance high-interest debt.

Answer (A) is incorrect because callable bonds sometimes pay a slightly higher rate of interest. Investors may demand a greater return because of the uncertainty over the true maturity date. Answer (B) is incorrect because conversion is at the option of the investor. Answer (D) is incorrect because the call premium is the amount in excess of par that the issuer must pay when bonds are called.

44. A major use of warrants in financing is to

A. Lower the cost of debt.

B. Avoid dilution of earnings per share.

C. Maintain managerial control.

D. Permit the buy-back of bonds before maturity.

The correct answer is (A). *(CMA, adapted)*

REQUIRED: The major use of warrants in financing.

DISCUSSION: Warrants are long-term options that give holders the right to buy common stock in the future at a specific price. If the market price goes up, the holders of warrants will exercise their rights to buy stock at the special price. If the market price does not exceed the exercise price, the warrants will lapse. Issuers of debt sometimes attach stock purchase warrants to debt instruments as an inducement to investors. The investor then has the security of fixed-return debt plus the possibility for large gains if stock prices increase significantly. If warrants are attached, debt can sell at an interest rate slightly lower than the market rate.

Answer (B) is incorrect because outstanding warrants dilute earnings per share. They are included in the denominator of the EPS calculation even if they have not been exercised. Answer (C) is incorrect because warrants can, if exercised, result in a dilution of management's holdings. Answer (D) is incorrect because a call provision in a bond indenture, not the use of warrants, permits the buyback of bonds.

Questions 45 and 46 are based on the following information. The current market price of Action Pharmaceutical's common stock is $34. A 6-month call option has been written on the stock. The option has an exercise price of $40 and a market value of $4. A financial analyst estimates that, at the end of 6 months, the expected value of the stock is $42.

45. What is the value just prior to expiration of the option if the stock closes at $42 at the end of 6 months?

A. $4.00

B. $0

C. $6.00

D. $2.00

The correct answer is (D). *(CMA, adapted)*

REQUIRED: The value of a call option just prior to its expiration.

DISCUSSION: A call option permits a holder to purchase stock at a certain price (the exercise price) regardless of the current market price. The value of the option just prior to its expiration will be the difference between the exercise price and the current market price ($42 – $40 = $2.00), assuming that the market price is higher. If the exercise price is higher than the market price just prior to the expiration date, the call option will have no value. A call option permits an investor to share in a price rise by making only a small investment. Hence, the downside risk is small because it is limited to the cost of the option.

Answer (A) is incorrect because $4 was the market price at the beginning of the exercise period. Answer (B) is incorrect because the call option has some value if the market price exceeds the exercise price. Answer (C) is incorrect because $6.00 exceeds the difference between the market price and exercise price.

46. What is the theoretical value of exercising the option on the date it is granted?

A. $4.00

B. $0

C. $6.00

D. $8.00

The correct answer is (B). *(CMA, adapted)*

REQUIRED: The theoretical value of exercising the call option on the date it was granted.

DISCUSSION: Theoretically, the call option had no exercise value on the date of grant because it permitted the purchase of a $34 stock at $40. No reasonable person would exercise such an option.

Answers (A), (C), and (D) are incorrect because the theoretical exercise value is zero when the exercise price exceeds the market price.

47. Which one of the following is a disadvantage of the use of convertible bonds as a form of financing?

A. Less restrictive covenants in bond indentures would usually be more acceptable to investors in convertible bonds than to investors in nonconvertible bonds.

B. Convertible bonds defer equity financing until the stock price is higher.

C. Convertible bonds carry a lower interest rate at issuance than if the bond were not convertible.

D. The investor may choose not to convert the convertible bonds.

The correct answer is (D). *(CMA, adapted)*

REQUIRED: The disadvantage of convertible bonds as a form of financing.

DISCUSSION: A conversion feature permits bondholders to convert their bonds into common stock at some future time if the stock price rises. This provision is sometimes incorporated into a bond contract to entice investors to lend money to the issuer at a lower interest rate. Another purpose of issuing convertible bonds is to obtain equity financing at a time when market prices are unfavorable. Issuing convertible bonds is tantamount to selling the stock at a higher price, assuming that bondholders eventually exercise their option to convert. The disadvantage to the corporation is that stock prices may never reach the conversion price, and bondholders will not convert their bonds into stock. The corporation will then have to make interest and principal payments.

Answer (A) is incorrect because an advantage of convertible bonds is that covenants in the bond indentures are often less restrictive. Answer (B) is incorrect because an advantage of convertible bonds is that they defer equity financing until the stock price is higher. Answer (C) is incorrect because an advantage of convertible bonds is that they carry a lower interest rate at issuance.

48. All of the following may reduce the coupon rate on a bond issued at par except a

A. Sinking fund.

B. Call provision.

C. Change in rating from Aa to Aaa.

D. Conversion option.

The correct answer is (B). *(CMA, adapted)*

REQUIRED: The item that will not reduce the coupon rate on a bond issued at par.

DISCUSSION: A bond issued at par may carry a lower coupon rate than other similar bonds in the market if it has some feature that makes it more attractive to investors. For example, a sinking fund reduces default risk. Hence, investors may require a lower risk premium and be willing to accept a lower coupon rate. Other features attractive to investors include covenants in the bond indenture that restrict risky undertakings by the issuer and an option to convert the debt instruments to equity securities. The opportunity to profit from appreciation of the firm's stock justifies a lower coupon rate. An improvement in a bond's rating from Aa to Aaa (the highest possible) also justifies reduction in the risk premium and a lower coupon rate. However, a call provision is usually undesirable to investors. The issuer may take advantage of a decline in interest rates to recall the bond and stop paying interest before the bond's maturity.

Answers (A), (C), and (D) are incorrect because a sinking fund, an improved rating, and a conversion option are features attractive to investors that may result in their acceptance of a lower coupon rate.

49. The characteristics of venture capital include all of the following except

A. Initial private placement for the majority of issues.

B. A minimum holding period of 5 years for new securities.

C. The use of common stock for most placements.

D. A lack of liquidity for a period of time.

The correct answer is (B). *(CMA, adapted)*

REQUIRED: The item that is not a characteristic of venture capital.

DISCUSSION: The concept of venture (risk) capital applies to new enterprises that might not be able to obtain funds in the usual capital markets because of the riskiness of new products. Such companies sometimes try to place securities normally common stock, with venture capital firms. These are normally private placements of the securities and thus not subject to SEC regulation. The venture capitalists risk low liquidity for their investments until the young corporation becomes successful. The payoff may be substantial if the company does succeed. There is no minimum holding period for venture capital investments.

Answer (A) is incorrect because venture capital investments are typically private placements. Answer (C) is incorrect because common stock is usually a part of most venture capital deals. Venture capitalists want large payoffs in exchange for the risk assumed. Answer (D) is incorrect because venture capital investments typically are not liquid for a substantial time after the investment is made.

50. Shelf registration of a security is a procedure allowing a firm to

A. Register an issue price on its securities for a specified period of time.

B. Control both the issue price and the secondary market price of its securities by registering these prices for a specified period of time.

C. Register a security for a specified period of time and then sell the securities on a piecemeal basis.

D. Freeze the market price of its new issues of securities for a specified period of time.

The correct answer is (C). *(CMA, adapted)*

REQUIRED: The purpose of shelf registration.

DISCUSSION: SEC Rule 415 allows corporations to file registration statements covering a stipulated amount of securities that may be issued over the 2-year effective period of the statement. The securities are placed on the shelf and issued at an opportune moment without the necessity of filing a new registration statement, observing a 20-day waiting period, or preparing a new prospectus. The issuer is required only to provide updating amendments or to refer investors to quarterly and annual statements filed with the SEC. Shelf registration is most advantageous to large corporations that frequently offer securities to the public.

Answers (A) and (B) are incorrect because prices are not registered. Answer (D) is incorrect because the market price of securities is not frozen by shelf registration.

D. Dividend Policy

51. In practice, dividends

A. Usually exhibit greater stability than earnings.

B. Fluctuate more widely than earnings.

C. Tend to be a lower percentage of earnings for mature firms.

D. Are usually changed every year to reflect earnings changes.

The correct answer is (A). *(CMA, adapted)*

REQUIRED: The true statement about dividends and their relation to earnings.

DISCUSSION: Dividend policy determines the portion of net income distributed to shareholders. Corporations normally try to maintain a stable level of dividends, even though profits may fluctuate considerably, because many shareholders buy stock with the expectation of receiving a certain dividend every year. Thus, management tends not to raise dividends if the payout cannot be sustained. The desire for stability has led theorists to propound the information content or signaling hypothesis: a change in dividend policy is a signal to the market regarding management's forecast of future earnings. This stability often results in a stock that sells at a higher market price because shareholders perceive less risk in receiving their dividends.

Answers (B) and (D) are incorrect because most companies try to maintain stable dividends. Answer (C) is incorrect because mature firms have less need of earnings to reinvest for expansion; thus, they tend to pay a higher percentage of earnings as dividends.

Questions 52 and 53 are based on the following information. A firm's dividend policy may treat dividends either as the residual part of a financing decision or as an active policy strategy.

52. Treating dividends as the residual part of a financing decision assumes that

A. Earnings should be retained and reinvested as long as profitable projects are available.

B. Dividends are important to shareholders, and any earnings left over after paying dividends should be invested in high-return assets.

C. Dividend payments should be consistent.

D. Dividends are relevant to a financing decision.

The correct answer is (A). *(CMA, adapted)*

REQUIRED: The assumption made when dividends are treated as a residual part of a financing decision.

DISCUSSION: According to the residual theory of dividends, the amount (residual) of earnings paid as dividends depends on the available investment opportunities and the debt-equity ratio at which cost of capital is minimized. The rational investor should prefer reinvestment of retained earnings when the return exceeds what the investor could earn on investments of equal risk. However, the firm may prefer to pay dividends when investment opportunities are poor and the use of internal equity financing would move the firm away from its ideal capital structure.

Answer (B) is incorrect because a residual theory assumes that investors want the company to reinvest earnings in worthwhile projects, not pay dividends. Answer (C) is incorrect because dividend payments will not be consistent under a residual theory. The corporation will pay dividends only when internal investment options are unacceptable. Answer (D) is incorrect because dividends would not be important to a financing decision under the residual theory.

53. Treating dividends as an active policy strategy assumes that

A. Dividends provide information to the market.

B. The firm should pay dividends only after investing in all investment opportunities having an expected return greater than the cost of capital.

C. Dividends are irrelevant.

D. Dividends are costly, and the firm should retain earnings and issue stock dividends.

The correct answer is (A). *(CMA, adapted)*

REQUIRED: The assumption made when dividends are treated as an active policy strategy.

DISCUSSION: Stock prices often move in the same direction as dividends. Moreover, companies dislike cutting dividends. They tend not to raise dividends unless anticipated future earnings will be sufficient to sustain the higher payout. Thus, some theorists have proposed the information content or signaling hypothesis. According to this view, a change in dividend policy is a signal to the market regarding management's forecast of future earnings. Consequently, the relation of stock price changes to changes in dividends reflects not an investor preference for dividends over capital gains but rather the effect of the information conveyed.

Answer (B) is incorrect because the residual theory of dividends assumes that the firm should pay dividends only after investing in all investment opportunities having an expected return greater than the cost of capital. Answer (C) is incorrect because an active dividend policy suggests management assumes that dividends are relevant to investors. Answer (D) is incorrect because an active dividend policy recognizes that investors want dividends.

54. Residco Inc. expects net income of $800,000 for the next fiscal year. Its targeted and current capital structure is 40% debt and 60% common equity. The director of capital budgeting has determined that the optimal capital spending for next year is $1.2 million. If Residco follows a strict residual dividend policy, what is the expected dividend-payout ratio for next year?

A. 90.0%

B. 66.7%

C. 40.0%

D. 10.0%

The correct answer is (D). *(CMA, adapted)*

REQUIRED: The expected dividend-payout ratio assuming a strict residual dividend policy.

DISCUSSION: Under the residual theory of dividends, the residual of earnings paid as dividends depends on the available investments and the debt-equity ratio at which cost of capital is minimized. The rational investor should prefer reinvestment of retained earnings when the return exceeds what the investor could earn on investments of equal risk. However, the firm may prefer to pay dividends when investment returns are poor and the internal equity financing would move the firm away from its ideal capital structure. If Residco wants to maintain its current structure, 60% of investments should be financed from equity. Hence, it needs $720,000 (60% x $1,200,000) of equity funds, leaving $80,000 of net income ($800,000 NI – $720,000) available for dividends. The dividend-payout ratio is therefore 10% ($80,000 ÷ $800,000 NI).

Answer (A) is incorrect because 90% is the reinvestment ratio. Answer (B) is incorrect because 66.7% is the ratio between earnings and investment. Answer (C) is incorrect because 40% is the ratio of debt in the ideal capital structure.

55. A stock dividend

A. Increases the debt-to-equity ratio of a firm.

B. Decreases future earnings per share.

C. Decreases the size of the firm.

D. Increases shareholders' wealth.

The correct answer is (B). *(CMA, adapted)*

REQUIRED: The true statement about a stock dividend.

DISCUSSION: A stock dividend is a transfer of equity from retained earnings to paid-in capital. The debit is to retained earnings and the credits are to common stock and additional paid-in capital. Additional shares are outstanding following the stock dividend, but every shareholder maintains the same percentage of ownership. In effect, a stock dividend divides the pie (the corporation) into more pieces, but the pie is still the same size. Hence, a corporation will have a lower EPS and a lower book value per share following a stock dividend, but every shareholder will be just as well off as previously.

Answers (A), (C), and (D) are incorrect because a stock dividend has no effect except on the composition of the shareholders' equity section of the balance sheet.

56. Brady Corporation has 6,000 shares of 5% cumulative, $100 par value preferred stock outstanding and 200,000 shares of common stock outstanding. Brady's board of directors last declared dividends for the year ended May 31, 1995, and there were no dividends in arrears. For the year ended May 31, 1997, Brady had net income of $1,750,000. The board of directors is declaring a dividend for common shareholders equivalent to 20% of net income. The total amount of dividends to be paid by Brady at May 31, 1997, is

A. $350,000

B. $380,000

C. $206,000

D. $410,000

The correct answer is (D). *(CMA, adapted)*

REQUIRED: The total amount of dividends to be paid given cumulative preferred stock.

DISCUSSION: If a company has cumulative preferred stock, all preferred dividends for the current and any unpaid prior years must be paid before any dividends can be paid on common stock. The total preferred dividends that must be paid equal $60,000 (2 years x 5% x $100 par x 6,000 shares), and the common dividend is $350,000 ($1,750,000 x 20%), for a total of $410,000.

Answer (A) is incorrect because $350,000 is the common stock dividend. Answer (B) is incorrect because $380,000 omits the $30,000 of cumulative dividends for 1996. Answer (C) is incorrect because $206,000 is based on a flat rate of $1 per share of stock.

57. A 10% stock dividend most likely

A. Increases the size of the firm.

B. Increases shareholders' wealth.

C. Decreases future earnings per share.

D. Decreases net income.

The correct answer is (C). *(CMA, adapted)*

REQUIRED: The most likely effect of a stock dividend.

DISCUSSION: A stock dividend is a transfer of equity from retained earnings to paid-in capital. The debit is to retained earnings, and the credits are to common stock and additional paid-in capital. Additional shares are outstanding following the stock dividend, but every shareholder maintains the same percentage of ownership. In effect, a stock dividend divides the pie (the corporation) into more pieces, but the pie is still the same size. Hence, a corporation will have a lower EPS and a lower book value per share following a stock dividend, but every shareholder will be just as well off as previously.

Answers (A), (B), and (D) are incorrect because a stock dividend has no effect except on the composition of the shareholders' equity section of the balance sheet.

58. When a company desires to increase the market value per share of common stock, the company will implement

A. The sale of treasury stock.

B. A reverse stock split.

C. The sale of preferred stock.

D. A stock split.

The correct answer is (B). *(CMA, adapted)*

REQUIRED: The transaction that increases the market value per share of common stock.

DISCUSSION: A reverse stock split decreases the number of shares outstanding, thereby increasing the market price per share. A reverse stock split may be desirable when a stock is selling at such a low price that management is concerned that investors will avoid the stock because it has an undesirable image.

Answer (A) is incorrect because a sale of treasury stock increases the supply of shares and could lead to a decline in market price. Answer (C) is incorrect because a sale of preferred stock will take dollars out of investors' hands, thereby reducing funds available to invest in common stock; therefore, market price per share of common stock will not increase. Answer (D) is incorrect because a stock split increases the shares issued and outstanding. The market price per share is likely to decline as a result.

59. Arch Inc. has 200,000 shares of common stock outstanding. Net income for the recently ended fiscal year was $500,000, and the stock has a price-earnings ratio of eight. The board of directors has just declared a three-for-two stock split. For an investor who owns 100 shares of stock before the split, the approximate value (rounded to the nearest dollar) of the investment in Arch stock immediately after the split is

A. $250

B. $1,333

C. $2,000

D. $3,000

The correct answer is (C). *(CMA, adapted)*

REQUIRED: The value of an investment after a stock split given the P-E ratio.

DISCUSSION: EPS equals $2.50 ($500,000 NI ÷ 200,000 pre-split shares). Thus, 100 shares had a value of $2,000 (100 shares x 8 P-E ratio x $2.50 EPS) before the split. This value is unchanged by the stock split. Although the shareholder has more shares, the total value of the investment is the same.

Answer (A) is incorrect because $250 represents the annual earnings on 100 shares. Answer (B) is incorrect because $1,333 assumes that the value of the total investment declines after the split. Answer (D) is incorrect because $3,000 assumes that the value of the investment as well as the number of shares increases by 50%.

E. Business Contraction/Expansion

60. The purchase of treasury stock with a firm's surplus cash

A. Increases a firm's assets.

B. Increases a firm's financial leverage.

C. Increases a firm's equity.

D. Increases a firm's interest-coverage ratio.

The correct answer is (B). *(CMA, adapted)*

REQUIRED: The true statement about treasury stock.

DISCUSSION: A purchase of treasury stock involves a decrease in assets (usually cash) and a corresponding decrease in shareholders' equity. Thus, equity is reduced and the debt-to-equity ratio and financial leverage increase.

Answer (A) is incorrect because assets decrease when treasury stock is purchased. Answer (C) is incorrect because equity (assets – liabilities) declines. A treasury stock purchase is equivalent to a special dividend because assets are paid out to one or more shareholders. Answer (D) is incorrect because a firm's interest-coverage ratio is unaffected. Earnings, interest expense, and taxes will all be the same regardless of the transaction.

61. If a firm is to be purchased entirely for cash, which of the following items would the purchaser consider?

I. The incremental future after-tax cash flow from operations
II. Cash paid to the seller's shareholders
III. The present value of the seller's liabilities

A. I and II.

B. I and III.

C. I, II, and III.

D. I.

The correct answer is (C). *(CMA, adapted)*

REQUIRED: The items considered when a firm is to be purchased entirely for cash.

DISCUSSION: If a company is being purchased for cash, the buyer needs to determine the net investment or gross cash requirement (after adjustments for taxes and recoveries from sales of existing assets) and the incremental future after-tax cash flows from operations to calculate a rate of return on the investment. The cash flow calculation is a function of reliable estimates of revenues, cost savings, etc. The future returns will be compared with the initial investment, which consists of the cash paid to the seller's shareholders and the present value of any liabilities assumed by the buyer.

Answers (A), (B), and (D) are incorrect because the present value of any liabilities assumed, the cash paid to the seller's shareholders, and the incremental future cash flows must be known.

62. An example of a "poison pill," a form of takeover defense, is

A. The selling off of profitable units in an attempt to dissuade the hostile corporate raider.

B. The issuance of rights that allow shareholders to purchase stock in the proposed merged company at a substantial discount.

C. The act of substantially increasing a company's debt.

D. An agreement to buy back from the hostile raider a large block of stock at a premium.

The correct answer is (B). *(CMA, adapted)*

REQUIRED: The example of a poison-pill.

DISCUSSION: A target corporation's charter, bylaws, or contracts may include a wide variety of provisions that reduce the value of the target to potential tender offerors. For example, a valuable contract may terminate by its terms upon a specified form of change of ownership of the target. A poison pill is typically a right to purchase shares, at a reduced price, in the merged firm resulting from a takeover. A corporation may issue warrants to shareholders that permit purchase of stock at a small percentage (often half) of market price in the event of a takeover attempt. In the event of a friendly tender offer, the outstanding stock rights can be repurchased for a few cents per share, thereby facilitating the combination. In many cases, these rights are not issued in certificate form because they are not immediately exercisable and are not traded separately from common stock.

Answer (A) is incorrect because a crown jewel transfer is the selling off of profitable units in an attempt to dissuade the hostile corporate raider. Answer (C) is incorrect because simply increasing debt may not be disadvantageous to the raider unless the corporation distributes the new assets as dividends. Answer (D) is incorrect because greenmail is an agreement to buy back a large block of stock from a hostile raider.

Use Gleim's ***CMA/CFM Test Prep*** for interactive testing with **over 2,000 additional multiple-choice questions!**

STUDY UNIT 7: RISK

17 pages of outline
54 multiple-choice questions

A. Investment Risk
B. Financing Risk
C. Corporate Insurance

Risk is the possibility of an unfavorable event. This study unit covers the identification, measurement, and management of risks that must be considered in decisions concerning both working capital finance and capital structure finance. Thus, questions on risk will be included in the 24 to 36 questions in Part 1 that are devoted to the prior two study units.

A. Investment Risk

1. **Investment risk** is analyzed in terms of the probability that the actual return on an investment will be lower than the expected return. Accordingly, the concepts of probability distributions and expected value are basic to risk measurement. They are discussed in Part 4, Study Unit 4.
   a. The risk of an investment may be considered in isolation. It may also be viewed from the perspective of its inclusion in a portfolio of investments chosen to minimize the riskiness of the whole.
2. **Specific Types of Risks**
   a. **Interest-rate risk** is the risk of fluctuations in the value of an asset due to changes in interest rates.
      1) In general, interest-rate risk is greater the longer the maturity of the asset.
      2) One component of interest-rate risk is **price risk**. Thus, the value of bonds declines when interest rates increase.
      3) A second component of interest-rate risk is **reinvestment-rate risk**. If interest rates decline, lower returns will be available for reinvestment of interest and principal payments received.
   b. **Purchasing-power risk** is the risk that a general rise in the price level will reduce what can be purchased with a fixed sum of money. Accordingly, required returns include an inflation premium.
   c. **Default risk** is the risk that a borrower will be unable to repay debt. Hence, the higher the default risk, the higher the return required by an investor.
   d. **Market risk** is the risk that changes in price will result from changes that affect all firms. Prices of all securities, even the values of portfolios, are correlated to some degree with broad swings in the economy caused by recession, inflation, high interest rates, etc. Market risk is also known as systematic risk or nondiversifiable risk.
   e. **Nonmarket risk** or **company-specific risk** is the risk that is influenced by an individual firm's policies and decisions. Nonmarket risk is diversifiable because it is specific to each firm. Thus, it is also known as diversifiable or unsystematic risk.
   f. **Portfolio risk** is the risk remaining after allowing for the risk-reducing effects of combining securities into a portfolio.

g. **Total risk** is the risk of a single asset, whereas market risk is its risk if it is held in a large portfolio of diversified securities.

h. **Liquidity risk** is the possibility that an asset cannot be sold on short notice for its market value. If an asset must be sold at a deep discount, it is said to have a substantial amount of liquidity risk.

i. **Business risk** is the risk of fluctuations in earnings before interest and taxes or in operating income when the firm uses no debt. It is the risk inherent in its operations that excludes **financial risk**, which is the risk to the shareholders from the use of financial leverage. Business risk depends on factors such as

   1) Demand variability
   2) Sales price variability
   3) Input price variability
   4) Amount of operating leverage

j. **Exchange-rate risk** is the risk that a foreign currency transaction will be negatively exposed to fluctuations in exchange rates.

3. Whether the expected return on an investment is sufficient to entice an investor depends on its risk, the risks and returns of alternative investments, and the investor's attitude toward risk.

   a. Most serious investors are risk averse. They have a diminishing marginal utility for wealth. In other words, the utility of additional increments of wealth decreases. The utility of a gain for serious investors is less than the disutility of a loss of the same amount.

   b. Due to this risk aversion, risky securities must have higher expected returns.

4. **Portfolio Management.** An investor wants to maximize expected return and minimize risk when choosing a portfolio of investments. A feasible portfolio that offers the highest expected return for a given risk or the least risk for a given expected return is an **efficient portfolio**. A portfolio that is selected from the efficient set of portfolios because it is tangent to the investor's highest indifference curve is the **optimal portfolio**.

   a. An indifference curve represents combinations of portfolios having equal utility to the investor. Given that risk and returns are plotted on the horizontal and vertical axes, respectively, and that the investor is risk averse, the curve has an increasingly positive slope. As risk increases, the additional required return per unit of additional risk also increases.

      1) The steeper the slope of an indifference curve, the more risk averse an investor is.

      2) The higher the curve, the greater is the investor's level of utility.

      3) In the diagram on the next page, A, B, C, D, and E are indifference curves. A represents the highest level of utility and E the lowest. On a given curve, each point represents the same total utility to a risk-averse investor. For example, points 1, 2, and 3 are different combinations of risk and return that yield the same utility. The investor is indifferent as to which combination is chosen.

   b. Two important decisions are involved in managing a company's portfolio:

      1) The amount of money to invest
      2) The securities in which to invest

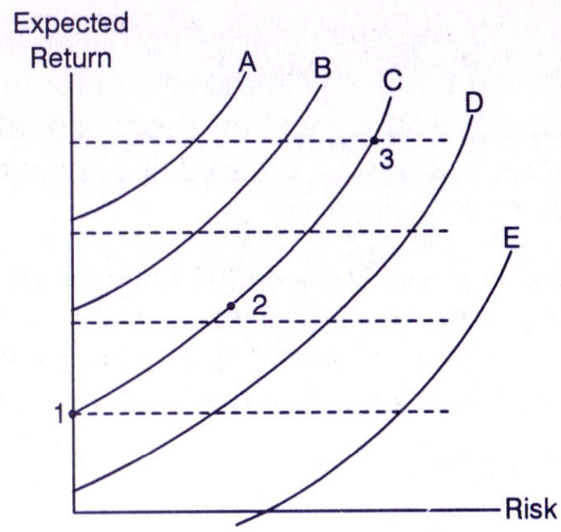

c. The investment in securities should be based on expected net cash flows and cash flow uncertainty evaluations.

1) Arranging a portfolio so that the maturity of funds will coincide with the need for funds will maximize the average return on the portfolio and provide increased flexibility.

a) Maturity matching ensures that securities will not have to be sold unexpectedly.

2) If its cash flows are relatively uncertain, a security's marketability and market risk are important factors to be considered. Transaction costs are also a consideration.

a) Higher-yield long-term securities provide less certainty.

3) When cash flows are relatively certain, the maturity date is a paramount concern.

d. **Financial instruments**. Financial managers may select from a wide range of financial instruments in which to invest and with which to raise money.

1) Ranked from the lowest rate of return to the highest, the following is a short list of widely available long-term financial instruments:

a) U.S. Treasury bonds
b) First mortgage bonds
c) Second mortgage bonds
d) Subordinated debentures
e) Income bonds
f) Preferred stock
g) Convertible preferred stock
h) Common stock

2) These instruments also are ranked according to the level of security backing them. An unsecured financial instrument is much riskier than an instrument that is secured. Thus, the riskier asset earns a higher rate of return. Mortgage bonds are secured by assets, whereas common stock is completely unsecured. Accordingly, common stock will earn a higher rate of return than mortgage bonds. For more on long-term financing, see Study Unit 6.

3) Short-term financial instruments increase the liquidity of an entity. For discussion of short-term instruments, see Study Unit 5.

e. **Portfolio theory** concerns the composition of an investment portfolio that is efficient in balancing the risk with the rate of return of the portfolio.

1) The expected rate of return of a portfolio is the weighted average of the expected returns of the individual assets in the portfolio.

2) The variability (risk) of a portfolio's return is determined by the correlation of the returns of individual portfolio assets.

a) To the extent the returns are not perfectly positively correlated, variability is decreased.

b) In principle, diversifiable risk should continue to decrease as the number of different securities held increases. However, in practice, the benefits of diversification become extremely small when more than 30 to 40 different securities are held. Moreover, commissions and other transaction costs increase with greater diversification.

3) **Company-specific (investee-specific) risk** or **unsystematic risk** is associated with a specific company's (investee's) operations: new products, patents, acquisitions, competitors, activities, etc.

a) This risk can be largely eliminated by proper diversification.

b) The relevant risk of an individual security held in a portfolio is its contribution to the overall risk of the portfolio.

c) When much of a security's risk can be eliminated by diversification, its relevant risk is low.

4) The risk of an individual security that is unaffected by diversification is **market** or **systematic risk** and is measured by the **beta coefficient**.

a) According to the capital asset pricing model, beta measures the volatility of the returns of a security relative to the returns on the market portfolio (a portfolio of all securities). An average-risk stock has a beta of 1.0 because its returns are perfectly positively correlated with those on the market portfolio. For example, if the market return increases by 20%, the return on the security increases by 20%.

b) A beta of less than 1.0 means that the security is less volatile than the market; e.g., if the market return increases by 20% and the security's return increases only 10%, the security has a beta of .5.

c) A beta over 1.0 indicates a volatile security; e.g., if the return increases 30% when the market return increases by 15%, the security has a beta of 2.0.

d) The word **beta** is derived from the regression equation for regressing the return of an individual security (the dependent variable) to the overall market return. The beta coefficient is the slope of the regression line.

i) The beta for a security may also be calculated by dividing the covariance of the return on the market and the return on the security by the variance of the return on the market.

e) Beta is the best measure of the risk of an individual security held in a diversified portfolio because it determines how the security affects the risk of the portfolio.

i) The beta of a portfolio is the weighted average of the betas of the individual securities.

5. **Other Risk Management Methods**

   a. **Hedging.** A financial manager can protect a firm against adverse changes in prices and interest rates by hedging in the futures market. Hedging is the process of using offsetting commitments to minimize or avoid the impact of adverse price movements.

      1) Long hedges are futures contracts that are purchased to protect against price increases.

      2) Short hedges are futures contracts that are sold to protect against price declines.

      3) EXAMPLE: In the commodities market, a company might have a contract with a farmer to buy soybeans at a future date. The price is agreed upon as the current price. The company would lose money if the soybean prices declined before the soybeans were delivered. To avoid any loss (or gain), the company could sell soybeans in the future at today's price. If the price of soybeans does decline before the delivery date, the company will lose money on the soybeans bought from the farmer, but it will gain money on the soybeans sold through the futures contract by buying cheap soybeans in the future to cover the delivery.

         a) Because commodities can be bought and sold on margin, considerable leverage is involved. This high degree of leverage is most beneficial to the speculator who is looking for large returns and is willing to bear the risk to get them. For hedgers, however, the small margin requirement is useful only because the risk can be hedged without tying up a large amount of cash.

   b. **Interest rate futures contracts** involve risk-free securities such as Treasury bonds, T-bills, and money-market certificates.

      1) The quantity traded is either $100,000 or $1,000,000, depending on which market is used.

      2) EXAMPLE: If a corporation wants to borrow money in 6 months for a major project, but the lender refuses to commit itself to an interest rate, the interest rate futures market can be used to hedge the risk that interest rates might increase in the interim. The company agrees to sell Treasury bonds in 6 months. If interest rates do increase over the period, the value of the Treasury bonds will decline. The company can buy Treasury bonds in 6 months and use them to cover the delivery that it had promised in the futures contract. Because the price of Treasury bonds has declined over the period, the company will make a profit on their delivery. The interest rates that the company will have to pay on the upcoming loan will be higher, however. It has cost the company money to wait 6 months for the loan. The profit from the futures contract should approximately offset the loss resulting from the higher interest loan. If interest rates had declined, the company would have had the benefit of a lower interest loan but would have lost money on the Treasury bonds. The goal of any such hedging operation is to break even on the change in interest rates.

         a) By hedging, the financial manager need not worry about fluctuations in interest rates but can concentrate instead on the day-to-day operations of the company.

c. **Duration hedging** involves hedging interest-rate risk by matching the duration of assets with the duration of liabilities. **Duration** is the weighted average of the times to interest and principal payments. If duration increases, the volatility of the price of the debt instrument increases.

1) Duration is lower if the nominal rate on the instrument is higher because more of the return is received earlier. The formula for duration is as follows if C_T is the interest or principal payment, T is the time to the payment, n is the time to maturity, r is the yield to maturity, and V is the value of the instrument:

$$\sum_{T=1}^{n} \left(\frac{C_T \times T}{(1 + r)^T} \right) \div V$$

2) The goal of duration hedging is not to equate the duration of assets and the duration of liabilities but for the following relationship to apply:

$$(Value\ of\ assets) \times (Duration\ of\ assets) = (Value\ of\ liabilities) \times (Duration\ of\ liabilities)$$

a) The firm is immunized against interest-rate risk when the total price change for assets equals the total price change for liabilities.

d. **Swaps** are contracts to hedge risk by exchanging cash flows.

1) In an **interest-rate swap**, one firm exchanges its fixed interest payments for a series of payments based on a floating rate. If a firm has debt with fixed charges, but its revenues fluctuate with interest rates, it may prefer to swap for cash outflows based on a floating rate. The advantage is that revenues and the amounts of debt service will then move in the same direction, and interest-rate risk will be reduced.

2) A **currency swap** is an exchange of an obligation to pay out cash flows denominated in one currency for an obligation to pay in another. For example, a U.S. firm with revenues in francs has to pay suppliers and workers in dollars, not francs. To minimize exchange-rate risk, it might agree to exchange francs for dollars held by a firm that needs francs. The exchange rate will be an average of the rates expected over the life of the agreement.

6. Stop and review! You have completed the outline for this subunit. Study multiple-choice questions 1 through 14 beginning on page 278.

B. Financing Risk

1. The **financial structure** of a firm encompasses the right-hand side of the balance sheet, which describes how the firm's assets are financed. Capital structure is the permanent financing of the firm and is represented primarily by

a. Long-term debt

1) Most firms renew (roll over) their long-term obligations. Thus, long-term debt is often effectively permanent.

b. Preferred stock

c. Common shareholders' equity

1) Common stock
2) Additional paid-in capital
3) Retained earnings

2. The following factors influence financial structure:
   a. Growth rate and stability of future sales
   b. Competitive structures in the industry
   c. Asset makeup of the individual firm
   d. Attitude toward risk of owners and management
   e. Control position of owners and management
   f. Rating agencies' and lenders' attitudes toward the industry and a particular firm
   g. Tax considerations

3. **Leverage** is the relative amount of the fixed cost of capital, principally debt, in a firm's capital structure. Leverage, by definition, creates financial risk, which relates directly to the question of the cost of capital. The more leverage, the higher the financial risk, and the higher the cost of debt capital.
   a. Earnings per share will ordinarily be higher if debt is used to raise capital instead of equity, provided that the firm is not over-leveraged. The reason is that the cost of debt is lower than the cost of equity because interest is tax deductible. However, the prospect of higher EPS is accompanied by greater risk to the firm resulting from required interest costs, creditors' liens on the firm's assets, and the possibility of a proportionately lower EPS if sales volume fails to meet projections.
   b. **The degree of financial leverage (DFL)** is the percentage change in earnings available to common shareholders that is associated with a given percentage change in net operating income. (The second formula below can be derived from the first, but the steps in the process are not shown.)
   c. $DFL = \dfrac{\%\ \Delta \text{ in net income}}{\%\ \Delta \text{ in net operating income}} = \dfrac{EBIT}{EBIT - I}$
      1) Net income means earnings available to common shareholders.
      2) Operating income equals earnings before interest and taxes (EBIT).
      3) I equals interest expense. If the company has preferred stock, the formula is further modified as follows (if P = preferred dividends and T is the tax rate):

$$\frac{EBIT}{EBIT - I - [P \div (1 - T)]}$$

      4) The greater the DFL, the riskier the firm.
   d. If the return on assets exceeds the cost of debt, additional leverage is favorable.
   e. Operating leverage concerns the extent to which fixed costs are used in the production process. A company with a high percentage of fixed costs is more risky than a firm in the same industry that relies more on variable costs to produce.
      1) **The degree of operating leverage (DOL)** is the percentage change in net operating income associated with a given percentage change in sales. (The second formula below can be derived from the first, but the steps in the process are not shown.)
      2) $DOL = \dfrac{\%\ \Delta \text{ in net operating income}}{\%\ \Delta \text{ in sales}} = \dfrac{\text{Contribution margin}}{\text{Contribution margin} - \text{fixed costs}}$
         a) EXAMPLE: If operating income increases 20% with a 10% increase in sales, DOL is 2.0.

f. **The degree of total leverage (DTL)** combines the DFL and the DOL. It equals the degree of financial leverage times the degree of operating leverage. Thus, it also equals the percentage change in net income that is associated with a given percentage change in sales.

1) $$DTL = DFL \times DOL = \frac{\%\ \Delta \text{ in net income}}{\%\ \Delta \text{ in sales}}$$

a) EXAMPLE: If net income increases 15% with a 5% increase in sales, DTL is 3.0.

2) Firms with a high degree of operating leverage do not usually employ a high degree of financial leverage and vice versa. One of the most important considerations in the use of financial leverage is operating leverage.

a) EXAMPLE: A firm has a highly automated production process. Because of automation, the degree of operating leverage is 2. If the firm wants a degree of total leverage not exceeding 3, it must restrict its use of debt so that the degree of financial leverage is not more than 1.5. If the firm had committed to a production process that was less automated and had a lower DOL, more debt could be employed, and the firm could have a higher degree of financial leverage.

4. **Cost of Capital**. Managers must know the cost of capital in making investment (long-term funding) decisions because investments with a return higher than the cost of capital will increase the value of the firm (shareholders' wealth). The theory underlying the cost of capital applies to new, long-term funding because long-term funds finance long-term investments. Short-term funds are used to meet working capital and other temporary needs. Cost of capital is of less concern for short-term funding.

a. The cost of capital is a weighted average of the various debt and equity components. The **weighted-average cost of capital** weights the percentage cost of each component by the percentage of that component in the financial structure.

1) The **cost of debt** equals the interest rate times one minus the marginal tax rate because interest is a tax deduction. Hence, an increase in the tax rate decreases the cost of debt.

2) The **cost of retained earnings** is an opportunity cost. It is the rate that investors can earn elsewhere on investments of comparable risk. The cost of internally generated funds is an imputed cost.

3) The **cost of new external common equity** is higher than the cost of retained earnings because of stock flotation costs.

a) Providers of equity capital are exposed to more risk than are lenders because the firm is not obligated to pay them a return. Also, in case of liquidation, creditors are paid before equity investors. Thus, equity financing is more expensive than debt because equity investors require a higher return to compensate for the greater risk assumed.

4) The **cost of preferred stock** equals the preferred dividend divided by the net issuance price. No tax adjustment is necessary because preferred dividends paid are not deductible.

b. Standard financial theory states that an **optimal capital structure** exists.

1) The optimal capital structure minimizes the weighted-average cost of capital and thereby maximizes the value of the firm's stock.

a) The optimal capital structure does not maximize EPS. Greater leverage maximizes EPS but also increases risk. Thus, the highest stock price is not reached by maximizing EPS.

2) The optimal capital structure usually involves some debt but not 100% debt.

3) The relevant relationships are depicted below.

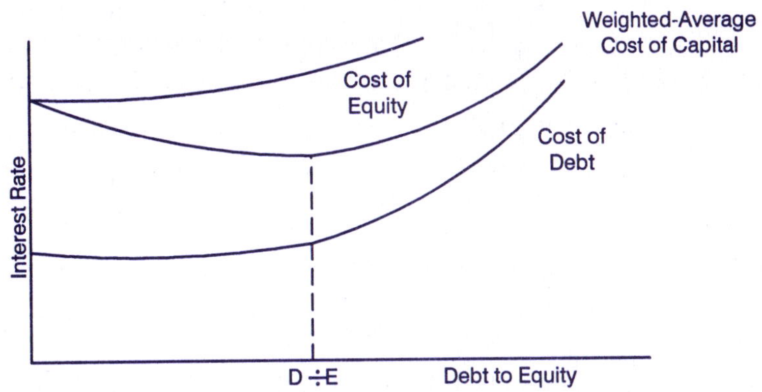

a) D ÷ E represents the lowest weighted-average cost of capital and is therefore the firm's optimal capital structure.

4) Ordinarily, firms cannot identify this optimal point precisely. Thus, they should attempt to find an optimal range for the capital structure.

c. The required rate of return on equity capital (R) can be estimated as follows.

1) The **capital asset pricing model** (CAPM) adds the risk-free rate (determined by government securities) to the product of the beta coefficient (a measure of the firm's risk) and the difference between the market return and the risk-free rate. Below is the basic equilibrium equation for the CAPM.

$$R = R_F + \beta(R_M - R_F)$$

a) The **market risk premium** ($R_M - R_F$) is the amount above the risk-free rate required to induce average investors to enter the market.

b) The **beta coefficient (β)** of an individual stock is the correlation between the volatility (price variation) of the stock market and the volatility of the price of the individual stock.

i) EXAMPLE: If an individual stock rises 10% and the stock market 10%, the beta coefficient is 1.0. If the stock rises 15% and the market only 10%, beta is 1.5.

c) EXAMPLE: Assuming a beta of 1.20, a market rate of return of approximately 17%, and an expected risk-free rate of 12%, the required rate of return on equity capital is .12 + 1.20 (.17 – .12), or 18%.

d) The graph of this equation (with interest rates plotted on the vertical axis and betas on the horizontal axis) is the **Security Market Line**. The slope of the SML equals the market risk premium, and the y-intercept is the risk-free rate.

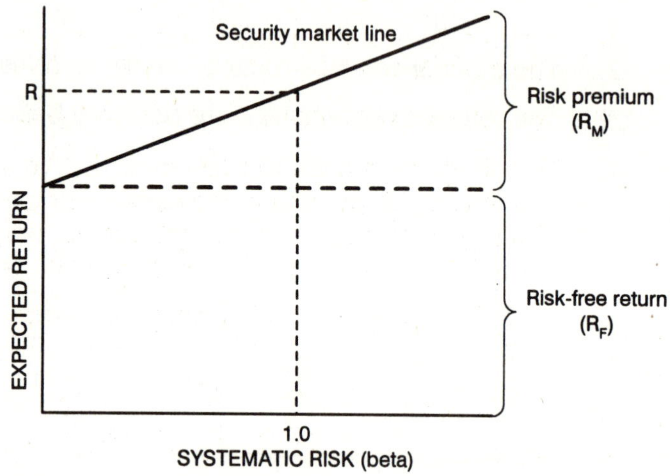

e) **Risk premium** is the difference in expected rates of return on a risky asset and a less risky asset.

2) **Arbitrage pricing theory (APT)** is based on the assumption that an asset's return is based on multiple systematic risk factors. In contrast, the CAPM is a model that uses just one systematic risk factor to explain the asset's return. That factor is the expected return on the market portfolio, i.e., the market-valued weighted-average return for all securities in the market.

a) The difference between actual and expected returns on an asset is attributable to systematic and unsystematic risks. **Unsystematic risk** (also called company-specific risk or diversifiable risk) is specific to a particular asset and can be eliminated by sufficient diversification. However, **systematic risk** (also called market risk or nondiversifiable risk) affects many assets and is undiversifiable. Thus, investors must be paid a risk premium to compensate for systematic (market) risk.

b) Accordingly, APT provides for a separate beta and a separate risk premium for each systematic risk factor identified in the model. Examples of the many potential systematic risk factors are the gross domestic product (GDP), inflation, and real interest rates. The APT for a three-factor model may be formulated as follows:

$$R = R_F + \beta_1 k_1 + \beta_2 k_2 + \beta_3 k_3$$

If: R = expected rate of return
R_F = risk-free rate
$\beta_{1,2,3}$ = individual factor beta coefficients
$k_{1,2,3}$ = individual factor risk premiums

c) EXAMPLE: Assume $R_F = 9\%$
$K_1 = 2\%$ $\beta_1 = .6$
$K_2 = 5\%$ $\beta_2 = .4$
$K_3 = 8\%$ $\beta_3 = .2$

Applying the above values, the expected rate of return is .09 + (.6)(.02) + (.4)(.05) + (.2)(.08), or 13.8%.

3) R may also be estimated by adding a percentage to the firm's long-term cost of debt.

a) A 3% to 5% premium is frequently used.

4) The **dividend growth model** estimates the cost of retained earnings using the dividends per share, the expected growth rate, and the market price. To justify retention of earnings, management must expect a return at least equal to the dividend yield plus a growth rate.

a) The formula for calculating the cost of retained earnings is

$$R = \frac{D_1}{P_0} + G$$

If: P_0 = current price

D_1 = next dividend

R = required rate of return

G = growth rate in dividends per share (but the model assumes that the dividend-payout ratio, retention rate, and therefore the EPS growth rate are constant).

i) EXAMPLE: If a company's dividend is expected to be $4 while the market price is $50 and the dividend is expected to grow at a constant rate of 6%, the required rate of return would be $4 ÷ $50 + .06, or 14%.

b) To determine the cost of new common stock (external equity), the model is altered to incorporate the flotation cost. As the flotation cost rises, R increases accordingly.

$$R = \frac{D_1}{P_0\ (1 - \textit{Flotation cost})} + G$$

c) The dividend growth model is also used for stock price evaluation. The formula can be restated in terms of P_0 as follows:

$$P_0 = \frac{D_1}{R - G}$$

d) The stock price is affected by the dividend-payout ratio because some investors may want capital gains, but others may prefer current income. Thus, investors will choose stocks that give the proper mix of capital gains and dividends.

d. The **marginal cost of capital**. The cost of capital to the firm for the next dollar of new capital increases because lower-cost capital sources are used first.

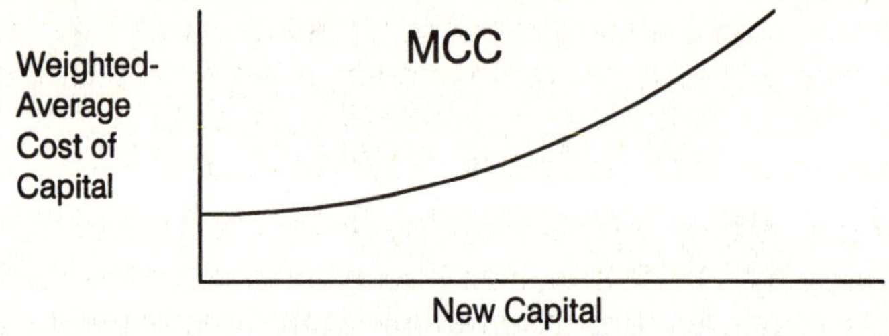

1) The **marginal efficiency of investment**. The return on additional dollars of capital investment decreases because the most profitable investments are made initially.

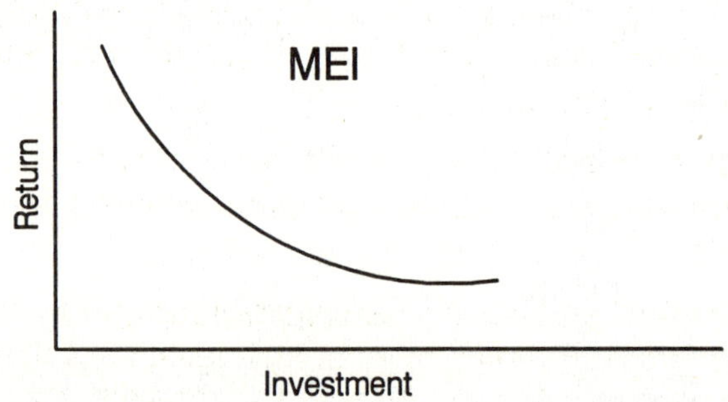

2) Combining the MCC and MEI schedules (graphs) produces the equilibrium investment level for the firm (Q*) at a particular interest rate (I) and the capital budget.

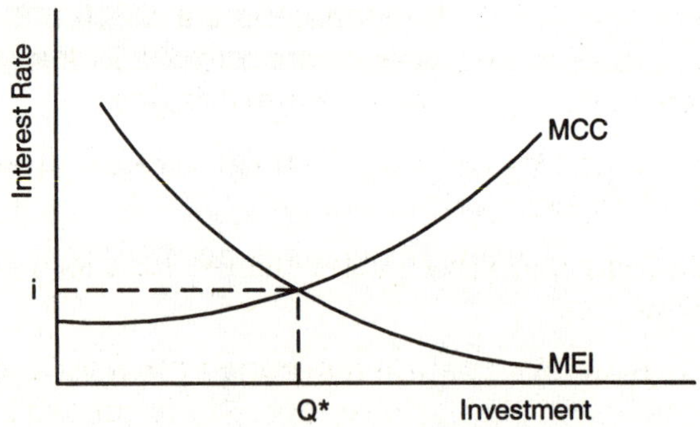

5. Stop and review! You have completed the outline for this subunit. Study multiple-choice questions 15 through 43 beginning on page 282.

C. Corporate Insurance

1. An insurance contract (policy) must satisfy the usual requirements of offer and acceptance, consideration, legality, and capacity of the parties. Furthermore, the insured must have an insurable interest in the subject matter of the contract. In the contract, the insurer makes a promise to pay a stated amount for loss or injury incurred as a result of a contingent event. Payment for the actual loss is called indemnity.
2. **Types of Insurance**. An insurance policy is a legal contract to shift the risk of financial loss caused by certain specified occurrences from the insured to the insurer in exchange for a payment called a **premium**. Insurance may protect a business from virtually any type of liability. The following list is not comprehensive, but it contains many types of insurance commonly encountered by a business person. Life, property, and liability insurance will be discussed in greater depth later in this subunit.
    a. **Property insurance** protects the owner of real or personal property (or another party with an insurable interest in the property, such as a secured creditor) against loss resulting from damage to, or destruction of, property by fire and other specified perils.

    b. **Life insurance** is a contract for the payment of a specified amount to the named beneficiary or to the estate of the insured if the insured dies while the policy is in effect.

    c. **Accident and health insurance** (commonly referred to as medical insurance) covers accidental injury or sickness, as well as other specified perils, under explicit conditions. Accident and health insurance is designed to pay at least a portion of an insured's expenses that arise from injury or sickness, disability, and hospitalization.

    d. **Disability insurance** provides income to those who become physically or mentally disabled and are unable to perform the tasks of their chosen occupation. While medical insurance covers a person's hospital and medical expenses during illness, disability insurance provides a source of income for a person during the time of the disability.

        1) Disability coverage usually covers only a percentage of a person's former income.

    e. **Title insurance** repays the insured for a loss arising from defects in the title to real property.

    f. **Business interruption insurance** provides benefits to cover losses due to interruptions in business operations caused by a specified and insured peril.

    g. **No-fault insurance** provides coverage to the insured and others protected under the policy regardless of any fault or liability of the parties. This type of insurance plan often applies to automobiles.

    h. **Credit insurance** protects both the creditor and the debtor by providing for payment of the debt of the insured in the event of his/her death. Credit insurance is typically used to insure payment of mortgage indebtedness, for both personal- and business-use property.

i. **Workers' compensation insurance** requires employers to compensate workers who are injured while on the job (even if an employee is injured because of an act of another employee).

1) Workers' compensation laws are not based on negligence or fault by the employer; rather, employers are held strictly liable for injuries that occur in the workplace.

2) The employers are the purchasers of workers' compensation insurance.

3) An employer **self-insures** when it does not purchase workers' compensation insurance but instead uses company assets to pay for any claim.

3. **Life insurance** is a contract for the payment of a specified sum to a named beneficiary or to the estate of the insured when the insured dies.

a. Life insurance protects against the **risk of mortality**, the financial uncertainty associated with dying.

1) Life insurance transfers the mortality risk to the insurance company.

b. Life insurance may be obtained by a corporation to insure the life of a key employee. A key employee is an employee whose death would cause the company to suffer substantial economic loss. The company is entitled to the life insurance proceeds if it is named as the beneficiary.

c. Life insurance takes the following principal forms:

1) **Whole life insurance.** Whole life or ordinary life insurance is designed to remain in force for the entire life of the insured and ordinarily requires the payment of premiums until the insured's death.

a) Whole life is often considered a form of savings or investment because the insured has a right to borrow from the insurer an amount not to exceed the cash surrender value of the policy.

i) The **cash surrender value** of a policy is the amount the insurance company will pay on a given life insurance policy if the policy is canceled prior to the death of the insured.

b) **Limited-payment whole life** requires the payment of premiums for only a fixed number of years.

c) **Single-premium whole life** allows for prepayment of the entire premium in one lump sum. The policy remains in force until either it is cashed in or proceeds are paid to the beneficiary upon the death of the insured.

2) **Term insurance.** Term life insurance is a contract that furnishes life insurance protection for a fixed term.

a) Under **level term** policies, the benefits payable on the insured's death remain level during the term of the policy.

b) Term insurance does not build up cash surrender value or loan value. Thus, term insurance is the least expensive form of insurance.

i) Term insurance can usually be renewed for additional periods until the insured reaches age 65.

ii) The cost of term insurance may increase rapidly with each renewal because the risk of death increases with the increased age of the insured.

3) **Endowment insurance**. An endowment contract pays a stated amount if the insured dies during a specified period of time, or pays the same amount if the insured is living at the end of the period.

   a) Endowment policies build up cash value. The cash value gradually increases until, at the end of the endowment period, it equals the face amount of the policy.

   b) Endowment policies are written for a variety of periods, such as 20, 25, or 30 years. They are also written to endow at a stated age.

   c) Endowment insurance is a form of forced savings protected by life insurance. Insureds who live until their policies mature (endow) complete their savings goals by means of their premium payments. Moreover, the protection aspect of the policy assures them that their savings goal will be completed whether or not they live to complete it themselves.

   d) Endowment contracts are very expensive.

4) **Hybrids**. One of the cornerstones of whole life insurance is that coverage both provides protection and represents a kind of forced savings.

   a) Insurers were quick to respond to the public's interest in the investment element of life insurance. (Life insurance cash values build up income tax free.) A number of companies offer hybrid financial products that possess basic insurance protection combined with an increased return on tax-free buildup of cash value.

      i) **Variable life** insurance permits the policyholder to participate in the investment expertise of the insuring company.

      NOTE: To the dismay of many purchasers, the policyholder also has the dubious privilege of participating in decreases in value of the investments.

      ii) **Universal life insurance** combines the features of an investment that earns current money market interest rates with a term insurance policy.

d. Life insurance policies become incontestable after a stated period established by law or in the policy. The purpose is to protect the insured against stale defenses by insurers. They are also more freely assignable than other policies.

4. **Property Insurance**. Fire or property insurance protects the owner of, or another person with an insurable interest in, real or personal property against loss resulting from damage to, or destruction of, insured property by certain specified perils.

   a. A **loss** is an unexpected destruction, reduction, or disappearance of economic value.

      1) Insured losses are unintended. They do not include

         a) Normal depreciation of property used in a trade or business
         b) Damage that is intentionally inflicted on property by the insured

   b. A **peril** is the cause of a loss. A single peril can cause more than one type of loss. Commonly insured perils include fire, theft, explosion, and illness.

c. A **hazard** is a condition that increases likelihood of loss due to a particular peril.

1) EXAMPLE: Fireworks are a hazard because they increase the likelihood of the peril of a fire, which would cause a loss.

d. Property or fire insurance is distinct from casualty insurance.

1) **Casualty insurance** typically covers loss due to damage or destruction of personal property by various causes other than fire or the elements.

2) At one time companies licensed to write fire insurance and other property lines of insurance could not write casualty insurance and vice versa. The law now permits multi-line insurers, enabling a single company to provide any or all lines of property-casualty insurance.

e. Property insurance may be provided by two principal means.

1) Under a **specified-perils contract**, the insurer indemnifies only for losses resulting from one or more specified perils.

2) Under an **all-risk contract**, the insurer indemnifies the insured for loss resulting from any perils except those specifically excluded by the contract.

a) All-risk contracts are useful when the exact nature of the perils is difficult to predict.

5. **Fire Insurance**. Fire insurance is one of the most common types of property insurance.

a. Fire insurance is a contract by which the insurer agrees to pay the insured a specified amount for property loss or property damage due to fire.

b. Most states recognize the standard fire policy, which is a standard contract of insurance prescribed by statute or administrative rule or regulation.

1) Frequently, fire insurance policies also insure against damage from wind, hail, and other forces of nature, as well as faulty plumbing or smoke damage.

c. Fire insurance policies are usually limited to cover loss from hostile fires, not friendly fires.

1) A **friendly fire** is one that is contained where it is intended to be, e.g., a fire in a fireplace, furnace, or stove.

2) A **hostile fire** is any other fire that is unintended or not in its usual place.

6. **Co-Insurance**. A co-insurance clause is used by many property and casualty insurers to encourage policyholders to insure commercial property for an amount that is near to its full replacement cost.

a. If a policyholder does not insure the property for an amount close enough to its full replacement cost, the policyholder must bear a proportionate part of any loss.

1) The co-insurance requirement applies only to partial losses, i.e., the amount required to repair or replace the damage. Total losses result in recovery of the face amount of the policy.

b. Thus, co-insurance is a method of sharing risk between the insurer and the insured.

c. A co-insurance clause typically provides that, if the owner of property insures his/her property for at least a stated percentage (usually 80%) of its actual cash value, any loss will be paid in full up to the face amount of the policy.

d. A building insured for less than the stated percentage (e.g., less than 80% of fair value) will not be fully insured, even for a small loss. For example, if a $100,000 building is insured for $60,000, given an 80% requirement, the owner will be a co-insurer with the insurance company. Any loss will be covered only to the extent of 75% of that loss, calculated as follows:

$$\frac{\textit{Face amount of policy } (\$60{,}000)}{\textit{Co-insurance requirement } (\$80{,}000)} = 75\%$$

7. **Liability Insurance**. Liability insurance provides the insured with money (policy proceeds) to cover losses (injuries) suffered by others for personal injury or property damage if the insured is held liable.

   a. Liability insurance protects against tort liability only, not criminal liability.

      1) Insurers routinely exclude intentional torts from insurance coverage.

   b. **Personal liability**. Personal liability coverage typically protects the policyholder against the financial risk of injuries or damage to the property of others that might occur in the course of the policyholder's personal activities.

      1) The primary purpose of this liability coverage is to insure against the policyholder's negligence.

      2) Personal liability protection is usually part of a homeowner's or renter's insurance policy, but it can be purchased as a separate personal liability policy.

      3) Liability coverage under a homeowner's policy usually applies only to personal activities, not to business or professional activities.

   c. **Business liability**. Businesses may insure against their own negligence by obtaining either comprehensive general liability insurance or specific insurance, e.g., product liability or dramshop coverage (for sellers of alcoholic beverages).

   d. **Professional liability**. Most professionals, e.g., doctors, lawyers, accountants, and architects, can obtain malpractice insurance to shift risk of loss due to their negligence to the insurance carrier.

      1) Most professional liability policies are written on either a claims-made basis or an occurrence basis.

         a) On a **claims-made basis**, the insurer is responsible only for claims filed during the policy period.

         b) On an **occurrence basis**, the insurer is responsible for all events occurring during the policy period regardless of when any claims are filed.

8. Stop and review! You have completed the outline for this subunit. Study multiple-choice questions 44 through 54 beginning on page 293.

MULTIPLE-CHOICE QUESTIONS

A. Investment Risk

1. Catherine & Co. has extra cash at the end of the year and is analyzing the best way to invest the funds. The company should invest in a project only if

A. The expected return on the project exceeds the return on investments of comparable risk.

B. The return on investments of comparable risk exceeds the expected return on the project.

C. The expected return on the project is equal to the return on investments of comparable risk.

D. The return on investments of comparable risk equals the expected return on the project.

The correct answer is (A). *(Publisher)*

REQUIRED: The rule for deciding whether to invest in a project.

DISCUSSION: Investment risk is analyzed in terms of the probability that the actual return on an investment will be lower than the expected return. Comparing a project's expected return with the return on an asset of similar risk helps determine whether the project is worth investing in. If the expected return on a project exceeds the return on an asset of comparable risk, the project should be pursued.

Answers (B), (C), and (D) are incorrect because a project should be pursued only if its expected return exceeds the return on investments of similar risk.

2. Which of the following are components of interest-rate risk?

A. Purchasing-power risk and default risk.

B. Price risk and market risk.

C. Portfolio risk and reinvestment-rate risk.

D. Price risk and reinvestment-rate risk.

The correct answer is (D). *(Publisher)*

REQUIRED: The components of interest-rate risk.

DISCUSSION: Interest-rate risk is the risk of fluctuations in the value of an asset due to changes in interest rates. One component of interest-rate risk is price risk; for example, the value of bonds declines as interest rates increase. Reinvestment-rate risk is another component of interest-rate risk. If interest rates decline, lower returns will be available for reinvestment of interest and principal payments received.

Answer (A) is incorrect because purchasing-power risk concerns inflation, and default risk concerns nonpayment by the debtor. Answer (B) is incorrect because market risk concerns price changes in the overall securities markets. Answer (C) is incorrect because portfolio risk is the risk remaining in a portfolio after diversifying investments.

3. The type of risk that is not diversifiable and affects the value of a portfolio is

A. Purchasing-power risk.

B. Market risk.

C. Nonmarket risk.

D. Interest-rate risk.

The correct answer is (B). *(Publisher)*

REQUIRED: The term for the type of risk that is not diversifiable.

DISCUSSION: Prices of all stocks, even the value of portfolios, are correlated to some degree with broad swings in the stock market. Market risk is the risk that changes in a stock's price will result from changes in the stock market as a whole. Market risk is commonly referred to as nondiversifiable risk.

Answer (A) is incorrect because purchasing-power risk is the risk that a general rise in the price level will reduce the quantity of goods that can be purchased with a fixed sum of money. Answer (C) is incorrect because nonmarket risk is the risk that is influenced by an individual firm's policies and decisions. Nonmarket risk is diversifiable since it is specific to each firm. Answer (D) is incorrect because interest-rate risk is the risk that the value of an asset will fluctuate due to changes in the interest rate.

4. The risk that securities cannot be sold at a reasonable price on short notice is called

A. Default risk.

B. Interest-rate risk.

C. Purchasing-power risk.

D. Liquidity risk.

The correct answer is (D). *(CIA, adapted)*

REQUIRED: The term for the risk that securities cannot be sold at a reasonable price on short notice.

DISCUSSION: An asset is liquid if it can be converted to cash on short notice. Liquidity (marketability) risk is the risk that assets cannot be sold at a reasonable price on short notice. If an asset is not liquid, investors will require a higher return than for a liquid asset. The difference is the liquidity premium.

Answer (A) is incorrect because default risk is the risk that a borrower will not pay the interest or principal on a loan. Answer (B) is incorrect because interest-rate risk is the risk to which investors are exposed because of changing interest rates. Answer (C) is incorrect because purchasing-power risk is the risk that inflation will reduce the purchasing power of a given sum of money.

5. When purchasing temporary investments, which one of the following best describes the risk associated with the ability to sell the investment in a short period of time without significant price concessions?

A. Interest rate risk.

B. Purchasing power risk.

C. Financial risk.

D. Liquidity risk.

The correct answer is (D). *(CMA, adapted)*

REQUIRED: The risk associated with the ability to sell investments in a short period of time without significant price concessions.

DISCUSSION: Liquidity risk is the possibility that an asset cannot be sold on short notice for its market value. If an asset must be sold at a high discount, it is said to have a substantial amount of liquidity risk.

Answer (A) is incorrect because interest rate risk is caused by fluctuations in the value of an asset as interest rates change. Its components are price risk and reinvestment-rate risk. Answer (B) is incorrect because purchasing power risk is the risk that a general rise in the price level (inflation) will reduce what can be purchased with a fixed sum of money. Answer (C) is incorrect because financial risk is the risk borne by shareholders, in excess of basic business risk, that arises from use of financial leverage (issuance of fixed income securities, i.e., debt and preferred stock).

6. O & B Company, a U.S. corporation, is in possession of accounts receivable denominated in German deutsche marks. To what type of risk are they exposed?

A. Liquidity risk.

B. Business risk.

C. Exchange-rate risk.

D. Price risk.

The correct answer is (C). *(Publisher)*

REQUIRED: The risk to which a business is exposed when accounts receivable are denominated in a foreign currency.

DISCUSSION: Exchange-rate risk is the risk that a foreign currency transaction will be negatively exposed to fluctuations in exchange rates. Because O & B Company sells goods to German customers and records accounts receivable denominated in deutsche marks, O & B Company is exposed to exchange-rate risk.

Answer (A) is incorrect because liquidity risk is the possibility that an asset cannot be sold on short notice for its market value. Answer (B) is incorrect because business risk is the risk of fluctuations in earnings before interest and taxes or in operating income when the firm uses no debt. Answer (D) is incorrect because price risk is a component of interest-rate risk.

7. Business risk is the risk inherent in a firm's operations that excludes financial risk. It depends on all of the following factors except

A. Amount of financial leverage.

B. Sales price variability.

C. Demand variability.

D. Input price variability.

The correct answer is (A). *(Publisher)*
REQUIRED: The factor not affecting business risk of a firm.
DISCUSSION: Business risk is the risk of fluctuations in earnings before interest and taxes or in operating income when the firm uses no debt. It depends on factors such as demand variability, sales price variability, input price variability, and the amount of operating leverage. Financial leverage affects financial risk and is not a factor affecting business risk.
Answers (B), (C), and (D) are incorrect because they are all factors affecting business risk.

8. A feasible portfolio that offers the highest expected return for a given risk or the least risk for a given expected return is a(n)

A. Optimal portfolio.

B. Desirable portfolio.

C. Efficient portfolio.

D. Effective portfolio.

The correct answer is (C). *(Publisher)*
REQUIRED: The term for a portfolio that offers the highest expected return for a given risk.
DISCUSSION: A feasible portfolio that offers the highest expected return for a given risk or the least risk for a given expected return is called an efficient portfolio.
Answer (A) is incorrect because an optimal portfolio is a portfolio selected from the efficient set of portfolios because it is tangent to the investor's highest indifference curve. Answer (B) is incorrect because a desirable portfolio is a nonsense term. Answer (D) is incorrect because an effective portfolio is a nonsense term.

9. The marketable securities with the least amount of default risk are

A. Federal government agency securities.

B. U.S. Treasury securities.

C. Repurchase agreements.

D. Commercial paper.

The correct answer is (B). *(CMA, adapted)*
REQUIRED: The marketable securities with the least default risk.
DISCUSSION: The marketable securities with the lowest default risk are those issued by the federal government because they are backed by the full faith and credit of the U.S. government and are therefore the least risky form of investment.
Answer (A) is incorrect because securities issued by a federal agency are first backed by that agency and secondarily by the U.S. government. Agency securities are issued by agencies and corporations created by the federal government, such as the Federal Housing Administration. Answer (C) is incorrect because repurchase agreements could become worthless if the organization agreeing to make the repurchase goes bankrupt. Answer (D) is incorrect because commercial paper is unsecured.

10. From the viewpoint of the investor, which of the following securities provides the least risk?

A. Mortgage bond.

B. Subordinated debenture.

C. Income bond.

D. Debentures.

The correct answer is (A). *(CIA, adapted)*
REQUIRED: The least risky security from the viewpoint of the investor.
DISCUSSION: A mortgage bond is secured with specific fixed assets, usually real property. Thus, under the rights enumerated in the bond indenture, creditors will be able to receive payments from liquidation of the property in case of default. In a bankruptcy proceeding, these amounts are paid before any transfers are made to other creditors, including those preferences. Hence, mortgage bonds are less risky than the others listed.
Answer (B) is incorrect because a debenture is long-term debt that is not secured (collateralized) by specific property. Subordinated debentures have a claim on the debtor's assets that may be satisfied only after senior debt has been paid in full. Debentures of either kind are therefore more risky than mortgage bonds. Answer (C) is incorrect because an income bond pays interest only if the debtor earns it. Such bonds are also more risky than secured debt. Answer (D) is incorrect because unsecured debt is riskier than a mortgage bond.

11. Which of the following classes of securities are listed in order from lowest risk/opportunity for return to highest risk/opportunity for return?

A. U.S. Treasury bonds; corporate first mortgage bonds; corporate income bonds; preferred stock.

B. Corporate income bonds; corporate mortgage bonds; convertible preferred stock; subordinated debentures.

C. Common stock; corporate first mortgage bonds; corporate second mortgage bonds; corporate income bonds.

D. Preferred stock; common stock; corporate mortgage bonds; corporate debentures.

The correct answer is (A). *(CIA, adapted)*

REQUIRED: The correct listing of classes of securities from lowest to highest risk/opportunity for return.

DISCUSSION: The general principle is that risk and return are directly correlated. U.S. Treasury securities are backed by the full faith and credit of the federal government and are therefore the least risky form of investment. However, their return is correspondingly lower. Corporate first mortgage bonds are less risky than income bonds or stock because they are secured by specific property. In the event of default, the bondholders can have the property sold to satisfy their claims. Holders of first mortgages have rights paramount to those of any other parties, such as holders of second mortgages. Income bonds pay interest only in the event the corporation earns income. Thus, holders of income bonds have less risk than shareholders because meeting the condition makes payment of interest mandatory. Preferred shareholders receive dividends only if they are declared, and the directors usually have complete discretion in this matter. Also, shareholders have claims junior to those of debtholders if the enterprise is liquidated.

Answer (B) is incorrect because the proper listing is mortgage bonds, subordinated debentures, income bonds, and preferred stock. Debentures are unsecured debt instruments. Their holders have enforceable claims against the issuer even if no income is earned or dividends declared. Answer (C) is incorrect because the proper listing is first mortgage bonds, second mortgage bonds, income bonds, and common stock. The second mortgage bonds are secured, albeit junior, claims. Answer (D) is incorrect because the proper listing is mortgage bonds, debentures, preferred stock, and common stock. Holders of common stock cannot receive dividends unless the holders of preferred stock receive the stipulated periodic percentage return, in addition to any averages if the preferred stock is cumulative.

12. A measure that describes the risk of an investment project relative to other investments in general is the

A. Coefficient of variation.

B. Beta coefficient.

C. Standard deviation.

D. Expected return.

The correct answer is (B). *(CIA, adapted)*

REQUIRED: The measure of the risk of an investment relative to investments in general.

DISCUSSION: The required rate of return on equity capital in the capital asset pricing model is the risk-free rate (determined by government securities), plus the product of the market risk premium times the beta coefficient (beta measures the firm's risk). The market risk premium is the amount above the risk-free rate that will induce investment in the market. The beta coefficient of an individual stock is the correlation between the volatility (price variation) of the stock market and that of the price of the individual stock. For example, if an individual stock goes up 15% and the market only 10%, beta is 1.5.

Answer (A) is incorrect because the coefficient of variation compares risk with expected return (standard deviation ÷ expected return). Answer (C) is incorrect because standard deviation measures dispersion (risk) of project returns. Answer (D) is incorrect because expected return does not describe risk.

13. An asset with high risk will have a(n)

A. Low expected return.

B. Lower price than an asset with low risk.

C. Increasing expected return.

D. High standard deviation of returns.

The correct answer is (D). *(Publisher)*

REQUIRED: The characteristic of an asset with high risk.

DISCUSSION: The greater the standard deviation of returns, the greater the risk is for an asset. The expected return can vary anywhere between the large standard deviation of returns, creating the risk that the actual return is significantly low in the range of the standard deviation of returns.

Answer (A) is incorrect because an asset with high risk will have a high expected return to compensate for the additional risk. Answer (B) is incorrect because an asset with high risk will have a higher price than an asset with low risk due to the high expected return. Answer (C) is incorrect because an asset with high risk will have a constant expected return, not an increasing expected return.

14. When a firm finances each asset with a financial instrument of the same approximate maturity as the life of the asset, it is applying

A. Working capital management.

B. Return maximization.

C. Financial leverage.

D. A hedging approach.

The correct answer is (D). *(CMA, adapted)*

REQUIRED: The technique used when a firm finances a specific asset with a financial instrument having the same approximate maturity as the life of the asset.

DISCUSSION: Maturity matching, or equalizing the life of an asset and the debt instrument used to finance that asset, is a hedging approach. The basic concept is that the company has the entire life of the asset to recover the amount invested before having to pay the lender.

Answer (A) is incorrect because working capital management is short-term asset management. Answer (B) is incorrect because return maximization is more aggressive than maturity matching. It entails using the lowest cost forms of financing. Answer (C) is incorrect because financial leverage is the relationship between debt and equity financing.

B. Financing Risk

15. A firm must select from among several methods of financing arrangements when meeting its capital requirements. To acquire additional growth capital while attempting to maximize earnings per share, a firm should normally

A. Attempt to increase both debt and equity in equal proportions, which preserves a stable capital structure and maintains investor confidence.

B. Select debt over equity initially, even though increased debt is accompanied by interest costs and a degree of risk.

C. Select equity over debt initially, which minimizes risk and avoids interest costs.

D. Discontinue dividends and use current cash flow, which avoids the cost and risk of increased debt and the dilution of EPS through increased equity.

The correct answer is (B). *(CIA, adapted)*

REQUIRED: The financing arrangement that should be selected to acquire additional growth capital while attempting to maximize earnings per share.

DISCUSSION: Earnings per share will ordinarily be higher if debt is used to raise capital instead of equity, provided that the firm is not over-leveraged. The reason is that the cost of debt is lower than the cost of equity because interest is tax deductible. However, the prospect of higher EPS is accompanied by greater risk to the firm resulting from required interest costs, creditors' liens on the firm's assets, and the possibility of a proportionately lower EPS if sales volume fails to meet projections.

Answer (A) is incorrect because EPS is not a function of investor confidence and is not maximized by concurrent proportional increases in both debt and equity. EPS is usually higher if debt is used instead of equity to raise capital, at least initially. Answer (C) is incorrect because equity capital is initially more costly than debt. Answer (D) is incorrect because using only current cash flow to raise capital is usually too conservative an approach for a growth-oriented firm. Management is expected to be willing to take acceptable risks to be competitive and attain an acceptable rate of growth.

16. The theory underlying the cost of capital is primarily concerned with the cost of

A. Long-term funds and old funds.

B. Short-term funds and new funds.

C. Long-term funds and new funds.

D. Short-term funds and old funds.

The correct answer is (C). *(CMA, adapted)*

REQUIRED: The true statement about the theory underlying the cost of capital.

DISCUSSION: The theory underlying the cost of capital is based primarily on the cost of long-term funds and the acquisition of new funds. The reason is that long-term funds are used to finance long-term investments. For an investment alternative to be viable, the return on the investment must be greater than the cost of the funds used. The objective in short-term borrowing is different. Short-term loans are used to meet working capital needs and not to finance long-term investments.

Answer (A) is incorrect because the concern is with the cost of new funds; the cost of old funds is a sunk cost and of no relevance for decision-making purposes. Answer (B) is incorrect because the cost of short-term funds is not usually a concern for investment purposes. Answer (D) is incorrect because the cost of old funds is a sunk cost and of no relevance for decision-making purposes. Similarly, short-term funds are used for working capital or other temporary purposes, and there is less concern with the cost of capital and the way it compares with the return earned on the assets borrowed.

17. A higher degree of operating leverage compared with the industry average implies that the firm

A. Has higher variable costs.

B. Has profits that are more sensitive to changes in sales volume.

C. Is more profitable.

D. Is less risky.

The correct answer is (B). *(CMA, adapted)*

REQUIRED: The effect of a higher degree of operating leverage (DOL).

DISCUSSION: Operating leverage is a measure of the degree to which fixed costs are used in the production process. A company with a higher percentage of fixed costs (higher operating leverage) has greater risk than one in the same industry that relies more heavily on variable costs. The DOL equals the percentage change in net operating income divided by the percentage change in sales. Thus, profits become more sensitive to changes in sales volume as the DOL increases.

Answer (A) is incorrect because a firm with higher operating leverage has higher fixed costs and lower variable costs. Answer (C) is incorrect because a firm with higher leverage will be relatively more profitable than a firm with lower leverage when sales are high. The opposite is true when sales are low. Answer (D) is incorrect because a firm with higher leverage is more risky. Its reliance on fixed costs is greater.

18. When calculating the cost of capital, the cost assigned to retained earnings should be

A. Zero.

B. Lower than the cost of external common equity.

C. Equal to the cost of external common equity.

D. Higher than the cost of external common equity.

The correct answer is (B). *(CIA, adapted)*

REQUIRED: The cost assigned to retained earnings when calculating cost of capital.

DISCUSSION: Newly issued or external common equity is more costly than retained earnings. The company incurs issuance costs when raising new, outside funds.

Answer (A) is incorrect because the cost of retained earnings is the rate of return shareholders require on equity capital the firm obtains by retaining earnings. The opportunity cost of retained funds will be positive. Answers (C) and (D) are incorrect because retained earnings will always be less costly than external equity financing. Earnings retention does not require the payment of issuance costs.

Questions 19 through 21 are based on the following information. Carlisle Company currently sells 400,000 bottles of perfume each year. Each bottle costs $.84 to produce and sells for $1.00. Fixed costs are $28,000 per year. The firm has annual interest expense of $6,000, preferred stock dividends of $2,000 per year, and a 40% tax rate. Carlisle uses the following formulas to determine the company's leverage.

$$\text{Operating leverage} = \frac{Q(S - VC)}{Q(S - VC) - FC}$$

$$\text{Financial leverage} = \frac{EBIT}{EBIT - I - [P \div (1 - T)]}$$

$$\text{Total leverage} = \frac{Q(S - VC)}{Q(S - VC) - FC - I - [P \div (1 - T)]}$$

If:
Q = Quantity
FC = Fixed cost
VC = Variable cost
S = Selling price
I = Interest expense
P = Preferred dividends
T = Tax rate
EBIT = Earnings before interest and taxes

19. The degree of operating leverage for Carlisle Company is

A. 2.4

B. 1.78

C. 1.35

D. 1.2

The correct answer is (B). *(CMA, adapted)*

REQUIRED: The degree of operating leverage.

DISCUSSION: Operating leverage is the percentage change in operating income resulting from a percentage change in sales. It measures how a change in volume affects profits. Companies with larger investments and greater fixed costs ordinarily have higher contribution margins and more operating leverage. The degree of operating leverage measures the extent to which fixed assets are used in the production process. A company with a high percentage of fixed costs is more risky than a firm in the same industry that relies more on variable costs to produce. Based on a contribution margin of $.16 per unit ($1 – $.84 variable cost), the degree of operating leverage is

$$(400{,}000 \times \$.16) \div [(400{,}000 \times \$.16) - 28{,}000] = 1.78.$$

Answer (A) is incorrect because 2.4 could be obtained only by overstating the contribution margin or the fixed costs. Answer (C) is incorrect because 1.35 includes a nonoperating expense (interest) and dividends on preferred stock as fixed costs. It is the degree of financial leverage, not operating leverage. Answer (D) is incorrect because 1.2 is obtained by understating the $64,000 contribution margin or understating the $28,000 of fixed costs.

20. If Carlisle Company did not have preferred stock, the degree of total leverage would

A. Decrease in proportion to a decrease in financial leverage.

B. Increase in proportion to an increase in financial leverage.

C. Remain the same.

D. Decrease but not be proportional to the decrease in financial leverage.

The correct answer is (A). *(CMA, adapted)*

REQUIRED: The true statement about the degree of total leverage if the company did not have preferred stock.

DISCUSSION: The degree of total leverage is equal to the degree of operating leverage times the degree of financial leverage. Thus, a decrease in either of these ratios results in a decrease in total leverage. If the company had no preferred stock, the DFL and the DTL would be lower because the pretax income necessary to pay the preferred dividends [P ÷ (1 – T)] is subtracted from the denominator of the DFL.

Answer (B) is incorrect because the increases would not be proportional. Answer (C) is incorrect because the elimination of preferred stock would change the equation. Answer (D) is incorrect because the decrease would be proportional.

21. The degree of financial leverage for Carlisle Company is

A. 2.4

B. 1.78

C. 1.35

D. 2.3

The correct answer is (C). *(CMA, adapted)*

REQUIRED: The degree of financial leverage.

DISCUSSION: The degree of financial leverage is the percentage change in earnings available to common shareholders that is associated with a given percentage change in net operating income. Operating income equals earnings before interest and taxes. The more financial leverage employed, the greater the degree of financial leverage, and the riskier the firm. Earnings before interest and taxes equal \$36,000 [\$400,000 sales – (\$.84 x 400,000 units) VC – \$28,000 FC]. Using the given formula, the calculation is as follows:

$$\frac{\$36,000}{\$36,000 - \$6,000 - (\$2,000 \div .6)} = \frac{\$36,000}{\$26,667} = 1.35$$

Answer (A) is incorrect because 2.4 could be obtained only by overstating the contribution margin or the fixed costs. Answer (B) is incorrect because 1.78 is the degree of operating leverage, not financial leverage. Answer (D) is incorrect because 2.3 is derived by overstating the \$64,000 contribution margin or the \$28,000 of fixed costs.

22. If Brewer Corporation's bonds are currently yielding 8% in the marketplace, why is the firm's cost of debt lower?

A. Market interest rates have increased.

B. Additional debt can be issued more cheaply than the original debt.

C. There should be no difference; cost of debt is the same as the bonds' market yield.

D. Interest is deductible for tax purposes.

The correct answer is (D). *(CMA, adapted)*

REQUIRED: The reason a firm's cost of debt is lower than its current market yield.

DISCUSSION: Because interest is deductible for tax purposes, the actual cost of debt capital is the net effect of the interest payment and the offsetting tax deduction. The actual cost of debt equals the interest rate times (1 – the marginal tax rate). Thus, if a firm with an 8% market rate is in a 40% tax bracket, the net cost of the debt capital is 4.8% [8% x (1 – .4)].

Answer (A) is incorrect because the tax deduction always causes the market yield rate to be higher than the cost of debt capital. Answer (B) is incorrect because additional debt may or may not be issued more cheaply than earlier debt, depending upon the interest rates in the market place. Answer (C) is incorrect because the cost of debt is less than the yield rate given that bond interest is tax deductible.

23. In general, it is more expensive for a company to finance with equity capital than with debt capital because

A. Long-term bonds have a maturity date and must therefore be repaid in the future.

B. Investors are exposed to greater risk with equity capital.

C. Equity capital is in greater demand than debt capital.

D. Dividends fluctuate to a greater extent than interest rates.

The correct answer is (B). *(CMA, adapted)*

REQUIRED: The reason equity financing is more expensive than debt financing.

DISCUSSION: Providers of equity capital are exposed to more risk than are lenders because the firm is not obligated to pay them a return. Also, in case of liquidation, creditors are paid before equity investors. Thus, equity financing is more expensive than debt because equity investors require a higher return to compensate for the greater risk assumed.

Answer (A) is incorrect because the obligation to repay at a specific maturity date reduces the risk to investors and thus the required return. Answer (C) is incorrect because the demand for equity capital is directly related to its greater cost to the issuer. Answer (D) is incorrect because dividends are based on managerial discretion and may rarely change; interest rates, however, fluctuate daily based upon market conditions.

24. A preferred stock is sold for $101 per share, has a face value of $100 per share, underwriting fees of $5 per share, and annual dividends of $10 per share. If the tax rate is 40%, the cost of funds (capital) for the preferred stock is

A. 4.2%

B. 6.2%

C. 10.0%

D. 10.4%

The correct answer is (D). *(CMA, adapted)*

REQUIRED: The cost of capital for a preferred stock issue.

DISCUSSION: Because the dividends on preferred stock are not deductible for tax purposes, the effect of income taxes is ignored. Thus, the relevant calculation is to divide the $10 annual dividend by the quantity of funds received at the time the stock is issued. In this case, the funds received equal $96 ($101 selling price – $5 underwriting fee). Thus, the cost of capital is 10.4% ($10 ÷ $96).

Answer (A) is incorrect because the 4.2% figure can be obtained only by incorrectly treating the dividends as deductible. Answer (B) is incorrect because the 6.2% figure can be obtained only by treating the dividends as deductible. Answer (C) is incorrect because 10% can be obtained only by basing the calculation on par value instead of funds received.

25. Osgood Products has announced that it plans to finance future investments so that the firm will achieve an optimum capital structure. Which one of the following corporate objectives is consistent with this announcement?

A. Maximize earnings per share.

B. Minimize the cost of debt.

C. Maximize the net worth of the firm.

D. Minimize the cost of equity.

The correct answer is (C). *(CMA, adapted)*

REQUIRED: The consistent corporate objective.

DISCUSSION: Financial structure is the composition of the financing sources of the assets of a firm. Traditionally, the financial structure consists of current liabilities, long-term debt, retained earnings, and stock. For most firms, the optimum structure includes a combination of debt and equity. Debt is cheaper than equity, but excessive use of debt increases the firm's risk and drives up the weighted-average cost of capital.

Answer (A) is incorrect because the maximization of EPS may not always suggest the best capital structure. Answer (B) is incorrect because the minimization of debt cost may not be optimal; as long as the firm can earn more on debt capital than it pays in interest, debt financing may be indicated. Answer (D) is incorrect because minimizing the cost of equity may signify overly conservative management.

26. In referring to the graph of a firm's cost of capital, if e is the current position, which one of the following statements best explains the saucer or U-shaped curve?

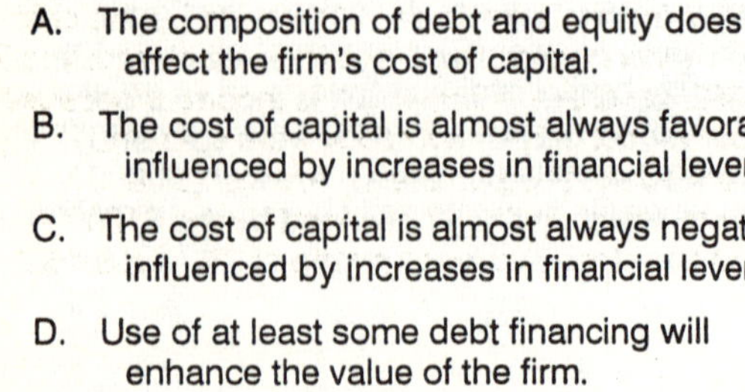

A. The composition of debt and equity does not affect the firm's cost of capital.

B. The cost of capital is almost always favorably influenced by increases in financial leverage.

C. The cost of capital is almost always negatively influenced by increases in financial leverage.

D. Use of at least some debt financing will enhance the value of the firm.

The correct answer is (D). *(CMA, adapted)*

REQUIRED: The best explanation of the U-shaped curve in a cost-of-capital graph.

DISCUSSION: The U-shaped curve indicates that the cost of capital is quite high when the debt-to-equity ratio is quite low. As debt increases, the cost of capital declines as long as the cost of debt is less than that of equity. Eventually, the decline in the cost of capital levels off because the cost of debt ultimately rises as more debt is used. Additional increases in debt (relative to equity) will then increase the cost of capital. The implication is that some debt is present in the optimal capital structure because the cost of capital initially declines when debt is added. However, a point is reached at which debt becomes excessive and the cost of capital begins to rise.

Answer (A) is incorrect because the composition of the capital structure affects the cost of capital since the components have different costs. Answer (B) is incorrect because the cost of debt does not remain constant as financial leverage increases. Eventually, that cost also increases. Answer (C) is incorrect because increased leverage is initially favorable.

Questions 27 through 30 are based on Williams, Inc., which is interested in measuring its overall cost of capital and has gathered the following data. Under the terms described below, the company can sell unlimited amounts of all instruments.

- Williams can raise cash by selling $1,000, 8%, 20-year bonds with annual interest payments. In selling the issue, an average premium of $30 per bond would be received, and the firm must pay flotation costs of $30 per bond. The after-tax cost of funds is estimated to be 4.8%.
- Williams can sell 8% preferred stock at $105 per share. The cost of issuing and selling the preferred stock is expected to be $5 per share.
- Williams' common stock is currently selling for $100 per share. The firm expects to pay cash dividends of $7 per share next year, and the dividends are expected to remain constant. The stock will have to be underpriced by $3 per share, and flotation costs are expected to amount to $5 per share.
- Williams expects to have available $100,000 of retained earnings in the coming year; once these retained earnings are exhausted, the firm will use new common stock as the form of common stock equity financing.
- Williams' preferred capital structure is

Long-term debt	30%
Preferred stock	20
Common stock	50

27. The cost of funds from the sale of common stock for Williams, Inc. is

A. 7.0%

B. 7.6%

C. 7.4%

D. 8.1%

The correct answer is (B). *(CMA, adapted)*

REQUIRED: The percentage cost of capital from the sale of common stock.

DISCUSSION: According to the Gordon growth model, the three elements required to calculate the cost of equity capital are (1) the dividends per share, (2) the expected growth rate, and (3) the market price of the stock. If flotation costs are incurred when issuing new stock, they are deducted from the market price to arrive at the amount of capital the corporation will actually receive. Accordingly, the $100 selling price is reduced by the $3 discount and the $5 flotation costs to arrive at the $92 to be received for the stock. Because the dividend is not expected to increase in future years, no growth factor is included in the calculation. Thus, the cost of the common stock is 7.6% ($7 dividend ÷ $92).

Answer (A) is incorrect because the 7.0% figure would be correct only if $100 were received from the sale of the stock. Answer (C) is incorrect because 7.4% would be correct only if the stock could be sold without giving a $3 discount. Answer (D) is incorrect because 8.1% would be correct only if the amount received were about $86 or if some growth factor were assumed.

28. The cost of funds from retained earnings for Williams, Inc. is

A. 7.0%

B. 7.6%

C. 7.4%

D. 8.1%

The correct answer is (A). *(CMA, adapted)*

REQUIRED: The percentage cost of funds from using retained earnings as a capital source.

DISCUSSION: The three elements required to calculate the cost of equity capital are (1) the dividends per share, (2) the expected growth rate, and (3) the market price of the stock. Because growth is not expected, the calculation is simply to divide the dividend of $7 by the $100 market price of the stock to arrive at a cost of equity capital of 7%.

Answer (B) is incorrect because 7.6% would be the cost of new equity capital from selling stock if the stock resulted in proceeds of $92 per share. Answer (C) is incorrect because 7.4% would be correct only if new stock were sold and resulted in proceeds of $95 per share. Answer (D) is incorrect because dividing the $7 dividend by the $100 market price of the stock produces a ratio of 7%, not 8.1%.

29. Refer to the information preceding question 27. If Williams, Inc. needs a total of $200,000, the firm's weighted-average cost of capital would be

A. 19.8%

B. 4.8%

C. 6.5%

D. 6.8%

The correct answer is (C). *(CMA, adapted)*

REQUIRED: The weighted-average cost of capital assuming that the firm needs a total of $200,000.

DISCUSSION: Williams' preferred capital structure is 50% common stock. However, $100,000 of retained earnings (50% of the required $200,000 of capital) will be used before any common stock is issued. Thus, the weighted-average cost of capital will be determined based on the respective costs of the bonds, preferred stock, and retained earnings. The cost of the bonds is given as 4.8%, the cost of the preferred stock is 8%, and the cost of the retained earnings is 7% ($7 dividend ÷ $100 market price of the common stock). These three costs are then weighted by the preferred capital structure ratios:

30% × 4.8%	= 1.44%
20% × 8.0%	= 1.60%
50% × 7.0%	= 3.50%
Total	6.54%

Rounding to the nearest tenth produces the correct answer of 6.5%.

Answer (A) is incorrect because 19.8% represents the unweighted sum of each of the three elements of cost. Answer (B) is incorrect because 4.8% is the cost of the long-term debt. All funding will not be obtained from debt because the firm wants to maintain a capital structure in which debt represents only 30% of the total capital. Answer (D) is incorrect because the 6.8% figure can only be obtained if new stock is sold. New stock will not be sold because the retained earnings can be used at a lower cost, and there is no need to sell stock when the total capital required is only $200,000.

30. Refer to the information preceding question 27. If Williams, Inc. needs a total of $1,000,000, the firm's weighted-average cost of capital would be

A. 6.8%

B. 4.8%

C. 6.5%

D. 27.4%

The correct answer is (A). *(CMA, adapted)*

REQUIRED: The weighted-average cost of capital if the firm needs $1,000,000 in total capital.

DISCUSSION: The cost of the bonds is given as 4.8%. The cost of the preferred stock is 8% ($8 dividend ÷ $100), the cost of new common stock is 7.6% ($7 dividend ÷ $92 proceeds), and the cost of the retained earnings is 7% ($7 dividend ÷ $100 market price). These four costs are then weighted by the preferred capital structure ratios, a process that requires subdividing the common stock portion into retained earnings of $100,000 (10% of capital) and new common stock of $400,000 (40% of capital):

30% × 4.8%	= 1.44%
20% × 8.0%	= 1.60%
40% × 7.6%	= 3.04%
10% × 7.0%	= .70%
Total	6.78%

Rounding to the nearest tenth results in the correct answer of 6.8%.

Answer (B) is incorrect because 4.8% is the cost of the long-term debt. Answer (C) is incorrect because 6.5% would be correct only if the equity capital were obtained totally from retained earnings. Because only $100,000 of retained earnings is available, the remainder of equity capital must come from sales of new stock. Answer (D) is incorrect because 27.4% represents the unweighted total of each of the four elements of cost.

31. According to the capital asset pricing model (CAPM), the relevant risk of a security is its

A. Company-specific risk.

B. Diversifiable risk.

C. Systematic risk.

D. Total risk.

The correct answer is (C). *(CIA, adapted)*

REQUIRED: The relevant risk of a security according to the capital asset pricing model.

DISCUSSION: The relevant risk of a security is its contribution to the portfolio's risk. It is the risk that cannot be eliminated through diversification and is synonymous with market risk and systematic risk. The relevant risk results from factors, such as inflation, recession, and high interest rates, that affect all stocks.

Answer (A) is incorrect because company-specific risk can be eliminated through portfolio diversification. Answer (B) is incorrect because diversifiable risk can be eliminated through portfolio diversification. Answer (D) is incorrect because only the systematic component of total risk is relevant to security valuation.

32. An investor uses the capital asset pricing model (CAPM) to evaluate the risk-return relationship on a portfolio of stocks held as an investment. Which of the following would not be used to estimate the portfolio's expected rate of return?

A. Expected risk premium on the portfolio of stocks.

B. Interest rate for the safest possible investment.

C. Expected rate of return on the market portfolio.

D. Standard deviation of the market returns.

The correct answer is (A). *(CIA, adapted)*

REQUIRED: The item not used to estimate the portfolio's expected rate of return.

DISCUSSION: The expected rate of return of a portfolio is the weighted average of the expected returns of the individual assets in the portfolio.

Answer (B) is incorrect because the interest rate for the safest possible investment is directly used in the capital asset pricing model. Answer (C) is incorrect because the expected rate of return on the market portfolio is the one systematic risk factor in the model. Answer (D) is incorrect because the standard deviation of the market returns is used to compute the beta coefficients for each security held in the investment portfolio and the beta coefficient for the market portfolio.

Questions 33 through 35 are based on the following information. DQZ Telecom is considering a project for the coming year that will cost $50 million. DQZ plans to use the following combination of debt and equity to finance the investment.

- Issue $15 million of 20-year bonds at a price of 101, with a coupon rate of 8%, and flotation costs of 2% of par.
- Use $35 million of funds generated from earnings.
- The equity market is expected to earn 12%. U.S. Treasury bonds are currently yielding 5%. The beta coefficient for DQZ is estimated to be .60. DQZ is subject to an effective corporate income tax rate of 40%.

---

33. The before-tax cost of DQZ's planned debt financing, net of flotation costs, in the first year is

A. 11.80%

B. 8.08%

C. 10.00%

D. 7.92%

The correct answer is (B). *(CMA, adapted)*

REQUIRED: The before-tax cost of the planned debt financing, net of flotation costs.

DISCUSSION: Proceeds are $14,850,000 [(1.01 x $15,000,000) – (.02 x $15,000,000)]. The annual interest is $1.2 million (.08 coupon rate x $15,000,000). Thus, the company is paying $1.2 million annually for the use of $14,850,000, a rate of 8.08% ($1,200,000 ÷ $14,850,000).

Answer (A) is incorrect because the contract rate is 8% annually. Answer (C) is incorrect because 10.00% is the sum of the coupon rate and the flotation rate. Answer (D) is incorrect because 7.92% ignores the 2% flotation costs.

34. Refer to the information preceding question 33. Assume that the after-tax cost of debt is 7% and the cost of equity is 12%. Determine the weighted-average cost of capital.

A. 10.50%

B. 8.50%

C. 9.50%

D. 6.30%

The correct answer is (A). *(CMA, adapted)*

REQUIRED: The weighted-average cost of capital given the costs of debt and equity.

DISCUSSION: The 7% debt cost and the 12% equity cost should be weighted by the proportions of the total investment represented by each source of capital. The total project costs $50 million, of which debt is $15 million, or 30% of the total. Equity capital is the other 70%. Consequently, the weighted-average cost of capital is 10.5% [(7%)(30%) + (12%)(70%)].

Answer (B) is incorrect because 8.50% reverses the weights. Answer (C) is incorrect because 9.50% assumes debt and equity are equally weighted. Answer (D) is incorrect because the weighted-average cost cannot be less than any of its components.

35. Refer to the information preceding question 33. The capital asset pricing model (CAPM) computes the expected return on a security by adding the risk-free rate of return to the incremental yield of the expected market return, which is adjusted by the company's beta. Compute DQZ's expected rate of return.

A. 9.20%

B. 12.20%

C. 7.20%

D. 12.00%

The correct answer is (A). *(CMA, adapted)*

REQUIRED: The expected rate of return using the capital asset pricing model (CAPM).

DISCUSSION: The market return (R_M), given as 12%, minus the risk-free rate (R_F), given as 5%, is the market risk premium. It is the rate at which investors must be compensated to induce them to invest in the market. The beta coefficient (β) of an individual stock, given as 60%, is the correlation between volatility (price variation) of the stock market and the volatility of the price of the individual stock. Consequently, the expected rate of return is 9.20% [$R_F + \beta (R_M - R_F) = .05 + .6(.12 - .05)$].

Answer (B) is incorrect because 12.20% equals the risk-free rate plus 60% of market rate. Answer (C) is incorrect because 7.20% results from multiplying both the market rate premium and the risk-free rate by 60%. Answer (D) is incorrect because 12.00% is the market rate.

36. The difference between the required rate of return on a given risky investment and that on a riskless investment with the same expected return is the

A. Risk premium.

B. Coefficient of variation.

C. Standard deviation.

D. Beta coefficient.

The correct answer is (A). *(CIA, adapted)*

REQUIRED: The difference between the required rate of return on a given risky investment and that on a riskless investment with the same expected return.

DISCUSSION: The required rate of return on equity capital in the capital asset pricing model is the risk-free rate (determined by government securities) plus the product of the market risk premium times the beta coefficient (beta measures the firm's risk). The market risk premium is the amount above the risk-free rate that will induce investment in the market. The beta coefficient of an individual stock is the correlation between the volatility (price variation) of the stock market and that of the price of the individual stock.

Answer (B) is incorrect because the coefficient of variation is the standard deviation of an investment's returns divided by the mean return. Answer (C) is incorrect because the standard deviation is a measure of the variability of an investment's returns. Answer (D) is incorrect because the beta coefficient measures the sensitivity of the investment's returns to market volatility.

37. Which of the following is directly applied in determining the value of a stock when using the dividend growth model?

A. The firm's capital structure.

B. The firm's cash flows.

C. The firm's liquidity.

D. The investor's required rate of return on the firm's stock.

The correct answer is (D). *(CIA, adapted)*

REQUIRED: The factor directly applied in determining the value of a stock using the dividend growth model.

DISCUSSION: The dividend growth model is used to calculate the cost of equity. The simplified formula is

$$R = \frac{D_1}{P_0} + G$$

R is the required rate of return, D_1 is the next dividend, P_0 is the stock's price, and G is the growth rate in earnings per share. The equation is also used to determine the stock price.

$$P_0 = \frac{D_1}{R - G}$$

Answers (A), (B), and (C) are incorrect because the model uses the growth rate in dividends and the investor's required rate of return.

38. Assume that nominal interest rates just increased substantially but that the expected future dividends for a company over the long run were not affected. As a result of the increase in nominal interest rates, the company's stock price should

A. Increase.

B. Decrease.

C. Stay constant.

D. Change, but in no obvious direction.

The correct answer is (B). *(CIA, adapted)*

REQUIRED: The effect on a company's stock price of an increase in nominal interest rates.

DISCUSSION: The dividend growth model is used to calculate the price of stock.

$$P_0 = \frac{D_1}{R - G}$$

If:
P_0 = current price
D_1 = next dividend
R = required rate of return
G = EPS growth rate

Assuming that D_1 and G remain constant, an increase in R resulting from an increase in the nominal interest rate will cause P_0 to decrease.

Answers (A), (C), and (D) are incorrect because a higher interest rate raises the required return of investors, which results in a lower stock price.

39. A firm seeking to optimize its capital budget has calculated its marginal cost of capital and projected rates of return on several potential projects. The optimal capital budget is determined by

A. Calculating the point at which marginal cost of capital meets the projected rate of return, assuming that the most profitable projects are accepted first.

B. Calculating the point at which average marginal cost meets average projected rate of return, assuming the largest projects are accepted first.

C. Accepting all potential projects with projected rates of return exceeding the lowest marginal cost of capital.

D. Accepting all potential projects with projected rates of return lower than the highest marginal cost of capital.

The correct answer is (A). *(CIA, adapted)*

REQUIRED: The determinant of the optimal capital budget.

DISCUSSION: In economics, a basic principle is that a firm should increase output until marginal cost equals marginal revenue. Similarly, the optimal capital budget is determined by calculating the point at which marginal cost of capital (which increases as capital requirements increase) and the marginal efficiency of investment (which decreases if the most profitable projects are accepted first) intersect.

Answer (B) is incorrect because the intersection of average marginal cost with average projected rates of return when the largest (not most profitable) projects are accepted first offers no meaningful capital budgeting conclusion. Answer (C) is incorrect because optimal capital budgeting assumes that the most profitable projects will be accepted first and that the marginal cost of capital increases as capital requirements increase. Thus, it is possible for the optimal capital budget to exclude profitable projects as lower cost capital goes first to projects with higher rates of return. Answer (D) is incorrect because accepting projects with rates of return lower than the cost of capital is not economically rational business.

Questions 40 through 43 are based on the following information. Rogers Inc. operates a chain of restaurants located in the Southeast. The first restaurant was opened in 1981, and the company has steadily grown to its present size of 48 restaurants. The board of directors recently approved a large-scale remodeling of the restaurant, and the company is now considering two financing alternatives.

- The first alternative would consist of
  - Bonds that would have a 9% coupon rate and would net $19.2 million after flotation costs
  - Preferred stock with a stated rate of 6% that would yield $4.8 million after a 4% flotation cost
  - Common stock that would yield $24 million after a 5% flotation cost
- The second alternative would consist of a public offering of bonds that would have an 11% coupon rate and would net $48 million after flotation costs.

Rogers' current capital structure, which is considered optimal, consists of 40% long-term debt, 10% preferred stock, and 50% common stock. The current market value of the common stock is $30 per share, and the common stock dividend during the past 12 months was $3 per share. Investors are expecting the growth rate of dividends to equal the historical rate of 6%. Rogers is subject to an effective income tax rate of 40%.

40. The after-tax cost of the common stock proposed in Rogers' first financing alternative would be

A. 16.00%

B. 16.53%

C. 16.60%

D. 17.16%

The correct answer is (D). *(CFM Sample Q. 7)*

REQUIRED: The after-tax cost of a proposed common stock issuance.

DISCUSSION: To determine the cost of new common stock, the dividend growth model is adjusted to include flotation cost as follows:

$$R = \frac{D_1}{P_0(1-\mathit{Flotation})} + G = \frac{\$3.18}{\$30.00(.95)} + .06 = 17.16\%$$

Answer (A) is incorrect because 16% ignores the increase in dividends and flotation costs. Answer (B) is incorrect because 16.53% ignores the increase in the next dividend. Answer (C) is incorrect because 16.6% ignores the flotation costs.

41. Assuming the after-tax cost of common stock is 15%, the after-tax weighted marginal cost of capital for Rogers' first financing alternative consisting of bonds, preferred stock, and common stock would be

A. 5.4%

B. 6.25%

C. 10.285%

D. 11.700%

The correct answer is (C). *(CFM Sample Q. 8)*

REQUIRED: The weighted marginal cost of the first financing alternative.

DISCUSSION: The cost of the bonds equals the interest rate times one minus the tax rate, or 5.4% [9% x (100% – 40%)]. The cost of preferred stock equals the preferred dividend divided by the net issuance price. No tax adjustment is necessary because preferred dividends paid are not deductible. The cost of the preferred stock is therefore 6% of the par value of the preferred stock {[$4,800,000 net issuance price ÷ (100% – 4% flotation cost)] = $5,000,000} divided by the net issuance price, or 6.25% [(6% x $5,000,000) ÷ $4,800,000]. The cost of the common stock is given as 15%. These costs are weighted as follows:

	Weight		
Bonds	40% × 5.4%	=	2.160%
Preferred stock	10% × 6.25%	=	.625
Common stock	50% × 15%	=	7.500
			10.285%

Flotation costs are ignored for the bonds because the face value must be repaid at the maturity date, which is not the case for preferred stock.

Answer (A) is incorrect because 5.4% is the cost of the bonds. Answer (B) is incorrect because 6.25% is the cost of the preferred stock. Answer (D) is incorrect because 11.700% is a nonsensical number.

42. The after-tax weighted marginal cost of capital for Rogers' second financing alternative consisting solely of bonds would be

A. 5.13%

B. 5.40%

C. 6.27%

D. 6.60%

The correct answer is (D). *(CFM Sample Q. 9)*

REQUIRED: The weighted marginal cost of the second financing alternative.

DISCUSSION: The cost of the bonds equals the interest rate times one minus the tax rate, or 6.60% [11% x (100% – 40%)].

Answer (A) is incorrect because 5.13% is 5.40% reduced by the 5% stock flotation costs. Answer (B) is incorrect because 5.40% is 60% of 9%. Answer (C) is incorrect because 6.27% is 6.60% reduced by the 5% stock flotation costs.

43. The interest rate on the bonds is greater for the second alternative consisting of pure debt than it is for the first alternative consisting of both debt and equity because

A. The diversity of the combination alternative creates greater risk for the investor.

B. The pure debt alternative would flood the market and be more difficult to sell.

C. The pure debt alternative carries the risk of increasing the probability of default.

D. The combination alternative carries the risk of increasing dividend payments.

The correct answer is (C). *(CFM Sample Q. 10)*

REQUIRED: The reason increases in debt financing relative to equity financing increase the interest rate.

DISCUSSION: As a larger proportion of an entity's capital is provided by debt, the debt becomes riskier and more expensive. Hence, it requires a higher interest rate.

Answer (A) is incorrect because the diversity decreases, not increases, risk. Answer (B) is incorrect because $50,000,000 is minuscule in the debt markets. Answer (D) is incorrect because the combination alternative maintains the same debt-equity mixture, which would not warrant a rate increase in the cost of debt or equity.

C. Corporate Insurance

44. Insurance may best be defined as

A. A system for transferring risk through risk avoidance or loss control.

B. Any contract that conveys an insurable interest.

C. A form of pure risk called gambling.

D. A means of combining many loss exposures so that losses are shared by all participants.

The correct answer is (D). *(Publisher)*

REQUIRED: The best definition of insurance.

DISCUSSION: Insurance is a method of spreading losses that arise from risks to which many persons are subject. Loss is an unanticipated diminution in economic value as opposed to normal depreciation. Risk is uncertainty about the occurrence or the amount of loss. For example, buildings are subject to the risk of loss by fire. If the owners all pay small fees (premiums) for insurance coverage, every participant bears part of the loss instead of a few bearing all the loss.

Answer (A) is incorrect because risk avoidance and loss control do not transfer risk of loss. Answer (B) is incorrect because an insurable interest is merely a potential for economic loss if an event occurs. Answer (C) is incorrect because there must be an insurable interest, which is basically potential for loss if an event occurs. Gambling occurs when only a bet is at risk.

45. Which of the following is the best functional definition of insurance?

A. A legal contract by which the insurer, in return for consideration, agrees to pay another person if a stated loss or injury occurs.

B. A legal contract by which an insurance company, in return for premiums, agrees to pay the policyholder if a certain event occurs.

C. A written promise by the insurer to pay the beneficiary if loss occurs from the occurrence of a contingent event.

D. A writing issued by an insurance company, for a consideration, that promises to indemnify a beneficiary for a loss from an existing risk or one which arises later.

The correct answer is (A). *(Publisher)*

REQUIRED: The best functional definition of insurance.

DISCUSSION: Insurance contracts must satisfy the usual requirements: offer and acceptance, consideration, legality, and capacity of the parties. The insured must have an insurable interest in the subject matter of the contract. The subject matter generally must exist at the time of contracting. The insurer promises to pay a stated amount for loss or injury incurred as a result of a contingent event.

Answer (B) is incorrect because the payee may be a stranger to the contract. Answer (C) is incorrect because there is no general requirement that an insurance contract be written. Answer (D) is incorrect because the contract may often be oral, and, if the risk is not already in existence, the transaction is in essence a wager, not insurance.

46. In which way does the formation of an insurance contract differ from any other contract?

A. The requirement that the insured must have an insurable interest.

B. The insurance contract is not valid unless written.

C. Consideration is not needed for the formation of an insurance contract.

D. In insurance, only the insured can commit a breach.

The correct answer is (A). *(Publisher)*

REQUIRED: The manner in which the formation of an insurance contract differs from other contracts.

DISCUSSION: An insurance contract is very similar to any other contract. However, an additional requirement is that the insured must have an insurable interest.

Answer (B) is incorrect because there is no general requirement that an insurance contract be written. Oral binders are given every day in the insurance business. Answer (C) is incorrect because consideration is needed for the initial formation of an insurance contract. The premium may be paid immediately, or a promise to pay is required. Answer (D) is incorrect because the insurance company can also commit a breach by refusing to pay the proceeds of the policy upon the occurrence of the event.

47. Life insurance

A. Is a contract of indemnity.

B. Usually has short-term policies.

C. Covers only the mortality risk.

D. Generally has no cash value.

The correct answer is (A). *(Publisher)*

REQUIRED: The correct statement about the characteristics of life insurance.

DISCUSSION: Life insurance is a contract for the payment of a specified amount to the named beneficiary or to the estate of the insured if the insured dies while the policy is in effect. Payment for the actual loss is called indemnity. Hence, life insurance is a contract of indemnity.

Answer (B) is incorrect because life insurance is customarily long-term, if not for life. Answer (C) is incorrect because, unlike other forms of insurance, life insurance does not attempt to reimburse for the actual amount of a loss since loss of life is not measurable. Life insurance is intended to replace economic benefits lost by a person's death. Answer (D) is incorrect because, except for term policies, life insurance differs from other kinds of coverage in providing cash value.

48. Jon Berstock is an employee of PR, Inc. During his employment, the corporation's earnings have doubled, largely because of Jon's ability to attract new accounts. PR therefore insured his life for a substantial sum. If Jon dies, will PR be able to collect the insurance proceeds?

A. Yes, because a corporation has an insurable interest in all its employees.

B. Yes, because PR has an insurable interest in Jon's continued life.

C. No, because PR will continue to exist after Jon's death.

D. No, because Jon was not a shareholder or officer of PR, Inc.

The correct answer is (B). *(Publisher)*

REQUIRED: The correct statement about a corporation's insurance on an employee's life.

DISCUSSION: When one person insures the life of another, the policyholder must have an insurable interest in the insured. That interest is found among persons who have a close family relationship or expect to suffer substantial economic loss from the death. Business entities are thus permitted to insure key people in their organizations whose death might have an adverse effect on profits.

Answer (A) is incorrect because a corporation has an insurable interest only in its key employees, i.e., those whose death would cause loss to the firm. Answer (C) is incorrect because the required loss need not be so great as to cause cessation of business. Answer (D) is incorrect because one need not be an owner or an officer to be insurable as a key person.

49. Life insurance is offered in several forms. The kind that offers no investment feature is

A. Whole life.

B. Endowment.

C. Straight life.

D. Term.

The correct answer is (D). *(Publisher)*

REQUIRED: The kind of life insurance not offering an investment feature.

DISCUSSION: Term life insurance provides protection for a specified period. Premiums are level throughout the period. When the term ends, the insured receives no payment. Term insurance may be renewable (possibly at higher premiums) or convertible to another form. It is the cheapest kind of life insurance.

Answer (A) is incorrect because whole life furnishes lifetime insurance protection with a cash surrender value. Answer (B) is incorrect because an endowment policy provides life insurance protection for its duration. A cash payment is made (the policy endows) at the end of the term. Premiums for endowment policies are higher than for whole life insurance. Answer (C) is incorrect because a straight life or ordinary policy is whole life insurance with level premiums payable for life.

50. Which of the following is a characteristic of fire insurance?

A. It is more standardized than life insurance.

B. It is written for a relatively short period but usually includes an incontestability clause.

C. A policy must be valued and contain a pro rata clause.

D. The insurable interest must be an ownership interest in the property itself.

The correct answer is (A). *(Publisher)*

REQUIRED: The characteristic of fire insurance.

DISCUSSION: Fire insurance is the most standardized kind of insurance. Following the lead of New York, almost all states have enacted a standard policy either by legislative or administrative action.

Answer (B) is incorrect because, given that fire insurance is usually written for a 1- to 3-year period, an incontestability clause is not necessary. Such a clause bars insurer defenses after a period specified by law or the policy. Answer (C) is incorrect because a policy may state a definite value of the insured property or simply a maximum amount of coverage that is not conclusive as to valuation when loss occurs. A policy may thus be valued or open (unvalued). A pro rata clause is often included (but not required) which requires the loss to be shared pro rata when there is more than one insurer. Answer (D) is incorrect because the insurable interest merely requires the person, e.g., mortgagee, bailee, etc., to suffer a loss if the event insured against occurs.

51. A fire insurance policy ordinarily indemnifies for losses arising from

A. Friendly, but not hostile, fires.

B. Hostile, but not friendly, fires.

C. Both hostile and friendly fires.

D. Smoke produced by friendly or hostile fires.

The correct answer is (B). *(Publisher)*

REQUIRED: The losses caused by fire that will be indemnified.

DISCUSSION: Ordinarily, smoke, water, or other damage caused by hostile, but not friendly, fires will be indemnified under a fire insurance policy. Hostile fires are those ignited in places where they are not meant to be. A friendly fire is one that burns where it is intended to burn, such as a fireplace or furnace. For example, if a friendly fire is kept within its usual container, damage caused by smoke from it will not be reimbursed.

Answers (A), (C), and (D) are incorrect because fire insurance usually indemnifies for loss caused by hostile, but not friendly, fires.

52. Which of the following wrongful acts prevents recovery under a policy of fire insurance?

A. Arson by the insured's employees or agents.

B. Arson by third persons unrelated to the insured.

C. An act by the insured intended to cause the damage.

D. Gross negligence but not amounting to recklessness and willful misconduct.

The correct answer is (C). *(Publisher)*

REQUIRED: The wrongful act preventing an insurance recovery.

DISCUSSION: Arson, fraud, or another intentional act of the insured calculated to cause the damage insured against will preclude recovery. The parties to an insurance contract have an implied duty not to bring about the very event that is the subject matter of the policy.

Answer (A) is incorrect because agency rules do not apply; i.e., the intentional act of an agent will not be imputed to the insured under the doctrine of *respondeat superior*. Arson by an agent without the actual knowledge or conspiracy of the insured will not preclude recovery. Answer (B) is incorrect because arson is compensable unless intended by the insured. Answer (D) is incorrect because negligence without fraud will not prevent recovery by an insured who has acted in good faith.

53. Which of the following is not a type of insurance policy that provides liability insurance?

A. Malpractice insurance.

B. Homeowners insurance.

C. Automobile insurance.

D. Fire insurance.

The correct answer is (D). *(Publisher)*

REQUIRED: The type of insurance policy not providing liability coverage.

DISCUSSION: Fire insurance generally protects the insured from damage to the insured property as a result of fire. It does not cover the insured for causing a fire on someone else's property.

Answer (A) is incorrect because malpractice insurance is a special form of liability insurance protecting professionals from lawsuits by third parties for negligence. Answer (B) is incorrect because homeowners insurance generally contains a liability section in the event guests are injured on the premises. Answer (C) is incorrect because a primary purpose of automobile insurance is to protect the owner or driver from liability in the event (s)he is responsible for injury to another person or damage to property.

54. The purpose of a co-insurance clause is to

A. Encourage policyholders to bear a proportionate part of any loss.

B. Encourage insurers to pay the face amount of the policy in the event of a partial loss on the part of the insured.

C. Encourage policyholders to insure commercial property for an amount that is near to its full replacement cost.

D. Encourage policyholders to insure commercial property for an amount that is significantly less than its full replacement cost.

The correct answer is (C). *(Publisher)*

REQUIRED: The purpose of a co-insurance clause.

DISCUSSION: Co-insurance is a method of sharing risk between the insurer and the insured. A co-insurance clause typically provides that, if the policyholder insures his/her property for at least a stated percentage (usually 80%) of its actual cash value, any loss will be paid in full up to the face amount of the policy. Thus, a co-insurance clause is used by many property and casualty insurers to encourage policyholders to insure commercial property for an amount that is near to its full replacement cost.

Answer (A) is incorrect because, if a policyholder does not insure the property for an amount close enough to its full replacement cost, the policyholder must bear a proportionate part of any partial loss. Answer (B) is incorrect because the co-insurance requirement applies only to partial losses. Total losses result in recovery of the face amount of the policy. Answer (D) is incorrect because a co-insurance clause encourages policyholders to insure commercial property for an amount that is near to its full replacement cost.

Use Gleim's ***CMA/CFM Test Prep*** for interactive testing with **over 2,000 additional multiple-choice questions!**

STUDY UNIT 8: ORGANIZATIONAL THEORY

26 pages of outline
61 multiple-choice questions

The relative weight range assigned to organizational structures, management, and communication in Part 1 is 20% to 30%. We cover this major topic in the following study units:

Study Unit 8: Organizational Theory
Study Unit 9: Motivation and the Directing Process
Study Unit 10: Communication

Thus, you should expect 24 to 36 questions on these three study units.

A. Overview of Management

1. Management can be characterized in many ways, each view reflecting one or more aspects of the development of management theory:
   a. Management is accomplishing work through people.
   b. Management is the process of planning, organizing (staffing), directing, and controlling resources to reach organizational goals.
   c. Management is a set of scientific tools used to produce rational solutions to organizational problems in a changing environment.
   d. Management is making and implementing decisions in an organizational setting.
   e. In *Management*, 6th ed. (Boston: Houghton Mifflin Company, 1995, p. 4), Robert Kreitner defines management as "the process of working with and through others to achieve organizational objectives in a changing environment. Central to this process is the effective and efficient use of limited resources."
      1) Thus, management is a social process that attempts to use scarce resources to achieve organizational objectives while anticipating environmental changes and balancing effectiveness against efficiency.
         a) The physical, social, political, moral, and informational environments external to the organization are the sources of change that managers must anticipate.
      2) Kreitner (pp. 20-22) also states that the variables in the basic formula for effective management are ability, motivation, and opportunity. Ability is the "capacity to achieve organizational objectives both effectively and efficiently." Motivation is "a persistent desire to move ahead." Opportunity has two components according to Kreitner: a suitable job in management and a supportive climate.

2. The management function is universal.
   a. Managers at every level of every organization perform four functions:
      1) **Planning**
      2) **Organizing**
      3) **Directing**
      4) **Controlling**
3. The amount of time spent on each function varies by level of manager.
   a. The higher the level, the more planning and organizing
   b. The lower the level, the more directing
   c. All levels of management must spend time controlling.
4. The proportionate time also varies with the size of the organization. Larger entities must make long-range plans, whereas smaller ones can be more flexible. Large amounts of invested assets often cannot respond to change as quickly.
5. Managers can be classified variously.
   a. An executive or general manager, such as a chair of the board, has policy-making as well as operational authority. A general manager has responsibility for multiple operational functions in a specific organizational unit.
   b. A functional manager has authority over a specific operational area (e.g., accounting) and is responsible for intermediate planning with a time line of approximately 6 months to 1 year.
   c. A first-line or middle manager directly supervises employees who are not managers. These managers deal with day-to-day operations.
6. Henry Mintzberg disagreed with the functional method of describing management's roles. He observed that the actual activities of managers could be classified as follows:
   a. **Interpersonal roles**
      1) Figurehead or ceremonial symbol of legal authority
      2) Leader who motivates subordinates
      3) Liaison in both horizontal and vertical chains of communication
   b. **Informational roles**
      1) Nerve center or focal point of nonroutine information and a recipient of all kinds of information
      2) Disseminator of information to subordinates
      3) Spokesperson who transmits information to outsiders
   c. **Decisional roles**
      1) Entrepreneur who devises and brings about organizational change
      2) Disturbance handler who takes nonroutine corrective action
      3) Resource allocator who determines who receives what
      4) Negotiator with outside parties who protects the organization's interests

7. The **scientific school of management** was the first major school to develop.

   a. Scientific management focuses on the production process and ways to make it more efficient. It is based on the work of Frederick W. Taylor, who advocated a systematic quantitative approach oriented towards individual job design.

      1) Taylor's four principles of scientific management are

         a) Scientific analysis of work

         b) Scientific selection, training, and development of workers

         c) Cooperation between work planners and operators

         d) Equal sharing of responsibility by labor and management, who perform the tasks for which they are best suited

      2) Taylor also pioneered the use of time and motion analysis, stopwatch measurement, and systematic shop management.

      3) Scientific management holds that there is one best way to do each job. Management should discover the best way and teach it to workers.

         a) Each job/task should be designed for maximum efficiency.

         b) Management should teach workers new habits. Old habits are often inefficient.

      4) Taylor designed incentive programs based on the prevailing management philosophy that the best way to get worker cooperation in performing the job in the prescribed efficient manner was to offer monetary rewards.

         a) If workers produce more, they should share in benefits.

         b) Productivity increased because the workers' incremental bonus usually was less than their productivity increase.

      5) Separation of tasks into simple subtasks, close supervision, and reliance on economic motivation are all characteristics of the scientific school later attacked by human relations researchers.

8. The **administrative school of management** emphasized principles, concepts, and ideas from past organizational experience. It paralleled the scientific school of management in seeking one best way to organize, but its focus was on the overall organization. In contrast, the scientific school focused on shop management and individual workers.

   a. It attempted to distill universal principles from practical experience. A principle is a statement of valid causal relationships that is useful in predicting the outcome of a pending relationship. The administrative school believed in the existence of certain valid principles of organization, such as the following:

      1) **Principle of span of control**. The number of subordinates a superior can effectively supervise is limited.

      2) **Principle of unity of command**. Each subordinate should have only one superior (though a superior may have as many subordinates as allowed by the superior's span of control). Violation of this principle (unity of command) leads to confusion and frustration for the subordinate.

b. The value of a management principle is to give the manager guidelines for improving decisions, minimizing inefficiency, and reducing unnecessary conflict.

c. Principles based on successful practices or careful observation did help managers learn to apply useful knowledge about organizational design.

d. The administrative school of management is considered mechanistic in that it seeks to build static models of organizations and the people in them (as opposed to organic or dynamic models).

e. It reflects the same lack of concern with human relations as the scientific school.

f. It assumes away the need of the organization to adapt to human, social, and technological changes.

g. The difficulty with administrative school of management principles is that they do not always hold true in actual organizations. For example, different organizations use different spans of control and are still successful.

9. Henri Fayol (a Frenchman publishing in 1916), sometimes called the father of administration, advocated the separation of administration from technical, commercial, financial, and accounting operations.

a. Fayol's **functions of management** listed below form the foundation for the modern functional or process approach to classifying a manager's activities.

1) Planning
2) Organizing
3) Commanding
4) Coordinating
5) Controlling

10. The **behavioral school** views management as accomplishing results through people, both as individuals and in groups. Thus, the stress is on applying findings from psychology, anthropology, and sociology.

a. Elton Mayo (working in the 1920s and 1930s) is referred to as the father of human relations. His initial experiments studied the relationship of workshop lighting levels to levels of productivity.

1) These experiments, conducted at the Hawthorne plant of Western Electric from 1927 to 1932, are known as the Hawthorne experiments. The results astounded researchers by revealing that increased worker productivity resulted from the workers' willingness to cooperate, not from the level of lighting. The researchers concluded that

a) The workers' individual needs and their social relationships with peers on the job were more important to productivity than the physical working conditions.

b) Work is a group activity.

c) Informal relationships are important parts of organizational systems.

b. Key elements recognized by the behavioral school include

1) Participation

a) Permits more involvement of subordinates in the organization

b) Encourages communication up as well as down the organizational hierarchy

c) Leads to better decisions

2) Group influences

a) Informal communication processes are important.

b) Group pressure shapes individual behavior, beliefs, values, and job attitudes.

3) Individual needs

a) Individuals are not solely motivated by financial incentives.
b) People get bored doing routine, simple, and repetitive jobs.
c) People have a variety of needs that the job setting should satisfy.

11. The **systems school** stresses interrelationships and interdependence of managerial problems. It emphasizes chains of events and how components relate to one another. The systems school is considered the modern approach to management.

a. An organizational system is a group or set of things that are interrelated or interdependent so as to form a part of a larger whole. The systems school recognizes that understanding an organization is impossible without considering the larger context or system of which it is a part.

1) It also considers both human relations and structural issues.

2) Systems may be closed or open. **Closed systems** are closed to the external environment. Few systems are truly closed, but boundaries may be artificially drawn to facilitate analysis by treating a system as if it were closed.

a) Classical viewpoints treated management as a closed system and ignored most things external to the organization. Such policy is limited and dangerous in that effective management of a social system is not deterministic or mechanistic.

3) **Open systems** are open to and have interaction with an external environment. The system boundaries are drawn to reflect external inputs and system outputs.

a) A closed system suffers entropy, but an open system seeks replenishment through its boundaries with the larger system (environment).

b) Closed-systems management writers viewed the environment as beyond their concern; open-systems writers see the environment as vital.

b. The **contingency approach**, derived from systems thinking, stresses that the search for answers to organizational problems depends on contingencies that can be discovered and studied.

1) Because this approach argues for situationally determined answers to management concerns, the key is finding the relevant factors in the organization's environment.

2) The same argument applies to individuals' motivations, needs, and wants because people are subsystems within the larger organizational system.

c. Management should be studied as an open social system because of its continual interaction with its external environment.

1) Technological change
2) Social responsibilities to other social institutions
3) Relationships of employee needs and organizational requirements
4) Organizational growth and development
5) Individual and organizational reasons for resisting change

d. The recognition of social responsibilities is a logical outgrowth of systems thinking. If the organization is part of a larger social system, it must recognize its subordination to and interdependence with this larger system. This recognition requires accepting the responsibility to make decisions with thoughtful consideration of their impact on society, the larger system.

e. Managers who recognize the interrelatedness of the business environment also recognize and take advantage of the principle of **synergy** -- the joint action of two or more parties that, taken together, enhances each other's effectiveness.

12. The emergence of the **total quality management (TQM)** concept is one of the most significant developments in recent years. TQM recognizes that quality improvement can increase revenues and decrease costs significantly.

    a. TQM is a comprehensive approach to quality. It treats the pursuit of quality as a basic organizational function that is as important as production or marketing.

    b. TQM is the continuous pursuit of quality in every aspect of organizational activities through a philosophy of doing it right the first time, employee training and empowerment, promotion of teamwork, improvement of processes, and attention to satisfaction of customers, both internal and external.

    c. TQM emphasizes the supplier's relationship with the customer, identifies customer needs, and recognizes that everyone in a process is at some time a customer or supplier of someone else, either within or without the organization.

13. Stop and review! You have completed the outline for this subunit. Study multiple-choice questions 1 through 7 beginning on page 323.

B. The Organizing Process

1. Kreitner [*Management*, 6th ed. (Boston: Houghton Mifflin, 1995), pp. 264-265] classifies organizations as follows:

    a. Businesses are engaged in economic activities with the intent to make a profit.

    b. Nonprofit service organizations, such as charities and universities, serve particular groups of clients. Money may come from donations, appropriations, or grants.

    c. Mutual benefit organizations are groups that exist to serve their members, e.g., labor unions or political parties.

    d. Commonweal entities provide a standard service to all members of a population. A public school system is an example.

2. Organizing is the design and structuring of tasks and roles to accomplish organizational goals.

    a. The roles define the relationships among individuals and groups of individuals within an organization.

    b. The structuring reflects the division of activities into subactivities.

    c. Structuring also coordinates or integrates these divided activities into a cohesive whole.

3. The **traditional approach** (also known as classical, structural, or formal) emphasizes authority, responsibility, tasks, hierarchy, span of control, etc.

    a. The traditional approach to organizing sets up prescribed (or dictated) relationships and then places people in them.

    b. "The person is selected to fill the job."

4. The **behavioral approach** emphasizes the limits, strengths, availability, and interests of the people available.
   a. The participants provide feedback in the role-definition process.
   b. This approach is less deterministic than the traditional approach because group dynamics and the feelings of subordinates are included in the process.
   c. "The job is designed to fit the person."
5. The **modern (contingency) approach** emphasizes the tailoring of the organization to its unique situation.
   a. It combines classical and behavioral principles of organization.
   b. "The job and the person must fit each other."
6. **Reengineering** involves starting from scratch to redesign a company's core processes rather than attempting to improve the current system. Reengineering is not merely downsizing or continuous improvement but a complete change in a company's ways of doing business.
   a. In the modern highly competitive business environment, a company may need to adapt quickly and radically to change. Thus, reengineering is usually a cross-departmental process of innovation requiring substantial investment in information technology and retraining. Successful reengineering may bring dramatic improvements in customer service and the speed with which new products are introduced.
7. The relationships present in the structure of an organization include authority, responsibility, and accountability. Classical theory stresses the need for balance between authority and responsibility.
   a. **Authority** is the right to direct and exact performance from others, including the right to prescribe the means and methods by which the work will be done. The right to direct should be distinguished from the ability (the power) to accomplish tasks.
      1) Under the classical approach, the right to exercise authority is deemed to be vested in the position. Based on objective criteria, the organization rationally determines where a decision is best made, gives the authority to make the decision to that position, and fills the position with the most suitable person.
      2) Under the behavioral approach, the right to direct is deemed to be only as good as the receiver's willingness to accept direction from another.
         a) It emphasizes the willingness of followers to be directed as opposed to the classical focus on the right of a leader to command.
         b) Belief in this approach necessitates a change in the attitude of the leader toward subordinates by focusing on the leader's need to secure compliance from followers rather than an assumption of blind obedience to commands.
      3) **Power** is the ability to influence employees to do what they would not ordinarily do. Power and influence may be wielded informally. Thus, power sources include
         a) Legitimate or position power (the power of the person with formal status)
         b) Expertise

c) Referent power (derived from the leader's charisma or employees' identification with the leader)

d) Control of rewards

e) Ability to punish (coercive power)

4) The greater the sources of power possessed by a manager, the more likely an employee will be inclined to accept his/her authority.

b. **Responsibility** is the obligation to perform.

1) In the classical view, this obligation is formally imposed by a superior and is inherent in any job.

2) In the behavioral view, responsibility must and should be delegated; there is a successive dividing and passing down of obligation.

a) The appropriate amount of authority or power must be delegated with the responsibility.

b) However, a higher position cannot escape ultimate responsibility.

c. **Accountability** is the duty to account for the fulfillment of the responsibility. In practice, accountability is

1) The duty to report performance to one's superior

a) The principle of single accountability or unity of command means that each subordinate should report to only one superior.

b) Unity of command permits more than one person to act as a subordinate's superior only when coordination of plans is so complete that no conflicting instructions are given.

2) The physical means for reporting or being able to substantiate performance, i.e., record keeping

8. **Unity of Objective**. An organizational structure is effective if it facilitates the contribution of individuals toward the attainment of enterprise objectives. Hence, organizational objectives must have been clearly formulated in the planning process.

a. In other words, the purpose of organizing is goal congruence, ensuring that all individuals in the organization are working toward the same organizational goals.

b. Organizing also allows management to perform a monitoring function by determining when goals are not achieved and where the problems exist within the organization.

1) Organizing is the beginning of control.

9. **Efficiency**. An organizational structure is efficient if it facilitates the accomplishment of organizational objectives with minimum resources and fewest unsought consequences. An efficient organizational structure

a. Maximizes output for a given amount of input
b. Provides all resources required, whether physical, financial, or human

10. **Effectiveness**. An organization that reaches its goals is effective. However, effectiveness does not consider the cost-benefit criterion. Thus, a process may be both very effective and very inefficient.

a. Goals usually include being efficient and may include social responsibility.

b. Effectiveness in meeting organizational objectives and social expectations should occur in the near future, the intermediate future, and the distant future.

11. **Decision Making**. The formal decision-making process in organizations is essential to organizing. For coverage of this process, see Study Unit 5 in Part 3.

12. **Elements of Organizational Structure**. Structure can be defined in terms of complexity, formalization, and centralization.

    a. The following are three kinds of differentiation that contribute to complexity:

        1) **Vertical differentiation** concerns the depth of the organizational hierarchy. The greater the number of levels, the more complex the organization, the greater the potential for information distortion, the more difficult the coordination of management activities, and the slower and less effective the response to changing conditions.

        2) **Horizontal differentiation** concerns the extent to which tasks require special skills and knowledge. The greater the diversity of skills and knowledge, the greater the organizational complexity, and the more difficult communication and coordination become.

        3) **Spatial differentiation** concerns the extent of the geographical separation of the organization's operations.

    b. **Formalization** concerns the extent to which job performance is standardized by job descriptions and clear procedures that define how tasks are to be accomplished. Low formalization enhances worker discretion.

    c. **Centralization** (See the subunit on Centralization and Decentralization.)

13. **Mechanistic versus Organic Structures**. The extremes of the structural continuum are mechanistic and organic organizations.

    a. A **mechanistic structure** is appropriate for organizations focusing on a cost-minimization strategy through tight controls, extensive division of labor, high formalization, and centralization. The information network is limited, and employees rarely participate in decision making.

    b. An **organic structure** is characterized by low complexity, low formalization, and decentralization. It has an extensive information system, and employees participate in decision making. Organic organizations tend to be flexible and adaptive to change.

14. Structure is a function of the organization's fundamental strategy.

    a. An **innovation strategy** concentrates on developing important new products or services. An organic structure provides the flexibility for this strategy.

    b. A **cost-minimization strategy** imposes tight controls over expenditures and attempts to reduce prices of products. The mechanistic structure is appropriate.

    c. An **imitation strategy** is not adopted by true innovators but rather by companies that move into new markets only after smaller competitors have demonstrated the potential for success. Imitation strategies are best suited to a structure that combines mechanistic and organic components.

15. Structure is also a function of

    a. **Organizational size**. Larger organizations tend to be mechanistic because greater formalization is needed. Strategies also change as organizations change size. Growing organizations often expand their activities within their industry.

b. **Technology**. An organic structure may be best for coping with nonroutine technology because formalization is low.

1) Joan Woodward classifies technology as follows:

a) Job shop
b) Mass production
c) Continuous process

2) Woodward concluded that organizations with more complex technology have more management levels, more administrative and clerical personnel, more coordination by committees, and a larger span of control at the chief-executive level.

c. **Environment**. In general, the more stable the environment, the more mechanistic the organization. A mechanistic structure is also appropriate when the environment has little capacity for growth. Dynamic environments require an organic structure because of their unpredictability. Moreover, a complex environment (e.g., one with numerous and constantly changing competitors) also requires the flexibility and adaptability of an organic structure.

1) Every organization's environment has three key dimensions: capacity, volatility, and complexity. Capacity is the degree of growth an environment can support. Volatility concerns the relative instability in the environment. Complexity refers to the amount of heterogeneity and concentration in the environment; e.g., an industry with a few very large firms is homogeneous and concentrated.

NOTE: Uncertainty is not a specific environmental factor. Rather, the foregoing factors determine the level of uncertainty present in the environment. However, entities that cope with high uncertainty or rates of change have design strategies different from those of stable organizations.

d. **Stage in life cycle**. Older organizations have structures different from those of newer ones.

16. According to Henry Mintzberg, an organization has five components. Depending on which is in control, one of five different structures will evolve. The five organizational components include the

a. **Operating core** -- workers who perform the basic tasks related to production

b. **Strategic apex** -- top managers

c. **Middle line** -- managers who connect the core to the apex

d. **Technostructure** -- analysts who achieve a certain standardization in the organization

e. **Support staff** -- indirect support services

17. Mintzberg's five organizational structures include the following:

a. A **simple structure**, such as that of a small retailer, has low complexity and formality, and authority is centralized. Its small size and simplicity usually precludes significant inefficiency in the use of resources. The strategic apex is the dominant component.

b. A **machine bureaucracy** is a complex, formal, and centralized organization that performs highly routine tasks, groups activities into functional departments, has a strict chain of command, and distinguishes between line and staff relationships. The technostructure dominates.

c. A **professional bureaucracy** (e.g., a university or library) is a complex and formal but decentralized organization in which highly trained specialists have great autonomy. Duplication of functions is minimized. For example, a university would have only one history department. Thus, the operating core is in control.

d. A **divisional structure** is essentially a self-contained organization. Hence, it must perform all or most of the functions of the overall organization of which it is a part. It is characterized by substantial duplication of functions compared with more centralized structures. The middle line dominates.

e. An **adhocracy** (an organic structure) has low complexity, formality, and centralization. Vertical differentiation is low and horizontal differentiation is high. The emphasis is on flexibility and response. Thus, the support staff dominates.

18. Stop and review! You have completed the outline for this subunit. Study multiple-choice questions 8 through 30 beginning on page 325.

C. Departmentation

1. Division of labor breaks complex processes into their simpler components. However, dividing labor creates a need for efficient coordination of those performing the separate tasks. One response to the problem is departmentation, which is a form of organizational integration intended to promote coordination. It is the grouping of related activities into significant organizational subsystems.

   a. **Departmentation by function** is the most widely used. It is found in almost every organization at some level whether profit-making or nonprofit. The most common departments in profit-making organizations are marketing, production, and finance (though other terms may be used). These often extend upward in the organizational chart to the level below the chief executive.

      1) Advantages include occupational specialization, simplified training, and representation of primary functions at the top level of the organization.

      2) Disadvantages include lack of coordination between primary functions and absence of profit centers within the organization.

   b. **Departmentation by territory** is favored by national or multinational firms and government agencies with scattered offices or plants.

      1) Advantages include quicker reaction to local market changes, greater familiarity with local problems or unique geographic concerns, and logistical savings in freight costs and travel time.

      2) Disadvantages include more delegation of authority to regional managers, problems of control for headquarters, and duplication of service functions (personnel, purchases, etc.).

   c. **Departmentation by product** is growing in importance for multiline, large-scale enterprises. It is often an outgrowth of functional departmentation and permits extensive authority for a division executive over a given product or product line.

      1) Advantages include better use of specialized capital and skills, ease of coordination, simpler assignment of profit responsibility, compatibility with a decentralization strategy, and a basis for allocating capital efficiently to products likely to achieve the best returns.

      2) Disadvantages include the requirement for a greater number of persons with managerial ability, duplication of staff functions, and difficulty in maintaining top management control over operations.

d. **Departmentation by customer** allows for service to a particular customer to be provided under the management of a department head. This form of departmentation seldom appears at the top level of an organizational structure, but it is often found at middle levels (e.g., the loan officer of a large bank who handles one account exclusively). Customer departmentation is often found within the sales department of a firm organized by function.

   1) Advantages include increased customer service as a result of the expertise gained in that customer's business and ease in identifying contributions to profit made by different types and locations of customers.

   2) Disadvantages include difficulties in coordination with other units in the organization and pressure to give preferential treatment to any given manager's customers.

e. **Project departmentation** is appropriate for experimental or one-time activities, e.g., the construction of a ship, a large building, or a major design project (such as a military weapons system).

   1) Advantages include specialization and ease of communication and coordination of efforts required within a particular project.

   2) Disadvantages include need for reorganization at the end of the project, problems of recruitment at the start of the project, and difficulty of maintaining control at the central office.

f. **Matrix organization** is a combination of any of the abovementioned approaches to departmentation. For example, a manager for each product may be appointed to supervise personnel who simultaneously report to a manager for each function. This form is used in R&D and in project management.

   1) The emphasis of the arrangement is on the result or the product.

   2) The functional organization remains, while parts of it are temporarily lent or assigned to a given project.

   3) The project may be to make a product indefinitely or to accomplish a limited but lengthy task, such as construction of a submarine.

   4) Matrix organization provides the security and accountability of the functional form while providing expert personnel to the project only when needed and only to the extent required. It allows personnel as well as functions to be most effectively and efficiently used.

   5) Technical ability of employees is better appraised by the functional managers than by the project manager.

   6) Practical applications skills can be appraised by the project manager on-site.

   7) Unnecessarily large swings in levels of personnel and equipment are minimized.

      a) The major disadvantage is that the principle of unity of command is violated. Hence, the authority, responsibility, and accountability of the parties involved must be clearly defined to avoid confusion and employee dissatisfaction.

      b) A second disadvantage is the possible inefficient use of employees. Individuals may be idle while waiting for project assignments that require their specific talents.

8) It is difficult for large organizations to use matrix organization because they typically have many levels (both vertical and horizontal), thus slowing communications.

g. The method of departmentation chosen is contingent upon

1) Organizational plans, programs, policies, and purposes
2) Environmental constraints
3) Training and preferences of available personnel

2. Stop and review! You have completed the outline for this subunit. Study multiple-choice questions 31 through 35 beginning on page 332.

D. Line and Staff Relationships

1. Major Approaches to Line and Staff Distinctions

a. The classical approach views **line** activities as those directly responsible for the primary function, product, or service of the organization, whereas staff members provide support services.

1) Production is ordinarily classified as a line activity, although more current writers include sales (marketing) and sometimes finance, depending on the goals of the organization.

2) **Staff** activities are those necessary to the organization but secondary or peripheral to the line functions. These functions assist or advise the line function.

3) Confusion arises from this concept because most staff activities are, in fact, essential to the accomplishment of the organization's purpose as recognized in modern (systems) theory.

4) Because early classical writers were describing production organizations, the holders of formal line authority were those producing the product.

5) Staff were merely hired hands to take the burden of secondary tasks off the shoulders of the production people.

b. Behavioral theorists' concerns with authority and its acceptance distinguish their approach to line and staff relationships.

1) The behavioral school sees exercise of informal authority as a very important constraint on formal chains of command.

2) Advice offered by senior staff members is akin to a command because they have access to top management and can exercise more informal authority than a junior-level line manager.

3) Staff assistants may be perceived as spies rather than assistants.

4) Even the classical school acknowledged the dilemma of how to ensure adoption of specialized staff advice without subverting line authority.

a) If line management refuses to accept staff's advice, what can top management do?

5) A staff group with **advisory** authority can only offer suggestions, prepare plans for consideration by line managers, and study and evaluate organizational performance.

a) A staff member often has an area of technical expertise, such as law, industrial labor relations, operations research, or personnel.

b) Line managers are not obligated to follow staff advice.

c) The staff member's goal is the approval (or rejection) of a complete recommended solution, but a line manager may want a quick fix to a problem rather than a complete solution.

d) Consultation by staff members with line personnel while preparing a solution is essential.

e) The concept of completed staff work requires that all loose ends be tied down by the staff member.

6) A staff group may be given **concurrent** authority, meaning that line management is required to induce the staff experts in specified areas to agree to an action or decision.

a) EXAMPLE: A line production manager may be required to obtain a second signature on a lease agreement from the law department, which must concur with terms in the lease.

7) A staff group may be given complete authority in a specialized area, and its specialized activities are separated from line.

a) Unlike advisory activities, the line manager must use the services of the staff organization.

b) Examples include information systems, purchasing, and personnel.

8) A staff group may occasionally be given **control** authority. Thus, line authority may be superseded by that of the specialist staff designated by higher levels of management to make certain decisions in the area of staff expertise.

a) Control staff authority appears to violate classical principles of unity of command.

b) Ideally, however, there is no violation because the control staff act as agents for the higher-level line manager, who has delegated authority to the staff.

i) EXAMPLE: Quality-control inspectors have the authority to reject marginal products, but because this authority is exercised on behalf of the manufacturing manager, the chain of command actually remains intact.

9) If the organization adopts TQM concepts with an emphasis on internal as well as external service, line managers and staff personnel may be viewed as having a customer-service provider relationship.

2. A hybrid of the control authority relationship of staff and line is called a **functional** relationship.

a. Functional authority exists when an individual is given authority outside the normal chain of command for certain specified activities. The individual may be either a line or a staff manager who is a specialist in a particular field.

1) EXAMPLE: The vice president in charge of sales may be given functional authority over manufacturing executives in scheduling customer orders, packaging, or making service parts available.

b. Functional authority may be created for numerous reasons when a line manager is not the person best suited to oversee a given activity. Examples are a lack of special knowledge, a lack of ability to supervise processes, a danger of diverse interpretations of policies, etc.

   1) EXAMPLE: The vice president for industrial labor relations may have functional authority over the production manager for the purpose of negotiating a new labor contract, though no line relationship exists at other times.

c. Functional specialists have the authority to determine the appropriate standards in their own field of specialization and to enforce those standards.

   1) EXAMPLE: The chief engineer of an airline may have the authority to remove airplanes from service, overriding the wishes of the vice president for operations.

3. **Line and Staff Conflicts**

   a. Conflict between line and staff personnel is almost inevitable given the considerable difference in their backgrounds and activities.

      1) These individuals tend to have different training and education, perspectives on the organization, and career and other objectives.

      2) Line and staff personnel also tend to have different temperaments.

         a) Line managers are immediately responsible for operating activities. Thus, they place an emphasis on decisive action.

         b) Staff members have a preference for thorough research and analysis of problems.

   b. Operating executives with line authority often see a high potential for harm in staff activity. A staff member with vaguely defined authority from a chief executive effectively usurps the authority of departmental managers.

   c. Staff are not responsible for the success of a line department but only for generating suggestions. If an implemented suggestion fails,

      1) Line managers will blame the suggestion.
      2) Staff will blame the poor implementation of the suggestion.

   d. Setting staff apart from line responsibilities gives them the time and environment in which to think.

      1) Unfortunately, this separation can also lead to thinking in a vacuum and resultant impracticable or inappropriate suggestions by staff.

   e. Excessive staff activity may violate the principle of unity of command.

      1) Subordinates may become confused and wonder whether they are primarily responsible to the staff member or to their line manager.

4. Line-staff conflicts may be minimized by

   a. Clearly defining areas of activity and authority

   b. Sharply defining the nature and place of line and staff. For example,

      1) Line may have authority and responsibility.
      2) Staff may be required to sell their ideas to line.

   c. Stressing the systems approach to all employees, whether line or staff, to encourage them to work together towards organizational goals

d. Minimizing areas of possible conflict, e.g.,
   1) Keeping functional authority to a minimum
   2) Providing feedback to staff of line's reaction to proposals
e. Using the concept of completed staff work if possible
   1) Recommendations should be complete enough to make possible a simple yes-or-no response from line managers.
   2) Staff members should be problem solvers, not problem creators.
      a) Incomplete or vague advice creates problems for line managers.
   3) The essential task of staff is to make the line manager involved look good. This result cannot be accomplished by staff members who insist on taking credit for the success of their ideas.

5. The modern approach to line and staff is based on systems thinking.
   a. Every position and every task must contribute to the organizational purpose or it should not exist.
   b. Distinctions between producers and helpers are therefore irrelevant.
   c. The changing nature of work environments from predominantly production firms to predominantly service providers makes it harder to pinpoint who exactly is responsible for producing.
      1) EXAMPLE: At a motor inn with the purpose of people pleasing, who is line and who is staff?
6. Stop and review! You have completed the outline for this subunit. Study multiple-choice questions 36 through 39 beginning on page 334.

E. Span of Control

1. **Span of control** (span of management or span of authority) is an upper limit to the number of subordinates who can be effectively supervised by one person. Beyond a certain number of subordinates, the effectiveness and efficiency of supervision decreases.
2. The classical view holds that the universal span of control is five or six subordinates.
3. The behavioral school advocates expanding the span of control if possible. The advantages are
   a. Increasing the autonomy and morale of individual workers by reducing the time available to a manager to direct them (the more subordinates per manager, the less time available per subordinate)
   b. Decreasing communication problems by reducing organizational levels (given a fixed number of employees, the narrower the span of control, the taller the organization, and the greater the number of levels)
4. The modern or contingency approach to span of control identifies the situational variables that determine the span of control, including
   a. The supervisor's training, interests, abilities, personality, time available to supervise, etc.
   b. The subordinates' interests, drives, commitment to the job, training, attitudes, aptitudes, etc.

c. The work situation, including the technological process used (job shop, mass production, continuous process), frequency of change in job method, complexity of the task, dependence on the work of others, and supervision required

d. The organization's environment, including how rapidly it is compelled to change by technological innovation or market pressure and the amount of uncertainty in the environment

NOTE: Current research indicates that the appropriate span of control varies widely depending on the situation as defined by the factors previously listed.

5. The number of levels in an organization will be greatly influenced by the span of control.
   a. **Flat** organizational structures have relatively few levels from top to bottom. Thus, they have wide spans of control.
      1) Flat structures provide fast information flow from top to bottom of the organization and increased employee satisfaction.
   b. **Tall** organizational structures have many levels between top and bottom. Hence, they have relatively narrow spans of control.
      1) Tall structures are faster and more effective at problem resolution than flat structures because of increased frequency of interaction between superior and subordinate and the greater order imposed by the hierarchical structure.
   c. Studies do not indicate great advantages for either flat or tall structures.
6. Stop and review! You have completed the outline for this subunit. Study multiple-choice questions 40 through 48 beginning on page 336.

F. Centralization and Decentralization

1. Centralization concerns the concentration of authority in an organization and the degree and levels at which it occurs.
2. Centralization and decentralization are relative terms. Absolute centralization or decentralization is impossible.
3. Classicists view decentralization with some distrust because they seek to avoid any dilution of control by top managers.
4. Behavioralists view decentralization in the same way as delegation, that is, as a good way to improve motivation and morale of lower-level employees.
5. The modern or contingency view is that neither centralization nor decentralization is good or bad in itself. The degree to which either is stressed depends upon the requirements of a given situation.
   a. Information. Decisions cannot be decentralized to those who do not have necessary information, e.g., knowledge of job objectives or measures for evaluation of job performance.
   b. Ability. Decisions cannot be decentralized to people who do not have training, experience, knowledge, or ability to make them.
   c. Timeliness. Decisions requiring a quick response should be decentralized to those near the action.

   d. Degree of coordination. Decentralization should not occur below the organizational level at which coordination must be maintained (e.g., each supervisor on an assembly line cannot be allowed to decide the reporting time for employees).
   e. Significance of decision. Decisions that are of critical importance to the survival of the organization should not be decentralized.
   f. Morale. Decentralization has a positive influence on morale.

6. Decentralization is a philosophy of organizing and managing. Careful selection of which decisions to push down the hierarchy and which to hold at the top is required. There will be a greater degree of decentralization if
   a. The greater number of decisions are made lower down the management hierarchy.
   b. The more important decisions are made lower down the management hierarchy.
   c. Most functions are affected by decisions made at lower levels.
   d. Review or prior approval is required before implementation of a decision.

7. **Implementing Decentralization**
   a. Decentralized structures typically use **return on investment** (ROI) or **profit center** accounting methods.
      1) ROI gives an objective measure of the performance of individual managers of decentralized units.
      2) ROI allows monitoring of performance through **management by exception**.
      3) ROI permits comparison of performance of decentralized divisions.
      4) ROI facilitates allocation of resources and rewards to the decentralized divisions.
      5) ROI measures for decentralized divisions have some limitations, as do other profit-center approaches.
         a) ROI measures encourage short-run performance to the detriment of long-run survival.
         b) They encourage division managers to maximize subunit goals to the possible detriment of the total organization.
         c) Transfer prices between units may be unjust.
         d) Top management may adversely influence divisional performance by indirect cost allocation decisions.
         e) Some parts of an organization do not lend themselves to 1-year evaluations (e.g., new product divisions).
         f) Annual profit objectives in a cyclical industry or economy may be difficult to determine.
         g) It is frequently impossible to assign responsibilities for deviations from profit objectives beyond the manager's control.
   b. Decentralization is most easily implemented in organizations with product departmentation based on clearly divisible units.
      1) Eliminates extensive transfer-price problems
      2) Easier to allocate and isolate overhead

8. **Advantages of Decentralization**

   a. Allows greater speed in making operational decisions

   b. Encourages better communication

   c. Necessitates understanding of goals throughout the organization (goal congruence)

   d. Enables identification and training of good decision makers at lower levels

   e. Builds a large pool of experienced management talent

   f. Provides many behavioral advantages

      1) Gains advantages of participation in management
      2) Gives responsibility and authority to lower-level managers

         a) Job autonomy is desired by many employees.
         b) Specific feedback is important for goal-directed people.

      3) Provides objective feedback

   g. Frees top management from operating problems, thus allowing them to concentrate on long-term strategy

   h. Provides a mechanism for allocating resources to profit centers based on ROI applications

   i. Permits determination of a single comprehensive figure, e.g., ROI or net income, that measures the financial status of the decentralized unit

9. **Disadvantages of Decentralization**

   a. Strong tendency to focus on short-run results to the detriment of long-run health

   b. Increased risk of loss of control by top management

   c. More difficulty in coordinating highly interdependent units

      1) EXAMPLE: A conglomerate that is highly decentralized, i.e., operates its divisions as totally separate companies, will find it difficult to establish a transfer price for goods manufactured in one division and consumed in another. The consuming division will not believe market prices are equitable, and the producing division will not want to sell for less.

   d. Greater danger of **satisficing** decisions (those that satisfy or suffice but are not optimal) made by a manager who is unable or unwilling to see overall organizational goals and is rewarded for maximizing the performance of the decentralized unit

   e. Less cooperation and communication between competing unit managers

10. **Delegation of authority** is the formal process of passing power downward from one individual to a subordinate. Delegation is similar to decentralization in philosophy, process, and requirements.

   a. The classical approach is to avoid delegation because the superior is deemed to be both responsible and knowledgeable. Under that view, delegation avoids responsibility.

   b. The behavioral view sees delegation as useful in every organization because no one has time to make every decision, and subordinates like to make decisions affecting their work.

c. The modern approach is to view delegation as dependent on the situation and the people involved. Delegation requires

1) Skill, self-confidence, and knowledge of organizational goals
2) A feedback system to allow objective assessment of performance
3) Faith in subordinates' abilities
4) Clear recognition of the basic need to delegate
5) Willingness to accept risk
6) Desire to develop and train subordinates

d. The delegation process involves

1) Determination of results expected
2) Assignment of tasks and responsibilities
3) Delegation of authority for accomplishing these tasks
4) Recruitment of responsible subordinates for the accomplishment of tasks
5) Clear communication of what is expected in objective terms to subordinates
6) Follow-up because ultimate responsibility still resides with the delegator

e. Under the **Scalar Principle**, employees should respect the chain of direct authority relationships from superior to subordinate throughout the organization (the chain of command). The clearer the line of authority from top management to every subordinate position, the more effective the responsible decision making and organizational communication will be. Failure to define the chain of command with care leads to inefficiency.

11. Stop and review! You have completed the outline for this subunit. Study multiple-choice questions 49 through 54 beginning on page 338.

G. Groups

1. A **committee** is a group that considers a particular problem or class of problems. The committee's objective is to educate, to inform, or to make a decision. The committee is one of the most universal, and most controversial, devices of the organization. Other names include task force, team, commission, and board.

a. The classical position is to avoid the committee. The behavioral position is to encourage its use because of positive morale benefits. The modern position is to determine both the type and the nature of committees by situational factors.

b. Committees may

1) Undertake managerial functions

2) Make decisions or participate in one or more parts of the decision process (e.g., identifying problems, searching for alternatives, evaluating alternatives, making recommendations, helping to implement choices)

3) Be formed merely to receive information, without making decisions or recommendations

4) Be either line or staff, depending upon authority

5) Be formal, if designated as part of the organizational structure

a) Formal committees can be standing (permanent) or ad hoc (temporary), i.e., formed to consider a one-time situation.

6) Be informal, if organized without specific delegation of authority

a) Informal committees are often formed by individuals desiring input for decision making in the form of advice from other managers or specialists.

c. **Principles for the use of committees**

1) **Balance**. Members should be selected to obtain optimum input bearing on the problem; the selection entails consideration of members' knowledge, time, and communication skills.

2) **Efficiency**. The benefits should exceed the cost.

3) **Time**. Scheduling and time away from regular work should be considered.

4) **Objective**. The objective should guide the committee and limit its actions in solving a problem, coordinating activities, selling an idea, educating, etc.

5) **Leadership**. The chair should act as a moderator and not be considered threatening or overbearing by the members.

6) **Groupism**. A tendency toward mediocrity and compromise should be avoided. **Groupthink**, i.e., the tendency to conform and ignore relevant individual input that is at variance with the perceived group opinion, is to be avoided. At the same time, consensus is desirable.

7) **Size**. The size of a committee is determined by its needed input, but in any event it should be kept small. Five members are often considered maximum for effective work.

8) **Individualism**. An overriding question is whether an individual should make the decision rather than the committee.

d. Misuse of committees has caused some organizations to neglect this form of management. The following abuses of committees should be avoided:

1) The committee should not be used as a managing device. Leadership is essentially a quality of individuals rather than groups. Clear, prompt decisions subject to unquestioned responsibility are better made by individuals.

2) Use of the committee for research or study is ineffective. The primary purpose of a committee is to discuss or exchange views on information already known to the members. A committee may use a research staff if research and study are needed.

3) Unimportant decisions are not appropriate for the committee forum. The feeling that time is being wasted on insignificant matters frustrates and alienates intelligent managers and specialists.

4) One of the most common abuses of committees is to make decisions that are beyond the authority of the participants. Delays occur while matters are referred to the appropriate superior authority, and much of the advantage of group decision making is lost.

5) The consolidation of divided authority is better accomplished through changes in the organizational structure than through the use of committees.

2. **Informal groups**, ignored by classical school writers, were the major focus of the behavioral school.
    a. People naturally seek association and group acceptance and tend to form both formal and informal groups as a result. Thus, effective managers recognize, accept, and take advantage of informal organization.
        1) Informal groups are created within organizations because of
            a) Authority interrelationships that cannot be charted
            b) Unwritten rules of conduct
            c) Group preferences
    b. **Characteristics of informal groups** (informal organization)
        1) Almost all employees, including managers, are members of some informal group(s).
        2) Members of informal groups react to the pressures of these groups.
            a) These pressures are difficult to resist, and most members do tend to conform.
        3) These groups tend to be small and
            a) Are often very complex
            b) Tend to develop their own leaders
            c) Exist to fill the needs of the members
            d) Usually result from the frequent interaction among individuals in the course of their work
    c. **Favorable effects of informal groups**
        1) Reduce tension and encourage production
        2) Improve coordination and reduce supervision required
        3) Aid in problem-solving situations
        4) Provide another channel of communication (in addition to the formal ones)
            a) The grapevine is the informal, unofficial communication system found in every kind of organization. The emergence of computer networks in the workplace has only served to strengthen the grapevine.
        5) Provide social satisfactions that supplement job satisfactions
    d. **Some potentially unfavorable effects of informal groups**. They can
        1) Work to circumvent managerial actions
        2) Serve to reduce production levels (slowdowns caused by counterproductive social interactions)
        3) Generate dissension in the formal organization
        4) Spread rumors and distort information
        5) Add to the cost of doing business
        6) Form subgroups that hinder group cohesiveness
        7) Pressure members to adopt group norms that may be contrary to the main goals of the organization
        8) Develop dominant members

3. **Quality circles** are groups, usually of five to ten employees (management or subordinates), doing similar work who volunteer to meet at a specified time (e.g., once a week) to discuss and solve problems associated with their work areas.

   a. The objectives of quality circles are to use employee capabilities more fully, build a more congenial workplace, and contribute to the improvement and development of both the company and individual employees.

   b. The mechanics of a quality circle include the following problem-solving steps:

      1) Circle members bring problems before the group.

      2) The problems or projects are analyzed.

      3) Solutions are developed and presented to management.

      4) Management follows up on the suggestions by either approving or disapproving the ideas, with feedback to circle members.

   c. **Advantages of quality circles**

      1) Easy implementation without major organizational change
      2) More efficient and effective operation of the company
      3) Better-quality products
      4) Improved employee morale and better cohesion among coworkers

   d. **Disadvantages of quality circles**

      1) Objections from unions

      2) Reduced morale if suggestions are not accepted by management and management fails to adequately explain nonacceptance

      3) Potential loss of management control

   e. **Self-managed teams** are a facet of TQM. They are autonomous groups that go beyond quality circles because they represent a major organizational change.

      1) Team members are not volunteers but have been assigned to the teams.

      2) Teams are assembled to produce a complete product or service. Accordingly, they are empowered to perform traditional management tasks, such as scheduling, ordering materials, and even hiring.

      3) The benefits of teams flow from the principle that employee self-management is the best management.

         a) Motivation is improved because decision making is decentralized. The increased authority of autonomous work groups is intended to create a sense of ownership in the work product. Better decision making, productivity, quality, and goal congruence should be the results.

         b) An advantage of cross-functional teams is improved communication because all members have a better understanding of all facets of team activities.

         c) If teams are staffed appropriately and have the necessary resources and support from management, they should be able to improve the processes of production. The individuals who perform the work have the power to make decisions about the way it is done.

4. Stop and review! You have completed the outline for this subunit. Study multiple-choice questions 55 through 58 beginning on page 340.

H. More on Organizational Theory

1. Organizational Charts

a. Organizational charts, used to represent the organizational structure, often resemble a pyramid, with the chief executive on top and the operating workforce on bottom. Recent trends in management, including increased span of control and decreased hierarchy, have resulted in flatter organizational charts. The typical organizational chart can be designed to

1) Reflect classical, formal authority channels (chain of command)
2) Show reporting relationships and task groupings (departmentation)
3) Describe communication channels
4) Identify location of sources of organizational expertise
5) Show promotional or career tracks
6) Depict span of control and number of organizational levels
7) Show major functions and their respective relationships

b. Shortcomings of organizational charts

1) Limited presentation of information, a shortcoming that can be overcome by supplementing the chart with a detailed manual
2) Tendency to become quickly obsolete because of rapid change
3) Failure to show informal communication, influence, power, or friendships
4) Tendency to ignore informal job trade-offs between titles on the chart
5) Possibility of misleading management by giving an appearance of structure and order that might not exist
6) Possibility that position titles do not reflect actual functions

2. **Organizational change** anticipates expected changes in circumstances or may be a reaction to the unexpected. The nature of the change may be incremental, or it may entail a strategic alteration of the structure or purpose of the organization.

a. Organizational and procedural changes often are resisted by the individuals and groups affected. Resistance may be caused by simple surprise or by inertia, but it also may arise from fear of

1) Personal adjustments that may be required
   a) Concern about usefulness
   b) Apparent disregard for workers' feelings
   c) Deviations from past procedures for implementing change (especially if procedures used are less participative than before)
   d) Downgrading of job status
2) Social adjustments that may be required
   a) Potential violation of the behavior norms of informal groups
   b) Disruption of the social situation within groups
3) Economic adjustments, e.g., potential economic loss and insecurity based on perceived threats to jobs
4) In general, any perceived deterioration in the work situation that is seen as a threat to needs -- economic, social, or psychological

b. Resistance may be overcome by a participative management approach that
   1) Communicates fully to reduce fear of adjustments
   2) Avoids arbitrary, capricious, or prejudicial actions
   3) Times the change so ample notice is given, including the reasons for the change, the precise nature of the change, and expected outcomes or results of the change
   4) Allows participation in the implementation of changes by those affected
   5) Includes informal and formal conferences and problem-solving groups
   6) Provides express guarantees against economic loss
   7) Anticipates and accommodates the perceived impact of a change on the needs -- economic, social, or psychological -- of those involved
c. Nadler and Tushman developed a model for categorizing organizational changes.
   1) Change is either anticipatory or reactive.
      a) Anticipatory changes are systematically planned changes intended to take advantage of expected situations.
      b) Reactive changes are necessitated by unexpected environmental events or pressures.
   2) The scope of change is either incremental or strategic.
      a) Incremental changes involve subsystem adjustments needed to keep the organization on its chosen path.
      b) Strategic changes alter the overall shape or direction of the organization.
   3) Tuning is an incremental anticipatory change. Preventive maintenance and continuous improvement (kaizen) are examples.
   4) Adaptation is an incremental reactive change. An example is a change in the styling of an automobile to meet competition.
   5) Reorientation is a strategic anticipatory change. It is "frame bending" because it is a redirection. For example, some fast-food companies are offering their products in dramatically different locations, such as department stores.
   6) Re-creation is a strategic reactive change. It is risky because it is "frame breaking." Moving into an entirely new business is an example.

3. **Network Corporations.** The relative independence of the various firms in a network differentiates it from a vertically integrated organization.
   a. A network is not based on the price mechanism or on a hierarchical relationship but on coordination through adaptation.
   b. It is a long-term, strategic relationship based on implicit contracts without specific legal ties.
   c. A network allows member firms to gain a competitive advantage against competitors outside the network.

d. A network corporation can be viewed as a group of activities involving suppliers and customers that add value. Each activity can be performed internally at an internal cost or subcontracted at an external cost.

1) When an activity is subcontracted, a transaction cost will be incurred.

2) A technological restriction on the existence of a network is that external costs must be less than internal costs. The firms in the network must be able to reduce the transaction costs so that the combination of external and transaction costs is less than internal costs.

3) The difference between a network and a normal market is that transaction costs in the market are low enough for any player.

a) In a network, the participating firms reduce initially high transaction costs through cooperative efforts.

e. A network corporation is an ultimate expression of **outsourcing**, which entails obtaining goods or services from outside sources that could be acquired internally. For example, a firm may choose to outsource its computer processing or legal work, and a manufacturer may buy rather than make components.

4. **Strategic partnerships** (joint ventures or strategic alliances) are associations to accomplish a specific business purpose or objective. The association is often organized for a single transaction. For example, U.S. and Japanese automobile companies may form an alliance to develop a new vehicle.

a. A strategic partnership allows each joint venture to reap advantages from the other's strengths. Furthermore, such an arrangement may be the only way to do business in a foreign country.

5. **Multinational Issues**. The home country benefits from multinational operations because of improved earnings and exports of products to foreign subsidiaries. A multinational company may also be better able to obtain scarce resources than a domestic corporation. The existence of multinationals tends to benefit everyone to the extent they foster more international trade, freer trading policies, a better international monetary system, and improved international understanding.

a. The home country, however, may suffer adverse balance of payments effects as a result of investment in foreign nations. Jobs may be lost to foreign subsidiaries, unions weakened, and tax revenues diminished. The multinational may also have a competitive advantage over domestic rivals. Furthermore, multinationals incur greater risk of expropriation and reduced flexibility of operation in a foreign political system.

b. The host country for a multinational operation reaps the advantages of the investment of capital, technology, and management abilities. Output and efficiency often improve along with exports and the balance of payments. The presence of a multinational may stimulate competition and increase tax revenues, and living standards usually rise.

1) But payment of royalties, dividends, and profits can result in a net capital outflow. Multinationals sometimes establish economically unreasonable transfer prices among subsidiaries so that profits will be earned where taxes are lowest or restrictions on export of profits are least stringent. Moreover, multinationals may engage in anticompetitive activities, such as formation of cartels.

6. Stop and review! You have completed the outline for this subunit. Study multiple-choice questions 59 through 61 beginning on page 341.

MULTIPLE-CHOICE QUESTIONS

A. Overview of Management

1. "The process of working with and through others to achieve organizational objectives in a changing environment" is a good definition of

A. Referent power.

B. Management.

C. Informal leadership.

D. Motivation.

The correct answer is (B). *(CIA, adapted)*

REQUIRED: The term defined as the "process of working with and through others to achieve organizational objectives in a changing environment."

DISCUSSION: In *Management*, 6th ed. (Boston: Houghton Mifflin Company, 1995, p. 4), Robert Kreitner defines management as "the process of working with and through others to achieve organizational objectives in a changing environment. Central to this process is the effective and efficient use of limited resources." Thus, management is a social process that attempts to use scarce resources to achieve organizational objectives while anticipating environmental changes and balancing effectiveness against efficiency. The physical, social, political, moral, and informational environments external to the organization are the "sources of change" that managers must anticipate.

Answer (A) is incorrect because referent power is the influence that a person has over those who identify with him/her if they comply on that basis alone. Answer (C) is incorrect because informal leadership is influencing others to pursue unofficial objectives that may or may not serve the organization's interest. Answer (D) is incorrect because motivation, an important part of the manager's job, is the psychological process that gives behavior purpose and direction.

2. Which level of management is most concerned with determining how specific tasks can be accomplished with available resources by a given date?

A. First-line manager.

B. Department head.

C. General manager.

D. Chief executive officer.

The correct answer is (A). *(CIA, adapted)*

REQUIRED: The level of management most concerned with determining how specific tasks can be accomplished with available resources.

DISCUSSION: A first-line or lower-level manager directly supervises employees who are not managers. Operational planning is a type of short-range or tactical planning performed by lower management. It involves the development of action plans by which strategies and policies are executed. According to Kreitner, it is "the process of determining how specific tasks can best be accomplished on time with available resources."

Answer (B) is incorrect because a department head is a middle manager and is concerned with intermediate planning. Answer (C) is incorrect because a general manager is a member of top management and is concerned with strategic planning. Answer (D) is incorrect because the chief executive officer is the most senior manager in an organization and focuses on strategic planning.

3. A lumber mill must carefully plan production for 160 different varieties of plywood. To do this, a linear programming model is used to generate a 6-month production schedule that is adapted to a weekly plan. The level of management responsible for this type of planning is

A. The board of directors.

B. Top management.

C. Middle management.

D. First-line supervision.

The correct answer is (C). *(CIA, adapted)*

REQUIRED: The level of management responsible for tactical planning.

DISCUSSION: Middle managers, such as department heads and functional managers, are responsible for intermediate planning with a time line of approximately 6 months to 2 years. Thus, the manager of the production function should be responsible for the 6-month production schedule.

Answer (A) is incorrect because the board of directors is not involved in operations. Answer (B) is incorrect because top management is responsible for strategic planning. Answer (D) is incorrect because first-line supervision is involved in day-to-day operations.

4. Henry Mintzberg believed that the functional approach for describing what managers do was inadequate. He developed a system based on managerial roles. The three basic role categories defined by Mintzberg are

A. Planning, organizing, and controlling.

B. Interpersonal, informational, and decisional.

C. Decision making, staffing, and communicating.

D. Motivation, leadership, and delegation.

The correct answer is (B). *(CIA, adapted)*

REQUIRED: The three basic role categories defined by Mintzberg.

DISCUSSION: The interpersonal roles (figurehead, leader, liaison) are necessary because, given his/her authority and status, a manager has substantial interpersonal contacts, particularly with peers and subordinates. The informational roles (nerve center, disseminator, spokesperson) reflect the importance of information to organizational activity. Managers must receive and transmit information to parties both within and outside the organization. The decisional roles require managers to make choices and balance divergent interests. Decisions involve developing strategies and implementing them.

Answers (A), (C), and (D) are incorrect because each lists functional categories.

5. An example of an appropriate interpersonal role carried out by a manager in an organization would be

A. Designing and initiating changes within the organization.

B. Transmitting selected information to subordinates.

C. Participating in negotiating sessions with other parties (vendors, unions, etc.).

D. Motivating subordinates to get the job done properly.

The correct answer is (D). *(CIA, adapted)*

REQUIRED: The example of an interpersonal role carried out by a manager.

DISCUSSION: Mintzberg describes three categories of managerial roles: interpersonal, informational, and decisional. By reason of their status and authority, managers have substantial interpersonal contact. A figurehead plays a symbolic role, for example, by performing such ceremonial functions as signing documents and receiving visitors. A leader motivates employees to perform jobs properly. A liaison serves as a link in both vertical and horizontal chains of communication.

Answer (A) is incorrect because designing and initiating change is an example of the entrepreneurial-decisional role of a manager. Answer (B) is incorrect because transmitting information to subordinates is an example of the disseminator-informational role of a manager. Answer (C) is incorrect because participating in negotiations is an example of the negotiator-decisional role of a manager.

6. All of the following are examples of the management function of decision making except

A. Participating in negotiating contracts with vendors.

B. Motivating subordinates to get the job done properly.

C. Taking corrective action in nonroutine situations.

D. Allocating organizational resources.

The correct answer is (B). *(CIA, adapted)*

REQUIRED: The activity not an example of decision making.

DISCUSSION: According to Mintzberg, the decisional roles of managers include entrepreneur, disturbance handler, resource allocator, and negotiator. However, the leader role of motivating subordinates to get the job done properly is one of the interpersonal roles.

Answer (A) is incorrect because participating in negotiating contracts with vendors is a decisional role. Answer (C) is incorrect because taking corrective action in nonroutine situations is a decisional role. Answer (D) is incorrect because allocating organizational resources is a decisional role.

7. The managerial role of the CEO in communicating selected information regarding the cost-cutting measures to the stock market analysts would be categorized as

A. Liaison.

B. Spokesperson.

C. Leader.

D. Figurehead.

The correct answer is (B). *(CIA, adapted)*

REQUIRED: The managerial role of the CEO.

DISCUSSION: According to Mintzberg, managerial roles may be categorized as interpersonal, informational, and decisional. The informational role of the CEO in providing selected information to outsiders, i.e., to stock market analysts, is that of a spokesperson.

Answer (A) is incorrect because the director is a liaison who provides the link in the vertical chain of communication, i.e., from the highest level (CEO) down to the lowest level (staff level). Answer (C) is incorrect because the interpersonal role of the leader is to motivate subordinates. Answer (D) is incorrect because the interpersonal role of the figurehead is the symbol of legal authority and the one who performs certain ceremonial duties, e.g., signing documents and receiving visitors.

B. The Organizing Process

8. A manager can use power and authority to accomplish objectives. The relationship between these two important concepts is best explained as follows:

A. Power is the right to do things, while authority is the ability to do things.

B. Authority is the right to do things, while power is the ability to do things.

C. Power and authority are both required to accomplish a task.

D. Power and authority are simply two words that describe the same concept--how to get things done in organizations.

The correct answer is (B). *(CIA, adapted)*

REQUIRED: The relationship between power and authority.

DISCUSSION: Authority is the officially sanctioned privilege to direct others. A clear hierarchy of authority enhances coordination and accountability. Power is the ability to marshal organizational resources to obtain results. A manager may have both authority and power, or one without the other.

Answers (A) and (D) are incorrect because authority is the right to do things, and power is the ability to do things. Answer (C) is incorrect because a manager may accomplish a task without having formal authority.

9. A company's decisions are made solely by Ed Smith, the president and major shareholder. Which of the following powers is Smith least likely to have over the other shareholders to whom he has delegated some authority?

A. Coercive power.

B. Legitimate power.

C. Referent power.

D. Reward power.

The correct answer is (C). *(Publisher)*

REQUIRED: The power that Smith is least likely to have over the other shareholders.

DISCUSSION: A person who is the head of a company may exert influence through five types of power. Referent power is the capacity for the individual's personality and style to cause others to identify with or like him/her.

Answer (A) is incorrect because coercive power is the ability of the individual to make others cooperate by applying pressure. Answer (B) is incorrect because legitimate power is the leader's right to expect cooperation from others. Answer (D) is incorrect because reward power is the individual's ability to influence others because they expect good behavior to be rewarded.

10. Organizational productivity can be defined as the ratio of an organization's total output to its total input, adjusted for inflation, for a specified period of time. For a number of years, Japan's productivity has been held out as an example to emulate. Japan's higher productivity has been mostly attributed to

A. Abundant raw materials and excellent human and financial resources.

B. Better management and the ability to do more with less.

C. Constant refurbishing of the country's infrastructure.

D. A superior educational system that emphasizes creativity.

The correct answer is (B). *(CIA, adapted)*

REQUIRED: The reason for Japan's high productivity.

DISCUSSION: Much of the credit for Japan's success has been given to its management systems and the ability to be efficient with limited resources. Japanese society and behavior is highly structured, which is conducive to effectiveness and efficiency.

Answer (A) is incorrect because Japan has very limited raw materials. Answer (C) is incorrect because the infrastructure has not been constantly refurbished, and frequent change is not conducive to efficiency. Answer (D) is incorrect because the Japanese educational system does not emphasize creativity.

11. A new manager of a production department has been asked to assess the effectiveness of that department. The organization needs to satisfy both internal and external constituents and takes a broad approach to effectiveness. In order to complete the assignment successfully, the manager should

A. Measure the daily productivity of the department.

B. Do a survey of employee morale, as it is often a major underlying factor in productivity.

C. Compare the past year's production against annual goals.

D. Consider short-, medium-, and long-term effectiveness.

The correct answer is (D). *(CIA, adapted)*

REQUIRED: The approach to assessing departmental effectiveness.

DISCUSSION: Kreitner (6th ed., pages 279-80) states, "Organizational effectiveness can be defined as meeting organizational objectives and prevailing societal expectations in the near future, adapting and developing in the intermediate future, and surviving in the distant future. In the near term (about one year), it should be effective in achieving its goals, efficient in its use of resources, and a source of satisfaction to its constituencies (owners, employees, customers, and society). In the intermediate term (2 to 4 years), it should adapt to new possibilities and obstacles and develop its abilities and those of its members. In the long term (5+ years), the organization should be able to survive in an uncertain world.

Answer (A) is incorrect because daily productivity relates to short-term effectiveness only. Answer (B) is incorrect because a survey of employee morale may contribute to assessing effectiveness, but it is not sufficient for assessing overall effectiveness. Answer (C) is incorrect because comparing production against goals is a measure of short-term effectiveness.

12. For the past several years, many organizations have attempted to reduce administrative costs and respond more rapidly to customer and competitive demands. One method is to eliminate layers of middle management. The element of organizational structure affected by such reductions is

A. Spatial differentiation.

B. Formalization.

C. Vertical differentiation.

D. Formalization of jobs.

The correct answer is (C). *(CIA, adapted)*

REQUIRED: The element of organizational structure affected by eliminating layers of middle management.

DISCUSSION: Vertical differentiation concerns the depth of the organizational hierarchy. The greater the number of levels, the more complex the organization, the greater the potential for information distortion, the more difficult the coordination of management activities, and the slower and less effective the response to changing conditions.

Answer (A) is incorrect because spatial differentiation refers to the degree of geographic dispersion of facilities and personnel. Answers (B) and (D) are incorrect because formalization refers to the degree of job standardization through descriptions and rules.

13. The term for the organizational design strategy favored by the classical school of management is

A. Mechanistic.

B. Organic.

C. Project management.

D. Contingency.

The correct answer is (A). *(Publisher)*

REQUIRED: The term for the traditional method of organizing.

DISCUSSION: The traditional approach to organizing the structure of roles to facilitate the achievement of goals emphasizes authority, responsibility, tasks, hierarchy, etc. Because this approach tends to set up prescribed or dictated relationships, it has been called mechanistic.

Answer (B) is incorrect because an organic organization has few hierarchical levels, low reliance on positional authority, and few dictated relationships among members. Answer (C) is incorrect because the matrix form of organization is used for project management since it temporarily combines product and functional structure for the duration of the project. Answer (D) is incorrect because the contingency or modern organizational structure is based on the particular situation, including environmental influences, technical considerations, and the size and age of the organization.

14. Routine tasks, which have few exceptions and problems that are easy to analyze, are conducive to

A. Formalized structure, in which procedures manuals and job descriptions are common.

B. Decentralized decision making, in which decisions are pushed downward in the organization.

C. Organic structures that emphasize adaptability and flexibility to changing circumstances.

D. High degrees of job satisfaction on the part of the employees performing them.

The correct answer is (A). *(CIA, adapted)*

REQUIRED: The structure best suited to routine tasks.

DISCUSSION: Technology has been viewed in terms of two dimensions: task variability and problem analyzability, or the exceptions encountered in work and the search procedures for responding to the exceptions, respectively. Routine tasks have few exceptions, and the search for solutions is well defined. Because routine tasks change little over time, they are well suited to a mechanistic structure. One characteristic of such a structure is high formalization.

Answer (B) is incorrect because decentralized decision making is not suited to routine tasks but to organic structures. Answer (C) is incorrect because organic structures are best when problems are poorly defined. Answer (D) is incorrect because job satisfaction is often low in routine and repetitive tasks.

15. A large company uses assembly line techniques to manufacture a single product. Its choice of relatively mechanistic organizational design was more likely based on its

A. Need for rapid response to environmental change.

B. Primary concern for operational efficiency.

C. Low fixed technology requirements.

D. Project management emphasis.

The correct answer is (B). *(Publisher)*

REQUIRED: The most likely basis for choice of a relatively mechanistic organizational design.

DISCUSSION: Mechanistic organizations have vertical structures with duties and authority clearly defined by position in the hierarchy, a stringent set of formal controls, and a centralized staff. Such organizations tend to emphasize efficiency and operate in a stable environment with well-established technology. Large firms in basic industries (autos, utilities) often adopt this structure.

Answers (A), (C), and (D) are incorrect because each is characteristic of an organic organization. This arrangement often works best when the fixed asset base is relatively small because the company must respond rapidly to frequent environmental change.

16. A small engineering consulting firm accepts special projects from customers in a variety of fields. Its choice of an organic organizational design was most likely based on its

A. Lack of concern for self-fulfillment of employees.

B. Preference for formal communication.

C. Adoption of directive leadership style.

D. Participative decision making processes.

The correct answer is (D). *(Publisher)*

REQUIRED: The most likely basis for choice of an organic organizational design.

DISCUSSION: The organic structure is best suited to a company that emphasizes operational efficiency less than the flexibility needed to respond quickly to changes in its environment and the creativity to find solutions to new problems. Decision making in this context tends to rely on input from many sources and requires multi-directional communication. Hence, a horizontal or flat structure typified by project or matrix management will be appropriate.

Answers (A), (B), and (C) are incorrect because each is characteristic of a mechanistic organization with a rigid vertical or chain-of-command structure. This design may be best when the jobs to be done require little creativity and personal fulfillment is correspondingly low, leadership is directive rather than participative, and communication is vertical rather than multi-directional.

17. When an organization depends to a great extent on its environment, which of the following statements best characterizes the relationship among an organization's environment, the level of uncertainty it faces, and its structure? The more dynamic and complex the environment, the

A. More uncertainty the organization will face and the more organic the structure should be.

B. More uncertainty the organization will face and the more mechanistic the structure should be.

C. Less uncertainty the organization will face and the more autocratic the structure should be.

D. Less uncertainty the organization will face and the more organic the structure should be.

The correct answer is (A). *(CIA, adapted)*

REQUIRED: The statement best characterizing the relationship among an organization's environment, the level of uncertainty it faces, and its structure.

DISCUSSION: A dynamic and complex organizational environment faces constant change, so the level of uncertainty increases. The more uncertainty an organization faces, the more organic the structure should be. Organic organizations tend to be flexible and adaptive to change.

Answers (B), (C), and (D) are incorrect because a dynamic and complex environment is more uncertain, so it requires a flexible structure.

18. The relationship between organizational structure and technology suggests that, in an organization using mass production technology (for example, automobile manufacturing), the best structure is

A. Organic, emphasizing loose controls and flexibility.

B. Matrix, in which individuals report to both product and functional area managers.

C. Mechanistic, that is, highly formalized, with tight controls.

D. Integrated, emphasizing cooperation among departments.

The correct answer is (C). *(CIA, adapted)*

REQUIRED: The best structure for an organization using mass production technology.

DISCUSSION: According to Joan Woodward's work on the relationship of technology and structure in manufacturing, companies may be categorized as engaged in unit production (units or small batches), mass production (large batches), or process production (continuous processing). Mass production is most effective if the entity has a mechanistic structure characterized by moderate vertical differentiation, high horizontal differentiation, and high formalization. This structure is one in which tasks are well-defined, most communication is downward, and control is tight.

Answer (A) is incorrect because an organic structure is flexible and therefore not suited to mass production. Answer (B) is incorrect because matrix is not a type of structure but rather a type of departmentation. Answer (D) is incorrect because an integrated structure is a nonsense term in this context.

19. The structure of an organization generally follows its overall strategy. At one end are loosely structured, organic organizations. At the other end are highly centralized, tightly controlled, mechanistic organizations. Consider the overall strategy of a company that is a pioneer in the combination of laser and robotic technologies. The company's scientists and engineers hold many patents. They are continually looking for ways to improve their products as well as to introduce new ones. Identify the most appropriate structural option for this organization.

A. Mechanistic.

B. Imitative.

C. Organic.

D. Bureaucratic.

The correct answer is (C). *(CIA, adapted)*

REQUIRED: The most appropriate structural option for a company that is continually improving old products and developing new ones.

DISCUSSION: Organizational structure depends on the company's overall strategy. This organization has adopted an innovation strategy. It introduces major new products or services. The structure that provides the flexibility required for major innovation is organic, a form of organization characterized by a loose structure, low division of labor, low formalization, and decentralization.

Answer (A) is incorrect because a mechanistic structure is appropriate for organizations focusing on cost minimization through tight controls, extensive division of labor, high formalization, and centralization. Answer (B) is incorrect because an imitation strategy is not adopted by true innovators but rather by companies that move into new markets only after smaller competitors have demonstrated the potential for success. Imitation strategies are best suited to a structure that combines mechanistic and organic components. Answer (D) is incorrect because bureaucracies are mechanistic, not organic.

20. Discount stores and sellers of generic grocery products keep prices low and innovate only when there are low-risk, high-payback projects. They are pursuing a(n)

A. Innovation-minimization strategy.

B. Imitation strategy.

C. Cost-minimization strategy.

D. Initiation strategy.

The correct answer is (C). *(CIA, adapted)*

REQUIRED: The strategy pursued by discount stores.

DISCUSSION: Research suggests that organizational structure follows strategy. A cost-minimization strategy tightly controls costs, avoids unnecessary innovation or marketing expenses, and cuts prices in selling a discount product. The sellers of generic grocery products pursue this strategy.

Answer (A) is incorrect because innovation minimization is not a type of strategy. An innovation strategy emphasizes the introduction of new products or services. Answer (B) is incorrect because an imitation strategy seeks to introduce new products or enter new markets only after their viability has been proven. Answer (D) is incorrect because there is no initiation strategy.

21. As an organization increases the number of employees, its structure becomes more complex. Rules become more formalized and more supervisors are hired to direct the increased numbers of subordinates. What is the nature of the size-structure relationship?

A. The size-structure relationship is linear.

B. The structure becomes fixed once an organization attains a level of about 200 employees.

C. The size-structure relationship is concave.

D. None of the answers are correct.

The correct answer is (D). *(CIA, adapted)*

REQUIRED: The nature of the size-structure relationship in an increasingly complex organization.

DISCUSSION: As an organization increases in size, its structure tends to become more formal and mechanistic. More policies and procedures are necessary to coordinate the increased number of employees, and more managers must be hired. However, the relationship between size and changes in structure is linear only within a certain range. For example, adding 100 employees to a company with 100 employees is likely to cause significant structural change, but adding the same number to a workforce of 10,000 is likely to have little impact. By the time a company reaches a certain size (1,500 to 2,000 or more), it usually has most of the qualities of a mechanistic structure.

Answers (A), (B), and (C) are incorrect because the size-structure relationship is likely to be linear but only within a narrow range.

22. In general, as organizations grow in size, their strategies

A. Become more ambitious, and they often expand their activities within their industry.

B. Focus on vertical integration, and their structures consequently must become more centralized.

C. Change from a focus on a diverse set of products to a focus on a single product line.

D. Follow and are determined by their internal structures.

The correct answer is (A). *(CIA, adapted)*

REQUIRED: The effect of growth on strategies.

DISCUSSION: The strategies of larger organizations tend to be more ambitious and complex. Thus, a company may expand from one product line to many. The result is a need for more complicated coordination methods.

Answer (B) is incorrect because a company with diversified products may decide to create independent, decentralized divisions. Answer (C) is incorrect because focusing on a single product line rather than a diverse set of products is not a strategy for a growing company. Answer (D) is incorrect because structure follows strategy.

23. A characteristic of a bureaucratic organizational structure is that

A. It is small and simple.

B. Work assignments are rarely delegated.

C. There is no hierarchy to follow when communicating.

D. The divisions of labor are distinct.

The correct answer is (D). *(Publisher)*

REQUIRED: The characteristic of a bureaucratic structure.

DISCUSSION: Organizational structure is the order and disposition of lines of responsibility. A bureaucracy is an organizational structure in which tasks are specialized under a given set of rules and a hierarchy of authority. Division of labor is the separation of work loads into small segments to be performed by one or more people.

Answer (A) is incorrect because bureaucratic organizations are usually large and complex. Answer (B) is incorrect because in a bureaucratic organization, efficiency is most likely to be achieved through a high degree of task delegation. Answer (C) is incorrect because a bureaucratic organization is characterized by a hierarchy of authority, which is typically adhered to when communicating.

24. Which of the following is an advantage of bureaucratic organizational structures?

A. The routine activities and performance methods related to a particular task are invariable and clearly defined to the employee.

B. Open positions are filled by individuals recruited from outside the firm to bring in new perspectives and backgrounds.

C. The organizations are typically decentralized to allow a subunit manager to make more timely decisions.

D. The minimization of the opportunity for social interaction enhances efficiency.

The correct answer is (A). *(Publisher)*

REQUIRED: The advantage of a bureaucratic organizational structure.

DISCUSSION: Each employee's job description defines the related activities and procedures, which do not vary over time. The result is certainty and consistency with regard to the routines and procedures of a job function.

Answer (B) is incorrect because open positions are usually filled by employees of the firm through promotion. Answer (C) is incorrect because centralization is typical of bureaucratic organizations. Answer (D) is incorrect because the impersonality of bureaucracy reduces the human and social processes that promote individual employee growth.

25. A disadvantage of a bureaucratic organizational structure is that

A. The quantity of paperwork prepared is minimal.

B. Employee behavior is not controlled because the organization is too flexible.

C. Creativity within the organization is low.

D. Organizational goals are de-emphasized because the work environment is personalized.

The correct answer is (C). *(Publisher)*

REQUIRED: The disadvantage of bureaucratic organizational structure.

DISCUSSION: In a bureaucracy, tasks are assigned through the division of labor. A set of outlined procedures exists for each job. Because these procedures are invariable, the tasks assigned for each job become routine for the employee.

Answer (A) is incorrect because the system of checks and balances within a bureaucracy requires elaborate paperwork that limits the action and reaction time of the organization. Answer (B) is incorrect because a bureaucracy's inflexibility promotes control but inhibits creativity. Answer (D) is incorrect because the work atmosphere of a bureaucracy is impersonal, which limits individual employee growth.

26. A likely effect of a bureaucratic structure on employee motivation is that

A. Employee performance will be mediocre because of inflexible standards and impersonal surroundings.

B. An employee will pursue organizational goals because of his/her participation in establishing them.

C. Morale will be high because of each employee's feeling of belonging and ownership.

D. Job enrichment will be high because of each employee's involvement in developing and adapting his/her job description and required tasks.

The correct answer is (A). *(Publisher)*

REQUIRED: The effect of a bureaucratic structure on employee motivation.

DISCUSSION: In a bureaucracy, standards for evaluating job performance do not fluctuate because required tasks never change. The work environment is impersonal, which limits individual growth of employees because no incentive for extraordinary performance is present.

Answer (B) is incorrect because employees of a bureaucracy do not participate in decision making. Answer (C) is incorrect because employees are usually unsatisfied since they lack a sense of ownership and belonging. Answer (D) is incorrect because each job's description and tasks are invariable. The employee has no input in the development of his/her function.

27. With the shift in some countries' economies toward service industries, a new form of organization has developed. This organization structure is referred to as the professional bureaucracy. While this structure resembles the machine bureaucracy (which relies on standardized work processes) in several respects, it is different in one key aspect. This significant difference is that in a professional bureaucracy

A. Senior management has had to give up a substantial amount of control.

B. Tasks are accomplished with a high degree of efficiency.

C. There is strict adherence to rules.

D. There is a tendency for subunit conflicts to develop.

The correct answer is (A). *(CIA, adapted)*

REQUIRED: The distinctive trait of a professional bureaucracy.

DISCUSSION: A professional bureaucracy (e.g., a university or library) is a complex and formal but decentralized organization in which highly trained specialists have great autonomy. The jobs performed by these professionals require years of education and training. By their nature, such jobs can be performed effectively only if the employees are afforded substantial autonomy.

Answer (B) is incorrect because both a machine bureaucracy and a professional bureaucracy can accomplish routine tasks in a highly efficient manner. Answer (C) is incorrect because both organizational structures thrive on rules. Answer (D) is incorrect because subunit conflicts are typical of bureaucracies. Specialization tends to result in a focus on subunit rather than organizational objectives.

28. A substantial duplication of functions characterizes which of the following structures?

A. Simple structure.

B. Divisional structure.

C. Machine bureaucracy.

D. Professional bureaucracy.

The correct answer is (B). *(CIA, adapted)*

REQUIRED: The structure with substantial functional duplication.

DISCUSSION: A division is essentially a self-contained organization. Hence, it must perform all or most of the functions of the overall organization of which it is a part. It is characterized by substantial duplication of functions when compared with more centralized structures.

Answer (A) is incorrect because a simple structure has low complexity and formality, and authority is centralized. Its small size and simplicity usually precludes significant inefficiency in the use of resources. Answer (C) is incorrect because a machine bureaucracy is a complex, formal, and centralized organization that performs highly routine tasks, groups activities into functional departments, has a strict chain of command, and distinguishes between line and staff relationships. Answer (D) is incorrect because a professional bureaucracy (e.g., a university or library) is a complex and formal but decentralized organization in which highly trained specialists have great autonomy. Duplication of functions is minimized. For example, a university would have only one history department.

29. An adhocracy is most likely to be found in what kind of organizational structure?

A. Mechanistic.

B. Organic.

C. Bureaucratic.

D. Classical.

The correct answer is (B). *(Publisher)*

REQUIRED: The structure most likely to contain an adhocracy.

DISCUSSION: The organic structure is at the opposite end of the design continuum from a mechanistic organization. An organic structure has groupings of similar persons and resources in subunits (horizontal specialization); relatively few policies, procedures, and rules; less stringent formal controls; decentralized staff; and matrix or divisional departmentation.

Answers (A), (C), and (D) are incorrect because the mechanistic (bureaucratic or classical) model emphasizes clear definition of duties and authority by position in the hierarchy (vertical specialization); numerous, well-documented policies, procedures, and rules; a complex formal control structure; and centralized staff. The strong centralized control in this model is inconsistent with adhocracy.

30. An organization that combines strict adherence to the unity of command with high division of labor may cause problems for customers trying to obtain information. Of the following, which is the most probable type of internal environment this structure creates?

A. Networked and formal.

B. Compartmentalized and informal.

C. Networked and informal.

D. Compartmentalized and formal.

The correct answer is (D). *(CIA, adapted)*

REQUIRED: The internal environment with a strict unity of command and high division of labor.

DISCUSSION: A high division of labor results in specialization. Unity of command clarifies authority and responsibility relationships. An organizational structure with a high division of labor and a strict unity of command is a classic bureaucracy. Thus, it is compartmentalized and formal.

Answers (A), (B), and (C) are incorrect because the structure is formal and compartmentalized.

C. Departmentation

31. Departmentation is the grouping of organizational subsystems. The greatest advantage of functional departmentation is that it

A. Provides the benefits of specialization.

B. Facilitates communication between primary functions.

C. Helps to focus on achievement of organizational goals.

D. Is appropriate for geographically dispersed companies.

The correct answer is (A). *(Publisher)*

REQUIRED: The greatest advantage of functional departmentation.

DISCUSSION: Departmentation by function is the most widely used method and is found in almost every enterprise at some level. The most common departments are selling, production, and finance (though other terms may be used). These often extend upward in the organizational chart to the level below the chief executive. If persons within a department have similar knowledge, skills, and interests, they can specialize in the solution of particular problems. Thus, problem solving becomes more efficient.

Answer (B) is incorrect because departmentation by function facilitates communication within rather than between departments. Answer (C) is incorrect because the focus may tend to be on departmental, not organizational, goals. Answer (D) is incorrect because territorial departmentation may be preferable for these companies.

32. The form of departmentation that most readily lends itself to use of profit centers is

A. Project.

B. Functional.

C. Product.

D. Matrix.

The correct answer is (C). *(Publisher)*

REQUIRED: The form of departmentation most appropriate for use of profit centers.

DISCUSSION: Departmentation by product is growing in importance for multiline, large-scale enterprises. It is often an outgrowth of functional departmentation and permits extensive authority for a division executive over a given product or product line. Its advantages include better use of specialized resources and skills, ease of coordination of the activities for a given product, and simpler assignment of profit responsibility. It is also compatible with a decentralization strategy and provides, through product profit centers, a basis for allocating capital more efficiently.

Answer (A) is incorrect because a profit center is an organizational unit responsible for costs and revenues on an ongoing basis, not just for a one-time activity. Answer (B) is incorrect because the profitability of a single function is difficult to measure. Answer (D) is incorrect because a matrix is used for a specific project or for R&D.

33. Dual reporting is most characteristic of which method of departmentation?

A. Territorial.

B. Functional.

C. Product.

D. Matrix.

The correct answer is (D). *(Publisher)*

REQUIRED: The method of departmentation of which dual reporting is most characteristic.

DISCUSSION: A matrix organization consists of a project team formed with people from various functional areas within the organization. These specialists report simultaneously to the project manager and the managers of their functional departments. At the end of the project, the team is disbanded.

Answers (A), (B), and (C) are incorrect because departmentation by territory, function, or product does not require violation of the unity of command principle.

34. Which particular type of organization structure will likely have unity-of-command problems unless there is frequent and comprehensive communication between the various functional and project managers?

A. Line and staff.

B. Strategic business unit.

C. Centralized.

D. Matrix.

The correct answer is (D). *(CIA, adapted)*

REQUIRED: The structure with unity-of-command problems in the absence of frequent communication among managers.

DISCUSSION: The matrix allows authority to flow both vertically and horizontally. A manager is appointed for each project and draws on personnel who are organized by function and report to a manager for each function. This violates the principle of unity of command, which states that each subordinate should have only one superior.

Answer (A) is incorrect because a line and staff structure is designed to maximize unity of command by giving only line managers the authority to make decisions affecting those in their chain of command. Answer (B) is incorrect because a strategic business unit is a subunit that is treated as an independent business. Thus, unity of command is not an issue for a strategic business unit. Answer (C) is incorrect because a centralized structure need not have unity-of-command problems if management is organized in a line and staff fashion.

35. In what form of organization does an employee report to multiple managers?

A. Bureaucracy.

B. Matrix.

C. Departmental.

D. Mechanistic.

The correct answer is (B). *(CIA, adapted)*

REQUIRED: The organization in which an employee reports to multiple managers.

DISCUSSION: A matrix organization (project management) is characterized by vertical and horizontal lines of authority. The project manager borrows specialists from line functions as needed. This manager's authority is limited to the project, and the specialists will otherwise report to the line managers.

Answer (A) is incorrect because, in a bureaucracy, each subordinate reports to a single manager. Answer (C) is incorrect because departmental organization structures represent the typical organization with unified and clear single lines of authority. Answer (D) is incorrect because mechanistic organization structure is another term for a bureaucracy.

D. Line and Staff Relationships

36. A line position

A. Is indirectly responsible for achieving the organization's basic objectives.

B. Makes administrative and operating decisions.

C. Advises and assists staff positions.

D. Is indirectly involved with the organization's product(s) and/or services.

The correct answer is (B). *(Publisher)*

REQUIRED: The characteristic of a line position in the organization.

DISCUSSION: A line position is in the direct chain of command and is responsible for administering policy and making operating decisions. People in line positions have direct responsibility for achieving the organization's basic objectives and thus have formal or legitimate authority.

Answer (A) is incorrect because a line position is directly responsible for achieving objectives. Answer (C) is incorrect because a line position receives advice and assistance from staff positions in the organization. Answer (D) is incorrect because a line position is directly related to the organization's product(s) and/or service(s).

Questions 37 and 38 are based on the following information:

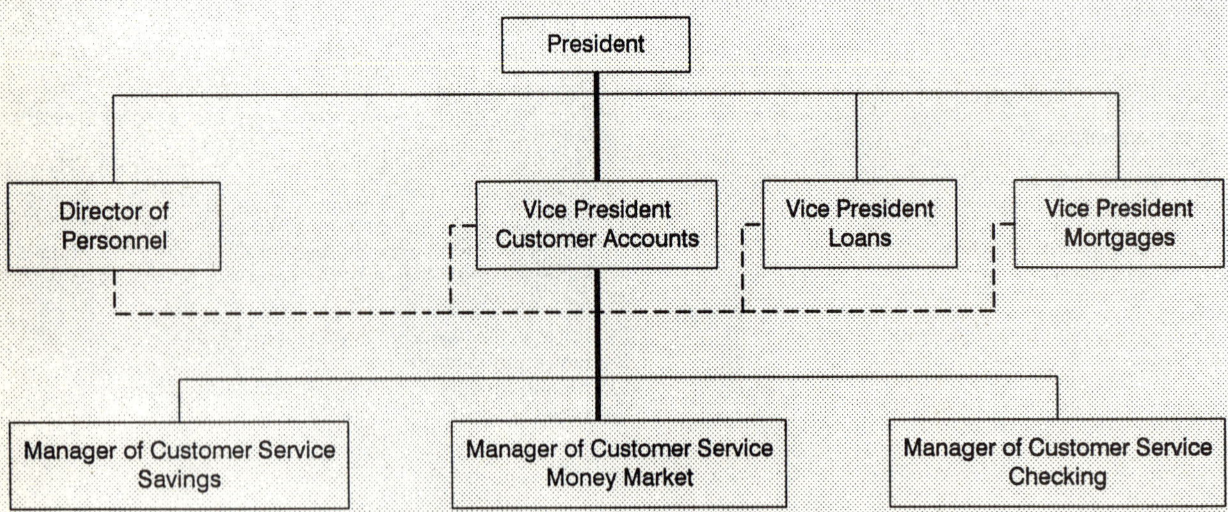

Partial Organizational Chart of the Fisher Bank

37. Which of the following is a staff position in the Fisher Bank (see organizational chart on the previous page)?

A. The manager of customer service-checking, the department that handles checking account inquiries and transactions.

B. The director of personnel, the department that handles the hiring, firing, promotion, etc., of all employees.

C. The chief loan officer, who is in charge of final approval of all loans.

D. The vice president in charge of the mortgage department, which handles mortgages on business and residential property.

The correct answer is (B). *(Publisher)*

REQUIRED: The example of a staff position in a bank.

DISCUSSION: Staff positions in any organization advise and support the line positions. They indirectly help to achieve the organization's basic objective. Each staff position's authority is, at most, functional. Such authority is exercised only over activities related to the staff's function or specialty.

Answers (A), (C), and (D) are incorrect because they are examples of line positions that are directly involved in the achievement of the organization's objectives. Line positions are directly related to the service(s) and/or product(s) offered by the firm.

38. The manager of customer service checking at Fisher Bank (see organizational chart on the previous page) is most likely to encounter conflict(s) because of

A. The department's reliance on the savings manager and the money market manager.

B. His/her providing services for customers who do not have checking accounts.

C. The requirement that (s)he must report directly to both the president and the vice president for customer accounts.

D. A potential disagreement with the director of personnel about a subordinate's performance appraisal.

The correct answer is (D). *(Publisher)*

REQUIRED: The conflict most likely to be encountered by a line manager.

DISCUSSION: The director of personnel (DP) must coordinate all employee evaluations. Although the manager of checking services is in a line position that is not under the DP, (s)he works with the DP when hiring, dismissing, transferring, or evaluating employees.

Answer (A) is incorrect because the manager of checking is a line position which does not rely on the other customer service managers. Answer (B) is incorrect because the department only provides services for the customers with checking accounts. Answer (C) is incorrect because the manager of checking reports to the president indirectly through a vice president.

39. Line and staff positions are most likely to be in conflict because

A. Line managers have no authority over staff employees.

B. Staff managers consider line managers' functional authority threatening to their own authority.

C. Line managers believe that staff managers are resistant to their advice.

D. Staff managers dislike relying on line expertise.

The correct answer is (A). *(Publisher)*

REQUIRED: The cause of conflict between line and staff positions.

DISCUSSION: Line managers are directly responsible for achieving the organization's objectives, but staff managers are not directly accountable. However, line managers may have no authority to influence staff behavior when it is inconsistent with the achievement of objectives.

Answer (B) is incorrect because staff managers may have functional authority that line managers perceive as threatening. Answer (C) is incorrect because staff managers give line managers advice, not vice versa. Answer (D) is incorrect because line managers are likely to become reliant on staff expertise.

E. Span of Control

40. Which of the following factors is least likely to affect a manager's direct span of control?

A. Frequency of supervisor-subordinate contact.

B. The manager's willingness to delegate authority.

C. The manager's training and communication skills.

D. Number of people in the corporation.

The correct answer is (D). *(CIA, adapted)*

REQUIRED: The factor least likely to affect a manager's direct span of control.

DISCUSSION: The optimal span of control is the number of subordinates that a given manager can effectively supervise. It is a function of many situational factors. However, the total number of people in an organization has no bearing on the optimal span of control of a particular manager.

Answer (A) is incorrect because managers who can contact subordinates frequently are able to control more people than those who have relatively infrequent contact with subordinates. Answer (B) is incorrect because managers who delegate authority have more time to control the subordinates who report to them. These individuals can therefore supervise more people than managers who prefer not to delegate authority. Answer (C) is incorrect because managers who have received effective training and are skillful communicators are equipped to control more individuals than managers who are untrained and/or have deficient communication skills.

41. When determining the appropriate span of control, the most important consideration is

A. The set of policies and procedures currently in effect.

B. The typical span of control used by other entities.

C. The preference of the company's creditors.

D. That all departments will be evaluated, whether or not they will be affected.

The correct answer is (A). *(Publisher)*

REQUIRED: The factor that is most important when choosing a span of control.

DISCUSSION: The most important factors to consider are the employees' and manager's preferences and skills, the firm's culture, the tasks involved, physical location of the department, and established policies and procedures.

Answer (B) is incorrect because, although examining similar entities may be useful, it is not one of the most important considerations. Answer (C) is incorrect because this consideration would only be necessary if required by an agreement with the creditors. Answer (D) is incorrect because this is not normally considered in a span-of-control decision.

42. The difference between a tall organization structure and a flat organization structure is that in the former

A. The communication process takes longer and is of poorer quality.

B. Maintenance of the organization is less costly.

C. The morale of lower-level employees is generally higher.

D. A higher degree of coordination and cooperation is created.

The correct answer is (A). *(CIA, adapted)*

REQUIRED: The difference between tall and flat organization structures.

DISCUSSION: "Flat" organizational structures have relatively few levels from top to bottom. "Tall" organizational structures have many levels between top and bottom. Flat structures have the advantages of fast information flow from top to bottom of the organization and increased employee satisfaction. Tall structures are faster and more effective at problem resolution because of the increased frequency of interaction between superior and subordinate, and the greater order imposed by the hierarchy. Studies do not indicate great advantages for either flat or tall structures.

Answers (B), (C), and (D) are incorrect because each is an advantage of a flat structure.

43. The most likely span of control to apply over 14 data-entry clerks who do essentially the same job and work in the same office would be

A. Close.

B. Narrow.

C. Moderate.

D. Wide.

The correct answer is (D). *(CIA, adapted)*

REQUIRED: The span-of-control category that would be most applicable.

DISCUSSION: In any situation, underlying variables influence the number of subordinates a manager can supervise. In general, if jobs are similar, procedures are standardized, and physical dispersion is minimized, a wide span of control is most effective.

Answer (A) is incorrect because close is not a span-of-control category. Answer (B) is incorrect because a narrow span of control is useful when jobs are dissimilar, procedures are not standardized, and subordinates are more dispersed. Answer (C) is incorrect because a moderate span of control is useful in situations that have some characteristics of both extremes, wide and narrow.

44. A flat organization structure is one with relatively few levels of hierarchy and is characterized by wide spans of management control. A tall organization has many levels of hierarchy and narrow spans of control. Which of the following situations is consistent with a flat organization structure?

A. Tasks require little direction and control of subordinates.

B. Work areas are geographically dispersed.

C. Tasks are highly complex and varied.

D. Subordinates perform distinctly different tasks.

The correct answer is (A). *(CIA, adapted)*

REQUIRED: The situation consistent with a flat organization structure.

DISCUSSION: Flat structures have the advantages of fast information flow from top to bottom of the organization and increased employee satisfaction. Tall structures are faster and more effective at problem resolution because of the increased frequency of interaction between superior and subordinate and the greater order imposed by the hierarchy. For a flat structure to be successful, employees must be able to work without supervision much of the time because a manager with many employees has little time for each one.

Answer (B) is incorrect because geographically dispersed work areas are very difficult for a manager with many subordinates to control. Answer (C) is incorrect because tasks that are highly complex and varied are more appropriate for a narrow span of control. Answer (D) is incorrect because a narrow span of control (a tall structure) is more appropriate when subordinates perform distinctly different tasks.

45. The optimal span of control of a manager is contingent upon several situational variables. For instance, a manager supervising workers within the same work area who are performing identical tasks that are simple and repetitive would best be able to supervise

A. An unlimited number of employees.

B. Only a few workers (a narrow span of control).

C. A relatively large number of employees (a wide span of control).

D. Fewer workers than if the workers were geographically dispersed.

The correct answer is (C). *(CIA, adapted)*

REQUIRED: The optimal span of control of a manager supervising workers within the same work area who are performing identical tasks that are simple and repetitive.

DISCUSSION: In any situation, there are underlying variables that influence the number of subordinates a manager can supervise. In general, if jobs are similar, procedures are standardized, and physical dispersion is minimized, a wide span of control is most effective.

Answer (A) is incorrect because, although a manager under these conditions would be able to supervise a large number of employees, an upper limit must exist. Answer (B) is incorrect because the conditions described support a wide rather than a narrow span. Answer (D) is incorrect because geographical dispersion would decrease rather than increase the span of control.

46. Which of the following is an advantage of a tall organizational structure?

A. The flow of communications from top to bottom and bottom to top is improved.

B. The organization's overall objectives are familiar to all employees.

C. More opportunity to advance.

D. Labor expenses are reduced.

The correct answer is (C). *(Publisher)*

REQUIRED: An advantage of tall organizational structure.

DISCUSSION: The organizational structure consists of the order, disposition, and relationships of positions and lines of responsibility within an entity. In a tall organizational structure, decision-making responsibility is shared by many levels.

Answers (A), (B), and (D) are incorrect because they are advantages of a flat organizational structure, which concentrates decision-making power at one level.

47. Which of the following is a disadvantage of a flat organizational structure?

A. Employees are not encouraged to be creative.

B. The input of fresh ideas from outside the company is limited because employee turnover is low.

C. Managers spend too much time training individuals and not enough time supervising.

D. Employees may not be performing work tasks properly.

The correct answer is (D). *(Publisher)*

REQUIRED: The disadvantage of a flat organizational structure.

DISCUSSION: A flat organizational structure concentrates decision-making authority at one level. Tasks and performance objectives may be unclear to employees because of a lack of supervision.

Answer (A) is incorrect because the lack of supervision increases employee flexibility. Answer (B) is incorrect because the number of management levels limits the opportunity for advancement, which may cause high employee turnover. Answer (C) is incorrect because managers spend too much time supervising, and employees do not receive enough supervision.

48. Which of the following is a likely effect of a narrow span of control?

A. The manager closely supervises employees.

B. Each employee is given more responsibility.

C. The organizational structure is flexible.

D. The manager's control over employees is limited.

The correct answer is (A). *(Publisher)*

REQUIRED: The effect most likely to result from a narrow span of control.

DISCUSSION: The span of control is the number of subordinates for which a manager or supervisor is responsible. When the span of control is narrow, a few subordinates are tightly controlled. A narrow span of control is typical of tall organizational structures.

Answers (B), (C), and (D) are incorrect because they are likely effects of a wide span of control, which is likely to be found in flat organizational structures.

F. Centralization and Decentralization

49. Centralization and decentralization are defined according to the relative delegation of decision-making authority by top management. Many managers believe that decentralized organizations have significant advantages over centralized organizations. A major advantage of a decentralized organization is that

A. Decentralized organizations are easier to control.

B. Decentralized structures streamline organizations and eliminate duplication of resources.

C. Decentralized organizations have fewer managers than centralized organizations.

D. Decentralized organizations encourage increased initiative among employees.

The correct answer is (D). *(CIA, adapted)*

REQUIRED: The major advantage of a decentralized organization.

DISCUSSION: A decentralized organization allows lower-level employees to participate in decision making. This increased involvement encourages initiative and creative thinking and is especially appropriate in complex and rapidly changing environments.

Answer (A) is incorrect because decentralized organizations are more difficult to control. Answer (B) is incorrect because centralized structures streamline organizations and eliminate duplication of resources. Answer (C) is incorrect because the number of managers is not related to the degree of centralization or decentralization but is a function of the span of control.

50. A claimed advantage of decentralizing is

A. Concentration of authority.

B. Manager development.

C. Elimination of duplication of effort.

D. Departmentalization.

The correct answer is (B). *(CIA, adapted)*

REQUIRED: The advantage of decentralizing an organization.

DISCUSSION: When an organization changes from a centralized to a decentralized structure, top management is delegating more authority to middle and lower levels. Thus, managers at these lower levels are usually hired and developed more rigorously than under the centralized structure.

Answer (A) is incorrect because authority is more concentrated in centralized management structures. Answer (C) is incorrect because some effort will inevitably be duplicated under decentralization, of which departmentalization is a moderate form. Answer (D) is incorrect because departments are formed when one manager can no longer supervise the entire organization; departmentalization is therefore a characteristic of centralized as well as decentralized organizations.

51. Which of the following is a benefit of decentralization?

A. The head of the company is aware of and can influence all decisions before they are made.

B. The company is operated as one unit.

C. Specialists for a particular product have no authority but advise the company's top management.

D. Decisions are made on a more timely basis.

The correct answer is (D). *(Publisher)*

REQUIRED: The benefit of decentralization.

DISCUSSION: Decentralization is the extent to which decision-making power is delegated within an entity. When approval from upper-level management is not required, lower-level managers can make more timely decisions because they are closer to the necessary sources of information.

Answers (A) and (B) are incorrect because each typifies a highly centralized entity. Answer (C) is incorrect because decentralization would give these specialists more authority.

52. Which of the following is a reason for delegating?

A. The manager wants to make more decisions.

B. Subordinates lack initiative.

C. The manager wants to remain the sole expert in his/her field.

D. Subordinates have too many responsibilities.

The correct answer is (B). *(Publisher)*

REQUIRED: The reason for delegating authority within a firm.

DISCUSSION: Delegation is the assignment of a manager's authority and/or workload to his/her subordinates. By increasing subordinates' responsibilities, the manager gives them more opportunity to exercise judgment and become more confident.

Answer (A) is incorrect because delegation passes some decision-making power to subordinates. Answer (C) is incorrect because delegation gives subordinates the opportunity to increase their expertise. Answer (D) is incorrect because delegation gives subordinates more responsibilities.

53. Which of the following is a reason that a manager may be reluctant to delegate?

A. The manager fears being held accountable for the subordinate's performance.

B. The manager fears (s)he may fail because of some lack of knowledge.

C. The manager did not monitor the subordinate's work.

D. The manager fears unknown goals.

The correct answer is (A). *(Publisher)*

REQUIRED: The reason a manager is reluctant to delegate.

DISCUSSION: Managers fear delegating because of insecurity, mistrust, insufficient planning, and/or aversion to the risk of being responsible for subordinates' actions.

Answers (B) and (D) are incorrect because these are fears that subordinates have about delegation. Answer (C) is incorrect because it states a potential implementation problem.

54. The most effective way for a supervisor to delegate a task to an employee would be to

A. Define the desired outcome and the approach precisely and in writing.

B. Define the desired outcome precisely, discuss possible approaches with the employee, and reach agreement on the approach to be taken.

C. Let the employee try to perform the task for a defined period of time and then meet to critique the approach, clarifying the assignment as needed.

D. Give the assignment in very general terms, have the employee develop the desired outcome and approach, and then review and critique the employee's decisions.

The correct answer is (B). *(CIA, adapted)*

REQUIRED: The most effective way for a supervisor to delegate a task to an employee.

DISCUSSION: The supervisor's expectations should be clear. The employee should also be involved in determining how to reach the desired outcome, thereby increasing both acceptance and understanding of the assignment.

Answer (A) is incorrect because defining the approach decreases both acceptance and understanding of the assignment. The employee should participate in the decision and be able to discuss and clarify the assignment. Answer (C) is incorrect because this approach almost guarantees that the employee will feel that (s)he failed to perform well. Answer (D) is incorrect because the significant risk is that the employee will not define an outcome and an approach with which the supervisor agrees.

G. Groups

55. The president of an organization assigned the chief information officer (CIO) the task of developing a disaster recovery plan for the organization. The recovery plan was to encompass all activities of the organization, not merely information systems. Therefore, the CIO needed to draw on the expertise of specialists from all over the organization. Identify the type of organizational structure that would be best to successfully complete this project.

A. Focus group.

B. Reengineering process team.

C. Matrix organization.

D. Ad hoc committee.

The correct answer is (D). *(CIA, adapted)*

REQUIRED: The best structure for a project requiring specialists from throughout the organization.

DISCUSSION: An ad hoc committee is the structure best suited for specialized, one-of-a-kind projects that require diverse specialists to work in small teams. It is simple, informal, decentralized, and temporary. It has no hierarchy, permanent departments, standard procedures for accomplishing routine tasks, or formal rules. Consequently, an ad hoc organization is flexible and responsive.

Answer (A) is incorrect because a focus group includes a small number of consumers brought together by marketing researchers to discuss a given topic. Answer (B) is incorrect because a reengineering process team is assembled to search for and implement a radical redesign of basic business activities. Answer (C) is incorrect because a matrix organization is characterized by dual lines of authority and a combination of functional and product departmentation. It puts similar specialists together.

56. Which one of the following is generally not beneficial to group decision making in an organization?

A. More information.

B. Acceptance.

C. More knowledge.

D. Dominant members.

The correct answer is (D). *(CMA, adapted)*

REQUIRED: The item that is not beneficial to group decision making in an organization.

DISCUSSION: Group decision making, such as by a committee, works better when the committee is small and the members accept each other as contributing parts of the group. A dominant member is not desirable. The chair should act as a moderator and not be considered threatening or overbearing by the other members.

Answer (A) is incorrect because a group decision, like an individual decision, is better when based on sufficient information. Answer (B) is incorrect because acceptance of each member of the committee and the goals of the committee is essential. Answer (C) is incorrect because the more knowledge that group members possess, the better the ultimate decision is apt to be.

57. Which one of the following is least likely to contribute to group cohesiveness in an organization?

A. Goal consensus.

B. Subgroup formation.

C. Leadership acceptance.

D. Interpersonal trust.

The correct answer is (B). *(CMA, adapted)*

REQUIRED: The item that is least likely to contribute to group cohesiveness in an organization.

DISCUSSION: People naturally seek association and group acceptance. Members of groups react to pressures of the group. Groups are often complex, develop their own leaders, exist to fill the needs of the members, and result from the frequent interaction among individuals in the course of their work. In a sense, group members typically have an experience of togetherness. Members develop interpersonal trust for other group members. The formation of small subgroups, however, can splinter the harmony of the large group.

Answer (A) is incorrect because agreement about goals facilitates group harmony. Answer (C) is incorrect because leadership acceptance contributes to group cohesiveness by helping to define roles within the group. Answer (D) is incorrect because interpersonal trust enhances the ease with which a group is formed and functions.

58. Which one of the following statements about quality circles is false?

A. A quality circle is typically composed of a group of 8 to 10 subordinates and supervisors.

B. Part of the quality circle concept includes teaching participants communication skills, quality strategies, and problem analysis techniques.

C. Quality circles meet on the company premises and on company time.

D. The quality circle has the final control over implementation of recommended solutions.

The correct answer is (D). *(CIA, adapted)*

REQUIRED: The false statement about quality circles.

DISCUSSION: Use of quality circles is a form of participative management. A quality circle is a group of up to 10 individuals (managers and subordinates) who do similar work and who volunteer to meet weekly to discuss and solve work-related problems. However, management retains the right to make the final decisions.

Answer (A) is incorrect because a quality circle is a small group of subordinates and supervisors, usually eight to 10 people. Answer (B) is incorrect because each member is responsible for the success of the circle, and success depends on the ability of members to analyze and solve problems. Answer (C) is incorrect because quality circles are used by companies to accomplish objectives. Participation is part of each worker's job.

H. More on Organizational Theory

59. The organizational chart

A. Is used only in centralized organizations.

B. Is applicable only to profit-oriented companies.

C. Depicts only line functions.

D. Depicts the lines of authority linking various positions.

The correct answer is (D). *(CMA, adapted)*

REQUIRED: The true statement about an organizational chart.

DISCUSSION: An organizational chart is used to represent the organizational structure of an entity. It normally resembles a pyramid, with the chief executive on top and the operating work force on the bottom. Lines show reporting relationships, lines of authority, and task groupings. An organizational chart depicts promotional or career tracks and illustrates the span of control and the number of organizational levels.

Answer (A) is incorrect because an organizational chart can be used in decentralized as well as centralized organizations. Answer (B) is incorrect because not-for-profit agencies use organizational charts for the same reasons as profit-oriented companies. Answer (C) is incorrect because both staff and line functions are depicted on organizational charts.

60. A printing company changes its type of ink to a nontoxic variety due to unfavorable publicity by a local environmental group. This is an example of an organizational change called

A. Anticipatory.

B. Reactive.

C. Incremental.

D. Strategic.

The correct answer is (B). *(CIA, adapted)*

REQUIRED: The organizational change due to unfavorable publicity by a local environmental group.

DISCUSSION: Reactive changes are necessitated by unexpected environmental events or pressures. They may be incremental or strategic. In the Nadler-Tushman model (Kreitner, Robert, *Management*, 6th ed., Houghton Mifflin, 1995, pp. 498-499), adaptation is an incremental reactive change, and re-creation is a strategic (and risky) reactive change.

Answer (A) is incorrect because anticipatory changes are systematically planned changes intended to take advantage of expected situations. In the Nadler-Tushman model, tuning is an incremental anticipatory change, and re-orientation is a strategic anticipatory change. Answer (C) is incorrect because incremental changes involve subsystem adjustments needed to keep the organization on its chosen path. Answer (D) is incorrect because strategic changes alter the overall shape or direction of the organization.

61. If a company makes a fundamental change in its organizational structure, resistance by employees

A. Is likely to be minimal if affected persons suffer no economic loss.

B. Can be minimized by adopting a participative management approach.

C. Can be minimized by adopting an autocratic management approach.

D. Will be greatest if they receive notice long before the change is implemented.

The correct answer is (B). *(Publisher)*

REQUIRED: The true statement about resistance to change.

DISCUSSION: Resistance to change may be caused by fear of the personal adjustments that may be required. Employees may have a genuine concern about the usefulness of the change, perceive a lack of concern for workers' feelings, fear the outcome, worry about downgrading of job status, and resent deviations from past procedures for implementing change (especially if new procedures are less participative than the old). Social adjustments also may be required that violate the behavioral norms of informal groups or disrupt the social status quo within groups. Economic adjustments may involve potential economic loss or insecurity based on perceived threats to jobs. In general, any perceived deterioration in the work situation that is seen as a threat to economic, social, and/or psychological needs will produce resistance. The various adjustments required are most likely to be resisted when imposed unilaterally by higher authority. However, employees who share in finding solutions to the problems requiring change are less likely to resist because they will have some responsibility for the change.

Answer (A) is incorrect because fear of personal and social adjustments may lead to resistance. Answer (C) is incorrect because imposed change will meet the greatest resistance. Answer (D) is incorrect because adequate notice helps reduce resistance.

Use Gleim's ***CMA/CFM Test Prep*** for interactive testing with **over 2,000 additional multiple-choice questions!**

STUDY UNIT 9: MOTIVATION AND THE DIRECTING PROCESS

25 pages of outline
60 multiple-choice questions

The relative weight range assigned to organizational structures, management, and communication in Part 1 is 20% to 30%. We cover this major topic in the following study units:

Study Unit 8: Organizational Theory
Study Unit 9: Motivation and the Directing Process
Study Unit 10: Communication

Thus, you should expect 24 to 36 questions on these three study units.

A. Individual and Group Dynamics

1. Individual dynamics is concerned with the psychological model of a single personality, in contrast to group dynamics, which attempts to explain the behavior of people in groups.
   a. Abraham Maslow (1940s and 1950s) presented one of the most widely cited theories of motivation. He saw human needs as a hierarchy, from lowest to highest. Lower-level needs must be satisfied before higher-level needs can influence the individual. He concluded that as the set of needs on each level was satisfied, those needs ceased to be a motivator.
   b. **Maslow's hierarchy of needs** is listed below, from lowest to highest:
      1) **Physiological needs** are the basic requirements for sustaining human life, such as water, food, shelter, sleep, and sexual satisfaction. Maslow took the position that until these needs are satisfied to the degree needed to maintain life, higher-level needs will not serve as motivators.
      2) **Security or safety needs** are freedom from physical danger, or from loss of job, property, food, or shelter.
      3) **Affiliation or acceptance needs** are the needs of people as social beings to belong to groups and be accepted by others.
      4) **Esteem** is the need to be valued, including the need to be esteemed by both one's self and others. These needs are satisfied by power, prestige, status, and self-confidence.
      5) **Self-actualization** is the highest need in the hierarchy. It is the desire to become what one is capable of becoming, to realize one's potential and accomplish to the limit of one's ability.

c. Research does not support the concept of a strict hierarchy in all situations (beyond the requirement that biological needs must be satisfied before other needs begin to serve as motivators).

   1) Physiological and safety needs tend to decrease in importance as managers advance in organizations, whereas needs for acceptance, esteem, and self-actualization tend to increase.

   2) Higher-level needs, esteem and self-actualization, are variable in their identity, depending upon the individual.

d. Maslow's hierarchy does not apply equally to all situations. It is dependent on the social, cultural, and psychological backgrounds of the people involved.

   1) People of different cultures respond differently.

   2) Professional workers, skilled workers, and unskilled workers react differently.

   3) Other social, ethnic, and cultural factors make people react differently.

   4) The hierarchy is not a smooth, step-by-step path; it is a complicated, intermingled, and interdependent set of relationships.

      a) However, the tendency to move upward as lower needs are satisfied does exist.

e. According to **David McClelland**, motivation is based on the needs for achievement, power, and affiliation.

   1) The **need for achievement** is the drive to succeed in relation to a set of standards. Thus, high achievers wish to do something better than it has been done before. They thrive when the job provides for personal responsibility, feedback, and moderate risks. They avoid very easy or very difficult tasks, and they do not like to succeed by chance.

   2) The **need for power** is a desire to compel others to behave in certain ways, to influence or control others. Individuals with a high need for power are concerned with prestige and status and prefer to be in charge.

   3) The **need for affiliation** is the need for close, amicable interpersonal relationships. Individuals with a high need for affiliation seek friendship, cooperative rather than competitive situations, and mutual understanding.

f. The **ERG theory** developed by Clayton Alderfer states that the core needs are existence (physiological and security needs), relatedness (affiliation and external esteem needs), and growth (self-actualization and internal esteem needs).

   1) ERG theory argues that multiple needs may serve as motivators at the same time.

   2) Frustration of a higher need may lead to regression to a lower need. For example, frustration of growth needs through inability to find more fulfilling work may result in a heightened need to make money.

g. **Individual values**

   1) Values are specific to each individual person and involve moral and personal issues.

   2) Values are learned from family, friends, school, and life experience in general.

3) Values can be modified throughout life but ordinarily tend to stay the same.

4) It is important to reward good values in a corporation to prevent fraud, theft, and deception and improve worker morale.

a) The value structure is an important part of the corporate culture.

5) Personal beliefs, such as those on religious and political matters, cannot be the basis of personnel actions. Discrimination on the basis of personal beliefs could expose the organization to legal action.

h. **Human defense mechanisms**

1) Defense mechanisms come into play when an employee feels jeopardized or threatened. Some of the most common methods of defense are listed below.

a) Rationalization entails giving more acceptable reasons for behavior than the actual ones.

b) Regression involves reversion to child-like behavior.

c) Repression eliminates stressful items from working memory.

d) Projection is the attribution of one's own ideas, feelings, or attitudes to others, especially the externalization of blame, guilt, or responsibility as a defense against anxiety.

e) Compensation attempts to offset bad qualities with good qualities.

f) Withdrawal is simply avoidance.

g) Aggression involves a direct attack on the perceived causes of the problem.

2. **Group Dynamics**

a. Many problems in management stem from group behavior patterns, attitudes, and desires.

1) Any organized enterprise is also a social structure that includes a number of subunits.

a) Each social structure is a complex of interacting attitudes, pressures, and conflicts arising from the cultural background of the individuals making up the subunit.

2) Some problems arise from the work group (inside the enterprise).

3) Other problems result from the differing backgrounds of people (outside of the enterprise), i.e., attitudes they bring with them to work. Examples are the prejudices people have about race or religion.

b. Kurt Lewin (late 1930s) identified **group dynamics** as a working model for describing human behavior. He stressed studying people where they were, not where someone believed they ideally should have been.

1) Lewin's work provided the theoretical framework for modern **sensitivity training** and training laboratories.

c. Several common characteristics of groups influence behavior.

   1) Leadership. All groups have leaders, formal and/or informal, who initiate interrelationships and act as communication centers.

   2) Norms. From earliest observations, groups have been found to be guided by self-set standards of performance and behavior, usually based on a composite of the personal and social backgrounds of the individuals on the job as well as those of people outside the group and outside the job.

   3) Status systems. There is a ranking within the group; it may be based on skill, age, ethnic background, seniority, and/or personality.

   4) Roles. Certain behavior patterns are expected of the individual by the group.

   5) Goals. The group becomes an entity and develops its own goals, its own survival and recognition needs, etc.

   6) Activity. Action by the members of the group identify them as a group.

   7) Bias. The group shares common beliefs and values about the world in which the group operates.

d. **Group behavior** is a distinct phenomenon. It is not merely the sum of the behaviors of the individuals making up the group. However, groups conceal the relationship between individual effort and outcome.

   1) A group as a whole tends to be riskier and more emotional than most of its individuals.

   2) A group has values of its own, as expressed by group behavior.

   3) Groups tend to normalize behavior, bringing deviant individuals into line through pressure to conform to group norms.

      a) The strength of this normalizing pressure is correlated to group cohesiveness. Increased cohesiveness may either increase or decrease productivity.

      b) Workers who exceed the group norm will also be pressured to conform so as not to embarrass the other group members.

      c) Workers who produce below the norm will be pressured to improve so as not to overburden the others.

      d) Cohesiveness in the organization of a labor union may allow the group to halt production completely until their demands are met.

   4) Work groups have a positive effect on the organization if management arranges for congruence between group goals and organizational goals. Management may encourage the development of a **corporate or organizational culture**, that is, a sense of shared customs, values, rituals, history, and style. It may operate through both formal procedures and implicit means of social control.

      a) An organizational culture should enhance stability, goal congruence, morale, and performance.

      b) Organizational socialization is the formal or informal process of training new employees to conform to the organizational culture.

e. Commitment to a group depends on its attractiveness and cohesiveness.

  1) Attractiveness is a favorable view from the outside.

  2) Cohesiveness is the tendency of members to adhere to the group and resist outside influences.

  3) Factors that enhance group attractiveness and cohesiveness are prestige, status, a cooperative relationship, a high degree of interaction, small size, the similarity of members, a superior public image, and a common threat in the environment.

  4) The process of group development proceeds through a succession of stages in which conflicts over power, authority, and interpersonal relationships must be overcome.

    a) Groups that evolve into the acceptance stage of group development tend to be both effective and efficient. This stage is characterized by personal and mutual understanding, tolerance of individual differences, constructive conflict about substantive matters, realistic expectations about group performance, and acceptance of the authority structure. The resulting trust engenders cohesiveness and a free exchange of information between group members.

f. **Role playing** is an important concept that emerged from the group dynamics theory. A role is the behavior expected of a person who occupies a particular position. Everyone is expected to play or assume different roles in different situations.

g. **Role conflict** emerges when two or more roles, making conflicting demands, are simultaneously expected of, or imposed on, a person.

  1) For example, a manager may expect an employee to work late (employee role) on the night of his/her child's birthday party (parent role). An example of conflict between an employer role and a coworker role occurs when a person is promoted to supervisor (employer role) of a department in which (s)he was previously on the same level with other employees (peer or coworker role).

  2) Types of role conflict

    a) Conflict between role and self occurs when personal characteristics are incompatible with the expected role.

    b) Interrole conflict involves having different roles, each with different behavioral expectations.

    c) Intersender conflict results from being expected to behave differently by different people, although having the same role, e.g., a manager who has to be a leader (of subordinates) and a follower (of top management).

    d) Intrasender conflict arises from being sent different **messages** (roles) by the same person (e.g., a manager who expects an employee to behave one way one day and another the next).

h. Ambiguous or contradictory role demands cause stress to the individual. Recognition of the causes of role conflict helps to minimize its effect.

3. Stop and review! You have completed the outline for this subunit. Study multiple-choice questions 1 through 9 beginning on page 368.

B. Motivation

1. Motivation is a general term used to describe an entire class of drives, desires, needs, fears, and similar forces that cause behavior.
   a. The ideal management action motivates subordinates by structuring situations and requiring behaviors of subordinates that will simultaneously satisfy both the subordinates' needs and the organization's requirements.
   b. There is no reason that the organization's needs and those of the individual **must** conflict.
   c. Level of motivation is determined by individuals' opportunity to satisfy their needs and wants within the organizational setting (i.e., the greater the ability to satisfy these needs, the greater the motivational level).
      1) The inducements that an organization offers an individual member should be matched with the contributions expected from that individual (i.e., each is willing to give up something to get something it wants).
      2) The task of a leader is to make available the kinds and amounts of inducements an individual requires as a trade for the kinds and amounts of contributions the organization requires.
2. **Classical views** stress fear and economics as motivators, i.e., the carrot-and-stick approach. For example,
   a. Economic incentive programs or bonuses (carrots)
   b. Losing one's job or being demoted (sticks)
3. **Behavioralists** believe that these motivational strategies are effective only for the short run or for people who don't have job alternatives. The behavioralist approach focuses on participation and personal involvement in the work situation as motivational factors.
4. **Chris Argyris** (1964) proposed a theory of motivation that involves integrating the needs of the individual with those of the organization.
   a. Conflict arises when a mature, independent adult who seeks self-actualization joins a highly structured, demanding, and limiting organization.
      1) EXAMPLE: A highly competent aeronautical engineer who takes a job with the federal government may find his/her attempts to pursue technical excellence through intellectual effort stifled by the rules and procedures that are characteristic of a bureaucracy.
      2) Self-actualization is the process of accomplishing goals to the limit of one's ability because of the personal need to excel.
5. **Douglas McGregor's Theory X and Theory Y** (1960s) are simplified models that define the extremes of managers' views on employee conduct. They permit a manager to evaluate his/her own tendencies.
   a. **Theory X** is the viewpoint of the autocratic manager. It is thought to be very common.
      1) "Average human beings have an inherent dislike of work and will avoid it if possible."
      2) "Because of this dislike for work, most people must be coerced, controlled, directed, and threatened with punishment to get them to put forth adequate effort toward the achievement of organizational objectives."
      3) "Average human beings prefer to be directed, have relatively little ambition, and want security above all."

b. **Theory Y** is the extreme opposite of Theory X. The permissive manager assumes that

1) "The expenditure of physical and mental effort in work is as natural as play or rest -- to average human beings."

2) "External control and the threat of punishment are not the only means for bringing about individual effort toward organizational objectives. Employees will exercise self-direction and self-control in their efforts to accomplish goals thought to be worthwhile."

3) "Commitment to objectives is proportional to the rewards associated with their achievement."

4) "Average human beings learn, under proper conditions, not only to accept responsibility, but to seek it."

5) "The capacity to exercise a relatively high degree of imagination, ingenuity, and creativity in the solution of organizational problems is widely, not narrowly, distributed in the population."

6) "Under the conditions of modern industrial life, the intellectual potentialities of the average human being are only partially realized."

c. McGregor did not suggest that Theory Y was the only correct managerial behavior. He suggested these theories as starting points from which a manager can examine his/her own views about human nature.

6. **Frederick Herzberg's two-factor theory of human behavior** (late 1950s) postulated that there are two classes of factors in the job situation.

a. **Dissatisfiers (maintenance or hygiene factors)**. These factors are found in the job context. Their presence will not especially motivate people, but their absence will lead to diminished performance. They include company policy and administration, supervision, working conditions, interpersonal relations, salary, status, and job security.

b. **Satisfiers (motivational factors)**. These factors relate to job content. Their absence will not diminish performance, but their addition or availability will motivate employees. These include achievement, recognition, challenging work, advancement, growth in the job, and responsibility.

c. If Herzberg is correct, considerable attention should be given to upgrading job content through the use of job enrichment strategies.

d. Herzberg's work has not gone unchallenged. Other researchers have found hygiene factors to be potent in yielding both satisfaction and dissatisfaction and therefore motivation. Nevertheless, Herzberg's ideas have been well received by practicing managers because many of them hold similar beliefs about motivation.

1) Based on Herzberg's analysis, some jobs obviously do not contain many motivators, whereas others have more than are being fully used by management. For example,

a) Routine, low-status work such as mail sorting has few motivators.

b) A company that may be paying above the industry average (maintenance factor) could also increase satisfaction by openly acknowledging sales or other efforts by initiating a salesperson of the week recognition program.

7. **Rensis Likert** (1967) stressed participation as the key to motivation. The manager is the **supportive mechanism** or device used in building toward the environment most conducive to participation and a resulting increase in productivity.

   a. He outlined four systems of management, the effects of which range from low productivity to high productivity.

      1) System 1 -- Exploitive-authoritative
      2) System 2 -- Benevolent-authoritative
      3) System 3 -- Consultative
      4) System 4 -- Participative

   b. As the management style moves from System 1 to System 4 (from autocratic to participative), some of the following shifts in variables are observed:

      1) Motivational forces move from security, fear, threats, conflict of goals, responsibility felt only at the top, and subservience to group processes in goal setting, a high level of satisfaction, feelings of responsibility, and high satisfaction with achievement.

      2) Communications move from little, all downward, inaccuracy, and no questioning to up-and-down freely, initiated by all levels as needed, accuracy, and no need for supplementary means.

      3) Personal interaction (influence) moves from little interaction, fear, distrust, and no teamwork to friendliness, trust and confidence, and much teamwork. Effective participation is impossible if either party feels threatened.

      4) Decision making moves from decisions made at the top without lower-level input, made by individuals only, or made at too-high levels to decision making spread throughout the organization, full information input, and group decisions.

      5) Goal setting moves from goals by edict and orders from the top and rejection by many to group participation, input from all levels, and full acceptance.

      6) Control processes move from a top-heavy concentration and inaccurate measurements to concern felt throughout the organization and widespread responsibility.

8. **Job Enrichment vs. Job Enlargement**

   a. Job enrichment attempts to apply the findings of Maslow, Likert, and McGregor by structuring the job so that each worker participates in planning and controlling. The purpose is to maximize the satisfaction of both social and ego needs and avoid the disadvantages of routine, highly specialized work. Job enrichment includes

      1) Allowing and encouraging more worker discretion over work methods, sequence, and pace.

      2) Encouraging interactions between workers

      3) Giving workers a feeling of personal responsibility for their tasks

      4) Making sure workers understand how their tasks contribute to the finished product

      5) Giving people feedback on their job performance

      6) Involving workers in changes in physical aspects of the work environment

b. Job enlargement is primarily a technique for combating boredom at repetitive or highly paced jobs through the assignment of a wide variety of tasks. Job enrichment may result from job enlargement.

9. **Quality of Work Life (QWL)**. According to Robert Guest (*Harvard Business Review*, Vol. 57, July-August 1979, pp. 76-77), quality of work life (QWL) is "a process by which an organization attempts to unlock the creative potential of its people by involving them in decisions affecting their lives."

   a. The domain of QWL includes pay, employee benefits, job security, alternative work schedules, occupational stress, participation, and workplace democracy.

   b. The major categories of QWL programs are flexible work schedules, participative management, and workplace democracy.

10. **Expectancy theory** (Victor Vroom, 1960s) is a commonsense notion that people have expectations of rewards derived from their unique personal motive structure (achievement, affiliation, power, etc.), from their beliefs as to what is important (a trip to Acapulco, a gold watch, a pat on the back), and from their expectations of getting these incentives if they exert effort (probability assessments, such as, "If I do this, will I get that reward?").

   a. High effort expended, ability, and accurate role assessment will lead to a high performance level (i.e., putting the effort into the task and having the right amount of ability to do it will lead to high performance).

      1) Insufficient ability will impede performance despite effort.

      2) Executing a task that is not desired or is improperly performed according to role definition will impede performance despite effort or ability.

   b. Motivation is a product of the values an individual seeks and his/her estimation of the probability that a certain action will lead to those values. This relationship can be expressed as the following equation:

$$\textit{Motivation} = \textit{Valence} \times \textit{Expectancy}$$

   c. **Valence** is the strength of an individual's preference for one outcome in relation to others. Valence is a personal value unique to each employee that cannot be controlled by management.

   d. **Expectancy** results from past experiences and measures the strength of belief that a particular act will be followed by a specific outcome.

   e. Management is more able to control the expectancy factor than the valence factor because expectations are based on past experiences. A consistent management policy will reinforce employee expectations.

   f. Performance leads to rewards.

      1) Individuals evaluate rewards on the basis of equity ("Did I get what I deserved for what I did?") compared with others in similar jobs.

      2) If inequity exists, individuals react, usually negatively.

   g. Perception of the equity of rewards leads to satisfaction ("I got what I earned.")

   h. Level of satisfaction or dissatisfaction feeds back into the next cycle's estimates of reward values, individual abilities, and role perceptions.

11. **Satisfaction and Productivity**

    a. The proposition that "a happy worker is a good worker" has **not** been supported by research. Evidence tends to indicate that increased rewards bring increased satisfaction, but not necessarily increased productivity.

    b. Increased productivity, when followed by increased rewards, has been shown to produce increased satisfaction. Productivity is affected by many factors other than satisfaction; that is, there is no direct relationship between satisfaction and productivity.

    c. Job satisfaction has an economic importance only indirectly related to productivity. Satisfied workers exhibit lower rates of absenteeism and turnover, and reduced tardiness, apathy, and sabotage.

    d. Nevertheless, it remains a basic belief of the human relations position that satisfaction and productivity must bear some relationship despite the lack of empirical evidence.

12. **Goal-setting theory** is another attempt to explain motivation. According to Edwin Locke's goal-setting theory, specific, difficult goals to which the employee is committed provide the best motivation tool.

    a. Performance improves when goals are specific rather than general, difficult rather than easy, and self-set rather than imposed by others.

    b. Furthermore, feedback, especially self-generated feedback, also improves performance compared with lack of feedback.

    c. Commitment to goals, that is, a determination not to reduce or abandon them, and self-efficacy, that is, a belief in one's ability to accomplish the task, are additional qualities that result in better performance.

13. **Job Characteristics Model.** The JCM (developed by J.R. Hackman and G.R. Oldham) defines five core job characteristics and their relationship to behavioral outcomes.

    a. The first three of the following five job dimensions determine the meaningfulness of work.

        1) Skill variety
        2) Task identity (requires completion of a whole, identifiable unit of work)
        3) Task significance
        4) Autonomy (worker discretion in carrying out the work)
        5) Feedback

    b. High motivation, performance, and satisfaction and low turnover and absenteeism result when the worker views the job as important, feels responsible for outcomes as a result of autonomy, and knows how effectively (s)he performed because of clear feedback.

    c. The model computes a **motivating potential score** (MPS) as follows:

$$\left[\frac{\textit{Skill Variety} \times \textit{Task Identity} \times \textit{Task Significance}}{3}\right] \times \textit{Autonomy} \times \textit{Feedback}$$

14. **Behavior modification** is the management of environmental factors to encourage desirable behavior and to discourage undesirable behavior.

    a. Environmental factors include antecedents and consequences of behavior. Antecedents are cues that encourage but do not cause a given behavior. Barriers to good performance should be eliminated and replaced with helpful aids.

b. Consequences include the following:

1) **Positive reinforcement** provides rewards for certain responses. It focuses on desirable rather than undesirable behavior. Theorists regard positive reinforcement as the most effective approach.

a) Examples are the awarding of merit-based salary bonuses or paying on a sliding scale relative to production.

b) Continuous reinforcement rewards every occurrence of a desirable new behavior, and intermittent reinforcement provides occasional rewards for an established behavior.

c) Variable-interval schedules of intermittent reinforcement lead to better performance. Employees are more alert because of the uncertainty involved, and performance and reward are connected. Fixed-interval schedules of reinforcement do not clearly link performance and reward.

2) **Negative reinforcement** is the withdrawal of an existing unpleasant condition when the desired behavior occurs.

3) **Extinction** discourages a behavior by ignoring it (not reinforcing it).

4) **Punishment** discourages a behavior by immediately following it with a negative consequence.

15. **Equity theory** states that employee motivation is affected significantly by relative as well as absolute rewards. An employee compares the ratio of what (s)he receives from a job (outcomes such as pay or recognition) to what (s)he gives to the job (inputs such as effort, experience, ability, or education) with the ratios of relevant others.

a. If the ratios are equal, equity exists, but if they are unequal, equity tension exists, and the employee will be motivated to eliminate the tension.

b. The referent chosen (the employee's experience inside or outside the organization or the experiences of others inside or outside the organization) tends to be affected by the employee's job tenure, education, and salary level. For example, better-educated employees are more likely to make comparisons with outsiders, and longer-tenured employees may rely on coworkers.

c. Equity tension leads to changes in inputs or outcomes, distorted perceptions of one's effort or of the referent, choice of a different referent, or abandonment of the job.

16. **Cognitive evaluation theory** holds that intrinsic rewards (such as competence, responsibility, and achievement) tend to be reduced when extrinsic rewards (such as higher pay, promotion, and better working conditions) are provided for superior performance.

a. The reason may be that the individual perceives a loss of control over his/her behavior. However, research suggests that the negative effects of extrinsic rewards on motivation do not apply when a job provides either a very high or a very low level of intrinsic rewards. In the latter case, extrinsic rewards may actually increase intrinsic motivation.

17. Stop and review! You have completed the outline for this subunit. Study multiple-choice questions 10 through 30 beginning on page 370.

C. Leadership

1. Leadership is the act or process of influencing people so they will strive willingly toward the achievement of group goals.
   a. The classical position focused on the idea that authority, decision making, and responsibility may all be decentralized in the organization to some extent, but leadership is a characteristic of the individual's personality and cannot be subdivided.
   b. **The traitist approach** was characteristic of studies before 1949, in which attempts were made to identify traits possessed by leaders. Starting with the theory that leaders are born, not made, attempts were made to identify the physical, mental, and psychological traits of various leaders. The traitist approach has produced such a long list of leadership traits that, in effect, it identifies nothing. A few traits do seem to have significant correlation with a leader's effectiveness, however.
      1) Intelligence
      2) Maturity
      3) Social participation and interest
      4) Socioeconomic status (in comparison to nonleaders)
2. With so little useful guidance from the leader characteristics approach, behavior-oriented researchers examined **leader behavior** to see if leaders conducted themselves in certain ways.
   a. Styles of leadership are emphasized in behavioral approaches.
      1) These styles have been characterized as
         a) **Autocratic**. The manager dictates all decisions to the employees.
         b) **Consultative**. The manager takes the employee's view into account but still makes the decisions.
         c) **Participative** (also known as democratic). The employee has a definite input into decision making, and the manager must include subordinates' views in the decision.
            i) But not all employees are willing to participate.
         d) **Free-rein**. The employees make their own decisions.
      2) The behaviorists feel that leadership traits are not hereditary, except for physical characteristics like stature or health.
   b. **Employee vs. task orientation**. A greater concern for people than for task accomplishment (although a certain degree of task orientation is vital) is felt to be more productive. The leader must balance the personal needs of subordinates with task accomplishment.
   c. **Initiating structure vs. consideration** behavior. Two behavior patterns that are consistently found in the study of leadership are the initiation of structure and the initiation of consideration by the leader (production-centered versus employee-centered behavior).
      1) Initiating structure behavior is directed towards accomplishing tasks. Structure includes
         a) Defining duties
         b) Establishing procedures
         c) Planning and organizing the work

2) Consideration behavior is the establishment of a personal relationship between the leader and the subordinate. High consideration by the leader includes

   a) Warmth toward the employee as a person
   b) Psychological support for the employee
   c) Helpfulness with problems in the work

3) Both structure initiation and consideration behavior are present in all job situations, and the relative amounts of each must be appropriate to the situation.

   a) EXAMPLES:

      i) A highly structured situation (like assembly-line work) may respond negatively to further structure initiated by the manager but positively to increased consideration.

      ii) A manager of research and development may find the initiation of structure much more productive than increased consideration. Creative personnel working on a disorganized project may find a better-defined project plan much more satisfying than a demonstration of concern by the manager.

3. The modern view follows a **contingency approach** in looking for even better answers to the questions, "What is an effective leader?" and "How do we train and identify leaders?"

   a. According to Fred E. Fiedler's contingency theory, people become leaders not only because of personality attributes but also because of various situational factors and the interaction between the leaders and the situation.

      1) Thus, the right person at the right time may rise to a position of leadership if his/her personality and the needs of the situation complement each other. The same person might not become a leader in different circumstances because of failure to interact successfully with that situation.

      2) There are three dimensions to the contingency theory model:

         a) **Position power** is a function of the formal authority structure and is the degree to which the position held enables a leader to evaluate, reward, sanction, or promote the group members independent of other sources of power, such as personality or expertise.

         b) **Task structure** is how clearly and carefully the worker's responsibilities for various tasks are defined. Quality of performance is more easily controlled when tasks are clearly defined.

         c) **Leader-member relations** reflect the extent to which group members like and trust and are willing to follow a leader.

            i) Relationship to group members is the most important dimension from the leader's point of view, since position power and task structure may be largely under the control of the enterprise.

            ii) The "least preferred coworker" test is one way to assess the optimal arrangement of group members by asking the leader to rank possible subordinates from least to most preferred. Previously unrecognized biases may surface that the leader can evaluate and learn to deal with.

3) Fiedler's research showed two types of leaders:

a) Task-oriented style is most effective when the situation is very favorable or very unfavorable.

b) Relationship-oriented style is most effective in the middle, less extreme situations.

4) The most effective leadership style is contingent upon the definition of the three dimensions.

5) Leadership is therefore as much a responsibility of the organization's placement of leaders as it is of the leaders themselves. An organization should identify leadership situations and its managers' leadership styles and engineer the job to suit the manager if necessary.

b. According to Hersey and Blanchard's **situational leadership theory**, the appropriate leadership style depends on followers' maturity, which is their degree of willingness to be responsible for directing their behavior.

1) Maturity includes both job and psychological maturity. For example, experienced and knowledgeable workers who are highly motivated need little external direction.

2) The dimensions of leadership involve task and relationship behaviors.

a) One leadership style is participative. Task emphasis should be low, but relationship emphasis should be high. The leader's primary activities are facilitating and communicating, and decisions should be shared.

b) The delegating style does not emphasize tasks or relationships.

c) The selling style emphasizes both tasks and relationships.

d) A directive (telling) leadership style is characterized by a high task, low relationship emphasis.

c. **Path-goal theory** combines the research on initiating structure and consideration with expectancy theory.

1) According to path-goal theory, two groups of contingency factors affect the relationship between leadership behavior and outcomes (performance and satisfaction).

a) Environmental factors are those beyond subordinates' control (task structure, the formal authority system, and the work group).

b) Subordinate factors include the subordinate's locus of control, experience, and perceived ability.

2) A leadership style should be chosen that complements but does not duplicate the factors in the environment and is consistent with subordinates' characteristics.

a) The **directive** leader lets subordinates know what is expected of them, schedules work to be done, and gives specific guidance on how to accomplish tasks.

i) A directive style is most effective when the subordinate's locus of control is external, tasks are ambiguous or stressful, and substantial conflict exists in the work group. Thus, a directive style is appropriate when subordinates do not have high perceived ability or experience.

b) The **supportive** leader is friendly and shows concern for the needs of the subordinates.

i) Supportive style is best when tasks are highly structured and the authority relationships are clear and bureaucratic.

ii) This approach depends on people who want to work, grow, and achieve.

c) The **participative** leader consults with subordinates and uses their suggestions before making a decision.

i) Participative style is most useful when subordinates believe they control their own destinies, that is, when they have an internal locus of control. Such individuals may be resentful if they are not consulted.

d) The **achievement-oriented** leader sets challenging goals and expects subordinates to perform at their highest level.

i) Achievement-oriented leadership is appropriate when tasks are nonrepetitive and ambiguous and employee competence is high.

4. **Influence** is an attempt to change the behavior of others in the workplace, whether they are superiors, subordinates, or coworkers. The following categories of influence tactics have been identified:

   a. **Consultation** permits the other person(s) to participate in the decision or change.

   b. **Rational persuasion** tries to convince others by reliance on a detailed plan, supporting evidence, and reason.

   c. **Inspirational appeals** are calls to superordinate goals. They are appeals to emotions, values, or ideals.

   d. **Ingratiating tactics** attempt to raise the other person's self-esteem prior to a request.

   e. **Coalition tactics** seek the aid of others to persuade someone to agree.

   f. **Pressure tactics** involve intimidation, threats, and demands.

   g. **Upward appeals** are based on the formal or informal support of higher management.

   h. **Exchange tactics** entail an exchange of favors, a reminder of a past favor, or an offer of a personal sacrifice.

5. Stop and review! You have completed the outline for this subunit. Study multiple-choice questions 31 through 41 beginning on page 377.

D. Management and Organizational Development

1. **Management development** is a progressive process designed to improve the abilities of a manager. Higher-level managers are responsible for providing mentoring or coaching to their subordinates as part of their directing function.

   a. Managers benefit from the preparation and presentation to subordinates.
   b. Training provided by managers can be tailored to employees' needs and abilities.

2. Some of the techniques used include the following:
   a. **Planning a career progression**. The general path expected for a manager's progress in the enterprise is laid out in advance at the hiring or the first promotion. This schedule is geared to the short term rather than the long term. Advantages accrue from the increased knowledge of what is expected, both from the manager's point of view and from that of superiors.
   b. **Job rotation**. A manager's knowledge and skills are broadened when (s)he serves in a number of different capacities. Though popular with managers, this technique often suffers from lack of continuity, both for the subordinates and for superiors, and from confusion about the training process.
   c. **Formal management training programs**. Certain managerial positions, which are a regular part of the organizational structure, are designated for training purposes and are filled by a succession of managerial trainees.
      1) In-house training programs may be geared toward passing national certification examinations, e.g., the CIA, CMA, and CPA examinations.
   d. **Special assignments**. These appointments, such as acting manager or project management responsibilities, may be temporary.
   e. **Special training**
      1) Regional or national conferences give managers exposure to other ideas and approaches and develop skills in presentation and interaction.
      2) Continuing education may be necessary to maintain professional certification.
      3) Refresher courses are offered by professional groups, for example, the management development seminars offered by the American Management Association for practicing managers.
   f. **Mentoring** (coaching) entails the assignment of an experienced individual to advise and encourage a junior colleague.
3. Sensitivity training (also known as **encounter groups**, **T-group training**, or **laboratory training**) has been an effective tool in psychological therapy for many years.
   a. Sensitivity training has as its objective the development of **awareness** of the feelings of oneself and others.
   b. Techniques, especially adapted to managerial development, vary widely, but they have some common aspects.
      1) Groups of managers (not necessarily from the same department or even the same company) meet with a person trained in the techniques.
      2) There may be no agenda and little or no directive guidance.
      3) The group members interact and then gain an understanding of how they appear to others from the feedback they receive from the trainer and the rest of the group.
4. **Assessment centers** provide a technique for evaluation and/or selection of managers and are usually run by a highly trained and objective outside group that subjects managers and managerial candidates to a variety of tests and exercises.
5. **Organizational development (OD)** is a contemporary expression that refers to planned change in an organization. These changes are massive and long term. OD is an attempt to make earlier behavioral approaches (such as sensitivity training) more pragmatic and relevant to business situations.

a. It requires a commitment by top management to conscious, planned, directed, structured change, with special emphasis on behavioral issues. Moreover, the behavioral approach is the focal point in implementing any change.

b. Grid training is a popular method of organizational development.

1) This method was developed by Robert Blake and Jane Mouton who postulated two dimensions of managing on a 9 x 9 grid. The two dimensions are the

a) Concern for production on the X axis, and the
b) Concern for people on the Y axis.

2) Most people tend to be either too concerned with one while ignoring the other or not concerned enough about either.

3) Organizational development training develops maximum concern for both dimensions (a 9 by 9 manager).

6. Stop and review! You have completed the outline for this subunit. Study multiple-choice questions 42 and 43 beginning on page 380.

E. Management by Objectives (MBO)

1. MBO is a behavioral, communications-oriented, responsibility approach to self-direction.

a. MBO is based on the philosophy that employees

1) Want to work hard if they know what is expected
2) Like to understand what their jobs actually entail
3) Are capable of self-direction and self-motivation

b. MBO requires

1) Top management participation and commitment to the program. They must

a) Determine overall direction and objectives for the organization

b) Communicate these effectively in operational or measurable terms

c) Coordinate subordinate managers' goals with overall goals

d) Follow up at end of time period to reward performance and review problems

2) Integration of the objectives for all subunits into a compatible, balanced system directed toward accomplishment of the overall goals

3) Provisions for regular periodic reporting of performance toward attainment of the objectives

4) Free and honest communications between manager and subordinate

5) A commitment to a Theory Y philosophy on the part of managers

6) An organizational climate that encourages mutual trust and respect

2. The early definition of MBO was by **Peter Drucker** (1954). He emphasized that

a. Objectives are needed in every area where performance and results directly and vitally affect the survival and prosperity of the business.

b. The performance that is expected of the manager must be derived from the performance goals of the business.

c. A manager's performance should be measured by the contribution (s)he makes to the success of the enterprise.

d. Traditional systems were inadequate in fulfilling the two major requirements of a good performance appraisal program.

   1) Performance appraisals should identify good performers for rewards and promotions.

   2) Performance appraisals should serve as a feedback mechanism to show employees' strengths and weaknesses.

   3) Evaluations used as a basis for compensation frequently conflict with use as objective feedback, and, consequently, they become merely documents to justify pay or promotion decisions.

e. Traditional appraisals are inadequate because

   1) They focus on past events rather than future direction.

   2) Trait appraisals measure traits, not job performance.

   3) They focus on personal traits that are irrelevant to what an employee needs to know to correct actual job performance deficiencies (e.g., a poor score on the **trait** "appearance" may be of little use to an employee who is seeking information on job **behavior**).

   4) Traditional trait appraisals do not easily encourage the employee and the manager to communicate about job performance expectations, career development needs, or job context and objectives (how the subordinate's job fits into the big picture).

   5) Traditional appraisal systems encourage the manager to "look over the subordinates' shoulders to see how they are doing" rather than clarifying what to accomplish and letting them do it on their own.

f. MBO fulfills the need for a new method by

   1) Allowing employee self-direction with specific tasks and concrete feedback

   2) Encouraging the manager to be a facilitator rather than a director

   3) Promoting positive morale by allowing participation, good communication, mutual trust, and job autonomy

3. **The Steps Necessary to Implement an MBO Program**

   a. First, ask for the subordinate's own job objectives and the specific actions (s)he would like to take over the next time period to help reach those job objectives.

   b. Review the subordinate's goals and activities within the context of the goals at higher levels.

   c. When the subordinate's goals are at odds with upper-level goals, initiate a coaching session to review them.

      1) The review frequently represents the acid test of the MBO because the manager must avoid dictating the subordinate's goals if the spirit of participation is to be preserved.

      2) If the subordinate's goals are deemed by the supervisor to be inappropriate, and the subordinate cannot be **coached** out of them, the supervisor can either

         a) Let the subordinate learn by failing in doing the job his/her way, or
         b) Overrule on this particular issue.

3) Commitment to Theory Y, trust in subordinates, and the supervisor's job security (the confidence to allow subordinates still more latitude) will play important roles.

4) The clearer the definition of job objectives and organizational purposes and the greater the degree of trust and communication between supervisor and subordinate, the easier it is to avoid these dilemmas in implementing MBO.

d. Mutually set and agree on a realistic program of activities that can be accomplished by the end of the period.

e. Maintain flexibility during the period to accommodate unforeseen changes.

f. Review the results, analyzing and discussing differences, and using the discussion as learning and performance feedback (not as correctional, disciplinary, etc.).

g. Repeat the process to set new goals and objectives.

4. Stop and review! You have completed the outline for this subunit. Study multiple-choice questions 44 through 47 beginning on page 381.

F. Managing Human Resources

1. Human resource planning consists of forecasting future employment requirements. It includes the hiring, training, and monitoring of employees.

2. **Job analysis** is the first step. It entails interviewing employees about the way they accomplish their tasks, analyzing work flows, and studying the methods used to achieve work-unit objectives.

a. Has the nature of the job changed? If so, the job description should be rewritten.

b. If the job's nature remains the same, the job specifications should be written from the job description and sent to personnel to be advertised.

c. A **job description**, based on job analysis, should list basic duties. For higher-level positions, reporting relationships may also be included.

1) EXAMPLE: For an accounting clerk, the job description might include

a) Preparing payroll checks
b) Maintaining inventory ledgers
c) Preparing invoices

d. **Job specifications**, based on the job description, should list the abilities needed by a person hired for that job.

1) EXAMPLE: The job specifications for an accounting clerk might list

a) 10-key facility

b) Typing ability at a specified number of correct words per minute

c) Experience in a similar position for a specified number of years

d) Bondable

e) Education to a specified level and, perhaps, in specified types of courses

2) For other jobs, other factors may be pertinent:

a) Physical characteristics, e.g., strength, stamina

b) Personal characteristics, e.g., personality, communication skills

3. **Recruitment**

   a. Sources of personnel

      1) Advertising in media (e.g., newspapers)

      2) Word-of-mouth referral by current employees

      3) Walk-ins

      4) Internal job posting and computerized staff inventories of existing employees

      5) Targeted recruiting sources, e.g., colleges and universities

      6) Temporary placement and part-time employees

   b. Governmental constraints and restrictions on recruiting practice

      1) Title VII of the 1964 Civil Rights Act, including its subsequent amendments, prohibits discrimination on the basis of race, color, religion, sex, or national origin by private employers of 15 or more persons, unions, employment agencies, joint labor-management committees controlling apprenticeships or training programs, state and local governments, and educational institutions.

         a) Discrimination is permissible on the basis of a **bona fide occupational qualification**; e.g., clergy can be selected on the basis of religious faith.

         b) The Equal Employment Opportunity Commission has the right to bring discrimination suits against employers in federal courts.

      2) The Age Discrimination in Employment Act of 1967 prohibits discrimination on the basis of age (as amended in 1978). This act applies to the 40 and older age group.

      3) Governmental reviews evaluate compliance with employment law by checking

         a) Sources of employees recruited for each job category

         b) Advertising

         c) Estimates of employees needed for coming year

         d) Statistics on number of applicants processed by sex, race, etc., for each job category and level

      4) The following cannot be done in recruiting interviews:

         a) Make notation of sex

         b) Ask marital status (may ask after hiring for insurance purposes)

         c) Ask for number of children (may ask after hiring for insurance purposes)

         d) Ask for height and weight

         e) Ask for criminal record (only for security clearance)

         f) Ask type of military discharge

         g) Ask age

5) Summary of compliance criteria

a) Does the employment practice have an unequal impact on the groups covered by law?

b) Is the practice justified by job-related (bona fide occupational qualification) requirements or is it otherwise legally defensible as necessary to the organization?

4. Using **temporary or part-time workers** gives management the flexibility to adjust quickly to changing market conditions.

   a. Such workers can often be paid lower salaries and given fewer benefits than full-time workers.

   b. Disadvantages of hiring temporary or part-time workers include the lack of long-term benefits to the company from training programs and less employee loyalty to the firm.

   c. These workers can improve the morale of permanent employees, however, by relieving overtime pressures or by performing the more tedious and less desirable tasks.

      1) On the other hand, they may reduce the morale of permanent employees who might desire more overtime work or who might feel that their jobs are threatened.

   d. Leasing employees has a variety of administrative benefits because the lessor prepares payrolls, pays the employees, files tax returns, etc. (S)he also assumes liability for unemployment claims.

      1) However, the behavioral disadvantages of directly hiring temporary or part-time workers also apply to employee leasing.

5. **Employee Selection**. Requirements should come from job specifications developed from each job description and include education; experience; physical characteristics, e.g., strength and stamina; and personal characteristics, e.g., personality, confidence, and skills.

   a. All requirements, to be legal, must be based on their relationship to the ability to perform successfully in a specific job category.

6. **Employee Testing**. Testing applicants for jobs with quantifiable output (e.g., jobs requiring clerical skills or manual dexterity) is easier than testing for positions with a less tangible work product (e.g., public relations director or human resource manager).

   a. All tests must be validated in each organization and for minority and nonminority groups before they can be predictive of successful performance.

   b. Tests must be given to all applicants for the same job category.

   c. It is not easy or inexpensive to validate a test.

   d. Test validity is the capacity to measure accurately what it was designed to measure.

   e. Test reliability is the ability of a test to obtain the same scores in repeated administrations, regardless of validity.

   f. Lie detector tests and drug tests are currently significant issues. The validity and legality of these tests have not yet been determined.

7. **Orientation** is the introduction to the workplace. The employees get their first formal information about
    a. Overall organizational objectives
    b. Overall organizational chart, i.e., the pecking order
    c. Benefits, e.g.,
        1) Retirement plan
        2) Attendance regulations
        3) Vacation and sick leave
    d. Organizational procedures, e.g.,
        1) Grievance procedures
        2) Safety rules (e.g., fire drills, etc.)
8. **Training and Development**
    a. Training consists of organizational programs to prepare employees to perform currently assigned tasks (e.g., on-the-job training or formal off-site programs).
        1) On-the-job or experiential training, for example, by job rotation, apprenticeships, and mentoring arrangements, is usually less costly than off-the-job training but may disrupt the workplace and result in increased errors. It is suited to requisition of technical skills.
        2) Off-the-job training, for example, in classroom lectures, film study, and simulations, is well suited to development of problem solving and interpersonal abilities and to teaching of complex skills.
    b. Development includes organizational programs to prepare people to perform future tasks and acquire new skills.
        1) The focus is mostly on management and organizational development to develop human relations skills.
9. **Evaluation**
    a. An important aspect of management is the evaluation of employees.
        1) Evaluations are important to the employee, the employer, and the company as a whole.
        2) Evaluations provide an opportunity for growth of the employee and, when done properly, can be instrumental in the prevention of future disputes.
            a) Documentation must be complete, accurate, and consistent.
            b) Employees should be notified of appraisals and given an opportunity to discuss them.
            c) Different techniques are necessary to accommodate different employee performance levels.
    b. **Purposes of evaluation**
        1) Uses performance criteria to identify job-related abilities necessary to do the job
        2) Uses performance goals to help employees direct their energies toward what the organization expects without constant supervision
        3) Uses performance outcomes to allow employee satisfaction in knowing when jobs are completed and done well

4) Distinguishes effective from ineffective job performance

5) Helps employer and organization develop employee strengths and identify weaknesses

c. **Problems of evaluation**

1) Design of appraisal system can be faulty if the

a) Criteria for evaluations are poor or inappropriate.

b) Technique is cumbersome or not understood by users.

c) Criteria focus on wrong attributes causing emphasis on wrong things (e.g., personal appearance rather than job accomplishments).

d) Top management does not lend support.

2) Evaluation-based problems

a) **Halo effect**. Manager's judgment on one trait (either negative or positive) affects rating on other traits.

b) **Central tendency**. All personnel are rated within the same narrow range; e.g., "All my people are good."

c) **Recency effect**. Most recent behavior overshadows overall performance.

d) **Differing standards**. Some managers have stricter standards than others, making cross-departmental comparisons difficult.

e) **Personal bias**. Traits may not reflect actual job performance, so appraisal can be biased by the degree to which the manager likes the subordinate.

f) Traits like dependability or industriousness may have very little to do with the job expected of an employee and are too subjective to be measured.

g) Trait scales tend to equate subjectively both pertinent and nonperformance traits (e.g., quality of work and appearance get equal points toward total appraisal score on many scales).

h) The once-a-year process tends to affect the usefulness and accuracy of any job-related information.

i) According to **attribution theory**, people attempt to determine whether observed behavior is internally or externally caused.

i) Behavior that is unusual for a particular individual is perceived to be externally caused. If it is not unusual, causation is ordinarily perceived to be internal.

ii) If everyone in similar circumstances behaves in a certain way, causation is believed to be external. Otherwise, causation is deemed to be internal.

iii) However, biases may distort attributions.

- **Fundamental attribution error** is a bias in judgments about the behavior of other people. This bias is a tendency to overestimate internal factors and underestimate external factors.
- **Self-serving bias** is the tendency to attribute one's successes to internal factors (e.g., diligence and talent) and failures to external factors (e.g., bad luck).

d. **Major types of appraisals**

1) **Rating scales** on personal traits

2) **Management by objectives (MBO)** -- behavioral, communications-oriented, responsibility approach to employee self-direction

a) MBO is based on the philosophy that

i) Employees want to work hard if they know what is expected.
ii) Employees like to understand what their jobs actually entail.
iii) Employees are capable of self-direction and self-motivation.

3) **Critical incident technique** -- list of critical aspects of job which evaluator uses to evaluate employee performance

4) **Behaviorally anchored rating scales (BARS)** -- similar to critical incident technique in which descriptions of good and bad performance are developed for a number of specific job-related behaviors and then used for evaluation of employees

e. **Characteristics of effective evaluation systems**

1) Relevant. Criteria should be reliable and valid. They should relate to employee functions, that is, to activities over which the employees exert control.

2) Unbiased. Systems should be based on performance of job, not on unrelated personal characteristics.

3) Significant. Systems should focus on the important part of the job rather than whatever is convenient to evaluate. This avoids misdirection or confusion of employee effort.

4) Practical. System should be as objective, easy to use, clearly understood, and efficient as possible.

f. **Criteria for effective appraisal**

1) Employees must understand the appraisal.
2) They must feel the appraisal is fair.
3) They must feel it is important to them and their job.

g. A manager can make appraisals easier and more effective by being involved in employee affairs.

1) Spending a little time with each employee each day and offering praise as well as constructive criticism facilitates acceptance of appraisals.

10. **Compensation and benefits** are extrinsic rewards. They should satisfy individual needs, encourage positive expectations (see expectancy theory), be equitable, and be related to performance. Compensation and benefits take many forms, each with its own advantages and disadvantages. Cost and ease of administration are also considerations.

a. Hourly wages and annual salaries, including overtime and holiday pay

b. Sales commissions

c. Piece rate pay plans

d. Merit pay

e. Profit sharing

f. Sharing of productivity gains or cost savings

g. Payments for skill mastery or degrees earned

h. Stock-based compensation

i. Flextime, telecommuting, job sharing, compressed work weeks (e.g., a four-day, 10-hour-per-day week), and family and medical leave

j. Fringe benefits

k. Pensions and other postretirement employee benefits

l. Cafeteria plans offering individually designed packages of compensation and benefits

11. **Human Resource Planning**

    a. A human resource audit evaluates the department's compliance with laws and regulations, determines whether the department is run efficiently, and considers the company's recruitment and salary and benefit programs.

    b. It is a thorough analysis of the human assets of the organization that permits

        1) Scheduling of training to develop experienced staff as needed
        2) Appropriate promotion decisions
        3) Analysis of staffing needs

    c. Information should be compiled about employees' education, experience, work histories, and compensation histories.

    d. Human resource or human asset accounting attempts to measure the value, and the changes in value, of the organization's investment in human assets.

12. **Downsizing** results from organizational decline, changes in the business cycle, or business combinations. The objectives are cost reduction, improved efficiency, and higher profits.

    a. These purposes are often not achieved because many companies follow cycles of hiring, firing, and rehiring that do not yield the expected benefits to offset the harm to terminated employees, the loss of morale of the survivors, and the damage to communities.

    b. Downsizing also tends to have a disproportionate effect on women and members of minorities, who tend to be the last hired and first fired.

    c. The more enlightened view is that employees are not readily disposable commodities but rather valuable resources who should be terminated only as a last resort. This view seeks alternatives to involuntary termination.

        1) Redeployment involves retraining or transferring employees.

        2) Voluntary retirement programs offer accelerated retirement benefits, severance allowances, or other compensation.

        3) Employees may be shifted to lower-level positions.

        4) All employees may be asked to accept reduced hours or pay.

        5) Outplacement assists laid-off employees in finding new jobs.

        6) Federal law requires companies with 100 or more employees to give 60 days' notice of facilities' closings or layoffs.

13. Stop and review! You have completed the outline for this subunit. Study multiple-choice questions 48 through 60 beginning on page 382.

MULTIPLE-CHOICE QUESTIONS

A. Individual and Group Dynamics

1. Maslow's theory of motivation is based on a hierarchy of human needs. The need satisfied by greater income is

A. Self-actualization.

B. Safety.

C. Participation.

D. Authority.

The correct answer is (B). *(Publisher)*
REQUIRED: The need satisfied by greater income.
DISCUSSION: Maslow saw human needs as a hierarchy and held that lower-level needs (physiological and safety needs) must be satisfied before higher-level needs (acceptance by peers, esteem, self-actualization) can influence the individual. Safety needs involve protection not only from physical harm but also from economic insecurity. Job and income security help to satisfy the need for safety.
Answer (A) is incorrect because, according to Maslow, the highest need in the hierarchy is self-actualization. It is the desire to become what one is capable of becoming, to realize one's potential, and to accomplish to the limit of one's ability. Answers (C) and (D) are incorrect because neither is part of Maslow's hierarchy.

2. People with a high need for achievement usually do not

A. Perform best when they perceive risks are high.

B. Seek situations in which they can attain personal responsibility for problem solving.

C. Function effectively as salespeople.

D. Prefer frequent and unambiguous feedback.

The correct answer is (A). *(CIA, adapted)*
REQUIRED: The item characteristic of people with a high need for achievement.
DISCUSSION: People with a high need for achievement prefer tasks of intermediate difficulty. They want success or failure to be the result of their own actions. High achievers avoid easy tasks because of the lack of challenge and difficult tasks because of the low probability of success.
Answer (B) is incorrect because personal responsibility is a prerequisite for recognition of achievement. Answer (C) is incorrect because sales positions provide the individual autonomy, personal responsibility, rapid feedback, and opportunity for moderate challenge needed by achievers. Answer (D) is incorrect because frequent and unambiguous feedback allows high achievers to determine improvement.

3. A manager has a small team of employees, but each individual is self-motivated and could be termed a "high achiever." The manager has been given a particularly difficult assignment. Even for a high achiever, the probability that this job can be completed by one individual by the required deadline is low. Select the best course for the audit manager.

A. Assign one individual since high achievers thrive on high risks.

B. Assign two employees to moderate the risk of failure.

C. Assign all employees to ensure the risk of failure is low.

D. Ask company management to cancel the job.

The correct answer is (B). *(CIA, adapted)*
REQUIRED: The best course of action for a manager whose team consists of high achievers.
DISCUSSION: High achievers wish to do something better than it has been done before. According to McClelland's theory of needs, high achievers thrive when the job provides for personal responsibility, feedback, and moderate risks. They avoid very easy or very difficult tasks, and they do not like to succeed by chance. Accordingly, one high achiever should not be assigned a job when the probability of its successful completion is very low.
Answers (A), (C), and (D) are incorrect because high achievers perform best given moderate risks.

4. Which of the following statements is correct with respect to a change in values?

A. Values are neither stable nor enduring.

B. The process of questioning values will result in a change.

C. Values are not fixed, and when they change, they change quickly.

D. Values are established in early years and are unlikely to change.

The correct answer is (D). *(CIA, adapted)*
REQUIRED: The true statement about values.
DISCUSSION: Values are specific to each individual and involve moral and personal issues. They tend to be learned in childhood from parents, friends, and others. Values can be modified throughout life but ordinarily stay the same.
Answer (A) is incorrect because values are stable and enduring. Answer (B) is incorrect because questioning values may result in their reinforcement. Answer (C) is incorrect because values are relatively fixed and change only slowly.

5. Which of the following is not an advantage of teamwork compared with work performed by individuals?

A. Teams provide support to the team members.

B. Teams make decisions that are more easily accepted.

C. Teams provide a clear link between effort and outcome.

D. Teams control and discipline members.

The correct answer is (C). *(CIA, adapted)*

REQUIRED: The item that is not an advantage of teamwork.

DISCUSSION: In a culture that strongly emphasizes individual identity and competition, the preference tends to be for a clear link between effort and outcome. However, teams tend to submerge individual identity and responsibility and therefore to blur the link between individual effort and its results.

Answers (A), (B), and (D) are incorrect because teams support team members, make better decisions than individuals, and control and discipline members.

6. There has been an increased emphasis on group decision making in organizations. Which of the following statements has been found to hold true in studies of individual decision making as compared with group decision making? Individual decision making tends to

A. Be more conservative.

B. Evaluate more complete information.

C. Generate more alternatives.

D. Increase the perceived legitimacy of the decision.

The correct answer is (A). *(CIA, adapted)*

REQUIRED: The true comparison between individual and group decision making.

DISCUSSION: Group decision making is often characterized by greater acceptance of risk because of the dispersal of accountability. Individual decision making tends to be more conservative because accountability can be specifically assigned.

Answer (B) is incorrect because a group has greater resources of knowledge and experience than an individual. Answer (C) is incorrect because a group has a wider diversity of views and should be able to offer a wider range of solutions. Answer (D) is incorrect because group decisions are more likely to be accepted by those affected.

7. There are numerous factors that enhance or detract from a group's attractiveness and cohesiveness. Select the factor that enhances cohesiveness.

A. Favorable view from the outside-looking-in.

B. Wide variety of members.

C. A common threat in the environment.

D. Moderately large size.

The correct answer is (C). *(CIA, adapted)*

REQUIRED: The factor that enhances group cohesiveness.

DISCUSSION: Commitment to a group depends on its attractiveness and cohesiveness. The latter quality is the tendency of members to adhere to the group and resist outside influences. Factors that enhance group attractiveness and cohesiveness are prestige, status, a cooperative relationship, a high degree of interaction, small size, the similarity of members, a superior public image, and a common threat in the environment.

Answer (A) is incorrect because a favorable view from the outside is a definition of attractiveness. Answer (B) is incorrect because the similarity of members aids cohesiveness. Answer (D) is incorrect because a relatively small size enhances cohesiveness.

8. The key ingredient to group effectiveness is

A. Challenge.

B. Trust.

C. Norms.

D. Roles.

The correct answer is (B). *(CIA, adapted)*

REQUIRED: The key ingredient of group effectiveness.

DISCUSSION: Groups in the acceptance stage of group development tend to be effective and efficient. This stage is characterized by personal and mutual understanding, tolerance of individual differences, constructive conflict about substantive matters, realistic expectations about group performance, and acceptance of the authority structure. The resulting trust engenders cohesiveness and a free exchange of information between group members.

Answer (A) is incorrect because challenge and conflict within the group are threats to cohesion. Answer (C) is incorrect because norms are general standards of conduct for group members. They are important to group effectiveness, but violation of norms is not as immediately damaging as mistrust. Answer (D) is incorrect because a role is a social scheme for behavior in a specific position. All group members develop their roles as the group evolves.

9. A new production team has been formed by taking experienced high achievers from existing teams within the factory. The members of the new team have not been required to learn any new skills, and the machines used are identical to those used in their former teams. The team's production supervisor is a longtime employee of the organization but has not previously worked with any members of the new team. Despite the abilities and previous individual achievements of the individual team members, management is surprised by the mediocre performance of the new team. The best approach for the production supervisor to improve performance would be to

A. Increase pressure on the team through higher goals and reprimands.

B. Replace these individuals on the team.

C. Provide opportunities for the team members to socialize with each other.

D. Do nothing now because it is too soon to draw any conclusions.

The correct answer is (C). *(CIA, adapted)*

REQUIRED: The best approach for improving team performance.

DISCUSSION: As the team members work and socialize with each other, cohesiveness will be enhanced because of the opportunity to talk with each other, to discover commonalities, and to share experiences. However, performance may or may not improve as cohesiveness increases. Improvement is also contingent on the group's performance norms. A cohesive group enforces norms. Thus, if norms are high, greater cohesiveness should result in better performance.

Answer (A) is incorrect because external pressure sometimes increases group cohesiveness and improves performance. However, these team members do not know each other well, and they may perceive that the team will not respond adequately to adversity. Answer (B) is incorrect because group cohesiveness has not had sufficient opportunity to develop. Starting over will be counterproductive. Answer (D) is incorrect because cohesiveness will probably improve over time, but the supervisor can speed the process by encouraging social interaction.

B. Motivation

10. A Theory X manager most likely believes that employees

A. Require little supervision.

B. Are creative and imaginative.

C. Need direction and security.

D. Solve problems outside their immediate control.

The correct answer is (C). *(Publisher)*

REQUIRED: The characteristic a Theory X manager attributes to employees.

DISCUSSION: In the 1960s, Douglas McGregor developed two theories to describe the extremes of managers' views of human nature. Theory X is a negative view of people and the way they interact with the organization. Theory X assumes that people dislike work, must be threatened with punishment to work toward organizational objectives, require close supervision, avoid responsibility, and crave security.

Answers (A), (B), and (D) are incorrect because they are characteristics that McGregor's Theory Y and MBO managers attribute to their employees.

11. Frederick Herzberg postulated a two-factor theory of human behavior that included satisfiers and dissatisfiers. Which of the following is a dissatisfier?

A. Promotion to another position.

B. Salary.

C. Challenging work.

D. Responsibility.

The correct answer is (B). *(CIA, adapted)*

REQUIRED: The item that is a dissatisfier.

DISCUSSION: Frederick Herzberg's two-factor theory of human behavior postulates that there are two classes of factors in the job situation. Maintenance or hygiene factors (dissatisfiers) are those the presence of which will not especially motivate people but the absence of which will diminish performance. These factors are extrinsic to the work itself. They include supervision, working conditions, interpersonal relations, salary, and status. Motivational factors (satisfiers) are those the absence of which will not diminish performance but the addition or availability of which will motivate employees. Intrinsic to the work itself, these include achievement, recognition, challenging work, advancement, growth in the job, and responsibility.

Answer (A) is incorrect because recognition and status are satisfiers. Answer (C) is incorrect because challenging work is a satisfier. Answer (D) is incorrect because responsibility is a satisfier.

12. Both Maslow and Herzberg have developed popular motivational theories. Which statement best distinguishes Herzberg's theory?

A. Job performance improves as job satisfaction increases.

B. Job performance improves as physiological needs are met.

C. Job esteem improves as physiological needs are met.

D. Job esteem improves as job satisfaction increases.

The correct answer is (A). *(CIA, adapted)*

REQUIRED: The statement that best distinguishes Herzberg's theory.

DISCUSSION: Frederick Herzberg's two-factor theory of human behavior postulates that there are two classes of factors in the job situation. Maintenance or hygiene factors are those whose presence will not especially motivate people but whose absence will diminish performance. These factors are extrinsic to the work itself. They include supervision, working conditions, interpersonal relations, salary, and status. Motivational factors are those the absence of which will not diminish performance but the addition or availability of which will motivate employees. Intrinsic to the work itself, these include achievement, recognition, challenging work, advancement, growth in the job, and responsibility.

Answer (B) is incorrect because physiological needs are at the base of Maslow's hierarchy of needs. Answer (C) is incorrect because Maslow's theory is that higher needs emerge as lower needs are met. Answer (D) is incorrect because esteem and satisfaction are almost synonymous.

13. Some behavioral models stress employee participation as a key to motivation. A limitation of the participative approach is

A. Workers are intrinsically lazy and must be driven.

B. A number of dissatisfiers must be present in order for the approach to work.

C. It is difficult to elicit the participation of all employees.

D. Unresolvable conflicts arise when a mature, capable, creative person joins a structured, demanding, and limiting organization.

The correct answer is (C). *(CIA, adapted)*

REQUIRED: The limitation of the participative approach.

DISCUSSION: For a participative management approach to succeed, the parties must have sufficient time, the issues must be relevant to employees' interests, employees must have the abilities (training and communication skills) to participate, and the company culture should support participation. Accordingly, a limitation of the participative approach is that it is unlikely that all employees are willing to participate in decision making.

Answer (A) is incorrect because the participative approach assumes that workers are positively motivated. Answer (B) is incorrect because the presence of dissatisfiers is not consistent with the participative approach. Answer (D) is incorrect because such conflicts arise when the needs of individuals are not integrated with the needs of the organization.

14. Job enrichment is a motivational approach used by management that

A. Emphasizes the need for close supervision.

B. Is based on Maslow's analysis of survival needs.

C. Is based on Herzberg's analysis of factors extrinsic to the work.

D. Applies the principle of worker participation.

The correct answer is (D). *(Publisher)*

REQUIRED: The true statement about job enrichment.

DISCUSSION: Job enrichment increases the scope of boring, repetitive tasks by using more of the employee's skills and allowing the employee more power to make decisions concerning the job, such as order of tasks, etc. Thus, it encourages worker participation in decisions previously made by management.

Answer (A) is incorrect because job enrichment is based on the assumption that employees who have qualitatively improved jobs need less supervision. Answer (B) is incorrect because survival needs are at the bottom of Maslow's hierarchy. Job enrichment seeks to meet the higher-level needs (affiliation, esteem, self-actualization). Answer (C) is incorrect because the intrinsic factors (challenge, growth, responsibility, etc.) are relevant to job enrichment.

15. Job design involves not only the intentional planning of the characteristics of a job but also of the work environment. The purpose is to increase workers' intrinsic job motivation so as to improve performance. It is an approach that explicitly considers workers' ego and social needs. The aspect of job design that should have the greatest motivational effect is

A. Job enlargement.

B. Job rotation.

C. Job enrichment.

D. Job simplification.

The correct answer is (C). *(Publisher)*

REQUIRED: The method of job design that should have the greatest motivational effect.

DISCUSSION: Job enrichment is an attempt to apply the findings of Herzberg (two-factor theory of behavior), Maslow (hierarchy of human needs), Likert (participation), and McGregor (Theories X and Y) by structuring the job so that each worker participates in the planning and controlling so as to maximize the satisfaction of both social and ego needs and avoid the disadvantages of routine, highly specialized work. Job enrichment includes allowing and encouraging more worker discretion in deciding work methods, work sequence, and work pace. It encourages interactions between workers, gives workers a feeling of personal responsibility for their tasks, makes sure workers understand how their tasks contribute to the finished product, provides feedback on job performance, and involves workers in changes in the physical aspects of the work environment.

Answer (A) is incorrect because job enlargement increases the number of tasks assigned to one worker but does not necessarily make those tasks more challenging or interesting. Answer (B) is incorrect because job rotation merely shifts workers among different jobs. Answer (D) is incorrect because job simplification clearly defines and may reduce the complexity of tasks through standardization of the job.

16. Job enlargement is typified by

A. Horizontal loading of the job.

B. Vertical loading of the job.

C. Increased worker control of tasks.

D. More rapid performance feedback.

The correct answer is (A). *(Publisher)*

REQUIRED: The characteristic of job enlargement.

DISCUSSION: Job enlargement is a quantitative (horizontal) extension of the job. It does not necessarily involve any greater worker control, responsibility, or challenge. An example is job rotation through assignment to duties requiring similar skills.

Answer (B) is incorrect because vertical loading is a term used in management literature to describe qualitative job enhancement (enrichment). It entails greater control and responsibility and increased chances for growth. Answers (C) and (D) are incorrect because each is typical of job enrichment.

17. In many jobs, excessive specialization can eventually lead to poor motivation, boredom, and alienation. In order to cope with the potential problems in such a situation, managers should

A. Focus on their employees' higher-level needs in order to help them achieve self-actualization.

B. Remove dissatisfiers such as low salary, bad supervision, lack of job security, and poor working conditions.

C. Implement an optimal organizational rewards system and provide all needed training to keep employees up to date on technology.

D. Change the jobs to fit the employees' needs or rotate employees to jobs that satisfy their needs.

The correct answer is (D). *(CIA, adapted)*

REQUIRED: The approach to cope with employee boredom, poor motivation, and alienation.

DISCUSSION: Job design theories of motivation specifically address the issue of overspecialization. These theories focus on the match between the person and the job as the key to motivation. The recommendation for dealing with the potential problems of overspecialization and boredom is either to enrich the job or to move the employee to a job that provides the appropriate level of challenge.

Answer (A) is incorrect because focusing on employees' higher-level needs in order to help them achieve self-actualization is a recommendation based on Maslow's hierarchy of needs that does not address the job itself as a source of motivation. Answer (B) is incorrect because removing dissatisfiers does not address the issue of overspecialization, although it may remove some of the obstacles to motivation. Answer (C) is incorrect because implementing an optimal organizational rewards systems and providing extensive training to keep employees up to date do not address the job and the issue of overspecialization.

18. The basic underlying principle of the quality-of-work-life view of motivation suggests that an organization should unlock the creative potential of its people by

A. Involving them in decisions affecting their lives and providing them with more control over their work.

B. Providing fair and equitable reward systems that are clearly linked to the employees' effort and performance.

C. Focusing on employees' higher-level needs.

D. Using job enrichment techniques that increase skill variety, task identity and significance, autonomy, and feedback.

The correct answer is (A). *(CIA, adapted)*

REQUIRED: The way an organization should unlock the creative potential of its people.

DISCUSSION: According to Robert Guest (*Harvard Business Review*, Vol. 57, July-August 1979, pp. 76-77), the quality of work life (QWL) is "a process by which an organization attempts to unlock the creative potential of its people by involving them in decisions affecting their lives." The domain of QWL includes pay, employee benefits, job security, alternative work schedules, occupational stress, participation, and workplace democracy.

Answer (B) is incorrect because providing fair and equitable reward systems that are clearly linked to the employees' effort and performance is one of the keys to motivation. However, it is merely one part of the domain of QWL. Answer (C) is incorrect because focusing on employees higher-level needs relates to Maslow's needs hierarchy, not QWL concepts. Answer (D) is incorrect because the emphasis of QWL is not on job enrichment but on participation and workplace democracy.

19. Victor Vroom's expectancy theory is based on the intuitively appealing idea that people have expectations of rewards derived from their unique personal motive structure, from their beliefs as to what are important rewards to them, and from their expectations of getting these incentives if they exert effort. The perceived equity of rewards leads to satisfaction or dissatisfaction and thus feeds into the next cycle's expectancies. For example, an employee who believes (s)he is compensated less well than another worker performing the same task with the same degree of skill may become dissatisfied. An important concept in the expectancy theory is

A. Theory X and Theory Y.

B. Motivation = Valence × Expectancy.

C. The two-factor theory of behavior.

D. The management grid.

The correct answer is (B). *(Publisher)*

REQUIRED: The important concept in the expectancy theory.

DISCUSSION: Victor Vroom's expectancy theory holds that the force with which an individual is motivated is a function of the valence of a motivator (whether it has a positive or negative value to the individual) and the expectancy, which is that individual's estimation of the probability that a particular action will lead to a desired outcome. Thus, motivation equals the valence times the expectancy.

Answer (A) is incorrect because Theory X and Theory Y were used by McGregor to signify the extremes of managers' beliefs about employee conduct. Answer (C) is incorrect because Herzberg believed that maintenance factors (such as wages) must be present to avoid diminished performance but that motivational factors (such as challenge and recognition) are necessary to stimulate better performance. Answer (D) is incorrect because the grid approach arrays two dimensions of managing (concern for production and concern for people) on a 9-by-9 grid.

20. As a manager, you should be striving for a high level of job satisfaction for your staff for all the following reasons except

A. A happy, satisfied worker is a more productive worker.

B. High job satisfaction results in lower turnover.

C. Dissatisfied employees are less healthy.

D. None of the answers are correct.

The correct answer is (A). *(CIA, adapted)*

REQUIRED: The item that is not a reason to strive for high employee job satisfaction.

DISCUSSION: Studies have shown that worker satisfaction does not necessarily lead to improved productivity. In fact, studies indicate that it is more likely that a productive worker is a happy worker.

Answer (B) is incorrect because satisfaction is negatively correlated with turnover. However, level of performance is a moderating factor on the relationship. Superior performers have lower turnover in part because management makes stronger efforts to retain them. Answer (C) is incorrect because job satisfaction is directly correlated with good health and longevity. Answer (D) is incorrect because a happy worker is not necessarily a more productive worker.

21. According to the behavioral theory of management,

A. Employees are motivated to fulfill needs.

B. Morale problems are not goal related.

C. Compensation is a universal motivator.

D. Productivity is not correlated with job satisfaction.

The correct answer is (A). *(Publisher)*

REQUIRED: The behavioral theory of management.

DISCUSSION: The behavioral theory of management holds that all people (including employees) have complex needs, desires, and attitudes. The fulfillment of needs is the goal toward which employees are motivated. Effective leadership matches need-fulfillment rewards with desired behavior (tasks) that accomplishes organizational goals.

Answer (B) is incorrect because management's role in the directing process is to motivate people to contribute toward accomplishment of organizational goals. Answer (C) is incorrect because, although management theories differ as to the motivational value of wages, compensation is not a motivator for all persons at all times. Answer (D) is incorrect because, while research has indicated that satisfaction and productivity are not directly related, behavioral theorists believe that they must have some relationship.

22. Two managers were discussing the merits of goal setting to improve employee performance. One manager felt that specific goals should not be established and that, to provide for flexibility, only generalized goals should be used. The other manager felt that specific, difficult goals produce the best results. As the discussion continued, other methods of goal setting were identified. Select the best method for setting goals.

A. The manager should provide generalized goals.

B. The manager should select specific, difficult goals.

C. The employee should develop generalized goals and obtain management concurrence.

D. The employee should develop specific, difficult goals and obtain management concurrence.

The correct answer is (D). *(CIA, adapted)*

REQUIRED: The best method for setting goals.

DISCUSSION: According to Edwin Locke's goal-setting theory, specific, difficult goals to which the employee is committed provide the best motivation tool. Performance improves when goals are specific rather than general, difficult rather than easy, and self-set rather than imposed by others. Feedback, especially self-generated feedback, also improves performance compared with lack of feedback. Commitment to goals, that is, a determination not to reduce or abandon them, and self-efficacy, that is, a belief in one's ability to accomplish the task, are additional qualities that result in better performance.

Answers (A) and (C) are incorrect because specific, difficult goals provide more motivation than generalized goals. Answer (B) is incorrect because employee involvement in goal setting provides better assurance that employees will be committed to the goals.

23. According to management literature, worker absenteeism, turnover, and error rates are likely to be greatest

A. When workers alternate in performing different jobs.

B. In simplified assembly-line jobs.

C. In job sharing situations.

D. When flexible working hours are provided.

The correct answer is (B). *(Publisher)*

REQUIRED: The instance in which worker turnover, absenteeism, etc., are greatest.

DISCUSSION: The literature tends to support the theory that, while job satisfaction has an economic importance only indirectly related to productivity, satisfied workers exhibit lower rates of absenteeism, turnover, tardiness, apathy, and sabotage. Organizations with more organic or flexible organization structures may use more of the worker's skills and present a greater variety of work challenges, thus improving morale. Mass production technology usually involves repetitious, boring tasks.

Answers (A), (C), and (D) are incorrect because each should improve job satisfaction.

24. A production manager is working on a plan to increase employee motivation at a local plant by comparing results of employee interviews to those from employees at a higher-performing plant. The manager is puzzled about the results of two sets of employee interviews. The employees interviewed performed identical jobs. Local employees thought their jobs were boring and unfulfilling while the other plant's employees were very satisfied. Even new employees at the local plant indicated they quickly lost enthusiasm. Identify the primary element the manager must overcome to enhance performance.

A. Negative job perception.

B. Inadequate job autonomy.

C. Lack of skill variety.

D. Low task significance.

The correct answer is (A). *(CIA, adapted)*

REQUIRED: The element to be overcome to enhance performance.

DISCUSSION: The tasks and environment for both sets of employees are the same. Thus, the individuals' perceptions are the key to the problem.

Answers (B), (C), and (D) are incorrect because both sets of employees have the same degree of autonomy, exhibit the same skill variety, and perform the same tasks.

25. Which of the following is not an example of positive reinforcement of behavior?

A. Paying a bonus to employees who had no absences for any 4-week period.

B. Giving written warnings after only every other absence.

C. Assigning a mentor to each employee.

D. Having a lottery every month in which 10% of the employees with no absences receive a $200 bonus.

The correct answer is (B). *(CIA, adapted)*

REQUIRED: The action not an example of positive reinforcement.

DISCUSSION: Negative reinforcement removes an unpleasant condition when the desired behavior occurs, whereas positive reinforcement rewards the desired behavior. Thus, attending class is reinforced by the removal of something unpleasant, i.e., the receipt of a written warning. Because a warning is given after every other absence, the reinforcement is intermittent, not continuous.

Answer (A) is incorrect because paying a bonus is a positive reinforcement. Answer (C) is incorrect because assigning a mentor is a positive reinforcement. The firm is attempting to link each individual with a positive role model. Answer (D) is incorrect because holding a lottery is an intermittent positive reinforcement.

26. The punishing of employees is made less effective by

A. Stating the offending behavior specifically.

B. Postponing the start of disciplinary procedures.

C. Permitting employees to challenge their culpability.

D. Focusing the discussion on the offending behavior instead of the offender.

The correct answer is (B). *(CIA, adapted)*

REQUIRED: The action that renders the discipline process less effective.

DISCUSSION: Effective discipline requires immediate corrective action to eliminate the negative effects of the undesirable employee conduct and to establish and reinforce appropriate behavior. Delay merely invites more serious consequences. Moreover, the punishment should be commensurate with the offense, and the employee should clearly perceive the relationship between the punishment and the behavior.

Answer (A) is incorrect because stating the undesirable behavior clarifies for the employee the link between conduct and consequences. Answer (C) is incorrect because, in U.S. legal culture, the accused has the right to be heard in his/her defense. Answer (D) is incorrect because focusing on the offense rather than the offender is less likely to engender fear and resentment on the part of the employee.

27. A manager believes that positive reinforcement is the most appropriate way to deal with employees. Which of the following actions demonstrates the principle of positive reinforcement?

A. Employees are given 2-day suspension without pay if errors exceed a predefined level.

B. Employees are praised when the detected error rate in their work stays below a predefined level.

C. Time budgets, which have forced employees to rush and consequently make errors, are eliminated.

D. Employees are not required to work overtime if errors stay below a predefined level.

The correct answer is (B). *(CIA, adapted)*

REQUIRED: The action that demonstrates positive reinforcement.

DISCUSSION: Positive reinforcement is a behavior modification technique that provides rewards for certain responses. It focuses on desirable rather than undesirable behavior. The practice of praising employees when the detected error rate in their work stays below a predefined level demonstrates positive reinforcement.

Answer (A) is incorrect because suspending employees is punishment. Answer (C) is incorrect because eliminating time budgets is extinction, which is the elimination of reinforcement that is maintaining a behavior. Answer (D) is incorrect because not requiring employees to work overtime is negative reinforcement, which is the elimination of something unpleasant when a desired behavior occurs.

28. When supervising employees, the behavior most likely to attain long-term positive results for a manager would be to

A. Discipline employees immediately using oral reprimands, written warnings, and temporary suspensions.

B. Hold weekly meetings during which employees are reminded of work procedures and are praised for the week's accomplishments.

C. Praise employees on a random schedule and link rewards to performance.

D. Tell employees that working overtime now will result in a better evaluation in 6 months.

The correct answer is (C). *(CIA, adapted)*

REQUIRED: The supervisory behavior most likely to have long-term positive results.

DISCUSSION: Variable-interval schedules of reinforcement lead to higher performance. Employees are more alert because of the uncertainty involved, and performance and reward are connected.

Answer (A) is incorrect because punishment leads only to short-term suppression of the behavior and may cause the employee to avoid the manager, who is seen as punishing rather than helpful. Answer (B) is incorrect because fixed-interval reinforcement schedules do not clearly link performance and rewards. Answer (D) is incorrect because 6 months is too long an interval for linking performance and reward.

29. Which of the following conditions would motivate employees to improve performance under a merit pay system?

A. Ideal goals are stressed.

B. The company's culture emphasizes outstanding performance.

C. Different levels of performance have minimal differences in pay.

D. Job descriptions are invariably set with the required tasks clearly outlined.

The correct answer is (B). *(Publisher)*

REQUIRED: The condition that would best motivate employees under a merit pay system.

DISCUSSION: A merit pay system rewards good conduct or behavior with salary increases. To motivate employees under this system, management should be visibly committed to the system, develop a culture that emphasizes above-average performance, implement a policy of following up on unacceptable performance reviews, and establish an employee appeal process for unfavorable reviews.

Answer (A) is incorrect because an emphasis on currently attainable goals better motivates employees under a merit pay system. Answer (C) is incorrect because a significant difference in pay for different levels of performance would motivate employees to improve performance. Answer (D) is incorrect because employees are more motivated when job descriptions are frequently reviewed and opinions are heard.

30. An employee with little educational background but many years of experience knows that others at the same level receive higher pay because of educational qualifications. He is often asked for help by others because of his years of experience. The most likely behavioral effect is that the employee will

A. Become less productive.

B. Continue to help the other, more educated employees.

C. Request a transfer.

D. Seek a new job.

The correct answer is (A). *(Publisher)*

REQUIRED: The effect on an employee of believing that performance is not equitably rewarded.

DISCUSSION: When an employee is aware that others at the same level are paid more because of superior education rather than performance, the perceived inequity is likely to have several effects; e.g., (s)he is likely to become less productive, be less cooperative, have a negative effect on subordinates' output, and be reluctant to help colleagues.

Answer (B) is incorrect because the employee will probably be reluctant to help colleagues since they have higher salaries. Answers (C) and (D) are incorrect because an employee whose leading attribute is long experience with the company is more likely to reduce his/her productivity than to seek possibly inferior employment elsewhere.

C. Leadership

31. According to the contingency theory of leadership, a manager will be most effective when (s)he

A. Consistently initiates structure.

B. Adapts his/her style to specific circumstances.

C. Is task-oriented.

D. Is relationship-oriented.

The correct answer is (B). *(Publisher)*

REQUIRED: The most effective management approach according to contingency theory.

DISCUSSION: Fred E. Fiedler's contingency theory of management holds that no single style of directing is best for all occasions. A successful director (leader) must, for each situation, balance his/her formal authority, the task structure, and the leader's relationships with the pertinent group members.

Answers (A) and (C) are incorrect because a relationship (employee)-oriented approach may be preferable when tasks are highly structured. Answer (D) is incorrect because, when tasks are ill-defined, the more effective manager may be one who concentrates on defining and organizing the jobs to be done rather than on motivating employees.

32. Leadership situations vary with regard to the degree to which the leader can determine what subordinates will do, how they will do it, and what the results will be. According to Fiedler's contingency theory, a leader with a relationship-oriented management style will be most effective when (s)he exerts

A. Great control.

B. Moderate control.

C. Little control.

D. Great or little control.

The correct answer is (B). *(Publisher)*

REQUIRED: The situation in which a relationship-oriented management style will be most effective.

DISCUSSION: A relationship-oriented manager is employee centered. His/her self-esteem is strongly affected by personal interactions with subordinates. Fiedler indicated that such a manager is most effective when not faced with the extremes of high or low control situations. High control follows from strong position power, a structured task, and good leader-member relations. A low control situation has just the opposite characteristics. In a high-control environment, a concern for personal relations may be unimportant. In a low-control situation, the relationship-oriented leader may be unable to provide the needed task structuring. Thus, the moderate control situation is best. An example is an assembly-line situation (a structured task) in which leader-member relations are poor.

Answers (A), (C), and (D) are incorrect because the task-oriented leader is least effective in these situations.

33. If a supervisor uses a supportive management approach, evidenced by positive feelings and concern for subordinates, a problem might result because

A. An approach based on pure power makes it difficult to motivate staff.

B. This approach depends on material rewards for the worker.

C. This approach depends on people who want to work, grow, and achieve.

D. The manager must believe in the teamwork approach.

The correct answer is (C). *(CIA, adapted)*

REQUIRED: The problem that could result from using a supportive management approach.

DISCUSSION: Supportive management techniques orient workers toward performance rather than obedience or happiness. The leader should have positive feelings for his/her employees and should attempt to encourage participation and involvement. This approach is effective when used with employees who are motivated to work, improve themselves and their abilities, and accomplish goals.

Answer (A) is incorrect because an approach based on pure power is an autocratic style of leadership, not a supportive approach. Answer (B) is incorrect because the custodial model depends on material rewards for the worker. This model is predicated on the belief that a happy worker is a productive worker. Answer (D) is incorrect because the manager's beliefs are not sufficient. The workers must also believe in the system.

Questions 34 through 37 are based on the following information. The following questions present scenarios in which a manager needs to decide what leadership style to use to obtain employee satisfaction and effective employee performance. For the purposes of these questions, the manager has a choice of four styles.

- The directive leader lets subordinates know what is expected of them, schedules work to be done, and gives specific guidance on how to accomplish tasks.
- The supportive leader is friendly and shows concern for the needs of the subordinates.
- The participative leader consults with subordinates and uses their suggestions before making a decision.
- The achievement-oriented leader sets challenging goals and expects subordinates to perform at their highest level.

34. The workers in a factory have been told that their machines are obsolete and will be replaced by new, computer-assisted machines. The workers must be retrained and are eager to learn everything about the new machines. The manager was recently hired from a company where the new machines were extensively used and is very familiar with them. In this case, what is the best leadership style for the manager?

A. Directive.

B. Supportive.

C. Participative.

D. Achievement-oriented.

The correct answer is (A). *(CIA, adapted)*

REQUIRED: The best leadership style for the manager when workers must be retrained and are eager to learn.

DISCUSSION: According to path-goal theory, two groups of contingency factors affect the relationship between leadership behavior and outcomes (performance and satisfaction): environmental factors beyond subordinates' control (task structure, the formal authority system, and the work group) and subordinate factors. The latter include the subordinate's locus of control, experience, and perceived ability. A leadership style should be chosen that complements but does not duplicate the factors in the environment and is consistent with subordinates' characteristics. A directive style is most effective when the subordinate's locus of control is external, tasks are ambiguous or stressful, and substantial conflict exists in the work group. Thus, a directive style is appropriate when subordinates do not have high perceived ability or experience.

Answer (B) is incorrect because subordinates who are neither competent nor confident are best led using the directive style. Answer (C) is incorrect because subordinates with an internal locus of control need a leader with a participative style. Answer (D) is incorrect because achievement-oriented leadership is appropriate when tasks are nonrepetitive and ambiguous and employee competence is high.

35. A production team has been together for several years and has worked well together. However, severe arguments have recently occurred between two members of the group, and other members have begun to take sides. This problem has had a negative effect on production performance. The best leadership style for the manager in this situation is

A. Directive.

B. Supportive.

C. Participative.

D. Achievement-oriented.

The correct answer is (A). *(CIA, adapted)*

REQUIRED: The best leadership style for the manager given substantive internal conflict.

DISCUSSION: Directive leadership provides highest subordinate satisfaction when a team encounters substantive internal conflict. Thus, directive leadership is the appropriate complement to the environmental factors. The leader should intervene to compensate for the stress and strife in the workplace.

Answer (B) is incorrect because supportive style is best when tasks and authority relationships are highly structured. Answer (C) is incorrect because participative style is most useful when subordinates believe they control their own destinies. Answer (D) is incorrect because achievement-oriented leadership is appropriate when tasks are nonrepetitive and ambiguous and employee competence is high.

36. The manager of a team of actuaries has been asked to develop the basic pricing structure for a new health insurance product. The team has successfully designed other pricing structures in recent years. The manager was assigned to the team 6 months ago. What is the best leadership style for the manager of this team?

A. Directive.

B. Supportive.

C. Participative.

D. Achievement-oriented.

The correct answer is (C). *(CIA, adapted)*

REQUIRED: The best leadership style for a new manager of a team that has successfully completed similar projects.

DISCUSSION: Participative style is most useful when subordinates believe they control their own destinies, that is, when they have an internal locus of control. Such individuals may be resentful if they are not consulted.

Answer (A) is incorrect because directive leadership provides highest subordinate satisfaction when a team encounters substantive internal conflict, when tasks are ambiguous, and when subordinates' locus of control is external. Answer (B) is incorrect because supportive style is best when tasks are highly structured and the authority relationships are clear and bureaucratic. Answer (D) is incorrect because achievement-oriented style will increase subordinates' expectations that high performance will result from their best efforts.

37. A manager in a government agency supervises a section of clerical employees who review license applications for approval or denial. The clerical jobs are well defined procedurally and are covered by government regulations. In this case, what is the best leadership style for the manager?

A. Directive.

B. Supportive.

C. Participative.

D. Achievement-oriented.

The correct answer is (B). *(CIA, adapted)*

REQUIRED: The best leadership style for the manager of clerical workers.

DISCUSSION: Supportive style is best when tasks are highly structured and the authority relationships are clear and bureaucratic.

Answer (A) is incorrect because supportive style is best when tasks are highly structured and the authority relationships are clear and bureaucratic. Answer (C) is incorrect because participative style is most useful when subordinates believe they control their own destinies. Answer (D) is incorrect because achievement-oriented leadership is appropriate when tasks are nonrepetitive and ambiguous and employee competence is high.

38. A manager implementing the directive leader approach should

A. Closely supervise each employee.

B. Display confidence in each employee's ability.

C. Work with the employee when developing goals.

D. Clearly signal that the employee is expected to be successful.

The correct answer is (A). *(Publisher)*

REQUIRED: The action that should be taken by a manager using the directive leader approach.

DISCUSSION: The situational approach to leadership (called path-goal theory) allows a manager to choose one of four approaches for implementing his/her leadership style. One of these is the directive leader approach in which a manager provides close guidance to the employee through the use of specific rules, policies, and procedures.

Answers (B), (C), and (D) are incorrect because these actions would be taken when implementing the achievement-oriented leader approach.

39. Which of the following is a benefit of implementing the achievement-oriented leader approach rather than the directive leader approach?

A. Employee development is enhanced.

B. The structured environment allows employees to better achieve the organization's goals.

C. Closer supervision is provided for those who perform better in a structured work atmosphere.

D. Employees have more opportunities to develop creativity and meet challenges.

The correct answer is (D). *(Publisher)*

REQUIRED: The benefit of using the achievement-oriented leader approach.

DISCUSSION: The benefits to the company of the achievement-oriented leader approach include greater employee confidence and commitment, more employee decision making, increased employee creativity, more challenging objectives, and reduced supervision for employees who work best independently.

Answer (A) is incorrect because employee development is also enhanced under the directive leader approach. Answers (B) and (C) are incorrect because these benefits result from the directive leader approach. A structured environment and close supervision are not characteristics of the achievement-oriented leader approach.

40. Rupert is a manager who believes that his department's most valuable resource is the employees' time. He enforces a set of rigid rules for employees. A characteristic of this leadership style is that

A. Employees are encouraged to participate in decision making.

B. Personal interaction among employees is limited.

C. Organizational objectives are coordinated with each employee's goals.

D. The manager's perceptions are similar to McGregor's Theory Y.

The correct answer is (B). *(Publisher)*

REQUIRED: The characteristic of a leadership style based on the importance of time and a set of rigid rules.

DISCUSSION: The characteristics of a leadership style based on deadlines and strict rules include an emphasis on relatively inflexible congruence with the organization's overall goals, perceptions related to McGregor's Theory X, and limitations on interaction and communication among employees.

Answer (A) is incorrect because employee participation is decreased by this leadership style. Answer (C) is incorrect because organizational goals are strongly emphasized, whereas individual employee goals are de-emphasized. Answer (D) is incorrect because Theory Y is optimistic about employees' motivation, ability, and self-discipline. In this situation, the manager's perceptions are similar to Theory X, which suggests that employees dislike work and need constant direction and coercion.

41. Marianne is a manager who believes that positive employee attitudes are extremely important. She cooperates with employees in solving problems. A likely effect on employee behavior of this leadership style is

A. Mistrust of the manager.

B. A lack of extraordinary performance.

C. High employee turnover.

D. Increased employee creativity.

The correct answer is (D). *(Publisher)*

REQUIRED: The effect on employee behavior most likely to result from the described leadership style.

DISCUSSION: When a manager works to maintain a positive attitude among employees and cooperates with them in problem solving, employees are likely to be more motivated, confident, and creative. This leadership style should also improve communication and decrease absenteeism.

Answers (A), (B), and (C) are incorrect because these effects are more likely when the leadership style is to impose a set of strict rules and the manager has a Theory X approach.

D. Management and Organizational Development

42. Which of the following is most likely to provide for the continual development of managerial skills?

A. Organizational orientation sessions.

B. Job rotation.

C. Role playing.

D. Liaison committees.

The correct answer is (B). *(CIA, adapted)*

REQUIRED: The item that provides for the continual development of managerial skills.

DISCUSSION: A manager's knowledge and skills are broadened by serving in a number of different capacities. To a significant degree, research shows that managers learn to manage by managing.

Answer (A) is incorrect because, in an organizational orientation session, employees receive formal information about objectives, the organizational chart, benefits, and procedures. Answer (C) is incorrect because role playing is assuming different roles in different situations according to the expectations of the group. Answer (D) is incorrect because liaison committees facilitate understanding between management and employees.

43. The least effective method for an employee to learn computer skills is

A. Classroom training using equipment.

B. Video training.

C. Apprenticeships.

D. Case analysis.

The correct answer is (D). *(CIA, adapted)*

REQUIRED: The least effective method for an employee to learn computer skills.

DISCUSSION: According to Robbins (*Organizational Behavior*, pg. 565), simulation exercises, such as case analyses, role playing, experiential exercises, and group interaction sessions, best serve in developing problem-solving and interpersonal skills.

Answer (A) is incorrect because classroom training permits the employee to learn to use the actual job-related equipment in a training setting. Answer (B) is incorrect because videos provide the specific, technical details necessary to perform the job and can be viewed until the employee is comfortable with the material. Answer (C) is incorrect because apprenticeships place the employee with an experienced worker who serves as a model for the understudy to observe.

E. Management by Objectives (MBO)

44. MBO managers are most likely to believe that employees

A. Dislike their work.

B. Avoid responsibility whenever possible.

C. Work best when threatened with punishment.

D. Are self-motivated.

The correct answer is (D). *(Publisher)*

REQUIRED: The characteristic an MBO manager attributes to employees.

DISCUSSION: MBO managers believe that employees are committed to achieving objectives, working hard to receive the rewards of achievement, and striving for self-actualization. The MBO view is that employees enjoy work, need little supervision, seek responsibility, and are imaginative problem solvers.

Answers (A), (B), and (C) are incorrect because they are characteristics that Theory X managers attribute to their employees.

45. A company has a compensation system for its managers based on a management-by-objectives (MBO) approach. The essential premise of MBO is that

A. Compensation should be based on qualitative factors.

B. Employees should be concerned with routine matters, and managers should attend to exceptions.

C. Employees should participate in setting goals.

D. Managers should establish goals for their employees.

The correct answer is (C). *(Publisher)*

REQUIRED: The essential premise of MBO.

DISCUSSION: The hallmark of MBO is the mutual setting of goals by the superior and the subordinate as a basis for performance evaluation. Based on the Theory Y philosophy that employees want to work hard if they know what is expected, MBO requires top management participation and commitment to the program, integration of the objectives for all subunits into a compatible system directed toward accomplishment of overall goals, provision for regular reporting of performance, and free and honest communication between superior and subordinates. Subordinates must make careful assessments of their abilities and their interests, and managers must "coach" subordinates rather than dictate their proper goals. Both sides must maintain flexibility to accommodate unforeseen changes, and the review and analysis of results before setting the next round of goals is a vital part of the process.

Answer (A) is incorrect because MBO goals may be set in terms of quantitative measures (such as sales dollars) or qualitative ones (such as improved service). Answer (B) is incorrect because it describes management by exception. Answer (D) is incorrect because goal setting should be participative.

46. Which of the following is a weakness of using MBO for motivating employees?

A. Employees may believe that they control situations that arise in the company.

B. Employees may be forced to place too much emphasis on quantitative factors.

C. Employees may participate too much in the goal-setting process.

D. Employees may become too trusting and too dependent on the "team" to get things done.

The correct answer is (B). *(Publisher)*

REQUIRED: The weakness of using MBO to motivate employees.

DISCUSSION: MBO is the process by which a manager and his/her subordinate(s) work together to formulate the objectives and goals of the subordinate(s). One of the weaknesses of MBO is that emphasis on quantitative factors may cause employees to focus on ends rather than means. Thus, MBO may jeopardize the quality of the organization's output.

Answer (A) is incorrect because, when an employee believes that (s)he is in control, (s)he feels more responsible for achieving goals. Answer (C) is incorrect because employee participation in goal setting helps clarify goals and motivate the employee. Answer (D) is incorrect because an employee's trust in the team approach helps make the work atmosphere more positive.

47. What is the first step to take when implementing MBO in a department accustomed to Theory X?

A. Teach the employees about MBO.

B. Set up individual goals with each employee on a one-to-one basis.

C. Discuss overall organizational goals with the employees.

D. Verify that top management supports MBO.

The correct answer is (D). *(Publisher)*

REQUIRED: The first step in implementing MBO.

DISCUSSION: When making a change of policy as great as from Theory X to MBO, ascertaining that top management is committed to the change is the essential first step. Establishing and communicating organizational goals, obtaining the trust of subordinates, educating employees about MBO, assisting individuals in goal setting, ensuring that employees have needed resources, conducting informal reviews, making performance evaluations, and establishing new employee goals are additional steps an MBO manager might take.

Answers (A), (B), and (C) are incorrect because they are not as important as obtaining top management support.

F. Managing Human Resources

48. The protected group under the Age Discrimination in Employment Act of 1967, as amended, is defined as anyone in which age group?

A. 35 and 60.

B. 40 and 75.

C. 40 and older.

D. 45 and older.

The correct answer is (C). *(CMA, adapted)*

REQUIRED: The protected age group under the Age Discrimination in Employment Act.

DISCUSSION: The Age Discrimination in Employment Act is designed to protect individuals aged 40 and older from employment discrimination. The act has been amended to eliminate the mandatory retirement age. However, certain managerial employees are not protected by this amendment.

Answers (A), (B), and (D) are incorrect because the act provides protection for individuals who are aged 40 and older.

49. Evaluating performance is not done to

A. Determine the amount of nondiscriminatory benefits that each employee deserves.

B. Assess the available human resources of the firm.

C. Motivate the employees.

D. Determine which employees deserve salary increases.

The correct answer is (A). *(Publisher)*

REQUIRED: The statement that is not a purpose of performance evaluations.

DISCUSSION: There are many reasons for evaluating performance. Evaluations reinforce accomplishments, help in assessing employee strengths and weaknesses, provide motivation, assist in employee development, permit the organization to assess its human resource needs, and serve as a basis for wage increases. Nondiscriminatory benefits are given to everyone in the organization in equal amounts regardless of title, pay, or achievement of objectives.

Answers (B), (C), and (D) are incorrect because they are purposes of a performance evaluation.

50. When a manager generalizes from the evaluation of one or a few traits to the employee's total performance, (s)he has made

A. A judgmental evaluation.

B. An evaluation subject to the halo effect.

C. A projection.

D. An objective evaluation.

The correct answer is (B). *(Publisher)*
REQUIRED: The type of evaluation that generalizes from an evaluation of a few of an employee's traits.
DISCUSSION: The halo effect occurs when the appraiser judges one or a few employee traits and carries over this judgment to the evaluation of the employee's other traits. The halo effect can be positive or negative.
Answer (A) is incorrect because a judgmental evaluation is based on nonverifiable, subjective criteria. Answer (C) is incorrect because projection is the process of attributing one's own traits to another person. Answer (D) is incorrect because an objective evaluation uses verifiable, often quantitative criteria.

51. A manager discovers by chance that a newly hired employee has strong beliefs that are very different from the manager's and from those of most of the other employees. The manager's best course of action would be to

A. Facilitate the reassignment of the new hire as quickly as possible before this situation becomes disruptive.

B. Ask the rest of the team for their reaction and act according to the group consensus.

C. Take no action unless the new hire's behavior is likely to cause harm to the organization.

D. Try to counsel the new hire into more reasonable beliefs.

The correct answer is (C). *(CIA, adapted)*
REQUIRED: The manager's best course of action when a new employee has strong beliefs that are very different from the manager's.
DISCUSSION: The only legitimate grounds on which the supervisor may take action is the employee's behavior. Personal beliefs, such as those on religious and political matters, cannot be the basis of personnel actions. Discrimination on the basis of personal beliefs could expose the organization to legal action.
Answers (A), (B), and (D) are incorrect because personal beliefs alone are not an appropriate basis for managerial action.

52. A company allows each of its departments to develop its own system for evaluating performance. Linda Ward, the personnel director, should communicate appraisal information to a new employee by

A. Presenting anything that is pertinent to the listener's situation.

B. Providing an overview of all systems within the company.

C. Describing how her own performance is evaluated.

D. Discussing each department's evaluation system in detail.

The correct answer is (A). *(Publisher)*
REQUIRED: The best method of discussing performance evaluations with a new employee when evaluations are departmentalized.
DISCUSSION: The personnel director should tailor the discussion to the listener by describing how the employee's department evaluates performance and what is expected of him/her. The director should also obtain feedback from the employee to determine if everything is clearly understood.
Answers (B), (C), and (D) are incorrect because they may confuse the new employee.

53. A disadvantage of separating performance evaluations from wage-increase decisions is that

A. Not enough emphasis is placed on short-run performance.

B. Financial rewards may lose their motivational effect.

C. Employees may not be motivated by good appraisals.

D. The employee's performance evaluation does not consider the financial status of the company overall.

The correct answer is (C). *(Publisher)*
REQUIRED: The disadvantage of separating performance appraisals from wage increases.
DISCUSSION: The employee may not be motivated immediately by a good appraisal because of the delay in receipt of any monetary reward. The evaluation may also not be taken as seriously by the employee if compensation is not correlated with performance.
Answer (A) is incorrect because an advantage of separating appraisals from wage increases is that more emphasis is placed on long-term objectives and goals. Answer (B) is incorrect because this separation does not deprive money of its motivational power, but it does emphasize other rewards, such as feelings of achievement and the recognition of superiors. Answer (D) is incorrect because an advantage of separating performance evaluations from wage-increase decisions is that the employee's good performance can be separated from the overall company's bad financial performance.

54. A company that wishes to improve its rate of retention of its experienced employees might

A. Abolish its hire-from-within policy.

B. Improve its fringe benefit package.

C. Initiate job simplification programs.

D. Set a mandatory retirement age.

The correct answer is (B). *(Publisher)*

REQUIRED: The way to improve employee retention.

DISCUSSION: Fringe benefits (e.g., pensions and profit-sharing plans) may be contingent on duration of employment. Accordingly, they motivate employees to remain with the company.

Answer (A) is incorrect because reduced opportunity for advancement may motivate employees to find jobs elsewhere. Answer (C) is incorrect because job simplification may result in boredom, lessened job satisfaction, and a higher turnover rate. Answer (D) is incorrect because abolition of a mandatory retirement age would be more appropriate.

55. A company that formerly paid certain management employees on a salary plus commission basis decided to compensate a test group solely with commissions. Performance of these employees declined. The most likely explanation for this result is that

A. The employee received special attention.

B. Compensation was a motivational factor.

C. Compensation was not a hygiene factor.

D. Increased concerns about security made the employees risk averse.

The correct answer is (D). *(Publisher)*

REQUIRED: The most likely reason for the performance decline.

DISCUSSION: A straight salary with commissions rewarded increased efforts while providing security and reduced anxiety. Satisfaction of the need for security may have permitted the employees to adopt promising and profitable but more risky strategies. Since people concerned about security needs tend to be risk averse, the change in compensation method probably caused the performance decline.

Answer (A) is incorrect because the famous Hawthorne studies suggest that the employees' knowledge of their special status would improve their output. Answer (B) is incorrect because Herzberg defines a motivational factor as one whose absence will not diminish performance but whose presence will be a motivator. Answer (C) is incorrect because a performance decline followed a reduction in the security of compensation; hence, money was probably a hygiene (maintenance) factor according to Herzberg's two-factor theory of motivation.

56. The human resource department of an organization observed that accounting staff turnover was unusually high. Exit interviews indicated that the accounting department work schedule was highly restrictive for accountants who had young children. To improve the retention of skilled employees in the accounting department, the best solution would be to

A. Implement a program of job rotation within the accounting department.

B. Promote job enlargement for the positions experiencing the greatest turnover.

C. Provide job sharing and flextime opportunities for accounting department employees.

D. Enrich the jobs of accounting department employees.

The correct answer is (C). *(CIA, adapted)*

REQUIRED: The best way to improve employee retention.

DISCUSSION: Job sharing and flextime allow employees to adjust their work schedules and hours to better achieve personal objectives. These programs can increase worker loyalty and motivation.

Answers (A), (B), and (D) are incorrect because job rotation, job enlargement, and job enrichment would not adequately address the scheduling issue.

57. The factor that would not contribute to retention of experienced employees would be

A. Initiation of job enrichment programs.

B. Adherence to federal regulations regarding sex discrimination in paying and promoting workers.

C. Paying new employees more than older ones.

D. Adoption of flextime rules.

The correct answer is (C). *(Publisher)*

REQUIRED: The factor not contributing to employee retention.

DISCUSSION: When old employees discover that newcomers are being hired at higher salaries, the group hired first will be unhappy, feeling that their greater experience should warrant greater reward. In the short run, the newcomers will be satisfied. But it is possible that next year's newcomers will be hired at still higher salaries, contributing to the overall dissatisfaction. Thus, such a policy will provide incentives for experienced workers to leave the company.

Answer (A) is incorrect because a more intrinsically satisfying job will improve the retention rate. Answer (B) is incorrect because employees subject to discrimination may be strongly motivated to find other jobs. Answer (D) is incorrect because greater freedom in determining his/her hours may enable a worker to remain with the company when other responsibilities (e.g., child care) might have compelled him/her to leave.

58. The value of retaining employees is determined by

A. Human asset accounting.

B. Financial accounting.

C. Cost accounting.

D. Human resource planning.

The correct answer is (A). *(Publisher)*

REQUIRED: The method used to determine the value of retaining employees.

DISCUSSION: Human resource or human asset accounting attempts to measure the value, and the changes in value, of the organization's investment in human assets. Although this "asset" is enormously valuable (sometimes estimated at two or three times the annual payroll), it is not shown in balance sheets or accounted for in earnings statements. One experimental measurement approach is a sort of "present value" of human resources. Another is a "cost" approach, with dollar investments (training, customer goodwill, etc.) offset by reductions (e.g., retirement).

Answers (B) and (C) are incorrect because traditional accounting methods do not value the organization's human assets. Answer (D) is incorrect because human resource planning merely audits the skills of the current employees and forecasts needs.

59. An employee with a good background and years of experience earns a salary at the top of his/her range. Under the company's compensation program, the employee can increase his/her salary above the usual annual increase only by earning a promotion. Which of the following is most likely to be an effect on his/her behavior?

A. The employee may refuse new duties or tasks.

B. The employee may become less productive.

C. The employee may not be motivated to improve performance.

D. The employee may seek a position with another company.

The correct answer is (D). *(Publisher)*

REQUIRED: The effect on the employee's behavior of the limitation on possible rewards.

DISCUSSION: When an employee can earn a desired salary increase only through a promotion, (s)he is likely to be motivated to perform better. If this does not result in a promotion, (s)he will probably look for another job.

Answers (A), (B), and (C) are incorrect because these behaviors would undermine the employee's chance for a promotion.

60. A company's compensation program does not allow for salary increases based on above-average performance after an employee reaches the top of a position's salary range. It also pays some employees higher salaries because of their educational qualifications. This company could improve the program by

A. Allowing each manager to set up his/her own system of salary increases.

B. Providing only monetary compensation.

C. Developing a system that equates years of experience with education.

D. Decreasing the annual percentage increase in each salary range.

The correct answer is (C). *(Publisher)*

REQUIRED: The improvement in the described compensation program.

DISCUSSION: A company with a compensation program that stops rewarding above-average performance at the top of each salary range and rewards education with higher compensation could improve the system in several ways. These include starting a bonus program for above-average performance, refusing to hire a person at the top of a salary range unless (s)he will be promoted quickly, and equating experience and education so that employees are treated fairly.

Answer (A) is incorrect because the company should administer a uniform system of salary increases. Answer (B) is incorrect because the company could improve its system if it provided other compensation, such as assisting with an employee's tuition or recognizing an employee who has given many years of service. Answer (D) is incorrect because the company would please all employees by increasing this percentage.

Use Gleim's ***CMA/CFM Test Prep*** for interactive testing with **over 2,000 additional multiple-choice questions!**

ADDENDUM: COMPUTATIONAL PRACTICE QUESTIONS

Questions A7 and A8 are presented below. Please see pages 64, 172, and 473 for additional questions. The study unit on which the question is based is indicated in bold after the source code for each question.

A7. A firm has daily cash receipts of $300,000. A bank has offered to provide a lockbox service that will reduce the collection time by 3 days. The bank requires a monthly fee of $2,000 for providing this service. If money market rates are expected to average 6% during the year, the additional annual income (loss) of using the lockbox service is

A. ($24,000)

B. $12,000

C. $30,000

D. $54,000

The correct answer is (C). (*Publisher*) **SU 5**

REQUIRED: The amount a company will gain or lose by hiring a bank lockbox service to process cash collections.

DISCUSSION: Because collections will be accelerated by 3 days at a rate of $300,000 per day, the company will have an additional $900,000 to invest. At a rate of 6%, the interest earned will be $54,000 per year. However, the bank will charge $24,000 (12 months × $2,000 per month) for its services. Thus, the firm will increase its income by $30,000 ($54,000 – $24,000).

Answer (A) is incorrect because ($24,000) ignores the additional interest revenue from investing the increased funds. Answer (B) is incorrect because $12,000 is based on 2 days of accelerated inflows rather than 3. Answer (D) is incorrect because $54,000 ignores the $24,000 bank service charge.

A8. Management of a company does not want to violate a working capital restriction contained in its bond indenture. If the firm's current ratio falls below 2.0 to 1, technically it will have defaulted. The firm's current ratio is now 2.2 to 1. If current liabilities are $200 million, the maximum new commercial paper that can be issued to finance inventory expansion is

A. $20 million.

B. $40 million.

C. $240 million.

D. $180 million.

The correct answer is (B). (*Publisher*) **SU 5**

REQUIRED: The amount of commercial paper that can be issued to finance inventory without violating the bond indenture.

DISCUSSION: If current liabilities are $200 million and the current ratio (current assets ÷ current liabilities) is 2.2, current assets must be $440 million (2.2 × $200 million). If X amount of commercial paper is issued to finance inventory (current assets), thereby increasing both current assets and current liabilities by X, the level of current assets at which the new current ratio will be 2.0 is $480 million ($440 million + $40 million of commercial paper).

$$(\$440 + X) \div (\$200 + X) = 2.0$$
$$\$440 + X = 2(\$200 + X)$$
$$\$440 + X = \$400 + 2X$$
$$\$440 = \$400 + X$$
$$X = \$40$$

Answer (A) is incorrect because $20 million ignores the increase in current assets. This answer would be appropriate if noncurrent assets were being financed. Answer (C) is incorrect because $240 million is the amount of working capital both before and after the issuance of commercial paper. Answer (D) is incorrect because $180 million is a nonsense answer.

Study Unit 10: Communication

12 pages of outline
60 multiple-choice questions

The relative weight range assigned to organizational structures, management, and communication in Part 1 is 20% to 30%. We cover this major topic in the following study units:

Study Unit 8: Organizational Theory
Study Unit 9: Motivation and the Directing Process
Study Unit 10: Communication

Thus, you should expect 24 to 36 questions on these three study units.

Being a good communicator does not ensure that a person will be a good manager, but virtually every good manager is a good communicator. Communication should not be viewed as a separate managerial activity. Every aspect of management requires effective communication.

A. Nature of Communication

1. **Communication** is the process of conveying meaning or understanding from one person to another. It permeates all segments of an organization and moves in many directions.
   a. Because all managerial functions require communication, it is the secret to the success of any manager. A manager's ability to understand other people and their ability to understand the manager are crucial to accomplishing organizational objectives. Communication is the link that ties an organization together and transforms a diverse group of people into a cohesive whole.
   b. An organization's internal communications network is designed to facilitate decision making among managers, promote goal congruence among employees, integrate the efforts of all employees, and build high morale and mutual trust.
   c. **Formal communication** is conducted through the formal structure of the organization, e.g., budgets, bonus programs, memoranda, or technical manuals.
   d. Informal communication (the **grapevine**) operates outside of formal structural channels.
      1) The grapevine exists wherever there are people.
      2) Grapevines can exist in several patterns. For example, one person may tell one other person who tells one other person, etc.; one person may tell all people in a group; individuals may tell selected others; or individuals may tell others at random.
      3) Although the grapevine is usually accurate, it can carry gossip and rumor. Managers can minimize the damage that a grapevine can cause by transmitting accurate and timely information and maintaining open channels of communication.
      4) The effective manager stays tuned in to the grapevine and uses it constructively.

e. **Written communication** provides a permanent record of the message and tends to be accurate but can be time consuming to prepare. An inherent weakness of written communication is that it inhibits feedback because the sender and the receiver are not in simultaneous communication.

f. **Oral communication** is less formal and less accurate than written communication but permits immediate feedback. It also permits messages to be transmitted rapidly. Most managers spend more of their time in oral than in written communication.

g. **Electronic communication**. Modern technology (e.g., voice mail, fax, and e-mail) blurs the distinction between written and oral communications. The benefits of electronic communication include better control of information, more timely information, elimination of tedious tasks, improvement of competitiveness due to improved technology, standardization of procedures by computer programs, assistance for strategic planning, and optimization of organizational resources to improve productivity.

2. **Directions of Communication**

a. **Downward communication** (from superior to subordinate) is vertical communication consisting of orders, instructions, notices, memos, bulletins, newsletters, handbooks, loudspeakers, and the chain of command.

b. **Upward communication** is vertical communication consisting of morale surveys, grievance procedures, interviews, and conferences. Upward communication must overcome more barriers and is slower than downward communication.

c. **Horizontal (lateral) communication** is from one peer to another.

3. The communication process has five elements (the mnemonic is SSMRF).

a. **Sender**, who originates the message

b. **Symbols**, in which the message is encoded

c. **Medium**, the channel through which the message flows

d. **Receiver**, the person who decodes the message and interprets the sender's meaning

e. **Feedback**, acknowledging to the sender that the message was correctly understood

f. EXAMPLE

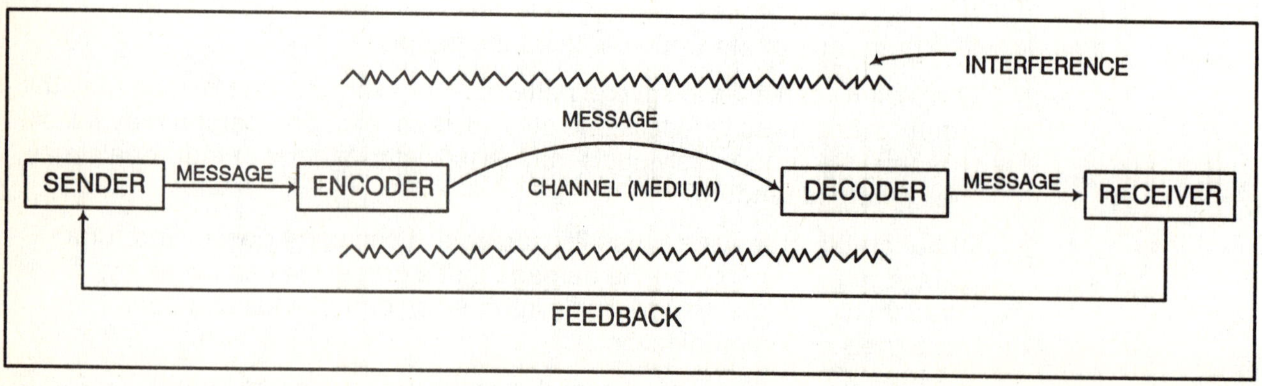

4. The effectiveness of communication can be determined only when the sender seeks feedback and observes the impact of the communication on the receiver.
   a. The sender is obligated to solicit feedback to ensure the communication process is complete.
   b. The receiver is obligated to give feedback to the sender.
   c. The importance of feedback to check on the effectiveness of the communication process indicates the limitations of one-way communications (e.g., memos).
5. Managers must consider the nature of the message receiver. Receivers vary in their perception of messages because of language, education, culture, attitudes toward the sender and job, etc. This variance may result in communication distortion.
   a. EXAMPLES:
      1) In some cultures, to move toward a person while speaking is expected; in others, it is considered an act of aggression.
      2) In some cultures, consistently being late to appointments means laxness, lack of concern, discourtesy, and disinterest; in others, it is normal and expected, and carries no particular meaning.
6. **Traditional or classical management** stresses the sending of one-way communications from top management down to the subordinates. This military model of organization is autocratic or mechanistic and ignores the need for feedback.
7. **Participative management** stresses multidirectional communication. All parts of the organization are allowed and expected to communicate with each other, and not merely along lines of authority.
8. **Systems theory** stresses the importance of feedback in determining the effectiveness of communications. Without a channel from the receiver back to the sender, the sender has no idea how the information has affected the performance or actions of the receiver, if at all.
9. Research shows that communications networks have various characteristics.
   a. A **wheel** network, which is a fast and accurate means of information flow, channels all communication to a central supervisor.
      1) The result is lower satisfaction among participants, but the circumstances favor the emergence of a leader.
   b. Extensive cross-communication in an **all-channel network** results in moderate accuracy but with
      1) Free-flow
      2) More innovation
      3) Member satisfaction
   c. **Chain-type** communication is slower.
      1) Accuracy is high, but member satisfaction is moderate.

10. **Nonverbal Communication**

    a. **Nonverbal signals** occur in clusters, whether or not accompanied by verbal communication. They include such nonverbal nuances as

        1) Vocal characteristics such as tone of voice
        2) Facial expressions and eye contact
        3) Hand and body gestures and other movements
        4) Breathing, sighs, and other noises that are not words
        5) Physical distance between the sender and the receiver
        6) Posture and other aspects of physical appearance
        7) Touch
        8) Mode of attire
        9) Decoration and layout of rooms

    b. Nonverbal communication is easily misunderstood because

        1) Different cultures and languages employ different nonverbal signals.
        2) Clarifying the ambiguities inherent in nonverbal communication is difficult.

    c. Interpreting nonverbal communication requires the establishment of the norms in a particular person's nonverbal repertoire.

        1) For example, folded arms may signify resistance or inflexibility, or may simply be a habit.

        2) People should not be judged solely on established or learned norms of nonverbal communication but instead on an individual basis.

11. Stop and review! You have completed the outline for this subunit. Study multiple-choice questions 1 through 19 beginning on page 399.

B. Problems in Communication

1. **Poorly Encoded Messages**

    a. Inappropriate choice of words or phrases for the receiver

        1) For example, using technical language (jargon) in speaking with a lay person

    b. Careless omissions of key ideas

    c. Lack of coherence in forming the message

    d. Inconsistency between verbal and nonverbal messages

    e. Incomplete ideas or ideas out of the receiver's context

    f. **Projection**, which is the tendency of the sender to attribute his/her traits, values, and emotions to the receiver, and vice versa

    g. **Filtering** the message so that it reflects more favorably on the sender, a typical problem in upward communication

2. **Faulty Channel Selection**

    a. Trying to speak while a loud airplane flies overhead
    b. Gesturing to someone who cannot see the gesture

3. **Noise in the communications channel** is an outside disruption that impedes the flow of a message, for example,
   a. Asking for a raise during discussion of an operational problem
   b. Random events that cause a breakdown in communication (lost mail, phone service disruption, etc.)
   c. Use of technical language by the sender that is unlikely to be understood by a receiver trained in a different discipline
4. **Perceptual Problems**
   a. Sender's dislike of receiver or vice versa
   b. Distortion created by personal enthusiasm for embellishing good news and downplaying the bad, or vice versa
   c. Status differences between people that impede free and open communication
      1) Few people are secure enough to tell a superior that what was just said was not understood.
   d. Perceptual errors can be minimized with feedback from the receiver concerning his/her perceptions and interpretations of the message, understanding of the sender's perspective by the receiver, the sender's sensitivity to the receiver's problems, and implementation of a company-wide training program to improve communication skills.
   e. **Selective perception** arising from the receiver's needs, motives, projections, experiences, and expectations
      1) People tend to interpret what they see and hear in the light of their own needs, etc., and to regard that interpretation as reality.
      2) Moreover, people necessarily must narrow their perception to avoid sensory overload. Such screening is required to organize and interpret experience.
   f. **Stereotyping** is the attribution to another person of traits that are commonly associated with a category or group to which that person belongs.
5. **Use of Communication Channels for Enhancement of Personal Status**
   a. Some lower-level employees who have the ear of management become influential among their peers.
6. **Loss in Transmission and Poor Retention**
   a. As much as 30% of the information in oral communication is lost in each transmission. Even written communications are subject to some loss. After passing through a chain of command, little of the message may have been retained.
   b. Poor retention. One study found that as little as 50% of communicated information was retained by employees.
7. **Nonreception**. The receiver commonly fails to receive any communication.
   a. Inattention or disinterest in the message
   b. Information overload. The receiver is already receiving so many messages that (s)he cannot process what (s)he is hearing.
   c. Confusing messages. The sender is not sending enough information to fully communicate thoughts, and the receiver must allocate too much time to interpreting what the sender is saying.

8. **Formal Organization Channel Breakdowns**
   a. EXAMPLE: Omissions from mailing lists
9. **Solutions to Communications Problems**
   a. The message should be in the context of the receiver's perceptions.
      1) Explaining an accounting concept to a nonaccountant will require terms different from those used with someone who has an accounting background.
   b. The sender must monitor channels to ensure they are free from distortion or breakdown.
   c. The sender must actively solicit feedback to ensure reception and understanding.
   d. The organizational climate should encourage the elimination of interpersonal barriers to communication.
   e. The sender should look for nonverbal cues or feedback (such as body language).
   f. The sender must remember that it is his/her responsibility to deliver the communication with appropriate symbols over appropriate channels and never to make assumptions about the receiver's reaction.
   g. Two-way communication should be used whenever possible to permit ease of feedback.
   h. Communication can be improved through redundancy, that is, by repeating the message in several different formats and in several media.
10. Stop and review! You have completed the outline for this subunit. Study multiple-choice questions 20 through 32 beginning on page 405.

C. Listening and Other Forms of Communication

1. **Listening** is the responsibility of both the speaker (sender) and the listener (receiver). Listening is one of the problems in communication that can be improved by the manager. The art of listening must be exercised effectively to
   a. Gain more information about the work situation
   b. Have a positive effect on both superiors and subordinates through showing concern for their views
2. **Problems in Listening**
   a. People can listen several times faster than words can be spoken, which may result in inattention and mind-wandering.
   b. Prejudgment of the message, before or during the communication process, may reduce the ability to listen objectively.
   c. Concentration may be focused on the words used to the exclusion of the ideas.
3. **Guides to More Effective Listening**
   a. **Empathy** is the process of mentally putting oneself in another person's position to better understand his/her feelings, attitudes, and thoughts. Empathy
      1) Enables the sender and the receiver to take into account each other's backgrounds, biases, beliefs, and values
      2) Aids in anticipating others' reactions to messages

3) Aids in effective communication by guiding the choice of

a) Words used and their meanings
b) Word inflection and emphasis
c) Tone of voice and gestures

b. **Sensitivity training** gives managers a greater awareness of, or sensitivity to, their own attitudes, feelings, and beliefs. This understanding helps them perceive how their behavior affects the people with whom they communicate.

1) Such training is designed to result in better listening skills, tolerance for individual differences, and an awareness of the impact of one's personality on other people.

2) The disadvantage is that some managers may spend a disproportionate amount of time focusing on relationships rather than on the day-to-day problems of the job.

c. **Interpersonal communications training**. Supervisors and their subordinates receive formal training in how to give and receive both written and oral communication. The advantage is that everyone has the same training and can practice working together using specific problems.

4. **Other Forms of Communication**

a. **Audit reports** and other documents are forms of communication.

1) Internal audit reports are expected to communicate audit results to management and create desired actions.

2) Audit reports should be timely, clear, concise, objective, and constructive.

3) A corporate annual report is a one-way communication device.

a) Clarity and conciseness must be emphasized because no immediate feedback from readers is possible.

b) A logical organization of the report's contents facilitates transmission of the message.

b. **Employee handbooks and accounting manuals** are also forms of communication.

1) The employee handbook communicates company policies and provides employees and management with quick and consistent answers to employment-related questions.

a) It provides a store of knowledge and outlines the responsibilities and levels of authority within an organization.

b) It can be the basis of a contract between the company and its employees.

c) It should include information about

i) Benefit packages
ii) Holiday and vacation policies
iii) Sick pay provisions
iv) Severance policy
v) Retirement benefits
vi) Grievance procedures
vii) Promotion and transfer policies

2) An accounting manual promotes equitable and consistent treatment of similar transactions.
    a) It should define accounting and technical terms in language that all employees can understand.
3) Both employee handbooks and accounting manuals should be prepared so that revisions and updates are facilitated (e.g., kept in a ring binder).
    a) Specific individuals should be responsible for periodic updating of handbooks and manuals.

c. **Business memos**.

1) Memos vary in form and content, but often begin in the following way:

TO:	All employees
FROM:	Irv Gleim
SUBJECT:	Format and content of memos
DATE:	July 30, 1997

    a) Most companies have prepared stationery with a logo and their desired format.
    b) Memos may be signed or unsigned, convey good or bad news, or give information necessary to facilitate smooth daily business.
2) Memos should have the characteristics of good writing. They should avoid unnecessary verbiage, and readers should grasp the meaning quickly and easily. Good business writing style is concise, clear, coherent, correct, credible, natural, positive, interesting, and readable.
    a) It treats receivers with respect by sending a courteous message.
    b) It is also suitable to the medium of presentation and delivery.
    c) Good business writing style provides clear, developed ideas but avoids overstatement.
        i) It also conveys the message unobtrusively. The writing should not call attention to itself.
3) The details for a memorandum announcing a mandatory meeting include the purpose and goals of the meeting, a list of who must attend, the information or reports required for the meeting, the expected length of the meeting, and the person to contact regarding any questions or problems.
    a) The writer-chairperson should take preliminary actions after announcing the meeting including distributing the planned agenda, providing copies of information to prepare the participants, and calling the participants to remind them of their required attendance.
    b) During the meeting the writer-chairperson should state the purpose and objectives of the meeting, maintain a list of assignments decided on during the meeting, focus the discussion by giving direction, curtail repetition and triviality, encourage individual responses, and summarize and review the discussion at the meeting's conclusion.
    c) After the meeting, the writer-chairperson should follow-up the special assignments made to individuals at the meeting. A request for periodic reports on the status of these assignments may be made or the individuals can be contacted directly.

d. **Persuasive communications**

1) Persuasive communication, whether for internal or external purposes, requires clarity of presentation. Arguments should be focused on the ultimate objective, organized in a logical manner that leads inevitably to the desired conclusion, and shaped with regard to the attitudes, opinions, and information needs of the specific recipient. Unrelated and unnecessary subjects should be avoided.

a) The credibility of the message is also important in changing attitudes. Trust, competence, objectivity, and high ethical standards are persuasive.

b) Although objective evidence is important, emotional appeals may also be effective. However, they must be carefully designed to appeal to the recipient's emotional structure. Otherwise, they may backfire.

i) High connotation words should be used with care in persuasive communication because such language has strong but unpredictable effects. Emotion-laden words should be chosen to appeal to the particular recipient.

2) A typical sequence of arguments in a persuasive message places strong arguments first and last, with weaker arguments and refutations of opposing arguments in the middle. The reasons for this ordering are the primacy and recency principles. People tend to remember best what they read or hear first and last.

a) The middle section includes weaker arguments. It also is the appropriate location of counterarguments.

i) Selective choice of the opponent's arguments that can be successfully rebutted can be very effective. However, mention of the opponent's arguments that cannot be refuted will weaken the persuader's case.

e. **Telecommuting**. People who are computer literate have in recent years begun working from their homes. They correspond with their offices by means of telecommunication.

1) Problems associated with these employees include a tendency to fall behind in their fields of specialization, a lack of strong working relationships with other employees, a loss of career opportunities, and inadequate organizational socialization.

2) The primary strength of these individuals, however, has been their communication skills.

3) Many corporations have taken advantage of e-mail, file transfer protocol (ftp), the Internet, and various network configurations to make telecommuting more practical and useful.

5. Stop and review! You have completed the outline for this subunit. Study multiple-choice questions 33 through 45 beginning on page 409.

D. Negotiation and Conflict Management

1. **Negotiation** or bargaining strives for an exchange of goods or services and an agreement as to the rate of exchange.

   a. According to Walton and McKensie, *A Behavioral Theory of Labor Negotiations: An Analysis of a Social Interaction System*, the general approaches to negotiation are distributive bargaining and integrative bargaining.

      1) **Distributive bargaining** is typical of negotiators who are in a zero-sum situation, such as labor-management negotiations about wages. What one side gains, the other loses. Thus, the interests of the parties diverge because they are competing for shares of a fixed amount of resources.

         a) The negotiators in distributive bargaining operate with a maximum desired result and a minimum acceptable result in mind. If the ranges of feasible outcomes of the parties overlap, an agreement is possible.

      2) **Integrative bargaining** occurs in a positive sum situation; that is, the parties believe that a solution exists that permits both sides to win. The parties have shared interests, the amount of resources to be allocated is not fixed, and the relationship tends to be long-term.

         a) Integrative bargaining is the preferable mode within an organization because it fosters cooperation, minimizes conflict, and develops constructive long-term relationships. However, it works only when the negotiators are open, flexible, able to trust the other side, sympathetic to each other's concerns, and committed to finding creative solutions.

         b) Effective negotiators are good listeners, ask frequent questions, avoid defensiveness and attacks on the opponents, do not use language calculated to be irritating, and phrase their arguments clearly and directly.

            i) They also understand that reciprocity is often a characteristic of negotiation. A tough stance encourages a similar response, and concessions usually result in reciprocal concessions. In the latter case, however, the amount of concessions received will usually be less than those offered.

         c) Third parties as negotiators

            i) **Mediation** is an intervention between conflicting parties by a neutral and noncoercive agency to facilitate an agreement. A mediator offers solutions, facilitates communications, and presents arguments.

            ii) **Arbitration** is the hearing and determination of a case in controversy by a person chosen by the parties or appointed under statutory authority. The results of arbitration are binding although the process may be entered voluntarily or compulsorily (under law or contract).

            iii) **Conciliation** overlaps with mediation. A conciliator is a trusted individual who provides an informal communication link, interprets messages, etc.

iv) **Consultation** is performed by a neutral individual whose expertise is in conflict management. The consultant's function is less to arrive at a settlement than to improve interactions between the parties.

b. The benefits of negotiating include resolving an issue without litigation, recognizing that each party values the other party's needs and rights, and impartially treating tension while finding compromise solutions.

2. **Conflict Management**. Conflict may be constructive or destructive.

   a. Communication, structure, and personal variables are the broad categories of conditions that may result in conflict.

      1) Communication variables pertain to semantical issues, noise in communication channels, and other problems in communication that impair cooperation and cause misunderstanding.

      2) Structural conditions include the size of the work group, specialization of tasks, the clarity of lines of authority, leadership practices, compensation schemes, and the interdependence of groups.

      3) Personal variables include individual personality characteristics and value systems.

   b. Conflict triggers include ambiguous jurisdictions (unclear job boundaries); competition for scarce resources; status differentials; time pressures, personality clashes; unreasonable standards, rules, etc.; communication breakdowns; and unrealized expectations.

   c. **Interactionist theory** regards conflict as potentially beneficial. Functional conflict improves performance and helps the organization to achieve its objectives.

   d. Whether conflict is functional depends on the intentions of the parties.

      1) In **competition**, individuals display the maximum of assertiveness (behavior intended to achieve one's own objectives) and the minimum of cooperativeness (behavior intended to meet the concerns of others). Generally, this technique does not effectively resolve conflict.

      2) **Collaboration** is an attempt by all parties to the conflict to attain everyone's objectives.

      3) **Avoidance** is withdrawal from the conflict (the minimum of both cooperation and assertiveness).

      4) **Compromise** is a position in which each party to the conflict both gains and loses. It is characterized by moderate cooperation and moderate assertiveness.

      5) **Accommodation** is an intention that reflects a high degree of cooperation and a low degree of assertiveness.

   e. Conflict may result in better decision making, a reduction in complacency, more self-criticism, greater creativity, and solutions to problems. Functional conflict drives the change processes that all organizations need to survive and prosper.

1) Thus, intentional stimulation of conflict may be desirable. For example, management may intentionally trigger conflict by issuing threatening communications; by making changes in the organizational structure; by hiring new employees with different values, managerial styles, attitudes, and backgrounds; or by designating individuals to oppose the majority views of the group.

f. Conflicts may be resolved in a variety of ways.

1) **Problem solving** is a means of confronting the conflict and removing its causes. The emphasis is on facts and solutions, not personalities and assignment of blame. The disadvantage is that problem solving takes time.

2) **Smoothing** is a short-term avoidance approach. The parties in conflict are asked by management to submerge their differences temporarily.

3) **Forcing** occurs when a superior uses his/her formal authority to order a particular resolution of the conflict.

4) **Superordinate goals** are the overriding goals of the entity to which subunit and personal goals are subordinate. An appeal to these goals is another short-term solution.

5) **Compromise** entails negotiation by the parties in conflict. The conflict is avoided rather than solved through a process by which each side makes concessions. Thus, the parties both gain and lose.

6) **Expanding resources** resolves conflicts that result from scarcity.

7) **Avoidance** withdraws from and suppresses the conflict but does not solve the underlying problem.

8) **Changing the human element** involves use of behavioral techniques to change attitudes and behavior.

9) **Changing structure** alters formal organizational arrangements.

10) **Diffusion** is an approach to resolving conflict whereby critical issues are temporarily set aside while an attempt is made to reach an agreement on less controversial issues first.

11) The **public media** hinders communication because issues are addressed to the public, not the other party. However, the media may help resolve the problem through public pressure.

3. Stop and review! You have completed the outline for this subunit. Study multiple-choice questions 46 through 60 beginning on page 414.

MULTIPLE-CHOICE QUESTIONS

A. Nature of Communication

1. Communication is the process by which meaning is conveyed between people. According to communications theory

A. The process has three elements: sender, medium, receiver.

B. One-directional communication is usually most effective.

C. Communication is the message actually received, not what is transmitted.

D. Informal communications are usually to be avoided because of their inaccuracy.

The correct answer is (C). *(Publisher)*

REQUIRED: The true statement about communications.

DISCUSSION: The communication process has five elements: the sender, the symbols in which the message is encoded, the medium through which the message flows, the receiver, and feedback. Because the effectiveness of communication can be known only by its impact on the receiver and the perceived change in the receiver's behavior, the received message is what is communicated. The sent message may be garbled in encoding, in transmission, or in the receiver's decoding.

Answer (A) is incorrect because the process has the five elements listed above. Answer (B) is incorrect because effective communication requires feedback. Answer (D) is incorrect because informal communication (the grapevine) is often accurate, and effective managers use it constructively.

2. The basic purposes of an organization's internal communications network include all of the following except

A. Obtaining a common focus among employees.

B. Informing potential investors about company operations and financial results.

C. Aiding high-quality decision making.

D. Integrating the efforts of specialists.

The correct answer is (B). *(CMA, adapted)*

REQUIRED: The item not one of the basic purposes of an organization's internal communications network.

DISCUSSION: Because all managerial functions require communication, it is the secret to the success of any manager. A manager's ability to understand other people and their ability to understand the manager are crucial to accomplishing organizational objectives. Communication is the link that ties an organization together and transforms a diverse group of people into a cohesive whole. An organization's internal communications network is designed to facilitate decision making among managers, promote goal congruence among employees, integrate the efforts of all employees, and build high morale and mutual trust. Informing potential investors about company operations is a purpose of the external, not internal, communications network.

Answers (A), (C), and (D) are incorrect because basic purposes of an organization's internal communications network include establishing a common focus, aiding decision making, and integrating employee efforts.

3. Which one of the following is not an example of formal communication within an organization?

A. The grapevine.

B. Variance analysis.

C. The performance evaluation system.

D. A budget.

The correct answer is (A). *(CMA, adapted)*

REQUIRED: The item not an example of formal communication.

DISCUSSION: Formal communication is conducted through the officially established structure of the organization. Informal communication operates outside officially established structural channels. The grapevine is an example. Although the grapevine is usually accurate, it can also carry gossip and rumor.

Answers (B), (C), and (D) are incorrect because variance analysis, the performance evaluation system, and a budget are formal means of communication.

4. Which one of the following is not an example of formal internal communication?

A. Input for the yearly budget provided by the Purchasing Department to the director of budgeting.

B. Environmental impact statements.

C. Expense account reports.

D. Safety bulletins.

The correct answer is (B). *(CMA, adapted)*

REQUIRED: The item not a formal internal communication.

DISCUSSION: A formal communication is conducted through the formal structure of the organization. Informal communication operates outside of officially established channels. An internal communication is one that is both generated and received within the organization. An environmental impact statement is generated within the organization, but the recipient (a governmental body) is outside the organization.

Answers (A), (C), and (D) are incorrect because input for the yearly budget, expense reports, and safety bulletins are all forms of communication that are both generated internally and received by a person within the organization.

5. Which one of the following statements regarding communication along the grapevine in an organization is incorrect?

A. By maintaining open channels of communication, managers can minimize the damage the grapevine can do in an organization.

B. Attempts to totally eliminate the grapevine are unlikely to succeed.

C. The grapevine communication network can exist in several patterns.

D. The grapevine is rumor-mongering, and managers should not use it.

The correct answer is (D). *(CMA, adapted)*

REQUIRED: The false statement about communication along a grapevine.

DISCUSSION: A grapevine is the name of the informal communication channel that exists in all organizations. The grapevine exists wherever there are people. Although the grapevine is usually accurate, it can carry gossip and rumor. The effective manager stays tuned into the grapevine and uses it constructively.

Answer (A) is incorrect because managers can minimize the damage that a grapevine can cause by transmitting accurate and timely information and maintaining open channels of communication. Answer (B) is incorrect because attempts to eliminate the grapevine are likely to strengthen it. Answer (C) is incorrect because grapevines can exist in several patterns. For example, one person may tell one other person who tells one other person, etc.; one person may tell all people in a group; individuals may tell selected others; or individuals may tell others at random.

6. The biggest single drawback of written communication, when compared with oral communication, is that it

A. Is less time consuming.

B. Is relatively difficult.

C. Provides a permanent record.

D. Inhibits feedback.

The correct answer is (D). *(CMA, adapted)*

REQUIRED: The greatest single drawback of written communication compared with oral communication.

DISCUSSION: Written communication offers the advantage of providing a permanent record of the message. Written communication is also more accurate, but it can be time consuming to prepare. Its major disadvantage is that it inhibits feedback. The recipient of the message is not face-to-face with the sender.

Answer (A) is incorrect because written communications are time consuming to prepare. Answer (B) is incorrect because written communications are not particularly difficult for most people. Answer (C) is incorrect because a permanent record is an advantage of written communication.

7. All of the following statements about communication are correct except

A. Written communication inhibits feedback.

B. Managers spend more of their workday involved in oral communication than written communication.

C. Written communication provides a permanent record.

D. Written communication is usually better when the message is nonroutine and personal.

The correct answer is (D). *(CMA, adapted)*

REQUIRED: The false statement about communication.

DISCUSSION: Written communication is usually better when the message is routine and impersonal. A nonroutine message can be better communicated orally. Written communication also offers the advantage of providing a permanent record of the message, but it inhibits immediate feedback because the two parties are not in direct contact. Breakthroughs in electronic technology, such as computers that can recognize the human voice, may in the future blur the distinction between oral and written communication.

Answer (A) is incorrect because written communication does inhibit feedback. Answer (B) is incorrect because most managers do spend more time involved with oral than with written communication. Answer (C) is incorrect because written communication does provide a permanent record of the message.

8. Because communication is vital to effective management, managers spend most of their time communicating. Consequently, managers

A. Who are good communicators will be effective.

B. Mostly engage in oral communication.

C. Devote most of their time to formal, written communication.

D. Are essentially senders of messages.

The correct answer is (B). *(Publisher)*

REQUIRED: The true statement about managerial communication.

DISCUSSION: Because communication is the process of conveying meaning or understanding from one person to another, managers must spend most of their time communicating with subordinates, peers, and superiors. More of this communication is oral and informal than written and formal. Managers communicate lower-level results and problems upward, and coordinating information horizontally. Infrequently, communication may also be among peers or across organizational channels.

Answer (A) is incorrect because management involves more than communication skills. Answer (C) is incorrect because most communication is oral and informal. Answer (D) is incorrect because modern management theory stresses feedback and multi-channel communication, not the sending of one-way messages down to subordinates.

9. The benefits of electronic communication for a company and its employees include

A. More efficient use of resources to increase profitability.

B. Creation of redundant tasks that allow employees to develop expertise.

C. Constant development of new procedures.

D. Elimination of simulation models.

The correct answer is (A). *(Publisher)*

REQUIRED: The benefit of electronic communication for a company and its employees.

DISCUSSION: The benefits of electronic communication include better control of information, more timely information, elimination of tedious tasks, improvement of competitiveness due to improved technology, standardization of procedures by computer programs, assistance for strategic planning, and optimization of organizational resources to improve productivity.

Answer (B) is incorrect because electronic communication eliminates redundant tasks. Answer (C) is incorrect because procedures and operations are standardized by electronic communication. Answer (D) is incorrect because simulation is enhanced by computerization.

10. Communication must occur in various directions within an organization. The kind of communication that is the slowest is

A. Upward.

B. Downward.

C. Horizontal.

D. Diagonal.

The correct answer is (A). *(Publisher)*

REQUIRED: The kind of communication that is the slowest.

DISCUSSION: The directions of communication are upward, downward, horizontal, and diagonal. Upward communication is from a subordinate to a superior (morale surveys, grievance procedures, interviews, conferences). It is usually slower and must overcome more barriers than other directions of communication. Moreover, subordinates may be hesitant to communicate with superiors when interpersonal problems arise.

Answer (B) is incorrect because downward communication is easier than upward communication. It is initiated by the superior. Answer (C) is incorrect because horizontal communication occurs among peers or across organizational channels, so status differences are less of a concern, and the fear of criticism from a superior is not involved. Answer (D) is incorrect because sending a communication diagonally may be more rapid than transmittal along a traditional vertical and then horizontal path. An example is a plant manager's communicating a cost report directly to the accounting department instead of first conveying it vertically to the production vice president.

11. The marketing manager of Oakleaf Corporation wrote an interdepartmental memorandum to the budget manager concerning corrections to the sales forecast for the coming year. This is an example of

A. Downward communication.

B. Upward communication.

C. Informal communication.

D. Horizontal communication.

The correct answer is (D). *(CMA, adapted)*

REQUIRED: The type of communication represented by an interdepartmental memorandum.

DISCUSSION: An interdepartmental memorandum, as described, is a horizontal communication in that no superior-subordinate relationship is involved.

Answer (A) is incorrect because downward communication is from a superior to a subordinate. Answer (B) is incorrect because upward communication is from a subordinate to a superior. Answer (C) is incorrect because informal communication operates outside the formal structural channels of the organization; an example is the grapevine.

12. Nancy Ashburn is the cost accounting manager for Imperial Aluminum's extrusion plant. Her job involves coordinating and summarizing monthly production department variance reports that are prepared by various staff accountants. She then provides the relevant variances to her colleagues, the production departmental managers. The accounting reports communicated by Ashburn are an example of

A. Downward communication.

B. Hierarchical communication.

C. Informal communication.

D. Horizontal communication.

The correct answer is (D). *(CMA, adapted)*

REQUIRED: The type of communication represented by variance reports.

DISCUSSION: Communication can be downward (from superior to subordinate), upward (from subordinate to superior), or horizontal (from one peer to another). It may also be formal or informal. A variance report prepared in the accounting department and sent to production departments is a formal horizontal communication because it occurs among peers laterally through an officially established channel.

Answer (A) is incorrect because downward communication is from a superior to a subordinate. Answer (B) is incorrect because hierarchical communication is either upward or downward. Answer (C) is incorrect because informal communication operates outside of formal structural channels; a grapevine is an example.

13. Arthur Bell is the superintendent of a production department. Every month, Bell sends copies of his department's production variance reports to his supervisory staff asking them to explain variances that exceed certain prescribed limits. Bell's communication of variances to his supervisory staff and their explanation to him of the variances are examples of

A. Horizontal communication and upward communication, respectively.

B. Formal and informal communication, respectively.

C. Informal communication and the grapevine, respectively.

D. Downward communication and upward communication, respectively.

The correct answer is (D). *(CMA, adapted)*

REQUIRED: The types of communication represented by a supervisor's request for an explanation of variances and the subordinates' responses.

DISCUSSION: Communication can be downward (from superior to subordinate), upward (from subordinate to superior), or horizontal (from one peer to another). Bell's communication of variance reports to his subordinates is downward communication. The subordinates' replies are upward communications.

Answer (A) is incorrect because no communication among peers occurred. Answers (B) and (C) are incorrect because both forms of communication were within the formal organizational structure.

14. Which of the following devices translates the intended message into the sender's chosen communication form?

A. Transmitter.

B. Encoder.

C. Channels.

D. Decoder.

The correct answer is (B). *(Publisher)*

REQUIRED: The device that translates the original message into the communication form chosen by the sender.

DISCUSSION: The encoder is a device used to translate the sender's message into an appropriate form of communication. This communication form is selected by the sender of the message. The device may be verbal, written, or nonverbal, such as facial expressions or voice inflections. Computers are often used as encoders.

Answer (A) is incorrect because a transmitter is a device used by the encoder to send the message toward the receiver. Answer (C) is incorrect because channels are media along which the message travels, e.g., telephone lines. Answer (D) is incorrect because a decoder is a device used to translate the message into a form meaningful to the receiver. The human auditory system is a decoder.

15. Communication is most likely to be effective when

A. The sender carefully considers the receiver's needs.

B. Sender and receiver concentrate only on verbal messages.

C. It changes the receiver's attitude.

D. The receiver monitors the sender's behavior.

The correct answer is (A). *(Publisher)*

REQUIRED: The instance in which communication is most likely to be effective.

DISCUSSION: The needs, abilities, and skills of the receiver must be taken into account by the sender. The sender must fit the message to what the receiver can effectively receive or the message will be useless.

Answer (B) is incorrect because nonverbal cues (body language) may be vital in transmitting a message and in receiving feedback. Answer (C) is incorrect because effective communication changes behavior, not just attitudes. Answer (D) is incorrect because the sender should monitor the receiver's behavior or solicit feedback to determine the effectiveness of the message.

16. An advisable strategy for a participant in a meeting of the employees would be to

A. Read the agenda and supporting materials for the meeting during the early part of the meeting to prepare for later discussion.

B. Present strong opinions on one side of a proposal right away.

C. Present views as trial balloons that can be researched later.

D. Consider the opinions and information needs of other participants before speaking.

The correct answer is (D). *(CIA, adapted)*

REQUIRED: The strategy for a participant in a meeting of the employees.

DISCUSSION: Analyzing the audience assists a speaker to gather the right information for the meeting. Moreover, understanding the other participants' opinions and needs enables the speaker to express his/her ideas in the way best calculated to be persuasive.

Answer (A) is incorrect because the most effective meeting participants come to meetings prepared. The agenda and other materials should be read in advance. Answer (B) is incorrect because, unless the speaker is certain of others' opinions (or is the most powerful person in the organization), (s)he should not commit to a position until the degree of support for that view can be estimated. Answer (C) is incorrect because ideas should be researched in advance of the meeting so that the participant appears to be prepared and productive.

17. At Marshall Inc., accounting clerks log incoming invoices, and the controller determines the amount and timing of invoice payments. For this type of situation, the most efficient and accurate communication network is the

A. All-channel network.

B. Circle network.

C. Chain network.

D. Wheel network.

The correct answer is (D). *(CMA, adapted)*

REQUIRED: The best communication network to use for a system in which clerks log invoices and the controller determines the amount and timing of payments.

DISCUSSION: In the wheel form of communication network, the leader acts as a central conduit for all communications. Because the controller must process all payments, a wheel network offers the most efficient and accurate communication channel in these circumstances.

Answer (A) is incorrect because an all-channel network is inappropriate. All members of this group have no need to communicate with each other. Answers (B) and (C) are incorrect because a circle network and a chain network, are inappropriate. Each member of the group must communicate with the controller.

18. Nonverbal communication is a powerful but little-understood form of communication in organizations. All of the following represent forms of nonverbal communication except

A. The tone of voice a person selects.

B. The positioning of furniture in a person's office.

C. Prolonged eye contact.

D. A facsimile message from a business associate.

The correct answer is (D). *(CMA, adapted)*

REQUIRED: The item that is not a form of nonverbal communication.

DISCUSSION: Nonverbal communication consists of the nuances that accompany a verbal communication. For instance, the tone of a speaker's voice may communicate something totally different from the words being spoken. Similarly, body language (facial expressions, gestures, posture, and appearance) is a nonverbal communicator. Even the positioning or nature of furniture in an office may communicate something to a listener. A fax message, however, is a verbal communication to the extent that it contains words.

Answer (A) is incorrect because the tone of voice can be a nonverbal communication. Answer (B) is incorrect because the way people organize their offices can indicate a feeling of openness or a feeling of separateness. Answer (C) is incorrect because eye contact is usually considered to be a positive communication tool.

19. Nonverbal communication consists of messages conveyed by

I. The physical distance between the sender and the receiver
II. The facial expressions used when speaking
III. Electronic means of communication such as e-mail
IV. Unconscious actions of the speaker while speaking

A. III only.

B. IV only.

C. I and II only.

D. I, II, and IV.

The correct answer is (D). *(CIA, adapted)*

REQUIRED: The true statement(s) about nonverbal communication.

DISCUSSION: Physical distance and positioning convey many nonverbal messages that depend on cultural differences. For example, Americans tend to prefer a large personal space. Facial expressions provide almost limitless variations of meaning thanks to the dozens of facial muscles and the possibilities created by different contexts, cultures, and individual personalities. In addition to facial expressions, other unconscious actions of the speaker affect the message sent. They include gestures, posture, movement, touch, mode of dress, surroundings, and voice characteristics.

Answer (A) is incorrect because e-mail is electronic communication, not a nonverbal communication. Answer (B) is incorrect because the physical distance between the sender and the receiver and the facial expressions used when speaking are also nonverbal signals. Answer (C) is incorrect because the speaker's unconscious actions are part of nonverbal communication.

B. Problems in Communication

20. In which one of the following statements is the use of accounting jargon an impediment to communication between accountants and nonaccounting professionals?

A. "Labor standards tell us how much time workers should take to assemble a computer."

B. "I am trying to decide whether the million dollar disbursement should be expensed or capitalized."

C. "In carrying out variance analysis, I am seeking the possible reasons why the net income shown in the financial statements for the year 1996 is 20% less than expected."

D. "An accounting department in a factory is classified as a service because it allows the departments actually involved in the making of products freedom from bookkeeping chores."

The correct answer is (B). *(CMA, adapted)*

REQUIRED: The statement in which accounting jargon impedes communication.

DISCUSSION: The use of jargon leads to communication problems when a specialist tries to send a message to a nonspecialist. The use of the phrase "expensed or capitalized" is a use of jargon in that a nonaccountant might not understand the technical meaning of the terms. Thus, the recipient of the message may not be able to provide a clear answer.

Answer (A) is incorrect because this statement is straightforward in that it defines the technical term labor standards. Answer (C) is incorrect because the technical term is described in layman's terms. Answer (D) is incorrect because no technical accounting terms are used.

21. Which of the following perceptual errors is the tendency for one party to attribute his/her traits to the other party when communicating?

A. Expectancy.

B. Projection.

C. The halo effect.

D. Stereotyping.

The correct answer is (B). *(Publisher)*

REQUIRED: The perceptual error that occurs when one person assigns his/her traits to the other person when communicating.

DISCUSSION: Perception is the process used to adapt the message to the receiver during encoding or to interpret the message from the sender when decoding. Perceptual errors cause misinterpretation of the intended message. Projection is the tendency for the sender to attribute his/her traits, values, and emotions to the receiver and vice versa.

Answer (A) is incorrect because expectancy is the tendency to allow past experience to affect the individual's perception of the other party. Answer (C) is incorrect because the halo effect is the extrapolation of a judgment about one matter to other, possibly unrelated, issues. Answer (D) is incorrect because stereotyping is the attribution to another person of traits that are commonly associated with a category or group to which that person belongs.

22. Noise may disrupt communication during transmission. All of the following are examples of noise except

A. Selective perception.

B. Static on a telephone line.

C. A letter lost because it was interspersed with junk mail.

D. A participant in a conversation being called away for a meeting.

The correct answer is (A). *(CMA, adapted)*

REQUIRED: The item that is not an example of noise.

DISCUSSION: Noise in a communication channel is an outside disruption that impedes the flow of a message. It can vary from real noise, such as loud machines running and static on a phone line, to disruptions such as phone calls during a face-to-face conversation. Selective perception on the part of either the sender or the receiver of a message is not noise because it is not an outside disruption.

Answer (B) is incorrect because static on a phone line is noise that might affect the quality of a communication. Answer (C) is incorrect because a lost letter is a random event that can cause a disruption in communication. Answer (D) is incorrect because an interruption during a conversation disrupts the communication.

23. A manager found that instructions given to a subordinate were not followed. A review of the cause of the failure revealed that the manager was interrupted by several telephone calls while issuing the instructions. In terms of problems in the communications chain, the interruptions are

A. Noise.

B. Nonverbal feedback.

C. Semantics.

D. Closure.

The correct answer is (A). *(CIA, adapted)*

REQUIRED: The interruptions encountered in the communications process.

DISCUSSION: Noise in the communication channel refers to any disruption that impedes the encoding, sending, or receipt of a message, such as being interrupted by several telephone calls while issuing instructions.

Answer (B) is incorrect because nonverbal feedback, or body language, encompasses the facial expressions, gestures, and posture that send various messages. Answer (C) is incorrect because semantics is the study of meanings, especially connotative nuances. Answer (D) is incorrect because closure is the process of filling in the blanks of an incomplete message.

Questions 24 and 25 are based on the following information. A multinational firm was attempting to buy a controlling interest in a medium-sized ($10 million annual sales) Brazilian metal-working firm. Its negotiator in Brazil sent the following telegram: "They won't deal unless 51% ownership." The executive committee of the multinational firm, not wanting a minority interest, then canceled the deal. Upon returning to the multinational firm, the negotiator pointed out that the Brazilian firm wanted to sell no more than 51% ownership so they could retain at least 49%. Thus, the deal could have been made.

24. The telegram received by the executive committee was faulty. In terms of the links in the communications process, the error occurred because of

A. Noise in the communication chain.

B. The sender's perception.

C. Message encoding.

D. The choice of transmission medium.

The correct answer is (C). *(CIA, adapted)*

REQUIRED: The reason for the communications error.

DISCUSSION: Encoding is the sender's packaging of an idea for better understanding. It entails translating the message into symbols that can be transmitted through the chosen medium of communication and then decoded by the recipient. In this example, the sender's wording of the message was misleading.

Answer (A) is incorrect because the message was received exactly as transmitted. Answer (B) is incorrect because sender had the correct perception of the message as it was actually encoded. Answer (D) is incorrect because no transmission errors occurred.

25. The faulty telegram led to a communications error by the executive committee of the multinational firm. The error was in

A. Decoding of the message.

B. Choice of transmission medium.

C. Understanding of the message.

D. Response to the message.

The correct answer is (C). *(CIA, adapted)*

REQUIRED: The nature of the communications error.

DISCUSSION: Because of faulty encoding, the message was open to two different interpretations. The committee chose the wrong one.

Answer (A) is incorrect because words were properly decoded. Answer (B) is incorrect because the medium was capable of completing the exchange. Answer (D) is incorrect because the action matched the committee's understanding of the message.

26. Which of the following actions is most likely to minimize the effect of perceptual errors?

A. The sender should ensure that the receiver understands the message by allowing only one-way communication.

B. The receiver should consider how the sender decodes the message.

C. The sender alone should minimize noise in the flow of communication.

D. The receiver should try to understand the sender's perspective.

The correct answer is (D). *(Publisher)*

REQUIRED: The action that should be taken to minimize perceptual errors.

DISCUSSION: Perceptual errors can be minimized in several ways, including feedback from the receiver concerning his/her perceptions and interpretations of the message, understanding of the sender's perspective by the receiver, the sender's sensitivity to the receiver's problems, and implementation of a training program to improve communication skills throughout the company.

Answer (A) is incorrect because the sender should encourage feedback from the receiver through two-way communication. Answer (B) is incorrect because the sender encodes the message; the receiver decodes the message. Answer (C) is incorrect because both parties should make an effort to minimize noise.

27. Which one of the following statements about human perception and its role in the communication process is incorrect?

A. Perception is used to interpret information from the environment.

B. Perception can distort communication only at the end of the communication process.

C. Selective perception refers to the tendency to remember what we prefer and to forget what we are uncomfortable with.

D. Stereotyping is a form of perceptual organization.

The correct answer is (B). *(CMA, adapted)*

REQUIRED: The false statement about human perception and its role in the communication process.

DISCUSSION: Managers must always consider the perceptions of a message recipient. Recipients vary in their perception of messages because of background, language, education, attitudes toward the sender (such as stereotyping) and job, etc. This variance can result in communication distortion at any stage of the communication process.

Answer (A) is incorrect because perception is the process of giving meaning to the environment, e.g., to determine the meaning of messages. Answer (C) is incorrect because selectivity is the necessary process of filtering external stimuli. Answer (D) is incorrect because stereotyping is a way of organizing and interpreting experience. Unfortunately, it entails drawing inferences based on inadequate information.

28. Which one of the following statements about the nature of communication is correct?

A. Communication occurs only when we deliberately and consciously decide to communicate.

B. Accounting terms such as expense, revenue, net income, and variance mean the same to all users.

C. Because managerial accounting reports classify and summarize vast amounts of data, they do not add to the information overload within an organization.

D. Communication between departments is affected by the level of functional specialization within departments.

The correct answer is (D). *(CMA, adapted)*

REQUIRED: The true statement about the nature of communication.

DISCUSSION: Communication between departments is sometimes affected by the level of functional specialization within those departments. Noise of any sort can inhibit communication, and that noise can be physical or nonphysical. An example of nonphysical noise is the difference in expertise between the sender and the recipient. A sender must establish a climate that encourages the elimination of interpersonal barriers to communication.

Answer (A) is incorrect because communication can be unconscious, e.g., body language. Answer (B) is incorrect because accounting terms can mean different things to different people; that is why some companies use an accounting manual to promote consistent treatment of similar items. Answer (C) is incorrect because accounting reports can add to information overload, particularly for people who do not understand them.

29. "But, I mailed the order 4 weeks ago, giving the supplier plenty of time," said the parts manager when asked why a critical part was not available. The most likely reason for this failed communication between the parts manager and the supplier was

A. Lack of feedback.

B. Confusing language.

C. Inappropriate medium.

D. Perceptual selectivity.

The correct answer is (A). *(CIA, adapted)*

REQUIRED: The most likely reason for failed communication between the parts manager and the supplier.

DISCUSSION: The effectiveness of communication can be determined only by the sender's seeking feedback and observing the impact of the communication on the receiver. The sender is obligated to solicit feedback to ensure that the communication process is complete. The receiver should give feedback to the sender. The importance of feedback to check the effectiveness of the communication process indicates the limitations of one-way communications (e.g., memos). Effectiveness can be measured only when the sender perceives a change in the receiver's behavior. Thus, the parts manager (the sender) should have sought, and the supplier (the receiver) should have provided, feedback.

Answer (B) is incorrect because the facts do not suggest that the language used was confusing. Answer (C) is incorrect because the mail is an acceptable medium of transmission. Answer (D) is incorrect because the supplier had no reason to ignore (selectively screen out) an order. A supplier's perceptual selection obviously includes rather than excludes customer orders.

30. Which one of the following will not help overcome communication problems between the Accounting Department and other departments?

A. Interdepartmental task forces.

B. Cross training and job rotation.

C. Organization-wide social events.

D. A performance appraisal prepared by your immediate supervisor.

The correct answer is (D). *(CMA, adapted)*

REQUIRED: The item that will not help overcome communication problems between accounting and other departments.

DISCUSSION: Horizontal communication between departments is often subject to more problems than either upward or downward communication within a single department. Examples of these problems include the use of technical terms understood by only one side in the communication process, faulty channel selection, and interpersonal problems. To overcome these difficulties, the sender must encode the message in the context of the receiver's perceptions; that is, the sender must understand the receiver. The sender must establish an interpersonal climate that encourages the elimination of interpersonal barriers to communication. A performance appraisal prepared by the accountant's supervisor will not help the accountant understand the perceptions of people in other departments.

Answers (A), (B), and (C) are incorrect because interdepartmental task forces, cross training and job rotation, and organization-wide social events are excellent means of overcoming communication problems between departments.

Questions 31 and 32 are based on the following information. The supervisor of purchasing reviewed a memorandum prepared for a buyer in the department. The memo read, "Effective September 30, the corporation has determined that your functions will be absorbed into our parent company's small-unit purchasing function. This will reduce operating costs, improve communications, and facilitate production engineering changes. You will be provided with outplacement support." "That should cover the situation," thought the supervisor. "It's too bad that I am leaving on vacation before the buyer returns from vacation, but this memo will give the buyer the general idea."

31. What link in the communications chain is defective?

A. The meaning of the message would be unclear to the buyer.

B. The supervisor chose the wrong channel for the communication.

C. The supervisor should not be the source of this type of communication.

D. The supervisor did not account for the noise in the communication chain.

The correct answer is (B). *(CIA, adapted)*

REQUIRED: The link in the communications chain that is defective.

DISCUSSION: In the communications process, the medium is the channel through which the communication flows. The defect in this case was the channel chosen to inform the employee of his/her loss of job. The supervisor should have spoken directly with the employee.

Answer (A) is incorrect because the buyer will readily understand that (s)he has been fired. Answer (C) is incorrect because the buyer's supervisor should have conveyed the news of the termination. Answer (D) is incorrect because there is no noise (interference) in the communication channel.

32. Select an additional deficiency in the communication chain.

A. The receiver of the communication was inappropriate; the personnel department should have received the memorandum and then informed the buyer.

B. The message is improperly encoded because the buyer does not know why the termination is to be completed.

C. Because the supervisor and buyer have conflicting vacation schedules, no possibility exists for feedback.

D. The supervisor should not be the sender of the memorandum; the personnel department is the appropriate source.

The correct answer is (C). *(CIA, adapted)*

REQUIRED: The additional deficiency in the communications chain.

DISCUSSION: The communications process has five elements: (1) the sender of the message, (2) symbols used to encode the message, (3) the medium chosen to send the message, (4) the receiver of the message, and (5) feedback acknowledging interpretation of the message by the receiver. Because the supervisor and buyer have conflicting vacation schedules, no possibility exists for feedback, and the buyer is not referred to anyone else in the organization for any additional information.

Answer (A) is incorrect because, although the message should also be routed through the personnel department, the notification of a termination appropriately comes from the direct superior. Answer (B) is incorrect because the memorandum included the reasons for the termination. Answer (D) is incorrect because communication of a direct job-related impact should be transmitted by the employee's immediate superior.

C. Listening and Other Forms of Communication

33. Tolerating silence, asking open-ended questions, and paraphrasing are three aids to more effective

A. Meetings.

B. Listening.

C. Interviews.

D. Feedback.

The correct answer is (B). *(CIA, adapted)*

REQUIRED: The process rendered more effective by tolerating silence, asking open-ended questions, and paraphrasing.

DISCUSSION: Listening entails decoding and understanding the first message sent. The sender then becomes a listener with respect to the feedback. Hence, listening is necessary at both ends of the communication channel. Other aids to effective listening are using body language to encourage the speaker, showing appropriate emotion to signify sympathy, understanding and correcting for one's biases, avoiding making premature judgments, and briefly summarizing what has been said.

Answer (A) is incorrect because these methods may slow down a meeting. Answer (C) is incorrect because these methods may or may not help depending on the purpose of the interview. Answer (D) is incorrect because only paraphrasing relates to feedback.

34. A supportive behavior that a listener, such as an auditor or a supervisor, can use to encourage a speaker would be to

A. Look away from the speaker to avoid any intimidation.

B. Interject a similar incident or experience.

C. Stop other activity or work while the person is talking.

D. Not respond verbally until the speaker stops talking.

The correct answer is (C). *(CIA, adapted)*

REQUIRED: The supportive behavior that a listener can use to encourage a speaker.

DISCUSSION: An effective listener enhances the communication process by sending appropriate nonverbal signals to the speaker. Thus, even though a person can probably listen and do some routine work, a listener who wishes to convey a positive and encouraging message should stop other activities and focus complete attention on the speaker.

Answer (A) is incorrect because looking away is discouraging. Answer (B) is incorrect because interruptions devalue the speaker and the speaker's message. Answer (D) is incorrect because complete silence may appear disapproving.

35. Some studies show that managers spend 60 to 70% of their time communicating and that nearly 60% of that time is spent listening. Listening effectiveness is best increased by

A. Resisting both internal and external distractions.

B. Waiting to review key concepts until the speaker is through talking.

C. Tuning out messages that do not seem to fit the meeting purpose.

D. Factoring in biases to evaluate the information being given.

The correct answer is (A). *(CIA, adapted)*

REQUIRED: The best method to increase listening effectiveness.

DISCUSSION: Concentrating on what the speaker is saying is critical to effective listening. This result is best achieved by resisting internal and external distractions. Physical distractions such as noise, a tendency to be overly aware of the speaker's physical and other differences from the listener, focusing on interesting details at the expense of major points, or emotional reactions to a statement with which the listener disagrees should be avoided.

Answer (B) is incorrect because, given that a person listens faster than a speaker talks, (s)he can review the key concepts silently without waiting for the speaker to conclude. This process helps the listener remember them better without notes. Answer (C) is incorrect because seemingly unrelated information may be important. Answer (D) is incorrect because the listener should concentrate on the information while listening. Later, that person can allow for bias on both the listener's part and the speaker's part.

36. All of the following are true about business memos except

A. They are usually short.

B. They should be written in active voice.

C. The tone should be casual to get the reader's attention.

D. They should be concise, clear, and readable.

The correct answer is (C). *(CIA, adapted)*

REQUIRED: The false statement about business memos.

DISCUSSION: Memos can vary considerably in tone, depending on what they are about and how they will be circulated. Some are quite formal, while others are informal, depending on many factors (i.e., message, circulation, etc.).

Answer (A) is incorrect because memos are usually short, but some can be lengthy reports. Answer (B) is incorrect because passive voice is often wordier and more awkward than active voice, which is stronger and more vivid. Answer (D) is incorrect because memos should have the characteristics of good writing. They should avoid unnecessary verbiage, and readers should grasp the meaning quickly and easily.

37. All of the following are true about good writing styles used in business memos except

A. Draws positive attention to the writing style.

B. Treats all receivers with respect.

C. Suits the method of presentation and delivery.

D. Develops ideas without overstatement.

The correct answer is (A). *(CIA, adapted)*

REQUIRED: The false statement about good writing styles for business memos.

DISCUSSION: Good business writing style is concise, clear, coherent, correct, credible, natural, positive, interesting, and readable. It treats receivers with respect by sending a courteous message. It is also suitable to the medium of presentation and delivery. Good business writing style provides clear, developed ideas but avoids overstatement. It also conveys the message unobtrusively. The writing should not call attention to itself.

Answer (B) is incorrect because treating all receivers with respect is a characteristic of good business style. Answer (C) is incorrect because using a suitable writing style for the method of presentation and delivery is a characteristic of good business style. Answer (D) is incorrect because developing ideas without overstating is a characteristic of good business style.

38. A memorandum to announce an important, mandatory meeting should contain several details, including

A. A list of all of the people who may be affected by the meeting.

B. The expected length of the meeting.

C. A brief description of the topic of the next monthly meeting.

D. The person to contact if the employee has not received the memorandum.

The correct answer is (B). *(Publisher)*

REQUIRED: The detail to include in a memorandum announcing an important, mandatory meeting.

DISCUSSION: The necessary details for a memorandum announcing a mandatory meeting include the purpose and goals of the meeting, a list of who must attend, the information or reports required for the meeting, the expected length of the meeting, and the person to contact regarding any questions or problems.

Answer (A) is incorrect because such a list is not necessary in the memorandum and may result in information overload, which clouds the reader's understanding of the main points of the memorandum. Answer (C) is incorrect because the memorandum should cover only one subject, specifically the meeting it announces. Answer (D) is incorrect because an employee who has not received the memorandum may not be aware of it or need to receive it. In addition, (s)he could not find out whom to contact without receiving a memorandum or reading someone else's copy.

39. After writing a memorandum announcing a meeting but before the meeting occurs, the writer-chair should take several actions, including

A. Checking with his/her superior for approval to call the meeting.

B. Calling the participants to find out if they have any questions or problems.

C. Distributing a proposed agenda for the meeting to all participants.

D. Requesting an advance copy of all supporting information to be brought to the meeting by each participant.

The correct answer is (C). *(Publisher)*

REQUIRED: The preliminary action to be taken by the chair after announcing a meeting.

DISCUSSION: There are several preliminary actions the writer-chair should take after announcing the meeting, including distributing the planned agenda, providing copies of information that will prepare the participants for the meeting, and calling the participants to remind them of their required attendance.

Answer (A) is incorrect because approval should have been obtained prior to announcing the meeting. Answer (B) is incorrect because the name of the person to contact about questions and problems should have been included in the memorandum. Answer (D) is incorrect because allowing each person to choose the style of presentation may be preferable. In addition, the individual may not be able to distribute the information in advance.

40. A special, mandatory meeting was announced in a memorandum. What action should the chair take during the meeting to make it more productive?

A. Direct individual responses offered by participants.

B. Take the minutes.

C. Discuss at the beginning of this meeting the minutes from the last monthly meeting.

D. Discuss any topics relating to the special purpose of the meeting in the random order that they are introduced by participants.

The correct answer is (A). *(Publisher)*

REQUIRED: The action the chair of a special meeting could take to make it more productive.

DISCUSSION: The chair could state its purpose and objectives at the beginning of the meeting, maintain a list of assignments decided on during the meeting, focus the discussion by giving direction, curtail repetition and triviality, encourage individual responses, and summarize and review the discussion at the meeting's conclusion.

Answer (B) is incorrect because the chair would be too busy to take minutes and chair the meeting. (S)he should assign this task to another participant. Answer (C) is incorrect because the minutes for the last monthly meeting would normally be read at the next monthly meeting. This meeting was called for a special purpose. Answer (D) is incorrect because the meeting will run more smoothly if a preestablished agenda is distributed to all participants and followed.

41. Which of the following actions should a chair take following an important, mandatory meeting announced in a memorandum?

A. Place the minutes and any documented information shared at the meeting in a file to which (s)he alone has access.

B. Distribute a list of any individual assignments made during the meeting to all company personnel.

C. If any problems arise, call a follow-up meeting announced to all participants at a moment's notice.

D. Request status reports on projects assigned to individuals during the meeting.

The correct answer is (D). *(Publisher)*

REQUIRED: The action the chair should take after the meeting to enhance its results.

DISCUSSION: There are several actions the chair should take after a meeting. A follow-up of special assignments made to individuals at the meeting is appropriate. A request for periodic reports on the status of these assignments may be made or the individuals can be contacted directly.

Answer (A) is incorrect because the minutes, attendance list, and documented information from the meeting should be distributed to participants. Answer (B) is incorrect because it is unnecessary and costly to distribute such a list. Answer (C) is incorrect because, if at all possible, the participants should be informed of the time and location of the follow-up meeting with plenty of time to adjust their schedules, prepare, and plan.

42. In a persuasive message organized around rational arguments, a persuasive writer deals with the opposition's arguments by

A. Refuting some of their more vulnerable arguments in a subtle fashion.

B. Taking a representative sample of their arguments and agreeing that the strong ones are strong and refuting the weaker ones.

C. Attacking the character of the people who hold those opinions.

D. Refuting arguments at the end of the message to show that they are the least important.

The correct answer is (A). *(CIA, adapted)*

REQUIRED: The means of countering opposing arguments in a persuasive writing.

DISCUSSION: A typical sequence of arguments in a persuasive message places strong arguments first and last, with weaker arguments and refutations of opposing arguments in the middle. The reasons for this ordering are the primacy and recency principles. People tend to remember best what they read or hear first and last. The middle section includes weaker arguments. It also is the appropriate location of counterarguments. Selective choice of the opponent's arguments that can be successfully rebutted can be very effective. However, mention of the opponent's arguments that cannot be refuted will weaken the persuader's case.

Answer (B) is incorrect because attacking strong arguments may help the opponent. Refuting weaker arguments shows that the opposing position has weaknesses. Answer (C) is incorrect because an attack on the character of the opponent is not a rational business strategy. It may hurt the persuader more than it will help. Answer (D) is incorrect because the last part of the message should move readers or listeners to action.

43. In a written communication, which of the following is least likely to cause changes in attitudes?

A. Make sure that the message is credible.

B. Present as many different issues in as short a time as possible.

C. Appeal to the individual's emotions.

D. Shape the argument to the listener.

The correct answer is (B). *(CIA, adapted)*

REQUIRED: The item least likely to cause changes in attitudes.

DISCUSSION: Presenting many different issues in as short a time as possible will confuse the listener and cause the message to be lost or disregarded. To convey a persuasive message effectively, the communicator should make a clear presentation that focuses on the ultimate objective. The argument should be stated one idea at a time, and unrelated subjects and jumping from issue to issue should be avoided. The presentation should guide the recipient of the communication directly to the desired conclusion.

Answer (A) is incorrect because trust, competence, objectivity, and high ethical standards are important in changing attitudes. Answer (C) is incorrect because, although rational and objective evidence is important, one also should try to understand a person's loves, hates, fears, and frustrations. This information can then be used to design what to say and how to say it to effectively change the person's attitudes. Answer (D) is incorrect because effective persuasion demands flexibility so that arguments presented have a better chance of changing the person's attitudes.

44. Which of the following is a benefit of a holiday party as a communication link between employees and management?

A. Employees are given the opportunity to discuss issues with management in an informal setting.

B. Employees become more aware of the organizations' objectives.

C. Each employee may discuss concerns without fear of repercussions from management.

D. Outstanding employee performance is communicated in a formal, public atmosphere.

The correct answer is (A). *(Publisher)*

REQUIRED: The benefit of a holiday party for employees and management.

DISCUSSION: The benefits of a holiday party include establishing a controlled setting in which all levels of employees can interact equally, acknowledging that the company appreciates the employees, and providing an opportunity for discussions with management other than the immediate supervisor.

Answer (B) is incorrect because increased employee awareness of corporate objectives is more likely to be a benefit of written communication, such as a periodic newsletter. Answer (C) is incorrect because the opportunity to express concerns without repercussion is more likely to be a benefit of negotiating employee-supervisor differences. Answer (D) is incorrect because communication of outstanding performance is more likely to occur when recognizing employee achievements, which may not be done at a holiday party.

45. Telecommuting, working away from the office and communicating via electronic media, has become more widespread as advances in communication devices have made this more practical. All of the following are problems that are beginning to be associated with employees using telecommuting except that the telecommuting employees

A. Fall behind in their fields of specialization.

B. Lack strong working relationships.

C. Experience a loss of career opportunities.

D. Lack sufficient communication skills.

The correct answer is (D). *(CMA, adapted)*

REQUIRED: The item that is not a problem associated with employees who telecommute from their homes.

DISCUSSION: People who are computer literate have in recent years begun working from their homes via telecommunication devices. Problems include lack of reliable telephone lines, a potential increase in management's work load, the loss of in-office contributions, a tendency to fall behind in fields of specialization, a lack of strong working relationships with other employees, a loss of career opportunities, and inadequate socialization. The primary strength of these individuals, however, has been their communication skills.

Answer (A) is incorrect because telecommuters have tended to fall behind in their fields of specialization. Answer (B) is incorrect because telecommuters may be unable to form normal manager-employee and employee-employee relationships. Interaction with telecommuters poses obvious problems. Answer (C) is incorrect because telecommuters sometimes experience a loss of career opportunities as a result of not being in the office on a day-to-day basis.

D. Negotiation and Conflict Management

46. A construction manager is using a distributive-bargaining approach in negotiating the price of lumber with a supplier. The construction manager will

A. Concede to the supplier's asking price in order to maintain a positive working relationship.

B. Hire a mediator to negotiate the deal on behalf of the manager.

C. Attempt to get agreement on a price within the settlement range (that is, within both the manager's and supplier's aspiration ranges).

D. State the resistance point (that is, the highest price acceptable) and ask the supplier to concede.

The correct answer is (C). *(CIA, adapted)*

REQUIRED: The action based on a distributive-bargaining approach.

DISCUSSION: When using a distributive-bargaining approach, the negotiator operates with a maximum desired result (target point) and a minimum acceptable result (resistance point) in mind. If the ranges of feasible outcomes (aspiration ranges) overlap, an agreement is possible.

Answer (A) is incorrect because, when using a distributive-bargaining approach, the manager should negotiate a price that both the manager and the supplier can agree on. Answer (B) is incorrect because a mediator is not used when the distributive-bargaining approach is used to resolve a conflict. Answer (D) is incorrect because the manager should not reveal the resistance point (the minimum acceptable result). Instead, (s)he should negotiate to induce the supplier to agree to an amount closer to the target point.

47. As a conflict resolution strategy, optimizing (or a win-win strategy) is most appropriate when

A. The benefits being contested cannot be changed.

B. The relationship between the parties is likely to continue.

C. People are deeply committed to established habits and patterns.

D. Time is scarce and the manager's patience is wearing thin.

The correct answer is (B). *(CIA, adapted)*

REQUIRED: The circumstances in which optimizing is most appropriate.

DISCUSSION: Optimizing or problem solving entails addressing the source of conflict and finding alternative strategies that benefit all parties. It promotes cooperative, positive attitudes that transfer to other organizational behaviors. Hence, optimizing may be worth the expenditure of more resources than other strategies because it improves the future relationship of the parties.

Answer (A) is incorrect because optimizing can usually discover more benefits to divide. Answer (C) is incorrect because, to optimize, people need to think outside of established habits to find new benefits to divide. Answer (D) is incorrect because optimizing takes more time and energy than other conflict resolution strategies.

48. Two managers have been arguing about the distribution of money for capital investment projects affecting their respective production units. All of the projects are worthwhile and significantly exceed the organization's required rate of return. The approach that would create a win-win solution for the managers under these circumstances would be to

A. Smooth the differences of the two managers by emphasizing their common interests.

B. Alter the attitudes and behaviors of the managers so that agreement can be reached.

C. Force the managers to compromise by asking each of them to give up something.

D. Expand the resources available so that both manager's projects can be funded.

The correct answer is (D). *(CIA, adapted)*

REQUIRED: The conflict resolution method creating a win-win situation.

DISCUSSION: Expanding the pool of scarce resources, in this case, the money available for capital projects, permits both managers to achieve their objectives without having to give up anything of value. Thus, each side wins.

Answer (A) is incorrect because emphasizing common ground may resolve the conflict but does not allow each party to get what (s)he wants. Answer (B) is incorrect because altering attitudes and behaviors that cause conflict does not create a win-win situation. Answer (C) is incorrect because compromise forces each side to give up something of value.

49. Two managers have been informed that their units will be relocated to a new site. The units are to share space at the new office location. The managers have been arguing for several weeks over the allocation of space and the location of offices. This disagreement is threatening the relocation schedule and disrupting other projects. The managers' supervisor has now become involved in the conflict and must try to minimize the potential for hurt feelings while resolving the problem quickly. Identify the supervisor's best approach for this situation.

A. Sit down with the managers and determine a solution.

B. Design a floor plan and tell the managers who occupies what space.

C. Remind the managers that the company needs their cooperation in this effort so that costs can be reduced.

D. Tell the managers not to worry and that problems like this have a way of working themselves out.

The correct answer is (A). *(CIA, adapted)*

REQUIRED: The supervisor's best approach for resolving a conflict between managers.

DISCUSSION: Problem solving is a means of confronting the conflict and removing its causes. The emphasis is on facts and solutions, not personalities and assignment of blame. The disadvantage is that problem solving takes time. In this situation, a three-party negotiation stressing a win-win attitude is appropriate. Negotiation should be feasible because the parties have overlapping interests.

Answer (B) is incorrect because forcing does not resolve the basis for the conflict and can cause resentment to grow. Answer (C) is incorrect because superordinate goals can be achieved only by bringing conflicting parties together. This disagreement is over the allocation of scarce resources, office space. One party may not be inclined to cooperate unless the supervisor requires some form of compromise. Answer (D) is incorrect because avoidance merely postpones the inevitable face-to-face resolution of this disagreement.

50. While conducting field work, a strong conflict arises between two of your subordinates regarding possible scope expansion. You draw their attention to their shared views, downplaying the issues of contention. This technique for resolving conflict is called

A. Superordinate goals.

B. Smoothing.

C. Problem solving.

D. Compromise.

The correct answer is (B). *(CIA, adapted)*

REQUIRED: The technique for resolving conflict.

DISCUSSION: Smoothing is a conflict resolution technique in which differences are de-emphasized and common interests of the parties are emphasized. It has the disadvantage of not solving the underlying problems that created the conflict.

Answer (A) is incorrect because superordinate goals are shared goals that can be achieved only through cooperation. Answer (C) is incorrect because problem solving involves identifying and correcting the source of the conflict. Answer (D) is incorrect because compromise requires each party to give up something.

51. Which of the following is a benefit of the communication link represented by negotiating employee-supervisor differences?

A. Each employee perceives that management values his/her accomplishments.

B. A written communication link between the employees and management is provided.

C. Each employee is shown that management values his/her rights and needs.

D. The need for an informal grapevine is reduced.

The correct answer is (C). *(Publisher)*

REQUIRED: The benefit of negotiations between the employees and the supervisor.

DISCUSSION: The benefits of negotiating employee-supervisor differences include communicating both sides of an issue without litigation, recognizing employee concerns to indicate that management values each subordinate's needs and rights, and impartially treating tensions in the work environment while finding compromise solutions.

Answer (A) is incorrect because the perception that management values employee accomplishments is a benefit of recognition of employee achievements rather than negotiation. Answers (B) and (D) are incorrect because a written communication link and the reduced need for the informal grapevine are benefits of a device such as a periodic (e.g., monthly or quarterly) newsletter.

52. There are many types of third-party negotiations available to parties facing disagreement. If the goal is to be certain that settlement is reached, a negotiator with authority to make a decision should be selected. The best negotiator to select, given this goal, would be a(n)

A. Mediator.

B. Arbitrator.

C. Consultant.

D. Conciliator.

The correct answer is (B). *(CIA, adapted)*

REQUIRED: The best negotiator if the goal is to be certain that settlement is reached.

DISCUSSION: An arbitrator has the authority to impose an agreement. Arbitration may be requested by the parties or may be imposed by law or by the terms of a contract.

Answer (A) is incorrect because a mediator is a neutral third party who facilitates a negotiated solution by using persuasion and offering solutions. However, the mediator has no authority to make a decision. Answer (C) is incorrect because a consultant is skilled in facilitation and communication skills but does not have authority to make a decision. A consultant helps improve relations between the two disagreeing parties but does not offer specific solutions. Answer (D) is incorrect because a conciliator provides an informal communication link between the two parties but does not have authority to make a decision.

53. In a situation involving a disagreement between two parties, when one party's interests are more important than the other's (for example, a customer believes one product is most suitable while the seller disagrees, yet the seller's primary goal is to keep the customer satisfied), the best conflict-resolution strategy is

A. Accommodating.

B. Compromising.

C. Competing.

D. Challenging.

The correct answer is (A). *(CIA, adapted)*

REQUIRED: The best conflict-resolution strategy when one party's interest is more important than the other's.

DISCUSSION: Accommodating is a conflict handling intention. The dimensions of conflict handling intentions are assertiveness and cooperation. An intention is what mediates between one's actual behavior and one's emotions and perceptions. Accommodating entails placing another person's interests above one's own. It represents the minimum of assertiveness and the maximum of cooperation. For example, the seller should accommodate the customer by providing the product the customer wants.

Answer (B) is incorrect because, in a compromise, both parties give up something to reach accord. It represents moderate assertiveness and cooperation. Answer (C) is incorrect because, in a competitive situation, each party seeks to satisfy his/her own needs without regard to the other. It represents the maximum of assertiveness and the minimum of cooperation. Answer (D) is incorrect because challenging is not a conflict handling intention.

54. Many people think that conflict is inherently detrimental to an organization. However, studies and actual case experience demonstrate that some conflict is desirable if an organization is to thrive. Identify the technique that management could use to stimulate conflict.

A. Authoritative command.

B. Restructuring the organization.

C. Expansion of resources.

D. Creation of superordinate goals.

The correct answer is (B). *(CIA, adapted)*

REQUIRED: The technique for stimulating conflict.

DISCUSSION: The interactionist view is that conflict may be constructive as well as destructive because it encourages self-criticism, creativity, and necessary change. Accordingly, managers may decide to stimulate controlled conflict. Techniques for this purpose may include ambiguous or threatening communications; hiring outsiders with different values, managerial styles, attitudes, and backgrounds; designating an individual to argue against the majority opinions of the group; and restructuring the organization to disrupt the status quo.

Answers (A), (C), and (D) are incorrect because authoritative command, expansion of resources, and creation of superordinate goals are conflict resolution techniques.

55. Which one of the following techniques is not generally recognized as an effective conflict resolution technique for management to use in a dispute between employees?

A. Accommodation - management encourages a high degree of cooperation and a low degree of assertiveness.

B. Competition - management encourages the parties to seek their own interests, regardless of the effect on each other.

C. Reorganization - management transfers one of the disputants to another department.

D. Compromise - management persuades each party to make concessions.

The correct answer is (B). *(CIA, adapted)*

REQUIRED: The technique not ordinarily regarded as effective in conflict resolution.

DISCUSSION: Competition is a conflict-handling intention characterized by considerable assertiveness (the degree to which the party seeks to achieve his/her goals) and a low degree of cooperativeness (the degree to which the party attempts to satisfy the concerns of others). Encouraging competition stimulates conflict.

Answers (A), (C), and (D) are incorrect because accommodation, altering the structural variables, and compromise are conflict resolution techniques.

56. Which of the following would be the best approach for negotiating the purchase of a large number of microcomputers, assuming that both parties follow the same approach?

A. Review previous demands, concessions, and settlements (precedents).

B. Attempt to get personal information about the opposing negotiators.

C. Enter without preconceived ideas about what should be accomplished.

D. Ask as few questions as possible during negotiations.

The correct answer is (A). *(CIA, adapted)*

REQUIRED: The best negotiating approach.

DISCUSSION: The best approach to negotiating a large purchase, assuming that both parties follow the same approach, is to review previous settlements, demands, and concessions to determine what can be achieved. The history of past practices and interactions tends to define current standards of fairness in negotiations.

Answer (B) is incorrect because research indicates that personality traits have no material direct effect on the outcome of negotiation. Answer (C) is incorrect because negotiators should be prepared. They should know what they wish to gain and what their resistance point is. Answer (D) is incorrect because a skilled negotiator asks many questions, is a good listener, is not defensive, focuses arguments well, and avoids irritating the opponent.

57. Which of the following would not be considered a conflict trigger?

A. Ambiguous jurisdictions.

B. Competition for scarce resources.

C. Status differential.

D. Superordinate goals.

The correct answer is (D). *(CIA, adapted)*

REQUIRED: The item not a conflict trigger.

DISCUSSION: An appeal to superordinate goals is a means of resolving conflict. Superordinate goals are overriding, common goals of the parties. The conflict can be resolved if the individuals involved understand that it is preventing them from achieving more important, mutually held goals.

Answers (A), (B), and (C) are incorrect because conflict triggers include ambiguous jurisdictions (unclear job boundaries); competition for scarce resources; status differentials; time pressure; personality clashes; unreasonable standards, rules, etc.; communication breakdowns; and unrealized expectations.

58. To market effectively the internal auditing function to management, auditors must recognize that their roles may result in varying degrees of conflict. Conflict triggers must be understood and managed so that a dysfunctional situation does not develop. Select the answer that is not a conflict trigger.

A. Communication breakdowns.

B. Superordinate goals.

C. Personality clashes.

D. Status differentials.

The correct answer is (B). *(CIA, adapted)*

REQUIRED: The item not a conflict trigger.

DISCUSSION: Conflict triggers include ambiguous jurisdictions (unclear job boundaries); competition for scarce resources; status differentials; time pressures; personality clashes; unreasonable standards, rules, etc.; communication breakdowns; and unrealized expectations. However, an appeal to superordinate goals is a conflict resolution technique, not a conflict trigger.

Answer (A) is incorrect because communication breakdowns are conflict triggers. Two-way communication is a complex process that is fraught with maintenance problems. Answer (C) is incorrect because personality clashes between an auditor and auditee can destroy the auditor's usefulness if allowed to continue. Answer (D) is incorrect because some auditees may not respect a staff auditor if a significant disparity in organization status exists.

59. The behavioral science literature identifies diffusion as an effective approach to resolving conflict. An auditor effectively using diffusion in working with a confrontational auditee would

A. Set aside critical issues temporarily and try to reach agreement on less controversial issues first.

B. Emphasize differences between the parties.

C. Avoid the conflict situation.

D. Identify the sources of conflict and address them directly.

The correct answer is (A). *(CIA, adapted)*

REQUIRED: The action taken by an auditor using diffusion in working with a confrontational auditee.

DISCUSSION: Diffusion temporarily leaves the conflict unresolved. Smoothing (downplaying differences and emphasizing common interests) and compromise (requiring each party to make concessions) are diffusion approaches to conflict management. The disadvantage is that the underlying problems remain unresolved while the less controversial issues are being addressed first.

Answer (B) is incorrect because differences are downplayed while using a diffusion approach. Answer (C) is incorrect because diffusion addresses issues of conflict. Answer (D) is incorrect because directly addressing the conflict is a confrontational approach.

60. Which of the following results is most likely to occur when public media are used to resolve disputes between employees and management?

A. The company's image may be improved.

B. Public opinion may pressure the parties to resolve the dispute.

C. Communication between employees and management is improved.

D. The need for support from a union is increased.

The correct answer is (B). *(Publisher)*

REQUIRED: The result of using public media to resolve disputes between employees and management.

DISCUSSION: When public media are used as tools for resolving employee-management disputes, communication is hindered because the issues are addressed to the public rather than discussed with the other party. Moreover, compromise becomes difficult because the stated conclusions are solidified by public opinion. However, the need for union support is reduced because public pressure may help to resolve the negotiations.

Answer (A) is incorrect because, when public knowledge of the stated conclusions hinders the compromise process, the company's image may be distorted. Answer (C) is incorrect because, when issues are presented to the public rather than discussed by the two parties, communication is inhibited. Answer (D) is incorrect because the pressure from the public to resolve the situation may eliminate the need for union support.

Use Gleim's ***CMA/CFM Test Prep*** for interactive testing with **over 2,000 additional multiple-choice questions!**

APPENDIX A: ETHICS AS TESTED ON THE CMA/CFM EXAMS

6 pages of outline
14 multiple-choice questions

ETHICS

Questions containing ethical issues can appear on any part of the examination, presented within the context of specific subject areas. Candidates should be familiar with:

> *Statement on Management Accounting Number 1C (Revised),* "Standards of Ethical Conduct for Practitioners of Management Accounting and Financial Management," *Institute of Management Accountants, Montvale, N.J., 1997.*

Current references to business ethics are also found in recent periodicals and newspapers.

A. Ethics

1. Definitions

a. Corporate ethics -- an organization's policies and standards established to assure certain kinds of behavior by its members

b. Individual ethics -- principles of conduct adhered to by an individual

2. Increased Concern for Business Ethics

a. Electrical-equipment conspiracy cases in 1960 caused public concern and creation of the Business Ethics Advisory Council (BEAC) in 1961 under the Secretary of Commerce.

b. BEAC pointed out areas needing self-evaluation by the business community:

1) General business understanding of ethical issues

2) Compliance with laws

3) Conflicts of interest

4) Entertainment and gift expenses

5) Relations with customers and suppliers. Should gifts or kickbacks be given or accepted?

6) Social responsibilities

c. BEAC's recommendations generated business interest, especially from big business, in problems of ethical behavior.

3. **Factors That May Lead to Unethical Behavior**

    a. In any normal population, some people have less than desirable levels of ethics. If these people hold leadership positions, they will adversely influence subordinates.

    b. Organizational factors may lead to unethical behavior.

        1) Pressures for short-run performance in decentralized return on investment (ROI) centers may inhibit ethical behavior.

        2) Emphasis on strict adherence to chain-of-command authority may provide excuses for ignoring ethics when following orders.

        3) Informal work-group loyalties may subvert ethical behavior.

        4) Committee decision processes may make it possible to abstain from or dodge ethical obligations.

    c. External factors may lead to unethical behavior.

        1) Pressure of competition may compromise ethics in the interest of survival.
        2) Unethical behavior of others may force a compromise of ethics.
        3) Definitions of ethical behavior may vary from one culture to another.

            a) Bribes to overseas officials or buyers may be consistent with some countries' customary business practices, but such a practice is not considered ethical among U.S. purchasing agents.

                i) Bribes are now considered illegal under the Foreign Corrupt Practices Act.

            b) The propriety of superimposing our cultural ethical standards (by refusing to bribe) on another culture may be controversial.

4. **General Guides to Ethics**

    a. Golden Rule -- Do unto others as you would have others do unto you.

    b. Maximize good -- Act to provide the greatest good for the greatest number.

    c. Fairness -- Act in ways that are fair or just to all concerned.

    d. Maximize long-run outcomes -- Act to provide the best long-range benefits to society and its resources.

    e. General respect -- Act to respect the planet all humans share and the rights of others because corporate and individual decisions affect them.

5. **Simplified Criteria for Evaluating Ethical Behavior**

    a. Would this behavior be acceptable if people I respect knew I was doing this?

    b. What are the consequences of this behavior for myself, other employees, customers, and society?

6. Ethics are individual and personal, influenced by

    a. Life experiences (rewards for doing right, punishment for doing wrong)
    b. Friendship groups (professional associations, informal groups)
    c. Organizational pressures (responsibilities to superiors and the organization)

B. Codes of Ethical Conduct

1. An organization's code of ethical conduct is the established general value system the organization wishes to apply to its members' activities through
   a. Communicating organizational purposes and beliefs
   b. Establishing uniform ethical guidelines for members
      1) Including guidance on behavior for members in making decisions
2. Laws and written rules cannot cover all situations. However, organizations can benefit from having an established ethical code because it
   a. Effectively communicates acceptable values to all members
      1) Including recruits and subcontractors
   b. Provides a method of policing and disciplining members for violations
      1) Through review panels (formal)
      2) Through group pressure (informal)
   c. Establishes high standards against which individuals can measure their own performance
   d. Communicates to those outside the organization the value system from which the organization's members must not be asked to deviate
3. A typical code for accounting activities (note similarities to the Standards for the Professional Practice of Internal Auditing, GAAP, GAAS, etc.) holds that a financial manager must have
   a. Independence from conflicts of economic interest
   b. Independence from conflicts of professional interest
      1) Responsibility to present information fairly to shareholders/owners and not intentionally protect management
      2) Responsibility to present data to all appropriate managers and not play favorites with information or cover up bad news
      3) Responsibility to exercise an ethical presence in the conduct of professional activities
         a) Ensuring organizational compliance with spirit as well as letter of pertinent laws and regulations
         b) Conducting oneself according to the highest moral and legal standards
         c) Reporting to appropriate internal or external authority any illegal or fraudulent organizational act
   c. Integrity in not compromising professional values for the sake of personal goals
   d. Objectivity in presenting information, preparing reports, and making analyses

C. IMA Code of Ethics

1. The National Association of Accountants (now the Institute of Management Accountants or IMA), through its Management Accounting Practices Committee, issued a revised code of ethics for management accountants in April 1997. This code reflects the official position of the organization. Candidates are urged to study the provisions of the code closely because it is tested. The code is printed below and on the following page in its entirety. (Source: Statement on Management Accounting 1C (Revised), Objectives: Standards of Ethical Conduct for Practitioners of Management Accounting and Financial Management, April 1997, pp. 69-70). The mnemonic CCIO (competence, confidentiality, integrity, and objectivity) is useful. The final section, Resolution of Ethical Conflict, is especially significant.

STANDARDS OF ETHICAL CONDUCT FOR PRACTITIONERS OF MANAGEMENT ACCOUNTING AND FINANCIAL MANAGEMENT

Practitioners of management accounting and financial management have an obligation to the public, their profession, the organizations they serve, and themselves, to maintain the highest standards of ethical conduct. In recognition of this obligation, the Institute of Management Accountants has promulgated the following standards of ethical conduct for practitioners of management accounting and financial management. Adherence to these standards, both domestically and internationally, is integral to achieving the Objectives of Management Accounting. Practitioners of management accounting and financial management shall not commit acts contrary to these standards nor shall they condone the commission of such acts by others within their organizations.

Competence

Practitioners of management accounting and financial management have a responsibility to:

- *Maintain an appropriate level of professional competence by ongoing development of their knowledge and skills.*
- *Perform their professional duties in accordance with relevant laws, regulations, and technical standards.*
- *Prepare complete and clear reports and recommendations after appropriate analyses of relevant and reliable information.*

Confidentiality

Practitioners of management accounting and financial management have a responsibility to:

- *Refrain from disclosing confidential information acquired in the course of their work except when authorized, unless legally obligated to do so.*
- *Inform subordinates as appropriate regarding the confidentiality of information acquired in the course of their work and monitor their activities to assure the maintenance of that confidentiality.*
- *Refrain from using or appearing to use confidential information acquired in the course of their work for unethical or illegal advantage either personally or through third parties.*

Integrity

Practitioners of management accounting and financial management have a responsibility to:

- *Avoid actual or apparent conflicts of interest and advise all appropriate parties of any potential conflict.*
- *Refrain from engaging in any activity that would prejudice their ability to carry out their duties ethically.*
- *Refuse any gift, favor, or hospitality that would influence or would appear to influence their actions.*
- *Refrain from either actively or passively subverting the attainment of the organization's legitimate and ethical objectives.*
- *Recognize and communicate professional limitations or other constraints that would preclude responsible judgment or successful performance of an activity.*
- *Communicate unfavorable as well as favorable information and professional judgments or opinions.*
- *Refrain from engaging in or supporting any activity that would discredit the profession.*

Objectivity

Practitioners of management accounting and financial management have a responsibility to:

- *Communicate information fairly and objectively.*
- *Disclose fully all relevant information that could reasonably be expected to influence an intended user's understanding of the reports, comments, and recommendations presented.*

Resolution of Ethical Conflict

In applying the standards of ethical conduct, practitioners of management accounting and financial management may encounter problems in identifying unethical behavior or in resolving an ethical conflict. When faced with significant ethical issues, practitioners of management accounting and financial management should follow the established policies of the organization bearing on the resolution of such conflict. If these policies do not resolve the ethical conflict, such practitioners should consider the following courses of action:

- *Discuss such problems with the immediate superior except when it appears that the superior is involved, in which case the problem should be presented initially to the next higher managerial level. If satisfactory resolution cannot be achieved when the problem is initially presented, submit the issues to the next higher managerial level. If the immediate superior is the chief executive officer, or equivalent, the acceptable reviewing authority may be a group such as the audit committee, executive committee, board of directors, board of trustees, or owners. Contact with levels above the immediate superior should be initiated only with the superior's knowledge, assuming the superior is not involved. Except where legally prescribed, communication of such problems to authorities or individuals not employed or engaged by the organization is not considered appropriate.*
- *Clarify relevant ethical issues by confidential discussion with an objective advisor (e.g., IMA Ethics Counseling Service) to obtain a better understanding of possible courses of action.*
- *Consult your own attorney as to legal obligations and rights concerning the ethical conflict.*
- *If the ethical conflict still exists after exhausting all levels of internal review, there may be no other recourse on significant matters than to resign from the organization and to submit an informative memorandum to an appropriate representative of the organization. After resignation, depending on the nature of the ethical conflict, it may also be appropriate to notify other parties.*

D. Conflict of Interest

1. Conflict of interest is a conflict between the private and the official responsibilities of a person in a position of trust, sufficient to affect judgment, independence, or objectivity in conducting the affairs of the business.
2. **Examples of Conflict of Interest**
   a. Having a substantial financial interest in a supplier, customer, or distributor
   b. Using privileged information gained from one's official position to enter transactions for personal gain
3. **Methods for Control**
   a. Provide a code of conduct provision applying to conflicts of interest.
   b. Require full financial disclosure by managers.
   c. Require prior notification of any transaction that may raise conflict of interest.
   d. Prohibit financial ties to any supplier, customer, or distributor.
   e. Encourage adherence to strong ethical behavior through corporate actions, policies, and public communications.

E. Legal Aspects of Social Responsibility

1. The **Racketeer Influenced and Corrupt Organization (RICO) Act** was passed in 1970 as an attempt to combat the problem of organized crime and its infiltration of legitimate enterprises.
   a. Its goals were to eliminate organized crime by concentrating on the illegal monies through the use of civil and criminal forfeitures.
   b. Criminal penalties can be levied up to $25,000 and 20 years in jail. Civil penalties include the awarding of treble damages and attorney's fees to the successful plaintiff.
   c. RICO specifically makes the following activities unlawful:
      1) Using income derived from a pattern of racketeering activity to acquire an interest in an enterprise.
      2) Acquiring or maintaining an interest in an enterprise through a pattern of racketeering activity.
      3) Conducting the affairs of an enterprise through a pattern of racketeering activity.
      4) Conspiring to commit any of these offenses.
   d. RICO has been used against white-collar criminals, terrorists, Wall Street insider trading, anti-abortion protesters, local law enforcement agencies, and public accounting firms -- none of which was intended by Congress when the law was passed.
2. The **Foreign Corrupt Practices Act (FCPA) of 1977** regulates payments by U.S. firms operating in other nations.
   a. The act is a reaction to publicity over questionable foreign payments.
   b. The FCPA makes it a criminal offense to make payments to a foreign government or representative thereof to secure or retain business.
   c. It prohibits payments of sales commissions to independent agents, if the commissions are knowingly passed to foreign officials.
   d. Corporations are required to establish internal accounting controls to assure that all overseas payments are proper.
   e. The FCPA applies even if payment is legal in the nation where it is made.
   f. The rationale for the FCPA is that the international reputation of the United States is affected by its international business conduct, which should reflect the best of the United States' ethics.
3. The SEC mandates that the composition of boards of directors include outside directors.
   a. To create diversity and broaden the overview of a company's place in the market and in society
4. Courts are increasingly willing to hold boards of directors and auditors liable for problems.
5. Stop and review! The following 14 multiple-choice questions cover the topic of ethics as it may be tested on the CMA/CFM exams. They are not divided by subunits. We anticipate some "case" questions that describe situations and are followed by one or more questions; e.g., to whom should the financial manager report an ethics violation?

MULTIPLE-CHOICE QUESTIONS

1. If a financial manager/management accountant has a problem in identifying unethical behavior or resolving an ethical conflict, the first action (s)he should normally take is to

A. Consult the board of directors.

B. Discuss the problem with his/her immediate superior.

C. Notify the appropriate law enforcement agency.

D. Resign from the company.

The correct answer is (B). *(Publisher)*

REQUIRED: The proper ethical behavior by a financial manager/management accountant.

DISCUSSION: The Standards of Ethical Conduct for Practitioners of Management Accounting and Financial Management state that the financial manager/management accountant should first discuss an ethical problem with his/her immediate superior. If the superior is involved, the problem should be taken initially to the next higher managerial level.

Answer (A) is incorrect because the board would be consulted initially only if the immediate superior is the chief executive officer and that person is involved in the ethical conflict. Answer (C) is incorrect because unless "legally prescribed, communication of such problems to authorities or individuals not employed or engaged by the organization is not considered appropriate." Answer (D) is incorrect because resignation is a last resort.

2. Sheila is a financial manager who has discovered that her company is violating environmental regulations. If her immediate superior is involved, her appropriate action is to

A. Do nothing since she has a duty of loyalty to the organization.

B. Consult the audit committee.

C. Present the matter to the next higher managerial level.

D. Confront her immediate superior.

The correct answer is (C). *(Publisher)*

REQUIRED: The proper action when a financial manager/management accountant's immediate superior is involved in an ethical problem.

DISCUSSION: To resolve an ethical problem, the financial manager/management accountant's first step is usually to consult his/her immediate superior. If that individual is involved, the matter should be taken to the next higher level of management.

Answer (A) is incorrect because "practitioners of management accounting and financial management have an obligation to the public, their profession, the organization they serve, and themselves, to maintain the highest standards of ethical conduct." Answer (B) is incorrect because the audit committee would be consulted first only if it were the next higher managerial level. Answer (D) is incorrect because if the superior is involved, the next higher managerial level should be consulted first.

3. If a financial manager/management accountant discovers unethical conduct in his/her organization and fails to act, (s)he will be in violation of which ethical standard(s)?

A. "Actively or passively subvert the attainment of the organization's legitimate and ethical objectives."

B. "Communicate unfavorable as well as favorable information."

C. "Condone the commission of such acts by others within their organizations."

D. All of the answers are correct.

The correct answer is (D). *(Publisher)*

REQUIRED: The ethical standard(s) violated by failure to disclose unethical behavior.

DISCUSSION: A financial manager/management accountant displays his/her competence and objectivity and maintains integrity by taking the appropriate action within the organization to resolve an ethical problem. Failure to act would condone wrongful acts, breach the duty to convey unfavorable as well as favorable information, undermine the organization's legitimate aims, discredit the profession, and violate the duty of objectivity owed to users of the subordinate's work product.

Answers (A), (B), and (C) are incorrect because each standard is violated by a financial manager/management accountant who fails to act upon discovering unethical conduct.

4. Corporate social responsibility is

A. Effectively enforced through the controls envisioned by classical economics.

B. Defined as the obligation to shareholders to earn a profit.

C. More than the obligation to shareholders to earn a profit.

D. Defined as the obligation to serve long-term, organizational interests.

The correct answer is (C). *(Publisher)*

REQUIRED: The true statement about corporate social responsibility.

DISCUSSION: The concept of corporate social responsibility involves more than serving the interests of the organization and its shareholders. Rather, it is an extension of responsibility to embrace service to the public interest in such matters as environmental protection, employee safety, civil rights, and community involvement.

Answer (A) is incorrect because a perfectly competitive market was envisioned by classical economics. Answers (B) and (D) are incorrect because the concept embraces the public or societal interest.

5. A common argument against corporate involvement in socially responsible behavior is that

A. It encourages government intrusion in decision making.

B. As a legal person, a corporation is accountable for its conduct.

C. It creates goodwill.

D. In a competitive market, such behavior incurs costs that place the company at a disadvantage.

The correct answer is (D). *(Publisher)*

REQUIRED: The common argument against corporate involvement in socially responsible behavior.

DISCUSSION: Socially responsible behavior clearly has immediate costs to the entity, for example, the expenses incurred in affirmative action programs, pollution control, and improvements in worker safety. When one firm incurs such costs and its competitor does not, the other may be able to sell its products or services more cheaply and increase its market share at the expense of the socially responsible firm. The rebuttal argument is that in the long run the socially responsible company may maximize profits by creating goodwill and avoiding or anticipating governmental regulation.

Answer (A) is incorrect because such behavior may prevent governmental action. Answers (B) and (C) are incorrect because each is an argument for such behavior.

6. The IMA Code of Ethics requires a financial manager/management accountant to follow the established policies of the organization when faced with an ethical conflict. If these policies do not resolve the conflict, the financial manager/management accountant should

A. Consult the board of directors immediately.

B. Discuss the problem with the immediate superior if (s)he is involved in the conflict.

C. Communicate the problem to authorities outside the organization.

D. Contact the next higher managerial level if initial presentation to the immediate superior does not resolve the conflict.

The correct answer is (D). *(Publisher)*

REQUIRED: The proper action when organizational policies do not resolve an ethical conflict.

DISCUSSION: In these circumstances, the problem should be discussed with the immediate superior unless (s)he is involved. In that case, initial presentation should be to the next higher managerial level. If the problem is not satisfactorily resolved after initial presentation, the question should be submitted to the next higher level.

Answer (A) is incorrect because this course of action would be appropriate only for the chief executive officer or for his/her immediate subordinate when the CEO is involved in the conflict. Answer (B) is incorrect because the proper action would be to present the matter to the next higher managerial level. Answer (C) is incorrect because such action is inappropriate unless legally prescribed.

7. Financial managers/management accountants are obligated to maintain the highest standards of ethical conduct. Accordingly, the IMA Code of Ethics explicitly requires that they

A. Obtain sufficient competent evidence when expressing an opinion.

B. Not condone violations by others.

C. Comply with generally accepted auditing standards.

D. Adhere to generally accepted accounting principles.

The correct answer is (B). *(Publisher)*

REQUIRED: The conduct required of financial managers/management accountants.

DISCUSSION: The preamble to the IMA Code of Ethics states, "Practitioners of management accounting and financial management have an obligation to the public, their profession, the organizations they serve, and themselves, to maintain the highest standards of ethical conduct. In recognition of this obligation, the Institute of Management Accountants has promulgated the following standards of ethical conduct for practitioners of management accounting and financial management. Adherence to these standards, both domestically and internationally, is integral to achieving the Objectives of Management Accounting. Practitioners of management accounting and financial management shall not commit acts contrary to these standards nor shall they condone the commission of such acts by others within their organizations."

Answers (A), (C), and (D) are incorrect because each applies to external auditors. The IMA Code of Ethics does not expressly use such language.

8. Integrity is an ethical requirement for all financial managers/management accountants. One aspect of integrity requires

A. Performance of professional duties in accordance with applicable laws.

B. Avoidance of conflict of interest.

C. Refraining from improper use of inside information.

D. Maintenance of an appropriate level of professional competence.

The correct answer is (B). *(Publisher)*

REQUIRED: The aspect of the integrity requirement.

DISCUSSION: According to the IMA Code of Ethics, financial managers/management accountants must "avoid actual or apparent conflicts of interest and advise all appropriate parties of any potential conflict."

Answers (A) and (D) are incorrect because each states an aspect of the competence requirement. Answer (C) is incorrect because it states an aspect of the confidentiality requirement.

9. Under the express terms of the IMA Code of Ethics, a financial manager/management accountant may not

A. Advertise.

B. Encroach on the practice of another financial manager/management accountant.

C. Disclose confidential information unless authorized or legally obligated.

D. Accept other employment while serving as a financial manager/management accountant.

The correct answer is (C). *(Publisher)*

REQUIRED: The action explicitly proscribed by the IMA Code of Ethics.

DISCUSSION: Financial managers/management accountants may not disclose confidential information acquired in the course of their work unless authorized or legally obligated to do so. They must inform subordinates about the confidentiality of information and monitor their activities to maintain that confidentiality. Moreover, financial managers/management accountants should avoid even the appearance of using confidential information to their unethical or illegal advantage.

Answers (A) and (B) are incorrect because the code does not address these matters. Answer (D) is incorrect because other employment may be accepted unless it constitutes a conflict of interest.

10. A financial manager/management accountant discovers a problem that could mislead users of the firm's financial data and has informed his/her immediate superior. (S)he should report the circumstances to the audit committee and/or the board of directors only if

A. The immediate superior, who reports to the chief executive officer, knows about the situation but refuses to correct it.

B. The immediate superior assures the financial manager/management accountant that the problem will be resolved.

C. The immediate superior reports the situation to his/her superior.

D. The immediate superior, the firm's chief executive officer, knows about the situation but refuses to correct it.

The correct answer is (D). *(Publisher)*

REQUIRED: The situation in which the financial manager/management accountant must report to the audit committee and/or board of directors.

DISCUSSION: According to the IMA Code of Ethics, the financial manager/management accountant should "discuss such problems with the immediate superior except when it appears that the superior is involved, in which case the problem should be presented initially to the next higher managerial level. If satisfactory resolution cannot be achieved when the problem is initially presented, submit the issues to the next higher managerial level. If the immediate superior is the chief executive officer, or equivalent, the acceptable reviewing authority may be a group such as the audit committee, executive committee, board of directors, board of trustees, or owners."

Answer (A) is incorrect because, in this situation, the chief executive officer is the next higher managerial level. Answers (B) and (C) are incorrect because the immediate superior has promised or taken action toward satisfactory resolution.

11. In which situation is a financial manager/management accountant permitted to communicate confidential information to individuals or authorities outside the firm?

A. There is an ethical conflict and the board has refused to take action.

B. Such communication is legally prescribed.

C. The financial manager/management accountant knowingly communicates the information indirectly through a subordinate.

D. An officer at the financial manager/management accountant's bank has requested information on a transaction that could influence the firm's stock price.

The correct answer is (B). *(Publisher)*

REQUIRED: The situation in which a financial manager/management accountant may disclose information to those outside the firm.

DISCUSSION: According to the IMA Code of Ethics, financial managers/management accountants are responsible for observing the standard of confidentiality. Thus, the financial manager/management accountant should "refrain from disclosing confidential information acquired in the course of his/her work except when authorized, unless legally obligated to do so."

Answer (A) is incorrect because the IMA Code of Ethics states that "except where legally prescribed, communication of such [ethical conflict] problems to authorities or individuals not employed or engaged by the organization is not considered appropriate." Answer (C) is incorrect because the financial manager/management accountant should "inform subordinates as appropriate regarding the confidentiality of information acquired in the course of their work and monitor their activities to assure the maintenance of that confidentiality." Answer (D) is incorrect because the financial manager/management accountant is required to "refrain from using or appearing to use confidential information acquired in the course of his/her work for unethical or illegal advantage either personally or through third parties."

12. Which ethical standard is most clearly violated if a financial manager/management accountant knows of a problem that could mislead users but does nothing about it?

A. Competence.

B. Legality.

C. Objectivity.

D. Confidentiality.

The correct answer is (C). *(Publisher)*

REQUIRED: The ethical standard most clearly violated when a financial manager/management accountant does nothing about information that is misleading to users.

DISCUSSION: Objectivity is the fourth part of the IMA Code of Ethics. It requires that information be communicated "fairly and objectively," and that all information that could reasonably influence users be fully disclosed.

Answer (A) is incorrect because the competence standard pertains to the financial manager/management accountant's responsibility to maintain his/her professional skills and knowledge. It also pertains to the performance of activities in a professional manner. Answer (B) is incorrect because legality is not addressed in the IMA Code of Ethics. Answer (D) is incorrect because the confidentiality standard concerns the financial manager/management accountant's responsibility not to disclose or use the firm's confidential information.

13. The IMA Code of Ethics includes an integrity standard, which requires the financial manager/management accountant to

A. Identify and make known anything that may hinder his/her judgment or prevent satisfactory completion of any duties.

B. Report any relevant information that could influence users of financial statements.

C. Disclose confidential information when authorized by his/her firm or required under the law.

D. Refuse gifts from anyone.

The correct answer is (A). *(Publisher)*

REQUIRED: The action required of the financial manager/management accountant by the integrity standard.

DISCUSSION: One of the responsibilities of the financial manager/management accountant under the integrity standard is to "recognize and communicate professional limitations or other constraints that would preclude responsible judgment or successful performance of an activity."

Answer (B) is incorrect because the objectivity standard requires the financial manager/management accountant to "disclose fully all relevant information that could reasonably be expected to influence an intended user's understanding of the reports, comments, and recommendations presented." Answer (C) is incorrect because the confidentiality standard requires the financial manager/management accountant to "refrain from disclosing confidential information acquired in the course of his/her work except when authorized, unless legally obligated to do so." Answer (D) is incorrect because the integrity standard requires the financial manager/management accountant to "refuse any gift, favor, or hospitality that would influence or would appear to influence his/her actions."

14. The IMA Code of Ethics includes a competence standard, which requires the financial manager/management accountant to

A. Report information, whether favorable or unfavorable.

B. Develop his/her professional proficiency on a continual basis.

C. Discuss ethical conflicts and possible courses of action with an unbiased counselor.

D. Discuss, with subordinates, their responsibilities regarding the disclosure of information about the firm.

The correct answer is (B). *(Publisher)*

REQUIRED: The action required of the financial manager/management accountant by the competence standard.

DISCUSSION: One of the responsibilities of the financial manager/management accountant under the competence standard is to "maintain an appropriate level of professional competence by ongoing development of his/her knowledge and skills."

Answer (A) is incorrect because the integrity standard requires the financial manager/management accountant to "communicate unfavorable as well as favorable information and professional judgments or opinions." Answer (C) is incorrect because one of the suggestions from the "Resolution of Ethical Conflict" paragraph is to "clarify relevant ethical issues by confidential discussion with an objective advisor (e.g., IMA Ethics Counseling Service) to obtain a better understanding of possible courses of action." Answer (D) is incorrect because the confidentiality standard requires the financial manager/management accountant to "inform subordinates as appropriate regarding the confidentiality of information acquired in the course of their work and monitor their activities to assure the maintenance of that confidentiality."

APPENDIX B: TAXES AS TESTED ON THE CMA/CFM EXAMS

6 pages of outline
9 multiple-choice questions

A. Taxation
B. Fundamentals of Corporate Taxation

Taxes are tested in Parts 1, 2, and 4. The intended emphasis is on a user's point of view rather than a preparer's point of view.

Part 1 - The effect of tax provisions on financing and capital structure decisions, such as deductibility of payments for use of capital and after-tax cost of capital (i.e., debt vs. equity issues), is discussed in Study Unit 6, Capital Structure Finance, and Study Unit 7, Risk.

Part 2CMA - Accounting for deferred income taxes is a separate subunit in Study Unit 5, Liabilities.

Part 2CFM - Accounting for deferred income taxes is a subunit in Study Unit 2, Special Topics in Financial Statements.

The income tax code provisions that impact investment decisions are in Study Units 3 through 7 and cover advanced topics in corporate financial management.

- Deductibility of payments for use of capital
- After-tax cost of capital
- Tax shields from property transactions
- Transaction timing for favorable tax consequences

International tax considerations and their effect on international regulations on business are in Study Unit 8, Risk Management.

The tax implications of multinational corporations are in Study Unit 9, External Financial Environment.

Part 4 - The impact of income taxes on operational decisions, including operating income subject to income taxes, gains and losses subject to income taxes, and tax credits apply to Study Unit 1, Decision Analysis.

The impact of income taxes on investment decisions, including tax shields from sunk costs, transaction timing for favorable tax consequences, and tax elections apply to Study Unit 3, Capital Budgeting.

Important background for the above two study units appears in this appendix.

This appendix provides background and overview of taxes as tested on the CMA/CFM exams. Additional detail required in each part is provided as set forth above.

Obviously taxes are a major expense of doing business, and each business attempts to minimize taxes. Thus, financial managers and management accountants must be knowledgeable about taxes.

A. Taxation

1. Two Principles of Taxation

a. Benefits received. Individuals should pay a tax based on the benefits received from the services (e.g., paying for the use of a public park or swimming pool).

b. Ability to pay. Consumers should pay taxes based on their ability to pay them (e.g., taxes on income and wealth).

2. Three Classifications of Taxes Reflecting Ability-to-Pay Principles

a. **Progressive**. With a higher income, individuals pay a higher percentage of their income in taxes (e.g., income tax).

b. **Proportional**. At all levels of income, the percentage paid in taxes is constant (e.g., sales tax).

c. **Regressive**. As income increases, the percentage paid in taxes decreases (e.g., payroll or excise taxes).

1) EXAMPLE: An excise tax is regressive because its burden falls disproportionately on lower-income persons. As personal income increases, the percentage of income paid declines since an excise tax is a flat amount per quantity of the good or service purchased.

3. Taxes also may be classified as either direct or indirect.

a. **Direct taxes** are imposed upon the taxpayer and paid directly to the government, e.g., the personal income tax.

b. **Indirect taxes** are levied against others and thus only indirectly on the individual taxpayer, e.g., sales taxes and Social Security taxes paid by employers.

4. **Incidence of Taxation** -- the parties who actually bear a particular tax. For example, the person who actually bears the burden of an indirect tax may not be the same one who pays the tax to the government.

a. The incidence of taxation becomes important when a government wants to change the tax structure. Because taxation is a form of fiscal policy, the government needs to know who will actually bear the incidence of taxation, not just who will pay the tax.

b. EXAMPLE: Taxes such as the corporate income tax, the corporate property tax, and the excise tax are often shifted to the consumer in the form of higher prices.

c. EXAMPLE: Taxes such as windfall profits taxes are not shifted to the consumer via higher prices. This type of one-time-only tax levied on part of the output produced does not increase the equilibrium price of the taxed good.

5. In recent years, some authorities have supported a tax based on consumption -- a **value-added tax**.

a. Many major industrial nations have already adopted a value-added tax.

b. The tax is levied on the value added to goods by each business unit in the production and distribution chain.

1) The amount of value added is measured by the difference between a firm's sales and its purchases.

2) Each firm in the chain collects the tax on its sales, takes a credit for taxes paid on purchases, and remits the difference to the government.

3) The consumer ultimately bears the incidence of the tax through higher prices.

c. A value-added tax encourages consumer saving because taxes are paid on consumption only, not on savings.

1) Because the value-added tax is based on consumption, people in the lower income groups would spend a greater proportion of their income on taxes.

2) The value-added tax is thus regressive.

d. Only those businesses that make a profit have to pay income taxes. Under the value-added tax, however, all businesses have to pay taxes, regardless of income.

6. **Taxes** as a business expense (federal, state, local, and foreign) are an important consideration because they are frequently 25% to 50% of all costs.

a. They include income, use, excise, property, legal document, payroll, and others.

b. Thus, governmental services (national defense, fire, police, etc.) are an important and costly factor of production.

c. Tax planning is very important in investment and financing decisions.

1) Investment tax credits have at times provided direct reduction of taxes when assets were purchased for use in the business.

a) The net effect is to decrease the cost of the asset.

b) The amount of the credit and limitations on the tax credit on used equipment affect investment decisions.

c) Investment tax credit is currently available for solar and geothermal property (business energy credit), for rehabilitation of historic structures, and for certain reforestation property.

2) Accelerated depreciation is permitted on many types of business assets.

a) Accordingly, in the early periods of an asset's life, depreciation is higher, taxable income is lower, and the rate of return on investment is higher.

3) Corporate capital gains are taxed at regular rates, and the capital gains of individuals are taxed at a maximum rate of 28%.

4) Special loss carryforward and carryback rules permit businesses to deduct net operating losses incurred in one period against income earned in other periods.

5) A dividends-received deduction makes tax free 70% to 100% of dividends received by one company from investments in the stock of another company.

a) This deduction prevents or reduces double taxation.

b) It also encourages one company to invest in the stock of another company.

6) Interest is a tax-deductible expense of the debtor company.

a) But dividends on common or preferred stock are not deductible by the issuer.

d. Federal tax policy is fiscal policy that affects the overall economy, which in turn affects production and the finished-goods markets in which the company deals.

e. Government monetary policy determines the availability and cost of capital, which affects financing (and in turn, investing) decisions.

1) Monetary policy also affects overall economic activity.

7. Stop and review! You have completed the outline for this subunit. Study multiple-choice questions 1 through 3 on page 435.

B. Fundamentals of Corporate Taxation

1. A C corporation is subject to tax liability imposed on its income (S corporations are taxed as partnerships).

2. **Gross income** means all income from whatever source derived (unless excluded by statute).

   a. Income is considered realized when certain transactions occur.

      1) Mere increases in value (appreciation) do not create income.

         a) EXAMPLE: Land owned by a corporation increases in value from $5,000 to $20,000 per acre. There is no income until the land is sold or exchanged.

      2) Transactions are normally in the form of a sale, an exchange, or the rendering of services.

      3) Taxation of realized income may be excluded or deferred, for example, upon exchange of like-kind property.

      4) The term "recognized" is used when income is realized and also taxed.

      5) Nonresident aliens (including foreign corporations) are, generally, subject to federal income tax on U.S.-source income.

3. **Deductions** are those expenses and other statutorily prescribed items that are subtracted from gross income to determine taxable income.

   a. Deductions should be distinguished from **exclusions**. Exclusions are never included in gross income (e.g., interest on tax-exempt bonds).

4. **Taxable income** is gross income minus deductions.

   a. Taxable income is analogous to net income.
   b. The tax rates are applied to taxable income to determine the tax liability.

5. **Credits** are subtracted from the tax liability.

   a. Credits directly reduce taxes, while deductions reduce taxable income upon which the taxes are computed.

6. **Book Income vs. Taxable Income**

   a. CMA/CFM candidates (Parts 2) are required to understand the difference between book income and taxable income. Problems may begin with book income, list numerous transactions, and require the adjustments necessary to arrive at taxable income.

b. The following adjustments are necessary to adjust book income to taxable income:

   1) Add to book income

      a) Federal income tax

      b) Excess of capital losses over capital gains

      c) Taxable income not reported on books

      d) Expenses reported on books but not deducted on tax return (e.g., charitable contributions in excess of limit)

   2) Subtract from book income

      a) Income reported on books but not included on tax return (e.g., interest income from tax-exempt municipal bonds)

      b) Deductions on tax return but not reported on books (e.g., dividends-received deduction)

c. These adjustments are the fundamental differences between net income for financial accounting purposes (book income) and taxable income. The discussion of income and deductions that follows will concentrate on these differences and assume that candidates can already compute book (i.e., accrual accounting) income.

d. According to generally accepted accounting principles (SFAS 109), accounting for income taxes (interperiod tax allocation) is based on the asset and liability method.

7. **Temporary Differences**

   a. Depreciation expense arises from using different methods for tax and book purposes.

   b. To account for bad debt expense, the direct write-off method is used for tax purposes, and the allowance method (estimating expenses) is used for book purposes.

   c. For tax purposes, warranty expense is deductible only when paid, even if reserves based on estimates are used for book purposes.

   d. Charitable contributions exceeding 10% of corporate taxable income before charitable contributions and special deductions are deductible during the 5 succeeding tax years.

   e. Capital losses in excess of capital gains are not deductible in the current year. Instead, a net capital loss must be carried back 3 years (as a short-term capital loss) and applied towards any capital gains. Any loss remaining can be carried forward for 5 years. Capital losses can be used only to offset capital gains (i.e., ordinary income is unaffected).

   f. Prepaid rent income is included in taxable income when received. Prepaid rent expense is deductible in computing taxable income for the period to which it is attributable.

   g. The cost of certain intangibles (e.g., goodwill) acquired in connection with the conduct of a trade or business or income-producing activity is amortized over a 15-year period, beginning with the month in which the intangible is acquired.

   h. Amortization of organizational costs and business start-up costs can be elected for a period of not less than 60 months for tax purposes.

8. **Permanent Differences**

   a. Life insurance premiums paid on key persons are not deductible if the corporation is the beneficiary. Proceeds from the policy are not taxed.

   b. Seventy percent of dividends received from taxable domestic corporations are deductible by a distributee corporation that owns less than 20% of the stock of the distributing corporation. The percentage deductible is 80 if the distributee owns 20% to 80% of the distributing corporation. A 100% dividend-received deduction is permitted for dividends received among members of an affiliated group of corporations (80% ownership).

   c. Federal income tax expense is not deductible in computing taxable income.

   d. Tax-exempt interest is included in book income. Expense attributable to earning it is not deductible for tax purposes.

   e. Business gifts exceeding $25 are generally not deductible for income tax purposes.

   f. Compensation in excess of $1 million paid to the chief executive officer and certain other employees is not deductible in computing taxable income. Premiums, tax-free benefits, and compensation based on performance goals are excluded from the $1 million limit.

9. **Nonrecognition Transactions**. Certain types of transactions result in deferral or nonrecognition of gains. Examples are like-kind exchanges, involuntary conversions, and tax-free reorganizations.

   a. **Like-kind exchanges**. Sec. 1031 defers recognizing gain or loss to the extent that property productively used in a trade or business or held for the production of income (investment) is exchanged for property of like-kind.

   b. **Involuntary conversions**. A taxpayer may elect to defer recognition of gain, but not losses, if property is involuntarily converted (e.g., by fire, loss, or government condemnation for public use) into money or property that is not similar or related in use. Nonrecognition of gain is contingent on the involuntarily converted property being reinvested in qualified replacement property.

   c. **Tax-free reorganization**. A nontaxable reorganization of one or more corporations is considered a mere change in form of investment rather than a disposition of assets. For this reason, a general rule of nonrecognition of gain or loss applies to qualifying reorganizations. However, gain is recognized to the extent of receipt of cash or other nonqualifying payment.

10. **Taxation on Multinational Corporations**

    a. Multinational corporations frequently derive income from several countries. The government of each country in which a corporation does business may enact statutes imposing one or more types of tax on the corporation.

    b. To avoid double taxation, most countries have adopted treaties to coordinate or synchronize the effects of their taxing statutes.

11. Stop and review! You have completed the outline for this subunit. Study multiple-choice questions 4 through 9 beginning on page 436.

MULTIPLE-CHOICE QUESTIONS

A. Taxation

1. A regressive tax is a tax in which

A. Individuals with higher incomes pay a higher percentage of their income in tax.

B. The burden for payment falls disproportionately on lower-income persons.

C. The individual pays a constant percentage in taxes, regardless of income level.

D. Individuals with lower incomes pay a lower percentage of their income in tax.

The correct answer is (B). *(Publisher)*

REQUIRED: The statement that describes a regressive tax.

DISCUSSION: With a regressive tax, the percentage paid in taxes decreases as income increases. For example, excise taxes and payroll taxes are both regressive taxes. An excise tax is regressive because its burden falls disproportionally on lower-income persons. As personal income increases, the percentage of income paid declines because an excise tax is a flat amount per quality of the good or service purchased.

Answers (A) and (D) are incorrect because a progressive tax is a tax in which individuals with higher (lower) incomes pay a higher (lower) percentage of their income in tax. For example, income taxes are progressive. Answer (C) is incorrect because a proportional tax is a tax in which the individual pays a constant percentage in taxes, regardless of income level. A sales tax is a proportional tax.

2. Two examples of indirect taxes are

A. Taxes on business and rental property and personal income taxes.

B. Sales taxes and Social Security taxes paid by employees.

C. Sales taxes and Social Security taxes paid by employers.

D. Social Security taxes paid by employees and personal income taxes.

The correct answer is (C). *(CMA, adapted)*

REQUIRED: The two forms of indirect taxes.

DISCUSSION: Indirect taxes are those levied against someone other than individual taxpayers and thus only indirectly affect the individual. Sales taxes are levied against businesses and are then passed along to the individual purchaser. Social Security taxes are levied against both the employer and the employee. Those levied against the employee are direct taxes; those levied against the employer are indirect.

Answers (A), (B), and (D) are incorrect because personal income taxes and Social Security taxes levied against the employee are direct taxes.

3. When a fixed plant asset with a 5-year estimated useful life is sold during the second year, how would the use of an accelerated depreciation method instead of the straight-line method affect the gain or loss on the sale of the fixed plant asset?

	Gain	Loss
A.	Increase	Increase
B.	Increase	Decrease
C.	Decrease	Increase
D.	Decrease	Decrease

The correct answer is (B). *(CMA, adapted)*

REQUIRED: The effect of using an accelerated depreciation method instead of straight-line.

DISCUSSION: An accelerated method reduces the book value of the asset more rapidly in the early years of the useful life than does the straight-line method. Hence, the effect of an early sale is to increase the gain or decrease the loss that would have been recognized under the straight-line method.

Answers (A), (C), and (D) are incorrect because the effect is to increase gains and decrease losses.

B. Fundamentals of Corporate Taxation

Questions 4 and 5 are based on the following information. The Hando Communications Corporation (HCC) has just finished its first year of operations. For the year, HCC had $80,000 of income. HCC also earned $11,000 of interest on a tax-exempt bond, a $10,000 depreciation deduction, and an $8,000 tax credit. Assume that HCC has a 30% tax rate.

4. What is HCC's net tax liability?

A. $17,700

B. $15,300

C. $9,700

D. $2,000

The correct answer is (C). *(Publisher)*

REQUIRED: The net tax liability.

DISCUSSION: The first step in calculating HCC's net tax liability is to subtract the exclusion for tax-exempt interest from income, for a gross income amount of $69,000 ($80,000 – $11,000). Next, the deprecation deduction is subtracted from gross income, for a taxable income of $59,000 ($69,000 – $10,000). Then, the taxable income is multiplied by the tax rate, for a gross tax liability of $17,700 ($59,000 x 30%). Finally, net tax liability is computed by subtracting the tax credits from the gross tax liability. Therefore, HCC's net tax liability is $9,700 ($17,700 – $8,000).

Answer (A) is incorrect because $17,700 is the gross tax liability. Answer (B) is incorrect because $15,300 is the net tax liability found when incorrectly treating the tax credit as a direct reduction in taxable income. Answer (D) is incorrect because $2,000 is the net tax liability found when incorrectly treating the exclusion as a credit.

5. Which item reduces HCC's gross tax liability by the largest amount?

A. Gross income.

B. The tax-exempt interest exclusion.

C. The depreciation deduction.

D. The tax credit.

The correct answer is (D). *(Publisher)*

REQUIRED: The item that decreases HCC's gross tax liability by the largest amount.

DISCUSSION: Credits directly reduce taxes, while exclusions and deductions reduce income prior to the computation of the gross tax liability. Therefore, the credit reduces the gross tax liability on a dollar-for-dollar basis, or $8,000. An exclusion or deduction reduces gross tax liability by the amount of the exclusion or deduction x (1 – tax rate). Therefore, the exclusion will reduce HCC's gross tax liability by $7,700 [$11,000 x (1 – 0.30)], and the deduction will reduce HCC's gross tax liability by $7,000 [$10,000 x (1 – 0.30)]. Gross income does not reduce the gross tax liability; rather it increases the gross tax liability by $24,000 ($80,000 x 0.30). The tax credit reduction of $8,000 is larger than the exclusion and deduction reductions of $7,700 and $7,000, respectively.

Answers (A), (B), and (C) are incorrect because the tax credit will reduce HCC's gross tax liability by the largest amount.

6. None of the following items are deductible in calculating taxable income except

A. Estimated liabilities for product warranties expected to be incurred in the future.

B. Dividends on common stock declared but not payable until next year.

C. Bonus accrued but not paid by the end of the year to a cash-basis 90% shareholder.

D. Vacation pay accrued on an employee-by-employee basis.

The correct answer is (D). *(CMA, adapted)*

REQUIRED: The item that is deductible in the calculation of taxable income.

DISCUSSION: Sec. 162(a) states that a deduction is allowed for the ordinary and necessary expenses incurred during the year in any trade or business. A corporation may therefore deduct a reasonable amount for compensation. Accrued vacation pay is a form of compensation that results in an allowable deduction for federal income tax purposes.

Answer (A) is incorrect because warranty expenses are not deductible until paid. Answer (B) is incorrect because dividends on common stock are never deductible by a corporation; they are distributions of after-tax income. Answer (C) is incorrect because amounts accrued by an accrual-basis taxpayer to be paid to a related cash-basis taxpayer in a subsequent period are not deductible until the latter taxpayer includes the items in income. This rule effectively puts related taxpayers on the cash basis.

7. All of the following are adjustments/preference items to corporate taxable income in calculating alternative minimum taxable income except

A. All of the gain on an installment sale of real property in excess of $150,000.

B. Mining exploration and development costs.

C. A charitable contribution of appreciated property.

D. Sales commission earned in 1990 but paid in 1991.

The correct answer is (D). *(CMA, adapted)*

REQUIRED: The item that is not an adjustment or preference item in calculating the alternative minimum tax (AMT).

DISCUSSION: Taxable income is adjusted to arrive at alternative minimum taxable income. Some of the common adjustments include gains or losses from long-term contracts, gains on installment sales of real property, mining exploration and development costs, charitable contributions of appreciated property, accelerated depreciation, the accumulated current earnings adjustment, and tax-exempt interest on private activity bonds issued after August 7, 1986. A sales commission accrued in 1990 but paid in 1991 is not an example of an AMT adjustment.

Answer (A) is incorrect because the gain on an installment sale of real property in excess of $150,000 is an adjustment to taxable income for purposes of computing alternative minimum taxable income. Answer (B) is incorrect because mining exploration and development costs are adjustments to taxable income for purposes of computing alternative minimum taxable income. Answer (C) is incorrect because a charitable contribution of appreciated property is an adjustment to taxable income for purposes of computing alternative minimum taxable income.

8. Which one of the following factors might cause a firm to increase the debt in its financial structure?

A. An increase in the corporate income tax rate.

B. Increased economic uncertainty.

C. An increase in the federal funds rate.

D. An increase in the price-earnings ratio.

The correct answer is (A). *(CMA, adapted)*

REQUIRED: The factor that might encourage a firm to increase the debt in its financial structure.

DISCUSSION: An increase in the corporate income tax rate might encourage a company to borrow because interest on debt is tax deductible, whereas dividends are not. Accordingly, an increase in the tax rate means that the after-tax cost of debt capital will decrease. Given equal interest rates, a firm with a high tax rate will have a lower after-tax cost of debt capital than a firm with a low tax rate.

Answer (B) is incorrect because increased uncertainty encourages equity financing. Dividends do not have to be paid in bad years, but interest on debt is a fixed charge. Answer (C) is incorrect because an increase in interest rates discourages debt financing. Answer (D) is incorrect because an increase in the price-earnings ratio means that the return to shareholders (equity investors) is declining; therefore, equity capital is a more attractive financing alternative.

9. The deferral or nonrecognition of gains is not allowed for tax purposes when the transaction is a(n)

A. Reorganization that is a change in the form of investment.

B. Exchange of property that is used in a business for like-kind property.

C. Reorganization that is considered a disposition of assets.

D. Involuntary conversion of property into qualified replacement property.

The correct answer is (C). *(Publisher)*

REQUIRED: The statement that does not allow for the deferral or nonrecognition of gain.

DISCUSSION: Like-kind exchanges, involuntary conversions, and tax-free reorganizations are examples of transactions that result in the deferral or nonrecognition of gain. A reorganization is nontaxable when it is considered a mere change in investment, not a disposition of assets.

Answer (A) is incorrect because a reorganization that is a mere change in the form of investment is nontaxable. Answer (B) is incorrect because a like-kind exchange allows for the deferral of gain. Answer (D) is incorrect because an involuntary conversion allows for the deferral of gain.

APPENDIX C: IMA MEMBERSHIP, ICMA APPLICATION, AND EXAMINATION FORMS

A. *IMA Membership Application*
B. *Application for Admission to the ICMA*
C. *Examination Registration Form*

You must apply and become an IMA member in order to participate in the IMA Certification programs. The cost is $135 per year for Regular or International membership; $45 for the first year and $90 for the second year for Associate membership (for those within 2 years of completing full-time studies and who reside in the U.S. or Canada); $67.50 per year for Academic membership (full-time faculty in the U.S. and Canada); and $27 per year for Student membership (must carry at least 6 hours per semester and reside in the U.S. or Canada). The IMA offers two member interest groups at $75 per year: the Controllers Council and the Cost Management Group. Everyone except students and associates must pay a $15 IMA registration fee. See pages 439 and 440, which can be photocopied and used to apply for IMA membership, or call the IMA at (800) 638-4427 and ask for a CMA/CFM "kit."

The application for admission to the ICMA is on pages 441 and 442. This form is required for participation in the IMA Certification Programs. Completion of the registration form on page 443 is required in order to take any and all of the five examination parts.

Photocopy the following 5 pages and fill them out and mail them today! It will take you less than 10 minutes!

IMA MEMBERSHIP APPLICATION

INSTITUTE of MANAGEMENT ACCOUNTANTS
CERTIFIED MANAGEMENT ACCOUNTANT PROGRAM
CERTIFIED IN FINANCIAL MANAGEMENT PROGRAM

10 Paragon Drive, Montvale, New Jersey 07645-1760 • 1 (800) 638-4427

☐ Initial Application
☐ Reinstatement

PLEASE PRINT CLEARLY OR TYPE BATCH NUMBER:

PERSONAL INFORMATION

☐ Mr. ☐ Ms. ☐ Miss ☐ Mrs. ☐ Dr. | ☐ Male ☐ Female | Social Security Number - - | Date of Birth / / | Send IMA Mail To ☐ Home ☐ Business

First Name | Middle Initial | Last Name (Family Name) | Suffix

Home Street Address

City | State | Zip Code (9 digit)

Spouse's First Name | Middle Initial | Last Name

COMPANY INFORMATION

Company Name | SIC Code (See Reverse)

Street Address (Include room, suite and/or mail stop) | Job Title Code (See Reverse)

City | State | Zip Code (9 digit) | Responsibility Code (See Reverse)

CHAPTER AFFILIATION

Chapter Affiliation (Your Choice of Chapter/Student Chapter - see inside of booklet cover) | Chapter Number | ☐ Member-At-Large (Check here if no chapter affiliation desired)

EDUCATION HISTORY - BEGIN WITH CURRENT OR LAST SCHOOL

School Name	Major(s)	Date(s) Attended or Expected Graduation Date	Degree(s) or Expected Degree

Telephone Preference: ☐ Home ☐ Business

Home Telephone Number ( )

Business Telephone with Extension ( )

Fax Number ( )

e-mail

First Name or Nickname for IMA Badges (optional)

ADMISSION CRITERIA FOR MEMBERSHIP: INSTITUTE OF MANAGEMENT ACCOUNTANTS

I affirm that I meet the criteria for membership which I have checked. (See Reverse. Check only one.)

C: ☐ 1 ☐ 2 ☐ 3 ☐ 4 ☐ 5 ☐ 6

CPA Certificate Number: State: Year:

Have you ever been convicted of a felony: ☐ NO ☐ YES (see reverse side)

Are you required to report CPE hours annually? ☐ NO ☐ YES

PROFESSIONAL DESIGNATIONS EARNED (Check One)
☐ CPA ☐ CFA
☐ CIA ☐ Other:______

CHECK HERE TO RECEIVE INTRODUCTORY INFORMATION ABOUT BECOMING A PART OF IMA'S PRESTIGIOUS CERTIFICATION PROGRAMS.
☐ CMA ☐ CFM

MEMBERSHIP INFORMATION/DUES - FILL IN AS APPROPRIATE. ALL PAYMENTS MUST BE IN U.S. DOLLARS

☐ REGULAR MEMBERSHIP:	1 Year - $ 135.00	$
☐ INTERNATIONAL MEMBER-AT-LARGE: (You must reside outside the United States and Canada.)	$ 135.00	$
☐ ACADEMIC: (You must be a full-time faculty member and reside in the U.S. or Canada.)	$ 67.50	$
☐ ASSOCIATE: (You must apply within 2 years of completing full-time studies and reside in the U.S. or Canada.)	☐ 1ST Year - $ 45.00 ☐ 2ND Year - $ 90.00	$
☐ STUDENT: (You must have not less than 6 equivalent hours per semester and reside in the U.S. or Canada.)	$ 27.00	$
MEMBER INTEREST GROUPS (IMA Membership Required): ☐ Controllers Council	☐ 1 Year - $ 75.00 ea.	$
☐ Cost Management Group	☐ 1 Year - $ 75.00 ea.	$
OPTIONAL SERVICES (IMA Membership Required): ☐ Research Publication Service for 1 year (U.S. members)	$ 85.00	$
☐ Research Publication Service for 1 year (International members)	$ 120.00	$
REGISTRATION/REINSTATEMENT FEE: Applies to Regular, Academic & International Members, ONLY.		$ 15 00
	TOTAL DUE ➤	

PAYMENT INFORMATION

☐ Check enclosed. Make check payable in U.S. dollars to: Institute of Management Accountants, Inc.

☐ Charge my credit card: ☐ VISA ☐ MasterCard ☐ American Express

Credit Card Number:______ Expiration date: ____/____

I affirm that the statements on this application are correct and agree to abide by the Standards of Ethical Conduct.

Signature: X______ Date:______

Sponsor's Signature (if applicable): X______ Sponsor's Member Number: (if applicable)______
(Or Signature of Professor or Registrar for Student)

15

PLEASE READ BOTH SIDES NOTE: PAYMENT IN FULL MUST ACCOMPANY APPLICATIONS - FEES SUBJECT TO CHANGE REVISED 5/97

STANDARD INDUSTRY CLASSIFICATIONS (SIC)

AGRICULTURE, FORESTRY, FISHERIES
01 AGRICULTURAL PRODUCTION
07 AGRICULTURAL SVCS / HUNTING / TRAPPING
08 FORESTRY
09 FISHERIES

MINING
10 METAL MINING
11 ANTHRACITE MINING
12 BITUMINOUS COAL / LIGNITE MINING
13 CRUDE OIL / LIGNITE MINING
14 MINING / QUARRY NONMETALLICS

CONTRACT CONSTRUCTION
15 BLDG. CONSTRUCTION - GENERAL CONTRACTORS
16 CONSTRUCTION - OTHER
17 CONSTRUCTION - SPECIAL TRADE CONTRACTORS

MANUFACTURING
19 ORDINANCE / ACCESSORIES
20 FOOD / KINDRED PRODUCTS
21 TOBACCO MANUFACTURERS
22 TEXTILE MILL PRODUCTS
23 APPAREL / FINISHED FABRICS
24 LUMBER / WOOD PRODUCTS
25 FURNITURE / FIXTURES
26 PAPER / ALLIED PRODUCTS
27 PRINTING / PUBLISHING
28 CHEMICALS / ALLIED PRODUCTS
29 OIL REFINING / RELATED INDUSTRIES
30 RUBBER / MISC. PLASTICS PRODUCTS
31 LEATHER PRODUCTS
32 STONE, CLAY, GLASS / CONCRETE PRODUCTS
33 PRIMARY METAL INDUSTRIES
34 FABRICATED METAL PRODUCTS
35 MACHINERY, NONELECTRICAL
36 ELECTRICAL MACHINERY
37 TRANSPORTATION
38 PROFESSIONAL , SCIENTIFIC, CONTROL INSTRUMENTS
39 MISC. MANUFACTURING INDUSTRIES

TRANSPORTATION, COMMUNICATION & UTILITY SERVICES
40 RAILROAD TRANSPORTATION
41 LOCAL AND SUBURBAN TRANSPORTATION
42 MOTOR FREIGHT / WAREHOUSING
44 WATER TRANSPORTATION
46 PIPE LINE TRANSPORTATION
47 TRANSPORTATION SERVICES
48 COMMUNICATION
49 ELECTRIC, GAS / SANITARY SERVICES

WHOLESALE & RETAIL TRADE
50 WHOLESALE TRADE
52 BUILDING / HARDWARE / FARM EQUIP DEALERS
53 RETAIL TRADE - GENERAL
54 FOOD STORES
55 AUTO DEALERS / SERVICE STATIONS
56 APPAREL / ACCESSORY STORES
57 FURNITURE / FURNISHINGS / STORES
58 EATING / DRINKING PLACES
59 MISC. RETAIL STORES

FINANCE, INSURANCE & REAL ESTATE
60 BANKING
61 CREDIT AGENCIES NOT BANKS
62 SECURITY / COMMODITY BROKERS, AND SERVICES
63 INSURANCE CARRIERS
64 INSURANCE AGENTS, BROKERS
65 REAL ESTATE
66 COMBINATIONS OF REAL ESTATE, INSURANCE, LOANS LAW OFFICES
67 HOLDING, INVESTMENT COMPANIES

SERVICES
70 HOTELS / ROOMING HOUSES / CAMPS, ETC.
72 PERSONAL SERVICES
73 MISC. BUSINESS SERVICES
75 AUTO REPAIR, AUTO SERVICES / GARAGES
78 MOTION PICTURES
79 AMUSEMENT / RECREATION SERVICES
80 MEDICAL / HEALTH SERVICES
81 LEGAL SERVICES
82 EDUCATIONAL SERVICES
84 MUSEUM / ART GALLERIES / GARDENS
86 NONPROFIT MEMBERSHIP ORGANIZATIONS
88 PRIVATE HOUSEHOLDS
89 PUBLIC ACCOUNTING

GOVERNMENT
91 FEDERAL GOVERNMENT
92 STATE GOVERNMENT
93 LOCAL GOVERNMENT
94 INTERNATIONAL GOVERNMENT

JOB TITLE
01 OWNER
03 CHAIRMAN OF THE BOARD
05 CHIEF EXECUTIVE OFFICER
06 CHIEF FINANCIAL OFFICER
07 PRESIDENT
09 GROUP PRESIDENT
11 CORPORATE SECRETARY
13 CORPORATE TREASURER
15 EXECUTIVE VICE PRESIDENT
17 SENIOR VICE PRESIDENT
19 VICE PRESIDENT
21 ASSISTANT VICE PRESIDENT
23 GROUP VICE PRESIDENT
25 DIVISIONAL VICE PRESIDENT
27 CORPORATE CONTROLLER
29 ASST. CORPORATE CONTROLLER
31 DIVISIONAL CONTROLLER
33 PLANT CONTROLLER
35 DIRECTOR
37 GENERAL MANAGER
39 MANAGER
41 GENERAL SUPERVISOR
43 SUPERVISOR
45 CHIEF ACCOUNTANT
47 ACCOUNTANT
49 ECONOMIST
51 ANALYST
53 SYSTEMS ANALYST
55 PROGRAMMER
57 ADMINISTRATOR
59 AUDITOR
61 BOOKKEEPER
63 ACCOUNTING CLERK
65 DEAN
67 PROFESSOR
69 ASSOCIATE PROFESSOR
71 ASSISTANT PROFESSOR
73 INSTRUCTOR
75 CONSULTANT
77 PRINCIPAL
79 PARTNER
99 OTHER

RESPONSIBILITY AREA
01 GENERAL MANAGEMENT
05 CORPORATE MANAGEMENT
10 PUBLIC ACCOUNTING
15 GENERAL ACCOUNTING
20 PERSONNEL ACCOUNTING
25 COST ACCOUNTING
30 GOVERNMENTAL ACCOUNTING
35 FINANCE
40 RISK MANAGEMENT
45 BUDGET AND PLANNING
50 TAXATION
55 INTERNAL AUDITING
60 EDUCATION
65 INFORMATION SYSTEMS
70 STUDENT
75 RETIRED
80 OTHER

Management Accounting Magazine
subscription rates per year:
★ Members $20.00
(included in dues, nondeductible)
★ Student members: $13.00
(included in dues, nondeductible)

ADMISSION CRITERIA FOR MEMBERSHIP:

All persons residing within the United States, its possessions, or Canada, and who are otherwise qualified for membership under the Bylaws, are eligible for membership as Regular Members, Associate Members or Student Members as defined in Article II, Section 2 of the Bylaws, provided they meet the following minimum criteria:

(b) Effective January 1, 1996, all new IMA members except CMAs, Emeritus Life Associates, Emeritus Life Members, Retired Members, and Student Members, will be required to meet a minimum standard for continuing professional education (CPE) of 10 hours per year as a condition of membership; that beginning January 1, 1998, the minimum standard of continuing professional education will increase to 20 hours per year; that all CPE hours must meet the qualitative specifications as set forth by the Institute of Certified Management Accountants; that CMAs will continue to meet a minimum standard for CPE of 30 hours per year; that the Board may adopt policies regarding CPE for volunteer leaders.

(c) (1) Have a full four-year college degree, or

(2) Have a two-year college degree with a minimum of 15 semester hours in accounting plus four years of experience in a management accounting position at the time of admission, or

(3) Hold a CPA certificate, or an international certificate comparable to a CPA or CMA certificate, or

(4) Have six years of experience in management accounting, or

(5) Agree to complete 18 Continuing Professional Education (CPE) hours in IMA-approved programs (local or national) in each of the five consecutive years from the date of admission. A member not fulfilling the commitment will automatically be dropped from membership, or

(6) Be a college student carrying a minimum of six undergraduate or graduate hours (or equivalent) per semester within a school, college or university in the United States.

NOTE: Prior felony conviction - This application, with a brief explanation of circumstances, should be sent directly to the Executive Director of IMA at the address on the reverse side of this form in an envelope marked "Confidential."

APPLICATION FOR ADMISSION TO THE ICMA

Institute of Certified Management Accountants
10 Paragon Drive • Montvale, New Jersey 07645-1759
(201) 573-9000 • 1 (800) 638-4427 • FAX: (201) 573-8438
Endorsed by the Institute of Management Accountants

PLEASE CHECK THE PROGRAMS YOU WISH TO ENTER

CMA CFM

☐ CMA PROGRAM ☐ CFM PROGRAM

PERSONAL INFORMATION

TYPE OR PRINT CLEARLY

☐ Mr. ☐ Ms. ☐ Miss ☐ Mrs. ☐ Dr. ☐ Male ☐ Female

Social Security Number ☐☐☐-☐☐-☐☐☐☐

Date of Birth ☐☐-☐☐-☐☐

☐ I would like my mail sent to my home address

Last Name (Family Name)	First Name	Middle Name	Suffix

Home Mailing Address

City	State	Zip Code (9 digit)

Home Telephone Number (include area code)
(   )

☐ I would like my mail sent to my business address

Firm Name

Business Mailing Address

City	State	Zip Code (9 digit)

Business Telephone Number (include area code)	Extension
( )	

Are you a member of the Institute of Management Accountants? ☐ Yes ☐ No

If yes, please provide IMA Membership Number: ☐☐☐☐☐☐☐ IMA Chapter Name: ______________

If no, please note: IMA membership is required for acceptance into the ICMA. You must complete and return the IMA Application, and this application must include the appropriate dues payment.

EDUCATIONAL QUALIFICATIONS

A. College or University	Degree	Date Received/Expected
Undergraduate		
Graduate		

Name on transcript (if different than above)

B. Candidates with CPA License: State	Year	License Number

Check the appropriate box(es) and make arrangements for supporting documents to be forwarded to the ICMA. Verification must be received for examination authorization.

- ☐ **College Graduate.** Submit official transcript showing university degree conferred and official university seal or arrange for university to send proof of degree directly to the ICMA. If you have more than one degree, submit only one transcript. Candidates with foreign degrees must have their degree evaluated by an independent agency. Contact the ICMA for details.
- ☐ **GMAT or GRE scores.** Provide copy of scores to ICMA.
- ☐ **CPA.** Arrange to have proof of license sent directly from your State Board of Accountancy to the ICMA.
- ☐ **CPA Waiver for Part 2.** Arrange to have proof of CPA examination completion sent directly from your State Board of Accountancy to the ICMA. Enclose the waiver fee with this application or use space on reverse side to charge this fee to your credit card.
- ☐ **Applying as Student.** Be sure to provide, in the Character Reference Section on the reverse side of this form, the name of a professor who can verify student status. Upon graduation, be sure to arrange for an official copy of your transcript to be sent to the ICMA.
- ☐ **Applying as Faculty.** In addition to confirming your educational qualification, please provide a letter on school stationery affirming full-time teaching status.

PLEASE COMPLETE BOTH SIDES

CHARACTER REFERENCES

The names, addresses and telephone numbers of two character references must be supplied. One, your current employer, or current professor if you are a student; the other, a person neither employed by your firm nor a member of your family. The ICMA may contact the references as appropriate.

Name - Employer or Professor -(Circle one)			Name - Personal		
Title:			Address:		
Address:			Address:		
City:	State:	Zip Code:	City:	State:	Zip Code:
Phone number:			Phone number:		

Have you ever been convicted of a felony? ☐ Yes ☐ No If yes, please explain in an accompanying letter.

EXPERIENCE REQUIREMENT

Appropriate experience is required before the certification is awarded. The experience listed below will be used by the ICMA to identify candidates whose experience may not meet the requirements. For students and others who do not have accounting experience, but who expect to be employed in the accounting field, please check the following space: ☐ Not currently employed in the required field but expect to be in the future.

DATES (MONTH AND YEAR)	EMPLOYER	JOB TITLE	DUTIES & RESPONSIBILITIES
START DATE: END DATE:			
START DATE: END DATE:			

I agree to comply with the Standards of Ethical Conduct. I declare and affirm that the statements made in the foregoing application, including accompanying statements and transcripts, are true, complete, and correct. I authorize the investigation of all statements contained in this application.

I hereby attest that I will not divulge the content of the examination, nor will I remove any examination materials, notes, or other unauthorized materials from the examination room. I understand that failure to comply with this attestation may result in invalidation of my grades and disqualification from future examinations. For those already certified by the Institute of Certified Management Accountants, failure to comply with the statement will be considered a violation of the Standards of Ethical Conduct for Practitioners of Management Accounting and Financial Management and could result in revocation of the certification.

Signature of Applicant*: X____________________ Date:__________

*Original signature required; do not fax this form.

PAYMENT INFORMATION

☐ I am enclosing a check payable to the Institute of Certified Management Accountants ☐ $50. Credentialing Fee (required)**

☐ Charge my: ☐ VISA ☐ MasterCard ☐ American Express ☐ CPA Waiver Fee $80.**

Card Number: ☐☐☐☐☐☐☐☐☐☐☐☐☐☐☐☐ Expiration Date: ☐☐-☐☐

Signature of Applicant: X____________________ Date:__________

FEES SUBJECT TO CHANGE **After September 1, 1997. Not required for students. CPA Waiver Fee is $60. until September 1, 1997.

NOTE: A SEPARATE EXAMINATION REGISTRATION FORM IS REQUIRED.

OFFICE USE ONLY	BATCH NUMBER	PAYMENT BY CHECK # ☐ PERSONAL ☐ COMPANY	AMOUNT

Institute of Certified Management Accountants
10 Paragon Drive • Montvale, New Jersey 07645-1759
(201) 573-9000 • 1 (800) 638-4427 • FAX: (201) 573-8438
Endorsed by the Institute of Management Accountants

CMA® CFM®

EXAMINATION REGISTRATION FORM

PERSONAL INFORMATION

TYPE OR PRINT CLEARLY

☐ Mr. ☐ Ms. ☐ Miss ☐ Mrs. ☐ Dr. ☐ CMA ☐ CFM ☐ Certification Candidate

Social Security Number ☐☐☐-☐☐-☐☐☐☐

Last Name (Family Name) First Name Middle Name Suffix

Preferred Mailing Address ☐ Home ☐ Business

City State Zip Code (9 digit)

Daytime Telephone Number (include area code) Please Specify ☐ Home ☐ Business

The separate Application for Admission to the ICMA and an application to the IMA must accompany this Examination Registration Form unless they have been previously submitted.

PLACE A CHECK MARK IN THE BLANK SPACES BELOW FOR THE PART(S) YOU WISH TO TAKE AT THIS TIME

☐ PART 1 Economics, Finance, and Management

☐ PART 2CMA Financial Accounting and Reporting

☐ PART 2CFM Corporate Financial Management

☐ PART 3 Management Reporting, Analysis, and Behavioral Issues

☐ PART 4 Decision Analysis and Information Systems

TOTAL PARTS ________

X $ 80.00 Fee* .... $ ________

Add $ 40.00 .... $ ________
International Site Fee
(if applicable)

Less Student/Faculty Discount...... $ ________
(if eligible)

AMOUNT DUE .... $ ________

*The per part fee is $60 until September 1,1997

CONFIDENTIALITY STATEMENT & PAYMENT INFORMATION

I hereby attest that I will not divulge the content of this examination, nor will I remove any examination materials, notes, or other unauthorized materials from the examination room. I understand that failure to comply with this attestation may result in invalidation of my grades and disqualification from future examinations. For those already certified by the Institute of Certified Management Accountants, failure to comply with the statement will be considered a violation of the Standards of Ethical Conduct for Practitioners of Management Accounting and Financial Management and could result in revocation of the certification.

Signature: **X** ________________________________

☐ I am enclosing a check payable to the Institute of Certified Management Accountants ☐ Charge my: ☐ VISA ☐ MasterCard ☐ American Express

Card Number: ☐☐☐☐☐☐☐☐☐☐☐☐☐☐☐☐ Expiration Date: ☐☐-☐☐

Signature: **X** ________________________________ Date: ____________

CREDIT POLICY ON PAGE 9. FEES SUBJECT TO CHANGE

APPENDIX D
ICMA CONTENT SPECIFICATION OUTLINES

Authors' Note: This is reference material only. The ICMA's CSOs have been carefully analyzed and are incorporated in our Study Units 1 through 10 to provide more systematic and rational coverage of topics within each part of the exam. We believe we provide comprehensive coverage of the subject matter tested on the CMA/CFM exams. If, after you take the exam, you find topics, concepts, etc., tested that are not covered or are inadequately covered, please call, fax, or e-mail (irvin@gleim.com). We do not want information about CMA/CFM questions, only information/feedback about our books/software.

The content specification outlines presented below represent the body of knowledge that will be covered on CMA/CFM Part 1. Candidates are responsible for being informed on the most recent developments in the areas covered in the outline. This includes understanding of public pronouncements issued by accounting organizations as well as being up-to-date on recent developments reported in current accounting and business periodicals.

The content specification outlines serve several purposes. These purposes include

- Establishing the foundation from which each examination will be developed
- Providing consistent coverage on each examination over time
- Communicating to interested parties more detail as to the content of each exam part
- Aiding candidates in their preparation for each examination
- Providing information to those who offer courses designed to assist candidates in preparing for the examinations

Important additional information about the content specification outlines and the examinations:

1. The percentage range given for each major topic within each examination part represents the relative weight range given to that topic in an examination part. A candidate will be required to answer questions that equal the minimum relative weight but do not exceed the maximum relative weight for a topic.
2. Each examination will sample from the subject areas contained within each major topic area to meet the relative weight specifications. No relative weights have been assigned to the subject areas within each major topic. No inference should be made from the order in which the subject areas are listed or from the number of subject areas as to the relative weight or importance of any of the subjects.
3. Each major topic within each examination part has been assigned a coverage level designating the depth and breadth of topic coverage, ranging from an introductory knowledge of a subject area (Level A) to a thorough understanding of and ability to apply the essentials of a subject area (Level C). Detailed explanations of the coverage levels and the skills expected of candidates are presented on page 446.
4. The topics for each of the exam parts have been selected to minimize overlapping subject areas among parts. The topics within a part and the subject areas within topics may be combined in individual questions.
5. Questions containing ethical issues can appear on any part of the examination. The ethical issues will be addressed within the context of a specific subject area. For determining the relative weight distribution of an examination, the questions containing ethical issues will be counted in the major topic area in which the ethical issues are raised.

6. Federal income taxation issues will be divided into two categories and be contained in questions that relate to the two categories. (See also Appendix B.)
   a. Accounting for income taxes. The financial reporting requirements for income taxes including the proper treatment of deferred income taxes will be contained in questions in Part 2CMA and Part 2CFM.
   b. Tax implications for decisions. The tax code provisions that impact decisions will be contained in: (1) questions that require decision analysis regarding debt versus equity issues in Part 1, (2) questions in Part 2CFM, and (3) the decision analysis questions in Part 4.
7. Candidates for the CMA and CFM designations are expected to have a minimum level of business knowledge that transcends all examination parts. This minimum level would include knowledge of basic financial statements, time value of money concepts, and elementary statistics.

In order to more clearly define the topical knowledge required by a candidate, varying levels of coverage for the treatment of major topics of the content specification outlines have been identified and defined. The cognitive skills that a successful candidate should possess and that should be tested on the examination can be defined as follows:

Knowledge: Ability to remember previously learned material such as specific facts, criteria, techniques, principles, and procedures (i.e., identify, define, list).

Comprehension: Ability to grasp and interpret the meaning of material (i.e., classify, explain, distinguish between).

Application: Ability to use learned material in new and concrete situations (i.e., demonstrate, predict, solve, modify, relate).

Analysis: Ability to break down material into its component parts so that its organizational structure can be understood; ability to recognize causal relationships, discriminate between behaviors, and identify elements that are relevant to the validation of a judgment (i.e., differentiate, estimate, order).

Synthesis: Ability to put parts together to form a new whole or proposed set of operations; ability to relate ideas and formulate hypotheses (i.e., combine, formulate, revise).

Evaluation: Ability to judge the value of material for a given purpose on the basis of consistency, logical accuracy, and comparison to standards; ability to appraise judgments involved in the selection of a course of action (i.e., criticize, justify, conclude).

The three levels of coverage can be defined as follows:

Level A: Requiring an appreciation of the broad nature and fundamentals, the ability to recognize the existence of special features and problems in various business transactions, and the ability to apply this knowledge in new and concrete situations, i.e., requiring the skill levels of knowledge and comprehension.

Level B: Requiring a sound understanding of the broad aspects of practices and procedures and awareness of the problems relating to more detailed aspects, the ability to apply such board knowledge in new and concrete situations, the ability to analyze the components of the material and their relationships, and the ability to reformulate the components into a new whole, i.e., requiring the skill levels of knowledge, comprehension, application, and analysis.

Level C: Requiring a sound understanding of principles, practices, and procedures, the ability to analyze material so that its organizational structure can be understood, the proficiency to apply such knowledge to situations likely to be encountered, the ability to deal with all aspects of the situation without extensive recourse to technical research and assistance, and the ability to judge the value of material for a given purpose, i.e., requiring all six skill levels.

The levels of coverage as they apply to each of the major topics of the Content Specification Outlines are shown on the following pages with each topic listing. The levels represent the manner in which topic areas are to be treated and represent ceilings, i.e., a topic area designated as Level C may contain requirements at the "A," "B," or "C" level but a topic designated as Level B will not contain requirements at the "C" level.

Your authors have organized and presented study outlines and multiple-choice questions in anticipation of the ICMA's questions to appear on the exam. We expect to have 95+% of the questions on your exam explained in the study outlines and/or illustrated in our questions. After you take your exam, please send us your evaluation of this book and our *CMA/CFM Review Test Prep* software. We want to know the topics, concepts, etc., that need to be expanded or added to our CMA/CFM books and software. Remember to check our e-mail updates by e-mailing update@gleim.com with CMA/CFM Part 1 8-2 in the subject line.

CONTENT SPECIFICATION
Part 1 - Economics, Finance, and Management

*A. **Microeconomics (10% - 15%) (Level B)***

1. *Factors affecting the individual firm*
   - a. *Theory of demand*
   - b. *Theory of supply*
   - c. *Interaction of demand and supply to determine prices*
   - d. *The laws of demand and supply*
   - e. *Elasticity of demand and supply*
   - f. *Government intervention in market operations*
2. *Consumption of goods*
   - a. *Marginal utility theory*
   - b. *Indifference curve analysis*
3. *Production cost functions*
   - a. *Economic costs*
   - b. *Economic profits*
   - c. *Production costs in the short run*
   - d. *Production costs in the long run*
   - e. *Economies and diseconomies of scale*
4. *Market structures and pricing*
   - a. *Pure competition*
   - b. *Monopoly*
   - c. *Monopolistic competition*
   - d. *Oligopoly*
   - e. *Effects of boycotts and cartels on prices and output*
5. *The economy as a system of markets*
   - a. *Production and demand for economic resources*
   - b. *The labor market*

*B. **Macroeconomics (10% - 15%) (Level A)***

1. *Issues and controversies in macroeconomics*
   - a. *Inflation*
   - b. *Employment and unemployment*
   - c. *Economic growth*
2. *Business cycles*
   - a. *Nature and history of business cycles*
   - b. *Terminology used to explain business fluctuations*
   - c. *Reason for fluctuations*
   - d. *Leading economic indicators*
3. *Fiscal policy*
   - a. *Theory of fiscal policy*
   - b. *Tools of fiscal policy*
   - c. *Taxation policies*
4. *Money and monetary policy*
   - a. *Nature of money*
   - b. *The commercial banking system and the creation of money*
   - c. *Definition of the money supply and supply of and demand for money*
   - d. *Relation between money and national income*
   - e. *The central banking system and its actions to influence the money supply*
   - f. *The Federal Reserve Board and its actions to influence the money supply*
   - g. *Instruments and objectives of monetary policy*

C. ***International Business Environment (10% - 15%) (Level B)***

1. *Comparative advantages of trade*
2. *Free trade and protectionism*
3. *Barriers in international trade*
    a. *Tariffs*
    b. *Negotiated import and export restrictions*
    c. *Trigger pricing and antidumping rules*
    d. *International agreements on trade and tariffs*
    e. *Compatibility of domestic and international policies*
4. *Nature and theory of foreign exchange*
    a. *Balance of payments*
    b. *Fixed and flexible exchange rates*
    c. *World Bank and International Monetary Fund*
5. *Other global topics*
    a. *International capital investment*
    b. *Global standards*

D. ***Domestic Institutional Environment of Business (10%-15%) (Level A)***

1. *Legal forms of business*
    a. *Proprietorship*
    b. *Partnership*
    c. *Corporation*
2. *Impact on business of government intervention*
    a. *Employee, employer, and union relations*
    b. *Antitrust policies*
    c. *Social legislation and government agencies*
    d. *Other government regulation*
3. *Non-governmental intervention*
    a. *Consumer groups*
    b. *Environmental groups*
    c. *Financial institutions*
4. *Social responsibility*

E. ***Working Capital Policy and Management (10% - 15%) (Level C)***

1. *Nature of working capital policy and management*
    a. *Optimum level of current assets and current liabilities*
    b. *Balancing profitability and risk*
2. *Cash management*
    a. *Factors influencing the levels of cash*
    b. *Reasons for holding cash*
    c. *Synchronizing cash inflows and outflows*
    d. *Methods to speed cash collections*
    e. *Using the float*
    f. *Compensating balances*
    g. *Overdraft systems*
3. *Marketable securities*
    a. *Types of marketable securities*
    b. *Factors influencing the level of marketable securities*
    c. *Reasons for holding marketable securities*
    d. *Strategies for holding marketable securities*
    e. *Risk and return factors influencing the selection of marketable securities*
4. *Accounts receivable management*
    a. *Factors influencing the level of accounts receivable*
    b. *Reasons for carrying accounts receivable*
    c. *Variables and decisions regarding credit policy*
    d. *Credit instruments*

5. *Inventory management*

    a. *Factors influencing the level of inventory*
    b. *Reasons for inventory*
    c. *Costs of inventory*
    d. *Inventory management techniques*

6. *Short-term credit for financing current assets*

    a. *Alternative strategies for financing working capital*
    b. *Advantages and disadvantages of short-term credit*
    c. *Types of short-term credit*
    d. *Secured short-term credit*
    e. *Minimizing the cost of short-term credit*

F. ***Long-Term Finance and Capital Structure (10% - 15%) (Level B)***

1. *Identification, measurement, and management of risk*

    a. *Risk and the organization's attitude toward risk*
    b. *Operating and financial leverage*
    c. *Sales stability*
    d. *Growth rate*
    e. *Profitability*
    f. *Asset structure*
    g. *Control position of owners and management*
    h. *Management attitude and ability*
    i. *Lender and rating attitude*
    j. *Competitive position in the industry*

2. *Objectives and policies of long-term financing*

    a. *Amount and mixture of permanent assets*
    b. *Methods of financing permanent assets*
    c. *Policies used to acquire firms*
    d. *Defenses against takeovers*
    e. *Initial public offerings*

3. *The cost of capital*

    a. *Weighted average cost of capital*
    b. *Cost of individual capital components*
    c. *Calculating the cost of capital*
    d. *Marginal cost of capital*
    e. *Models used in determining cost of capital*

4. *Types and nature of long-term financing*

    a. *Bonds*
    b. *Intermediate term loans*
    c. *Term loans*
    d. *Loan covenants*
    e. *Lease financing*
    f. *Common stock*
    g. *Preferred stock*
    h. *Convertible securities*
    i. *Stock warrants and rights*
    j. *Stock options*
    k. *Employee stock ownership plans (ESOPs)*

5. *Dividend policy*

    a. *Theories of dividend policy*
    b. *Factors that influence dividend policy*
    c. *Dividend payment procedures*
    d. *Stock repurchases*
    e. *Stock dividends and stock splits*
    f. *Automatic dividend reinvestment plans (ADRP)*

In conjunction with the long-term financing and capital structure topic, the income tax code provisions that impact financing decisions

-- *Deductibility of payments for use of capital*
-- *After-tax cost of capital*

G. ***Organizational Structures, Management, and Communication (20% - 30%) (Level B)***

1. *Nature and process of decision making in the organizational environment*

2. *Structural evolution in organizations*

   a. *Departmentalization*
   b. *Line and staff authority*
   c. *Centralization versus decentralization*
   d. *Matrix management*
   e. *Reengineering*
   f. *Strategic partnering and outsourcing*

3. *Social and cultural characteristics of effective organizations*

   a. *Sources of power*
   b. *Informal power and influence*
   c. *Delegation of authority*
   d. *Managing change*
   e. *Multinational issues*
   f. *Diversity issues*

4. *Effective organization of jobs and teams*

   a. *Nature of jobs*
   b. *Job design*
   c. *Teams and team processes*

5. *Roles of managers*

   a. *Interpersonal roles*
   b. *Informational roles*
   c. *Decisional roles*

6. *Staffing and managing human resources*

   a. *Planning*
   b. *Human resource audit*
   c. *Recruitment*
   d. *Selection and orientation*
   e. *Training and development*
   f. *Mentoring and coaching*
   g. *Compensation and benefits management*
   h. *Employee performance evaluation and incentive systems*
   i. *Transfers, terminations, and outplacements*

7. *Leadership styles*

   a. *Task versus employee orientation*
   b. *Autocratic leadership*
   c. *Democratic leadership*

8. *Motivational theories and methods*

   a. *Maslow's hierarchy of needs*
   b. *Herzberg's two-factor theory*
   c. *McGregor's Theory X and Theory Y*
   d. *Expectancy theory*
   e. *Equity theory*
   f. *Reinforcement theory - organization behavior modification*
   g. *Other theories on motivation*

9. *Communication*

   a. *Communication models*
   b. *Organizational communications*
   c. *Deterrents to effective communication*
   d. *Managing communication and information content*
   e. *Negotiating skills*

The topics and subject areas above may include ethical considerations in economics, finance, and management of concern to management accountants.

Statement on Management Accounting No. 1C, "Standards of Ethical Conduct for Management Accountants"

-- *Competence*
-- *Confidentiality*
-- *Integrity*
-- *Objectivity*

APPENDIX E
ICMA SUGGESTED READING LIST

The ICMA suggested reading list that follows is reproduced to give you an overview of the scope of each part. You will not have the time to study these texts. Our *CMA/CFM Review* books and *CMA/CFM Test Prep* software will be all you need. For all five parts, candidates are expected to stay up-to-date by reading articles from journals, newspapers, and professional publications.

CMA/CFM PART 1 -- ECONOMICS, FINANCE, AND MANAGEMENT

Economics

An introductory economics book, such as:

Lipsey, Richard G., and Courant, Paul, *Economics*, 11th edition, Harper & Row, New York, N.Y., 1996, or

McConnell, Campbell R., and Brue, Stanley L., *Economics: Principles, Problems and Policies*, 13th edition, McGraw-Hill Book Co., New York, N.Y., 1996.

An international economics book, such as:

Root, Franklin R., *International Trade and Investment*, 7th edition, South-Western Publishing Co., Cincinnati, Ohio, 1994.

Government and Business

Frederick, William C., Post, James E., and Davis, Keith, *Business and Society: Corporate Strategy, Public Policy, Ethics*, 7th edition, McGraw-Hill Book Co., New York, N.Y., 1992.

Greer, Douglas F., *Business, Government, and Society*, 3rd edition, Macmillan Publishing Company, New York, N.Y., 1993.

Business Finance

Van Horne, James C., and Wachowicz, John M., Jr., *Fundamentals of Financial Management*, 10th edition, Prentice-Hall, Inc., Englewood Cliffs, N.J., 1998.

Weston, J. Fred, and Copeland, Thomas E., *Managerial Finance*, 9th edition, The Dryden Press, Chicago, Ill., 1992.

Organization and Management Theory and Communication

Books that cover organization and management theory, such as:

Griffin, Ricky W., *Management*, 4th edition, Houghton Mifflin Company, Boston, Mass., 1993.

Tosi, Henry L., Rizzo, John R., and Carroll, Stephen J., *Managing Organizational Behavior*, 2nd edition, Ballinger Publishing, Cambridge, Mass., 1990.

PART 2CMA -- FINANCIAL ACCOUNTING AND REPORTING

Financial Statements and Reporting Requirements

An intermediate accounting book, such as:

Kieso, Donald E., and Weygandt, Jerry J., *Intermediate Accounting*, 8th edition, John Wiley & Sons, Inc. New York, N.Y., 1995, or

Nikolai, Loren A., and Bazley, John D., *Intermediate Accounting*, 7th edition, South-Western Publishing Company, Boston, Mass., 1997.

An advanced accounting book that covers the principles of consolidations and related topics, such as:

Larsen, E. John, *Modern Advanced Accounting*, 6th edition, McGraw-Hill Book Co., New York, N.Y., 1994.

Also:

Skousen, K. Fred, *An Introduction to the SEC*, 5th edition, South-Western Publishing Co., Cincinnati, Ohio, 1991.

Analysis of Accounts and Statements

Gibson, Charles H., *Financial Statement Analysis*, 6th edition, South-Western Publishing Co., Cincinnati, Ohio, 1995.

External Auditing

A general book such as:

Boynton, William C., and Kell, Walter G., *Modern Auditing*, 6th edition, John Wiley & Sons, New York, N.Y., 1996, or

Arens, Alvin A., and Loebbecke, James K., *Auditing: An Integrated Approach*, 6th edition, Prentice-Hall Inc., Englewood Cliffs, N.J., 1994.

PART 2CFM -- CORPORATE FINANCIAL MANAGEMENT

Financial Management

A finance book, such as:

Ross, Stephen A., Westerfield, Randolph W., and Jaffe, Jeffrey F., *Corporate Finance*, 4th edition, Richard D. Irwin, Inc., Homewood, Ill., 1996.

Van Horne, James C., *Financial Management and Policy*, 10th edition, Prentice-Hall, Inc., Englewood Cliffs, N.J., 1995.

Van Horne, James C. and Wachowicz, John M., Jr., *Fundamentals of Financial Management*, 10th edition, Prentice-Hall, Inc., Englewood Cliffs, N.J., 1998.

Weston, J. Fred, and Copeland, Thomas E., *Management Finance*, 9th edition, The Dryden Press, Chicago, Ill., 1992.

Financial Environment

Greer, Douglas F., *Business, Government, and Society*, 3rd edition, Macmillan Publishing Company, New York, N.Y., 1993.

McConnell, Campbell R., and Brue, Stanley L., *Economics: Principles, Problems, and Policies*, 13th edition, McGraw-Hill Book Co., New York, N.Y., 1996.

Root, Franklin R., *International Trade and Investment*, 7th edition, South-Western Publishing Co., Cincinnati, Ohio, 1994.

Skousen, K. Fred, *An Introduction to the SEC*, 5th edition, South-Western Publishing Co., Cincinnati, Ohio, 1991.

Analysis of Financial Statements

Gibson, Charles H., *Financial Statement Analysis*, 6th edition, South-Western Publishing Co., Cincinnati, Ohio, 1995.

Financial Statements and Accounting Standards

Accounting books, such as:

Kieso, Donald E. and Weygandt, Jerry J., *Intermediate Accounting*, 8th edition, John Wiley & Sons, Inc., New York, N.Y., 1995.

Larsen, E. John, *Modern Advanced Accounting*, 6th edition, McGraw-Hill, Inc., New York, N.Y., 1994.

CMA/CFM PART 3 -- MANAGEMENT REPORTING, ANALYSIS, AND BEHAVIORAL ISSUES

Management Reporting and Analysis

A managerial cost accounting book, such as:

Horngren, Charles, Foster, George, and Datar, Srikant, *Cost Accounting: A Managerial Emphasis,* 9th edition, Prentice-Hall, Inc., Englewood Cliffs, N.J., 1997, or

Rayburn, Letricia Gayle, *Cost Accounting: Using a Cost Management Approach*, 6th edition, Richard D. Irwin, Inc., Homewood, Ill., 1996, or

Wolk, Harry I., Gerber, Quentin N., and Porter, Gary A., *Management Accounting: Planning and Control*, PWS-Kent Publishing Company, Boston, Mass., 1988.

Also:

Welsch, Glenn, Hilton, Ronald W., and Gordon, Paul N., *Budgeting: Profit Planning and Control*, 5th edition, Prentice-Hall, Inc., Englewood Cliffs, N.J., 1988.

Behavioral Issues

See appropriate material on cost, budgeting, and responsibility centers in the managerial accounting books listed above, i.e., Horngren, Rayburn, and Welsch.

CMA/CFM PART 4 -- DECISION ANALYSIS AND INFORMATION SYSTEMS

Decision Analysis and Quantitative Methods

A managerial cost accounting book, such as:

Horngren, Charles, Foster, George, and Datar, Srikant, *Cost Accounting: A Managerial Emphasis,* 9th edition, Prentice-Hall, Inc., Englewood Cliffs, N.J., 1997.

Rayburn, Letricia Gayle, *Cost Accounting: Using a Cost Managerial Approach*, 6th edition, Richard D. Irwin, Inc., Homewood, Ill., 1996.

A finance book that covers capital budgeting, such as:

VanHorne, James C., *Financial Management and Policy*, 10th edition, Prentice-Hall, Inc., Englewood Cliffs, N.J., 1995 (chapters on capital investment analysis).

Weston, J. Fred, and Copeland, Thomas E., *Managerial Finance*, 9th edition, The Dryden Press, Chicago, Ill., 1992 (chapters on capital investment analysis).

A tax reference, such as:

Sommerfield, Ray M., and Jones, Sally M., *Federal Taxes and Management Decisions*, 10th edition, Richard D. Irwin, Inc., Homewood, Ill., 1995.

Also:

Bierman, Harold, Jr., Bonini, Charles P., and Hausman, Warren H., *Quantitative Analysis for Business Decisions*, 8th edition, Richard D. Irwin, Inc., Homewood, Ill., 1991.

Information Systems

A business data processing book, such as:

Kroenke, David, and Hatch, Richard, *Business Computer Systems*, 5th edition, Mitchell Publishing, Inc., Santa Cruz, Calif., 1993.

O'Brien, James A., *Introduction to Information Systems*, 7th edition, Irwin Professional Publishers, Barr Ridge, Ill., 1994.

Also:

Romney, Marshall B., Steinbart, Paul J., and Cushing, Barry E., *Accounting Information Systems*, 7th edition, Addison-Wesley Publishing Company, Reading, Mass., 1997.

Moscove, Stephen A., Simkin, Mark G., and Bagranoff, Nancy A., *Core Concepts of Accounting Information Systems*, 5th edition, John Wiley & Sons, Inc., New York, N.Y., 1997.

Internal Auditing

An internal auditing book, such as:

Brink, Victor, and Witt, Herbert, *Modern Internal Auditing: Appraising Operations and Controls*, 4th edition, John Wiley & Sons, New York, N.Y., 1982, or

Sawyer, Lawrence, *Internal Auditing*, 4th edition, Institute of Internal Auditors, Inc., Altamonte Springs, Fla., 1996.

CMA/CFM REVIEW: PART 1, CPE

CONTINUING PROFESSIONAL EDUCATION

FIVE SEPARATE COURSES

Courses Available	Course Level	Average Comp. Time	CPE Credit
1. Economics	Basic	500 min.	5/10* hours
2. Business Environment	Basic	500 min.	5/10* hours
3. Finance	Basic	500 min.	5/10* hours
4. Risk and Organizational Theory	Basic	500 min.	5/10* hours
5. Motivation and Communication	Basic	500 min.	5/10* hours
	Total CPE Credit		25/50* hours

*Check with your accreditation agency to determine whether it gives credit for half or full completion time.

1. Registration: The cost of this CMA/CFM Review: Part 1, CPE program is $25.

   A. If you have made your payment, then you are preregistered and in addition to this book you have one machine-readable answer sheet that you can use to submit up to five CMA/CFM Review CPE courses at one time. Should you decide to take fewer than five courses, you will need to purchase an additional answer sheet for $25 in order to submit additional courses. Gleim's CMA/CFM Review CPE is sold separately by exam part; i.e., a separate bubble sheet is required for each exam part's CPE courses.

   B. If you are not preregistered as described in A. above, you can register to participate by photocopying and completing the form below and mailing it, along with a $25 remittance, to

      Gleim Publications, Inc.
      CPE Division
      P.O. Box 12848, University Station
      Gainesville, FL 32604

      1) If you are using a credit card, you can fax us at (352) 375-6940.

      2) Gleim Publications will process your registration and send you one machine-readable answer sheet that you can use to submit up to five CMA/CFM Review CPE courses at one time. Should you decide to take fewer than five courses, you will need to purchase an additional answer sheet for $25 in order to submit additional courses.

Gleim's CMA/CFM Review CPE Registration Form

Name of Participant ______________________________

Social Security No. (for record-keeping purposes) ______________________________

Mailing Address ______________________________

____

City ______________________ State ________ ZIP ______________

Daytime Telephone ______________ E-mail Address ______________

Remit $25 registration fee by check, money order, or VISA/MC/AMEX/DISC.

Credit Card No. ______-______-______-______ Exp. Date ___/______

Signature ______________________________

2. Follow the specific instructions on the next four pages that describe exactly what must be done to earn CPE credit for each of the five courses.

PROCEDURES TO OBTAIN CPE CREDIT

Follow the instructions presented at the opening of **each** course you have chosen. Also, read these introductory pages carefully. In general, the procedure listed below is recommended.

1. Enroll in the program by photocopying and completing the form on page 455 and submitting it along with the $25 registration fee. We will send you a CPE answer sheet, which you must use to submit your final exam answers for grading.
2. Study the outlines in *CMA/CFM Review: Part 1*. Make study notes in your book and work through all examples.
   a. Work through each multiple-choice question in the pertinent study units. Do not skip questions.
   b. Study the adjacent answer explanations for the questions you answered incorrectly or had difficulty answering.
3. When you complete the assigned material, turn to the appropriate course in this CPE section and take the open-book final exam.
   a. The best procedure is to answer the questions in the order they appear.
   b. If you are unsure of some answers, consult the outlines and answer explanations in *CMA/CFM Review: Part 1*, 8th Edition.
   c. Circle your answer for each CPE question. Wait until you have answered all of the questions for a course before **carefully transferring** your answers to our machine-readable answer sheet.
      1) Do not make a mistake in this transfer (i.e., skip a line, start on the wrong line, etc.). Read the instructions in the next section and at the beginning of each course, and follow them carefully.
4. When you are ready to submit completed courses in this program, mail the machine-readable answer sheet in the special pre-addressed protective envelope accompanying your answer sheet to Gleim Publications, Inc., CPE Division, P.O. Box 12848, University Station, Gainesville, FL 32604. You may take one or more courses at a time using the answer sheet provided when you purchased this program. **Additional answer sheets are available for $25 and may be used for additional courses not submitted on the single answer sheet provided with the purchase of this program.**
   a. Please complete the course evaluation sheet and send it with your answer sheet.
   b. **Same day grading service** available Monday through Friday: Send your materials and $50 prepayment ($100 if out of the U.S.) (check, VISA, MC, AMEX, DISC) via Federal Express (priority, so we receive it by noon) or UPS Next Day Letter Service to 4201 N.W. 95th Blvd., Gainesville, FL 32606. We will hand-grade your answer sheet and arrange to have the results in your hands by the following afternoon. Add $10 if you request Saturday delivery.

MACHINE-READABLE ANSWER SHEET

We have contracted with the Office of Instructional Resources at the University of Florida to read your answer sheet with optical scanning equipment that will record your responses. Computerization of the grading and grade analysis means that you must fill out the answer sheet carefully and correctly.

1. Fill out all of the required information on page 2 of the answer sheet completely. You must write in the required information **AND** darken appropriate circles. Note that the answer sheet is four pages long. On page 2, fill in the following data:
   a. Last name, first initial, middle initial. If your last name is over 15 characters long, use only the first 15 characters.
   b. Sex, so we can computer-generate a Mr. or Ms. in our correspondence
   c. Social Security number
   d. Course number(s)--**THIS IS VERY IMPORTANT**. Note the four-digit code in the following table for each CMA/CFM Review CPE course you will be asking us to grade on this answer sheet. "B" means leave that circle blank.

	Course	Code
1.	Economics	B 3 B 1
2.	Business Environment	B 3 B 2
3.	Finance	B 3 B 3
4.	Risk and Organizational Theory	B 3 B 4
5.	Motivation and Communication	B 3 B 5
	All Five Courses	B 3 B 1 2 3 4 5

   NOTE: If you wish to take all five courses, fill in 1, 2, 3, 4, and 5 in the fourth column.

   e. Total CPE credit hours for which you are applying on this answer sheet.
      1) You may ignore this. Your Certificate of Completion will automatically reflect the proper amount of credit (see page 459).
2. **Sign and date** the self-certification statement on page 1 of the machine-readable answer sheet.

- Self-certification: I confirm that I have studied all of the required material and answered all the required questions for the course(s) for which I am seeking CPE credit. I also have studied the answer explanations to questions I answered wrong or had difficulty understanding.

_______________________________ _______________
Signature *Date*

3. If your answer sheet is not completed properly, it will be returned to you for correction.

4. Again, a single answer sheet may be used to take as many courses in a program as you wish, but it may be submitted only once. CPE participants may **NOT** mix courses from different programs on the same answer sheet. If you decide to submit this answer sheet for grading of only one or a few courses, but you would like to take more CMA/CFM Review CPE courses in the future, simply enclose $25 with the answer sheet you submit for grading, and we will send you another blank answer sheet separately from the results of your CPE tests.

GRADING YOUR CPE EXAM FOR CPE CREDIT

After we receive the results from the machine grading,

1. We will send you a Certificate of Completion if you achieve at least a 70% score.
   a. For every question you answered incorrectly, we will send a synopsis of the concept tested.
   b. When you receive your results, take the time to read through these synopses to be sure you have no miscomprehension of basic concepts or principles.
2. If you do not get a score of at least 70%, we will return your answer sheet and a list of the question numbers incorrectly answered. A $25 regrading fee is payable upon resubmission of the corrected answer sheet. You cannot obtain credit until you obtain at least a 70% success rate.

RECORD RETENTION AND DUPLICATE CERTIFICATES

Gleim Publications, Inc. will retain your answer sheet(s) and a record of your course completions for 5 years. You must notify us **within 60 days** if you have not received your Certificate of Completion. After 60 days, we will charge $25 to send you a duplicate certificate.

You should retain your Certificate of Completion to document completion of your CPE course(s). You should also retain your *CMA/CFM Review: Part 1* book containing this CPE section, which has your completed answers and notes.

ADDITIONAL INFORMATION ABOUT THIS CPE PROGRAM

Prerequisites and Advance Preparation -- A participant must have an undergraduate major in business or an equivalent.

Program Objectives -- Upon completion of this program, the participant will have at least an entry-level knowledge of the basic principles in each area studied as well as familiarity with current pronouncements and management accounting/financial management philosophies.

Change of Address -- Please notify us of any changes in your shipping and/or mailing addresses by writing to

Gleim Publications, Inc.
CPE Division
P.O. Box 12848, University Station
Gainesville, FL 32604

Time Limit on Completion of This CPE Program -- You have at least 1 year from the date of purchase to complete the courses in this CPE program. We will notify you at your permanent address (see the discussion on the previous page) when the program goes out of date and/or is superseded by a replacement program. You will have 30 days after our mailing to submit your final answer sheet. Thus, while we will allow you to use this CPE program until, in our opinion, it is no longer current, you should plan on completing the courses you desire within 1 year. Our intent is to serve you better than the competition; i.e., if a CPE program is not out of date in 1 year, why cancel it? We are committed, however, to provide up-to-date CPE programs, a commitment which requires us to retire out-of-date courses as we develop new (current) editions.

Limit on Amount of Correspondence Course CPE Credit -- We are concerned that some individuals may misuse our program (as is probably the case for all CPE programs). While we have not instituted limits on the maximum number of hours available through this CPE program, we ask that you do not misuse our programs. In addition, some state boards of accountancy have placed limits on the number of hours of CPE credit that may be fulfilled through individual study or correspondence courses.

Additionally, our Certificate of Completion lists maximum credit for both formal self-study measurement principles: average completion time and one-half average completion time. Thus, if your time spent on any course is less than the "recommended maximum hours of CPE credit," we suggest that you **report your actual hours consistent with the rules and procedures of the agency or organization to which you are reporting**.

Our approach permits you to take simple courses or courses already familiar to you for review purposes "just to make sure." When you use less than the average time, you can so indicate. We have explained our approach to the various agencies/organizations requiring CPE.

FORMAL SELF-STUDY CPE PROGRAM CREDIT MEASUREMENT

The AICPA standard for measuring CPE credit for formal, noninteractive self-study CPE programs states that CPE credit should equal one-half of the average completion time, as determined by the program developer through pretesting. For example, a course that takes an average of 800 minutes to complete is recommended for 8 contact hours of CPE credit. The recommended credit we indicate is based on this AICPA standard.

Note, however, that about a third of CPE jurisdictions that require reporting of CPE credit will allow "full credit" for our programs; i.e., a course that takes an average of 800 minutes to complete is recommended for 16 contact hours of CPE credit. Thus, our Certificate of Completion lists both measures of credit, i.e., **average completion time** and **one-half average completion time**. We encourage you to verify the measurement standard (as it relates to Gleim's self-study courses) with your reporting jurisdiction(s) so you can properly report your credit.

Call us for assistance: **(800) 87-GLEIM**.

COURSE 1
ECONOMICS

This CPE course covers Study Units 1 and 2 of ***CMA/CFM Review: Part 1***, Eighth Edition. In addition to the introductory material, this course consists of 42 pages of outlines and text and 124 multiple-choice questions (16 of which constitute the final exam). As continuing professional education, 5 hours of CPE credit is recommended based on the AICPA's one-half the average completion time measurement principle. If any of the CPE agencies to which you report measures self-study CPE in terms of average completion time (rather than one-half average completion time), your certificate of completion will indicate 10 hours of maximum CPE credit.

Date Completed	Time (Minutes)	
		1. Study Unit 1:
________	________	a. Study the outlines on "Microeconomics" on pages 23 through 43.
________	________	b. Work through questions 1 through 60 on pages 44 through 63 after covering the answer explanations on the right-hand side of the page. Answer each question and circle your answer.
________	________	1. Uncover the answer explanations and study the adjacent answer explanations for the questions that you missed or that gave you difficulty.
		2. Study Unit 2:
________	________	a. Study the outlines on "Macroeconomics" on pages 65 through 85.
________	________	b. Work through questions 1 through 48 on pages 86 through 100 after covering the answer explanations on the right-hand side of the page. Answer each question and circle your answer.
________	________	1. Uncover the answer explanations and study the adjacent answer explanations for the questions that you missed or that gave you difficulty.
		3. Final Exam:
________	________	a. Take the final exam by answering questions 1 through 16 on the following pages.
		1. If you have difficulty, refer to ***CMA/CFM Review: Part 1***, or other sources. Remember, this is an open-book exam.
		4. Carefully transfer your answers for these 16 questions to the CPE final exam answer sheet. Be sure you use the circles numbered 1 through 16.
		5. Mark **B 3 B 1** (B means Blank) as the course number on page 2 of the answer sheet. See example at right.
		a. Refer to pages 455 and 456 in this section for instructions on how to complete the remainder of the machine-readable answer sheet.
		6. Please complete the accompanying course evaluation and submit it with your answer sheet.
Total Time	________	(Carry this amount to your CPE course evaluation form.)

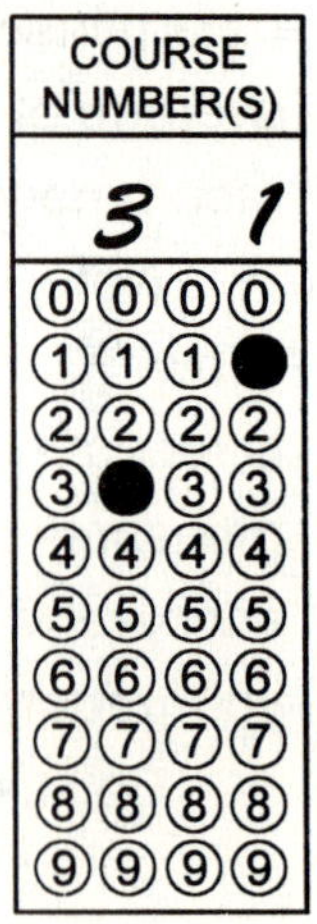

1. If the price of a commodity decreases, new buyers will enter the market and the commodity will be cheaper relative to other goods. This is a statement of

A. Say's law.

B. The substitution effect.

C. The law of diminishing returns.

D. The law of diminishing marginal utility.

2. Demand is defined as the amount of a good or service that consumers are willing and able to purchase at various prices during a specified period. A leftward shift in the demand curve itself may be caused by

A. A successful advertising campaign.

B. An expectation of future price increases.

C. A decrease in consumer income if the good is a normal good.

D. An increase in the price of a substitute good.

3. According to utility theory, utility is maximized when the budget constraint line is

A. Parallel to the highest possible indifference curve.

B. Parallel to the lowest possible indifference curve.

C. Tangent to the highest possible indifference curve.

D. Tangent to the lowest possible indifference curve.

4. If all else remains unchanged, a decrease in the price of steel will cause the supply curve for automobiles to

A. Become a horizontal line.

B. Move to the right.

C. Move to the left.

D. Remain unchanged.

5. The graph below illustrates market equilibrium between supply and demand. Which of the following is true?

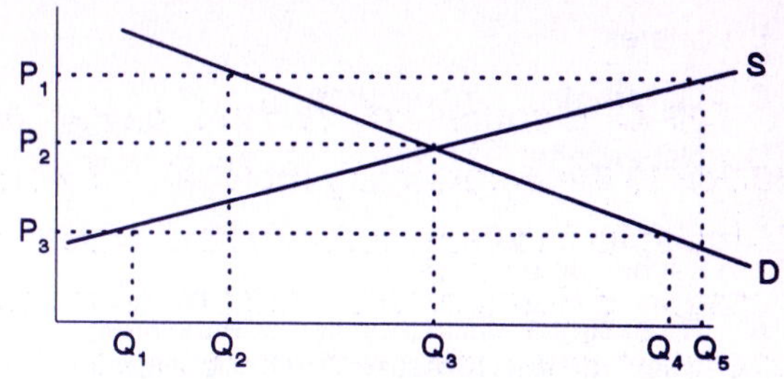

A. If the price (P_1) is established above the equilibrium price, a surplus equal to ($Q_3 - Q_2$) will develop.

B. If the price (P_1) is established above the equilibrium price, a shortage equal to ($Q_5 - Q_2$) will develop.

C. If the price (P_2) is established at the equilibrium price, either a shortage or a surplus will develop.

D. If the price (P_3) is established below the equilibrium price, a shortage equal to ($Q_4 - Q_1$) will develop.

6. Which of the following is an assumption underlying the model for perfect competition?

A. No control is exercised over prices.

B. The number of interdependent buyers and sellers is small.

C. The entry of other firms is relatively difficult.

D. Products are differentiated.

7. A monopolist maximizes profits by

A. Minimizing costs.

B. Equating marginal revenue and marginal cost.

C. Setting average revenue equal to average cost.

D. Maximizing total revenue.

8. As compared with pure competition, an oligopoly

A. Is characterized by a flat demand curve.

B. Permits greater ease of entering the market.

C. Has more firms in the market.

D. Consists of firms that tend to follow price decreases but not price increases.

9. Under the expenditure approach, gross domestic product (GDP) is measured as the sum of all the following except

A. Consumption.

B. Interest.

C. Government expenditures.

D. Net exports.

10. In Keynesian economics,

A. No essential distinction is made between savings and investment in understanding changes in the level of income.

B. The economy can be in equilibrium at less than full employment.

C. Price flexibility can be relied upon to provide full employment.

D. The equilibrium level of income provides full employment by definition.

11. Which of the following is a false statement about Keynesian economic theory?

A. As real interest rates increase, marginal investments are not undertaken, and total business investment is reduced.

B. As interest rates increase, the incentive to save is increased, and consumption is increased.

C. The major determinant of investment is profitability.

D. The major determinant of consumption is income.

12. Given that the production possibility frontier depicts all possible combinations of output of baubles and beads in a two-good world, all other things held constant,

A. The outer boundary cannot be shifted in the long run.

B. If the society is not producing on the outer boundary, it may be possible to produce more beads in the short run without giving up some baubles.

C. The outer boundary can be shifted in the short run only by a change in aggregate demand.

D. If the society is producing on the outer boundary, an increase in aggregate demand will have no effect on prices in the short run.

13. In Keynesian analysis, the supply and demand for money determine the interest rate. The liquidity preference schedule

A. Slopes downward because, at higher interest rates, people hold less cash.

B. Intersects with the fixed money supply to determine the inflation premium.

C. Is the supply curve for money.

D. Slopes upward, and the money supply curve is horizontal.

14. Assuming the banking system's excess reserves increase to $35,000 and no leakage occurs, what will be the increase in the money supply if the reserve requirement is 25%?

A. $140,000

B. $46,667

C. $26,250

D. $8,750

15. Which of the following is not an expansionary action of the Federal Reserve Board used to control the money supply?

A. Decreasing the discount rate.

B. Decreasing the legal reserve requirements.

C. Purchasing government securities.

D. Selling government securities.

16. Inflation is an increase in the general level of prices. Which of the following is not a true statement about inflation?

A. Modern macroeconomic theory suggests a strong relationship between inflation and unemployment in the long run.

B. Theoretically, inflation is caused by increased production costs.

C. Inflation helps debtors.

D. Inflation hurts creditors.

COURSE 2
BUSINESS ENVIRONMENT

This CPE course covers Study Units 3 and 4 of ***CMA/CFM Review: Part 1***, Eighth Edition. In addition to the introductory material, this course consists of 32 pages of outlines and text and 129 multiple-choice questions (16 of which constitute the final exam). As continuing professional education, 5 hours of CPE credit is recommended based on the AICPA's one-half the average completion time measurement principle. If any of the CPE agencies to which you report measures self-study CPE in terms of average completion time (rather than one-half average completion time), your certificate of completion will indicate 10 hours of maximum CPE credit.

Date Completed	Time (Minutes)	
		1. Study Unit 3:
________	________	a. Study the outlines on "International Business Environment" on pages 101 through 113.
________	________	b. Work through questions 1 through 50 on pages 114 through 130 after covering the answer explanations on the right-hand side of the page. Answer each question and circle your answer.
________	________	1. Uncover the answer explanations and study the adjacent answer explanations for the questions that you missed or that gave you difficulty.
		2. Study Unit 4:
________	________	a. Study the outlines on "Domestic Institutional Environment of Business" on pages 131 through 149.
________	________	b. Work through questions 1 through 63 on pages 150 through 171 after covering the answer explanations on the right-hand side of the page. Answer each question and circle your answer.
________	________	1. Uncover the answer explanations and study the adjacent answer explanations for the questions that you missed or that gave you difficulty.
		3. Final Exam:
________	________	a. Take the final exam by answering questions 17 through 32 on the following pages.
		1. If you have difficulty, refer to ***CMA/CFM Review: Part 1***, or other sources. Remember, this is an open-book exam.
		4. Carefully transfer your answers for these 16 questions to the CPE final exam answer sheet. Be sure you use the circles numbered 17 through 32.
		5. Mark **B 3 B 2** (B means Blank) as the course number on page 2 of the answer sheet. See example at right.
		a. Refer to pages 455 and 456 in this section for instructions on how to complete the remainder of the machine-readable answer sheet.
		6. Please complete the accompanying course evaluation and submit it with your answer sheet.

Total Time ________ (Carry this amount to your CPE course evaluation form.)

17. Assume there are only two countries and only two commodities. The only factor of production is labor, and the hours required to produce one unit of each product in both countries are as follows:

	Sprockets	Cogs
Gudenheim	3 hours	1 hour
Sandeen	2 hours	2 hours

These data show that

A. Gudenheim has an absolute advantage in both products.

B. Sandeen has an absolute advantage in both products.

C. Sandeen has an absolute advantage in sprockets only.

D. Sandeen has an absolute advantage in cogs only.

18. Assume there are only two countries and only two commodities. The only factor of production is labor, and the hours required to produce one unit of each product in both countries are as follows:

	Sprockets	Cogs
Gudenheim	3 hours	2 hours
Sandeen	1 hour	1.5 hours

Based on these data, which situation is the most advantageous to both countries?

A. Sandeen exports both products.

B. Sandeen imports both products.

C. Gudenheim exports sprockets and imports cogs.

D. Gudenheim imports sprockets and exports cogs.

19. For international trade to take place, the currencies involved must be easily convertible at some prevailing exchange rate.

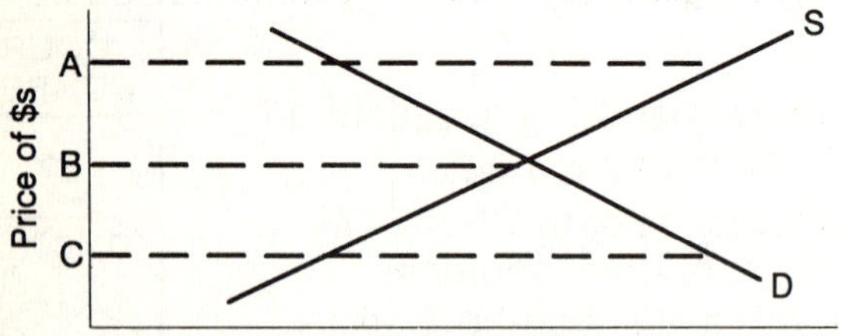

On the above graph,

A. At price C, the U.S. will have a deficit in its balance of payments.

B. At price C, a greater quantity of dollars is demanded than supplied (fewer U.S. exports, more imports).

C. At price A, a greater quantity of dollars is supplied by U.S. sources than demanded by foreigners (more U.S. imports, fewer exports).

D. At price A, the U.S. will have a surplus in its balance of payments.

20. Hedging is a means of avoiding the risk of exchange rate fluctuations. A company should

A. Sell forward exchange contracts to cover payables denominated in a foreign currency.

B. Buy forward exchange contracts to cover payables denominated in a foreign currency.

C. Sell the forward foreign currency at a premium if the nominal foreign interest rate is higher than the nominal domestic rate.

D. Sell the forward foreign currency at a discount if the nominal foreign interest rate is lower than the nominal domestic rate.

21. Assuming flexible exchange rates and no governmental intervention, the U.S. dollar would appreciate in relation to the Canadian dollar when

A. Inflation rates in Canada are below those in the U.S.

B. Interest rates in the U.S. are above those in Canada.

C. Canadians buy fewer goods from the U.S.

D. Direct investment by the U.S. in Canada increases.

22. The balance of payments account is treated as if it were a revenue or expense account. Which of the following is a debit to the account?

A. U.S. exports of goods.

B. Capital movements into the U.S.

C. Unilateral transfers of money from Americans to foreigners.

D. Unilateral transfers of money from foreigners to Americans.

23. Which of the following is a feature of the current international monetary system?

A. Intervention by governments to support their currencies as part of a managed float.

B. The convertibility of dollars into gold.

C. Fixed exchange rates.

D. Freely floating exchange rates.

24. Which of the following statements concerning the North American Free Trade Agreement (NAFTA) is false?

A. NAFTA should enable the U.S. to sell more goods to Mexico due to an increase in the disposable income of Mexicans.

B. Low technology industries in the U.S. may be faced with increased competition from cheaper Mexican products.

C. NAFTA has resulted in the creation of jobs in the U.S. due to the increased assembly operations in the U.S.

D. NAFTA will largely correct the disparities between the open markets of the U.S. and the relatively closed markets of Mexico.

25. Which of the following is a true statement about corporations?

A. The officers of the corporation elect the board of directors to whom they delegate the daily management of the firm.

B. Their formation and existence is entirely regulated by state law.

C. They are legal entities separate from their owners for all purposes except taxation.

D. A corporation created in one state must still incorporate in each state in which it wishes to do business.

26. The Securities Act of 1933

A. Prohibits insider trading on information not available to the public.

B. Requires a registration statement to be filed with the SEC for an initial issuance of securities.

C. Established the SEC.

D. Requires registration of stock exchanges, brokers, and dealers.

27. The Securities Exchange Act of 1934

A. Exempts intrastate issuances from its coverage if they meet certain requirements.

B. Exempts private placements from its coverage if they meet certain requirements.

C. Prohibits insider trading on information not available to the public.

D. Applies only to an initial issuance of securities.

28. The Occupational Safety and Health Act of 1970

A. Applies to all companies not specifically exempted if they affect interstate commerce.

B. Requires employers to provide hospitalization insurance to employees.

C. Is designed to protect the health and safety of workers in governmental entities and regulated businesses.

D. Provides for criminal but not civil sanctions.

29. The Employee Retirement Income Security Act (ERISA)

A. Requires immediate vesting of pension rights for all employees of a company.

B. Applies only to companies with pension fund assets exceeding $10,000,000.

C. Prohibits pension discrimination in favor of highly paid and key employees.

D. Requires employers to establish pension plans.

30. The Sherman Act of 1890

A. Makes illegal every contract, combination, or conspiracy in restraint of trade in interstate or foreign commerce.

B. Prohibits covenants not to compete.

C. Applies to intrastate commerce and unintended monopolies.

D. Prohibits a merger if the effect might be to lessen competition or create a monopoly.

31. The Clayton Act of 1914 as amended

A. Applies only to stock acquisitions.

B. Created the Federal Trade Commission.

C. Prohibits conglomerate mergers.

D. Prohibits sales that prevent the buyer from dealing with the seller's competitors.

32. The Environmental Protection Agency

A. Was created to maintain the safety of drugs, foods, and other products.

B. Sets the sliding tax charge that applies to those discharging effluents.

C. Sets effluent standards for the volume or quality of waste products that can be discharged.

D. Regulates firms only in specified industries.

COURSE 3
FINANCE

This CPE course covers Study Units 5 and 6 of ***CMA/CFM Review: Part 1***, Eighth Edition. In addition to the introductory material, this course consists of 43 pages of outlines and text and 142 multiple-choice questions (16 of which constitute the final exam). As continuing professional education, 5 hours of CPE credit is recommended based on the AICPA's one-half the average completion time measurement principle. If any of the CPE agencies to which you report measures self-study CPE in terms of average completion time (rather than one-half average completion time), your certificate of completion will indicate 10 hours of maximum CPE credit.

Date Completed	Time (Minutes)	
		1. Study Unit 5:
________	________	a. Study the outlines on "Working Capital Finance" on pages 173 through 191.
________	________	b. Work through questions 1 through 64 on pages 192 through 212 after covering the answer explanations on the right-hand side of the page. Answer each question and circle your answer.
________	________	1. Uncover the answer explanations and study the adjacent answer explanations for the questions that you missed or that gave you difficulty.
		2. Study Unit 6:
________	________	a. Study the outlines on "Capital Structure Finance" on pages 213 through 236.
________	________	b. Work through questions 1 through 62 on pages 237 through 260 after covering the answer explanations on the right-hand side of the page. Answer each question and circle your answer.
________	________	1. Uncover the answer explanations and study the adjacent answer explanations for the questions that you missed or that gave you difficulty.
		3. Final Exam:
________	________	a. Take the final exam by answering questions 33 through 48 on the following pages.
		1. If you have difficulty, refer to ***CMA/CFM Review: Part 1***, or other sources. Remember, this is an open-book exam.

4. Carefully transfer your answers for these 16 questions to the CPE final exam answer sheet. Be sure you use the circles numbered 33 through 48.

5. Mark **B 3 B 3** (B means Blank) as the course number on page 2 of the answer sheet. See example at right.

a. Refer to pages 455 and 456 in this section for instructions on how to complete the remainder of the machine-readable answer sheet.

6. Please complete the accompanying course evaluation and submit it with your answer sheet.

Total Time ________ (Carry this amount to your CPE course evaluation form.)

33. The objective of a firm that is most beneficial to shareholders is to maximize

A. Sales.

B. Profits.

C. The per-share price of stock.

D. Equity investment.

34. In acquisition-type combinations, either purchase or pooling accounting must be used. Which of the following is incorrect?

A. In a pooling, tax depreciation charges will usually decrease.

B. In a purchase, book but not tax depreciation charges will usually increase.

C. In a purchase, the assets and liabilities of the purchased company are recorded at fair value on the consolidated books.

D. In a pooling, the assets and liabilities of the purchased company are recorded at book value on the consolidated books.

35. The following information appears in TASK Company's financial statements at year-end:

	Year 1	Year 2
Cash	$ 49,500	$ 59,000
Marketable securities	110,000	100,000
Accounts receivable	875,000	139,000
Inventory	1,035,000	1,075,000
Accounts payable	625,000	455,000
Wages payable	30,000	65,000
Current portion of long-term debt	475,000	475,000
Noncurrent portion of long-term debt	1,025,000	750,000
Shareholders' equity	775,000	875,000

Sales increased by $250,000 in Year 2, and operating income increased by $30,000. What is the current ratio at the end of Year 2 (rounded to two decimal places)?

A. 1.38 to 1.

B. 1.94 to 1.

C. 2.06 to 1.

D. 2.42 to 1.

36. DAT Company had total sales for the year of $5,500,000. Cash sales were final and amounted to $950,000. Sales returns and allowances on credit sales were $90,000. The beginning and ending balances in accounts receivable were $950,000 and $1,280,000, respectively. DAT's accounts receivable turnover is

A. 3.55 times.

B. 4.00 times.

C. 4.93 times.

D. 5.20 times.

37. Which of the following is a method of accelerating cash inflows for a company doing business nationally?

A. Using check float.

B. Using zero-balance checking.

C. Maintaining compensating balances.

D. Using lockbox systems.

38. Effective management of marketable securities

A. Emphasizes maximization of yield.

B. In most companies results in maintaining a large balance as a cash substitute.

C. Is rarely influenced by concerns about inflation or taxation.

D. Minimizes interest rate risk.

39. Credit policies should be tightened and collection efforts should be increased until doing more becomes unprofitable. Thus,

A. Overdue accounts should be ignored.

B. Credit should be extended until the marginal benefit (profit) is maximized.

C. The accounts receivable turnover ratio should be maximized.

D. The average time receivables are held should be increased.

40. A firm's inventory policy should be designed to minimize inventory costs. Which of the following is true?

A. Offering quantity discounts to customers may reduce ordering costs.

B. Placing orders so that materials arrive when actually needed increases holding costs.

C. Inventory may be a good hedge against increasing holding costs.

D. The economic order quantity (EOQ) model helps minimize the sum of ordering and carrying costs.

41. Which of the following is an activity ratio?

A. Net income available to common shareholders ÷ average shares outstanding.

B. Net sales ÷ net fixed assets.

C. Dividend per share ÷ per-share market value.

D. Net income after taxes ÷ average total assets.

42. Capital structure finance concerns the amount and mixture of permanent assets used and the methods by which they are financed. The ratios used to evaluate capital structure include

A. Quick ratio.

B. Receivables turnover.

C. Inventory turnover.

D. Book value per share.

43. Which of the following is a true statement about the effects of securing long-term financing through the issuance of preferred stock?

A. Preferred stock is less flexible than bond issues.

B. Preferred stock dividends are deductible as a tax expense.

C. Underwriting costs are typically lower than for common stock issues.

D. The sale of preferred stock increases the creditworthiness of the firm.

44. Which type of bond pays interest only if the issuing company has earnings?

A. Mortgage.

B. Income.

C. Debenture.

D. Zero-coupon.

45. An option issued with a security to permit the investor to buy a certain number of shares at a specified price is a

A. Preemptive right.

B. Warrant.

C. Conversion feature.

D. Debenture.

46. Which of the following statements about the important dates relative to the declaration of dividends is true?

A. The ex-dividend date is established by the board of directors.

B. The declaration date is the date on which the corporation determines which shareholders will receive the declared dividend.

C. The dividend becomes a liability of the corporation on the date of record.

D. An individual who sells the stock after the ex-dividend date will receive the dividend.

47. Which of the following statements regarding treasury stock is true?

A. Treasury stock is an asset of a corporation.

B. Dividends are paid on treasury stock.

C. A company can buy treasury stock regardless of its retained earnings balance.

D. Treasury stock does not have voting rights.

48. Which of the following is true concerning a leveraged buyout?

A. An acquisition-minded investor offers to buy outstanding shares of an investee by tendering an open offer to all shareholders at a specified price.

B. The targeted company's assets are used as collateral for a loan to finance the purchase.

C. A leveraged buyout cannot be used by the targeted company's management or any of its employees.

D. Greenmail is a component of a leveraged buyout.

COURSE 4
RISK AND ORGANIZATIONAL THEORY

This CPE course covers Study Units 7 and 8 of ***CMA/CFM Review: Part 1***, Eighth Edition. In addition to the introductory material, this course consists of 43 pages of outlines and text and 131 multiple-choice questions (16 of which constitute the final exam). As continuing professional education, 5 hours of CPE credit is recommended based on the AICPA's one-half the average completion time measurement principle. If any of the CPE agencies to which you report measures self-study CPE in terms of average completion time (rather than one-half average completion time), your certificate of completion will indicate 10 hours of maximum CPE credit.

Date Completed	Time (Minutes)	
		1. **Study Unit 7:**
________	________	a. Study the outlines on "Risk" on pages 261 through 277.
________	________	b. Work through questions 1 through 54 on pages 278 through 296 after covering the answer explanations on the right-hand side of the page. Answer each question and circle your answer.
________	________	1. Uncover the answer explanations and study the adjacent answer explanations for the questions that you missed or that gave you difficulty.
		2. **Study Unit 8:**
________	________	a. Study the outlines on "Organizational Theory" on pages 297 through 322.
________	________	b. Work through questions 1 through 61 on pages 323 through 342 after covering the answer explanations on the right-hand side of the page. Answer each question and circle your answer.
________	________	1. Uncover the answer explanations and study the adjacent answer explanations for the questions that you missed or that gave you difficulty.
		3. **Final Exam:**
________	________	a. Take the final exam by answering questions 49 through 64 on the following pages.
		1. If you have difficulty, refer to ***CMA/CFM Review: Part 1***, or other sources. Remember, this is an open-book exam.

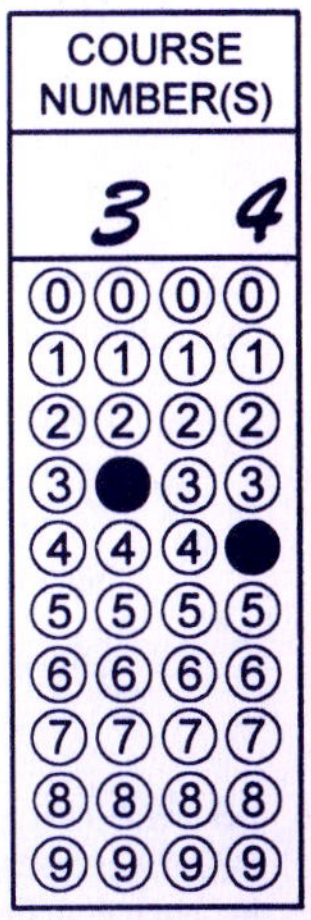

4. Carefully transfer your answers for these 16 questions to the CPE final exam answer sheet. Be sure you use the circles numbered 49 through 64.
5. Mark **B 3 B 4**(B means Blank) as the course number on page 2 of the answer sheet. See example at right.
   a. Refer to pages 455 and 456 in this section for instructions on how to complete the remainder of the machine-readable answer sheet.
6. Please complete the accompanying course evaluation and submit it with your answer sheet.

Total Time ________ (Carry this amount to your CPE course evaluation form.)

49. Portfolio theory concerns the composition of an investment portfolio that is efficient in balancing risk and returns. According to portfolio theory,

A. A beta coefficient of less than 1.0 indicates that the price of a security is less volatile than the market.

B. If the returns on the assets in the portfolio are correlated, the variability of the portfolio's return is decreased.

C. The expected rate of return of a portfolio is the sum of the expected returns of the individual assets in the portfolio.

D. Market risk can be eliminated by diversification.

50. The capital structure (permanent financing) of a firm is represented principally by

A. Accounts payable.

B. Retained earnings.

C. Long-term investments in marketable equity securities.

D. Short-term notes payable.

51. Leverage is the relative amount of the fixed cost of capital, principally debt, in a firm's capital structure. Which of the following statements about leverage is true?

A. The degree of financial leverage is the percentage change in net operating income associated with a given percentage change in sales.

B. The degree of operating leverage is the percentage change in net operating income associated with a given percentage change in sales.

C. The degree of total leverage is equal to the degree of operating leverage plus the degree of financial leverage.

D. The degree of total leverage equals the percentage change in net operating income times the percentage change in sales.

52. Standard financial theory states that the optimal capital structure

A. Involves no debt.

B. Maximizes cost of equity.

C. Minimizes the weighted-average cost of capital.

D. Disregards interest rates.

53. If a company's beta coefficient is 1.7, the market rate of interest is 6.5%, and the yield on T-bills is 5.0%, its required rate of return on equity capital is

A. 7.6%

B. 7.9%

C. 8.6%

D. 8.9%

54. The beta coefficient of a particular company's stock is the

A. Ratio of leverage employed.

B. Amount above the risk-free rate for which investors must be compensated.

C. Formula for calculating the cost of equity capital under the dividend growth model.

D. Correlation of the market price volatility of the individual stock to the volatility of the market as a whole.

55. BMF Co. paid its common shareholders a $2.00 per share cash dividend at the end of its last fiscal year. The shareholders expect a 7.5% growth rate in dividends, and BMF's common stock is currently selling at $50.59 per share. Ignoring flotation costs, the required rate of return on an issue of new common stock will be

A. 10.75%

B. 11.45%

C. 11.75%

D. 12.05%

56. The curves representing the marginal cost of capital and the marginal efficiency of investment intersect at the

A. Cost of debt.

B. Cost of equity.

C. Weighted-average cost of capital.

D. Equilibrium investment level.

57. According to Mintzberg, managers have various informational roles. This category encompasses which, if any, of the following specific roles?

	Disseminator	Resource Allocator	Spokesperson
A.	Yes	Yes	Yes
B.	No	No	Yes
C.	Yes	No	Yes
D.	No	No	No

58. The relationships inherent in the structure of an organization include authority, responsibility, and accountability. Which of the following is primarily a classical approach to these relationships?

A. The principle of unity of command means that each subordinate should report to only one superior.

B. The right to direct is only as good as the receiver's willingness to carry out the order.

C. Responsibility must and should be delegated.

D. The right to give the order is vested in the position.

59. Departmentation is the grouping of organizational subsystems. Which kind of departmentation is often found within the sales department of a firm organized by function?

A. Customer.

B. Territorial.

C. Matrix.

D. Project.

60. The systems approach to line and staff relationships

A. Gives staff members greater authority over line managers.

B. Views staff activities as secondary or peripheral to the line functions.

C. Treats line activities as those directly responsible for the primary function of the organization.

D. Recognizes that distinctions between producers and helpers are becoming irrelevant in the changing work environment.

61. Which of the following is a true statement about the principle of span of control?

A. Current research indicates that the maximum effective span of control is five or fewer subordinates.

B. Flat organizational structures speed informational flow and increase employee satisfaction.

C. Increasing the number of levels in an organization will decrease communication problems.

D. The classical view of management advocated broadening the span of control to improve employee morale.

62. Decentralized organizational structures typically

A. Improve control by top management.

B. Result in better communication between competing unit managers.

C. Push more operating problems upward to top management.

D. Use ROI or profit center accounting methods.

63. Which of the following is a favorable effect of encouraging informal groups in an organization?

A. Informal networks can move messages faster and more accurately than formal networks.

B. Informal groups may generate dissension in the formal organization.

C. Managerial talent can be developed among leaders of informal groups.

D. Informal groups improve coordination and reduce supervision required.

64. Resistance to organizational change may be overcome through

A. Centralized organizational structures.

B. Financial incentives for those affected by the change.

C. Conferences, consultations, and problem-solving groups.

D. Detailed organizational charts showing the change.

COURSE 5
MOTIVATION AND COMMUNICATION

This CPE course covers Study Units 9 and 10 of ***CMA/CFM Review: Part 1***, Eighth Edition. In addition to the introductory material, this course consists of 37 pages of outlines and text and 136 multiple-choice questions (16 of which constitute the final exam). As continuing professional education, 5 hours of CPE credit is recommended based on the AICPA's one-half the average completion time measurement principle. If any of the CPE agencies to which you report measures self-study CPE in terms of average completion time (rather than one-half average completion time), your certificate of completion will indicate 10 hours of maximum CPE credit.

Date Completed	Time (Minutes)	
		1. Study Unit 9:
________	________	a. Study the outlines on "Motivation and the Directing Process" on pages 343 through 367.
________	________	b. Work through questions 1 through 60 on pages 368 through 386 after covering the answer explanations on the right-hand side of the page. Answer each question and circle your answer.
________	________	1. Uncover the answer explanations and study the adjacent answer explanations for the questions that you missed or that gave you difficulty.
		2. Study Unit 10:
________	________	a. Study the outlines on "Communication" on pages 387 through 398.
________	________	b. Work through questions 1 through 60 on pages 399 through 418 after covering the answer explanations on the right-hand side of the page. Answer each question and circle your answer.
________	________	1. Uncover the answer explanations and study the adjacent answer explanations for the questions that you missed or that gave you difficulty.
		3. Final Exam:
________	________	a. Take the final exam by answering questions 65 through 80 on the following pages.
		1. If you have difficulty, refer to ***CMA/CFM Review: Part 1***, or other sources. Remember, this is an open-book exam.
		4. Carefully transfer your answers for these 16 questions to the CPE final exam answer sheet. Be sure you use the circles numbered 65 through 80.
		5. Mark **B 3 B 5** (B means Blank) as the course number on page 2 of the answer sheet. See example at right.
		a. Refer to pages 455 and 456 in this section for instructions on how to complete the remainder of the machine-readable answer sheet.
		6. Please complete the accompanying course evaluation and submit it with your answer sheet.
Total Time	________	(Carry this amount to your CPE course evaluation form.)

65. Maslow's theory of motivation holds that lower-level human needs cease to be motivators as they are satisfied and that higher-level needs will then influence the individual. The need in the hierarchy satisfied by realizing one's potential is

A. Esteem.

B. Affiliation.

C. Security.

D. Self-actualization.

66. Which of the following is a correct statement of an important tenet of Frederick Herzberg's two-factor theory of human behavior?

A. Productivity is greater when management moves from an exploitive-authoritative system to a participative system.

B. The organization should be analyzed in terms of the roles played by its members.

C. All groups have leaders, formal and informal, who initiate interrelationships and act as communication centers.

D. Certain factors in the job situation motivate people although their absence does not lead to poorer performance.

67. Job enrichment

A. Makes managers responsible for employee tasks.

B. Involves workers in changes in the physical aspects of the work environment.

C. Tends to reduce interaction among workers.

D. Is a technique for combating boredom through the assignment of a wide variety of tasks.

68. A contingency approach to the analysis of leadership would stress

A. Styles of leadership.

B. Interaction between the leaders and the situation.

C. The view that leaders are born, not made.

D. Personality traits of leaders.

69. Organizational development is planned change in an organization. It attempts to make earlier behavioral approaches more pragmatic and relevant to business situations. One method is

A. Matrix management.

B. Sensitivity training.

C. Grid training.

D. Management by objectives.

70. Management by objectives (MBO) is a managerial technique based on

A. A Theory X philosophy of management.

B. A Theory Y philosophy of management.

C. A consultative style of leadership.

D. An autocratic style of leadership.

71. Questions about which of the following can legally be asked in recruiting interviews?

A. Kind of military discharge.

B. Age.

C. Number of children.

D. Criminal record (but only for security clearance purposes).

72. The halo effect may diminish the accuracy of the evaluation of employees. Which of the following is an example?

A. A manager rates some employees as very good and some as very bad.

B. A manager's judgment of one trait affects his/her rating of other traits.

C. The most recent behavior overshadows overall performance.

D. All personnel who work together are rated within the same narrow range.

73. Which of the following is not one of the five elements of the communication process?

A. Feedback.

B. Symbols.

C. Medium.

D. Free flow.

74. Which of the following is a true statement about organizational communications?

A. Bonus programs are a means of informal communication within the organization.

B. The effective manager should ignore the grapevine.

C. Communications may be either vertical or horizontal.

D. The manager must ignore the nature of the message received and concentrate on the message.

75. Participative management stresses

A. Multidirectional communication.

B. Top-down communication.

C. Vertical communication.

D. Bottom-up communication.

76. Which of the following is a weakness in a communications network?

A. Absence of noise in the communication channel.

B. Extensive cross-communication.

C. Empathy by the receiver of a message.

D. Chain-type communications.

77. Trying to speak to someone while a loud radio plays nearby is an example of which type of communication problem?

A. Loss in transmission.

B. Interpersonal problems.

C. Faulty channel selection.

D. Noise in communication channel.

78. Which of the following is not a typical barrier to effective communication?

A. Redundancy.

B. Inconsistency between verbal and nonverbal messages.

C. Timing of communication.

D. Filtering.

79. Listening is the responsibility of both the speaker (sender) and the listener (receiver). Communications can be hindered by

A. Remembering that people can listen several times faster than they can speak.

B. Concentrating on the words used rather than the ideas they convey.

C. Noting nonverbal, as well as verbal, feedback.

D. Using one-way communication whenever possible.

80. A program that trains supervisors and subordinates to use techniques such as smoothing and compromise is

A. Matrix management.

B. Interpersonal communication training.

C. Conflict management.

D. Sensitivity training.

ADDENDUM: COMPUTATIONAL PRACTICE QUESTIONS

Questions A9 through A26 are presented beginning below. Please see pages 64, 172, and 386 for additional questions. The study unit on which the question is based is indicated in bold after the source code for each question.

A9. Assume that real gross domestic product (GDP), measured in 1986 dollars, rose from $3,000 billion in 1986 to $4,500 billion in 1998. Assume also that the price index rose from 100 to 200 during the same period. The GDP for 1986 expressed in terms of 1998 prices is

A. $1,500 billion.

B. $3,000 billion.

C. $4,500 billion.

D. $6,000 billion.

The correct answer is (D). (*Publisher*) **SU 2**

REQUIRED: The GDP for 1986 adjusted for inflation.

DISCUSSION: Between 1986 and 1998, the price index doubled (from 100 to 200). Thus, the nominal value of 1986 GDP ($3,000 billion) must also be doubled when restated in 1998 terms. The 1986 GDP in 1998 prices is $6,000 billion.

Answer (A) is incorrect because $1,500 billion assumes deflation rather than inflation from 1986 to 1998. Answer (B) is incorrect because $3,000 billion is the nominal value of the 1986 GDP. Answer (C) is incorrect because $4,500 billion is the actual 1998 GDP. The question asks about the restated 1986 GDP.

A10. If personal consumption expenditures increase from $720 billion to $760 billion when disposable income increases from $900 billion to $950 billion, the marginal propensity to consume equals

A. 0.20

B. 0.40

C. 0.60

D. 0.80

The correct answer is (D). (*Publisher*) **SU 2**

REQUIRED: The marginal propensity to consume given increases in personal expenditures and disposable income.

DISCUSSION: The marginal propensity to consume is the change in consumption divided by the change in income. The change in consumption is $40 billion, and the change in income is $50 billion. Hence, the marginal propensity to consume equals .8 ($40 billion ÷ $50 billion).

Answer (A) is incorrect because .2 is the marginal propensity to save. Answers (B) and (C) are incorrect because the marginal propensity to consume is .8.

A11. If personal consumption expenditures increase from $720 billion to $760 billion when disposable income increases from $900 billion to $980 billion, the marginal propensity to save equals

A. 0.20

B. 0.40

C. 0.50

D. 0.80

The correct answer is (C). (*Publisher*) **SU 2**

REQUIRED: The marginal propensity to save.

DISCUSSION: The marginal propensity to save is the change in savings divided by the change in income. The change in consumption is $40 billion, and the change in income is $80 billion. Thus, the change in savings is also $40 billion. The marginal propensity to save must therefore equal .5 ($40 billion ÷ $80 billion).

Answers (A) and (B) are incorrect because the increase in savings is equal to half of the increase in disposable income. Answer (D) is incorrect because the marginal propensity to save is only half of the increase in income.

A12. If an increase in government purchases of goods and services of $30 billion causes equilibrium GDP to rise by $120 billion, and if total taxes, investment, consumption, and net exports are constant, the marginal propensity to consume is

A. 0.25

B. 0.75

C. 4.00

D. 1.33

The correct answer is (B). (*Publisher*) **SU 2**

REQUIRED: The marginal propensity to consume.

DISCUSSION: A change (positive or negative) in investment, consumption, government spending, or net export spending will result in a multiplied change in equilibrium GDP. This multiplier phenomenon occurs because the initial change in spending has a ripple effect (the magnitude depends on the marginal propensity to consume). The multiplier in this case equals 4.0 ($120 billion increase in equilibrium GDP ÷ $30 billion increase in aggregate expenditures). Because the multiplier equals [1 ÷ (1 – MPC)], the marginal propensity to consume is .75.

$$4 = \frac{1}{1 - MPC}$$
$$4 - 4MPC = 1$$
$$4MPC = 3$$
$$MPC = .75$$

Answer (A) is incorrect because .25 is the marginal propensity to save, or the complement of the marginal propensity to consume. Answer (C) is incorrect because 4.0 is the multiplier. Answer (D) is incorrect because 1.33 is the multiplier assuming an MPC of .25.

A13. Given a deposit expansion model in which the required reserve ratio is 12.5%, a $100,000 purchase of government securities by the Federal Reserve will result in a maximum increase (decrease) in the money supply of

A. ($87,500)

B. $12,500

C. $87,500

D. $800,000

The correct answer is (D). *(Publisher)* **SU 2**

REQUIRED: The maximum change in the money supply given a purchase of securities and a specified reserve ratio.

DISCUSSION: This purchase of government securities provides $100,000 of excess reserves for member banks. The maximum effect of this transaction, that is, assuming no leakage of money except for required reserves, is to expand demand deposits (and the money supply) by an amount equal to the excess reserves times the money multiplier (1.0 ÷ the reserve ratio). Accordingly, the increase in the money supply is $800,000 [$100,000 × (1.0 ÷ .125)].

Answer (A) is incorrect because the money supply must increase when the Federal Reserve purchases government securities. Answer (B) is incorrect because $12,500 equals 12.5% of the increase in excess reserves. Answer (C) is incorrect because $87,500 equals the increase in excess reserves minus 12.5%.

A14. If the annual U.S. inflation rate is expected to be 3%, and the German mark is expected to depreciate against the U.S. dollar by 12%, a German firm importing from its U.S. parent can expect the costs of imports denominated in marks to

A. Decrease by about 12%.

B. Decrease by about 5%.

C. Increase by about 3%

D. Increase by about 17%.

The correct answer is (D). *(Publisher)* **SU 3**

REQUIRED: The effect on prices of imports given depreciation of the importing country's currency relative to the exporting country's.

DISCUSSION: Assuming the original exchange rate is $1 to 2 marks and that U.S. inflation is 3%, the cost in marks to purchase what once cost $1 will now be 2.06 marks (2 × 1.03). However, if the mark also depreciates by 12%, that is, if the mark is expected to be worth 88% of its current value, the exchange rate (before inflation) will be $1 to 2.2727 (2 ÷ .88) marks. At this rate, 2.3409 marks (2.2727 × 1.03) will be required to purchase $1. Costs in marks will therefore increase by just over 17% (.3409/2.00).

Answers (A) and (B) are incorrect because prices paid by the German buyer will increase. It must adjust payments in marks upward for both U. S. inflation and German monetary depreciation. Answer (C) is incorrect because prices would increase by 3% simply because of inflation. This answer disregards the effect of the currency depreciation.

A15. A firm often factors its accounts receivable. Its finance company requires a 6% reserve and charges a 1.4% commission on the amount of the receivables. The remaining amount to be advanced is further reduced by an annual interest charge of 15%. What proceeds (rounded to the nearest dollar) will the firm receive from the finance company at the time a $100,000 account due in 60 days is factored?

A. $92,600

B. $96,135

C. $90,285

D. $85,000

The correct answer is (C). *(Publisher)* **SU 5**

REQUIRED: The proceeds of factoring.

DISCUSSION: The factor will withhold $6,000 (6% × $100,000) as a reserve against returns and allowances and $1,400 (1.4% × $100,000) as a commission. The remaining $92,600 will be reduced by interest at the rate of 15% annually. The interest charge should be $2,315, assuming a 360-day year [($92,600 × .15) ÷ (60-day payment period ÷ 360 days)]. The proceeds to be received by the seller equal $90,285 ($92,600 – $2,315).

Answer (A) is incorrect because $92,600 ignores interest. Answer (B) is incorrect because $96,135 fails to deduct the 6% reserve. Answer (D) is incorrect because $85,000 assumes that the only amount withheld is a full year's interest on $100,000.

A16. If the average age of inventory is 60 days, the average age of the accounts payable is 30 days, and the average age of accounts receivable is 45 days, the number of days in the cash flow cycle is

A. 135 days.

B. 90 days.

C. 75 days.

D. 105 days.

The correct answer is (C). *(Publisher)* **SU 5**

REQUIRED: The length of the cash flow cycle.

DISCUSSION: The cash flow cycle begins when the firm pays for merchandise it has purchased and ends when the firm receives cash from the sale of the merchandise. Inventory is held for an average of 60 days prior to sale, but the average age of accounts payable is 30 days. Consequently, the average time between outlay and sale is 30 days. Receivables are collected an average of 45 days after sale, so the length of the cash flow cycle is 75 days (30 + 45).

Answer (A) is incorrect because the age of payables should be deducted from the sum of the other items. Answer (B) is incorrect because the payables are not added to the inventory period. They are deducted. Answer (D) is incorrect because 105 days equals the sum of the inventory cycle and the receivables cycle.

A17. DLF is a retail mail order firm that currently uses a central collection system that requires all checks to be sent to its Boston headquarters. An average of 6 days is required for mailed checks to be received, 3 days for DLF to process them, and 2 days for the checks to clear through its bank. A proposed lockbox system would reduce the mailing and processing time to 2 days and the check clearing time to 1 day. DLF has an average daily collection of $150,000. If DLF adopts the lockbox system, its average cash balance will increase by

A. $1,200,000

B. $750,000

C. $600,000

D. $450,000

The correct answer is (A). *(Publisher)* **SU 5**

REQUIRED: The average increase in cash after the adoption of a lockbox system.

DISCUSSION: Checks are currently tied up for 11 days (6 for mailing, 3 for processing, and 2 for clearing). If that period were reduced to 3 days, DLF's cash balance would increase by $1,200,000 (8 days × $150,000 per day).

Answer (B) is incorrect because the decrease is 8 days, not 5. Answer (C) is incorrect because $600,000 represents only a 4-day savings. Answer (D) is incorrect because the lockbox system will result in an additional 8 days of savings, not 3.

Questions A18 through A20 are based on the following information. Morton Company needs to pay a supplier's invoice of $60,000 and wants to take a cash discount of 2/10, net 40. The firm can borrow the money for 30 days at 11% per annum with a 9% compensating balance. Assume a 360-day year.

A18. The amount Morton Company must borrow to pay the supplier within the discount period and cover the compensating balance is

A. $60,000

B. $65,934

C. $64,615

D. $58,800

The correct answer is (C). *(Publisher)* **SU 5**

REQUIRED: The amount the company must borrow to pay the supplier within the discount period and cover the compensating balance requirement.

DISCUSSION: The company will need $58,800 (98% × $60,000) to pay the invoice. In addition, it will need a compensating balance equal to 9% of the loan. The equation is

$$Loan = \$58{,}800 + .09\ Loan$$

Thus, the loan amount needed is $64,615 ($58,800 ÷ .91).

Answer (A) is incorrect because $60,000 is the invoice amount. Answer (B) is incorrect because $65,934 assumes the amount paid to the supplier is $60,000. Answer (D) is incorrect because $58,800 is the amount to be paid to the supplier.

A19. Assuming Morton Company borrows the money on the last day of the discount period and repays it 30 days later, the effective interest rate on the loan is

A. 11%

B. 10%

C. 12.09%

D. 9.90%

The correct answer is (C). *(Publisher)* **SU 5**

REQUIRED: The effective interest rate when a company borrows to take a discount when the terms are 2/10, net 40.

DISCUSSION: The interest at 11% annually on a 30-day loan of $64,615 (see preceding question) is $592.30 [$64,615 × 11% × (30 ÷ 360)]. However, the company has access to only $58,800. The interest expense on usable funds is therefore at an annual rate of 12.09% [12 months × ($592.30 ÷ $58,800)].

Answer (A) is incorrect because 11% is the contract rate of interest. Answers (B) and (D) are incorrect because the effective rate is greater than the contract rate. The usable funds are less than the face amount of the note.

A20. If Morton fails to take the discount and pays on the 40th day, what effective rate of annual interest is it paying the vendor?

A. 2%

B. 24%

C. 24.49%

D. 36.73%

The correct answer is (C). *(Publisher)* **SU 5**

REQUIRED: The effective interest rate paid when a discount of 2/10, net 40 is not taken.

DISCUSSION: By failing to take the discount, the company is essentially borrowing $58,800 for 30 days. Thus, at a cost of $1,200, the company acquires the use of $58,800, resulting in a rate of 2.04081% ($1,200 ÷ $58,800) for 30 days. Assuming a 360-day year, the effective annual rate is 24.489% [2.04081% × (360 days ÷ 30 days)].

Answer (A) is incorrect because 2% is the discount rate for a 30-day period. Answer (B) is incorrect because 24% assumes that the available funds equal $60,000. Answer (D) is incorrect because 36.73% assumes a 20-day discount period.

Questions A21 through A26 are based on the following information. The FLF Corporation is preparing to evaluate capital expenditure proposals for the coming year. Because the firm employs discounted cash flow methods, the cost of capital for the firm must be estimated. The following information for FLF Corporation is provided:

- The market price of common stock is $60 per share.
- The dividend next year is expected to be $3 per share.
- Expected growth in dividends is a constant 10%.
- New bonds can be issued at face value with a 10% coupon rate.
- The current capital structure of 40% long-term debt and 60% equity is considered to be optimal.
- Anticipated earnings to be retained in the coming year are $3 million.
- The firm has a 40% marginal tax rate.

A21. The after-tax cost of the new bond issue is

A. 4%

B. 6%

C. 10%

D. 14%

The correct answer is (B). *(Publisher)* **SU 7**

REQUIRED: The after-tax cost of issuing bonds.

DISCUSSION: Because the bonds are issued at their face value, the pretax effective rate is 10%. However, interest is deductible for tax purposes, so the government absorbs 40% of the cost, leaving a 6% after-tax cost.

Answer (A) is incorrect because 4% assumes a 60% tax rate. Answer (C) is incorrect because 10% is the before-tax rate. Answer (D) is incorrect because the after-tax cost will be less than the effective before-tax rate.

A22. The cost of using retained earnings for financing is

A. 5%

B. 9%

C. 10%

D. 15%

The correct answer is (D). *(Publisher)* **SU 7**

REQUIRED: The cost of using retained earnings for financing.

DISCUSSION: The cost of internal equity capital equals the dividend yield (dividends per share ÷ market price) plus the dividend growth rate. Dividing the $3 dividend by the $60 market price results in a yield of 5%. Adding the 10% dividend growth rate produces a cost of 15% for retained earnings. No adjustment is made for taxes because dividends are not tax deductible.

Answer (A) is incorrect because 5% is the dividend yield; the growth rate is ignored. Answer (B) is incorrect because 9% would be the after-tax cost if dividends were deductible. Answer (C) is incorrect because 10% is the dividend growth rate; it ignores the dividend yield.

A23. If the company must assume a 20% flotation cost on new stock issuances, what is the cost of new common stock?

A. 6.25%

B. 15%

C. 16.25%

D. 10%

The correct answer is (C). *(Publisher)* **SU 7**

REQUIRED: The cost of new issuances of common stock given flotation costs.

DISCUSSION: This question is identical to the preceding question, except that the flotation costs must be incorporated into the calculation. The company will receive only 80% of the $60 market price, or $48. Consequently, the dividend yield is 6.25% ($3 ÷ $48). Adding the 10% growth rate produces a cost of new equity capital of 16.25%.

Answer (A) is incorrect because 6.25% ignores the dividend growth rate. Answer (B) is incorrect because 15% ignores the flotation costs. Answer (D) is incorrect because 10% is the dividend growth rate.

A24. The maximum capital expansion that can be supported in the coming year without resorting to external equity financing is

A. $2 million.

B. $3 million.

C. $5 million.

D. Cannot determine from the information given.

The correct answer is (C). *(Publisher)* **SU 7**

REQUIRED: The maximum capital expansion that can be supported without resorting to external equity financing.

DISCUSSION: The current optimal capital structure is 40% debt and 60% equity. The $3 million to be retained from earnings in the coming year represents the equity portion of the maximum new capital outlay. To retain the optimal capital structure, $2 million of debt must be added to the $3 million of retained earnings. Hence, the maximum capital expansion is $5 million.

Answer (A) is incorrect because $2 million is the amount of debt that must be added to maintain the optimal structure. Answer (B) is incorrect because $3 million is the amount of earnings retained. Answer (D) is incorrect because the amount of $5 million can be calculated.

Questions A25 and A26 are based on the following additional information. Without prejudice to your answers to the four preceding questions, assume that the after-tax cost of debt financing is 10%, the cost of retained earnings is 14%, and the cost of new common stock is 16%.

A25. If capital expansion needs to be $7 million for the coming year, what is the after-tax weighted-average cost of capital?

A. 11.14%

B. 12.74%

C. 13.6%

D. 16%

The correct answer is (B). *(Publisher)* **SU 7**

REQUIRED: The after-tax weighted-average cost of capital given the amount of the budget.

DISCUSSION: To maintain a capital structure of 40% debt and 60% equity, the $7 million total must consist of $2.8 million of debt and $4.2 million of equity. The equity will consist of $3 million of retained earnings and $1.2 million of new stock. The weighted-average cost of the three sources of new capital is determined as follows:

$3,000,000 ÷ $7,000,000 × 14% =	6.00%
$1,200,000 ÷ $7,000,000 × 16% =	2.74%
$2,800,000 ÷ $7,000,000 × 10% =	4.00%
	12.74%

Answer (A) is incorrect because 11.14% assumes a tax adjustment for the cost of debt, but the 10% rate is an after-tax amount. Answer (C) is incorrect because 13.6% assumes the equity consists solely of new common stock. Answer (D) is incorrect because 16% is the cost of new common stock.

A26. Based on the additional information preceding question A25, what is the marginal cost of capital for any projected capital expansion in excess of $7 million?

A. 10%

B. 12.74%

C. 13.6%

D. 16%

The correct answer is (C). *(Publisher)* **SU 7**

REQUIRED: The marginal cost of capital after projects exceed the capital budget.

DISCUSSION: For this calculation, the weighted-average cost of capital is based on the 16% cost of new common stock and the 10% cost of debt. Retained earnings will not be considered because the amount available has been exhausted. Thus, the weighted average of any additional capital required will be 13.6% [(60% × 16% cost of new equity) + (40% × 10% cost of new debt)].

Answer (A) is incorrect because 10% is the cost of debt capital. Answer (B) is incorrect because 12.74% is the weighted-average cost of capital calculated for a $7 million budget. Answer (D) is incorrect because 16% is the cost of new common stock.

Index

Gleim Publications, Inc.
P.O. Box 12848
Gainesville, FL 32604

TOLL FREE: (800) 87-GLEIM
LOCAL: (352) 375-0772
FAX: (888) 375-6940 (toll free)
INTERNET: http://www.gleim.com
E-MAIL: sales@gleim.com

Customer service is available:
8:00 a.m. - 7:00 p.m., Mon. - Fri.
9:00 a.m. - 2:00 p.m., Saturday
Please have your credit card ready or save time by ordering online!

CPA REVIEW *(97-98 Ed.)*	Books	Audiotapes	CPA Test Prep Software	
Auditing	☐ @ $24.50	☐ @ $75.00	☐ @ $35.00	$________
Business Law	☐ @ $24.50	☐ @ $75.00	☐ @ $35.00	________
TAX-MAN-GOV	☐ @ $24.50	☐ @ $75.00	☐ @ $35.00	________
Financial	☐ @ $24.50	☐ @ $75.00	☐ @ $35.00	________

☐ A System for Success (112 pp.) (FREE with any Gleim CPA Review book)

The Complete Gleim CPA System (save 15%) . . . . $457.00 ________
[5 books, 4 audio cassette albums (41 tapes), 4 CPA Test Prep diskettes, and bonus canvas book bag]

CMA/CFM REVIEW	Books	Audiotapes	CMA/CFMTP Software	CPE	
Part 1	☐ @ $22.95	☐ @ $60.00	☐ @ $35.00	☐ @ $25.00	$________
Part 2CMA	☐ @ $22.95	☐ @ $60.00	☐ @ $35.00	☐ @ $25.00	________
Part 2CFM	☐ @ $22.95	☐ @ $60.00	☐ @ $35.00	☐ @ $25.00	________
Part 3	☐ @ $22.95	☐ @ $60.00	☐ @ $35.00	☐ @ $25.00	________
Part 4	☐ @ $22.95	☐ @ $60.00	☐ @ $35.00	☐ @ $25.00	________

CIA REVIEW	Books	Audiotapes	CIATP Software	CPE	
Part I, Internal Audit Process	☐ @ $22.95	☐ @ $60.00	☐ @ $35.00	☐ @ $25.00	$________
Part II, Internal Audit Skills	☐ @ $22.95	☐ @ $60.00	☐ @ $35.00	☐ @ $25.00	________
Part III, Management Control and Information Technology	☐ @ $22.95	☐ @ $60.00	☐ @ $35.00	☐ @ $25.00	________
Part IV, The Audit Environment	☐ @ $22.95	☐ @ $60.00	☐ @ $35.00	☐ @ $25.00	________

"THE GLEIM SERIES" OBJECTIVE QUESTION AND EXPLANATION BOOKS & CPE

	Book Only	Book & CPE		
Auditing & Systems CPE	☐ $16.95	☐ $125.00	(49-98 hours)	$________
Business Law/legal Studies CPE	☐ $16.95	☐ $125.00	(48-96 hours)	________
Federal Tax CPE	☐ $16.95	☐ $125.00	(51-102 hours)	________
Financial Accounting CPE	☐ $16.95	☐ $125.00	(46-92 hours)	________
Managerial Accounting CPE	☐ $16.95	☐ $125.00	(41-82 hours)	________

Shipping (nonrefundable): **1 item = $3; 2 items = $4; 3 items = $5; 4 or more items = $6** . . . ________
Add applicable sales tax for shipments within Florida. . . . . ________
Fax or write for prices/instructions for shipments outside the 48 contiguous states. **TOTAL** $________

1. We process and ship orders daily, generally one day after receipt of your order.
2. Please PHOTOCOPY this order form for use by others.
3. No CODs. Orders from individuals must be prepaid. Library and company orders may be purchased on account.
4. Gleim Publications, Inc. guarantees the immediate refund of all resalable texts and unopened softwware and audiotapes if returned within 30 days. Applies only to items purchased direct from Gleim Publications, Inc. Our shipping charge is nonrefundable.

NAME (please print) ________________________________

ADDRESS ________________________________ Apt. ________
(street address required for UPS)

____

CITY ________________________ STATE ____ ZIP ________

____ MC/VISA/DISC/AMEX ____ Check/M.O. Daytime Telephone (____)____________

Credit Card No. ________ - ________ - ________ - ________

Exp. ___/___ Signature ________________________________
Mo. / Yr.

120

Printed 4/98. Prices subject to change without notice.

Please forward suggestions, corrections, and comments concerning typographical errors, etc., to **Irvin N. Gleim • c/o Gleim Publications, Inc. • P.O. Box 12848 • University Station • Gainesville, Florida • 32604**. Please include your name and address so we can properly thank you for your interest.

1. ______________________________

2. ______________________________

3. ______________________________

4. ______________________________

5. ______________________________

6. ______________________________

7. ______________________________

8. ______________________________

9. ______________________________

10. ______________________________

11. ______________________________

12. ______________________________

13. ______________________________

14. ______________________________

15. ______________________________

16. ______________________________

17. ______________________________

18. ______________________________

19. ______________________________

20. ______________________________

21. ______________________________

22. ______________________________

Remember for superior service: Mail, e-mail, or fax questions about our books or software. Telephone questions about orders, prices, shipments, or payments.

Name: ______________________________

Company: ______________________________

Address: ______________________________

City/State/Zip: ______________________________

Phone: ( ) __________ FAX: ( ) __________ E-mail: __________

Gleim Bookmark

Dr. Gleim's Recommendation: Cover the answers and explanations in our book with this bookmark to make sure you do NOT cheat yourself. Answers will not be alongside questions when you take your exam.

SOFTWARE

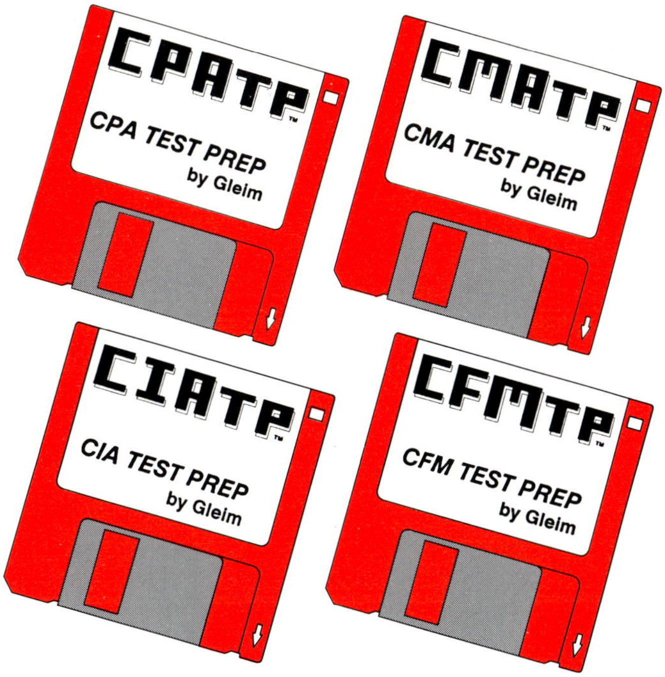

If you don't have it - GET IT!
Gleim's ***Test Prep*** software is
the most effective tool for
passing the CPA, CIA, CMA, and CFM exams.
One disk for each section of each exam
contains hundreds of questions
not found in the books.
Call today or download a
demo from our website.

BOOKS ◆ SOFTWARE ◆ AUDIOTAPES

(800) 87-GLEIM
www.gleim.com

GLEIM KNOWLEDGE TRANSFER SYSTEMS™

Gleim Bookmark

Dr. Gleim's Recommendation: Cover the answers and explanations in our book with this bookmark to make sure you do NOT cheat yourself. Answers will not be alongside questions when you take your exam.

SOFTWARE

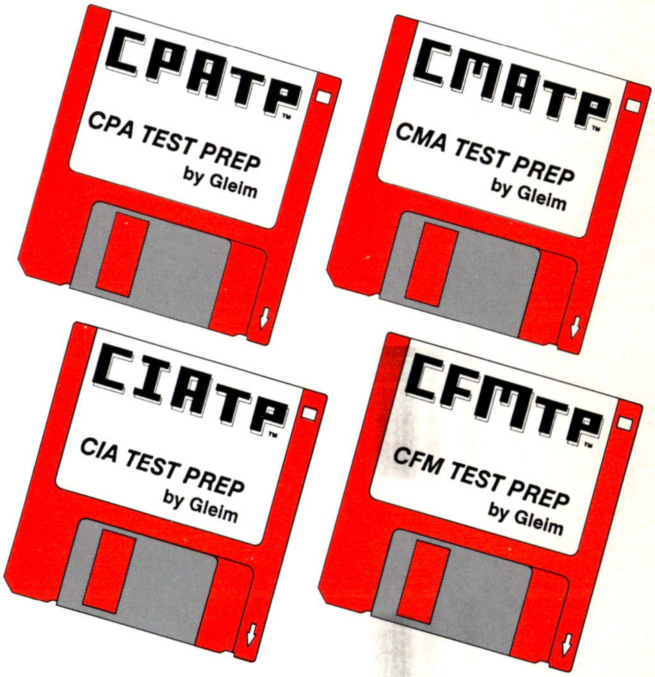

If you don't have it - GET IT!
Gleim's ***Test Prep*** software is
the most effective tool for
passing the CPA, CIA, CMA, and CFM exams.
One disk for each section of each exam
contains hundreds of questions
not found in the books.
Call today or download a
demo from our website.

BOOKS ◆ SOFTWARE ◆ AUDIOTAPES

(800) 87-GLEIM
www.gleim.com

GLEIM KNOWLEDGE TRANSFER SYSTEMS™